The Journal of English and

Germanic philology

(Volume XIII)

Gustaf E. Karsten, (Editor: Julius Goebel)

Alpha Editions

This edition published in 2020

ISBN : 9789354048319 (Hardback)
ISBN : 9789354048814 (Paperback)

Design and Setting By
Alpha Editions
www.alphaedis.com
email - alphaedis@gmail.com

TABLE OF CONTENTS

ZU ENTSTEHUNG, PROBLEM UND TECHNIK VON GOETHES 'WERTHER'

'Im ersten Theile des Werthers ist Werther Goethe selbst. In Lotte und Albert hat er von uns, meiner Frau und mir, Züge entlehnt. Viele von den Scenen sind ganz wahr, aber doch zum Theil verändert, andere sind, in unserer Geschichte wenigstens, fremd. Um des zweyten Theils Willen, und um den Tod des Werthers vorzubereiten, hat er im ersten Theile verschiedenes hinzugedichtet, das uns gar nicht zukömmt. Lotte hat z.B. weder mit Goethe, noch mit sonst einem andern, in dem ziemlich genauen Verhältniss gestanden, wie da beschrieben ist; . . . . . Es ist wahr, er hielt viel von meiner Frau; aber darin hätte er sie getreuer schildern sollen, dass sie viel zu klug und zu delicat war, als ihn einmal so weit kommen zu lassen, wie im ersten Theil enthalten. Sie betrug sich so gegen ihn, dass ich sie weit lieber hätte haben müssen, als sonst, wenn dieses möglich gewesen wäre. . . . . Sonst ist in Werthen viel von Goethe's Character und Denkungsart. Lottens Portrait ist im ganzen das von meiner Frau. Albert hätte ein wenig wärmer seyn mögen.

So viel vom ersten Theile. Der zweyte geht uns gar nichts an. Da ist Werther der junge Jerusalem; Albert der Pfälzische Legations-Secretair, und Lotte des letzteren Frau; was nämlich die Geschichte anbetrifft, denn die Charactere sind diesen drey Leuten grösstentheils nur angedichtet. Von Jerusalem wusste aber der Verfasser seine vorherige Geschichte vermuthlich nicht, darum schickte er die im ersten Theile voraus, und setzte verschiedenes hinzu, um den Erfolg des zweyten Theils wahrscheinlich zu machen, und diesem mehreren Anlass zu geben. Der Albert des zweyten Theils war freilich etwas eifersüchtig, aber stand doch nicht in dem Verhältniss mit seiner Frau, wie da beschrieben ist. Seine Frau ist ein sehr hübsches, sanftes, gutes Geschöpf; aber nicht das Leben in ihr, was ihr da beygelegt wird; sie war auch zu der kleinen Untreue nicht einmal fähig, und auch sie betrug sich viel eingezogener gegen Jerusalem, der sie freylich sehr liebte, aber doch im beleidigten Ehrgeiz, mehr als in der unglücklichen Liebe den Grund zu seinem letzten Entschlusse fand. Er beredete sich aber vielleicht selbst, dass das Letzte die Hauptursache sey, und die letzte Veranlassung ist die Liebe selbst gewiss gewesen. . . . .' [1]

So schildert Kestner die Entstehung des Werther in einem Briefe vom 7. November 1774 seinem Freunde von Hennings. Dass Kestner nicht gerecht sein kann in dieser Sache, ist ganz natürlich und Goethe hat klar den Grund dafür erkannt, wenn er ihm schreibt: "Ihr fühlt *ihn* nicht, ihr fühlt nur *mich* und *euch*, und was ihr *angeklebt* heisst—und truz euch—und andern—*eingewoben* ist—Wenn ich noch lebe, so bist du's dem ich's dancke—bist also nicht Albert—Und also—" [2]

Der Conceptionsprozess des Werther ist ausserordentlich kompliziert und kann für Kestner unmöglich durchsichtig sein, da er Goethes Arbeitsart nicht kannte, und da ausserdem noch Elemente hineinspielten, von denen er jedenfalls nichts wusste. Für jede Person haben wir mindestens zwei Vorbilder. In Werther verschmilzt Goethe und Jerusalem; in Albert: Kestner, Brentano und Herd; in Lotte: Lotte Buff, Maximiliane Brentano, Frau Herd und stellenweise wohl Fräulein von Ziegler, und selbst für "die Freundin seiner Jugend" wird Urania sowie Katharina von Klettenberg vorbildlich gewesen sein. Kestners Bericht über den Tod Jerusalems [3] liefert das Skelett der Erzählung. Von den Vorgängen im Hause Brentano wissen wir nicht genug, um sichere Schlüsse ziehen zu können. Lotte bekommt Maximilianes Augen, und vielleicht auch stammt von dort die leise Sentimentalisierung, die der wirklichen Lotte fremd, im Werther aber mit feinster Kunst *eingewoben* ist. Mir scheint, wenn man sehr genau zuzieht, kann man in den Briefen von 16. Julius, 24. November und 4. December das Portrait Maximilianes leise durchschimmern sehn: 'Sie hat ein Melodie, die sie auf dem Klavier spielt mit der Kraft eines Engels, so simpel und so geistvoll!' Freilich mag Lotte Buff *auch*

---

[1] Goethe und Werther, Briefe Goethes meistens aus seiner Jugend-Zeit etc. hrsg. v. A. Kestner, 3. Aufl. Stuttg. u. Berlin. o. J. (im folgenden citiert als GW) p. 106 f.

[2] 21 Nov. 1774.

[3] GW p. 47 ff.

einfache Lieder gespielt und gesungen haben, aber für sie sind die Menuetts und Contretänze bezeichnend, und am 1. December 1772 spielt Goethe noch auf einen Marsch an. Dagegen finden wir, dass er von der Max spricht als dem *Engel,* der mit den *simpelsten* und werthesten Eigenschaften alle Herzen an sich zieht.[4]

Dass Goethe Tagebuchaufzeichnungen und Briefe im Werther direkt eingeschmolzen habe, wie es gewöhnlich heisst, scheint mir sehr zweifelhaft oder zum mindesten unglücklich ausgedrückt. Jeder einzelne Brief Werthers ist dafür viel zu kunstvoll komponiert und im Tone von der im allgemeinen ziemlich sachlichen Korrespondenz Goethes verschieden. Seine Mitteilungen aus jener Zeit sind abrupter, statt Radotage die vielsagende Geste, einen lyrischen *matter of fact* Stil könnte man es nennen. Damit ist indessen nicht gesagt, dass er nicht eigne Erlebnisse benutzt habe; von rein Gegenständlichem ist uns folgendes zum Teil als wirklich vorgefallen bezeugt, zum Teil können wir es mit grösster Wahrscheinlichkeit annehmen : Topographie und Bevölkerung,[5] Spaziergänge nach Garbenheim, Vorfälle beim Zeichnen, der Ball (allerdings mit Kestner und ohne Ohrfeigen[6]) und Besuch am nächsten Tage, Homer, das Spielen mit den Kindern, Geschichte des Pfarrhofs zu St. . .[7] die kranke Freundin (eine wirkliche Begebenheit im Lichte der Lila-Urania Freundschaft[8]), vielleicht die Brunnenscene mit Malchen und vielleicht die Geschichte von dem 'geizigen, rangigen Filz'[9], Kestner-Alberts zurück-

[4] Anfg. Februar 1774, an Betty Jacobi.

[5] Darüber hauptsächlich: Heinrich Gloël, Goethes Wetzlarer Zeit. Berlin 1911.

[6] GW pp. 27 f., 120 f., 153.

[7] Deinet an Nicolai, 19. Nov. 74: 'Wer den Schlüssel zu Werthern hat, erschrickt über manche Satyre, die sich bloss in Frankfurt erschliesst. . . . .So ist der Brief vom 15. Sept. im 2ten Theil die Geschichte eines hiesigen Pfarrhauses, das ich nun aber freilich nicht öffentlich sagen möchte.' Citiert bei Morris, Der junge Goethe VI p. 417.

[8] Die Krankheit der Frau Rentmeister Rhodius in Atzbach, siehe GW p. 154. Über Lila und Urania: Erich Schmidt: Richardson, Rousseau u. Goethe, Jena 1875 pp. 281-9.

[9] Max Herrmann sieht darin wie auch in der Brunnenscene einen eingegangenen Lebensrest. Jubiläumsausgabe 16. p. 388.

haltendes Benehmen, Possen und verwirrtes Zeug (30. Julius), die Mahnung des Freundes (Merck-Wilhelms 'Entweder Oder'), Unterhaltung der Freunde über Lotte [10], der Tod von Lottens Mutter,[11] die fortgeworfenen Blumen (10. August),[12] Märchenerzählen, der Contrast zu Albert, der in den Akten begraben ist (22. August), die blassrote Schleife als Geschenk, Abschiedsgespräch, Überraschung durch Hochzeit, Ossian. Dass Goethe unter seinen Erlebnissen eine starke Auslese vorgenommen und fast nichts zugelassen hat, was nicht unbedingt sich der künstlerischen Absicht des Romans anpasste, geht daraus hervor, dass vieles, was wir aus seinen Briefen kennen und was also schon die Gedächtnisauslese passiert hat, im Roman keinen Platz fand; so das Bohnenschneiden und Beginnen der Geburtstagsfeier 'mit Thee und freundlichen Gesichtern',[13] der 'bunte Teppich des Tisches an dem sie sass und Filet machte, und ihr strohern Kistgen bey sich stehn hatte',[14] das blaugestreifte Nachtjäckchen Lottes,[15] der Brautstrauss,[16] Johannistraubenpflücken und Quetschenschütteln,[17] die Spaziergänge zu dreien, der Nadelcommerz mit Lottes Silhouette. Zumal alles, was Kestner betrifft ist eliminiert oder stark verändert: beim Balle ist er nicht zugegen; das Mondenmitternachtsgespräch an der Mauer [18] sowie die erste Begegnung mit ihm,[19] beides eminent poetische Motive, sind

[10] Kestner sagt in seinen Tagebuch, als er mit Goethe und andern Lotte aus Atzbach abgeholt:'. . . . gingen herein, vergnügt, dass wir *unser* L. wieder hatten.' GW p. 154.

[11] GW p. 139 f.

[12] GW P. 155 'seine Blumen . . . . . wurden gleichgiltig liegen gelassen, er empfand es, warf sie weg, redete in Gleichnissen; ich ging mit Göthe noch Nachts bis zwölf Uhr auf der Gasse spazieren; merkwürdiges Gespräch; wo er *voll Unmuth* war, und allerhand Phantasien hatte, worüber wir am Ende, im Mondschein an eine Mauer gelehnt lachten.'

[13] 27. August 1774.

[14] 15. Sept. 1773.

[15] 27. Oct; 1772, Oct. 1773; 31. Oct. 1773.

[16] 14. April 1773.

[17] 15. April 1773.

[18] Jan. 1773, siehe auch GW p. 155 wie oben citiert.

[19] GW p. 26 'Daselbst fand ich ihn im Grase unter einem Baume auf

nicht benutzt; die Tafelrunde im Kronprinzen liegt der Wertheratmosphäre völlig fern.

Das alles beweist die Eigenart der Konception und die Vorsicht, mit der einerseits Goethe beim Einschmelzen des Rohmaterials verfuhr, und mit der andrerseits Rückschlüsse auf diesen Prozess gemacht werden müssen. Der Werther zeigt, trotz Goethes Versicherung, ihn 'ziemlich unbewusst, einem Nachtwandler ähnlich'[20] niedergeschrieben zu haben, einen für die Sturm-und Drang Zeit fast unglaublichen Kunstverstand; kein falscher Ton läuft unter, mit Vorbereiten und Vordeuten von Brief zu Brief entwickeln sich die Vorgänge mit zwingender Gewalt.

Der Ton des ersten Teils, in den die Wetzlarer Erlebnisse eingingen, ist nicht der der Wetzlarer Zeit; denn trotz einiger Fälle, wo Goethe die Herrschaft über sich verliert und ihm das ἐπικρατεῖν δύνασθαι nicht gelingt, ist die Stimmung des Sommers 1772 kräftig und gesund, ohne ängstliche Spannung. Wo diese einmal entsteht, wird sie wohl gelöst wie im Mondenmitternachtsgespräch an der Mauer: der Unmut entlädt sich und man lacht, denn Kestner ist nicht Albert. Goethe hat zu viel Centrum in sich selbst, er spielt mit dem Feuer, aber als 'der Fuchs' bei ihm 'lebendig wird', weiss er ihn zu löschen. Das verschlägt nicht, dass er nacher, 'ein Mittelding zwischen dem reichen Mann und dem armen Lazarus',[21] Lotte dem Freunde 'im heiligen Sinne missgönnt'.[22] An Heiraten kann er nicht denken, Carlos Worte sind ihm sicher aus der Seele gesprochen: 'Und heurathen! heurathen just zur Zeit, da das Leben erst recht in Schwung kommen soll, sich häuslich niederlassen, sich einschränken, da

---

dem Rücken liegen, indem er sich mit einigen Umstehenden . . . . . unterhielt, und ihm recht wohl war. Er hat sich nachher darüber gefreuet, das ich ihn einer solchen Stellung kennen gelert.' 8. Jan. 1773: '. . . . . dachte an all unser Wesen, von dem ersten Lager in Garbenheim, biss zum Mondenmitternachtsgespräch an der Mauer, und weiter. Es war ein schönes Leben, auf das ich ganz heiter zurücksehe.'

[20] Dichtung und Wahrheit, Teil III Buch 13. Jubiläumsausg. 24 p. 169.

[21] 25. Dec. 1772.

[22] 15. April 1773.

man noch die Hälfte seiner Wanderung nicht zurückgelegt,
die Hälfte seiner Eroberungen gemacht hat.'[23]

Während der Wetzlarer Zeit schreibt Goethe die Recension
über die Gedichte des Polnischen Juden, in der sich der Di-
thyrambus auf Lotte befindet. Die Rezension über Sulzers 'Die
schönen Künste . . .', die am 18. Dezember erscheint, ist
wohl erst in Frankfurt entstanden und birgt möglicherweise
schon Assoziationen zu Jerusalems Schicksal in sich. Vorbereitet auf den Gedankengang der Recension war Goethe
dadurch, dass er schon früher 'die Natur im physikalischen
und moralischen Verstande zu seinem Haupt-Studium gemacht und von beyden die wahre Schönheit studirt hatte.'
Ich hebe hier die für uns wichtigsten Bestandteile der Besprechung heraus:

'Gehört denn, was unangenehme Eindrücke auf uns macht,
nicht so gut in den Plan der Natur als ihr Lieblichstes? Sind
die wütenden Stürme, Wasserfluthen, Feuerregen, unterir-
dische Glut, und Tod in allen Elementen nicht eben so wahre
Zeugen ihres ewigen Lebens, als die herrlich aufgehende
Sonne über volle Weinberge und duftende Orangenhaine.
Was würde Herr Sulzer zu der liebreichen Mutter Natur
sagen, wenn sie ihm eine Metropolis, die er mit allen schönen
Künsten, Handlangerinnen, erbaut und bevölkert hätte, in
ihren Bauch hinunterschlänge.

'Eben so wenig besteht die Folgerung: ''Die Natur wollte
durch die von allen Seiten auf uns zuströmenden Annehm-
lichkeiten unsre Gemüther überhaupt zu der Sanftmut und
Empfindsamkeit bilden''. *Überhaupt* thut sie das nie, sie
härtet vielmehr, Gott sey Dank, ihre ächten Kinder gegen die
Schmerzen und Übel ab, die sie Ihnen unablässig bereitet, so
dass wir den den glücklichsten Menschen nennen können, der
der stärkste wäre, dem Übel zu entgegnen, es von sich zu
weisen, und ihm zum Trotz den Gang seines Willens zu gehen.
Das ist nun einem grossen Theil der Menschen zu beschwer-
lich, ja unmöglich, daher retirien und retranchiren sich die
meisten, sonderlich die Philosophen, desswegen sie denn auch
überhaupt so adäquat disputiren. . . . .

'Was wir von Natur sehn, ist Kraft, die Kraft verschlingt,

---

[23] Clavigo Akt. I, Sc. I, d. j. G. IV p. 171.

nichts gegenwärtig, alles vorübergehend, tausend Keime zer-
treten jeden Augenblick tausend gebohren, gross und be-
deutend, mannigfaltig ins Unendliche; schön und hässlich,
gut und bös, alles mit gleichem Rechte neben einander exis-
tierend. Und die *Kunst* ist gerade das Widerspiel, sie ent-
springt aus den Bemühungen des Individuums, sich gegen
die zerstörende Kraft des Ganzen zu erhalten. Schon das Thier
durch seine Kunsttriebe *scheidet, verwahrt* sich; der Mensch
durch alle Zustände befestigt sich gegen die Natur, ihre
tausendfache Übel zu vermeiden, und nur das Maas von Gutem
zu geniessen; bis es ihm endlich gelingt, die Circulation aller
seiner wahr und gemachten Bedürfnisse in einen Pallast
einzuschliessen, so fern es möglich ist, alle zerstreute Schönheit und Glückseligkeit in seine gläserne Mauern zu bannen,
wo er denn immer weicher und weicher wird, den Freuden des
Körpers Freuden der Seele substituirt, und seine Kräfte von
keiner Widerwärtigkeit zum Naturgebrauche aufgespannt, in
Tugend, Wohltätigkeit, Empfindsamkeit zerfliessen.' [24]

Werther, der Philosoph, ist einer dieser Menschen, die sich
'retiriren und retranchiren', einer, dem es nicht gegeben ist,
sich durch seine Kunsttriebe gegen die zerstörende Kraft der
Natur zu verwahren. Auch er substituiert den Freuden des
Körpers die Freuden der Seele und zerfliesst bis zu einem gewissen Grade in Empfindsamkeit.

Am 11. September hat Goethe Wetzlar verlassen, am 10.
October empfängt er die Nachricht von Goués vermeintlichem
Tode, Anfang November die von Jerusalems. Vom 6.-10.
desselben Monats ist er in Wetzlar, vermutlich um genauere
Erkundigungen einzuziehen, am 28. November dankt er seinem Freunde 'für die Nachricht von des armen J (erusalems)
Todt,' von dem er 'das pragmatische Resultat seiner Re-
flecktionen' am 26. November bereits an Frau von La Roche
geschickt hat, zugleich mit Kielmannseggs Worten: ''das was
mir wenige glauben werden, was ich ihnen wohl sagen kann,
das ängstliche Bestreben nach Wahrheit und moralischer Güte,
hat sein Herz so untergraben, dass misslungene Versuche des
Lebens und der Leidenschafft, ihn zu dem traurigen Entschlusse hindrängten. Ein edles Herz und ein durchdrin-

[24] D. j. G. VI p. 222f.

gender Kopf, wie leicht von ausserordentlichen Empfindung-
en, gehen sie zu solchen Entschliessungen über, und das Leben
—was brauch, was kann ich *Ihnen* davon sagen.　Mir ists
Freude genug, dem abgeschiedenen Unglücklichen, dessen That
von der Welt so unfühlbar zerrissen wird, ein Ehrenmaal in
Ihrem Herzen errichtet zu haben.''

Trotz Goethes Beteurung in einem Briefe vom 10. October:
'Ich hoffe nie meinen Freunden mit einer solchen Nachricht
beschweerlich zu werden' beginnt der Selbstmordgedanke in
seinem Herzen Grund zu fassen.　Am 10. November hat er
'recht hängerliche und hängenswerthe Gedancken auf dem
Canapee . . . . . .', versichert einige Wochen später: 'erschiessen mag ich mich vor der Hand noch nicht' (28. Nov.)
und gedenckt Kestners mit den Worten 'Wie wohl euch ist und
nicht erschieserlich' (6. Dec.).　Der Beginn des nächsten Früh-
jahrs steigert seine Depression.　Ein Brief an Johanna Fahlmer
bezeugt einen ''Stand von Perturbation in dem es den Seelen,
sagen sie, nicht vorteilhafft ist aus der Welt zu gehn.''[25]
Und im April: 'Meine arme Existenz starrt zum öden Fels.
Diesen Sommer geht alles . . . . . und ich bin allein.
Wenn ich kein Weib nehme oder mich erhänge, so sagt ich habe
das Leben recht lieb . . . . .'' [26] Und an Frau von La
Roche: '. . . . . ich bin allein, und werd es täglich
mehr.' [27]　Er fürchtet also die Einsamkeit, die Jerusalems
Herz untergraben hat,[28] kann sich nicht mehr in einem
Freunde bespiegeln,[29] wie es 'das Schicksal der edelsten
Seelen ist, nach einem Spiegel ihres selbst vergebens zu
seufzen.' [30]　Tief trifft ihn der Tod Uranias.　'Heut früh
ward sie begraben und ich bin immer an ihrem Grabe,
und verweile, da noch meines Lebens Hauch und Wärme
hinzugeben, und eine Stimme zu seyn aus dem Steine
dem Zukünftigen.'[31]　'Auf dem Grabe—Ich will nicht davon

[25] März 1773.
[26] 21. April 1773.
[27] 12. May 1773.
[28] Anfg. Nov. 1772.
[29] 7. Dec. 1773.
[30] 20. Nov. 1772.
[31] 21. April 1773.

wissen will alles vergessen. Vergesst alles in Lottens Armen, und dann arbeitet euer Tagewerk.'[32]

Der Tod Jerusalems und sein eigenes Erleben stehen sicher in eigenartiger Wechselwirkung. Er sieht sein eignes Schicksal in Jerusalem, und das fremde Schicksal beeinflusst das Seine suggestiv. So beklagt er in dem Unglücklichen sich selber:—'die schändlichen Menschen, die nichts geniessen denn Spreu der Eitelkeit, und Götzen Lust in ihrem Herzen haben, und Götzen-dienst predigen, und hemmen gute Natur, und übertreiben und verderben die Kräffte sind schuld an diesem Unglück an unserm Unglück hohle sie der Teufel ihr Bruder. Wenn der verfluchte Pfaff sein Vater nicht schuld ist so verzeih mirs Gott dass ich ihm Wünsche er möge den Hals brechen wie Eli. Der arme iunge! wenn ich zurückkam vom Spaziergang und er mir begegnete hinaus im Mondschein, sagt ich er ist verliebt. Lotte muss sich noch erinnern dass ich drüber lächelte. Gott weis die Einsamkeit hat sein Herz untergraben''.[33] Ob die Wut über den Abt Jerusalem auf Zerwürfnisse mit dem einigen Vater schliessen lässt? wie sie auch der Brief von 10. November andeutet: "Der Brief meines Vaters ist da, lieber Gott wenn ich einmal alt werde, soll ich dann auch so werden. Soll meine Seele nicht mehr hängen an dem was liebenswerth und gut ist. Sonderbar, dass man da glauben sollte, ie älter der Mensch wird desto freyer er werden sollte von dem was irrdisch und klein ist. Er wird immer irrdischer und kleiner.'[34]

Liebe, Einsamkeit, edles Herz, durchdringender Kopf, ausserordentliche Empfindungen und das Elend des Lebens, alles das ist es, was des einen Schicksal dem andern gleich macht. Kestners Bericht hat ihn "so offt innig gerührt—und das gewissenhaffte Detail der Erzählung nimmt ganz hin.'[35] Die Vertrautheit mit dem Todesgedanken nimmt zu durch Uranias Hinscheiden. Und nun hat sich Lotte verheiratet und er lebt sich auch in *den* Teil des Jerusalemschen Schicksals ein. Wir spüren ein Anklingen der Erotik in den Briefen

[32] 25. April 1773.
[33] Anfang Nov. 1772.
[34] 10. Nov. 1772.
[35] 19. Jan. 1773.

nach der Hochzeit, wie überhaupt die Flamme noch einmal
aufschlägt. 'In der Ewigkeit aber hoffe er ihr einen Kuss
geben zu dürfen', hatte Jerusalem geschrieben.[36] Goethe erinnert sich des Abschiedsgesprächs vom Wiedersehn: 'Wir
redeten wie's drüben aussäh über den Wolcken, das weis ich
zwar nicht, das weis ich aber, dass unser Herr Gott ein sehr
kaltblütiger Mann seyn muss, der euch die Lotte lässt. Wenn
ich sterbe und habe droben was zu sagen ich hohl sie euch
warrlich.'[37] Und als Kestner den Spass übel nimmt, antwortet er: 'Mich einen Neider und Nexer zu heissen und
dergleichen mehr, das ist all nur seit ihr verheurathet seyd
. . . . . und das sag ich euch, wenn ihr euch ein-
fallen lasst eifersüchtig zu werden so halt ich mirs aus euch
mit den treffensten Zügen auf die Bühne zu bringen und
Juden und Cristen sollen über euch lachen.'[38] Und wie sehr
ihn sein Gedächtnis bei Ausführung einer solchen Drohung
helfen würde, zeigt der Satz: 'Ihre [Annchen Brandts] Gegenwart hat alles Andencken an Euch wieder aufbrausen gemacht, mein ganzes Leben unter euch, ich wollt alles er-
zählen biss auf die Kleider und Stellungen so lebhafft—.'[39]
Ein Traum aber, den er in einem Brief von 12. Juni berichtet,
mag vielleicht verraten, wie seine Phantasie Altes und Neues,
Wirkliches und in Wunsch oder Einbildung Erlebtes ver-
mischt: 'Heute Nacht hat mir's von Lotten wunderlich ge-
träumt. Ich führte sie am Arm durch die Allee, und alle
Leute blieben stehn und sahn sie an, Ich kann noch einige
nennen die stehen blieben und uns nachsahen. Auf einmal
zog sie eine Calesche über und die Leute waren sehr be-
treten/: Das kommt von Hansens Briefe der mir die Geschichte von Minden schrieb:/ Ich bat sie sie mögt sie doch
zurückschlagen das that sie. Und sah mich an mit den Augen
ihr wisst ia wies einem ist wenn sie einen ansieht. Wir gingen
geschwind. Die Leute sahen wie vorher. O Lotte sagt ich
zu Ihr, Lotte dass sie nur nicht erfahren dass du eines andern
Frau bist. Wir kamen zu einem Tanzplatz.''

[36] GW p. 53.
[37] 10. April 1773.
[38] 15. April 1773.
[39] ebenda.

Mitte Juli ''bearbeitet er seine Situation zum Schauspiel zum Trutz Gottes und der Menschen'', was jedenfalls nicht auf Werther sondern auf Prometheus zu deuten ist; denn Prometheus gleich schafft er in diesem eminent fruchtbaren Sommer Geschöpfe, die seine Einsamkeit beleben und erfreuen, 'wenn einem da der Genius nicht aus Steinen und Bäumen Kinder erweckte, man mögte das Leben nicht.'[40]

Das Jahr 1774 findet ihn mit neuem Mut und frischer Kraft und die Aussichten sind voll Sonne und Winterfreuden. 'Diese dritthalb Wochen her sind geschwärmt worden', heisst es am ersten Februar, 'und nun sind wir zufrieden und glücklich, als mans seyn kann. *Wir* sag ich, denn seit dem fünfzehnten jenner ist keine Branche meiner Existenz einsam. Und das Schicksaal mit dem ich mich herumgebissen habe so offt, wird ietzt höflich betittelt, das schöne, weise Schicksal, denn gewiss das ist die erste Gabe, seit es mir meine Schwester nahm, die das Ansehn eines Aequivalents hat. Die Max[41] ist noch immer der Engel—und das Gefühl das ich für Sie habe worinn ihr Mann nie Ursache zur Eifersucht finden wird, macht nun das Glück meines Lebens.' Ob diese Versicherung nicht ein wenig Selbstüberredung ist? Schon im März heisst es an Frau von La Roche: 'Ihre Lieben hab ich einige Zeit nicht gesehen. Ich hatte mein Herz verwöhnt. Nein, liebe Mama, Sie haben meine Hand darauf ich will brav seyn.'[42] Gleich darauf muss dann der Entschluss in ihm gereift sein, das Brentanosche Haus ganz zu meiden, wohl eher infolge von innern Vergängen in ihm und zwischen den Gatten selbst als etwa zwischen Goethe und Brentano.[43]

[40] An T. G. Röderer, Herbst 1773, vielleicht aber und mir wahrscheinlicher wegen einer Anspielung auf Merck, der ja von Mai bis Dezember nach Russland war, Frühling 1773. Siehe D. j. G. VI, 272.

[41] Kam Mitte Januar nach Frankfurt.

[42] D. j. G. No. 213, B. IV p. 12; in No. 210 'von ihrer Max kann ich nicht lassen solang ich lebe, und ich werde sie immer lieben dürfen.'

[43] 'Glauben Sie mir dass das Opfer das ich Ihrer Max mache sie nicht mehr zu sehn, werther ist als die Assiduität des feurigsten Liebhabers, dass es im Grunde doch Assiduität ist.' (16. Juni 1774) Und 'Wenn Sie wüssten was in mir vorgegangen ist eh ich das Haus mied, Sie würden mich nicht rückzulocken dencken liebe Mama, ich hab in denen

Inzwischen aber hat sich durch den leisesten Anstoss das lang in ihm Lebende krystallisiert. 'Das liebe Weibgen hat Ihnen was von einer Arbeit geschrieben die ich angefangen habe seit Sie weg sind, würklich angefangen, denn ich hatte nie die Idee aus dem Suiet ein einzelnes Ganze zu machen,'[44] meldet er Frau von La Roche, und im Mai: ''Meinen Werther musst ich eilend zum Drucke schicken.''

Goethe definiert das Problem seines Werkes in einem Briefe an Schönborn (vom 1-4 Juli 1774) folgendermassen: 'Eine Geschichte—darinn ich einen iungen Menchen darstelle, der mit einer tiefen reinen Empfindung, und wahrer Penetration begabt, sich in schwärmende Träume verliert, sich durch Spekulation untergräbt, biss er zuletzt durch dazutretende unglückliche Leidenschafften, besonders eine endlose Liebe zerrüttet, sich eine Kugel vor den Kopf schiesst.' Nehmen wir dazu das 'ängstliche Bestreben nach Wahrheit und moralischer Güte', von dem Kielmannsegg berichtet, und die Klagen Jerusalems 'über die engen Gränzen, welche dem menschlichen Verstande gesetzt wären'[45] sowie die engen Grenzen, die ihm im beruflichen Leben gezogen werden,[46] so haben wir alle

---

schröcklichen Augenblicken für alle Zukunft gelitten, ich bin ruhig und die Ruhe lasst mir.' Zweite Hälfte, Juli 1774. D. j. G. No. 232.
[44] Mitte Februar 1774. D. j. G. No. 208.
[45] 'wenigstens dem Seinigen; er konnte ausserst betrübt werden, wenn er davon sprach, was er wissen möchte, was er nicht ergründen könne etc.' GW p. 48.
[46] die Goethe auch kannte, siehe den Brief vom 15. Sept. 1773: 'Ich lieber Mann, lasse meinen Vater ietzt ganz gewähren, der mich täglich mehr in Stadt Civil Verhältnisse einzuspinnen sucht, und ich lass es geschehn. Solang meine Krafft noch in mir ist! Ein Riss! und all die siebenfache Bastseile sind entzwey.' und am 25. Dec. 1773: 'Mein Vater hätte zwar nichts dagegen wenn ich in fremde Dienste ginge, auch hält mich hier weder Liebe noch Hoffnung eines Amts—und so scheint es könnt ich wohl einen Versuch wagen, wieder einmal [zu sehen] wie's draussen aussieht. Aber Kestner, die Talente und Kräffte die ich habe, brauch ich für mich selbst gar zu sehr, ich bin von ieher gewohnt nur nach meinem Instinkt zu handeln, and damit könnte keinem Fürsten gedient seyn. Und dann biss ich politische Subordination lernte—Es ist ein verfluchtes Volk, die Frankf[ur]ter, pflegt der Präs. v. Moser zu sagen, man kann ihre eigensinnigen Köpfe nirgends hinbrauchen. Und wenn auch das nicht wäre, unter all meinen Talenten ist meine Jurisprudenz der geringsten eins.'

Züge beisammen, die Werther ins Verderben stürzen. Und dem allen borgt nun Goethe die Fülle seiner Liebe und seines eigenen Herzens.

Die Spekulation, die bei Jerusalem eine aufklärerisch-rationalistiche war,[47] wird ins Sturm-und Drangmässige verschoben; so berührt sich Werther mit Faust. Wie Faust sucht er zu erkennen 'was die Welt im innersten zusammenhält'; wie Faust sieht er 'die würckende Natur vor seiner Seele liegen'; selbst Töne des Osterspaziergangs werden hier schon angeschlagen, wenn er mit den Fittichen eines Kranichs sich aufzuschwingen sehnt, in der Phantasie Berge und Abgründe bis an das ungemessene Meer überschaut; nur einen Augenblick möchte er 'in der eingeschränkten Kraft seines Busens einen Tropfen der Seligkeit des Wesens fühlen das alles in sich und durch sich hervorbringt'; aber auch ihm bleibt es ein Schauspiel, und vor dem Geist des Ewigschaffenden, dem er nicht gleicht und der 'vom unzugänglichen Gebürge über die Einöde . . . . . bis ans Ende des unbekannten Ozeans' weht, sinkt er zusammen, erliegt 'unter der Gewalt der Herrlichkeit dieser Erscheinungen.' Diesem gefühls-mässigen Erfassen gegenüber steht das Wagnerische trockne Registrieren und kritische Bestreben: der junge V. . . . . ., der erst von Akademien kommt, 'sich eben weise dünkt,' und seinen Sulzer ganz durchgelesen hat; die 'gelassenen Kerls auf beyden Seiten des Ufers', die den Strom des Genies eindämmen, der pedantische Medikus, der Gesandte mit seiner Abneigung gegen Inversionen, der Fürst der 'mit einem gestempelten Kunstworte drein tölpelt', die Frau des neuen Pfarrers, die sich 'in die Untersuchung des Canons meliert, gar viel an der neumodischen, moralisch kritischen Reformation des Christenthums arbeitet', ja sogar Albert, der sich nicht in eines Menschen Seele versetzen kann und nicht begreifen 'wie ein Mensch so thörig seyn kann, sich zu erschiessen', und dem Einschränkung ein Weniger an Wissen, an Verstande ist.[48]

[47] Mendelsohns Phädon war seine liebste Lektüre . . . . . Leibnitzen's Werke lass er mit grossem Fleisse. GW p. 48.

[48] Brief vom 12. August: "Albert . . . . . wandte noch einiges ein. . . . ich habe nur von einem einfältigen Mädgen gesprochen, wie denn aber

Der Unterschied zwischen Werther und Goethe ist darin
zu finden, dass Goethe den Ausweg aus dem Kreis des Kerls,
der spekuliert, und die schöne grüne Weide findet; denn er
'verwahrt sich gegen die Natur' durch die Kunst. Erfassen
und wiedergeben, ἐπικρατεῖν δύνασθαι hat er gelernt während
des fruchtbaren Sommers von 1773. Werther dagegen ist
eigentlich kein wirklicher Künstler, wie ja Goethes Genie sich
auch nicht auf dem Gebiete der bildenden Kunst adäquat zu
äussern vermag. Werthers Kunst ist mehr ein Ausfluss seiner
Jugend, sein 'Wohlgefallen an der Natur ist kein ästhetisches,
sondern ein moralisches', 'es ist eine durch sie dargestellte
Idee', die er in ihr liebt, i. e. 'das stille schaffende Leben, das
ruhige Wirken aus sich selbst, das Daseyn nach eigenen Gesetzen, die innere Notwendigkeit.'[49] Es ist die Sehnsucht des
Sentimentalischen Menschen zum Naiven.

So sieht Werther und beneidet alle die, welche in harmon-
ischem Gleichgewicht von Wirken und Streben 'in der
glücklichen Gelassenheit so den engen Kreis' ihres Daseins
umschreiben und ausfüllen, die Mädchen, die am Brunnen
Wasser schöpfen, der Bauer, der sein Krauthaupt auf den
Tisch bringt, die Helden Homers, die Patriarchen und zumal
die Kinder, die ihn rühren, weil er 'zu der grenzenlosen Bestimmbarkeit in dem Kinde und zu seiner reinen Unschuld
hinaufsieht' aus der Beschränktheit seines Zustands (Schiller). Naiv ist auch Lotte, welcher *der* Autor der liebste ist,
in dem sie ihre Welt wiederfindet, und die sich in ihrem engen
Kreise glücklich fühlt, der 'freylich kein Paradies, aber doch
im Ganzen eine Quelle unsäglicher Glückseligkeit ist.'

> 'Wie vieles ist denn dein?
> Der Kreis den meine Würksamkeit erfüllt
> Nichts drunter und nichts drüber.'

So antwortet der schaffende Prometheus.

---

ein Mensch von Verstande, der nicht so eingeschränkt sey, der mehr
Verhältnisse übersähe, zu entschuldigen seyn möchte, könne er nicht
begreifen."

[49] Die Zitate sind aus dem Aufsatze Schillers, dem, wie mir scheint,
hauptsächlich am Werther der Unterschied von naiv und sentimentalisch
greifbar geworden ist.

Faust's Taumeln von Begierde zu Genuss und ewiges Ent-
täuschtsein spricht sich aus in dem Briefe, wo Werther klar
die immer wiederholte Unbefriedigtheit seines Sehnens ausdrückt: [50] Ich eilte hin! und kehrte zurück, und hatte nicht

[50] Goethes 'Wandrer' und 'Ganymed' zusammengenommen umfassen
schon das ganze Problem des Werther: im einen die 'Einschränkung'
im andern das Ausweiten des Individuums wie es spricht aus dem
'mache mir Raum in meiner engen Brust.' (10. Juli 72) Übrigens
scheint mir der Einfluss von Goldsmith's 'Traveller' auf Werther noch
nicht genügend gewürdigt zu werden. (Goethe Jahrbuch 1885. B. VI,
p. 281-298; Modern Language Notes 1902 H6 u. 7.) Man vergleiche z. B.
den Brief vom 21. Junius und den Brief vom 9. Mai (Wallfahrt)
mit den Versen:

> But me, not destined such delights to share,
> My prime of life in wandering spent, and care:
> Impell'd with steps unceasing, to pursue
> Some fleeting good, that mocks me with the view
> That like the circle bounding earth and skies,
> Allures from far, yet, as I follow, flies:
> My fortune leads to traverse realms alone,
> And find no spot of all the world my own.

Oder den Brief vom 22. Mai mit:

> Thus to my breast alternate passions rise,
> Pleased with each good that Heaven to man supplies
> Yet oft a sigh prevails, and sorrows fall,
> To see the sum of human bliss so small:
> And oft I wish, amidst the scene to find
> Some spot to real happiness consign'd
> Where my worn soul, each wandering hope at rest,
> May gather bliss to see my fellows blest.

Damit ist nicht gesagt, dass diese Ideen nicht schon Goethes Eigentum
gewesen seien, aber die ganze Stimmung des Goldsmith'schen Gedichtes
findet ihr Echo im Werther:

> Such are the charms to barren states assign'd,
> Their wants but few, their wishes all confined

and

> How small, of all that human hearts endure,
> That part which laws or kings can cause or cure!
> Still to ourselves in every place consign'd
> Our own felicity we make or find.

(Ach so **gewiss** ist's, dass unser Herz allein sein Glück macht) Aber
für Goldsmith ist noch reason, faith, conscience was für Werther
Gefühl ist, d. i. was keinem genommen werden kann und des Menschen
eigenstes ist.

gefunden was ich hoffte. O es ist mit der Ferne wie mit der
Zukunft! Ein grosses dämmerndes Ganze ruht vor unserer
Seele, unsere Empfindung verschwimmt darinne, wie unser
Auge, und wir sehnen uns, ach! unser ganzes Wesen hinzugeben, uns mit all der Wonne eines einzigen grossen herr-
lichen Gefühls ausfüllen zu lassen.—Und ach, wenn wir hin-
zueilen, wenn das Dort nun Hier wird, ist alles vor wie nach,
und wir stehen in unserer Armuth, in unserer Eingeschränktheit, und unsere Seele lechzt nach entschlüpftem Labsale.[51]
Und dass er schon als Kind die Keime des sentimentalischen
Menschen, des 'Zerfliessens in Empfindsamkeit' in sich hatte,
und *nicht,* wie man zuweilen annimmt, 'durchaus gesund',[52]
war, zeigt die Stelle, wo er auf seiner Wallfahrt der Jugend-
zeit gedenkt, da er schon als Knabe sich 'in dem Anschaun
einer unsichtbaren Ferne verlohr.'[53] So geht sein Streben
über die Grenzen der Menscheit hinaus, er 'überwächst sich'.[54]
In Stunden der Ruhe oder Niedergeschlagenheit kehren seine
Wünsche zur Erde zurück; aber auch da zeigt sich der Unterschied zwischen Faust und Werther: während der eine,
der unersättliche Forschergeist auch das Glück der Erde bis
zur Hefe auskostet, sich nicht 'retiriert und retranchiert', begnügt sich die zarter und idyllisch angelegte Jünglingseele,
das Kind zu spielen mit den Kindern, den Bauer, indem er
den Bauer idealisiert und dies Ideal nachahmt, dabei aber
seinen Homer liest oder seine Gedanken zu den Zeiten der
Patriarchen zurückwandern lässt. Bald will ihm auch hier
'Befriedigung nicht mehr aus dem Busen quillen'; denn so
wohl es ihm ist, dass er 'die simple harmlose Wonne des
Menschen fühlen', 'die Züge patriarchalischen Lebens—ohne

[51] Brief vom 21. Juni.

[52] Max Herrmann in der ausgezeichneten Einleitung der Jubiläumsausgabe, B. 16, p. VIII.

[53] Sein Gegenstück ist Herman in Goethes Epos:
'er streckte
schon als Knabe die Hände nicht aus nach diesem und jenem.
Was er begehrte, das war ihm gemäss; so hielt er es fest auch.'
(Hermann und Dorothea V. Vers 63 ff.)

[54] Karl Philipp Moritz's Ausdruck, der im Briefe vom 18. Aug. den
Mittelpunkt findet. cit. H. G. Gräf: Goethe über seine Dichtungen
T. I, B. II no. 987.

Affectation in seine Lebensart verweben kann'[55]—es ist eben doch nur ein gewaltsames Verweben, auch hier ein 'Schauspiel, aber ach ein Schauspiel nur.' Während die Kinder, die Landleute, die Altvorden, Lotte ihr Leben pflanzenhaft naiv dahinleben, ist Werthers patriarchalisches Leben immer ein Nachahmen, bei dem er Schauspieler und Zuschauer zugleich ist, eine Dualität, die den Genuss am Ende aufheben muss.

Das Unglück Werthers liegt darin begriffen; er kann sich nie zur Höhe eines Faust erheben, nie den Punkt erreichen, wo er durch Handeln, 'durch die mannigfaltigste Übung und Anwendung [seiner Kräfte]—zu dem ihm einzig gemässen Verhältnis mit der Natur' gelangt.[56] Denn er ist die Personification der Jugend, kann den Übergang zum Mannesalter nicht finden, den Goethe durch ihn fand. Mehr und mehr vernachlässigt er seine tätigen Kräfte; ganz Individualist,[57] will er auch sogleich Wirkungen seiner Tätigkeit sehn und kann sich nicht als Glied in das Getriebe einer Maschine fügen lassen. Die Tätigkeit, die ihm aufgedrängt wird, ist seiner Natur nicht gemäss; und damit zeigt sich wohl auch die Einschränkung, die dem Menschen des 18. Jahrhunderts aufgelegt ist und der Goethe durch ein wunderbares Geschick entrann. Vielleicht gälte von Werther, was Lavater von seinem grossen Freunde sagt: 'Goethe wäre ein herrliches handelndes Wesen bey einem Fürsten. *Dahin* gehört er. Er könnte König seyn. Er hat nicht nur Weisheit und Bonhomie, sondern auch Kraft.'[58] Ob er Kraft gehabt hätte?

Wir können die Faktoren, die Werthers Untergang herbei führen, nicht besser zusammenfassen, als es Schiller in dem bereits zitierten Aufsatze tut: 'Ein Charakter, der mit glühender Empfindung ein Ideal umfasst und die Wirklich-

[55] Brief vom 21. Juni.

[56] Siehe K. E. Schubarth über Werther, cit. H. G. Gräf Goethe über seine Dichtungen T. I, B. II no. 1046.

[57] 'Aktivität! Wenn nicht der mehr thut, der Kartoffeln stekt, und in die Stadt reitet, sein Korn zu verkaufen, als ich, so will ich zehn Jahre noch mich auf der Galeere abarbeiten, auf der ich nun angeschmiedet bin.'

[58] 20. Oktober 1774 D. j. G. IV p. 114.

keit flieht, um nach einem wesenlosen Unendlichen zu ringen, der, was er in sich selbst unaufhörlich zerstört, unaufhörlich ausser sich sucht, dem nur seine Träume das Reelle, seine Erfahrungen ewig nur Schranken sind, der endlich in seinem eigenen Daseyn nur eine Schranke sieht, und auch diese, wie billig ist, noch einreisst, um zu der wahren Realität durchzudringen—dieses gefährliche Extrem des sentimentalischen Charakters ist der Stoff eines Dichters geworden, in welchem die Natur getreuer und reiner als in irgend einem andern wirkt, und der sich unter modernen Dichtern vielleicht am wenigsten von der sinnlichen Wahrheit der Dinge entfernt.

'Es ist interresant zu sehen, mit welchem glücklichen Instinkt Alles, was dem sentimentalischen Charakter Nahrung gibt, im Werther zusammengedrängt ist; schwärmerische unglückliche Liebe, Empfindlichkeit für Natur, Religionsgefühle, philosophischer Contemplationsgeist, endlich, um nichts zu vergessen, die düstere, gestaltlose, schwermüthige Ossianische Welt. Rechnet man dazu, wie wenig empfehlend, ja wie feindlich die Wirklichkeit dagegen gestellt ist, und wie von Aussen her alles sich vereinigt, den Gequälten in seine Idealwelt zurückzudrängen, so sieht man keine Möglichkeit, wie ein solcher Charakter aus einem solchen Kreise sich hätte retten können.'

'Glücklicher Instinkt'—das ist der treffende Ausdruck für die schaffende Kraft, die Werther mit all den Zügen ausstattete oder die all den auseinanderliegenden Erlebnissen das geistige Band gab. Die Form aber setzt, wie schon einmal betont wurde, einen reifen Kunstverstand voraus.

Ob Goethe je ernstlich daran gedacht hat, den Werther oder einen Teil des 'Sujets'[59] in dramatischer Form zu geben, wie er Kestner androht, ist nicht gewiss. Mir ist es durchaus nicht unwahrscheinlich; wir wissen: 'Alles verwandelt sich gleich bey ihm ins Dramatische'[60] in jenem Sommer. Ich denke mir den Prozess ungefähr so: Die Einsamkeit, Selbstmordgedanken, angeregt durch Jerusalems Geschick, der Tod Uranias, die Kirchhofsstimmung ihres Begräbnisses hat seinem Herzen den Hamlet näher gebracht als zuvor, Scenen aus

[59] Siehe den Brief von Mitte Februar 1774. D. j. G. No. 208.
[60] Schönborn an Gerstenberg, 12. Okt. 1774. D. j. G. III, p. 389.

dem Hamlet erhalten plötzlich ganz neues, innerliches Leben.[61] Die bekannten Anklänge im Werther[62] bezeugen genugsam die endliche Näherung der beiden Werke. Und haben nicht beide den Gedanken gemeinsam, dass ihre Helden der Aufgabe, die auf ihre Seele gelegt ist, nicht gewachsen

[61] Ich möchte hier eine Vermutung aussprechen, deren Glaubwürdigkeit andre beurteilen mögen. Im Briefe vom 21. April 1773 heisst es: 'Der Tod einer teuer geliebten Freundinn ist noch um mich. Heut früh ward sie begraben und ich binn immer an ihrem Grabe, und verweile, da noch meines Lebens Hauch und Wärme hinzugeben, und eine Stimme zu seyn aus dem Steine dem Zukünftigen. Aber ach auch ist mir verboten einen Stein zu setzen ihrem Andencken, und mich verdriesst dass ich nicht streiten mag mit dem Gewäsch und Geträtsch.' Sollte ihm da—zumal wenn wir die Stelle in Dichtung und Wahrheit auf Urania beziehen dürfen, die von einer heimlichen Liebe für ihn spricht (III. 12, Jubiläumsausg. B. 24 p. 90)—nicht vielleicht der Vergleich mit Ophelias Begräbnis eingefallen sein: Die, welche die Würde der Leidtragenden in Anspruch nehmen, stehen der Toten nicht halb so nahe wie er. 'Woo't weep? Woo't fight? Woo't fast? Woo't tear thyself? etc'. Und des Königs 'This grave shall have a living monument' wird von Goethe beherzigt, er setzt es ihr im Werther (17. Mai und im Abschiedsbrief an Lotte 'Ich hatte eine Freundin . . . . .') Die Stelle im Briefe von 25. April ist zu unbestimmt, um irgend eine sichere Deutung zuzulassen: 'Auf dem Grabe—Ich will nicht davon wissen, will alles vergessen.'

[62] Brief vom 15. November: "Seyn und Nichtseyn." Brief vom 30. Nov. und die Stelle im letzten Briefe an Lotte: 'Sterben! Was heist das? Sieh wir träumen, wenn wir vom Tode reden. Ich habe manchen sterben sehen, aber so eingeschränkt ist die Menscheit, dass sie für ihres Daseyns Anfang und Ende keinen Sinn hat . . . . .' Und auch hier folgt in enger Verbindung damit die Stelle, die von Uranias Begräbnis spricht: 'Ich hatte eine Freundin . . . . .' Schon vorher: 'Den Vorhang aufzuheben und dahinter zu treten, das ist all! Und warum das Zaudern und das Zagen?—Weil man nicht weis, wie's dahinter aussieht?—und man nicht zurückkehrt? etc'. Brief vom 12. August: Der Gedanke an Hamlets Monolog liegt auch hier nahe. Das Schicksal des Mädchens, das sich ertränkt, erinnert im Zweiten Teil dieser episodischen Erzählung eher an Ophelia als an Gretchen; man vergleiche: 'Durch leere Vergnügungen einer unbeständigen Eitelkeit nicht verdorben, zieht ihr Verlangen grad nach dem Zwecke: Sie will die Seinige werden. . . . . Wiederholtes Versprechen, das ihr die Gewissheit aller Hofnungen versiegelt, kühne Liebkosungen, die ihre Begierden vermehren, umfangen ganz ihre Seele, sie schwebt in einem dumpfen Bewusstseyn, in einem Vorgefühl aller Freuden, sie ist bis auf den höchsten Grad gespannt, wo sie endlich ihre Arme ausstrekt, all ihre

sind. 'Ein schönes, reines, edles, höchst moralisches Wesen
ohne die sinnliche Stärke, die den Helden macht, geht unter
einer Last zu Grunde, die es weder tragen noch abwerfen
kann. . . . . Das Unmögliche wird von ihm gefordert,
nicht das Menschen Unmögliche, nein, das ihm Unmögliche!' [63]

Sollte die Verwandschaft der Idee nun Goethe nicht eine
Verwandschaft der Form suggeriert haben? Die Stelle im
'Wilhelm Meister', in der der Unterschied von Roman und
Drama diskutiert wird, passt auf den Werther fast so gut
wie auf den Hamlet: 'Der Unterschied beider Dichtungs-
arten [i. e. Roman und Drama] liegt nicht bloss in der
äussern Form, nicht darin, dass die Personen in dem einen
sprechen und dass in dem andern gewöhnlich von ihnen
erzählt wird. Leider viele Dramen sind nur dialogierte Ro-
mane, und es wäre nicht unmöglich, ein Drama in Briefen zu
schreiben.

'Im Roman sollen vorzüglich Gesinnungen und Begebenheiten vorgestellt werden; im Drama Charaktere und Taten.
—Das Drama soll eilen und der Charakter der Hauptfigur
muss sich nach dem Ende drängen und nur aufgehalten
werden. Der Romanheld muss leiden, wenigstens nicht im
hohen Grade wirkend sein; von dem dramatischen verlangt
man Wirkung und Tat.—Im Drama modelt der Held nichts
nach sich, alles widersteht ihm und er räumt und rückt die
Hindernisse aus dem Wege oder unterliegt ihnen. . . . .
dass hingegen das Schicksal, das die Menschen, ohne ihr Zutun, durch unzusammenhängende äussere Umstände zu einer
unvorgesehenen Katastrophe hindrängt, nur im Drama statt-

Wünsche zu umfassen—und ihr geliebter verlässt sie—u. s. w.' Und
über Ophelia in 'Wilhelm Meisters Theatralische Sendung' (Buch VI
Cap. 9) 'Reife süsse Sinnlichkeit! Ihre Neigung zu dem Prinzen,
auf dessen Hand sie Anspruch machen darf, ist so geradehin sich
selbst überlassen, dass Vater und Bruder beide fürchten, warnen. Der
Wohlstand wie der leichte Flor auf ihrem Busen kann die Bewegung
ihres Herzens nicht verbergen und wird vielmehr selbst ihr Verräther.
Ihre Einbildungskraft ist angesteckt, in stiller Bescheidenheit athmet
sie Verlangen, Liebe, und wenn die bequeme Göttin Gelegenheit das
Bäumchen schüttelt, so fällt die Frucht.'

[63] Wilhelm Meisters Theatralische Sendung, Buch VI Cap 8.

habe; dass der Zufall wohl pathetische, niemals aber tragische Situationen hervorbringen dürfe; das Schicksal hingegen müsse immer fürchterlich sein und werde im höchsten Sinne tragisch, wenn es schuldige und unschuldige, von einander unabhängige Taten in eine unglückliche Verknüpfung bringt.

'Diese Betrachtungen führten wieder auf den wunderlichen Hamlet und auf die Eigenheiten dieses Stücks. Der Held, sagte man, hat eigentlich auch nur Gesinnungen; es sind nur Begebenheiten, die zu ihm stossen, und deswegen hat das Stück etwas von dem Gedehnten des Romans: weil aber das Schicksal den Plan gezeichnet hat, weil das Stück von einer fürchterlichen Tat ausgeht und der Held immer vorwärts zu einer fürchterlichen Tat gedrängt wird, so ist es im höchsten Sinne tragisch und leidet keinen andern als tragischen Ausgang.'[64]

Werther hat etwas von dem Gedrängten des Dramas[65] und es ist wahrscheinlich, dass Goethe bei dem 'Drama in Briefen' wohl an seinen Roman dachte. Die eigentliche dramatische Form, wenn er sie überhaupt für den Werther in Erwägung gezogen hat, wird er bald aufgegeben haben. Sie passt für den idyllisch contemplativen Stoff nicht in ihrer völligen Reinheit. So giebt denn der Besuch Sophie von La Roche's von Mitte bis Ende Januar und Diskussionen mit ihr über 'Rosaliens Briefe' seinem Rad Schwung, die Form ist gefunden; was er darüber in Bezug auf 'Rosalie' im Briefe von Mitte Februar [66] sagt, führt er jetzt selber im Werther aus. Dramatisch ist das Werk geblieben in der Führung der Handlung, in der straffen immer nach Anfang und Ende deutenden Composition und in der Darstellung, indem wir gleichsam

[64] Wilhelm Meisters Lehrjahre, Buch V Cap. 7. Die Darstellung der Entstehung der Form des Werther, die Goethe in 'Dichtung und Wahrheit' (B. III Cap. 13 Jubiläumsausg. p. 155 ff.) giebt, ist sehr bestrickend, wohl aber mehr Dichtung als Wahrheit. Die Briefe hätten auf diese Weise nie ihre äusserst kunstvollen Wechselbeziehungen erhalten können. Passend ist der Absatz 'Wie nahe ein solches Gespräch im Geiste. . . . .' Vergleiche auch in Goethes 'Winckelmann'; 'Winckelmanns Briefe an Berendis'. (Jubiläumsausg. B. 34 p. 5.)

[65] Siehe auch Wolf Dohrn 'Die künstlerische Darstellung als Problem der Aesthetik. Hamb. u. Leip. 1907.

[66] D. j. G. IV, 8.

den Helden im beständigem Monologe vor uns sich mit *dem*
auseinandersetzen sehn, was ihm zustösst; ja selbst wo der
epische Bericht eintritt, wird er möglichst dramatisch gestaltet,
wie wir noch weiter unten ausführen wollen.

Die Teilung des Werkes in zwei Hälften ist nicht eigentlich
von der Handlung bedingt; sie tritt da ein, wo Goethes
Wetzlarer Erlebnisse und stärkerer biographischer Anteil
aufhören. Eine Dreiteilung wäre dem Sinne nach logischer,
indem die Zeit der vita activa ein unlyrisches Intermezzo
bildet. Wir könnten uns die zwei Schnitte auch so denken,
dass wirklich drei Akte eines Dramas entstehen: Der erste
Akt würde sich bis zur Mahnung des Freundes erstrecken. Albert ist angekommen, das resolute 'ich werde gehen' ist wieder
wankend geworden, und wir lassen nach dem Fallen des Vor-
hangs das 'wenn ich nur wüsste wohin? ich ginge wohl' in
uns nachklingen. Was wird er tun? In der zweiten Bearbeitung ist dieser Schnitt durch den Hinweis auf Werthers
Tagebuch verstärkt: Er blickt zurück und sieht wie er 'so
wissentlich in das alles, Schritt vor Schritt, hineingegangen'
ist. Der Höhepunkt des Aktes wäre dann die Ballscene.
Der zweite Akt, mit der Trennung als Klimax, geht bis zum
Ende der vita activa und Rückkehr zu Lotte. Und wieder
ist er durch einen Zusatz in der zweiten Bearbeitung stärker
abgeschlossen: 'Ja wohl bin ich nur ein Wandrer, ein Waller
auf der Erde! Seid ihr denn mehr?' Von da geht es ab-
wärts dem Ende zu im dritten Akte, nicht ohne auch den
dritten noch einmal leise zu halbieren mit dem 'Mir wäre besser, ich ginge' des Briefes vom 12. Dezember. Zählen wir die
Seiten der ersten Ausgabe, so finden wir in der Tat drei
ziemlich gleiche Stücke: 76, 67, 79 mit der Unterteilung:
45 + 31, 34 + 33, 31 + 48, Anfang und Ende also etwas
überwiegend.

Innerhalb der Akte bewegt sich die Handlung spiralen-
förmig, jede Seite von Werthers Wesen wird wieder und
wieder und jedesmal voller beleuchtet. 'Der Altar muss erst
gebaut, geziert und geweiht sein eh die Reliquien hineinver-
wahrt werden, und ich wünschte die ganze Stelle erst weiter
hinten, wenn der Charakter und der Sinn Rosaliens sich mehr
entfaltet haben, eingepflanzt zu sehn, wie ich denn auch mit

der süssen Melankolie von verirrter Empfindung die den ersten
Brief füllt, das Ganze gewürzt sehn möcht, und Sie bitte—
die ersten Briefe mit ganz simplem Detail wo Gefühl und
Geist nur durchscheint zu eröffnen.' So lauten die Rat-
schläge an Sophie von La Roche, die zur Richtschnur für
Werther geworden sind.

Der erste Brief zeigt uns einen jungen Menschen, dessen
Herz frei ist, dessen Seele, zur Melankolie neigend, mehr in
der Vergangenheit als Gegenwart lebt, der sein Streben 'nach
Wahrheit und moralischer Güte' dadurch zeigt, dass er den
Menschen gerecht zu werden trachtet (die Tante im Brief
von 4. Mai). Sein Verhältnis zur Natur tritt stark hervor
und wird charakterisiert durch seine Stellung zum englischen
Park. Dann gleich ein vollerer Akkord: Natur und philosophische Contemplation, Unfähigkeit des kräftigen künstlerischen 'Dreinpackens', ein idyllischer Nachklang in der Beschreibung des Brunnens. Bücher werden zurückgewiesen,
sein Herz braucht Ruhe, seine süsse Melancholie geht leicht
in verderbliche Leidenschaft über, und er ist nicht gewohnt,
seinem Herzen etwas zu versagen. Nun folgt eine Orien-
tierung gegen die Menschen nach oben und unten: nüchterne
Pedanten sowie verzerrte Originale sind ihm verhasst, seine
Sehnsucht geht nach den 'eingeschränkten Menschen', den
naiven, unbewussten. Aber er kann sich mit ihnen doch nur
'vergessen', er ist einsam, erst in der Bespiegelung mit einem
congenialen Geschöpfe fühlt er sich selbst. Erwähnung
Lottens!

22. May: Das Thema der Einschränkung wird aufgenommen
und ausgeführt, tätige und forschende Kräfte sind eingeschränkt; die ersteren richten sich nur noch auf 'die Befriedigung von Bedürfnissen, die wieder keinen Zweck haben
als unsere arme Existenz zu verlängern'; ein Vernachlässigen
des Gebrauchs der forschenden Kräft bedeutet 'nur träum-
ende Resignation.' So wendet er sich von der Wirklichkeit
zum Schaffen einer Welt in der eignen Seele, aber weder klar
spekulativ noch tätig künstlerisch, nur träumend gefühls-
mässig. Die Beschränkung der tätigen Kräfte wird illustriert
durch die Menschen, die durch das Zuckerbrot von Orden
und Titeln regiert werden, die der forschenden durch Ge-

lehrte und Philosophen, die ihren Lumpenbeschäftigungen prächtige Titel geben. Alles weist den Menschen in sich zurück.

So ergiebt sich Werther der freiwilligen Einschränkung eines idyllischen Lebens. Die Stellungnahme des Genies gegen Regeln und Convention in Liebe und Kunst deutet vor auf Lotte, Albert und die vita activa (26 May). Die Episode von der Bauernfrau betont von neuem das Glück der Einschränkung ('der Anblick eines solchen Geschöpfs, das in der glückichen Gelassenheit so den engen Kreis seines Daseyns ausgeht—'). Auch das ist eine Vordeutung auf den höheren Typus Lottes. Hier folgt dann in der zweiten Bearbeitung die Bauernbursch-episode, die auf die Liebe vorbereitet mit den Worten: 'ich, wie selbst davon entzündet, lechze und schmachte.'

Der Brief vom 16. Juni ist ganz dramatisch, ganz Vergangenheit in gegenwärtige Wirkung aufgelöst. Lotte stellt den Typus der bewussten Einschränkung dar, der Werther sofort anziehen *muss*. Eine böse Stimmung kann bei ihr nicht aufkommen, denn bei ihr ist die Kunst, wenn auch noch so primitiv, ein Schutz gegen das Leben. Naiv und unbewusst geht sie ganz im Tanze auf, versichert freimütig, 'dass sie herzlich gerne deutsch tanze' (wozu damals noch Mut gehörte[67]), während Werther nicht umhin kann zu bemerken, dass ein Mädchen, das er liebte, 'nie mit einem andern walzen sollte, als mit ihm.' Auch sie hat Sinn für die Erhabenheit der Natur und borgt sich den künstlerischen Ausdruck dafür von Klopstock. Albert, zweimal erwähnt, wird dennoch nicht eigentlich eine Realität für Werther. 'Die ganze Welt verliert sich um mich her', dieser doppeldeutige Ausdruck markiert den ersten Einschnitt.

Der Brief vom 21. Junius nimmt das Thema der Einschränkung vom neuem auf mit bewusster Anwendung auf Werther selbst, der sich als sentimentalische Natur charakterisiert (''Wenn das Dort nun Hier wird, ist alles vor wie nach, und wir stehen in unserer Armuth, in unserer Eingeschränktheit, und unsere Seele lechzt nach entschlüpftem Labsale''). Neue freiwillige Einschränkung in Nachahmung

[67] Jubiläumsausgabe 16. 386.

primitiver Naturen, Aufblick zur Unbegrenztheit der Bestimmbarkeit des Kindes, Einleben in Lottes Familie. Die Nussbaumepisode mit der Eifersucht des Herrn Schmidt deutet auf Albert vor, von dem Werther rühmt dass er 'wenig üble Laune' hat; Werther's Betragen zeigt seine ungeheure Erregbarkeit,[68] ebenso der Brief vom 6. Juli mit dem resignierten Ausklang, der zu der frohen Stimmung, die vorausgeht, in scharfen Kontrast steht. Das Wachsen der Leidenschaft, das bis jezt nur angedeutet ist, findet starken Ausdruck im Briefe vom 8. Juni und erfährt von nun an eine ängstliche Steigerung. Vorboten des Unglücks in seiner Hoffnung auf Gegenliebe, die durch die Erwähnung des Bräutigams in uns gleich zu nichte werden. Ein leises Hineinspielen physicher Anziehung am 16. Juli. Der Gedanke an Selbstmord ('zur Zeit, wo ich mir eine Kugel vor'n Kopf schiessen möchte,') ist vorbereitet durch Äusserungen unter dem 22. Mai und 1. Juli ('um deinetwillen muss ich leben') sowie die Idee des Gehens sich von 'Eure Idee—dass ich mit dem Gesandten nach—gehen soll' (20. Juli) steigert über 'ich werde gehen' (30. Juli), 'ich ginge wohl' (8. Aug.) 'ich muss fort' (3. Sept.) zu 'Ich gehe—Wir sehen uns wieder.' (10. Sept.) Der Gedanke an die vita activa, hier noch nicht der Seine, wird erst am 22. August von ihm ernstlich erwogen. Indessen nimmt die alles verschlingende Leidenschaft stetig zu trotz Alberts Ankunft.

Der zweite Akt mit dem Brief vom 12. August nimmt die Idee des Entweder Oder vom 8. August unmittelbar auf: 'durchstehlen' kann er sich nur mit dem Selbstmord, und die Diskussion [69] arbeitet mit den gleichen Mitteln der Illus-

---

[68] Interessant ist hier, wie offenbar die Gegenwart die Vergangheit (oder vice versa) beeinflusst. Die Kranke der Erinnerung ist jedenfalls Urania von Lila gepflegt; von diesem Bilde übertragen sich nun Züge auf Lotte.

[69] Die Diskussion, zwar auch vielleicht Goethes eignem Leben angehörend, mag zurückgehn auf Kestners: 'Mendelsohns Phädon war seine liebste Lectüre; in der Materie vom Selbstmorde war er aber immer mit ihm unzufrieden; wobey zu bemerken ist, dass er desselben auch bey der Gewissheit von der Unsterblichkeit der Seele, die er glaubte, für erlaubt hielt. . . . . Als neulich das Gerücht von Goué sich verbreitete, glaubte er diesen zwar nicht zum Selbstmorde fähig, stritt

trierung psychicher durch physischer Vorgänge. Im Briefe
vom 10. August deutet das Symbol der fortgeworfenen Blumen zurück auf das Degenabnehmen des 13. Juli; er ist jetzt
'all seiner Ehren und Würden entsetzt,' Albert wird ein Amt
erhalten: das bedeutet, er wird heiraten können. Die erste
Verstimmung zwischen den beiden Männern lässt uns einen
spätern Konflikt fürchten. Werther selbst formuliert klar
das Problem in dem Satze: 'Sieh den Menschen an in seiner
Eingeschränktheit, wie Eindrükke auf ihn würken, Ideen
sich bey ihm fest sezzen, bis endlich eine wachsende Leidenschaft ihn aller ruhigen Sinneskraft beraubt, und ihn zu
Grunde richtet!' Nun zeigt der 18. Juli deutlich, wie er sich
überwachsen hat, die Aussichtslosigkeit der Zukunft wird ihm
klar, die Kunst ist ihm seit der Entfernung von der Natur
nichts mehr, die Hoffnung auf vita activa wird rege ('Oft
beneid ich Alberten'), aber auch Zweifel, ob es nicht vielleicht
nur 'das Sehnen in ihm nach Veränderung des Zustands,
eine innre unbehagliche Ungeduld' ist. Ein Aufleuchten im
Geburtstagsbrief, dann aber überwältigt ein Umherirren in
der Natur und im Mondschein[70] und der verzweifelte Ausruf:
'Ich seh all dieses Elends kein Ende als das Grab.' Die Ab-
schiedscene mit der wundervollen symbolischen Geste des
Schlusses lässt nicht eigentlich eine Hoffnung in uns aufkommen, dass dies Aufraffen Werthers ihn retten wird. Trotzdem wird eine gewisse Erwartung rege, ob er imstande sein
wird, das 'Oder' durchzuführen.

Die vita activa beginnt nun in ähnlicher Weise wie der
erste Teil; die Menschen und die Atmosphäre werden gegeben, mit denen er kontrastiert wird: der Gesandte, das

---

aber in Thesi eifrig für diesen, wie mir Kiehmannsegge und viele, die
um ihn gewesen, versichert haben. GW p. 48.

[70] 'Er entzog sich allezeit der menschlichen Gesellschaft und den
übrigen Zeitvertreiben und Zerstreuungen, liebte einsame Spaziergänge
im Mondenscheine, gieng oft viele Meilen weit und hing da seinem
Verdruss und seiner Liebe ohne Hoffnung nach. Jedes ist schon im
Stande die erfolgte Wirkung hervorzubringen. Er hatte sich einst
in einem Walde verirrt, fand endlich noch Bauern, die ihn zurecht
wiesen, und kam um 2 Uhr zu Haus.' Kestner über Jerusalem GW
p. 48.

'Volk' mit dem glänzenden Elend und der Rangsucht[71] auf
der einen Seite, der Graf, den er achtet, auf der andern;
alles indessen weniger plastisch, weil ihm diese Welt selbst
völlig unreal ist. 'Selbstvertrauen und Genügsamkeit' wünscht
er sich und definiert den Vorstellungsprozess des Sentimentalischen Menschen gleich im ersten Briefe:

'Unsere Einbildungskraft, durch ihre Natur gedrungen
sich zu erheben, durch die phantastische Bilder der Dichtkunst
genährt, bildet sich eine Reihe Wesen hinauf, wo wir das
unterste sind, und alles ausser uns herrlicher erscheint, jeder
andre vollkommer ist. Und das geht ganz natürlich zu: Wir
fühlen so oft, dass uns manches mangelt, und eben was uns
fehlt, scheint uns oft ein anderer zu besizzen, dem wir denn
auch alles dazu geben was wir haben, und noch eine gewisse
idealische Behaglichkeit dazu, und so ist der Glükliche vollkommen fertig, das Geschöpf unserer selbst.' Die Berührung
mit der Wirklichkeit tut ihm in der Tat gut, indem sie sein
Selbstvertrauen hebt, weil ein Vergleich mit der Umgebung
vorteilhaft für ihn selbst ausfüllt. Aber er gesteht ihr im
Grunde keine 'raison d'être' zu so kann der Zusammenstoss
nicht ausbleiben: der Gesandte verklagt ihn bei Hofe,[72] der
Minister muss ihm einen Verweis erteilen, obwohl er ihn

---

[71] im Briefe vom 8. Jan. 'Vorige Woche gabs bey der Schlittenfahrt
Händel, und der ganze Spass wurde verdorben,' geht vielleicht auf
ein wirkliches Ereignis zurück. Gloël (Goethes Wetzlarer Zeit, Berlin 1911 p. 223) führt einen Brief von J. H. Günther vom 1 Januar
1779 an, der ähnliches berichtet: 'Oft stellte er [Graf v. Bassenheim]
allgemeine Schlittenfahrten an, aber auch da gab's gewöhnlich Händel.'
Günther mag indessen hier unter dem Einfluss Werthers stehen wie
auch in andern Briefen. Siehe Gloël p. 55.

[72] 'Jerusalem ist die ganze Zeit seines hiesigen Aufenthalts miss-
vergnügt gewesen, es sey nun überhaupt wegen der Stelle, die er hier be-
kleidete, und dass ihm gleich Anfangs (bey Graf Bassenheim) der
Zutritt in den grossen Gesellschaften auf eine unangenehme Art versagt
worden, oder insbesondere wegen des Braunschweigischen Gesandten,
mit dem er bald nach seiner Ankunft kundbar heftige Streitigkeiten
hatte, die ihm Verweise vom Hofe zuzogen. . . . . sein hiesiger Aufenthalt war ihm verhasst. . . . . GW p. 47.

schätzt.[73] Die einzige Seele, die ihn versteht [74] (und durch
die technisch Fühlung mit Lotte erhalten wird) ist durch
die verhassten Grenzen der Konvention von ihm getrennt.
Die Scene beim Grafen beendet seine Laufbahn, der Eindruck
seiner Unruhe und Rastlosigkeit ist durch das Wandern verstärkt und die Wallfahrt dient der Vertiefung der Idee: 'mit
wie viel fehlgeschlagenen Hoffnungen, mit wie viel zerstörten
Planen' er aus der Welt zurückkommt, in die er sich einst
in glüklicher Unwissenheit hinausgesehnt hat. Das Herz bekommt wieder seinen Willen (Brief vom 18. Juni), das
'Entweder' ist unmöglich, das 'Oder' ist missglückt.

Nun setzt die Enttäuschung auch in Lottes Nähe ein,
Schlag auf Schlag.[75] Seine letzte Hoffnung klammert sich
an den Gedanken, dass Albert Lotte nicht glücklich machen
kann. Von aussen werfen die Geschicke andrer (Bauernfrau,
Nussbäume) trübe Schatten in sein Herz, alles ist anders, alles
vergeht. Seinen Anzug muss er ablegen,[76] Ossian (erwähnt
beim ersten Aufflammen der Leidenschaft, 10. Juli) ersetzt
Homer; der Gedanke an das Ende nimmt überhand; die

[73] 'Der Gesandte, deucht mich, sucht auch die Aufmerksamkeit
ganz von sich, auf diese Liebesbegebenheit zu lenken, da der Verdruss
von ihm wohl zugleich Jerusalem determiniert hat; zumal da der Gesandte verschiedentlich auf die Abberufung des Jerusalem angetragen,
und ihm noch kürzlich starke reprochen vom Hofe verursacht haben
soll. Hingegen hat der Erbprinz von Braunschweig, der ihm gewogen
gewesen, vor kurzem geschrieben, dass er sich hier noch ein wenig
gedulden mögte, und wenn er Geld bedürfe, es ihm nur schreiben
sollte, ohne sich an seinen Vater, den Herzog, zu wenden.' GW p.
53. Dies letztere im Werther 19. April: 'Der Erbprinz hat mir zum
Abschiede fünf und zwanzig Dukaten geschickt, mit einem Wort, das
mich bis zu Thränen gerührt hat.'

[74] Fräulein B. ist Lila. Siehe Erich Schmidt, a. a. O.

[75] Der Brief von 20. Febr., dem ein erster Brief an Lotte vom 20.
Jan. vorausgeht, benutzt Züge und Ausdrücke aus Goethes Briefe vom
ca. 6. April 1773, aber auch wieder nur Züge. Das 'Es geht mir ein
Schauder durch den ganzen Körper, Wilhelm, wenn Albert sie um den
schlanken Leib fasst,' gegen den früheren 'Respekt' Kestner-Alberts
kontrastiert, mag auf die 'manières' (Merck 14 Febr. 74, D. j. G. IV
p. 76) des Brentano-Albert zurückdeuten.

[76] Nach Kestner's Bericht: "Er war in völliger Kleidung, gestiefelt,
im blauen Rock mit gelber Weste."

Natur ist ihm nur noch ein lackiertes Bildchen.[77] Die Briefe werden hastig und zerfliessend, so mutet in der lyrisch-dramatischen Umgebung uns die Episode des Irrsinnigen, wie Herrmann bemerkt, fast stilwidrig episch an.[78] Im Briefe vom 6. Dezember steigert sich die Sprache bis zu latentem freien Verse und Reim.

> Was ist der Mensch? der gepriesene Halbgott?
> . . . . .
> Und wenn er in Freude sich *aufschwingt*
> oder im *Leiden versinkt,*
> wird er nicht in *beyden*
> eben da *aufgehalten,*
> eben da wieder
> zu dem stumpfen *kalten*
> Bewusstseyn zurückgebracht
> . . . . .

Der Bericht Kestners, dessen Gebrauch wir schon in den Anmerkungen verfolgt haben, wird von nun an ausgiebiger benutzt. Es ist als ob er in kleine Streifen geschnitten und hier und da eingefügt wäre, aber so, dass *ein* Satz, *eine* Idee, *eine* Situation immer verdoppelt oder verdreifacht auftaucht, spiralisch, wie wir es bisher schon beobachtet haben, nur das Ende bleibt zusammen. Noch vor dem Herausgeberberichte ist im Briefe vom 8. Dez. (12. Dec. der zweiten Bearbeitung) Werthers: 'Ach mit offnen Armen stand ich gegen den

---

[77] 3. Nov. entsprechend den Naturbriefen 10. Mai, 18. August. Der Briefe vom 15. November mit seiner mehr der monotheistischen Gottesanschauung sich nähernden Stimmung ist meiner Meinung nach einer der uneingeschmolzenen Lebensreste. Der Brief an Lavater und Pfenninger vom 26. April 1774, der starke Anklänge aufweist, spricht dafür. Goethe weist Lavaters Ansicht, dass Bibel und Natur Zeugnisse für das Dasein Gottes seien, zurück mit dem: 'Nur so schätz, lieb, bet ich Zeugnisse an, die mir darlegen, wie tausende oder einer vor mir eben das gefühlt haben, das mich kräftiget und stärket.' Und der Wertherbrief wehrt Aussprüchen Lavaters, wie: "Entweder Atheist oder Christ", "ich habe keinen Gott als Jesus Christus";—"Sein Vater! Grosser Gedanke—ist *mir* nur in ihm; ist mir in allem—wäre mir nirgends, wär' er mir nicht in ihm". (1. Mai 1774): Deshalb verzichtet Goethe auf 'eine reine Experimental Psychologie seines Innersten' und verweist Pfenninger auf die 'Erläuterung in dem Mspt.' das er ihnen bald schicke.

[78] Jubiläumsausgabe 16. XVIII.

Abgrund, —' vielleicht angeregt durch Kestners: 'Man hat
ihn auch um diese Zeit eine ganze Weile am Fluss stehen
sehen, in einer Stellung, als wenn er sich hineinstürzen wolle'.
Anderseits wird Ossians 'seebespülter Felsen' hier sowie
später, wo man Werthers Hut 'auf einem Felsen, der an dem
Abhange des Hügels ins Thal sieht' findet, zur Scenerie bei-
getragen haben.

In Kestners Bericht sind die Ereignisse auf vier Tage verteilt: Am Dienstag Todesstimmung; am Mittwoch das Essen
mit Herd, der Besuch bei Frau Herd und die Liebesscene, der
Gang nach Garbenheim und unterdessen Herds Heimkehr
und Argwohn,[79] das Verlangen der Frau, Jerusalem das Haus
zu verbieten; am Donnerstag der Billetwechsel, die Bitte um
die Pistolen, Kramen in Papieren und Bezahlen von Schulden,
der italienische Sprachmeister, Ausgang auf die starke Weide
und an den Fluss, Vorbereitungen, Briefe an die Seinen und
an Herds; nach Mitternacht, also Freitag früh, der Schuss,
am Morgen die Entdeckung, am Abend das Begräbnis.

In Werther wird dasselbe auf Sonntag, Montag, Dienstag
und Mittwoch verteilt. Voraus geht eine knappe Konstatierung der Lage: 'Werthers Leidenschaft hatte den Frieden
zwischen Alberten und seiner Frau allmählig untergraben';
das entspricht dem Brief an Herds von Donnerstag;—'dass
er die Ruhe und das Glück seiner Ehe gestört und unter
diesem theuren Paar Uneinigkeit gestiftet'. Das Misstrauen
Alberts findet sich vorgebildet bei Herds Heimkehr am Mittwoch, doch dürfen wir hier natürlich auch Goethes Erfahrungen im Hause Brentano nicht vergessen. Das Einschränken
des Verkehrs resp. Aufgeben wird von *Frau* Herd gefordert.

Werthers Selbstmordidee ist natürlich bei Jerusalem als
treibende Kraft vorhanden und auch bei ihm ist es 'keine
übereilte, rasche That'. In der Rekapitulation zählt der Her-
ausgeber als Motive auf: 'Den *Verdruss* bei der Gesandt-
schaft (dasselbe Wort bei Jerusalem), gekränkte Ehre, wunderbare Empfind- und Denkensart, endlose Leidenschaft,
Verlöschen der stetigen Kraft, Einsamkeit und Umgang mit
Lotte. Dann am Sonntag ein Brief an Wilhelm und nun der

---

[79] Wir können wohl annehmen, dass Goethe auch den 'Nachtrag'
Kestners (GW p. 55/6) wenigstens dem Inhalte nach gekannt hat.

Besuch bei Lotte, die ihn bittet nicht vor Donnerstag wieder-
zukommen.[80] Diesen Abend geht er nicht aus, wie Jerusalem;
aber hier wie da der Bediente, der ihm die Stiefel ausziehn
will (bei Jerusalem allerdings dies erst am nächsten Tage).
Der Briefwechsel mit Herd fällt ganz fort, statt dessen beginnt Werther den Abschiedsbrief an Lotte, der am nächsten
Morgen (Montag) und Abend, Dienstag Morgen, Abend und
Nacht eingerückt wird. In dem Auftrage an den Bedienten
handelt es sich um dieselben Sachen: Fertigmachen zur
Reise, Schulden bezahlen, nur dass Goethe sich nicht entgehen
lässt, einen Beweis für Werthers Streben, 'nach moralischer
Güte' einzufügen durch den Befehl: 'einigen Armen, denen
er wöchentlich etwas zu geben gewohnt war, ihr Zugeteiltes
auf zwey Monathe voraus zu bezahlen.'' Werther wie Jerusalem essen zu Hause. Der Besuch beim Amtmann gehört
nur Goethe, ebenso der Brief an Lotte; hier dann erst der
Besuch bei Lotte, der zur Liebesscene führt, die bei Jerusalem
am Tage vorher stattgefunden hatte: 'Jerusalem habe sich
vor ihr auf die Knie geworfen und ihr eine förmliche Liebes-
erklärung thun wollen. Sie sey natürlicher Weise darüber
aufgebracht worden und hätte ihm viele Vorwürfe gemacht.' Das Kanapee ist wohl das Lottens, auf dem Goethe
einst hängerliche und hängenswerte Gedanken hatte. Der
Ausgang aus dem Stadtthor nach dem Felsen entspricht
Jerusalems Gang durchs Silbertor auf die Starke Weide, jener
verliert seinen Hut, dieser hat ihn 'tief in die Augen gedrückt.'

Dies waren die Vorgänge am Montag. Von dem entsprechenden Mittwoch im Kestnerbericht ist also die Liebesscene
herübergenommen, alles übrige ist vom letzten, dem Donners-
tage geborgt und wird nun im Werther am Dienstag wiederholt und variiert. Zuerst wird das Billet an Kestner fast
wortgetreu eingerückt, nachdem ein neuer Eintrag in Lottes
Brief gemacht ist, der mit dem Gedanken an ein Wiedersehn
droben endet. Das ist natürlich ein Zurückgehen auf den
Schluss des ersten Teils, mag aber zugleich angeregt sein

[80] 'Nein, Lotte, ich werde Sie nicht wieder sehn!': 'Liebe Frau Se-
cretairin, diess ist der letzte Kaffee, den ich mit Ihnen trinke.' GW p.
49.

durch Jerusalems: 'In der Ewigkeit aber hoffe er ihr einen
Kuss geben zu dürfen' und 'In jenem Leben sehen wir uns
wieder,' ehe er sich erschiesst. Nachgeholt wird die Erzählung von Lottes Befinden, die Heimkehr Alberts und ihr
und Lottes Verhalten: —'denn indem sie zitterte, er würde
das verweinte überwachte ihrer Augen und ihrer Gestalt
entdekken, ward sie noch verwirrter, bewillkommte ihn mit
einer heftigen Umarmung, die mehr Bestürzung und Reue,
als eine auffahrende Freude ausdrükte, und eben dadurch
machte sie die Aufmerksamkeit Albertens rege, der, nachdem
er einige Briefe und Pakets erbrochen, sie ganz trokken fragte,
ob sonst nichts vorgefallen, ob niemand dagewesen wäre.'
Das Hintenherum Alberts findet man bei Herd vorgebildet:
'Nachdem der Mann wieder kömmt, bemerckt er an seiner
Frau eine ausserordentliche Ernsthaftigkeit und bey Jerusalem eine Stille, welche beyde ihm sonderbar und bedencklich
geschienen, zumal da er sie nach seiner Zurückkunft so sehr
verändert findet. Jerusalem geht weg. Secret. H. . .macht
über obiges seine Betrachtungen; er fasst Argwohn, ob etwa in
seiner Abwesenheit etwas ihm nachteiliges vorgegangen sein
möchte, denn er ist sehr argwöhnisch und eyfersüchtig. Er
stellt sich jedoch ruhig und lustig; und will seine Frau auf
die Probe stellen. Er sagt—' (GW p. 55.)

Der Moment, wo der Knabe erscheint und die Pistolen holt,
der mit der grössten Meisterschaft von Goethe behandelt ist,
hat natürlich kein Vorbild; trozdem mag jedoch eine Suggestion gegeben sein durch das Benehmen des Italienischen
Sprachmeisters Kielmannsegg gegenüber: 'da er denn von
nichts als von Jerusalem, dessen Unruhe und Unmuth spricht,
*ohne jedoch von seiner Besorgniss zu erwähnen, indem er
geglaubt, man möge ihn deswegen auslachen.*' (GW p. 52.)[81]

Am Nachmittag gehen Jerusalem wie Werther kleine Schulden zu bezahlen, Werther wieder 'vor's Thor' und in den
gräflichen Garten, schweift 'weiter in der Gegend umher'
(mit nochmaliger Benutzung von Jerusalems Gang, 'vor das
Silberthor auf die starke Weide etc.') Dann der Brief an

---

[81] Diese Idee kommt allerdings erst eigentlich in der Bearbeitung
hinein, besonders durch die Stelle, die mit 'Noch ein sonderbarer Umstand kam dazu . . . . .' beginnt. Jubiläumsausgabe 16 p. 139.

Wilhelm und die Mutter und an Albert, die in der Vorlage
vor dem Schuss stehen. Hier 'in dem zweyten hat er H. . . . .
um Verzeihung gebeten, dass er die Ruhe und das Glück seiner
Ehe gestört, und unter diesem theuren Paar Uneinigkeit
gestiftet.' Dort: 'Ich habe dir übel gelohnt, Albert, und du
vergiebst mir. Ich habe den Frieden deines Hauses gestört,
ich habe Misstrauen zwischen euch gebracht.' Dann 'kramt'
Werther 'in seinen Papieren' wie Jerusalem am Nachmittag,
zereisst vieles, wie jener vor dem Schreiben der Briefe, lässt
im Ofen noch etwas nachlegen und sich einen Schoppen Wein
geben. Das, sowie die Bemerkung, dass der Diener sich mit
den Kleidern niedergelegt, weil um 6 Uhr die Abreise statt-
finden soll, ist beiden Berichten gemeinsam.

Und nun wird das Ende wieder ganz dramatisch gestaltet.
Der letzte Eintrag am Briefe ist ein Monolog, der die scen-
ischen Bemerkungen zum Teil einschliesst ('Ich trete ans
Fenster, meine Beste, und seh und sehe noch durch die stürm-
enden vorüberfliegenden Wolken einzelne Sterne des ewigen
Himmels!'). Und wie vermag uns der letzte Satz in die volle
Illusion des Theaters zu versetzen! 'Sie sind geladen—es
schlägt zwölfe! So sey's denn-Lotte! Lotte leb wohl! Leb
wohl!' Mit den Augen zwinkernd erwarten wir den Schuss
und glauben fast eine akustische Empfindung zu haben, so
dass die sachliche Bemerkung, die folgt, erlösend wirkt.
Die Überleitung, die Kestner giebt, dass man die Kugel nirgends finde, ist unbrauchbar, weil den dramatischen Gang
unterbrechend; 'der Franciskaner Pater Guardian' wird
zum einfachen Nachbar, der Nebensatz mit dem Perfectum
zum Hauptsatz mit dem Imperfect. Dass der Bediente sowie
die Leute nach hinten hinaus schliefen, ist mit Bedacht von
hier fortgenommen und bereits am Abend vorausgeschickt,
ganz beiläufig.[82] Kestners Vermutung, wie die Tat geschehn
sei, wird übersprungen, und der Bediente erlebt am Morgen

---

[82] Kestner: 'Der Bediente hatte die vorige Nacht wenig geschlafen
und hat sein Zimmer weit hinten hinaus, wie auch die Leute im Haus,
welche unten hinten hinaus schlafen.' Werther: ". . . . und nachdem
er um zehn Uhr im Ofen nachlegen und sich einen Schoppen Wein
geben lassen, schikte er den Bedienten, dessen Kammer wie auch die
Schlafzimmer der Hausleute weit hinten hinaus waren, zu Bette. . . . ."

die ganze Scene. Dass das Licht ausgebrannt war, ist auch
unbrauchbar, weil es eine Beschreibung des Vorgefallenen
ist. 'Er sieht Jerusalem auf der Erde liegen, bemerkt etwas
Nasses und meynt er möge sich übergeben haben; wird aber
die Pistole auf der Erde, und darauf Blut gewahr' wird mit
höchster künstlerischer Ökonomie zusammengezogen in: 'er
findet seinen Herrn an der Erde, die Pistole und Blut.' So
geht sprungweise das Erfassen des Vorgangs im Kopfe des
Dieners vor sich.[83] 'Er ruft: (Mein Gott, Herr Assessor, was
haben Sie angefangen;) er fasst ihn an (=schüttelt ihn),
(er giebt) keine Antwort, er (=und) röchelt nur noch.'
Nun bringt er die Nachricht zu Albert und Lotte, wo er in
Kestners Bericht 'zu Medicis' läuft. Was bei Kestner in-
direkte Erzählung Dr. Helds ist, wird hier zur direkten
Beobachtung des Arztes, auch hier zusammengedrängt. Die
Aufnahme des Tatbestandes, wie er gestorben sein muss, die
Kestner gleich nach dem Schuss giebt wird nun, ebenfalls
knapper, hier eingefügt:

Kestner:	Werther:
Es scheint sitzend in Lehnstuhl vor seinem Schreibtisch geschehen zu seyn. Der Stuhl hinten im Sitz war blutig, auch die Armlehnen. Darauf ist er vom Stuhl heruntergesunken, auf der Erde war noch viel Blut. Er muss sich auf der Erde in seinem Blute gewälzt haben; erst beym Stuhle war eine grosse Stelle von Blut; die Weste vorn ist auch blutig; er scheint auf dem Gesichte gelegen zu haben; dann ist er weiter, um den Stuhl herum, nach dem Fenster hingekommen, wo wieder viel Blut gestanden, und er auf dem Rücken entkräftet gelegen hat. (Er war in völliger Kleidung, gestiefelt, im blauen Rock mit gelber Weste.)	Aus dem Blut auf der Lehne des Sessels konnte man schliessen, er habe sizzend vor dem Schreibtische die That vollbracht. Dann ist er heruntergesunken, hat sich konvulsivisch um den Stuhl herum gewälzt, er lag gegen das Fenster entkräftet auf dem Rükken, war in völliger Kleidung, gestiefelt, im blauen Frack mit gelber Weste.

[83] Ich gebe im folgenden in Klammern die Erweiterungen bei Kestner; wo dieser abweicht, wird das mit (=. . . . .) bezeichnet.

Und weiterhin dann im Werther gleich anschliessend, bei Kestner nach der Konstatierung des Arztes:

Das Gerücht von dieser Begebenheit verbreitete sich schnell; die ganze Stadt war in Schrecken und Aufruhr. Ich hörte es erst um 9 Uhr, meine Pistolen fielen mir ein, und ich weiss nicht, dass ich kurzens so sehr erschrocken bin. Ich zog mich an und gieng hin. Er war auf das Bette gelegt, die Stirne bedeckt, sein Gesicht schon wie eines Todten, er rührte kein Glied mehr, nur die Lunge war noch in Bewegung, und röchelte fürchterlich, bald schwach, bald stärker, man erwartete sein Ende. Von dem Wein hatte er nur ein Glas getrunken. Hin und wieder lagen Bücher und von seinen schriftlichen Aufsätzen. Emilia Galotti lag auf dem Pult am Fenster aufgeschlagen; daneben ein Manuscript ohngefähr fingerdick in Quart, philosophischen Inhalts, der erste Theil oder Brief war überschrieben: *Von der Freiheit*, es war darin von der moralischen Freiheit die Rede . . . . .

Das Haus, die Nachbarschaft, die Stadt kam in Aufruhr.

Albert trat herein. Werthern hatte man auf's Bett gelegt, die Stirne verbunden, sein Gesicht schon wie eines Todten, er rührte kein Glied, die Lunge röchelte noch fürchterlich, bald schwach, bald stärker, man erwartete sein Ende.

Von dem Wein hatte er nur ein Glas getrunken. Emilia Galotti lag auf dem Pulte aufgeschlagen.

Dass die 'Emilia Galotti' zum Werther nicht passt, ist schon oft bemerkt; das 'Manuskript' dagegen hat Goethe verändert schon vor dem letzten Briefe eingefügt: 'Sie enthielten kleine Aufsätze, abgerissene Gedanken, deren ich verschiedene gesehen habe'. Auffallend ist, dass ihm die Diskrepanz des Lessingschen Dramas mit Werthers Denkart entgangen ist, wo er doch im Einklange mit Werthers unsystematischem Geist aus dem Manuskript 'Kleine Aufsätze' und, 'abgerissene Gedanken' macht!

Das Ende muss dann bis auf die Beschreibung von Werthers Beerdigung selbständig ausgeführt werden. Hier wird für 'Abends ¾ 11 Uhr', das einerseits wohl in der dialektischen Verschiedenheit der Berichterstatter bedingte, ander-

seits aber auch suggestivere und wegen der ungenaueren
Zeitangabe poetisch bessere 'Nachts gegen eilfe' eingesetzt.
Die Barbiergesellen werden zu Handwerken, das Kreuz fehlt.

Auf die zweite Bearbeitung des Romans will ich hier nicht
mehr eingehen, sie ist schon wiederholt untersucht [84] und die
Idee derselben, Werthers Tod noch unvermeidlicher erscheinen zu lassen, klar gezeigt. Erwähnen will ich nur noch
eins: durch die Wiederannäherung der Eheleute und Ver-
edlung Alberts ist auch, was der letzte Brief Werthers ('Sie
liebt mich! —Und was ist das, dass Albert dein Mann ist?
—u. s. w.') Peinliches haben könnte, in dem auch die Tragik
in *ihr* Leben hineingespielt, aber künstlerisch nicht weiter verfolgt wird, getilgt. Wir wissen nun, 'dass ihn wohl der leiden-
schaftliche Jüngling, aber doch der Leser nicht verkennt.' [85]
Damit ist die Verstimmung zwischen Albert und Lotte als
vorübergehend gekennzeichnet und der Werther in der That
'einige Stufen höher geschraubt'.

ERNST FEISE.

University of Wisconsin.

---

[84] Jubiläumsausgabe B. 16. p. XXXV. ff.; Fittbogen im Euphorion
XVII p. 556 ff.; Lauterbach in Quellen und Forschungen, Strassburg
1910.

[85] An Kestner, 2. May 1783.

A STUDY IN THE PRINCIPLES OF LINGUISTIC CHANGE [1]

The science of Philology or Linguistics has hitherto been, on the main, historically descriptive. The collection of a large mass of facts and materials in exhaustive detail, is the chief service which it has rendered to modern knowledge. This work had to be done before the vital interpretation of the phenonema of language could be attempted. However, Philology itself was not able to find this interpretation and to proceed from an accumulation of data and facts to the explanation of the vital processes of which they are the product. While the principle of organic evolution was fully recognized and applied in the scientific research of the last half-century, a thorough-going application of it to language was not in an adequate way accomplished by linguistic scholars. The non-performance of this most important task may appear excusable, in view of the comparatively recent discovery and perfection of the method by which alone it could be properly performed. The nature and development of language came to be rightly understood only when Wilhelm Wundt began to include language in his experimental psychophysical research. It would be unfair, therefore, and certainly unprofitable, to dwell at much length on the inability of philologists to deal satisfactorily with this side of their discipline. However, to review briefly the main errors of the earlier theories will enable us to form a better estimate of Wundt's work, and will serve to prepare the way for the particular aspect presented in this study.

What chiefly concerns us here is the question of the causes of linguistic change. The hypothesis by which Philology sought to explain sound change rests on the assumption that there are laws of sound, and that phonetic change proceeds in a regular way by laws inherent in sounds as such. The misconception, implied in this view, is just this, that a sound as such is thought to possess an immanent tendency to undergo change, independently of the fortunes which it has or may

[1] This study is largely based upon vols. I and II of W. Wundt's Völkerpsychologie, dealing with language. To this the reader is referred.

have as a sound element of a word. The sound is thus taken out of those relations with other sounds in which it always occurs; as a matter of fact it has no independent existence at all. To Wundt this notion appears to partake of something like mysticism. At any rate, the unexceptionable phonetic law is the grammarian's or the phonetician's abstraction and construction. The fact that sound-change is dependent on the context of sound, that it is the contact and association of a sound with other sounds which causes its modifications, had not become clearly evident to the philological mind. Furthermore, the inability to think in terms of evolution and of psycho-physical processes, is seen in the untenable general theories by which philologists tried to account for the variation and mutation in language, generally. To quote from Wundt: ''Here we find the assumption still widely current in linguistic science, that every general change in sound or meaning, is to be referred to one, individual deviation. While numerous other variations were lost, *one*, falling happily in with an existing tendency, became usual. This coöperative tendency itself is generally held to be totally independent of the individual origin of the change. It is sometimes ascribed to the interest in the novelty of the thing, but especially to the imitative instinct in human nature. Now, in as much as the original individual departures, especially in the domain of phonetic change, are supposed to be of purely accidental character, and owing to their absolutely incalculable nature, defy every attempt at ascertaining their conditions, this theory of the transition from the occasional to usual phenomena, manifestly evades the question of causation altogether. Or, instead of answering it, it points to the sociological law of imitation, according to which no individual can do anything striking or contrary to custom, without his associates succumbing to the suggestive influence of such an action. Under this theory of imitation, chance is literally made the creator of all social phenomena, and consequently of society itself. Now, to be sure, chance plays an accessory part in many cases, but it hardly ever assumes the principal rôle in the deeper and more incisive general changes of communal life and its products. On the contrary, wherever we are able to investigate the conditions of such changes, though the last and decisive cause be unknown, they are regularly found to be such as could not have started from an individual, or a limited number of individuals, but must depend upon influences which affect all members of a community, or, at least, the majority of them.''

The same failure to see the development of language as a vital thing, genetically, gave rise to theories of a teleological character. Thus, when it was assumed that there is an instinctive tendency toward ease, a desire to facilitate speech by following the line of least resistance, also a more or less conscious tendency to simplify, accompanied by an endeavor to make language uniform. Now, it is true that linguistic development has made articulation and expression simpler and easier, and it is really by this fact alone, that we are justified in regarding the history of language under the form of progressive evolutionary development. It is sentimental fogyism and a curious pessimism to speak of ''laziness'' and ''slovenliness'' as having caused a ''decay'' of words. What is really economy of effort and convenient systemization was, until quite recently, looked upon as a loss and corruption of the fancied greater beauty and virility of the older language. From the tendency toward uniformity, it was thought, arose the use of so-called ''false analogy'' which led to a decay of forms and a blurring of distinctions. This reprehensible drift toward ease and degeneration was, however, fortunately offset by a sort of instinctive purpose to preserve significant distinctions of sound and meaning. One is at a loss to understand why the idea of decadence should have commended itself so insistently to philological speculation. It seems paradoxical to think, that the function of speech is in any sense decadent, when the race is, intellectually, rapidly progressing and in no way decaying.

It is sufficiently clear from this cursory review that such theories are constructed upon wrong foundations. There are the two fatal errors, involving self-contradiction and wholly incompatible with the idea of growth: that language is consciously made, and again that it is a product of accident.

We can now pass on to an outline summary of Wundt's

views touching change in language. He begins by a very sane
caution: ''The question, how a nation in the course of centuries can change the phonology of a word beyond recognition cannot possibly be answered in a thoroughly satisfactory
and exhaustive manner. To do this we should have to account
for the nature and extent of all those changes which have
occurred through inner and outward circumstances in the
entire intellectual and physical nature of the speaking community. We can only say that such changes take place
irresistibly, receiving little attention when they first begin to
appear.''

There are, according to Wundt, three principal causes of
change, working more slowly or rapidly at different times:
(1) The influence of external or natural (physical) conditions. (2) The mixture of races and nations. (3) The
effects of culture and civilization. These factors may co-
operate. The first is naturally very slow. Race mixture is
connected with incisive historical events. It is to the influence
of culture that we must look for the causes of the steady
and slow permutations, which are always and everywhere
going on, even when external conditions may not seem to
change. Of these changes, language is, perhaps, the most
subtle manifestation.

At this point, a fundamental principle of evolution must
be introduced, for which we are indebted to biological research. It is based upon the observation that through the
gradual accumulation of slight changes, great sudden muta-
tions are prepared. Tendencies that were for a long time
more or less latent are apt to be liberated by sudden new influences, so that new varieties arise with surprising rapidity.
This law of mutation teaches us to regard a long period of
apparent stagnation as an interval of rest and incubation,
naturally and necessarily preceding greater advances. Now,
psychically, a significant advance in culture produces a great
mobility of ideas and emotions; there is a new wealth and
greater variety of thought, and such tension and stimulation
of mental life, that greater rapidity and ease of the combinative mental processes is bound to follow. It is hardly necessary to insist, at much length, on this point; it is a self-evident

fact. Now, it is quite certain that at all periods of history, marked by a pronounced cultural advance, language, too, enters into a new phase of development. So the high culture of the nobility in the twelfth century throughout Central Europe, the German Reformation, the Elizabethan period, the renewal of all intellectual and artistic life a hundred years ago in Germany, are epochs of language as well. At every cultural mutation, the language reshapes itself to meet the need of new and better expression, and the result is always greater flexibility, conciseness and vivacity. Wundt says: "On general principles it is not improbable that the rate of speech must keep a fairly even pace with the higher rate of psychological reactions caused among other things by growing culture." Lamprecht's interpretation of historical development, which rests upon the recognition of great psychological differences between the periods of history, places strong emphasis on the much higher nervous sensitiveness of the modern period, especially. We are, therefore, fully justified in concluding that the greater vivacity of thought, and the greater ease of our psychological adjustments, have caused the tempo of speech to become more rapid. This influence of the rate of speech Wundt pronounces "one of the most incisive factors in change, although it has received but little attention from philologists hitherto."

In the psychology of the individual, cerebration and the motor apparatus are so closely connected that the speed of articulation is in exact ratio with the force of stimulation. Slow, halting speech means a slow working of the brain; ready utterance is rapid, unimpeded thinking. Intelligent and imaginative persons are not only, as a rule, fluent speakers, but they are also very apt to have high vocal pitch; for it seems that a faster rate of speech generally produces and requires a higher tone, due to the quicker vibration of the vocal chords and to higher overtones. Strong sound-stress and word accent, too, naturally raise the pitch. Wundt mentions the well-known fact, that not only do we play the masters of classical music faster today, but the orchestral instruments are also keyed to a perceptibly higher pitch than a hundred years ago, and one might add that rapid parts are naturally assigned to the high instruments.

The purpose of this study in psycho-philology is to show that this acceleration in the psychological and mental processes, leading to more rapid articulation, can be set down as the strongest and most fundamental cause of linguistic change. To recognize it as a motive force, must logically imply acknowledging it as the principal psychological ground of change. When we compare modern English with the language of Malory and these again with Old English it is clear at once that the sum and substance of change in word-forms and in the manner of expression is a reduction and shortening. If this is due to the faster rate of speech, the question is, how does acceleration of tempo produce the effect? Wundt shows that it works mainly through sound-contact. The cogent proof of this theory is furnished simply enough by experimental reproduction of the whole process, i. e., most of the effects of sound-contact will occur at once when we accelerate articulation. We will in this way get assimilations of sound both regressive and progressive, which are the chief phenomena of phonetic change. "This evidence is all the more valuable as it extends over all known civilized languages and over the most various periods of linguistic and cultural development." Wundt gives the following examples: When Latin *supmus* passes into summus, sedla=sella; factus=fatto; fluctus=fiotto; habte=hatte; entfinden=empfinden, or progressively vulba=vulva; klimben=klimmen, the connection of these changes with accelerated articulation is proved by the very fact that all these words change very readily from the first to the second form when we articulate faster. All the phenomena of contraction, assimilation, dissimilation, all sound-induction can be readily explained as results of accelerated speech. The tendency of sounds to attract or repel increases with the rate of speech and is now vastly greater than in the slower, majestic pronunciation of the older language, evident from the length and full sound of the older words. Elision, contraction, and discarding of prefixes and suffixes, by which forms are much curtailed, cannot have had any cause other than the greater celerity of articulation. The fact that assimilation and contact-change are in the modern period mainly regressive, again appears as the result of the more rapid flow of speech, attending higher intelligence, causing a forward-bound movement of ideas, which is reflected in the regressive influence of a sound upon the preceding sound, by anticipation. In the slower speech of the older period, as also in the language of children, progressive assimilation is found to predominate.

At all events we must learn to regard every sound and every word as being under the influence of a great variety of assimilating forces. Thus in the series: Dach, Sache, poche, suche, Zeche, Sichel, the *ch* is a different spirant in every case. The organs of articulation are, in every one of these words in a different position when the spirant comes to be sounded, owing to the differing quality of the preceding vowel which is determined by the consonant preceding it as well as by the vowel of the following syllable. (cf. Wundt)

Naturally the variability of sounds is increased by differences in the place of articulation, duration, intensity, and pitch of sound. A clear illustration of the effect of accent-shifting is found in those Franco-English words in which the accent has been thrown back as far as possible, reducing the quantity and quality of all following syllables: ádmirable, éxecrable, ígnominy, ábsolutism.

A few general observations on speech-tempo may be added, in no strict order of arrangement. While in accordance with the law of mutation changes crop out suddenly and grow rapidly, a point of stand-still is naturally reached, even reversions are not excluded. The English of America shows signs of a return from the terseness of English accent to fuller and heavier pronunciation, e. g., librāry, hōtēl, bēfore, milk-mān, etc. The rise of round-about expressions, in place of forgotten concise English idioms is a similar phenomenon.

At any period of history, a nation which is in the lead intellectually, is very apt to exhibit the effects of speech-tempo at the most advanced point. So, at the beginning of the modern period, English and French had gone considerably farther in the process of reduction, and were far more concise in style than German, whose progress was retarded. Wundt points out that such bi-lingual men as Leibniz and Frederick the Great, must have thought and spoken faster in French than in German.

Differences in the rate of speech can be observed between young and old persons, between the old and young generations; between persons of higher and lower culture, or at the various stages of an individual's intellectual development; between persons of equal culture but of different temperament, also between times of greater vigor and better spirits and periods of fatigue and depression, when pitch will also be correspondingly higher and lower. We speak with greater ease and precision on topics with which we are conversant, than we do when we have to think hard to find our way through a question. It is hardly necessary to say that the rate of speech is by no means always a certain index of intelligence, as shallow people are often amazingly voluble and vice versa.

The known conservatism of language acts as a check on change. Perhaps our age of universal printed literature will tend to arrest language relatively longer at its present stage than ever before. A fully correct idea of the present state of phonetics cannot be derived from our present orthography, but only from exact phonetic transcriptions or records.

PHILIP SEIBERTH.

Washington University.

THE SOURCE OF AN EPISODE IN HEINRICH'S VON NEUSTADT APOLLONIUS [1]

Toward the close of the Apollonius Heinrich wove in a long episode based upon a motive which seems never to have found its way into any other work of a purely literary character and which, by reason of its source and of the witness it bears to the author's originality, should be of real interest.

The passage in question [2] tells that a maiden, Flordelise, appears while Ap. and his knights are sitting at the Round Table and accuses a certain Silvian of having attempted to violate her married sister and, failing in this, of having sent a slanderous report to the husband thus bringing the wife into disgrace. The maid demands that Silvian fight her. While the justice of her demand is recognized, the king is much perplexed because he does not know the proper conditions for such a combat. At length an old satrap, a bishop in the city, says he has read that in such cases the combat shall be arranged as follows:

The man shall stand in a narrow pit up to his navel and shall be clad in a shirt and coat. His right hand shall be bound behind his back, while in his left he shall have a fair sized stick an ell in length but no sharp weapon. The woman shall be outside the pit and shall be armed with a weight securely fastened in a linen cloth two ells long. If one kills the other, the case is settled. If the woman fails to overcome her opponent within a specified time he goes free. The text follows from Singer's edition:

> 20171 Es sol ain yeglicher man
> In ainer engen gruben stan,
> Das er halber dar inne sey.
> Scharffes wappen ist im nit frey;
> Das is recht uber das lant:
> Im sol auch di rechte hant
> Hinder sich gepunden sein;

[1] A large part of the material here offered is from the fourth chapter of the writer's unpublished dissertation: The Apollonius von Tyrland of Heinrich von Neustadt: A Study of the Sources. Harvard, 1910.

[2] Heinrich von Neustadt, Apollonius etc., ed. S. Singer, Berlin 1906; ll. 19856-20346: also p. 121ff. in J. Strobl's ed., Wien 1875.

Das ist das rechte urtail mein:
Man sol im ainen stecken geben,
20180   Da mit er were sein leben,
Noch ze gross noch ze kranck,
Er soll sein ainer elen langk.
Den gibt man im in di tencken hant,
Da mit sein wer ist bekant.
Ain plosser rock ist sein claid,
Uber ain hemde an gelayt.
Di frauwe soll hie aussen gan,
Ainen stauchen in der hende han
Mit riemen dar ein gepunden,
20190   Swer pey dreyn pfunden.
Di stauch soll wesen leynein
Und zwayr elen langk sein.
Von mitten morgen untz an den tag
Ob sy im nicht an gewynnen mag
So soll der man sein genesen
Und ledig von der frawen wesen.
Slecht aber sy in ze tod
Oder er sey, sy hat di not
Und ains das ander uberwunden:
20200   Sus ist das recht erfunden.

After some opposition from Silvian this program is followed out. Flordelise leaves him for dead but he revives and confesses, whereupon the crowd wishes to burn him alive.

In connection with this episode Singer and Bockhoff, in their study which appeared two years since,[3] correctly mention the reference in the Chronick von Bern[4] to a contest there in 1288 between a man and a woman, in which the woman was victorious. Although the conditions are not given, they may well have been similar to those in the Ap. and to those soon to follow, and the suggestion that Heinrich got his idea from a detailed account of this combat is not a bad one, even though the case can not be proved.

[3] A. Bockhoff u. S. Singer: Heinrich's v. N. Ap. V. T. und seine Quellen. Tübingen 1911, pp. 78-79.

[4] Justinger: Chronick von Bern, ed. Stierlin u. Wyss, Bern 1819, p. 38; the same, ed. G. Studer, Bern 1871, p. 296, cf. further Studer in Archiv d. hist. Vereins v. Bern V, 534; the same notice is found also in Joh. Stumpf's Gemeiner loblicher Eydgenoschafft Stetten, Landen und Völkeren Chronick, Zürich 1548, fol. Bk. VIII chap. VI, p. 250b.

Fortunately, however, there is abundant evidence to show that the episode is drawn from contemporary law. In at least two law-books conditions for this form of combat are set forth which agree substantially with those in the Ap. and the origin of each is geographically nearer Heinrich than is the chronicle case.

In Ruprecht's von Freisingen Bairisches Rechtbuch [5] §§134-135, entitled von der notnünft, state the conditions under which a woman may take action, then (§135) we read:

Ist dev frawe nicht magt gewesen so müs si in ansprechen mit einem kamph. oder mit den laeutten. ez sein frawn oder man. di zü dem Rüffe chomen sint do er die notnünft tan hat. unt mag dev frawe selb dritt war gemachen. hintz dem notnüfter. daz er si benött hab. ir eren. so sol man uber in richten. also daz man in sol haupten. wirt ir aver ein kamph ertailt. so sol man den notnüfter ein di erd begreben. untz an den nabel. also daz tzwischen und der Erd. ein wagen sail um gen mug. das er sich umb mug gereiben. und sol man im di tenken hant hintter den Rukke pinten. und sol im einen champhcholben ein dev hant geben. und sol einen rinch straen um in mit stro. ein der weit. daz er sei. mit dem cholben erlangen mug und sol man. der frawen einen stain. ein ir stauchen geben der ein pfunt hab. des gewaegs. daz ein markch tü. und sol ir den stauchen. inderhalb der hant untz in di Hant bewinden. daz er rog. und swes si den stauchen lasz hangen. so sol. der stain sweben. dar inne ob der Erd. einer gesatzten hant hoch. man sol in paiden griezwaertel geben. nach champhes recht gesigt di fraw. so sol man dem mann daz haubt abslahen. gesigt aver der man. so sol man der frawen newer di hant abslahen. Daz ist dar um gesetzet. daz nicht gewonleich ist daz ein fraw einem manne an gesiget . . . . .

Article **XXXI** of the Augsburger Stadtrecht vom Jahre 1276 (ed. C. Meyer, 1872) deals with the same subject. If the case is proven by witnesses, the offender is to be buried alive.

Ist aber, daz die notnumpht niemen gehoeret noh gesaehen hat, kumt diu frowe ce clage, so sol man den manne, den si der notnumphte zihet, dristunt furbieten als recht ist. Kumt

---

[5] Written 1332, ed. L. Westenrieder, München 1802.

er danne fur, so ist recht, daz er berede mit sin eines hant,
daz er unschuldic si. Wil aber diu frowe sins rechtes niht und
wilz im wern, daz muz si tun mit eime kamphe mit ir selbes
libe, also daz der man sol sin begraben unz an den nabel,
unde sol er in siner hant haben einen aichinen stap, der sol
einer dumellen lanch sin unde sleht ane gevaerde und hant-
vollic. So sol diu frowe ein roeclin an ir haben unde in ir
stuchen einen fustgrozzen stein. Gesigt danne dem man an,
so sol man uber in rihten also, daz man in laebendigen begraben sol. Gesigt aber der man der frowen an, so ist reht,
daz man si auch lebendig begraben sol.

The editor refers to the Freisingen Recht as the only other
occurrence of such conditions known to him, but there are at
least two other accounts, different in some important respects
but agreeing in other points even more closely with the Ap.

The first, contained in a Ms. at Wolfenbüttel, was summarized by Christian Thomasius.[6] Not having access to
Thomasius' work at this time, I can give only the following,
quoted by Friedrich Majer in his Geschichte der Ordalien
(Jena 1795, p. 271f.):

"Der Mann stehet in einer runden etwas weiten Gruben,
hat in der rechten Hand einen Kolben, mit dem er
nach der Frauen schlägt, er darf aber nicht heraus-
gehen, noch der Frauen nachlaufen, auch nicht einmal
mit der freyen Hand sich an die Grube oder das Erdt-
reich anhalten, bey Verlust des Sieges. Die Frau hat einen
Schleyer in der Hand, in welchem vornen ein Stein von
etlichen Pfunden geknüpft ist, vomit sie nach dem Mann
schlägt. Wenn die Frau dem Mann hinter den Rücken kommen kann, bemühet sie sich, dessen Kopf hinterwerts aus
der Grube zu ziehen und ihn zu würgen; parirt der Mann
den Schlag mit dem Schleyer mit dem Kolben aus, so umwickelt sich der Schleyer um den Kolben, und erlangt dadurch
die Frau Gelegenheit, dem Manne den Kolben aus der Hand
zu reissen. Parirt aber der Mann den Schlag mit dem lincken
und freyen Arm aus, so umwickelt sich der Schleyer um den
Arm, und hat der Mann also Gelegenheit die Frau zu sich an

[6] Diss. de occasione, conceptione et intentione instit. crimin. carolinæ,
Halle 1718, 4 §XIX not. r. pn. 22.

die Grube zu ziehen, da er dann trachtet, die Frau in der Mitte des Leibes zu fassen und sie in die Grube zu ziehen auch zuweilen umzuköpeln, etc.''

The tactics here described show marked resemblance to those employed in the poem:

> 20261   Si sprang umb in als ain kitz
>   Und slug im ains 'nu hab dir ditz!'
>   Ye doch der slag was nit gross:
>   Die schone lutzel sein genoss;
>   Wann der ungerte knabe
>   Slug ir aines mit dem stabe
>   Auff den leib und auff di wat
>   Da der ruck ain ende hatt,
>   Das sy mit lautter stymme sehre,
> 20270   Wann ir det der slag vil we.
>   Sy sprach 'du giltest mir den slag,
>   Es ensey dann das ich nit mag.'
>   Si hawt her und dar umb in.
>   Manigvalt was ir syn.
>   Da sy den slag zu im swayff,
>   Pey dem gern er sy pegraiff.
>   Er zoch sy pey dem claide
>   Zu im. do ward layde
>   Allen den di es sahen.
> 20280   Gemainklich sy jahen
>   'Flordelise di ist tod.'
>   Di magt was in grosser not.
>   Ir stauchen vaste umb wand:
>   Si slug im ains auff di hant,
>   Das im sein kampfstecke en viel.
>   Do slug sy im ains auff den schiel
>   Und dar nach ains auff den slaf,
>   Das er reret als ain schaff.
>   Volendet het sy ir not,
> 20290   Si liess in ligen da fur dot.

The second account is given by Ephraim Gerhard[7] and again I am forced to quote from Majer (p. 273):

Der Mann stehet in einer mitten im Kreise gemachten drei Schu weiten Grube bis an den Nabel, die Frau aber stehet zehn Schuhe weit davon. Ein jedes hat drei Stäbe. Die des Mannes sind ohngefähr eine Elle lang, und zwei Zolle dick im Durchmesser; die der Weibsperson sind von gleicher Länge

---

[7] Diss. de judicio duellico, Jena 1711, cap. III §6 und Anhang.

und Dicke, vorne aber ist an jeden derselben ein gewöhnlich drei Pfund schwerer Stein gebunden. Mit diesen Waffen greiffen die Kämpfer einander an. Schlägt der Mann nach der Frau, versieht es aber dabei und greifft mit der Hand an den Rand oder den Erdboden des Grabens, in welchem er steht, hat er einen von seinen Stöcken verloren. Übereilt sich aber die Frau, und schlägt, indem der Mann sich auf die ebengedachte Art vergehet, nach ihm, verliert sie ebenfalls einen von ihren Stöcken. Wer nun auf diese Art seine drei Stäbe zuerst einbüsst, der ist überwunden und wird für schuldig gehalten.

This account is even less like Heinrich's than the preceding yet it is of interest in as much as it may bear witness to the extent to which such laws existed and also by reason of the statement of the average weight of the stone allowed the woman. It certainly will be worth while to ascertain the time and place of the writing and also the character (probably legal) of both these Mss. which may contain more interesting material.

Whether or not Heinrich was led to insert this episode by some account of an actual combat, perhaps that at Berne, it is clear that some form of the law relating to die Notnunft lies at the bottom of the matter and the existence of such laws in Augsburg and especially in Freisingen—Heinrich occupied a house in Vienna which belonged to the Bishop of Freisingen—which show close correspondence with his account, even in the wording, makes the assumption plausible that he either drew his inspiration directly from the law or at least took over the conditions of the combat from that source.

The unparalleled choice and treatment of this bit of contemporary law proves conclusively that Heinrich possessed some degree of originality. This point should be borne in mind when considering the second part of Singer's study (cf. note 3) in which he gives his cleverly conceived theory of a lost Byzantine source for Heinrich's Ap. The present writer is inclined to attribute other additions to the Historia to Heinrich who may have had quite as ready access to the sources as the Byzantine author hypothecated by Singer.

R. W. PETTENGILL.

Harvard University.

THE FABLE *FROSCH UND MAUS* AS FOUND IN LUTHER AND HANS SACHS

On April 23, 1530 Kurfürst Johann of Saxony went to the Augsburg Reichstag. He would have been glad of Luther's presence there but did not venture to bring him over the borders of his own territory. That he might still be in the neighborhood however, he gave him as a residence his castle at Koburg. With characteristic diligence Luther planned to make use of this time for literary production. In a letter to Melanchthon he explains his project of erecting here three tabernacles "Psalterio unum, Prophetis unum et Aesopo unum."[1] Twice again in his letters from Koburg to Melanchthon on May 12 and to Wenzel Link on May 28 he mentions his projects.[2] From these references it can be safely assumed that the small collection of Luther's fables dates from his residence in Koburg, that is, between the dates of April 23 and October 5, 1530. Unfortunately his plan to make a complete collection of Aesop's fables was not destined to be carried out. His intimate friend and ardent champion, Johann Mathesius, refers to the writing of the 16 fables "mit einer sehr gelerten Vorrede." In reality there were only 13 fables, Mathesius's error here resting on a mistake in numbering that was also carried over into the printed editions.[3]

Luther's purpose in preparing this collection is plainly expressed in his introduction which was probably written at the same time as his fables. After explaining the value of fables as a means of instructing youth in an agreeable way he adds with regret in speaking of the fables then available "Darüber so schendliche unzüchtige Bubenstück darein gemischt, das kein züchtig, from Mensch leiden, zuuor kein jung Mensch, one schaden lesen oder hören kan. . . . . Darumb so bitten wir alle frome Hertzen, wollen denselben Deudschen schendlichen Esopum ausrotten, und diesen an sein stat gebrauchen."[4] His purpose in the work then, was to purify

[1] Enders, Luthers Briefwechsel VII p. 302.

[2] Enders, Luthers Briefwechsel VII pp. 332 and 346.

[3] For a scholarly treatment of the subject, see E. Thiele, "Luthers Fabeln" Neudrucke Literaturwerke des 16. und 17. Jahrhunderts. No. 76.

[4] Thiele, Luthers Fabeln, p. 20.

this branch of literature and make it again one which could really offer moral instruction. He had always recognized the value of thus coating a wholesome moral pill of reality with the sugar of unreality and employed this method on various occasions, 'in sermons, conversations, letters and as a means of instructing his own son.

In now turning directly to the fables of Aesop he was treating a material well-known to the reading world of his time. Various ones of the fables ascribed to Aesop had been appearing in the German literature of the Middle Ages since the time of Charlemagne. But however well-known individual stories may have been they were accessible to German readers as a complete collection in only one form, namely the translation by Heinrich Steinhöwel, printed in Ulm between 1476 and 1480.[5] It was this collection that had aroused the violent disapproval of the reformer and it was his wish now to produce a purified form of these immortal stories.

The work of Steinhöwel is in fact a curious mixture. The first part of the book presents the mythical biography of Aesop, which Maximus Planudes is said to have brought to Italy from Constantinople about 1327. The main part of this collection consists of the so-called fables of Romulus, a Latin paraphrase of Phaedrus, dating from the tenth century, 80 fables in four books. This is the basis of later collections of the so-called fables of Aesop and to this Luther refers when he speaks in praise of Aesop's fables. As an appendix, Steinhöwel added 17 stories designated as Extravaganzen, mostly animal fables, a selection of 27 fables of Avian, 16 parables from the "Disciplina Clericalis" of Petrus Alfonsus, and finally 6 stories taken from the "Facetiae" of Poggio. Such was the parti-colored volume known to the Germany of Luther as Aesop. But it was especially against the appendix that Luther's moral gorge rose. The tales of Alfonsus and above all of Poggio seemed to him by no means an appropriate medium for the conveying of moral truths.

Even before Luther was thus occupying some of his spare moments in the castle at Koburg with the remoulding of

[5] Bibliothek des literarischen Vereins in Stuttgart. Vol. 117. Ed. by H. Oesterley, 1873.

Aesop another German writer was attempting the same task. His plan was not expressed in such comprehensive terms but the quantity of his output in this field assumed far larger proportions than Luther's. His circle of influence and readers was infinitely smaller, but he was an ardent adherent of his great contemporary and known to him favorably as the author of the "Wittenbergisch Nachtigall", an inspiring poem announcing to Germany the dawn of the Reformation and assuring fame to its author, Hans Sachs.

Aesop as a source first occupied the attention of Sachs in 1520 when he used the material of the fable "Frosch und Maus"[6] as the basis of a mastersong. Up to and including the year 1530, when Luther's fables were written Sachs had treated six fables of Aesop in his mastersongs and one in his collection of Schwänke.

It is of interest to examine one of these more closely as showing a possible literary connection between Luther and Sachs. This is the fable mentioned above, "Frosch und Maus." It is the third one in Luther's collection and seems to have been a favorite one with Sachs as he treated it three times in metrical form, first as a mastersong in 1520, then as a Schwank May 1, 1528 and finally as a mastersong again November 10, 1546.[7] The mastersongs must here be left out of consideration as they appeared in print neither in the edition of Sachs's works nor in separate prints. The only possible connection then must be between the Schwank of Sachs and the prose fable of Luther. As the version of Sachs appeared in 1528 and that by Luther in 1530 it is evident that if one was influenced by the other Luther must have been in this case the recipient.

Luther was not in correspondence nor apparently in close touch with Sachs so he could hardly have had access to his manuscript. The first volume of Sachs's printed works appeared in 1558 so this must be left out of consideration. There was, however, another source of contact, the special printing of single poems. Many of Sachs's shorter poems

[6] Steinhöwel Aesop. Ed. Oesterley, p. 82.

[7] Sämtliche Fabeln und Schwänke von Hans Sachs. Ed. by E. Goetze. Neudrucke Vol. 1, No. 3; Vol. 3, No. 2; Vol. 4, No. 329.

thus attained a wider circulation and the general list of his
writings appearing in the first edition of his works shows that
this poem was one of the first to be so treated.[8]

The question now arises as to what probability there was
that Luther should know this version. "Die Wittembergisch
Nachtigall" had appeared in 1523, six years after Luther's
first public appearance in opposition to the sale of indulgences
and two years after the Diet of Worms. Its success was in-
stantaneous and it obtained a far larger audience than the
pulpit could command. Having thus taken his stand definitely on the side of the Reformation, Sachs entered the field
still more aggressively in the following year. In the first of a
series of dialogues he allows a shoemaker who is an adherent
of the Reformation to argue with and worst a Catholic canon.
Four of these dialogues were printed as pamphlets and attracted much attention.

Sachs's next attempt to aid the Reformation openly with
his pen was to be his last. Osiander, Protestant pastor in
Nürnberg, had undertaken the publication of a series of pictures attacking the Papacy and obtained the aid of Sachs to
furnish verses for the pictures. The print was entitled "Eine
wunderliche Weissagung von dem Papsttum" and appeared
early in 1527. It was a joy to the Lutherans and a torment to
their opponents. Luther's opinion we have in his own words
in a letter to Spalatin, April 29, 1527. "Ihr habt freilich
das Büchlein zu Nürnberg ausgangen mit den Figuren wohl
gesehen, darin des Papsttums ja nicht vergessen ist. Es ist
mit dem Antichrist auf die Hefen kommen und Christus
will sein ein Ende machen, desz sei Gott gelobt in Ewigkeit.
Amen."[9] It was not welcomed as eagerly by the Nürnberg
Council which saw in it only occasion for increasing the
already bitter attitude of the two parties and on March 6,
1527 issued a decree reprimanding Osiander and forbidding
Sachs to write further for publication. For a time he was
silent, but the Council seems to have meant this more as a
warning than as a permanent injunction. At any rate scarce-

[8] Goetze, Neudrucke, Fabeln und Schwänke, Vol. 1, p. 6 (note).

[9] Quoted in Kawerau, "Hans Sachs und die Reformation," Schriften
des Vereins für Reformationsgeschichte" Vol. 7, p. 70.

ly a year had elapsed before his next poem appeared in print and shortly after as the second poem to be so printed appeared the fable "Frosch und Maus." As these poems showed no polemical tendency the Council could plainly see that their warning had been heeded.

The Lutheran circle in Nürnberg would certainly hail with interest renewed literary activity on the part of the man who had suffered for championing the cause of their leader. With one of them at least Luther was in personal correspondence. This was Wenzel Link, an active worker in the Augustinian monastery which he won to Lutherism. It would not be surprising if this friend had kept Luther informed of the fortunes of his literary champion and also sent him the next productions of his pen especially as the fable in question has a moral teaching. It may even have stimulated his purpose to do something himself in this branch of literature.

But without internal evidence the conjecture of influence of one by the other would fall to the ground and examination of the two versions is necessary. Luther's fables as the manuscript shows were written with many corrections, filings and polishings. All the fables are brief, the first form of the one in question, number 3, containing the story in ten lines and the moral in six additional. Sachs extends his to 48 lines in rhyme. In the main story both have followed the Steinhöwel model closely, Sachs deviating more in details, as he often did from his source, and as the larger compass of his fable here demanded. The moral, "Hoist by his own petard", Steinhöwel expresses in one prosaic sentence devoid of any proverbs or figures of speech. Both Luther and Sachs use a wealth of proverbs in their writings and it is not surprising that they are found here to point the moral to this tale. It is interesting to note, however, that of the three proverbs found in Luther's manuscript version two are found in Sachs and one of these is by no means a common one.

Although both Sachs and Luther were interested in proverbs and proverbial phrases their common stock was very different. Luther made a collection of proverbs familiar to him.[10] Of the 489 proverbs here contained only 25 are found

[10] Luthers Sprichwörtersammlung. Ed. By E. Thiele, Weimar 1900.

in the fables, Schwänke and Shrovetide plays of Sachs, and when found only the general idea is the same. Practical similarity of words is scarcely found at all. Although Luther's collection does not exhaust the proverbs and popular expressions found in his writings, he must have picked them out as typical and appealing especially to him. In this connection it is worthy of note that the proverbs occurring in the fable "Von der maus und frosch" do not appear in his collection as they would have been likely to do if they had been such as readily occurred to his mind.[11]

A comparison of the texts will bring out the points mentioned above. Unless otherwise stated the quotations from Luther are from the first manuscript version.

Steinhöwel	Sachs	Luther
Von der mus, frosch und wyer.	Fabel mit dem Frosch und der Mausz.	[12]Von der maus und frosch
Ain mus wäre gern über ain wasser gewesen	Ein Mausz bey eynem Wasser sasz	[13]Vom frosch und der maus
	Gar geren sie hinüber was	Eine maus were gern uber ein wasser gewest
und begeret raut und hilff von einem frosch	(not found)	Da bat sie einen frosch umb trewen rat
(not found)	Der was untrewer liste voll	Der frosch war hemisch
		[13]Der frosch war ein Schalck
band den fuosz der mus an synen fuosz	Der band ein faden umb . . . . . der Mause Schwantz	Binde deinen fusz an meinen
Als er mitten in das wasser kam, tunket sich der frosch und zoch di mus under sich und wolt sie ertrencken	der Frosch zu stund Sich nieder ducket bisz zu grund Und zog die Mausz fast undter sich, Die Mausz die schrey: Frosch wilt du mich Ertrencken?	Da sie aber aufs wasser kamen, tauchet der frosch hinuntern und wolt die maus ertrencken.
Do des die ellend mus enpfand, widerstund sy	Da kam ein Storch geflogen hoch	Inn dem aber die maus sich weret und erbeit,

[11] E. Schröder in Anzeiger für deutsches Altertum 1901, Vol. 27, p. 101 ff., conjectures that Luther was trying to present a rival collection of proverbs to Agricola's, as explanation of the absence of many common ones.

[12] Manuscript.

[13] Printed edition.

dem frosch nach ieren krefften: in dem kompt ein wy geflogen und nimpt die mit synen klawen und den hangenden frosch mit ihr und asz sie baide	Und sach die Mausz im Wasser schweben. zeucht den frosch auch sie eben Und fürt sie mit im in sein nest Mit sampt den Frosch den er nicht west	fleuget ein Weyh daher und erhasschet die maus, Er schosz herab, er griff mit eraus und frisset sie alle beide

The parallel passages above show plainly that Steinhöwel was the original source for the two later writers. In Luther's only departure from Steinhöwel a precedent is found in Sachs. The passages that follow are the moral teachings of the fable and show striking similarities between Luther and Sachs in their divergence from Steinhöwel.

Steinhöwel	Sachs	Luther
Also beschicht auch denen, die ander lüt veruntrüwen wellent und versprechent hilff und begeren ze schedigen, das in offt gelyche bütt würt	So traff die untrew iren Herrn (Not found in Steinhöwel)	Doch schlegt untrew allzeit yhren herren
	Ich will dir zalen Dein untrew und dein *falsche* dück Überflüssig auff deinen rück Und must mir gelten mit der hewt Als du die Mausz hast veruntrewt (Not found in Steinhöwel)	und mus der *falsche* frosch ynn seiner untrew mit der maus verderben
(Not found)	Warumb sachst du nit basz für dich Warhaffte trew ist gar miszlich	Sihe fur dich trew ist misslich

The last sentence quoted above is the most striking of the similarities here shown as it is a proverb rarely met with in German literature. It is first found in slightly different wording in Brant's "Narrenschiff":

> Traw yedem wol, lûg doch für dich,
> dann worlich, truw ist yetz miszlich.[14]

Sachs uses it in the schwank in question but employs a different verb in the first member. Once more Sachs uses

[14] Ed. by Zarncke, Leipzig 1854. 69, 22.

it in a Schwank written on December 11, 1557,[15] illustrating
here his tendency to make use of a favorite phrase more than
once. Luther uses the same words as Sachs in a more condensed form. We also come across it again in Luther's
writings in the exposition of the tenth commandment from
the 20th chapter of Exodus. "Denn die Liebe helt das best
vom nehesten, Aber gleichwol sihe dich für, Trew is
mislich."[16] This commentary was written in 1529 the year
after the appearance of Sachs's fable and the year before
Luther prepared his brief collection. Although this phrase
is found recorded in such collections of proverbs as Wander,
Körte and Schottelius it was never widely employed and
could scarcely be called common literary property.[17]

In the parallel columns quoted above practically the entire
version as found in Steinhöwel and Luther has been given.
Only those passages from Sachs's longer version which show
similarities have been quoted. Luther uses one proverb not
found in either Sachs or Steinhöwel. In every other important variation from Steinhöwel, the same variation is
found in Sachs. Of significance too is the fact that the most
striking similarity with the latter version, the proverb just
treated, was written on the margin of the manuscript showing
that it was an addition from the very first form.

To sum up: Luther's version of the fable appeared two
years after the fable by Sachs. Luther could easily have become acquainted with this in its separately printed form and
it was very natural that friends in Nürnberg should send
him copies of poems produced by a man who had shortly
before done such signal service for the Reformation and was
still suffering under the bann of the authorities for this
activity. Internal examination shows that deviation from

---

[15] Goetze, Fabeln und Schwänke, Vol. I, No. 186, ll. 109-110.

[16] Luthers Schriften, Vol. 4. Jena 1560. 2nd Ed. p. 530[b].

[17] The fact that this proverb is found in Agricola together with
the other proverbs used in this fable by Luther admits the possibility
of his having drawn from the "Sprichwörtersammlung." This is offset
however by his well-known antipathy to Agricola and also by the fact
that of the 26 proverbs used by him in his other fables only 2 are
found in Agricola.

the original source, Steinhöwel, is largely in line with the version by Sachs. It is of course necessary to be cautious in any search for direct sources and in this case we must allow the possibility that the same expressions occurred to the two writers to illustrate the same moral truth. If so, it is in itself a most interesting case of literary and mental parallelism. It is certainly no more unreasonable to assume the possibility that aside from the Steinhöwel version, Luther also knew Sachs's fable "Frosch und Maus" in its separately printed form, the influence of Sachs appearing on the popular didactic side.

Eugene F. Clark.

Dartmouth College.

LANDSMAAL AND THE LANGUAGE MOVEMENT IN NORWAY*

The Viking Age and the following two centuries developed in Norway and Iceland a rich and beautiful language, a highly idiomatic native speech, free from Greek and Latin contamination in the matter of syntax. This language had its primary home in southwestern Norway. It is on the living dialects of the same promising linguistic regions that the modern Norwegian *Landsmaal,* the new speech of Norway, is built.

The old classical language of Norway and Iceland became, as we all know, the bearer of a rich, varied, and strikingly original literature. I shall merely mention the two Eddas, the Icelandic sagas, *Heimskringla* and the *Konungs Skuggsjá.*

Norway had her period of strength and greatness followed by one of almost unparalleled decline and calamities. Civil wars followed close upon one another. In place of the raids and expeditions into foreign lands for purposes of conquest or peaceful settlement, the descendants of the vikings fell to killing one another with an earnestness worthy of a better cause. From 1130 to 1240 Norwegian history is but a record of warring factions and intrigues of claimants to the throne.

This led ultimately to a decided weakening of Norway's most important class of citizens, the peasant nobles—I mean the proud, independent, headstrong Norwegian freeholders. The severe monarchy built up by King Sverre and his successors also tended in the same direction. In the midst of it all came the Black Death. This scourge appeared in Bergen in the year 1347 and spread rapidly through the adjacent country, depopulating whole districts. Denmark and Sweden also were affected, but these countries were able to recuperate in a comparatively short time. It is humiliating for us to review this period of our country's history. Norway, to use a figure, lay as a tempest-tossed vessel, storm-battered, rigging down, rudder lost, seams leaking—a veritable wreck at the mercy of wind and wave.

* For a bibliography on the linguistic situation in Norway see Publications of the Society for the Advancement of Scandinavian Study I, Nr. 4, where also a third type of *Landsmaal* is analyzed.

The union with Sweden lasted from 1319 to 1371. The linguistic center shifted from western to Eastern Norway and the border districts, that is, to the districts which by natural, native development were most closely related to Denmark and Sweden. For some time Swedish became fashionable among the higher classes in Norway, and Norwegians endeavored to learn to write the language. Of course the old classical language of Norway suffered by consequence. (See Noreen's *Altisländische und Altnorwegische Grammatik. Halle*, 1903, p. 13.

In the year 1380 came the union with Denmark, our plunge into more than Egyptian darkness. Our forefathers had run the ship of state on the rocks, and not a few of them seemed perfectly willing to dispose of the wreck to the highest bidder. The union with Denmark is the blot on the pages of Norway's history. It is the period of national shame and degradation, of ignorance, and general impoverishment, the decay of the native speech and the intrusion of a foreign tongue, the Danish. The feeling of nationality in the hearts of the Norwegians became well-nigh extinguished. People lost their sense of self-reliance, yes, almost the desire to be themselves. No able leaders appeared to save the land from bondage. Denmark drained the country of money and men. Danish kings pawned Norwegian islands in the Western seas; in quarrels with Sweden they lost the provinces of Baahuslän, Herjedalen, and Jämteland—all of them Norwegian territory. The Danish officials plundered churches, desecrated shrines, extorted possible and impossible things from the Norwegian peasants. And in return Denmark gave to Norway the Danish language!

The old Norwegian language ceased little by little to be used by the people in the cities and, as Norway's leading families died out or intermarried with Swedes and Danes, sank to the level of a number of country dialects. Danish became the language of fashion even as it became the language of the administration and, ere long, of the church.

It must be stated here, however, that Danish was not forced upon the Norwegians by the Danes, but Danish came in gradually to take the place of the retreating Norwegian language.

When Danish preachers at the time of the Reformation came to convert the Norwegians to the Lutheran faith, there was no longer a fully unified Norwegian speech which could be used in a Bible translation. Had there been any such language easily available, the Bible would no doubt have been translated into it. Iceland, on the other hand, which was likewise converted from Catholicism by Danes, was given an Icelandic translation. There was no longer a uniform Norwegian language to stem the Danish tide.

Danish became the official language of Norway in the year 1450. The last Bishop to use Norwegian was Gaute Ivarsson, who died in 1510. His successor was the Dane, Erik Valkendorf, and then the language of the church became fully Danish. The last persons to give up Norwegian, excepting, of course, the peasants, were the lawmen, for the laws were written in this language, and laws are adverse to violent changes in terminology and tradition.

One may perhaps be tempted to ask the question, how, in the light of this long sojourn of Danish in Norway, can there be any Norwegian language left at all? The answer is: the ruling class in church and state formed, as it were, a clique— a nation within a nation. Many of these officials were Danes or of other foreign origin. The peasants were looked upon as barbarians; the leading classes would have nothing to do with them. No intimate relation existed or could exist between the peasantry on the one hand and the professional classes and dwellers in the cities on the other. Of the peasantry only the men had direct dealings with Danish-speaking merchant, priest and judge. This left the women in the country districts almost entirely outside the pale of Danish influence. And the women of course reared the children and taught them the language as they knew it, that is, taught them Norwegian in the form of the local country dialect. The Norwegian common schools of later days naturally have tended to corrupt Norwegian by the use of Danish Bible History, Hymnal, and A. B. C., but the effect has not been so harmful as it might have been had the schools been well organized from the first. What country schools there were used, for the greater part until quite recently, local teachers, men of the people, who spoke the local dialect in the school room. It is fortunate therefore, from the point of view of the language, that popular education was so well neglected during the years of the union with Denmark, for had a strong educational system been in operation in city and country, mountain and glen, the Norwegian speech would have been wiped out everywhere even as it has been almost totally in the larger cities. Our national linguistic regeneration would then have become an impossibility.

However, Danish proved to be unable to destroy the Norwegian peasant dialects, but at the same time no Norwegian dialect had the opportunity, under the conditions of the time, to rise to the rank of a standard language. These dialects are yet today strong and fully living, though to some extent influenced by Danish. Some work in recording the native speech of Norway was done quite early, but only in a sporadic and unsystematic way. The first popular ballads were reduced to writing about 1640. Some Norwegian dialects produced somewhat of a literature in ballads and the like. Peter Dass, born in 1647, incorporated some things from Nordland dialects in his poems, but there was no conscious effort on the part of anyone to create a distinct Norwegian language. People had not yet come to a clear realization of the relation between the Norwegian peasant dialects and the language used by the Danish administration and by the cultured classes in Norway in general.

In 1772 was formed in Copenhagen, Det norske Selskab, a society of Norwegian students and literary men. As in the early days of the Viking Age, Norwegians from the different parts of Norway had met in foreign lands and fought side by side against a common foe, and in this co-operation created and strengthened the national feeling, so now Norwegians, meeting in the Danish capital, began to feel as brothers and as strangers in a strange land. Norway was waking out of its stupor. These young men began to feel that they were Norwegians and not Danes. Even before the separation from Denmark came a demand for a Norwegian university. As we know, the Danish king saw himself forced to yield, and in 1811 the University was granted. Two years later the modest little provincial university began its scholastic career.

Then came 1814, the historic year in the annals of Modern Norway. Denmark was forced to give Norway over to Sweden in the early part of that year. The Swedes unintentionally did us a great service when they forced us out of the union with Denmark. But to be given over to Sweden, that is, to Norway's traditional enemy, was too much even for long-suffering Norway. The war broke out, the outcome of which was that Norway secured for herself one of the world's freest constitutions, which constitution the king of Sweden accepted in the main on becoming joint king of Norway and Sweden. Long disputes followed, lasting almost a century. Sweden endeavored to make the union closer, but Norway opposed such moves. In all this the Norwegian national feeling was tested and trained as never before. Then came 1905, our crowning year politically. Norway has reached her goal: a free country with a descendant of Harold the Fairhaired on the throne!

But the awakening national feeling in Norway manifested itself in more ways than in the purely political. In some quarters appeared a more or less clearly defined desire for independence in other matters. It is the language, however, which chiefly concerns us here. The constitution of 1814 speaks very naïvely of Danish as Norwegian and demands among other things that the joint king of Norway and Sweden shall use Norwegian in his acts and documents pertaining to Norway. I have read some of these documents by the late Oscar II. They are written in Danish words with heavy German sentence structure. And yet it is called Norwegian!

The most important among the early language reformers in Norway was the poet, Wergeland. He had however no definite program. He was groping in the dark. He lacked the scientific and linguistic prerequisites for any far-reaching, well-planned reform. He voiced our awakening longing for cultural independence and maturity, and he prophesied that before the end of the century we should have a national language. His prophesy has not come true as yet, even though we passed the mile-stone of the century years ago. But there has been progress. In an article written in 1835, Wergeland advocated the use of certain native words in place of the corresponding Danish. He wrote some dialect poems himself. Much of what he did was good, much in rather bad taste. His work after all was only patchwork, somewhat like the work of K. Knudsen later in the interests of the *Riksmaal*.

Wergeland was of course not allowed to go on in peace in his work of Norwegianizing Danish as much as possible. He was bitterly opposed by the linguistic standpatters and self-appointed, self-anointed judges of taste. Welhaven was their chief spokesman. Johan Sverdrup said of him that if Welhaven could have had his way, the Norwegian lyre would not have had a single native string. Welhaven, with many more of his kind, drew his inspiration chiefly from literary Copenhagen, and he often felt his life in Norway a Babylonian captivity. He found the Norwegian peasants rough and untutored. So they undoubtedly were in many cases, but surely only by the fault of Welhaven, and others before him, who had neglected their traditions and their native language, to feed fat at the festal boards of the Danish capital.

The next big moment in the linguistic and cultural regeneration of Norway came with Jörgen Moe and Asbjörnsen. Perhaps I should rather use the word "emancipation" than "regeneration," for what was needed was to free the Norwegian spirit from the foreign yoke in order to enable Norway to reveal to the world its own treasures and resources. Moe and Asbjörnsen gave us our own Norwegian fairy tales. I do not mean fairy tales that necessarily originated in Norway. No, stories that bore the stamp of the Norwegian temperament, of our way of interpreting life and the world, our way of saying apt things in terse, aphoristic form. These fairy tales are delightfully Norwegian in spirit. We find the quick, straightforward presentation; short, snappy sentences; sly, unobtrusive humor; apt sayings, and the hard-headed sense of reality that belong to the best peasants. The only fault that some of us find with these stories by Asbjörnsen and Moe is that the language is too Danish. It seems very Norwegian to some who live in the cities and for whom Danish has become rather largely the mother tongue. But to those who speak a real Norwegian dialect, these stories are in the matter of language only too often quite un-Norwegian. We, then, who learned Norwegian

in our childhood homes, are glad to see that so many good
Norwegian words have been adopted in the language of these
stories; but we are grieved to see them for the greater part
thus translated into Danish and sent out among the Norwegians. One thing must be granted, the spirit of the language as well as the mode of presentation is thoroughly Norwegian.

In reality it was a great step forward toward things Norwegian that these men took. But it is not to be supposed that
they were not criticized for going so far in the use of words
that were not Danish! Harsh criticisms were bestowed upon
them here and there because the language was not pure
enough, that is, not Danish enough. To illustrate how zealous
some Norwegians were to keep their Danish language pure,
I will mention Lyder Sagen, (1777-1850). This teacher in
Bergen struck out ruthlessly whatever Norwegian idioms and
words appeared in the written work of his pupils. Or there
is the case of Landstad, the celebrated maker of our hymnal,
Landstads Salmebog. When Landstad had adapted some
Danish hymns, translated a number of German ones, and
written some very beautiful hymns himself, a commission
was appointed to examine the book. Landstad had used
words like *tagde,* and "I denne söde Juletid *tarv* man sig
ret fornöie." He was compelled to strike out *tarv,* "ought, has
reason to," and write *tör,* "to dare." This change destroyed
the meaning of course. Landstad intended, "In this blessed
Christmas time one has abundant reason to rejoice," or "one
ought to rejoice." In the changed version the sentence means
"In this blessed Christmas time one *dares* rejoice"! But
tarv was too Norwegian for the commission. Landstad answered not without some heat: "We ought to be ashamed to
be more hard to suit than is the Lord himself who has given
each people its language. He is no more offended by a Norwegian word in His holy house than by a coat of honest
homespun. It is possible to mock at all things, but this ought
not to be so. One ought to be careful not to make sport of
a people that has sustained the loss of a grand mother tongue
with its wonderful literature, a language that is fully on a
par with any other language whatsoever both in beauty and

richness and power of development, ... he reviles the people who makes light of the mother tongue.'' (*See*, Lars Eskeland—*Norsk Salmesong*, Oslo 1904, p. 10 ff.). This is the way Landstad felt about Norwegian, he who had been educated in Danish in common school and university. The commission made him change *makk*, 'worm,' to *orm*, which to a Norwegian means 'serpent.' He protested, but the commission held that the Norwegian word *makk* was too simple, too vulgar, too Norwegian, to be given a place in the church language of Norway. The hymnal was finally adopted after eight years of toning down and elimination of Norwegian words and idioms. The same year, 1869, in which the timid purists permitted Landstad's hymnal to pass, appeared by a strange coincidence *Nokre Salmar* by Blix—in *Landsmaal!* Old Landstad was right glad to see them.

And now let us turn to one of Norway's greatest men, poet, philologist, language reformer, patriot,—I mean Ivar Aasen. Ivar was born in 1813, the son of a peasant. The farm, Aasen, from which the surname is derived, lies in Söndmöre in Western Norway in the heart of the best Norwegian language region. Aasen had little formal schooling. He is a splendid example of what unswerving purpose, genius, and self-education can do. Language interested Aasen profoundly. Grammar was simply poetry to him. First he studied foreign languages somewhat; then he tried to get some fundamental knowledge of Scandinavian from existing Danish grammars. But as these grammars did not go far, he found it necessary to set to work for himself. He studied old Norse as a matter of course and also old Swedish. He investigated his own Söndmöre dialect and published a study of it in 1851 under the title *Söndmörsk Grammatik*. He came in due time to Bergen in order to show his work to the bishop. The bishop introduced him to Sophus Bugge, who happened to be in the city at that time. It did not take Bugge long to realize that he was face to face with a philological genius. Bugge helped Aasen to get financial aid to travel throughout Norway for the purpose of collecting dialect material. In 1848 appeared *Det norske Folkesprogs*

Grammatik. In 1850 Aasen published his *Ordbog over det norske Folkesprog.*

In doing all this work Aasen made a great discovery, or at least confirmed what may have been a mere surmise in his mind. It was generally held that Danish had completely driven out the Norwegian language, that the apparently rude and uncouth country dialects were mere corruptions of the noble speech of Denmark and of the speech of the cultured classes in Norway. Aasen soon found abundant proof to the contrary, proof that he was not dealing with corrupt Danish *patois* but with the healthy, vigorous direct descendants of the old language of Norway. He found that a great many of the Norwegians had never spoken Danish, never! These dialects were far from being as impoverished as was thought by the "cultured" of the cities. They were far from dissolution, these dialects, but perfectly healthy and sound. And when is a dialect or language sound and healthy? I should say, when it is able to form new words out of its own elements to meet whatever needs may arise, or is able to assimilate and make its own, whatever it may find necessary to borrow. These Norwegian dialects treat Danish as a distinctly foreign language. A Danish word has mental quotation marks around it when used in a Norwegian sentence. This is the way my dialect of Tysnœs treats Danish. These dialects retain to a remarkable degree the choice idioms and words of our ancient classical language. The statement is made by Aasen that in one part or another of Norway is found well-nigh all the words of the old Norse vocabulary. We have often found dialect words that have given us precious hints and aids in the interpretation of difficult passages of the Elder Edda. These dialects have, some of them, been more nobly conservative in the matter of phonology than has Icelandic, though they fall far below in the matter of the conservation of inflectional forms.

Here were rich dialects agreeing with one another in the main both as regards grammar and vocabulary, but lacking a central, unifying norm, a standard language to which they could furnish material and which in turn could keep them from running riot in the matter of individual development.

This large uniformity in the essentials of the various Norwegian dialects led Aasen to do a thing which has divided more than one household in Norway and turned mother against daughter and father against son. As the Primitive Germanic language had been scientifically reconstructed from converging lines of evidence, so Aasen set about to construct a central language out of the richest and most distinctly Norwegian dialects, that is, out of the dialects of Western Norway. With one difference, however, Aasen's language is made up, in its essentials, of real living forms, whereas the old Primitive Germanic has whole constellations of "starry" forms.

When Aasen had evolved his language, which is essentially normalized West Norwegian, he set about to write poems and sketches in this language to show its powers and possibilities. He gave us *Heimsyn,* a series of essays in which he treats the heavenly bodies, the air and climate, continents, life on earth, etc. The language is terse, pliable, rich, vital. (*See,* Aasen— *Skrifter i Samling,* Vol. II, 1912, 221ff.) It so happened that Ivar Aasen was not only a philological genius of the highest order, but a sincere patriot and a charming lyric poet as well. Some of his poems in *Landsmaal* belong to the finest ever written by a Norwegian. Some of his songs and charming lyrics are known and loved in every home in Norway, no matter what the occupants may think of Aasen's *Landsmaal.* Ivar had, moreover, the gift of making excellent definitions in his dictionaries, for saying striking things in defense of his language. He avoids invective and abuse. His presentation is calm, large and scholarly. He speaks with authority for he has earned the right by painstaking, careful study. He has great powers of generalization and can always master a mass of details by a powerful, shaping mind. The Norwegian dialects appeared to all a veritable chaos, but Aasen's creative mind turned them into a speech so truly Norwegian that we who have never spoken Danish find our own dialects vindicated, chastised and ennobled in Aasen's wonderful language. We accept unreservedly all that he has done and honor him as we can scarcely honor any other Norwegian. But however cool and calm the language discussions of Aasen are, one feels that below the surface there is a current of strong feeling. Aasen realizes keenly Norway's greatest shame, the use of the Danish language! (See, Aasen, *Skrifter i Samling,* 3 vol. Chr. 1912.)

Aasen soon found enthusiastic helpers. The Norwegian national feeling was awakening and to the extent that it was awake it approved Aasen's work. It has often been charged by the opponents of Aasen's language reform that the partisans of *Landsmaal* are merely a few faddists, and that their work is not supported by the Norwegian national feeling. If that charge had been true, how can one suppose that this language, starting as it did with apparently everything against it except its own just cause, could in a few short years have fought itself to a place of legal equality with Dano-Norwegian, which latter language has been in official use in Norway since 1450? There are many staunch defenders of *Landsmaal* who in speech and writing use Danish because that was the language taught them in the school. There are members in the Storthing who, in debates on the language question, have deplored the fact that Dano-Norwegian is the only language they master, but who say most emphatically that their children shall be given the opportunity to learn Norwegian. C. Bruun, for a number of years co-editor of *For Kirke og Kultur* has fought many a splendid battle for *Landsmaal,* but he always wrote in Danish. Once someone sneeringly remarked, ''You serve your cause, you do; write fervid articles in favor of *Landsmaal* but write in Danish!'' ''But,'' said Bruun, ''watch the students that come from the school in which I taught. You will find that they will both advocate and use *Landsmaal.''*

Now, Danish was by many, even in the early fifties of the last century, felt to be our most disgraceful badge of servitude. There were men who hated Danish with a large, sincere and splendid hatred. But what could they do before the great work of Aasen had been accomplished? On the one side was Danish firmly entrenched in church, in state, in school, and among the educated classes in general; on the other side were a great many country dialects very much alive but rather undisciplined. The malcontents had grumbled— in Danish. Aasen, however, now offered a means of salvation.

Here was a language—made by one man if you like [1]—but yet a language which was certainly not Danish, and which was much nearer to most of the Norwegian dialects than was the official Danish. A language rich in musical effect, was this *Landsmaal*. Danish has leveled under *e* well-nigh all the vowels of its older inflectional endings. Danish is consequently the least musically capable of the Scandinavian languages. With it compare the beauty of Swedish. Read, for instance, *Axel* by Tegner and glory in the melody thereof, then turn to any Danish poet and note the difference, and the endless succession of *e*'s; e. g.: *Og glemme stövets usle Frugt herneden.* Colorless, dull, and gray appears this language in comparison with Swedish, with the Norwegian dialects, or with *Landsmaal*. *Landsmaal* has nearly the richness and beauty of Swedish as far as the endings of the words are concerned, and it surpasses Swedish in having kept the diphthongal series *au, öy, ei* in the root syllables.

Among the early writers in *Landsmaal* may be mentioned, in addition to Aasen, Vinje, Fjörtoft, and Janson. Aasen's work as a language student and as a collector of dialect material had at first been received with enthusiasm and favor in all circles. But as soon as the majority of the cultured became aware of Aasen's enlarging plan and purpose, and noticed that he was beginning to have a following, the opposition arose. At first these apostles of good taste had been charmed by Aasen's simple country songs written in what appeared to them some peasant dialect, but when Aasen began to plan and advocate a more far-reaching and serious use of the *Landsmaal,* these men laughed condescendingly at what they considered Aasen's linguistic experiments, or scornfully dismissed the whole matter. Think, these men said, set a man-made paper-language, a rude peasant speech, an uncouth West Norwegian jargon, by the side of, or in the place of, Danish!

But *Landsmaal* was not a fad, hence it could not be howled down or laughed into silence. It was a profound and serious expression of the Norwegian will to live. Even its opponents today agree with it in its aim: a truly national language for

[1] Cp. Luther's work in German.

Norway. The difference of opinion comes in the choice of means to the desired end.

Landsmaal, however, gathered momentum. The Norwegian satirist and poet, Vinje, joined the movement after much deliberation and many a struggle. One can scarcely realize what it means to quit the official language of the land and take up one that is new and despised among the rich and influential. But Vinje took the step because he loved Norway and because he found in *Landsmaal* more of his mother's language and that of his own heart. As we know, he was a peasant-born man. Vinje began to publish in 1858 the famous *Dölen* (Valley-dweller, the man from the glen). This gave the *Landsmaal* men their organ. In this paper, Vinje used *Landsmaal* of course, however, not always according to Aasen's norm, but at times nearer his own Midland dialect of Telemarken, and at times nearer that of Eastern Norway. He wanted to be free to experiment in order to find the form that could unite most of Norway; the form that could embody most of the living dialects. He used, e. g.: *boki,* the book— later *boka,* the East Norwegian form. But however much he fluctuated, and part of this fluctuation was a psychological necessity with him regardless of language—he always moved within true Norwegian limits.

Finally we come to Arne Garborg, born 1851, who joined the *Landsmaal* movement at the age of twenty-seven. He was already becoming known as a writer of Danish-Norwegian. But while Ibsen sneered at the poor, struggling *Landsmaal* and Bjørnson blustered in provincial Danish, Garborg sat down and taught himself *Landsmaal,* that is, cast his lot with the despised patriots who were endeavoring to make the Norwegians wake up to the necessity of greater cultural independence. He was a most valuable addition to the ranks. His Danish and his *Landsmaal* are both admirable. (See, Garborg—*Den ny-norske Sprog- og Nationalitets Bevägelse.* Chr. 1877.) Garborg is from Jæderen in Western Norway. He has from childhood had a thorough knowledge of Norwegian, as he is a peasant's son.[2] Garborg is a keen

[2] And what a guiding norm such a dialect really is, is brought home to us most strikingly when we who know a dialect examine the well

critic. He has the gift of making his opponents appear delightfully ridiculous. One deft little turn of phrase becomes a telling blow. He is a poet of the purest type, and his lyrics are among our best. (See, Garborg—*Haugtussa*.) He has given us our greatest analysis of the morbid states of the religious consciousness, (See, Garborg—*Fred.*). And his every thought is for Norway: Improve its agriculture, reduce emigration, establish a national language, produce a saner religious attitude, revive the national feeling. (See, Garborg—*Knudaheibrev.*) He represents the deepest and sanest and truest in our nation. He is the veritable incarnation of the spirit of the New Norway.[3] And so Garborg joined the language movement with telling effect.

In the eighties there was started in the Storthing an agitation for granting *Landsmaal* some rights in Norway. And now the uproar began as one can well imagine! It was asked: are you going to introduce this language in the schools? It is hard enough to teach the children one language, without getting one more to contend with. And if you make this jargon the principal language of any school, are you not doing infinite harm to the children? Are you not shutting them out from culture and future usefulness in any career among the educated classes of Norway? And how about the literature? How about Holberg, Wessel, Ibsen, Björnson? You are mad! Well, perhaps we are mad, it was answered; perhaps, indeed, we are. But one thing is certain: We want a language of our own, or, at least, we want the Danish in Norway to become more Norwegian. Now, Danish in Norway is not going to become more Norwegian by some occult process. No, it must be brought into contact with Norwegian so that the Norwegian vocabulary and the *Sprachgefühl* of the best linguistic districts may be brought to bear on it. Peasants are largely

---

meaning attempts of city-bred people to write *Landsmaal*. We catch them sinning against the spirit of the Norwegian language in every line. They are used to the *s*-possessive of Danish and make the most unfortunate blunders in the use of our dialectal phrasal possessives.

[3] I shall elsewhere at a later time discuss more in detail the significance of Garborg's life-work.

ashamed of their language now. They affect a kind of Danish in the presence of city people and the cultured. We want to secure for the Norwegian dialects a better standing and recognition so that they may assert themselves more in the presence of the official language. And, moreover, we have had enough of our hyphenated existence: Politically we were Sweden hyphen Norway (Sweden-Norway), linguistically we are Denmark hyphen Norway! But there's no need for concern; Norway herself shall decide. Put *Landsmaal* to the test. Give it a chance. If it is not what is needed, it will die of itself. But the "cultured" continued to mock, the learned professors wrote long articles proving to their own satisfaction that no such language could long exist. A "paper-language"! Away with it! Look at your *Landsmaal*: Aasen uses one form, Fjørtoft another, and Vinje still another if not several. Bah!

It is true that there is a lack of strict uniformity in *Landsmaal*, but the same lack is found, though in a lesser degree, in Dano-Norwegian. Such a lack of uniformity, however, was part of the program of some of the language reformers, if not of all of them. Aasen's work was accepted as tentative. He located the gold mine and made the main shaft. Others must work too. Aasen's norm was in part accepted as something not absolutely definitive, but rather as a guiding principle which might indicate in a general way the direction in which the creation of a truly national speech for Norway ought to go. These reformers were themselves, and wanted others to be, profoundly influenced by their own particular dialects. In the moulding of the *Landsmaal* they wished to bring to it the wealth of the various dialects. This large treatment of the whole language question would, it was hoped, furnish an abundance of material from which usage could select the best as well as eliminate actual inconsistencies.

It must be admitted that *Landsmaal* was for a while rather chaotic. That was while Aasen's name did not have the commanding place it occupies now. Aasen's contemporaries found it harder to follow him than many of the present *Landsmaal* writers do. I suppose some jealousy entered in. If Ivar Aasen has a right to create a language for Norway, why can't I, A. O. Vinje, do as much? Why, indeed! But Aasen was a genius in addition to having a large and sound linguistic knowledge. He was not so likely to be lost in contradictions of detail as were the other men who attempted to use in writing a language different from Danish. There is noticeable a decided return to Aasen's form in late years, and of course his norm is used in the schools. Aasen is the venerated name and unifying influence which is felt more and more. He takes to some extent the place of a tradition.

The fight has, however, not been a sheer waste of time and energy as so many Norwegian-Americans, most of whom have not given the matter serious thought or study, are inclined to think. It has led to a clearer idea of what is really Norwegian. When I went to school at home, I did not realize that teacher and preacher were teaching me a foreign language as if it were my mother tongue. I thought they spoke the right and proper language and that *my* dialect was something to be ashamed of. It was refined and educated to say *hjem,* but vulgar to say *heim!* A great thing has been gained by all the bitterness and struggle of the language fight. All Norwegians at the present time want the language to become more Norwegian. The Danish of Denmark has ceased to be the accepted standard for Norway. If the Danes change their spelling, we no longer feel in duty bound to go and do likewise. The center of Danish-Norwegian has become the Norwegian capital. We who prefer the *Landsmaal* look upon the cultured speech of our Norwegian capital as provincial Danish, that is, Danish with enough Norwegian in it to spoil it as Danish, and make it a parody on real Norwegian. The *Riksmaal* is no longer good Danish, far from it; I and thousands with me are compelled by our Norwegian language feeling to reject this language as an uncouth hybrid, containing Danish elements and Christianiaisms which grammatically are to us perfect monstrosities. I shall merely mention that most astounding form, the neuter plural indefinite: *huser!*

But the Danish of Denmark has less influence on Danish-Norwegian than formerly. Years back it used to be so that when there was a choice between a known Danish word and an equally well known Norwegian word, the Danish word was given preference as a matter of course. The opposite is now true. The *Riksmaal* writers even go so far as to adopt an occasional word from their sworn enemy, the *Landsmaal*. Thus I come across words like *omsätning* for "oversättelse", and *nävnd* for "komite". But *Riksmaal,* so Danish in formative spirit and moulding power, has given to these words a Danish form. The more Norwegian and real *Landsmaal* forms are: *umsetjing* and *nemnd. Omsätning* and *nävnd* look like any other Danish words. There was a time—and not so very long ago either—when not a few of the most influential men of Norway considered it nothing short of crime to tamper with the Danish language, which they, of course, called Norwegian—in Norway. These men were purists to an extent unknown even in Denmark itself. They had the provincial's slavish respect for the language of the mother country. An example: When certain spelling reforms were being discussed in Norway, it was seriously considered to invite the Danes to make the same changes so as to keep the language alike in both realms. These men who wanted to keep Danish pure and undefiled were called by both *Riksmaal* and *Landsmaal* reformers, the *Donomaniacs*. There was another group, and these were actual, positive language reformers, who endeavored to reform without breaking with Danish. Björnson, the great agitator, belonged to this school. The professorial light was furnished by K. Knudsen. This man devoted his whole life to the cause of three voiceless consonants. Knudsen advocated the introduction of the co-called hard consonants in place of the corresponding Danish soft series *b-d-g.* This change, by the way, took place by law in 1907, or rather, the law gave its formal sanction to what was already a fact in the pronunciation of Danish-Norwegian.

We had, then, in Norway until quite recently, three groups or divisions in the language struggle: The ultra-conservatives, who desired to let well enough alone; the reformers within the "church", and lastly the "excommunicated" *Landsmaal* men. Aasen and his school considered Knudsen's work utterly futile. K. Knudsen said: "Let us reform, but reform within the Danish, and then gradually work out a language which shall satisfy the patriotic feeling of all Nor-

wegians.'' Aasen said: ''Let us once for all get a thoroughly
and solidly Norwegian foundation for ulterior linguistic
growth. Such retouching of Danish as Knudsen and
others of his kind are doing does not produce Norwegian.''
Danish is a language of long standing and as such has definite
laws of sound and syntax. It is able to shape, mould, trim,
lop off, transform whatever comes into it. It takes a Norwegian masculine or feminine noun, ''de-sexes'' it, and makes
it common gender. It normalizes the Norwegian words that
are taken into it: *Nemnd* becomes ''nävnd'', *spildrande* becomes ''spildrende.'' Aasen rightly maintained that Danish
is so contrary to the spirit of the Norwegian dialects that it
is well-nigh impossible to transfer into it their linguistic
wealth. Aasen's idea was to give Norway a befitting recep-
tacle into which the dialects could pour their valuable contributions.

All possible and impossible reasons have been urged against
Landsmaal. You cannot thus create a language; one man cannot do this. The answer is: Not unless he happens to give
direction and embodiment to the hopes and yearnings of a
goodly number of his fellow-countrymen. The national and
linguistic feeling of a growing number of Norwegians sanc-
tions Aasen's work. I find that my Norwegian dialect ap-
proves *Landsmaal* in all its essentials. And the rapid, phenomenal progress of Landsmaal proves that it is not a Uto-
pian impossibility.

Some have said: It would be impossible to obtain unity in
such a manufactured language; there would be no central
tradition to whip into line unruly writers and check individual tendencies to differences. This has been the favorite
line of attack with Professor Johan Storm. He pointed out
with gleeful satisfaction the differences and contradictions
in the *Landsmaal* writers. He made his case unduly strong
by dwelling fondly on real and imaginary differences and
passing over in silence large and essential elements of perfect
agreement. And if, perchance, he found it necessary to
mention some uniformity, it was only to condemn this self-
same uniformity as stagnation. He found nothing to praise
and everything to blame. The lack of uniformity he called

chaos; the presence of it, compulsory stagnation. Death alone could make *Landsmaal* whole.

Again, some objected that this new language was essentially a rural speech, poor in everything but the words for the most common and vulgar needs of life. But the answer to this was long ago furnished by Aasen and others. The West Norwegian dialects are rich, surprisingly rich. The West Norwegian farmer is an all-around man if ever there was one. He has bits of forest, hence he has all the terms that go with the work of the woodsman. He is a fisherman and sea-farer and consequently he has the rich vocabularies of these occupations. He is also a tiller of the soil—what little soil there is among the splendid rocks that Nature has so lavishly bestowed upon our land. To be a farmer in Western Norway, where division of labor is just beginning to make its appearance, means to be a shoemaker, painter, blacksmith, boatbuilder, cabinet-maker, tanner, cooper and what not. Of course the man knows the words involved. All these Norwegian farm-houses are veritable factories where an astonishing variety of things are made. The women spin and knit and weave, dye the cloth, make the clothes, embroider. And one can imagine how far the vocabulary of a plain city person would reach when put into these surroundings! No, the linguistic poverty lies very often on the other side.

In these country dialects are found, moreover, a wealth of excellent expressions of ethical and moral significance. I realized this, as never before, this last year when I began to examine systematically the vocabulary of my own dialect. I found a great many truly excellent terms of other than mere bread and butter significance. A certain peasant woman recognized as many as thirteen thousand of the dialect words in Vidsteen's *Ordbog over Bygdemaalene i Söndhordland.* In addition she knew of course the Danish of church and school. The *Landsmaal*, then, drawing upon these dialects for its form and substance, being endowed with their strength and vitality and wonderful power of word-creation, has the possibilities of becoming one of the richest of modern cultural languages. Many of these possibilities have now been turned into actualities. *Landsmaal* in the hands of Arne Garborg,

Professor Haegstad, Professor Gjelsvik, Hans Seland, Lars Eskeland, Vetle Vislie, Jens Tvedt, Pastor Hognestad, is second to no other Scandinavian language in any sense whatever. The opponents of *Landsmaal* are beginning to realize its ability to cope with the best of languages. As a consequence we hear less about the unfitness of *Landsmaal* to be a bearer of modern cultural ideas. That supposed inability used to be the great argument of the "cultured", *Riksmaal* was spoken of by its defenders as *kultursproget*, as though people who do not know Danish are shut out from culture.

Much work has been done in *Landsmaal* by men who have made the vindication of Norwegian speech the chief aim and object of their lives. Professor Marius Haegstad, following close in the footsteps of Aasen, has evolved an excellent Norwegian grammatical terminology. Pastor Hognestad has worked out the language of the church. Prof. N. Gjelsvik has brought forth a powerful, clear legal vocabulary. Many scientists have disciplined and enriched our language in lecture room and laboratory. *Landsmaal*, in the hands of one who has studied it long enough to be competent to handle it, is fully on a par with Danish in its ability to express anything ranging from your first baby's wee cry to abstruse cogitations on Oriental Philosophy. And it is infinitely superior to Danish in poetic beauty, in richness of tone-color, in variety of musical effect. It fits the Norwegian temperament. It is terse, direct, lively to a degree that can scarcely be reached by the flat, monotone Danish. Those who now take up *Landsmaal* enter into the labors of many. The hardest task is over. *Landsmaal* has assumed its character to a large extent; it has its spirit, its moulding power, its classics. What it needs now to reach success is a grim determination to make no concessions whatsoever to Danish-Norwegian.

Again it is said that the children of the cities cannot understand *Landsmaal;* that it is as difficult for them to understand this language as it would be to understand Swedish. There is much truth in this statement. But, say the partisans of *Landsmaal,* you of the cities have for the greater part substituted Danish for Norwegian. We admit that Danish is essentially your mother tongue; that it is the language of your mind and hearts. But more's the pity! You cannot help that you learnt Danish. You were not in sheltered nooks and valleys as we were, but lived in the centers of Danish influence where you were forced to learn Danish in order to transact business. Then it is objected that *Landsmaal* is essentially normalized West Norwegian. This objection is only partly true. East Norwegians themselves say that their dialects are one in spirit with *Landsmaal*. (*See,* Tov Flatin— *Flesbergmaalet.* Kongsberg, 1910. p. 3, and Sven Moren— *Austland og Vestland.*) In the lecture cited here which Sven Moren delivered at a national meeting of language reformers and others at Voss in 1908, we are told: "A 'West Norwegian language!'—you can imagine how strange such a term applied to *Landsmaal* appears to me who have grown up in the district farthest east, and who have built my Norwegian written language on the language spoken in my neighborhood. As far as I am concerned, the *Landsmaal* cannot be called a 'West Norwegian language'! *Landsmaal* is to me the most natural way of writing my own country dialect!"

But after all it must be admitted that *Landsmaal* has a decided West Norwegian appearance. And so it is asked by unpatriotic East Norwegians: "Why should we learn that language from the West, which is harder for us to learn than Danish?" But, of course, the Danish is called *Riksmaal*, our Norwegian language, in those regions, so when these people refuse to accept *Landsmaal*, they say: The choice is not between Norwegian and Danish but between your West Norwegian and our East Norwegian. Arne Garborg gave these people something to think about years ago. He wrote: It is impossible for a Norwegian to write Danish. He may learn to write German, or English, or French, and what he writes is called respectively German, or English, or French. But the minute a Norwegian attempts to write Danish, no matter how well he does the work, the result is—Norwegian. Now, it would seem reasonable to suppose that Norwegians, if they be Norwegians in the true sense, would prefer to learn a West Norwegian language rather than to continue the use of a language that was more or less forced upon the land in the days of national helplessness. Western Norway has infinitely more to contribute toward a national speech than the Eastern low-lands where Swedish and Danish influence has been much more potent than in the distant regions of the west coast.

The charge that *Landsmaal* would shut out culture, Aasen answered long ago: "I shall likewise say that I have never had in mind to expel the ideas along with the words [Danish and other foreign words], as there surely could be found a way to keep alive the ideas even though the names were slightly changed." (*Skrifter i Samling,* p. 58).

Aasen considers those dialects best that are most like the Old Norse and that have the largest number of native words. The best system is to select a *norm* to guide one in the use of the dialect material.

I shall give here the following quotations from Aasen's *Skrifter i Samling,* Vol. III, p. 95, to show you his "laboratory" method of word selection. "One must necessarily have such a model form before him each time there is a question of determining the right form of a word which is different in the various dialects. When, for instance, we consider the word which in Danish is *lys,* and in Norwegian dialects *ljos, ljös, lös, jos, jös,* we find after closer examination that the right Norwegian form is *ljos.*" That is, Aasen selects the form that is the nearest to the Old Norse. His dictum is, "The Old Norse must be our guide in the essentials." (i hovedsagen have det gamle sprog til mönster.).

One cannot get a language that will conform to the details of all the dialects. "A few words would have a somewhat different shape in a normalized Norwegian form than the shape they now have in the different districts. Such a thing is unavoidable. But if the teaching of Norwegian were conducted with half the time and energy devoted to teaching Danish, the people would soon understand *Landsmaal* better than Danish." And here Aasen speaks from his heart of hearts: "The old inheritence is yet in existence, the rightful heirs likewise, and it is within their power to enter into the enjoyment of the inheritence and to repair it fully. And no outsider has a right to interfere." (*loc. cit.* vol. III, p. 104)

Aasen says that *Landsmaal* is more rich and melodious than Danish, in fact a beautiful language. But one must use it with great care at first; it can easily be ruined in less competent hands. He who would reform a language cannot adopt everybody's ideas. Most people lack a clear outlook, a comprehensive understanding of the language itself and its relation to kindred tongues. If these very sane and sensible words of Aasen had been taken to heart by all the *Landsmaal* writers, we would have had less of the unfortunate confusion and contradictions that we find at present.

Let us here turn briefly to the work of K. Knudsen (1812-1895). Knudsen devoted his whole life to making the Danish used in Norway more Norwegian in sentence structure and vocabulary. He considered the form of the word, including the inflectional endings, as matters of less, even small, importance. His program is set forth clearly in his book, *Hvem skal vinne?* Chr. 1886. According to his view Danish is not a foreign language but the Danish version of the old common language of Scandinavia (fällesmaalet). Knudsen believes that Danish will gradually be influenced by Norwegian; he is himself trying to make it more "native". He has little or nothing to say in favor of the striking and genuine Norwegian element contained in the dialects. While the forms may be the same as those in the Danish language, the Norwegian language may have a spirit of its own, with certain differences in spelling. This ought, thinks he, to be sufficient to give Norway a national language! On page 73 we are told that "the language in Denmark is in reality the same as that of Norway, only in a different stage of development." By the same reasoning one could prove that Spanish is really not different from French, for French has in many cases passed through the Spanish stage of the words to get to its present form, even as Danish has passed through what is often yet the Norwegian forms. Knudsen's program for future linguistic endeavor (främtidsmaalsträv) is contained in the following quotation: "And now we come to the old differences between the two Norwegian languages, the questions concerning the feminine gender, the *a's* and the diphthongs. Any other far-reaching traces of Danish we have not. Concerning these 'traces', I have above expressed the opinion that they will not prove themselves so altogether ineffaceable when we only make our improvement along Danish-Norwegian lines, one by one and incidentally. The feminine gender is little by little gaining (*boka*—the book), *au-öy-ei* likewise, for the first in the root of the word: *Naut, graut, kaut, laus, löyse, blöyte, flöyte* (timber), *veik*, etc. Only let us not go too fast and antagonize the inhabitants of the cities." (*Hvem skal vinne?* p. 168ff.). Knudsen rather condemns the ending -*het* (-hed), preferring the more Norwegian ending -*skap*. He uses such Norwegian words as *navngjetne, gnag, kapaat, spildrende* (*spildrande*), en *bate*, "advantage." I cite the following as a sample of his Danish-Norwegian: "En *annen sak* var det, om de *hadde bygd* paa et enkelt *landskaps* maal, paa sönmörsk . . . . . ti da *hadde* de *hat* et virkelig talt maal . . . . ." (I have put the striking forms in italics.) Now, after all, this is good as far as it goes, but it does not go far enough in the direction of true Norwegian speech.

The chief ideas and methods of attack of Johan Storm may be found in the following books and articles: "Det Norske Maalsträv," *Nordisk Tidskrift*. 1878 pp. 405-430 and 526-550. *Det nynorske Landsmaal*, Kb. 1888. *Landsmaalet som Kultursprog*, Chr. 1903.

The prevailing spirit in these publications is that of a man who is completely at home in Danish, who looks upon Danish, with slight changes of pronunciation, as his mother tongue, as the Norwegian national language. He dwells fondly on the difference between the East and West Norwegian. Aasen made the *Landsmaal* out of West Norwegian dialects. Why should the East Norwegians accept it? There is no place where *Landsmaal* is spoken. There is a lack of uniformity. Vinje had five different language forms from 1858 to 1870. Now he uses *boki*, now East Norwegian *boka*, now regular Telemarken language, now more the Aasen form. To make a language one must base it on some one living dialect. Storm shows us that the language which the Höyem brothers used was in the main their Throndhjem dialect. (Fjørtoft defended the right of the dialects as over against Aasen's norm). Storm shows how Garborg and Mortenson use the so-called Midland form. He prophesies that greater confusion will follow later, when more districts become interested. He claims that forms like *bokjo, bojo, boko, bogo, boki, boka, bokja,* will all clamor for recognition in the same capacity, feminine singular definite. Then he speaks of the difficulties of all types—feminine nouns, neuters, use of datives, the plural of verbs. He deplores the lack of the s-possessive although he well knows, as professor of Romance philology, that the Romance languages get along splendidly without any such form.

As to the *Riksmaal;* the one drawback to this language is that its tradition goes straight back to Copenhagen—the farther back, the more Danish it becomes. Its classics tend in a foreign direction. Holberg, Wessel, Welhaven, Björnson, Ibsen, all exert to a greater or less degree a Danish influence when used as classics in the school-room. *Riksmaal,* if it is to make good progress in the direction of Norwegian idioms and vocabulary, must partly renounce its tradition, its classics. *Riksmaal* has been called Danish so much, that just now it is very eager to prove how genuinely Norwegian it can be. But its ancestry and traditions are there. The *Landsmaal* writers have an easier task. They say, Björson, Ibsen, Welhaven, etc., were Norwegians who wrote in Danish. We do not include them in our tradition, in our literature.

But the *Riksmaal* has become more Norwegian in sentence structure, idiom, vocabulary, and, to a limited extent, in the form of the words. Asbjörnsen and Moe, as I have said elsewhere in this article, wrote a language that is in spirit truly Norwegian. Björnson's peasant novels, though containing much Danish, have also many thoroughly Norwegian elements in the language. Ibsen, too, wrote well; *Peer Gynt,* for instance. I find in this play much that my dialect can sanction fully; many good Norwegian words and idioms. Of the current literature I shall merely mention the charming stories of Aanrud.

The opponents of *Landsmaal* have not always realized that the language movement, which came with the Romantic period in Norway and has lived through realism and naturalism, is rightly or wrongly a manifestation of the Norwegian *will to live.* If *Landsmaal* had been a mere fad, it would have been dead long ago. The *Landsmaal* movement has brought about as an indirect effect, a rapid change in Danish-Norwegian in the direction of the spoken Norwegian. And *Riksmaal*, which seems so Danish to some of us, is in reality more Norwegian than we realize at times. In 1907 the hard consonants were introduced into *Riksmaal*. In place of saying or writing *pibe*, for *Landsmaal pipa*, Danish-Norwegian now writes *pipe*. Other examples are *bok* for *bog*, *sandhet* for *sandhed*. But this change, good as it is, does not distinguish it from Swedish. The Swedes have the hard consonants in the same places as the Danish-Norwegian now has them. What then distinguishes Norwegian most clearly from both Danish and Swedish? The old diphthongs. Norwegian says *stein, höy, blaut,* for Danish *sten, hö, blöd.* Other differences I shall not touch upon.

The present status of *Landsmaal* in Norway is briefly this: It is legally on a par with Danish-Norwegian. It is taught in every school in the realm. The people in each school district may decide which language shall be the principal one. By *principal* is meant the language in which instruction in written work is given. One language shall thus be the principal language, and the other one shall be taught so that the pupils may be able to read it readily. As regards the churches, the congregations may by vote decide which language shall be used in the services. The laws of Norway are published in both languages, and the records of the proceedings of the Norwegian Storthing appear in both.

There are at the present time two main forms of *Landsmaal*. The first and by far the most important is that used by Haegstad, Liestöl, Gjelsvik, Jens Tvedt, Hans Seland and others. This is essentially the standard form of *Landsmaal* which is taught in the schools of Norway. This school norm is a modernized, toned-down form of Aasen's original *Landsmaal*. In my opinion, it is the form which with some changes will become the national language of Norway.

The form which is next in importance is that used by Arne Garborg for the last fifteen years. It is based on the Midland dialects of Norway—hence the name of *Midland* form of *Landsmaal*. One marked difference between this and the Aasen *Landsmaal* is that the Midland form has infinitives with long root syllables ending in *e* and with short root syllables ending in *a* (except a few words, as *sjaa, spy,* etc.), whereas in Aasen's language all infinitives end in -*a* in harmony with most West Norwegian dialects.

A vast majority of periodicals and newspapers are yet in Danish-Norwegian. Many of them print articles in both languages, however. About twenty publications in all Norway are completely in *Landsmaal*, but most of them are small. This state of affairs has nothing surprising in it. The present journalists of Norway were to a man educated in schools that used Danish as the only language. A change for the better will come when those who are now being educated in *Landsmaal* grow up.

Four professors at the University use *Landsmaal* in their courses. These are Hägstad, Liestöl, Koht, and Gjelsvik. Several other professors are in favor of the movement, but have not as yet changed language. A majority of the public school teachers the country over are in favor of *Landsmaal;* about fifteen per cent of the school children are taught it as the principal language. Many teachers use it regularly in all their work, and many more lend the language their moral support. In certain Normal schools, Notodden, for example, only *Landsmaal* is used.

In the church the *Landsmaal* has made slow progress. About twenty years ago the poet-preacher Anders Hovden began to conduct services in it. At the present time some thirty pastors use *Landsmaal* occasionally or exclusively.

The young people of Norway are for the greater part in favor of *Landsmaal*. And herein lies the hope of the new speech. It has been well said that for every old person that dies, Danish-Norwegian loses a supporter, and it is hard to find one to take the place. The young peoples' societies of Norway—a national organization of about 40,000 members—are nearly all in favor of restoring the Norwegian language.

About 250,000 to 300,000 people now use *Landsmaal*. These are mostly outside the cities and in West Norway. The following figures regarding *Landsmaal* in the bishopric of Bergen may be of interest. And let me say here that this bishopric out of the six in Norway is beyond compare the best *Landsmaal* region. Out of 1,020 school districts, 756 were Danish-Norwegian, and 264 *Landsmaal,* in 1907. In 1911 the same 1,020 school districts stood as follows: 480 were Danish-Norwegian, and 612 were *Landsmaal.* That is, *Landsmaal* gained 132 per cent in four years. (*See Yversyn yver Maalstoda i Bergens Bispedøme,* 1911, Aalesund, 1911.)

Norway has made progress. It has obtained political independence. Commerce is in a flourishing condition, emigration is decreasing, education is as good and abundant as in any other country. The national feeling is growing stronger. Fewer mothers are now glad to get their sons to America in time to escape the Norwegian military service, and fewer men are now so low in the scale of patriotism, as to be able to say that it matters little after all whether the Norwegians speak Norwegian or Danish. And, finally, Norway is well on the way toward acquiring a truly national speech; a speech that shall be the pride of all Norwegians; a speech that shall voice their joy and sorrow, their despair and hope, down through the years and years to come.

INGEBRIGT LILLEHEI.

University of Illinois.

MODERN IMITATIONS OF THE POPULAR BALLAD

It is extremely difficult in a study of modern imitations of the popular ballad to limit properly the scope of the investigation. During the last two hundred years at least, many poems whether they do or do not resemble the traditional poetry of the non-literary classes have been termed ballads by their authors. In addition, many poems which have no indication of the fact in their titles have more or less likeness to the popular ballad. To separate the imitations of the ballad from the poems which, although they may be called ballads, owe nothing actually to that literary form, is the first aim of this paper.[1]

In classifying the material, one is forced to rely upon his judgment alone to a considerable degree—too great a degree, indeed, for absolute accuracy. Many of the poems which have been considered contain only a few stanzas, or even lines, which suggest an attempt at reproducing the language or spirit of the traditional ballad. Others are a mixture of the lyric [2] and the ballad. Others have ballad themes and ballad diction in a complicated metrical structure, while still other poems have the structure of the ballad and little else that recalls it. It is not an easy task, then, to distinguish between the two primary classes which have been formed: poems showing no evidence internally of an attempt at imitation, and those that do show evidences of such an attempt. An avoidance of over-rigidity as to the exclusion or inclusion of doubtful poems has been attempted in this paper with the probable result that pieces of verse have been admitted which are only remotely indebted to the ancient ballad. Some certainly differ

---

[1] The following are examples of poems called ballads by their authors, which show no evidences of imitation of the popular ballad: *The Ballad of the Beard*, by W. H. Ainsworth; *Louisa, a Ballad*, by Robert Anderson; *Ballad, My Father was a Farmer*, by Robert Burns; *Caledonia, a Ballad*, by Robert Burns; *The Whistle, a Ballad*, by Robert Burns; *Ballad on the American War*, by Robert Burns; *The Country Clergyman's Trip to Cambridge, an Election Ballad*, by Lord Macaulay; *The Volunteer, a Ballad*, by Mrs. G. Sewell; *A Ballad*, by Mrs. G. Sewell; *The Devil's Walk, A Ballad*, by P. B. Shelley.

[2] "Lyric" in this paper is to be understood as meaning "subjective".

greatly in essence from the popular ballad, but show its influence in one way or another.

Three tests have to a certain extent been used in determining the poems to be considered. The first of these is stanzaic form. Comparatively few poems have been admitted which are not in the so-called ballad stanza, rhyming a b c b. This, of course, is a test not to be too rigorously applied, since stanzas of more or less than four lines in length occur in old ballads, as *Glasgerion, Earl Brand,* and *Fair Janet.* Likewise, the rhyme-scheme is not invariable, but may be, for instance, a a b b, as in *King John and the Bishop,* a a, as in *Gil Brenton,* or a b c b d b, as in *Lady Maisry,* stanza 17, version B. Little attention has been paid to metre, since that is variable in the popular ballad, although the commonest measure, which may be regarded as typical, exhibits four and three accents in alternating lines. As a second test the element of narration has been selected. No poem of a wholly subjective nature has been admitted. Of course, it has been impossible to bar subjectivity entirely; had it been done, few poems would have survived the test. Many ballads contain a certain amount of subjectivity which is subordinated to the generally narrative or objective quality of the poem. Furthermore, simple language, either naïve or archaic, is obviously necessary in the imitation ballad. This test, like the others, cannot be strictly applied, since there is in the majority of these poems a constant fluctuation between simplicity and bookishness, between antiquity and modernity. Upon these three tests or, more accurately, aids, the primary classifications of this discussion depend, except perhaps in case of the poems which are included in type A. In them obvious resemblance in subject-matter has determined the fact of imitation.

The brief classification contained in this paper makes no pretensions to completeness, aiming rather to be suggestive than exhaustive, and to serve as an introduction to an interesting phase of romanticism which has hitherto been partially neglected.

Although reputable poets wrote imitations of the popular

ballad[3] and persons published ballad collections before that date,[4] 1765 has been chosen as the most convenient and the most proper point of departure for this study. The publication of Percy's *Reliques of Ancient English Poetry* in that year marks the beginning of an interest in the popular ballad which has had no need of an apology for its existence,[5] and which has steadily increased up to the present time.

For the sake of convenience it is necessary to divide the poems which show evidence of being imitations of the ballad into certain groups, according to subject matter and treatment. In making these distinctions, one is confronted by the same difficulty as when distinguishing the poems which are imitative of the popular ballad from those which are not— that is, the various classes blend into each other to such a degree as to make definite classification in some cases almost impossible. In these cases a note suggesting an alternative classification has been appended to the ballad in question.

    A.   Imitations of the Plots of Specific Ballads.
    B.   Imitations of the Tone and Temper of the Border Ballad.
    C.   Ballads dealing with the Supernatural or Weird.
    D.   Ballads based on History or Tradition.
    E.   Ballads dealing with Religious Subjects.
    F.   Humorous Ballads.
    G.   Ballads Founded on Sentiment.

Certain poems which fall under none of these heads have been placed in a "Miscellaneous" class (H).

Type A—Imitations of Specific Ballads—includes those poems which are clearly either imitations or re-workings of certain popular ballads, or else close imitations of certain ballad types. Ballads, translated from foreign languages

---

[3] *Hardyknute*, by Lady Wardlaw, *William and Margaret*, by David Mallet, *Jemmy Dawson*, by William Shenstone, *Molly Mog*, by John Gay, *The Thief and Cordelier*, by Matthew Prior are imitations of the popular ballad before 1765.

[4] For example, *A Collection of Old Ballads*, three vols. 1723-25, edited probably by Ambrose Phillips.

[5] See the prefaces to the three volumes of the *Collection* cited in the preceding note.

which fulfill the general requirements are considered under this head. The following poems fall in this class:—

1. *Mother and Son* (William C. Bennett); an imitation of *Edward, Cambridge Ballads*, 13.[6] 2. *Lady Mary Ann* (Robert Burns); an imitation of a song heard by Burns in the Highlands. Cf. 155, *Cambridge Ballads*. 3. *Lord Gregory, A Ballad* (Robert Burns); founded on *The Lass of Roch Royal, Child's Ballads*, 76, B, or I. It is almost a lyric. 4. *The Song of the Western Men* (R. S. Hawker); an imitation of the old song of the same name. 5. *Jack Johnstone the Tinkler* (James Hogg); an imitation of *Robin Hood and the Tinker, Cambridge Ballads*, 127. 6. *Sir David Graeme* (James Hogg); an imitation of *The Twa Corbies, Cambridge Ballads*, p. 45. Cf. *Lord William, ibid.*, 254. 7. *The Sea-Wife* (Rudyard Kipling); an imitation of *The Wife of Usher's Well. Cambridge Ballads*, 79. 8. *The Last Rhyme of True Thomas* (Rudyard Kipling); an imitation of *Thomas the Rhymer, Minstrelsy*, Vol. IV, p. 86.[7] See also *Child's Ballads*, 37. 9. *The Water King* (M. G. Lewis); an imitation of *Lady Isabel and the Elf-Knight, Cambridge Ballads*, 4 B. 10. *Courteous King Jamie* (M. G. Lewis); an imitation of *King Henry, Child's Ballads*, 32. 11. *The Fause Ladye* (William Motherwell); an imitation of *Lady Isabel and the Elf-Knight, Cambridge Ballads*, 48. 12. *The Child of Elle* (Thomas Percy); an imitation and conclusion of *The Child of Elle, Reliques*, Vol. I, Bk. 1, 11.[8] See also *Earl Brand, Child's Ballads*, 7. 13. *The Marriage of Sir Gawaine* (Thomas Percy); a completion of the ballad of the same name. *Reliques*, Vol. II, bk. 7, 1. See *Child's Ballads*, 31. 14. *The Duke of Alba* (Edward Quillinan); a translation of the Spanish ballad *O Duque D'Alba*, imitating the English popular ballad. 15. *Thomas the Rhymer* (Sir Walter Scott); an imitation and completion of *Thomas the Rhymer, Minstrelsy*, Vol. IV. p. 86. See also *Child's Ballads*, 37. 16. *Alice Brand* (Sir Walter Scott); an imitation of *Tam Lin, Cambridge Ballads*, 39.

[6] *English and Scottish Popular Ballads.* Edited from the Collection of Francis James Child by Helen Child Sargent and George Lyman Kittredge. Boston and New York, 1904.

References have been made whenever feasible to this excellently selected volume of ballads, because of its being more accessible to some readers than the monumental collection of Professor Child.

[7] *Minstrelsy of the Scottish Border.* Edited by T. J. Henderson. Edinburgh. Four vols. Edinburgh, 1902.

[8] *Reliques of Ancient English Poetry.* By Thomas Percy. Edited by J. V. Pritchard. Two vols. New York, n. d.

17. *Young Lochinvar* (Sir Walter Scott); an imitation of *Katherine Jaffray, Child's Ballads*, 221, and closest to versions C, D, and F. 18. *Proud Maisie* (Sir Walter Scott); an imitation of the ballad in which a lady converses with a bird, such as *Young Hunting, Cambridge Ballads*, 68. 19. *The Bloody Son* (A. C. Swinburne); an imitation of *Edward, Cambridge Ballads*, 13. 20. *The Sea Swallows* (A. C. Swinburne); an imitation of the question and answer type of ballad. Cf. 1, 2, 4, 5, 46, *Cambridge Ballads*.

Type B—Imitations of the tone and temper of the Border Ballad—includes certain imitations of the ancient popular ballad the scenes of which are laid in the lowlands of Scotland, or in the north of England and especially about the borders of the two countries. Their themes are chiefly love or war. In this class are included:—

1. *Earl Walter* (James Hogg). 2. *The Laird of Lairiston* (James Hogg). 3. *Gilmanscleuch* (James Hogg). 4. *The Tweeddale Raide* (Robert Hogg). 5. *Kenneth* (Henry Mackenzie). 6. *Duncan* (Henry Mackenzie); almost too bookish and modern. 7. *The Slayne Menstrel* (William Motherwell). 8. *Christie's Will* (Sir Walter Scott). 9. *The Reiver's Wedding* (Sir Walter Scott). 10. *Elspeth's Ballad* (Sir Walter Scott). 11. *Jock of Haseldean* (Sir Walter Scott). 12. *Cadyow Castle* (Sir Walter Scott); almost too bookish. 13. *The Eve of St. John* (Sir Walter Scott). 14. *The Lord Herries, his Complaint* (C. K. Sharpe). 15. *The Murder of Caerlaveroc* (C. K. Sharpe). 16. *Lady Jean* (Robert White).

Type C—Ballads dealing with the Supernatural or Weird—includes those imitations of the ancient ballad which have as their primary purpose the inspiring of horror, fear, or wonder in the reader through the use of supernatural characters or gruesome incidents. The following poems fall in this class:—

1. *The Legend of the Lady of Rookwood* (W. H. Ainsworth); somewhat bookish in diction. 2. *The Old Oak Coffin* (W. H. Ainsworth); [9] somewhat bookish in diction. 3. *The Elden Tree, an Ancient Ballad* (Joanna Baillie). 4. *Malcolm's Heir, a Tale of Wonder* (Joanna Baillie); somewhat literary in language. 5. *Lord John of the East, a Ballad* (Joanna Baillie). 6. *Screaming Tarn* (Robert Bridges); only a few stanzas show an imitation of the popular ballad. 7.

[9] 1 and 2 occur in Ainsworth's *Rookwood*, pp. 94 and 149, respectively.

The Spectre Boat (Thomas Campbell). 8. *Ballad of the Dark Ladie* (S. T. Coleridge) ; somewhat subjective in nature. 9. *The Rime of the Ancient Mariner* (S. T. Coleridge). 10. *Lord Robert* (Sidney Dobell) ; a rather peculiar stanzaic structure and runs into the subjective. 11. *Keith of Ravelstone* (Sidney Dobell) ; somewhat literary in diction and contained in another poem—*A Nuptial Eve*—which is not in ballad form. 12. *The Doom-Well of St. Madron* (R. S. Hawker). 13. *The Witch of Fife* (James Hogg). 14. *Lyttil Pynkie* (James Hogg) ; the spelling is perhaps the chief evidence of an attempt at imitating the ancient ballad. 15. *May of the Moril Glen* (James Hogg). 16. *Lord Derwent* (James Hogg). 17. *The Pedlar* (James Hogg). 18. *Mess John* (James Hogg). 19. *The Keylan Rowe* (James Hogg).[10] 20. *The Dream of Eugene Aram* (Thomas Hood). 21. *The Fairies of the Caldon Low* (Mary Howitt). 22. *La Belle Dame sans Merci* (John Keats). 23. *The Priest's Heart* (Charles Kingsley). 24. *The Weird Lady* (Charles Kingsley). 25. *Bothwell's Bonny Jane* (M. G. Lewis) ; rhymes a b a b, and only a few stanzas recall the ancient ballad. 26. *The Gay Gold Ring* (M. G. Lewis). 27. *Bertrand and Mary-Belle* (M. G. Lewis) ; rhymes a b a b. 28. *The Cout of Keeldar* (John Leyden). 29. *Lord Soulis* (John Leyden) ; based to some extent on *John Thomson and the Turk, Child's Ballads*, 226, B. 30. *The Elfin King* (John Leyden). 31. *The Ring, a Tale* (Thomas Moore) ; almost too literary for consideration. 32. *The Tune of Seven Towers* (William Morris) ; almost a lyric. 33. *Elfinland Wud* (William Motherwell). 34. *Lord Archibald, a Ballad* (William Motherwell) ; the lines are fourteeners, rhyming a a b b. 35. *The Ettin of Sillarwood* (William Motherwell). 36. *May Margaret* (John Payne). 37. *The Legend of St. Meinrad* (Edward Quillinan) ; rather bookish. 38. *Sister Helen* (D. G. Rossetti) ; not in the common ballad metre. 39. *Rose Mary* (D. G. Rossetti) ; not in the usual ballad metre. 40. *St. Swithin's Chair* (Sir Walter Scott). 41. *Ballad in Rokeby* (*And Whither Would You Lead Me Then?*) (Sir Walter Scott). 42. *The Castle of the Seven Shields* (Sir Walter Scott). 43. *St. Edmund's Eve* (P. B. Shelley).[11] 44. *Sister Rosa* (P. B. Shelley) ; more or less literary diction. 45. *The Old Woman of Berkeley* (Robert Southey). 46. *The King's Daughter* (A. C. Swinburne). 47. *King Charles's Vision* (Lord Tennyson).

[10] 19 occurs in *The Brownie of Bodsbeck and Other Tales*. Two vols. Edinburgh, 1818. Vol. II, p. 320.

[11] 43 is found in *Original Poems by Victor and Cazire*. Edited by Richard Garnett. London, 1898. P. 37.

Type D—Imitations based on History or Tradition—includes those imitations of the popular ballad which take their subjects from history or from tradition and which are not treated in other classes. The following poems are grouped under this head:—

1. *The Custom of Dunmow* (W. H. Ainsworth); not in a common ballad metre. 2. *The Barber of Ripon and the Ghostly Basin* (W. H. Ainsworth);[12] see 1. 3. *The Heart of the Bruce* (W. E. Aytoun). 4. *The Lay of Talbot the Troubador* (W. L. Bowles). 5. *The Harp of Hoel* (W. L. Bowles). 6. *The Song of the Cid* (W. L. Bowles). 7. *Mucklemouth Meg* (Robert Browning). 8. *Charlie, he is my Darling* (Robert Burns). 9. *The Bristowe Tragedy* (Thomas Chatterton). 10. *The Cid's Departure into Exile* (Felicia Hemans). 11. *The Cid's Deathbed* (Felicia Hemans); rhymes a b a b. 12. *The Fray of Elibank* (James Hogg). 13. *Hengist and Mey* (W. J. Mickle). 14. *Rich and Rare were the Gems She Wore* (Thomas Moore). 15. *The White Ship* (D. G. Rossetti); some stanzas do not suggest the ancient popular ballad. 16. *The King's Tragedy* (D. G. Rossetti). 17. *The Gray Brother* (Sir Walter Scott). 18. *The Horn of Egremont Castle* (William Wordsworth); contains a considerable amount of the simplicity of the ballad.

Type E—Ballads dealing with religious subjects—includes those imitations of the popular ballad which are based on Biblical episodes, or which have to do with the Church, or with religion and the religious in general. Under this head fall the following poems:—

1. *The Rising at Aix* (Cecil Frances Alexander). 2. *The Ballad of Mary the Mother* (Robert Buchanan); certain stanzas resemble the popular ballad fairly closely. 3. *The Ballad of Judas Iscariot* (Robert Buchanan); this poem has the qualities of Type C to a considerable degree. 4. *The Ballad of Monk Julius* (P. B. Marston). 5. *Queen Orraca and the Five Martyrs of Morocco* (Robert Southey).

Type F—Humorous Ballads—includes ballads which are humorous either in subject matter or in treatment, or, it may be, in both. The following poems may be placed in this class:—

1. *Old Grinrod's Ghost* (W. H. Ainsworth); not many ele-

[12] 1 and 2 occur in *The Flitch of Bacon*, pp. 67 and 156, respectively, the *Novels* of W. Harrison Ainsworth, London, n. d. On p. 251 occurs *The Ballad of the Beard*, mentioned in note 1.

ments of the popular ballad. 2. *The Knight of Malta* (W. H. Ainsworth) ; form not that usually found in the popular ballad. 3. *Will Davis and Dick Turpin* (W. H. Ainsworth) ;[13] rhymes a a a a. 4. *A Lay of St. Nicholas* (R. H. Barham). 5. *Nell Cook, a Legend of the Dark Entry* (R. H. Barham). 6. *To the Weaver's Gin Ye Go* (Robert Burns). 7. *The Battle of Sherramuir* (Robert Burns) ; this poem may be placed here or under Type A, as it is an imitation of an old ballad of the same name. 8. *The Braes of Killiecrankie* (Robert Burns). 9. *The Five Carlins, an Election Ballad* (Robert Burns) ; allegorical and satirical to some extent. 10. *Kellyburn Braes* (Robert Burns) ; *The Farmer's Old Wife* is the source (see 278, *Cambridge Ballads.*) The poem might be placed under Type A. 11. *Striking* (C. S. Calverley). 12. *Ballad* (*The Auld Wife Sat at Her Ivied Door*) (C. S. Calverley). 13. *The Freere of Orderys Whyte* (Thomas Chatterton) ; the title suggests Percy's *Friar of Orders Gray,* and although the resemblance is confined to the titles, it may be a parody of Percy's sentimental ballad. 14. *The Diverting History of John Gilpin* (William Cowper). 15. *The Gude Grey Katt* (James Hogg) ; the imitation of the traditional ballad is chiefly in the spelling. 16. *The Powris of Moseke* (James Hogg) ; see 15. 17. *The Fall of Jock Gillespie* (Rudyard Kipling) ; this poem parodies one of the conventional opening paragraphs of the popular ballad, and the use of question and answer (See 161, 178, *Cambridge Ballads* for the first point. Citations are not necessary for the second.). 18. *Archie Armstrong's Aith* (John Marriott) ; this poem might be placed under Type C.

Type G—Ballads Founded on the Sentiments—includes those ballads which gain their effect chiefly through their appeal to love, pity, and the like.[14] The following poems may be listed under this head :—

1. *Sir Maurice, a Ballad* (Joanna Baillie). 2. *Bonnie Jean* (Robert Burns) ; not far from being purely subjective. 3. *The Lament of Mary Queen of Scotts* (Robert Burns) ; is more a lyric than a ballad, but it has some of the ballad elements in it. 4. *Lord Ullin's Daughter* (Thomas Campbell). 5. *Lady Mary, a Ballad* (Janet Hamilton) ; much that is sub-

---

[13] 1 is found in *The Flitch of Bacon,* p. 152, and 2 and 3 in *Rookwood,* pp. 180 and 274, respectively.

[14] This class in general approaches the purely subjective more closely than any one of the other classes which have been formed.

jective. 6. *O Falmouth is a Fine Town* (W. E. Henley).
7. *The Liddel Bower* (James Hogg). 8. *The Young Knight*
(Charles Kingsley); the rhyme-scheme (a a a b) is unusual.
9. *A New Forest Ballad* (Charles Kingsley); this poem might
almost be placed under Type C. 10. *The Song of the Little
Baltung* (Charles Kingsley). 11. *The Gift of the Sea* (Rudyard Kipling). 12. *Soldier, Soldier* (Rudyard Kipling); very
close to Type F. 13. *The Three Maidens* (George Meredith);
rhymes a b a b. 14. *Margaret's Bridal Eve* (George Meredith); rhymes a b a c. 15. *Love's Reward* (William Morris);
some stanzas recall the popular ballad. 16. *Welland River*
(William Morris). 17. *The Sailing of the Sword* (William
Morris). 18. *The Rose and the Fair Lilye* (William Motherwell). 19. *True Love's Dirge* (William Motherwell). 20.
Love from the North (Christina Rossetti). 21. *Stratton Water* (D. G. Rossetti). 22. *An Old Song Ended* (D. G. Rossetti). 23. *Song in Rokeby—O, Brignall Banks are Wild and
Fair*—(Sir Walter Scott). 24. *Allan-a-Dale* (Sir Walter
Scott); rhymes a a b b c c. 25. *The Orphan Maid* (Sir Walter
Scott); rhymes a b a b. 26. *The Fire King* (Sir Walter
Scott); this poem which is close to Type B, rhymes a a b b.
27. *Albert Graeme* (Sir Walter Scott). 28. *Glenkindie* (William B. Scott); some slight imitation of *Glasgerion, Child's
Ballads*, 67. 29. *The Ballad of Oriana* (Lord Tennyson); the
structure is unusual, and it is close to the purely subjective.
30. *Edward Gray* (Lord Tennyson); some characteristics of
the popular ballad are discernible. 31. *The Sisters* (Lord
Tennyson).

Type H—Miscellaneous Ballads—includes those imitations
of the popular ballad which cannot be placed under any of the
types, owing either to a lack of the elements necessary for
classification, or to such a mixture of elements as to make
classification an altogether too arbitrary matter. The following poems may be included in this group:—

1. *John Barleycorn* (Robert Burns).[15] 2. *Thirlestane*
(James Hogg). 3. *The Boar he would a-wooing go* (James
Hogg). 4. *Meg Merrilies* (John Keats). 5. *Scotch Song*

---

[15] This poem is founded upon *Sir John Barleycorn*, reprinted in Vol.
II, *Early Popular Poetry of Scotland and the Northern Borders*, edited
by David Laing, and reëdited by W. C. Hazlitt. The version of the
poem here printed is said by the editor to be from a "common stall copy
printed in the year 1781." This is probably a reprint or a version of
one of the following: *Sir John Barleycorne*, entered in the Stationers'
Register at London, December 14, 1624; *The Little Barleycorn*, entered

(Charles Kingsley); close to Type G. 6. *The Ballad of Earl Haldan's Daughter* (Charles Kingsley). 7. *Two Red Roses Across the Moon* (William Morris). 8. *Boy Johnny* (Christina Rossetti); close to Type G. 9. *The Staff and Scrip* (D. G. Rossetti); a question whether the religious, the sentimental, or the warlike predominates. 10. *William and Helen* (Sir Walter Scott); a translation of Bürger's *Lenore* in imitation of the popular ballad. 11. *May Janet* (A. C. Swinburne). 12. *Leonora* (Anonymous);[16] a translation of Bürger's *Lenore* in imitation of the popular ballad. The diction resembles that of the ancient ballad more closely than does that of 10.

R. S. FORSYTHE.

Columbia University.

November 23, 1832; *Sir John Barlicorne,* entered as "a Pamplett," March 22, 1633-4. It is not impossible that all four are garbled versions of a popular ballad. There is a blackletter version in the Pepysian collection.

[16] For 12 see Vol. II, p. 233, Lewis's *Tales of Wonder,* New York, 1801.

INDIAN DANCES IN *"THE TEMPEST"*

The relation of "The Tempest" to contemporary interest in American discovery and settlement was first suggested by Malone in his "Essay on the Chronological Order of Shakespeare's Plays," published in 1790. The surmise that the play may have been based upon "some particular and late misfortune at sea" Malone later confirmed by a pamphlet, "An Account of The Incidents from which The Title and Part of The Story of Shakespeare's Tempest were derived; and its True date Ascertained," published in 1808. In the advertisement the author states that he had conceived the discovery his own until the publication of Douce's "Illustrations of Shakespeare" " within these few days," in which the editor had pointed out the value of the Jourdan and Strachey pamphlets not only for determining the date of "The Tempest" but also as having suggested material for the play. Malone in this last pamphlet (reprinted in Boswell's Malone, 1821) names fourteen publications dating from 1602-1612, of which Boswell reprints thirteen, and states that he believes the list far from complete. In his discussion on the relation of "The Tempest" to these accounts of voyages, the author first makes the details of the famous wreck of the ship of Sir George Somers and Sir Thomas Gates clear, by quoting freely from Stith's "History of the first discovery and settlement of Virginia." Then for particular details to compare with "The Tempest" he quotes from the "True Declaration" issued by the Council, 1609-10, and from Jourdan's pamphlet, 1610, pointing out correspondences both in incident and in details of the setting. Strangely enough, he omits discussion of Strachey's "True Repertory" or letter of July 15, 1610. Although he does not quote from the Rosier pamphlet, he emphasizes the interest of the Earl of Southampton in voyages of discovery and settlement, the expedition under Captain George Weymouth, fitted out by Southampton and Lord Arundel and the interest of Southampton in the new charter of 1609, leading to the expedition under Somers and Gates. Of the pamphlets of 1612, Malone makes no use; for he had "certain knowledge" of the existence of "The Tempest" in

1611. Although Malone's work has since been proved not wholly accurate, his conclusions have been on the whole accepted.

Other early editors,[1] Theobald, Warburton, Johnson, Capell, Farmer, and Steevens used the pamphlets to explain certain allusions in the play, but they did not see that "The Tempest" had been based directly on Elizabethan interest in this voyage, reflected in conversation and printed pamphlets.

Furness in the Variorum edition of "The Tempest," 1892, summarized Malone's results and quoted freely from the Jourdan narrative. He suggested that if we could push the date of "The Tempest" on to 1613, the earliest date for which we have positive evidence, we could include a Strachey pamphlet of 1612, the identity of which he left confused. Furness then mentioned the possible acquaintanceship of Strachey and Shakespeare, surmised by Meissner from the fact that Strachey had written some poetry and that his pamphlet on "The Colony in Virginea Brittania" was issued "From my lodging in the blacke Friers."

The first real addition to Malone's discussion of the subject was made by Mr. Luce in the appendix to the Arden edition of "The Tempest", 1906. Mr. Luce has simplified the matter by giving a fairly complete list of pamphlets on American discovery, issued from 1608-1613, discussing the most significant at some length. He has also cleared away the confusion in regard to the various Strachey manuscripts and publications. In this summary Mr. Luce notices particularly: The Despatch sent by De la Warre in charge of Gates July 15, 1610; Strachey's Letter or "Repertory" written to some 'excellent lady' in England and probably carried by the same ship; Jourdan's, "A Discovery of the Bermudas, otherwise called the Ile of Devils . . . . .," written soon after the author landed in England; and "A True Declaration of the estate of the Colonies in Virginia . . . . . Published by Advise and direction of the Councell of Virginia, 1610." From the last three accounts, Mr. Luce has cited a large number of parallelisms, both in thought and phrasing, between the pamphlets and the play, the cumulative evidence of which is rea-

---

[1] Furness Variorum Ed. p. 308.

sonably convincing that Shakespeare based "The Tempest" in part on contemporary accounts of travel.

Mr. Luce, however, in his very thorough summary of the pamphlets related to "The Tempest", does not consider Shakespeare's possible indebtedness to these pamphlets for descriptions of the Indian dances, which may have furnished suggestive material for portions of the masque element of the play. In enumerating the various publications, Mr. Luce begins with those of 1608, thereby omitting the account of the Weymouth expedition fitted out by the Earl of Southampton and Lord Arundel, published in 1605. To this Shakespeare, on account of his friendship for Southampton, would naturally be attracted and from it the practical craftsman may have gleaned a bare suggestion for the strange burden of Ariel's Song, Act I, Sc. 2, which in the 1623 Folio reads:

> Come unto these yellow sands,
>   and then take hands:
> Curtsied when you have and kist
>   the wilde waves whist;
> Foote it featly heere, and there, and sweete
>   sprights beare the burthen. BURTHEN DISPERSEDLY
> Harke, harke, bowgh wawgh; the watch-dogges
>   barke, bowgh-wawgh.
> Ar. Hark, hark, I heare, the straine of
>   strutting chanticlere cry cockadidle-dowe.

The pamphlet thus describes an Indian dance on the shore: "Griffin which lay on Shoare, reported unto me their manner, and (as I may tearme them) the ceremonies of their Idolatry, which they perform thus. One among them (the eldest of the company as he judged) riseth right up, the rest sitting still, and *so sodainely cryed, Bowh, waugh;* then the women fall downe, and lye upon the ground, and the men altogether answering the same, fall a stamping round about with both feet as hard as they can, making the ground shake, with sundry loud outcries and change of voice and sound." [2]

Indian music and dances are among the features of Indian life most enthusiastically described in the accounts and may easily have caught Shakespeare's attention.

In the Strachey publication of 1612, "The Proceedings of

[2] Purchas, his Pilgrims (Glasgow 1906) Vol. XVIII, p. 344.

the English Colony in Virginea taken faithfully out of the writings of Thomas Studly Cape-Merchant, Anas Todkill, Doctor Russell, Nathaniel Powell . . . .; and since enlarged out of the Writings of Captain John Smith . . . . ." we find a complete description of a dance given by the women of Powhatan's camp before Captain John Smith, which again may have furnished a basis for the strange "living Drolerie" which contributes to the pageantry of "The Tempest" in Act III, Sc. 3. To this supposition there is of course the obstacle of the uncertainty of the date of "The Tempest". If the list of plays in the famous Cunningham Account Books of the Revels Office for the years 1604-5 and 1611-12 are forgeries, then there is no necessity for dating "The Tempest" earlier than 1613, and Shakespeare may easily have seen the 1612 volume edited by Strachey. If, however, we accept Mr. Law's apparently sound argument,[3] proving the authenticity of the Cunningham manuscripts, we cannot date "The Tempest" later than October 31, 1611. In that case, nevertheless, the playwright may earlier have seen the individual accounts which Strachey compiled for the volume of 1612. Mr. Luce, emphasizing the fact that Strachey posed as general editor, says: "A note 'To the Reader' informs us that the various narratives mostly by 'Souldiers' chanced 'into my hands' to publish it. 'T. Abbay' ' ". Purchas in a marginal note on his material says: "I have many written Treatises lying by me written by Capt. Smith and others, some there, some here after there returne, but because these have alreadie seene the light and containe a full relation of Virginian affaires, I was loth to wearie the Reader with others of this time." It seems fairly probable then, that Shakespear before writing "The Tempest" may have seen either "The Proceedings" or some of the separate accounts of which the volume was composed.

The description of the dance mentioned is in "The Proceedings" and reprinted in "Purchas, his Pilgrims"[4] and reads as follows:

"In a faire plaine field they made a fire, before which he

---

[3] Law, Some supposed Shakespeare Forgeries, London, 1911.

[4] Purchas, his Pilgrims (Glasgow 1906) Vol. XVIII, p. 496.

sitting upon a mat; suddenly amongst the woods was heard
such a hideous noise and shriking that they betooke them to
their armes, supposing Powhatan with all his power came
to surprise them; but the beholders which were many, men,
women, and children, satisfied the captaine there was no such
matter, being presently presented with this *anticke*, thirty
yong women came naked out of the woods (only covered be-
hinde and before with a few greene leaves) their bodies all
painted, some white, some red, some blacke, some party
colour, but every one different, their leader had a faire paire
of Stagges hornes on her head and another Skinne at her
girdle, another at her arme, a quiver of Arrowes in her hand,
the next in her hand a Sword, another a Clubbe, another a
Pot-sticke, all horned alike, the rest every one with their
several devices.   These fiends with most hellish cries and
shouts rushing from amongst the trees cast themselves in a
ring about the fire, singing and dancing with excellent ill
variety, oft falling into their infernall passions and then solemnly againe to sing and dance.   Having spent neere an
houre in this *Maskarado, as they entred, in like manner they
departed.   Having reaccommodated themselves, they solemnly
invited* Smith to their lodging, but no sooner was hee
within the house, but these Nimphes more tormented him than
ever most tediously crying, Love you not mee? *This salutation ended; the feast was set,* consisting of Fruite in Baskets,
Fish and Flesh in woodden Platters, Beans and Pease there
wanted not (for twenty Hogges) nor any savage daintie
which their invention could devise *some attending, others
singing and dancing about them; this mirth and banquet
being ended* with Firebrands (instead of Torches) they conducted him to his lodging.''

This strange and grotesque dance, which the author calls
'this Anticke,' 'this maskarado' would have delighted an
Elizabethan audience and might well have been one of the
features of "The Tempest" which called forth the well-
known censure of Ben Jonson in the Induction to "Bartholomew Fair," 1614. The elements of the masque (Act III,
Sc. 3) which makes one suspect a relationship between it
and the pamphlet are: the strange musicke, the several

strange shapes, the Banket, the gentle actions of salutation inviting the King to eate. The fact that the Shapes enter, dance, depart and re-enter as they did in the Indian dance also seems significant. The conversation following the dumb show seems further to suggest that Shakespeare thought of the masque as a phenomenon of beyond sea.

Alo. Give us kind keepers; what were these?
Seb. A living Drolerie; now I will beleeve
       That there are Unicornes; that in Arabia
       There is one Tree, the Phœnix throne, one Phœnix
       At this houre reigning there.
Ant. Ile beleeve both:
       And what do's else want credit, come to me
       And Ile besworne 'tis true: Travelers nere did lye
       Though fooles at home condemne 'em.
Gon. If in Naples
       I should report this now, would they beleeve me?
       If I should say I saw such Islands;
       (For certes, these are people of the Island)
       Who though they are of monstrous shape yet note
       Their manners are more gentle, kinde, then of
       Our humaine generation you will find
       Many, nay almost any.

The two following masques in Act IV are much more conventional, introducing the classic and pastoral elements found in "Cymbeline" and "The Winter's Tale." This one is quite different and on the whole far more congruous with the wonders of the Inchanted Isle beyond the seas.

RACHEL M. KELSEY.

Milwaukee.

THE ORIGIN OF THE CUSTOM OF SITTING ON THE STAGE

A few years ago Professor C. W. Wallace advanced the novel statements that "the fad of sitting on the stage came into vogue with the Blackfriars in 1597", that it is first alluded to in 1598, and that it was "a custom in no other theatre in Elizabeth's reign".[1] The assertions were as unfortunate as they were novel, for in a short while after their appearance Professor C. R. Baskervill showed conclusively that the custom must have originated before 1597, hence not at the Blackfriars, and that it was by no means confined to private theatres.[2]

Very recently, however, Professor Feuillerat has found documents establishing the existence of a Blackfriars Theatre as early as 1577.[3] As a result of this important discovery the question may arise whether after all the custom of sitting on the stage did not originate at the Blackfriars. Indeed, W. J. Lawrence has already raised the question. Speaking of the size and structure of this early playhouse, and arguing that it possessed no galleries for spectators, he writes:[4] "One can readily surmise that when the house was in the meridian of its prosperity, say in 1582, when Gosson speaks of 'a great many comedies' being acted there, the supply of pit-seats would often be considerably less than the demand. Surely we have in this a clue to the origin of sitting on the stage. It seems reasonably well assured that that custom began in the private theatre, and it has already been demonstrated that it was in existence before the erection of the second Blackfriars. We have, therefore, fair grounds for assuming that it first came into force at Farrant's house. If this assumption could be taken as a certainty, it would of itself prove the absence of galleries in the earlier Blackfriars, as, most indubitably, it can only have been under the severest pressure that the custom was allowed to spring into existence."

[1] *Children of the Chapel at Blackfriars*, p. 130.
[2] *Mod. Philology, VIII*, 581-86.
[3] *Shakespeare Jahrbuch*, XLVIII, pp. 81 seq.
[4] *The Eliz. Playhouse and Other Studies*, p. 234.

Now several statements in the passage above demand our attention. In the first place, it can certainly be shown that long before Burbage opened his Blackfriars the English stage had "under the severest pressure" been utilized by spectators for the purpose of sitting. We are told, for example, that great things would have been done at Gray's Inn on Innocent's Night, 1594, "if the multitude of beholders had not been so exceeding great, that thereby was no convenient room for those that were actors." As a result of this multitude, we are further informed, "there arose such a disordered tumult and crowd upon the stage, that there was no opportunity to effect that which was intended: there came so great a number of worshipful personages upon the stage that might not be displaced, and gentlewomen whose sex did privilege them from violence." [5]

That such a practice was rather common at the University may be implied from a passage in Sir John Harington's *Apology* (1596) for his *Metamorphosis of Ajax* (p. 21). "But methinks," he writes, "you may say, that here is a marvellous restraint made of shewing this discourse of mine, not much unlike to our stage-keepers in Cambridge, that for fear lest they should want company to see their comedies, go up and down with vizors and lights, puffing and thrusting, and keeping out all men so precisely, till all the town is drawn by this revel to the place; and at last, tag and rag, fresh men and sub-sizers, and all to be packed in together so thick, as now is scant left room for the prologue to come upon the stage."

It is entirely conceivable, then, that similar circumstances at the earlier Blackfriars might have led to a similar invasion of stage regions, and that such a custom once established might have easily spread to other theatres. But even if we admit that the fad was in vogue at Farrant's house, we cannot say strictly that it originated there; for there is indisputable evidence that spectators at private performances before royalty occupied the stage long before Farrant conceived the idea of fitting up his private theatre. The origin of such a practice at private theatricals is probably twofold: the prom-

[5] *Gesta Grayorum*, Nichols, *Prog. of Eliz.*, ed. 1788, II, 14-17.

inence of the chief spectator, and the size and structure of
the stages, which at courtly entertainments seem, until rather
a late date, to have served for the masque following the play
as well as for the play itself.[6]

Whether Henry VIII [7a] ever occupied the stage on such
occasions, I am unable to say, but one passage perhaps implies
that he did. Writing to his brother in 1527, Spinelli thus
described the play given by Wolsey: "Supper being ended,
they proceeded to the first hall . . . . . where a very well designed stage had been prepared, on which the Cardinal's
gentlemen recited Plautus' Latin comedy entitled Menaech-
mi. On its conclusion all the actors, one after the other,
presented themselves to the King, and on their knees recited
to him, some more and some less, Latin verses in his praise." [7b]

Similarly the epilogues of early court plays must have been
spoken directly to royalty very near at hand; and there is
considerable evidence to show that the actors, instead of
descending from the stage and passing to the royal state or
canopy at the opposite end of the hall, where it was situated
in the later masques, really remained on the stage, and kneeling before the state very close at hand addressed the royal

---

[6] Cf. passages below, Reyher, *Les Masques Anglais*, Machyn, *Diary*,
p. 275, etc.

[7a] In connection with the origin of the custom of sitting on the stage
two or three passages should perhaps be noted. Writing about the
early indoor stage in Paris, Stuart, (*Stage Decoration in France*, p. 193)
refers to a miniature of Jean Fouquet showing "a second story of a
stage in which is found Paradise, the emperor, certain devils and some
spectators." What are these "spectators"? *Élégantes* on the stage
were unknown in France in the middle of the sixteenth century, says
Bapst (*Essai sur l'histoire du Théâtre*, p. 146). Albright in quoting
the stage direction accompanying the stage plan of the *Castle of Perseverance* defines *stytelerys* as auditors (*The Shakspearian Stage*, p. 14).
Furnivall, however, in his edition of the Macro Plays gives to the word
the meaning of *orderers, arrangers, managers*. There is no evidence,
says Rennert (*The Spanish Stage*, p. 65), that spectators occupied
the stage in Spain in the sixteenth century, although he affirms that one
might infer from a passage (latter half of sixteenth century) that
they occupied the platform at the presentation of the short *autos* or
farces (Ibid., note).

[7b] *Cal. State Papers, Venetian*, 1527-33, p. 2.

occupant. That this state was sometimes placed on the stage there can be no doubt. Such was the case at Cambridge in 1564. According to Feuillerat,[8] the "dais" of the Queen was on this occasion "contre l'un des murs latéraux" of King's College Chapel. It was situated *on* the stage, however, as the following passage shows: "For the hearing and playing whereof ['Aulularia Plauti'], was made, by her Highness surveyor and at her own cost, in the body of the Church, a great stage containing the breadth of the church from one side to the other, that the chappels might serve for houses. In the length it ran two of the lower chappels full, with the pillars on a side. Upon the south-wall was hanged a cloth of state, with the appurtenances and half-path for her Majesty . . . . . When all things were ready for the plays, the Lord Chamberlayn with Mr. Secretary came in, bringing a multitude of the guard with them, having every man in his hand a torch-staff, for the lights of the play (for no other lights were occupied); and would not suffer any to stand upon the stage, save a very few upon the north side. And the guard stood upon the ground by the stage side, holding their lights. From the quire doore unto the stage was made as 'twere a bridge, rayled on both sides: for the Queen's Grace to go to the stage: which was straightly kept." [9]

Now the significant thing about this arrangement is that it was designed by "her Highnes surveyor" and at her own cost. He was obviously reproducing, so far as possible, the conditions as he was acquainted with them at court performances. The invaders of the stage at Cambridge, as described at a later date by Harington, had royal precedent for their procedure.

The passage above is also significant in that it helps to clarify matters at Oxford in 1566. At the disputation there

[8] *Bureau des Menus Plaisirs,* p. 74.

[9] Nichols, *Prog. of Eliz.,* ed. 1788, I, 13-14. See also Robinsin's description (Ibid. III, 59). On this same stage *Dido* and *Ezechias* were also acted (Ibid., I, 17); and while *Dido* was "a handling, the Lo. Robert, steward to the universitie, and Mr. secretarie Cecil, chancellor, to signifye their good wille, and that things might be orderlye done, vouchsafed to hold both books on the scaffold themselves" (Ibid., III, 177).

on the occasion of the Queen's visit, the state apparently occupied the speakers' platform,[10] and in view of the passage above it is virtually certain that, as Feuillerat affirms (*Le Bureau*, p. 73), her Majesty occupied the stage when Edward's *Palamon and Arcyte* was presented on the same occasion. Durand's translation of the part of Bereblock's description which is of significance in this connection follows: "In the first place there was a remarkable proscenium there, with an approach thrown open from the great solid wall; and from it a hanging wooden bridge . . . . . stretched across to the great hall of the college . . . . . Through this bridge, without commotion and without contact with the pressing crowd, the Queen might hasten by an easy ascent to the play, when it was ready . . . . . On each side of the stage magnificent palaces and well equipped houses are built up for the actors in the comedies and for the masked persons (commœdis ac personatis). On high a seat had been fixed, adorned with cushions and tapestries and covered with a golden canopy; this was the place made ready for the Queen." [11]

Now if it is established that Queen Elizabeth actually occupied the stage at an early date, then the passages suggesting her proximity to the actors in later court plays must be given consideration. In *The Arraignment of Paris*, V, "the state being in place", the Fates "lay down their properties at the Queenes feete", while Diana "delivereth the ball of golde to the Queenes owne hands". In Trotte's introduction to *Misfortunes of Arthur* we have the direction: "Three Muses come upon the stage apparelled accordingly bringing five gentlemen students with them attyred in their usuall garments, whom one of the Muses presented to her Maiestie as captives."

In Lyly's *Sapho and Phao* the Prologue kneels before the Queen and speaks directly to her. In the same manner the prologue to *Gallathea*, the prologue and epilogue to *Endymion*, etc., would gain in point and effectiveness if they were spoken to the Queen actually on the stage. Finally, some light may possibly be thrown on the situation of the chief spec-

[10] Nichols, *Prog. of Eliz.*, III, Wood's account, pp. 110-111.
[11] *P. M. L. A.*, XIII, p. 505, cf. Plummer, *Eliz. Oxford*, pp. 123-24.

tators at court entertainments by Grove's rather indefinite description (1587) of the boor who on the occasion of a court entertainment

> "Dyd mynde (if that he myght) to get
>   and wryng into the hall:
> To take the vewe, this boyish clowne
>   dyd nothing aye appall,
> Though with sight of nobles store
>   his doltish eyes were fed,
> But loppeth to the *upper end,*
>   his cap upon his head."

He was promptly ejected by one of the "wayters" who remarked:

> "sirrha, to come *so nygh*
>   how darest thou be bolde." [12]

It is time to return to Farrant's Blackfriars. In view of the fact that the custom of sitting on the stage originated before 1577, is it entirely safe to assume that it came into force as a result of limited space and the absence of galleries at Farrant's house? In all probability the practice was in vogue at the early Blackfriars from which it spread to later houses, but in my opinion Elizabethan vanity as well as stage structure is at the basis of the introduction of the fashion into the regular theatres. The gentlemen who occupied the stage were paying for the privilege of sitting where they had seen their superiors sit at private performances; and this is only one of the various ways in which practices at court influenced the regular playhouses during the reign of Elizabeth.

T. S. GRAVES.

Trinity College, N. C.

[12] Grosart, *Occasional Issues,* VI, 122.

CHARACTERIZATION IN *CLARISSA HARLOWE*

During the hundred and fifty odd years since the publication of Richardson's masterpiece *Clarissa Harlowe*, there has been an interesting alternation of opinion on the part of his readers as to the realistic value of the character-drawing of this retiring, sentimental printer. We have before us interesting documetary evidence of various conspicuous parties to the discussion; we may compare the definite pronouncement of intention which the author himself makes in his meticulous preface to the novel, with the opinions of several friends and contemporaries recorded in his correspondence—a valuable literary record, edited by Mrs. Barbauld and published in 1804 (but unfortunately never reprinted)—and in the letters and diaries of Dr. Johnson and Lady Mary Wortley Montagu. And we may also bring forward for comparison the opinion of latter-day critics such as Hazlitt, Sir Leslie Stephen, Augustine Birrell, and W. D. Howells. The characters about whom opinion has been most positive and most diverse are, of course, Clarissa herself, Lovelace the villain, and Miss Howe, the confidante of the heroine.

Richardson, always ready to devote ample time to the portrayal of his characters, through dialogue, self-analysis, the comment of other characters, and footnotes by the author, surpasses all his other efforts in the fulness and exactness of his delineation of Clarissa's character. In addition to the solicitous attention given her throughout the course of the story, the author makes an additional effort in a "Postscript" to justify her according to the canons of real life, waiving as uncomprehending the criticism, which evidently existed even in his own day, that the "incomparable lady" was not entirely a product of this world. He writes with almost petulant insistence: "Some there are, and ladies too! who have supposed that the excellencies of the heroine are carried to an improbable and even an impracticable height in the History. But the education of Clarissa from *early childhood* ought to be considered as one of her very great advantages;

and indeed the very foundation of *all* her excellencies; and
it is hoped for the sake of the doctrine designed to be incul-
cated by it, that it will. . . . . It must be confessed that we
are not to look for Clarissa's among the constant frequenters
of Ranelagh and Vauxhall, nor among those who may be
called *daughters of the card table.* If we do the character
of the heroine may then indeed be justly thought not only
improbable, but unattainable. But we have neither room in
this place, nor inclination, to pursue a subject so invidious.
We quit it therefore after we have *repeated* that we *know*
there are *some,* and we hope there are *many* in the British
Dominion . . . . . who as far as occasion has called upon them
to exert the like *humble and modest* yet *steady* and *useful* virtues, have reached the perfection of Clarissa.'' [1]

Evidently from many devoted readers of his own time
Richardson secured a satisfactory conformity to his opinions.
The singular unanimity with which several famous literary
personages of the period unite in affirming that Clarissa is a
''natural character'' lead one to reflect on the possibility of
a higher level of behavior than the middle of the eighteenth
century is usually credited with, or a lower order of discernment.

Foremost and best known among these contemporary criticisms is Boswell's record of a conversation with Dr. Johnson
on the merits of Richardson and Fielding. Boswell writes:
''It always appeared to me that he (Johnson) estimated the
compositions of Richardson too highly, and that he had an unreasonable prejudice against Fielding. In comparing those two
writers, he used this expression: 'that there was as great
difference between them as between a man who knew how a
watch was made and a man who could tell the hour by looking
at the dial plate.' This was a short and figurative statement of
his distinction between drawing characters of nature and
characters only of manners. But I cannot help being of
opinion that the real watches of Fielding are as well constructed as the large clocks of Richardson, and that his dial
plates are brighter. Fielding's characters though they do not
expand themselves so widely in dissertation are just pictures

[1] *Clarissa Harlowe.* Tauchnitz Edition, IV, 499.

of human nature, and I will venture to say, have more striking features, and nicer touches of the pencil.''[2] Boswell's
judgment, indeed, accords with that of many a modern reader,
but Dr. Johnson, in this as in other matters, voiced the
general opinion of his own age.

The captious, critical Lady Mary Wortley Montagu, far-
traveler and writer of letters, a luckless friend of Pope and
avowedly not an admirer of Richardson, writes: ''The two
first tomes of Clarissa touched me as being very resembling
to my maiden days.''[3] Miss Sara Fielding, a loyal admirer and
correspondent of Richardson's, though the sister of his great
and unduly hated rival, writes to Richardson of Clarissa:
''When I read of her I am all sensation; my heart glows;
I am overwhelmed; my only vent is tears; and unless tears
could mark my thoughts as legibly as ink, I cannot speak half
I feel. I become like the Harlowe's servant, when he spoke
not; he could not speak; he looked, he bowed, and withdrew.''[4]
Perhaps this excessive veneration is hardly such as Miss
Fielding would accord to an individual of her own world,
yet the unreality of Clarissa's character is not so pronounced
in her mind as to destroy the illusion.

Mrs. Barbauld, Richardson's biographer, herself a prominent literary figure of the time, writes: ''We regard the
characters as real personages, whom we know and converse
with, and whose fate remains to be decided in the course of
events.'' Yet she goes on to say of the chief of these ''real
personages'': ''The character of Clarissa is all along very
highly wrought; she has all the grace of dignity and delicacy
of a finished model of female excellence.''[5] Thus, whoever
may have been the crude and undiscriminating ''some'' (''and
ladies too''!) for whose benefit Richardson wrote his defence
in the Postscript, the recorded judgment of his peers, with
the exception of the unassuming Boswell, evidently supported

---

[2] Boswell's Life of Samuel Johnson, Everyman's Library. 1, 343.

[3] Letters of Lady Montagu, Everyman's Library, p. 461.

[4] Barbauld, *Correspondence of Samuel Richardson* (London, 1804)
II, 60.

[5] *Correspondence*, I, LXXXII.

the author's own contention that the character of Clarissa bears the marks of reality.

Compare with these contemporary tributes certain comments of the nineteenth century. Hazlitt, in his lecture on "The English Novelists" in the series of lectures on "The English Comic Writer" delivered in 1818 says:

"I should suppose that never sympathy more deep or sincere was excited than by the heroine of Richardson's romance, except by the calamities of real life. The links in this wonderful chain of interests are not more finely wrought than their whole weight is overwhelming and irresistible. Who can forget the exquisite gradations of her long dying-scene, or the closing of the coffin-lid when Miss Howe comes to take her last leave of her friend; or the heartbreaking reflection that Clarrisa makes on what was to have been her wedding day? Well does a certain writer exclaim:

'Books are a real world, both pure and good,
Round which, with tendrils strong as flesh and blood,
Our pastimes and our happiness may grow.'"[6]

Sir Leslie Stephen, in the keen, comprehensive introductory essays in his edition of Richardson's complete works,[7] satirizes happily Miss Howe's glowing panegyrics upon the heroine; yet he himself goes on to sum up Clarissa's character prosaically, without suggestion of its unreality. He writes: "Miss Harlowe appears to us as, in the main, a healthy, sensible country girl, with sound sense, the highest respect for decorum, and an exaggerated regard for constituted, especially paternal authority." Perhaps, however, we may accept this description as a half facetious judgment, set, as it is, in a context of mingled satire and keenly critical analysis.

Augustine Birrell in an essay on Richardson in his volume *Res Judicatae,* compares Clarissa and Fielding's heroines to the great advantage of the former, accepting without cavil the effectiveness of her exalted excellence: "Sophia Western," he says, "was, as we have seen, a comely girl enough,

[6] Hazlitt, *Collected Works,* Ed. by A. R. Waller and A. Glover (London, 1903) VIII, 120.

[7] Complete Works of Samuel Richardson, edited by Sir Leslie Stephen, London, 1883. 12 vols.

but she was as much like Clarissa as a ship in dock is like a ship at sea and on fire."[8]

But Mr. Howells caps the climax of this serious commendation of Clarissa's naturalness when he writes in his *Heroines in Fiction*: "Clarissa Harlowe, in spite of her eighteenth century costume and keeping, remains a masterpiece in the portraiture of that ever-womanly, which is of all times and places. The form of the novel in which she appears, the epistolary form, is of all forms the most averse to the apparent unconsciousness of so fascinating a heroine, yet the cunning of Richardson (it was in some things an unrivalled cunning) triumphs over the form, and shows us Clarissa with no more pose than she would confront herself with in the glass."[9] One wonders whether Mr. Howells, in his preparation of these volumes for the holiday trade, found time to reread many of the seven volumes in which Clarissa achieves her task of self-revelation with such "apparent unconsciousness." Natural she may have seemed to contemporary readers, whose criteria were based upon the lofty ladies of Romance, the vaguely drawn heroine of the picaresque stories, and Fielding's women objectively portrayed; but it is hard to believe that a modern critic, familiar with realistic heroines from Elizabeth Bennet, Ethel Newcome, Maggie Tulliver, to the American girls of his own creating, could see in Clarissa "no more pose than she could confront herself with in the glass." Yet Mr. Howell's statement may contain a truth more true than he intended, for it seems probable that the looking-glass itself must reflect Clarissa the heroine, in stately pose, poised, ready for her pedestal!

Such is the consensus of opinion as represented by notable readers of the *History of Clarissa* up to the present time. Before the rising generation accepts, however, the testimony of leisurely critics of the past—for it is safe to assume that but a small number of present-day readers will seek complete first hand evidence on the character of Clarissa—let us test Richardson's heroine by certain possible prototypes.

[8] Birrill, *Res Judicatae* (New York, 1892) p. 23.

[9] Howells, *Heroines in Fiction*, (New York, 1901) I, 3.

To my mind, Clarissa is heir to the triumphant grandeur of the heroines of Heroic Tragedy in the seventeenth century, and the noble self-immolation of Sentimental Comedy of the early eighteenth. The delineation of her character is a piece of epic-heightening, achieved in accordance with former models, but adapted to an eighteenth century purpose. We can trace the kinship between Clarissa and the seventeenth century heroines of Scudéry and the French romancers, and the writers of English Heroic Tragedy—notably Dryden. Compare the raptures over Clarissa's beauty, with the minute descriptions of "the women of Granada" and the "Fair Semahris" in Scudéry's *Almahida, or the Captive Queen*,[10] and of Chrysalia and Claricia in *Clélie* by the same author. Almahida herself embodies many of Clarissa's most conspicuous virtues, "a noble pride," and a desire to be "at her own disposal to marry," a strong sense of paternal authority. Semahris, another heroine of the same romance, exhibits a decorous reserve which is described by her baffled lover much in the manner of Lovelace: "She must be very dainty indeed (answered Almador, finding himself nipped to the quick) that can brook nothing but what pleases her fancy; and would deprive herself of all things that are delightful to free herself from those things for which she has no kindness. This is indeed a mark of niceness of the fair Semahris' humour."

In *Clélia*, another Scudéry romance, we have a heroine who is a striking prototype of Clarissa in many points of character and situation. See, for instance, the condition resulting from her reception of a letter from the lover opposed by her father: "This letter gave much joy to Clelia, but withal it augmented her persecution; for Clelius [the father] understanding it, told her she was infinitely culpable for receiving it, that there could no longer be an innocent correspondence between her and Aronces, since himself prohibited it; and that Rome having daily greater obligations to Horatius, it behoov'd her to look upon him as the man that was infallibly to marry her at the end of the war. Clelia answered to this speech of her

[10] Scudéry, *Almahida, or the Captive Queen*, translated by J. Phillips, London, 1677.

father with her accustomed constancy; and though she said
nothing inconsistent with the respect she ow'd to such a relation, yet withal she said nothing prejudicial to the fidelity
she promised to her lover." [11] Later she is endangered through
abduction by one Sextus, and immediately she betrays that
decisive preference for death to dishonor, which all heroic
ladies are given opportunity to display. After parting with
her accepted lover, we see her in the attitude of a noble grief
characteristic of her kind: [12] "Never was seen so sad a person
as she on this occasion; but her melancholy was accompanied
with so much discretion that it caused the greater compassion."
And finally she speaks before the Roman Senate "with so
resolute and generous an aspect, that all who beheld her,
judged she deserved greater honor than the senate had de-
creed her." Thus the exaltation of Clelia is accomplished by
universal commendation, much as that of Clarissa is achieved
through universal lamentation.

In the heroines of Dryden's heroic tragedies also we find
elements similar to Clarissa's character and situation. A
lofty contempt for unworthy love characterizes all these heroines, and growing out of it, an untempered scorn for the unworthy lover, and a glorious willingness to die in self-defense.
Almeyda in *Don Sebastian* says:

> "My virtue is a guard beyond my strength,
> And death, my last defense, within my call.
>
> . . . .
>
> I'll venture landing on that happy shore,
> With an unsullied body and white mind.
> If I have erred, some kind inhabitant
> Will pity a strayed soul to take me home." [13]

Compare this with Clarissa's attitude in the dramatic pen-
knife scene, which Lovelace recounts, beginning: " 'Stop
where thou art, O vilest and most abandoned of men! Stop
where thou art!' . . . . . She held forth a pen-knife in her
hand, the point to her own bosom, grasping resolutely the

[11] Scudéry, *Clélia*. Translated, London, 1670, page 598.

[12] Ibid., page 732.

[13] Dryden, *Poetical Works*, edited by Scott and Saintsbury, Edinburgh, 1882. III:364.

whole handle so that there was no offering to take it from her.''[14]

But more than the royally amorous ladies who people most of these tragedies, the cold, dispassionate Clarissa resembles the martyred Saint Catherine of *Tyrannic Love*. Compare Maximin's words,

''See where she comes with that high air and mien
    Which marks in bonds the greatness of a queen,'' [15]

with Lovelace's description of Clarissa's entrance: ''Then hear her step toward us and instantly see her enter among us, confiding in her own innocence, with a majesty in her person and manner that is natural to her; but which then shone out in all its glory.''

The heroine of *Tyrannic Love* also utters many sententious moral reflections in keeping with her high religious faith, which remind us of Clarissa's preparation for death, as does her anxiety to divorce herself from earthly ties and seek a heavenly recompense. Both heroines feel the same responsibility to live up to their high calling, to set a worthy example to a waiting world.

The same elements of mind and temperament, the elevation of diction, the tragic extravagance of feeling, the conscious integrity of virtue, which marks these tragic heroines of high degree, remote in time and place, the writers of Sentimental Comedy translated into the mode of human life. The scene is changed from Rome and Granada in the early Christian era, to London of the early eighteenth century; the hero is no longer an emperor or a triumphant general, but a perfect gentleman, as regal and as victorious as his predecessors. The virtuous heroine is no longer reserved for a tragic death, but now is destined to a fit reward on earth; yet she mourns in early life an unkind fate [16] and ''wraps herself up in the integrity of her own heart'' until chance and paternal sanction present a lover of honourable intent. This type of comedy, which is a link between the Heroic Drama of the seven-

[14] Clarissa Harlowe III, 271.

[15] Dryden, *Op. Cit.*: III, 403.

[16] Steele, Richard, *The Conscious Lovers.* Mermaid Series, New York, 1894, p. 312.

teenth century, and the realistic Laughing Comedy of the later eighteenth, suggests the relation of Richardson's work to the early romancers and to the novels of Fielding, Smollett, Goldsmith, and the later realists. Richardson, too, set his scenes in the contemporary life he knew; the majority of his characters he chose from the middle class world about him; but, like the writers of Sentimental Comedy, his heroine, Clarissa, he deliberately exalted above the rest. Her character he drew from nobler models; her mind and her situation exhibit the virtues of those older heroines; her diction is of the same elevated style; her appearance and her actions command a similar reverence; and her death, anticipated with a similar delight, redounds equally to her glory.

This exaltation of Clarissa's character I maintain was premeditated, consistent, and sustained to suit the author's purpose. Richardson himself tells us in his preface that "the principal of these two young ladies is proposed to us as an exemplar to her sex." In a footnote [17] he repeats this statement, and the same idea is conspicuous in his correspondence. The problem, then, resolves itself into a question whether a heroine can be drawn intentionally as a model of virtue and an example of supreme excellence, and yet be realistic. In answer let us see in what manner she is portrayed in the course of the narration. In her first letter Miss Howe describes Clarissa as "A young lady whose distinguished merits have made her the public care," as excelling all her sex, as one whom every eye is fixed upon, "with the expectation of an example." Mrs. Howe is reported as saying, "Miss Clarissa Harlowe is an admirable young lady; wherever she goes she confers a favor; whomever she leaves she fills with regret." [18] Aunt Hervey addresses her reverently: "Rise, my noble-minded niece! charming creature! . . . . . kneel not to me." [19]

Lovelace himself declares: "No age from the first to the present, ever produced, nor will the future to the end of the world, I dare aver, ever produce a young blooming lady, tried as she has been tried, who has stood all the trials as she has

[17] *Clarissa Harlowe* IV, 430.

[18] *Clarissa Harlowe* I, 44.

[19] *Clarissa Harlowe* I, 217.

done—let me tell you, sir, that you never saw, never knew, never heard of such another woman as Miss Harlowe." [20] And indeed we are most of us willing to agree heartily with Lovelace, and in this agreement lies our common faith in the incredibility of such a character. Rare, miraculous, isolated by her virtue, as her friends declare her to be; justified in all her actions by her own revelations and the careful notes of the author; established as a fountain-head of wisdom and excellent discernment by the counsel she gives, the meditations she writes, and the sententious utterances that are quoted from her; she is still further exalted by her suffering, and finally transfigured in the manner of her death. In his correspondence, in a letter to Miss Highmore, Richardson admits his deliberate intention of enhancing Clarissa's merit by means of her suffering. "You will be the less surprised, madam, that these strict notions are mine, when you will recollect, that in the poor ineffectual History of Clarissa, the parents are made more cruel, more implacable, more punishable in short, in order to inculcate this very doctrine that the want of duty on one side enhances the merit on the other, when it is performed, and you see how Clarissa shines in hers; nor loses sight of her gratitude and love, cruel as they were in the nineteenth year of her life, for their kindness and favour to her in the preceding eighteen." [21] Surely here is no true intention of realistic portraiture. Richardson is not drawing from life but from an ideal, loath as he is to admit it.

Lovelace is in some respects a more complicated problem for the author than Clarissa. As Sir Leslie Stephen points out, the difficulty lies in composing "a villain who shall be by nature a Devil and yet capable of imposing upon an angel." Richardson's solution of this problem brought with it a result he neither expected nor desired. The keynote of Lovelace's character is pride, with all its ramifications of vanity, self-love, love of power, disdain of opposition and control; on this fundamental trait is built the motives of his complicated villainy. But he is also endowed with a pleasing person, an amiable manner, a specious humility mixed with

[20] *Clarissa Harlowe* III, 441.
[21] *Correspondence* II:217.

reckless daring, and an insinuating need of reform which not
only attracted the lady of his choice, but also won the hearts
of many fair readers, to the infinite chagrin of the author.
Lady Bradshaigh writes to Richardson, "But you must know
(though I shall blush again) that if I was to die for it, I cannot help being fond of Lovelace. A sad dog! Why would you
make him so wicked and yet so agreeable? He says somewhere
or other he designs being a good man, from which words I
have great hope; and in excuse for my liking him, I must
say, I have made him so, up to my own heart's wish; a
faultless, faultless husband have I made him, even without
danger of a relapse. A foolish rake may die one; but a sensible rake must reform, at least in the hands of a sensible
author it ought to be so and will, I hope." [22] To this Richardson replies, "And did you not perceive that in the very first
letter of Lovelace, all those seeds of wickedness were thick
sown which sprouted up into action afterwards in his character? Pride, revenge, a love of intrigue, plot, contrivance;
and who is it that asks, *Do men gather grapes of thorns or
figs of thistles?* On this consideration it has been a matter
of surprise and indeed of some concern, that this character
has met with so much favour from the good and virtuous,
even as it stands from his two or three first letters; and in
some measure convinced me of the necessity of such a catastrophe as I have made." [23]

But Richardson need not have felt concern merely for
misplaced admiration on the part of the "good and virtuous,"
for about this time we find Colley Cibber writing to him in
a similar strain: "Lovelace's letter, page 52, has thrown out
such lively strokes of his uncommon and yet natural character, such almost justifiable sentiments of his intended treatment of Clarissa, that scarce a libertine reader will forbear
to triumph with him over the too charming and provoking
delicacy of his Clarissa. I am in the same rapture with Miss
Howe's reply to her narrator, page 60. I have not patience
to dwell on its particular parts that have seized upon my
approbation." [24]

[22] *Correspondence*, IV:180.
[23] *Correspondence*, IV:107.
[24] Ibid., II:167.

Miss Howe has a chance to be the most natural character in the book, because she escapes almost entirely any share of the author's purpose. Her function is to act as interlocutor, eulogist, and in between times, as an element of relief; hence she is permitted to develop her own personality without restraint. Vivacious, headstrong, ardent in her loyalties and antipathies, she is a realistically lovable character. She is portrayed, too, in a less obvious and more incidental way than either of the principals: by stray hints, glimpses of her home life, impulsive expressions of her friendly devotion, spirited reports of her fearless encounters with the forces of the enemy. And Richardson, too, seems to appreciate this by-product of his brain, for he writes to Lady Bradshaigh: "I love Miss Howe next to Clarissa; and I see very evidently in your letters that you are the true sister of that lady. And indeed I adore your spirit and your earnestness." [25] Lady Montagu, however, possibly piqued by the tribute of tears wrung from her by Clarissa's own character, writes scathingly of this minor heroine: "Richardson is as ignorant in morality as he is in anatomy, when he declares abusing an obliging husband or an indulgent parent to be an innocent recreation. Miss Anne Howe and Charlotte Grandison are recommended as patterns of charming pleasantry, and applauded by his saint-like dames who mistake pert folly for wit and humor, impudence and ill-nature for spirit and fire." [26]

Clarissa, Lovelace, and Miss Howe are the only characters portrayed subjectively. Belford is never fully realized, either in his early rakish days, or in the later days of his reforms, or in the future foretold him when the hand of Miss Montagu is his dubious reward. The other characters are all realized from without, and portrayed in broad, unshaded lines. The members of her family, Clarissa introduces to us early in none too favorable a light, and her unhappy evidence is reinforced by the comments of Miss Howe and Lovelace. There is nothing subtle or subjective in the delineation of these characters, and there need not be, for their rôle is crude and

[25] *Correspondence*, IV:194.
[26] Letters, page 465.

unconcealed. Mrs. Harlowe is a weak, unhappy soul, totally subject to the tyranny of her gouty lord. Taine delights in the brutality of what he considers typical Britishers and writes with picturesque gusto of father and son: "Above the outbursts of his voice we hear the loud wrath of his son, a sort of plethoric, over-fed bull-dog," and Arabella he describes as endowed with "the venomous bitterness of an offended, ugly woman."

Yet whether we of the present believe or disbelieve in the naturalness which Richardson's greatest admirers have claimed for his principal characters, we cannot but be impressed with the delight with which competent judges have read this tragedy, seven volumes long in the original edition and even now presented to us in four of goodly size. A writer of Richardson's own day, Edwards by name, the author of "Canons of Criticism," wrote to "the author of Clarissa,"—as Richardson was generally known—: "I have read, and as long as I have eyes will read, all your three most excellent pieces at least once a year." Lady Bradshaigh made a similar promise naïvely as a bribe to the author to save his heroine from the doom foretold. After the first four volumes of the novel had appeared, she opened her correspondence with Richardson under an assumed name, risking the invidious distinction of correspondence with an author to plead against this tragedy which she felt was imminent, concluding with a postscript: "If you should think fit to alter your scheme, I will promise to read your history over at least once in two years as long as I live; and my last words are—be merciful." [27]

Thus in its own day the book was popular both because of its didactic purpose and in spite of it. The plot commanded absorbing and anxious interest, the characters appealed intensely to personal sympathy and enthusiasm, the incident was as powerfully affecting as details out of real life. Why is it that today the book has taken rank among those that all should know about but few should read? Is it that to our taste, the technique is too weak, or is its purpose too strong? Or is it rather, that the temper of our time prevents

[27] *Correspondence,* IV:177.

our giving the book that just and leisurely attention for which it was designed? If we could but divest ourselves of our appetite for epitomized pleasure, of our habit of tense, impatient endeavor, our crude disdain of full, unhurried speech, we could perhaps judge with more righteous judgment such products of a more deliberate time, and find in the elongated novel of the eighteenth century the delight that Tennyson felt in "those great, still books," fulfilling more nearly Dr. Johnson's sanguine prophecy, that "Clarissa is not a performance to be read with eagerness and laid aside forever, but will be occasionally consulted by the busy, the aged, and the studious." [28]

HELEN SARD HUGHES.

Wellesley College.

[28] *Correspondence,* V:282.

REVIEWS AND NOTES

J. DRESCH: Le Roman Social en Allemagne. 1850-1900. Gutzkow, Freytag, Spielhagen, Fontane. (Paris Félix Alcan 1913) 389 pp.

M. Dresch's work is not a series of monographs but a well-organized work of the highest unity. The writer addresses himself primarily to his countrymen, seeking to make the four authors better understood by the French public at large. This is shown by the fact that the numerous and long quotations from the novelists treated invariably appear in the text in French translations.

The critic's impelling interests were social and political quite as much as literary. He defines with the utmost precision how Gutzkow, Freytag, Spielhagen and Fontane looked upon the revolution of 1848 and upon the war of 1870 with the events that preceded and followed it. He specifies the views of all four in regard to German unity, Prussian hegemony, to the "Junker", the middle class and the fourth estate, and gives a well-founded estimate of the reliability of all as historical witnesses. If followed with due caution M. Dresch's work will prove an invaluable guide to the novels of Gutzkow, Freytag, Spielhagen and Fontane for it interprets their novels in the light of their entire published works, their private letters and memoirs, their critical writings in regard to previous and contemporary literary models and regarding each other. The criticisms of the last named order are among the most instructive.

M. Dresch does not believe that "Tendenz" can be excluded from novels or from criticism and makes for himself no hypocritical claims to impartiality. In order rightly to make use of this excellent work it is important to ascertain just wherein this self-confessed "Tendenz" lies.

M. Dresch's personal bias exhibits itself most clearly in his treatment of Freytag. It must be admitted that in method and style his personal portrait of Freytag is a masterpiece not inferior to the work of a Thackeray. With ostensible impassionateness, with cool synthesis he combines out of Freytag's own words a startling confession of narrowness of mind, of prejudice and of self-satisfaction. He concedes at the outset that Freytag has an ideal and a patriotic one. Freytag wrote to Treitschke in 1863: "We are of those who live a little for themselves, a little for their friends and chiefly for their people."[1] It was Freytag's desire to contribute to

[1] *Gustav Freytag u. H. v. Treitschke im Briefwechsel* S. 5.

the national welfare by supporting the national ideal. Now according to Freytag the typical German was anti-Austrian, that is pro-Prussian. He was furthermore Protestant. Protestant and Prussian were nearly synonymous to his mind. Thirdly, the sound core of German life was the middle class. Freytag describes himself at the beginning of his "Erinnerungen" as Prussian, Protestant and belonging to the middle class and shows thus that he feels himself to be a German of the Germans. M. Dresch frequently returns to this point. For example, after surprising us with a laudatory description of the König family in the last volume of the "Ahnen" series, M. Dresch adroitly reminds us that Freytag was himself the model for Victor König. He remarks: "Cette longue série de romans aboutit à la famille de Freytag, à Freytag lui-même, qui aurait pu leur donner pour titre— *Mes Ancêtres.* En somme n'est il pas l'héritier de toutes les vertus germaniques?".[2] Dresch adds another trait to this picture of Freytag. That is tranquil joy. Real joy according to Freytag consists rather in the contemplation of the achieved than in anticipations of the future. This is true of the individual and of the community. Freytag's novels end leaving no doubt as to the tranquil happiness of the good characters and expressing no dissatisfaction with society as it exists. Freytag himself looked upon his own life work with a feeling of satisfaction. The course of his life had been marked by few failures. Throughout all his career he was popular with the people, praised by the predominant literary criticism and in accord with the prevailing political development, the rise of the power of Prussia. It is not strange that he formed the high opinion of his literary achievement which he expresses in a letter written to the Duke of Coburg, April 11, 1874, and cited by M. Dresch:[3] "Wie auch das Masz meiner Kraft sein mag, unter den lebenden Künstlern unseres Volkes erkenne ich keinen über mir, nicht viele als meinesgleichen".

M. Dresch's bias is equally marked in his concession to Freytag of two good qualities—honesty and simplicity. Freytag's civic honesty was shown, M. Dresch says, by his abhorrence of the idea of demanding an indemnity from France after the war of 1870-71. His civic simplicity was shown by his opposition to the assumption of imperial dignity on the part of the Prussian king. We find M. Dresch elsewhere taking the side of Freytag, wherever Freytag assumes an attitude of opposition to Bismarck.

[2] Dresch p. 160.

[3] Dresch p. 170.

M. Dresch appraises low the value of Freytag's novels as historical documents. Freytag does not even present, he says, a complete picture of the middle class. The chief joy of the middle class, domestic happiness, is absent. Futhermore his picture is one-sided in that it concedes none of the foibles of the middle class. Stout citizen though he was, Hans Sachs knew the weaknesses of his class, its narrowness, self-satisfaction and self-interest. These qualities escaped Freytag's notice completely. M. Dresch chiefly discredits Freytag's pictures of contemporary society, however, because the laboring class is omitted from them. Freytag asserted, it is well known, that the novel should be without "Tendenz". His idea of "Tendenz" apparently was dissatisfaction with the present, agitation for reforms in the future. To exclude from his novels the fermentation of unrest he excluded the laboring class and emphasized the agreeable side of the social organization of the recent past, in which the middle class had come to its heritage. M. Dresch asks pointedly whether this is absence of "Tendenz."

M. Dresch's strictures upon Freytag are by no means new. Kummer in his *Deutsche Literaturgeschichte d. 19. Jahrhunderts* mentions most of the points referred to by M. Dresch. The Frenchman's characterization is, however, the most realistic and convincing that has yet appeared and it will certainly leave its impress upon literary history. But however correct it may be in its essentials it is certainly open to criticism in some respects.

In the first place it is not correct to assume that Freytag believed that he had attained at least in *Soll und Haben* his ideal of freedom from "Tendenz". In a letter written to Geffken on the twenty-third of August 1856 he confesses: "Wenn das Publikum wohlwollend über die Unterhaltungsfähigkeit des Buches urteilt, so ist mir das schon recht, aber im Grunde lag mir während der Arbeit am meisten an der Tendenz und zwar an der politischen. Das mag für diese und künftige Kunstleistungen ein Übelstand sein, aber gern will ich auf den Dichterruhm verzichten, welcher nur durch eine vollständige Freiheit gegenüber den Erscheinungen des wirklichen Lebens erworben werden kann. Überall fühle ich mich in einem stillen Eifer, den ich am liebsten einen preuszischen nennen möchte."[4]

Then M. Dresch disregards too much the transitions in Freytag's development. Such a method necessarily leads to unsympathetic treatment. He minimizes Freytag's Young

[4] *Zeitschrift für Vergleichende Literaturgeschichte.* Neue Folge Bd. 13 (1889) S. 88-91.

German tendencies before the year 1848. This paves the way for a total disregard of the influence of the *Grenzboten* on the new Freytag of the post-revolutionary period. Critics have often seen in Fink in *Soll und Haben* the type of a Young German becoming "solid"[5] and have found in him much of Freytag himself. Strange that no critic has yet seen traits of Julian Schmidt in Fink's matter of fact co-worker, Anton. The two characters mutually influenced each other in much the same way as the two Grenzboten editors. The fact that the occupation of the father of both Anton and Julian Schmidt was similar may be more than a coincidence.[6] By giving more attention to the personal influences upon Freytag M. Dresch might have presented him in a less unfavorable light.

In the third place M. Dresch emphasizes too much Freytag's spirit of social caste as the reason for his exclusion of the laboring class from his novel. Freytag did not lack sympathy with the laboring classes. M. Dresch himself concedes this at one point though he denies it elsewhere.[7] The real reason, he says, manifests itself systematically in all his works. "Freytag s'est refusé à introduire la démocratie dans son roman parcequ'il trouvait en elle trop de laideurs et trop de confuses aspirations".[8] "Il ne veut pas tourner son attention vers un avenir incertain; il tient à s'arrêter au passé immédiat . . . . . C'est une activité 'reposée' qu'il s' attache à retracer, et non pas les débuts d'un industrialisme qu'il sent déjà fiévreux."[9] On the contrary the real reason for Freytag's omission of the fourth estate is one which M. Dresch here minimizes. Freytag followed, namely, the safe principle of writing from actual experience, not from superficial observation. He had had personal contact with the

[5] Robert Prutz first characterized Fink as a "solid gewordener Saalfeld" (see Prutz, *Die deutsche Literatur der Gegenwart*, 1859 S. 106. Saalfeld was the hero of Freytag's early play *Die Valentine*. Prutz was perhaps the first to recognize Freytag's close affinity with the Young German movement. See an article by him in the *Deutsches Museum*, 1858 II, pp. 441-458. In fairness of judgment and aptness of characterization this article has not been surpassed by later criticisms. Gustav Freytag's Young German tendencies have recently been systematically treated by O. Mayrhofer, *Gustav Freytag und das Junge Deutschland*. Marburger Dissertation 1907.

[6] Anton's father (see Freytag's *Gesammelte Werke* IV S. 5) was "königlicher Calculator" and Julian Schmidt's father (see *Allgemeine deutsche Biographie* XXXI p. 751) occupied a similar position. The relation of Julian Schmidt to Anton is treated at some length in an investigation of mine soon to be published.

[7] Dresch p. 110 and p. 164.

[8] Dresch p. 112.

[9] Dresch p. 108.

circles of society represented in *Soll und Haben* and *Die verlorene Handschrift*. He had associated with merchants, aristocrats, peasant proprietors and university professors. The laboring class, however, he did not thoroughly understand. To draw a picture of the laboring class without intimate knowledge thereof, to emphasize the elements of discontent without having a definite and practical program of betterment was to Freytag a profitless procedure. Gutzkow had, to his mind, already proved this. Such opinions as these are definitely expressed by Freytag in an article which he contributed to the *Grenzboten* in 1853.[10] Appearing thus at the time when Freytag was beginning his *Soll und Haben* the article may be justly regarded as the advance program of his novel. It was not included in his *Vermischte Aufsätze* (1903), in his *Gesammelte Aufsätze* (1888) nor in his *Gesammelte Werke* (1886-1888) and probably for this reason has escaped the attention of M. Dresch as well as of Freytag's previous critics and biographers. In this article Freytag declares that not the dilletante hero but the man at work should be the subject of the German novel; German life as it is is full of interesting and romantic realities. Trade and industry he suggests as proper backgrounds for the German novel. These opportunities have been neglected by the novelists hitherto and he asks why. ''Die Antwort darauf ist leider, weil unsere Romanschriftsteller in der Mehrzahl sehr wenig, ja zuweilen so gut wie gar nichts von dem Treiben der Gegenwart verstehen.''[11]Freytag commends them to the course of J. Gotthelf and above all of Walter Scott. First let them intimately know their social subject matter, then let them discuss it.

There is no better illustration of Freytag's early democratic tendencies than his fragment of 1884, *Der Gelehrte*.[12] In this work the title hero, who is in many respects Freytag himself, refuses a political career in the conservative ministry and refuses the editorship of a liberal paper, believing that neither party has solved the social problem. He determines to enter the ranks of the laboring class and learn from his

[10] Grenzboten 1853 I, 77-80. It was, however, recognized by Freytag as his own. See *Vermischte Aufsätze* II, S. 432.

[11] Grenzboten 1853 I, S. 78. We hear furthermore in these works an echo of Julian Schmidt's Grenzboten criticism. Through the pages of this journal between the years 1848 and 1853 we find the constant recommendation that the dilletante hero of the Wilhelm Meister type be supplanted by the hero of the life-long realistic occupation as in the English novel. This is what Freytag has attempted in *Soll und Haben* and we may say that it is the chief respect in which Freytag is more modern than Gutzkow.

[12] *Gesammelte Werke* Bd. II. S. 132.

fellows. With the words: ''Ich gehe in das Volk'' the dramatic fragment ends. ''Das Volk'' means here not the fourth estate, it is true, but rather the lower middle class, nevertheless Freytag shows in these words a quite notable freedom from prejudice. Gutzkow and the Young German writers were willing to instruct the working classes but not to learn from them. The abrupt close of the fragment with these words shows at once the willingness and the inability of Freytag to depict the social and political aspirations of the laboring class.

That Freytag in his novel *Soll und Haben* should have painted a picture of society and should have omitted to indicate the conflict between labor and capital as a main element seems to us now remarkable. But Germany was not so far advanced economically in 1850 as England and France. To the Germans it may well have appeared as if the question of the justification of an aristocratic class were the more important social problem. M. Dresch seems hardly to take these facts into consideration and passes judgment on the matter from the point of view of a Frenchman of today.

The economic Germany of 1870 was, it is true, much like the economic Europe of today. One might properly have expected Freytag to conclude his ''Ahnen'' series with a picture of modern economic life. There is no good reason for doubting the report of Freytag's wife, that he recognized it as incumbent upon him to do so.[13] That he did not publish such a work, however, is explicable. He was interested in the modern problems of labor but had not made the close acquaintance of the industrial laborer. He was too far advanced in years to learn fully and to comprehend the laborer's point of view. He was but following the principles of his entire literary career when he refrained from picturing a phase of life with which he was unfamiliar.

For many decades the unfavorable judgment of Julian Schmidt and of Treitschke was adopted in regard to Gutzkow. Political events seemed to sanction their views and the extensiveness of Gutzkow's work discouraged independent investigation. The growing interest in the fourth estate and in naturalism has reawakened an interest in this once despised forerunner of the modern movement, and time has mitigated certain political controversies and permitted a milder judgment of him. Except in the person of his confessed advocates Gutzkow has rarely found a better defender than M. Dresch.

The political and literary opposition between Freytag and Gutzkow is well known. The opposition of their social ideas

[13] See Ulrich *G. Freytags Romantechnik*, S. 27.

was no less pronounced. Freytag put his trust in the dominance of the middle class. Gutzkow stood for a leveling movement, which should do away with all class distinctions. The state should exist in order to protect labor. M. Dresch regards "Die Ritter vom Geist" as a social rather than a political work. In this novel Gutzkow represents the failure of statesmen of diverse parties but finds the hope of the future in a voluntary association of public-spirited men who agree to cast aside social differences and thus set an example of how the citizen may work for the public good.

"Der Zauberer von Rom" was born out of Gutzkow's hope for a Germany united religiously as well as politically, out of his hope, indeed, for a world-unity of religion. In religious dogma he found no hindrance to this hope. He believed if the papacy could be deprived of its temporal dominions this ideal could be realized. History has proved Gutzkow to be in the wrong but M. Dresch says: "La portée sociale n'en est point par là diminuée. Pour être le romancier de son temps, il faut en traduire aussi les pensées chimériques."[14] One cannot but approve of this tolerant criticism, but why should not the author have made a similar concession to the prejudices of Freytag in his *Soll und Haben*.

M. Dresch accepts Gutzkow's novel *Die neuen Serapionsbrüder* (1877) as a true picture of the general feeling of unrest, insecurity and discontent that prevailed in Germany after the war of 70-71 with France. In this work Gutzkow manifests his disgust at the hollow, materialistic results obtained by the war.

M. Dresch lays emphasis rather upon the differences than upon the similarities between Gutzkow and his French models. If he adopted the intricate mechanism of mystery of Eugene Sue, it was in order to carry the interest of the reader through long political discussions. He believed with Balzac in the important rôle that materialistic considerations play in life, yet he often attributed benevolent motives to his characters. A higher sense of unity led him to compose a *"Roman des Nebeneinanders"* rather than a *"Comédie humaine."* *Wilhelm Meister* was the novel that Gutzkow really took as his model. The combination of eighteenth century idealism with nineteenth century social interest in all classes appealed to him. The slow cumbersome movement, the humanitarian and didactic intent are common to both novels. In both symbolic and typical characters exist side by side with realistic ones. M. Dresch interprets a leading character, Hackert in the "Ritter vom Geist," as a symbol of democracy,[15] and

[14] Dresch p. 66.
[15] Dresch p. 42.

thus takes issue apparently unconsciously with Julian Schmidt, whose matter of fact mind protested against such an interpretation in a realistic work,[16] and who declared that the moral code of Hackert was in no sense representative of the time.[17]

It is to be regretted that M. Dresch did not join issue directly with some of the earlier critics in regard to Gutzkow's historical reliability. He admits that public characters and events are slightly distorted. This was due to the political condition of the time. Serious treatment of contemporary social and political affairs was forbidden, hence these subterfuges on Gutkow's part. Except for this inconsiderable reservation M. Dresch's claims in regard to Gutzkow are extreme. He characterizes Gutzkow as a "peintre exact et fidèle des choses de son temps." [18] A new and more favorable estimate of Gutzkow, is it is true, gaining ground but even so generally favorable a critic as R. M. Meyer finds it hard to believe that Gutzkow's novels present a true picture [19] while Gutzkow's contemporary, Julian Schmidt said: "Dasz Gutzkow ein Portrait der Zeit, wie seine Verehrer behaupten, nicht geliefert hat, wird der Unbefangene wohl von selbst erkennen." [20] The general tendency on the part of recent critics to do justice to the lost political cause of Young Germany is to be commended, but it would be disastrous if it should lead them to overestimate the historical reliability of the Young German novels.

M. Dresch's treatment of Freytag and of Gutzkow serves to show with what reservations his opinions need be accepted. It should be added that his judgments in regard to Spielhagen and Fontane have been less affected by social bias. It is easy for M. Dresch to be fair to both, for both sympathised with the strivings of the fourth estate, and both were aristocratic in their tastes, even though Spielhagen often attacked the nobility bitterly. M. Dresch finds a high merit in Spielhagen's attempt to reconcile naturalism and classicism, theoretically in his "Neue Beiträge zur Theorie und Technik der Epik und Dramatik" and practically in his last novels. He rejoices that Spielhagen's novels are regaining some of the popularity lost in the last decade of the nineteenth century.

[16] J. Schmidt *Geschichte der deutschen Literatur* 2te Auflage Bd. I, S. 91.

[17] J. Schmidt *Geschichte der deutschen Literatur* 2te Auflage Bd. III, S. 301.

[18] Dresch p. 20.

[19] Meyer *Deutsche Literatur im 19. Jht.* III Aufl. S. 227.

[20] Schmidt *Geschichte der deutschen Literatur.* 2te. Aufl. Bd. III. S. 311.

He regards Spielhagen's novels as valuable contributions to our knowledge of the times described, but agrees with Schian [21] and with Bleibtreu [22] that Gutzkow described more exactly the conditions and events of his period.

Fontane wins the favor of M. Dresch completely by the novels of his last years, wherein he holds up to view the narrowness of mind, the coldness, the purely formal morality of the self-satisfied middle class, thus emphasizing the features that Freytag had neglected in his picture and performing the function of a German Flaubert or Balzac. Fontane began to form his impressions of the Berlin middle-class citizen in 1866, while serving as an apprentice to a pharmacist. He was able to declare in 1898 that the average present day citizen possessed less false virtue and more real virtue than the citizen of sixty years ago.[23]

Perhaps it is due to a sympathy born of the kinship of race that M. Dresch's account of Fontane is the product of more enthusiasm and more industry than his account of Spielhagen. To reconcile Spielhagen's novelistic theory with his practice is not a task demanding originality. Spielhagen himself has done that thoroughly and will long remain the chief of Spielhagen authorities. Fontane's theory must, however, be carefully collated out of personal correspondence, daily dramatic criticism, reported conversations and memoirs. For performing this task M. Dresch will deserve the gratitude of later critics of Fontane. He has also accounted for the literary development of Fontane, explaining his transitions from revolutionary lyrics to old Prussian ballads, from travel correspondence to history, from the historical novel to the contemporary social novel in such a way as to make Fontane's literary career seem logical and consistent.

In some instances M. Dresch's judgments in regard to Fontane reveal his partiality a little too strongly. He cannot avoid the question, why Fontane with all his interest in the fourth estate never caused it to play a part in his novels. The answer he gives is: "Son âge avancé ne lui permettait guère d'aller étudier de près la vie de l'ouvrier." [24] In other words Fontane did not describe the fourth estate because he did not know it intimately. The explanation is simple and fair, but why could not it have been made in behalf of Freytag as well?

M. Dresch's nationalistic bias appears most strikingly in

[21] Schian *Der Deutsche Roman seit Goethe.* (1904). S. 86.

[22] Bleibtreu *Revolution der Literatur.* (Leipzig 1886) S. 28.

[23] *Von Zwanzig bis Dreiszig,* S. 12.

[24] Dresch p. 360.

his opposition to Bismarck. He takes no little satisfaction in pointing out that all four novelists, diverse as were their political and social opinions in other respects, were united in their discontent with the social conditions following the year 1870 and were unanimous in holding Bismarck responsible for the conditions which they condemned. In the case of three of the novelists this opposition is sufficiently well-known. Fontane, however, has usually been presented as a whole-souled admirer of Bismarck.

Fontane, M. Dresch says, always felt a strong admiration for the "Junker". Bismarck, at the beginning of his career, gave promise of becoming such a hero as Fontane's imagination loved to paint. Fontane could with difficulty reconcile himself to the later disappointments which Bismarck had in store for him. Thereafter there existed for Fontane two Bismarcks—his ideal Bismarck, whom he often permitted himself to celebrate in verse, and another Bismarck, whom he criticised unsparingly in his private letters. The attitude of Fontane to Bismarck is worthy of a special investigation, undertaken perhaps preferably not by a Frenchman. At any rate M. Dresch has performed a good service in emphasizing the fact that Fontane's admiration for Bismarck was not unmixed. He has, moreover, taken account of the laudatory lyrics, while such biographers as Servaes [25] and Ettlinger [26] have disregarded the condemnatory private letters.

In conclusion M. Dresch points out that all four of these novelists desired German unity, however different their ideals in regard to this united Germany. An earnest purpose led all to the novel. All sought in their own way to assist in the realization of their ideal. "Gutzkow a vu dans le roman le meilleur moyen d'initier une nation aux questions vitales dont dépend sa destinée. Freytag a tenté de faire l'éducation patriotique du peuple allemand. Spielhagen a mis dans ses livres tout l'idéalisme du XVIIIe siècle et sa conception si noble de l'humanité. Fontane a voulu que la société moderne, en se regardant vivre dans le roman, éprouvât le désir d'être moins vaine et plus sincère." [27] All four, however, presented incomplete pictures, "même Gutzkow et Spielhagen qui ont visé à la 'totalité.' Gutzkow manque d'art; il est si touffu que l'on a peine à voir clair dans une telle surabondance. Freytag ne comprend la solidarité sociale qu'en Prussien

[25] Servaes, Franz: *Th. Fontane* Berlin 1900. (Die Dichtung herausgegeben von Paul Remer.)

[26] Ettlinger, Josef: *Theodor Fontane* Berlin (Die Literatur herausgegeben von Georg Brandes).

[27] Dresch p. 388.

bourgeois et protestant. Spielhagen la marque plus large-
ment, mais d'une façon abstraite. Fontane la voit psycho-
logiquement, intimement, mais fragmentairement.''[28] It
would have required a Shakespeare to represent this era in
its totality, M. Dresch says, and Germany has had no such
Shakespeare. None of the four novelists could even be compared with Balzac or with Tolstoi.[28]

M. Dresch's work is full of such enlightening comparisons
as those just quoted. It presents in a systematic form a
modern and thoroughly independent estimate of the authors.
His judgments in regard to Spielhagen and Fontane are as
securely grounded and as nearly non-partisan as any that
had hitherto appeared.[29] All four portions are based on the
intensity of study required for a monograph, but mono-
graphic partiality is noticeable only in the case of Gutzkow,[30]
and if the critic's judgment of Freytag is too severe to be
final it is too well supported to be disregarded.

L. M. PRICE.

University of Missouri.

GÜNTHER JACOBY: HERDER ALS FAUST—Felix
Meiner. Leipzig 1911.

''Herder als Faust.'' Es liegt ein zum Widerspruche auf-
reizendes Moment in diesem Titel. Man hat das Gefühl, als
gelte es ein Attentat auf Goethes Genius. Ich gestehe, das
Buch zur Hand genommen zu haben, erfüllt von solchem
Geiste des Widerspruchs. Allein ich gestehe auch, es aus
der Hand gelegt zu haben im Gefühle, dass es mir möglich
gewesen ist, den Verfasser auf jedem seiner Schritte ver-
ständnissvoll zu begleiten, wenn ich mich auch nicht in der
Lage finde, von ihm hinsichtlich des wesentlichsten Punktes
rückhaltslos überzeugt worden zu sein. Dieser wesentlichste
Punkt ist die Behauptung, dass die Faustgestalt vom An-
fange des ersten Teils der Tragödie bis zur Schwelle von
Auerbachs Keller die Gestalt Herders ist, wie sie sich in
Goethes Phantasie projizierte. Ist diese Behauptung tatsäch-

[28] Dresch p. 387.

[29] Almost simultaneously with M. Dresch's work appeared the monograph of Dr. Victor Klemperer *Die Zeitromane Friedrich Spielhagens
und ihre Wurzeln* 179 Seiten (Weimar 1913) in *Forschungen zur neueren
Literaturgeschichte,* no. XLIII. This will supplement the French work
with its different points of view and different comparisons. The work
is as scholarly and perhaps more unbiased than M. Dresch's work but
its intricate style will cause it to be less used.

[30] M. Dresch is also the author of a monograph *Gutzkow et la jeune
Allemagne* Paris Cornely et Cie.

lich so ungeheuerlich, wie sie im ersten Augenblicke erscheint?

Man vergegenwärtige sich die Lage. Als Goethe den Keim zur Faustdichtung empfing, ist ihm, wie wir annehmen dürfen, unzweifelhaft gewesen, dass es sich bei seinen Gestalten nicht um den Faust des 16ten Jahrhunderts, sondern um eine Übertragung dieser Persönlichkeit in die Ideenkreise des 18ten Säkulums handelte, um einen Mann, der alles Wissen seiner Zeit in sich aufgenommen hatte und, überzeugt von der Eitelkeit solchen Wissens, mit glühender Seele nach Betätigung im praktischen Leben sich sehnte, der hinausstrebte aus der drückenden Enge der Gelehrtenstube in den wogenden Strom der Welt. Konnte der Jüngling Goethe, ob auch ausgerüstet mit höchster Genialität der Intuition, in sich die Erfahrungen gesammelt haben, welche ihn zur Gestaltung einer solchen Persönlichkeit befähigten? Wir werden diese Frage getrost mit ''nein'' beantworten können. Gerade aber im Augenblicke, da er seiner am dringendsten bedurfte, führte ihm das Schicksal einen Mann zu, der in wundersamster Weise die Bedingungen in sich vereinigte, deren Kenntniss allein Goethe zur Schöpfung seiner Faustgestalt in den Stand setzte. In klarer Weise hat es Jacoby, sich stets an Äusserungen Herders haltend, verstanden, des Mannes Seelenzustand in der Zeit unmittelbar vor seiner Berührung mit Goethe und während der Dauer ihres innigsten Freundschaftsbundes zu zeichnen. Ebenso erschöpfend sind des Verfassers Darlegungen über Herder in Goethes Urteil. Es ist rührend zu beobachten, mit welcher hingebenden Verehrung der in Wahrheit so viel Grössere emporblickt zu einer Persönlichkeit, welche er als eine sein eigenes Selbst gegenwärtig weit überragende zu erkennen meint, und welche dereinst zu erreichen, ihm als höchstes Ziel seines Lebens vorschwebt.

Das sind die grundlegenden Tatsachen, auf welchen der Verfasser das Gebäude seiner Beweisführung errichtet. So warm Jacoby auch für seine These eintritt, dass sich in Fausts Sehnen und Erleben das Sehnen und Erleben Herders, des Mannes ganzes Sein und Wesen, wenn auch in erhöhter verklärter Form, wiederspiegle: so hat er es doch bei dieser Beweisführung nirgends an dem für jede wissenschaftliche Arbeit notwendigen Masse von Objektivität fehlen lassen. Freilich sind wir nicht in der Lage, alle seine Argumente widerspruchslos hinzunehmen. Er sucht bei jedem Satze, ja mitunter bei jedem Worte der in Frage stehenden Szenen (Prolog im Himmel, Anfang des ersten Teiles bis einschliesslich der Schülerszene und Glaubensbekenntniss) die unmittelbar bildenden Einflüsse des Herderschen Geistes nachzuweisen und geht hier-

bei wie alle jene, welche ein neue Idee vertreten, zu weit, indem
er im Bestreben alles zu geben, mehr gibt als alles. Hier wird
die Kritik im einzelnen sichtend eingreifen müssen, ohne indessen, wie ich meine, den Gesammteindruck wesentlich ver-
wandeln zu können, den Eindruck nämlich, dass die in Frage
stehenden Abschnitte von Goethes Dichtung nicht nur erfüllt
und durchtränkt sind mit Herderschem Geiste, sondern dass
sich dieser Geist in festumrissener Form in Einzelzügen der
Faustgestalt niedergeschlagen hat. Was Jacobys Darlegung-
en eine solche Beweiskraft verleiht, ist der Umstand, dass sie
fast ausschliesslich in persönlichen Äusserungen Herders bestehen. Es ist selbstverständlich, dass sich's bei diesen Äusserungen Herders nur um solche handeln darf, welche der
Zeit des innigen Freundschaftsverkehrs mit Goethe oder der
kurz vorangegangenen Epoche im Leben des grossen Ostpreussen angehören. Dieser notwendigerweise zu fordernden
Beschränkung in der Auswahl seines Beweisstoffes hat sich
der Verfasser willig unterworfen. Beruft er sich dennoch
einmal auf ein Wort aus späteren Tagen, so sucht er gewissen-
haft nachzuweisen, dass es im Keime auf frühere Zeiten zu-
rückweist. Einzelheiten der ungemein eingehenden Beweisführung müssen hier unerörtert bleiben. Es sei aber gestat-
tet, auf einige Punkte hinzuweisen, welche, ob auch über das
im Titel angegebene Thema des Werkes hinausreichend, meines
Erachtens mindestens eine gleich hohe Bedeutung beanspruchen dürfen, denn Jacobys Buch gehört zu jenen seltenen
Gaben, welche mehr bieten als sie verheissen. Der Titel
lautet nur ''Herder als Faust''. Wir empfangen aber ein
geschlossenes Gesammtbild von Herders Persönlichkeit während des uns hier interessierenden Lebenabschnittes, ein Bild,
das wir—darin beruht sein bedeutender Wert und sein hoher
Reiz—als Selbstbildnis des so ungewöhnlich vielseitigen,
wundersam anregenden und in weiteren Kreisen immer noch
unterschätzten, ja nahezu unbekannten Ostpreussen betrachten dürfen. Denn was wir von ihm erfahren, erfahren wir
in seinen eigenen Worten. Wir lernen ihn kennen in seinem
ganzen Fühlen, Sinnen und Sehnen, in dem oft rhapsodischen
Schwunge seiner Prosa und der mitunter stammelnden Hilf-
losigkeit seiner Verse.

Noch mehr aber bietet Jacobys Buch. Wenn uns die
breiten Kanäle gezeigt werden, durch welche Gedanken Herders in das Gebiet des Faust herübergeleitet wurden, so erkennen wir plötzlich in diesem Gebiete Brücken und Zusammenhänge an Stellen, die uns sonst abgerissen und rät-
selhaft erschienen sind. So bietet Jacobys Argumentation
selbst für denjenigen, der nicht gewillt ist, alle ihr entnom-

menen Folgerungen gut zu heissen, gerade an einigen der
wichtigsten Stellen eine neue Quelle zur Erfassung von
Fausts Seelenleben. Wir werden bequem um sonst unüber-
windlich erscheinende Abgründe herumgeleitet und erblicken
gar manches z.B. in den Auseinadersetzungen mit Wagner in
einem völlig neuen ungewohnten Lichte. Auch andere Frag-
en der Faustforschung werden aufgerollt und z.T. in neu-
artiger Weise gelöst. So ist die schon früher vertretene
Auffassung, dass nicht wie in der gegenwärtigen Fassung
der Erdgeist, sondern der Weltgeist, der Geist des Makrokosmus Faust im ersten Auftritt erscheinen sollte, für den
Verfasser durch seinen Beweisstoff zu voller Gewissheit geworden. Ebenso ist es ihm unzweifelhaft, dass das Gedanken-
material, mit dem die sogenannte "grosse Lücke" ausgefüllt
worden ist, in seiner Urform der hier in Frage kommenden
Periode nächster geistiger Beziehungen zu Herder angehört.
Endlich entdeckt er in jener Herderschen Gedankenwelt auch
die Keime für die Gestaltung des zweiten Faustteiles, die also
vermutlich gleichzeitig mit denen der anderen Abschnitte in
Goethes Seele eingedrungen sind. So gewinnt er von einer
neuen Seite her einen Beweis für die Einheitlichkeit in der
Konzeption unserer grössten Dichtung. Endlich sei noch ein
Punkt erwähnt, dem ich besondere Wichtigkeit beimesse,
wenn sich's hierbei, wie der Verfasser zugeben muss, auch
nur um eine Vermutung handelt, um die Vermutung nämlich,
dass Goethe, durch Herder mit Lessings Absicht, eine Faustdichtung zu gestalten, bekannt gemacht, dieser Anregung
einen starken Anreiz zu eigenem Schaffen verdankt. Herder
besass, wie nachgewiesen wird, ziemlich genaue Kenntnis
von der durch Lessing vorgenommenen Behandlung des
Stoffes. Ob und wieweit eine vermutlich erfolgte Übermitt-
lung dieser Kentnisse an Goethe in des letzteren Werke
Wiederhall gefunden hat, werden wir kaum je erfahren, weil
uns Lessings Faust bis auf einige Szenen verloren gegangen
ist. Allein welcher Art die Beziehungen zwischen Lessing
und Goethe in diesem Punkte auch gewesen sein mögen, ein
Vorhandensein solcher Beziehungen böte eine Erklärung für
Lessings sonst unbegründetes unfreundliches Verhalten dem
jungen Goethe gegenüber. Wenn es voraussichtlich nicht
gelingen wird, in diesem Punkte über blosse Vermutungen
hinauszukommen, so dürfte doch der, meines Wissens neue
Hinweis auf den Anteil von dreien unserer grossen Geister
an der einzigen Dichtung reges Interesse beanspruchen.

Es wäre ungerecht, angesichts der zahlreichen Lichtseiten
des Buches die Schattenseiten zu übersehen, an denen es
naturgemüss nicht fehlt. Ich erwähnte bereits, dass ich nicht

allen beigebrachten Beweistoff als stichhaltig anerkennen
kann. Ich erwähnte auch das Gefühl der Opposition, welches
der Verfasser durch seinen Titel in des Lesers Gemüte ent-
fesselt. Beim ersten Punkte handelt sich's um ein blosses
Zuviel, hinsichtlich des zweiten meine ich, dass Jacoby nicht
in genügender Weise für die Zerstreuung dieses Widerspruchs
gesorgt hat, indem er es verabsäumte, seine Stellung zum
Problem des künstlerischen insonderheit des dichterischen
Schaffens darzulegen. Er hielt dies wohl für überflüssig,
weil im Grunde nicht zur Sache gehörig. Denn es ist ihm
natürlich wie jedem, der sich mit den Gesetzen des menschlichen Schaffens beschäftigt hat, hinlänglich bekannt, dass
es bei unserer Schöpfertätigkeit weniger auf die Gewinnung
neuer Gedanken als auf die Neugestaltung vorhandenen
Materials ankommt. Eine Dichtung wie Goethes Faust kann
für uns nicht das Mindeste von ihrem Werte einbüssen, wenn
wir auch erkannt haben sollten, dass ihrer Hauptgestalt ein
bestimmtes Vorbild zu Grunde liegt und dass die Mehrzahl
der in ihr enthaltenen Gedanken aus fremder Quelle in sie
geflossen ist; dagegen dürfen wir es als wirklichen Gewinn
an Erkenntnis betrachten, wenn wir diese Quellen kennen
lernen. Das Streben nach Erforschung solcher Quellen kann
sehr wohl verbunden sein mit dem Gefühle tiefer Ehrfurcht
vor dem schaffenden Genius. Dass dem Verfasser letztere
nicht fremd ist, beweisen mir die warm empfundenen Schluss-
worte seines Buches. Ja, ich meine sogar, die ganze Untersuchung war geeignet, diese Ehrfurcht nur um so tiefer in
das Herz des Forschenden zu pflanzen. Denn wenn er auf
Schritt und Tritt erkannte, wie ein Gedanke, bei Herder
oft in unklare Form und unbeholfenen Ausdruck geprägt, in
Goethes Dichtung durch Hoheit und Schönheit Ewigkeitswert
gewinnt, so musste er von aufrichtigster Bewunderung für
das Mysterium des dichterischen Schaffens erfüllt werden. Ob
diese Umprägung Herderscher Gedanken in Goethes Seele
sich bewusst oder unbewusst vollzogen hat, ob der jüngere
Freund dem älteren Genossen mit voller Absichtlichkeit in
seinem Werke ein Denkmal errichtet habe; diese Frage lässt
der Verfasser in der Schwebe. Ich selbst möchte nach meiner
Kenntniss der künstlerischen Psyche mit grösster Ent-
schiedenheit behaupten, ein solcher Vorgang könne nur unbewusst erfolgt sein. Wie man aber dieser Frage gegenüber
sich stellen mag, man darf Jacobys Buch wenn man es in
diesem Sinne liest, als wertvollen Beitrag zur Psychologie des
Dichters betrachten.

Natürlich liegt dem Verfasser die Annahme fern, als handle sich's bei dem von Herder auf Goethe übertragenen Ge-

dankenmaterial um des ersteren Originalbesitz. An vielen
Stellen sucht er selbst die Quellen festzustellen, aus denen
bestimmte Ideen zu Herder geflossen sind. Er meint also
nur, dass gewisse Gedankenkomplexe, die an sich schon Erb-
gut der Menscheit waren, auf Goethe in spezifisch Herderscher Formung übertragen worden sind. Diese Meinung des
Autors erhellt daraus, dass er auch ausserhalb der Faustgestalt in der Faustdichtung allerorten Herdersches Gut
wahrzunehmen meint. So erkennt er in Mephisto, namentlich in der Schülerszene Herdersche Züge. Das beweisst,
dass der Titel nicht in dem engen mathematischen Sinne
einer Gleichung aufzufassen ist. Denn mag Jacoby in der
Gestalt Faust so viele Elemente Herderschen Wesens erblicken,
dass er die Behauptung aufstellt: Herder ist Faust, so hat
er doch niemals seinen Satz umgekehrt in dem Sinne: Faust
ist Herder d.h. nur Herder. Er hat vielmehr, wie ich aus
einer Reihe von Äusserungen schliessen darf, niemals vergessen, dass Faust auch Goethe und dass Faust auch Faust
ist. Es hat ihm sicher nichts ferner gelegen als ein Attentat
auf Goethes Genius. Freilich hätte das alles zur Vermeidung
von Missverständnissen in Jacobys Buch breiter ausgeführt
werden sollen.

Solche Ausstellungen können aber die Bedeutung des
Werkes nicht beeinträchtigen. Die Darstellung, mag sie auch
noch so sehr ins Kleine gehen, versinkt niemals in Klein-
lichkeit. Sie ist getragen von wissenschaftlichem Ernste und
dabei erfüllt von warmer Hingebung an die Sache. Man
fühlt, das Buch wurde nicht nur mit dem Verstande sondern
auch mit dem Herzen geschrieben. Mag man sich des Verfassers Behauptungen und Beweisen gegenüberstellen wie
immer man wolle, man wird seine Arbeit als erwünschte
Bereicherung unserer Goethe-und Herder Literatur ansehen
müssen.

WILHELM V. OBERNITZ.

Berlin, Germany.

ELISE DOSENHEIMER, Friedrich Hebbels Auffassung vom
Staat. H. Haessel Verlag, Leipzig, 1912.

Hebbel's conception of the state is in essence Hegelian.
Unlike his great prototype, however, Hebbel does not pretend
to give a systematic study of the nature of the state and its
functions. He limits himself to a purely metaphysical contemplation of the abstract principles which, he believes, underlie state existence. To these he gives utterance in his dramas.
Nor are Hebbel's views the result of a thorough study of gov-

ernment and history or even of a long and varied political
experience; they represent merely an *a priori* conception, the
highest expression of his Weltanschauung. To a certain extent, his motive is similar to that of Hegel, who, in his philosophy of the state, attempted to solve what he conceived to
be a purely metaphysical problem and to apply his results
to actual conditions. In so far as Hebbel conceives of the
problem as a philosophic one we shall endeavor to follow him
into the nebulous realms of abstraction where he constructed
his phantom. But when the application of his results to
concrete phenomena comes into conflict with the actualities
of political existence, we shall feel obliged to apply the more
rigid tests of scientific political discussion.

Although the author of the present book acknowledges that
the basis of Hebbel's conception of the state represents nothing
original, she believes that he has made a contribution by the
fact that he has applied to the idea of the state his metaphysical *Weltauffassung*, effecting thereby, "a transposition
from the realm of the absolute to the limited, from the infinite to the finite." Hebbel's metaphysics rested upon a
peculiar duality of individual and All, a relation which the
author regards as felicitously expressed in the relation of the
individual to the state, the state symbolically representing
the *Weltall*, the *Weltgesetz*, which is, of course, to mean the
ethical law. The state, therefore, as the representative of the
ethical law stands above both good and evil, for from its
very nature it must serve the highest good. From this it follows that from the ethical point of view, the individual may
not attack the state without dissolving all the conditions of
his existence.

It seems strange that in spite of this theory of state-origin
that Hebbel should conceive of the state as existing only contemporaneously with man and as a restriction upon his individuality. The state, accordingly, is an unfortunate necessity which suppresses all spontaneity and destroys the self-
reliance of the individual. In fact Hebbel seems to look forward to a condition of society where the state will be totally
non-existent. But until the individual comes to a realization
of his relation to the universe and thereby ceases to be an individual, there can be no change in the status quo; he must
bow to the universal—the Idea, as represented in the state.
This, the author maintains, is the fundamental thought of
Agnes Bernauer.

Agnes Bernauer is the tragedy of the conflict of the individual human right with the universal right of the state. The
former is typified by Agnes who, by the mere fact of her ex-

istence and through no volition of her own, comes in clash with the Idea—the state, as represented in Duke Ernst and to a lesser extent in Albrecht, and by the inexorable law of the supremacy of the Idea she is fated to succumb to this power. It is not merely a tragic necessity that Agnes is sacrificed to the state. It is the subjection of the individual to the Idea.

It is apparent from this brief sketch of Hebbel's conception of the state, that his whole political thinking is characterized by an irreconcilable duality of individualistic and socialistic elements. It bespeaks a lack of true political feeling which is most astounding and which the author of the present essay tries in vain to explain. On one occasion she asserts by way of justification, that the point of departure of socialism is essentially a sort of individualism. This is characteristic of the hair splitting to which the apostles of Hebbel are obliged to resort in order to explain the incongruity of his so-called *Weltanschauung* with his actual modus operandi. But assuming for the moment that the philosophic basis of socialism is individualism, this does not alter the fact that as political phenomena, the two are as far apart as the two poles. The individualist conceives of the state as force. The socialist supports a view diametrically opposite. So, returning to Hebbel's conception, it is on the one hand distinctly individualistic in its treatment of the state as the manifestation of the Idea and, on the other hand, in its contemplation of the metaphysical duality of individual and state it is blatantly socialistic. The political irreconcilability of these two aspects of Hebbel's conception must be traced to a more fundamental fallacy.

The state as the universal law or as the manifestation of the Idea is an abstraction as far removed from political thought as it is from political reality. No publicist will be satisfied to regard the state as a power superimposed upon a will-less man, by some superhuman will, coincident with his sojourn in a state of ignorance, comparable to the state of sin, and eradicable by human progress. If the state is a power it is so because it has been forged by human will and is the cumulative result of long and patient human experience. Moreover, Hebbel's conception excludes the necessary subjective relation which must exist between the individual and the state, and without which a state is not a true state. It is true that we can conceive of a relation between state and individual which is one of pure objectivity. Such, for instance, is the relation between the state and the individual who, for some reason or other, has become *heimatlos* or *staatlos*. Such a person has lost both his subjective and his objective relation to his parent state, but he has acquired a new relation to the state of residence which is purely objective. At the same time he has absolutely no subjective rights. As cases of this sort are rare exceptions, one is justified in regarding Hebbel's concept as fundamentally wrong both in principle and in actuality.

An interesting point in connection with the Hebbelian conception is the question of where the sovereignty in his state would lie. On the basis of his metaphysical ideas, Hebbel manifestly could not take adequate consideration of this most important element of state existence, but as far as one is able to judge, he believed it to be vested in the highest executive, to wit, the king. Thus, Hebbel attributes to the ruler superhuman qualities and says that the ruler has less right to be an individual than any other man. This view is an echo of Hegel's glorification of the princely power which in turn smacks somewhat of oriental despotism, or at best of the early nineteenth century Prussian regime, where the king was regarded as the final and absolute depository of the sovereignty. This conception of the identity of king and sovereignty is the natural result of any view which attempts to inject into the theory of state-origins, the idea of a divine or superhuman interposition. To a certain degree this idea formed the basis of the arguments in favor of the divine right of kings which one is almost tempted to accuse Hebbel of favoring. Hopelessly archaic, however, is the view which seeks to place the sovereignty, both legal and political, in a single individual. Certainly Hebbel did not get this idea from Hegel, for even he was inclined to ascribe the ultimate sovereignty to the profanum vulgus.

This analysis of Hebbel's borrowed conception of the state as the manifestation of the Idea, and the consequent and necessary relation of pure objectivity of the individual to the state, will explain in some measure the other aspect of his conception, namely, the position of dominance which he accords the state over the individual. In terms of his metaphysics, the subjection of the individual to the Idea. As a general proposition, no one would deny that within the generally accepted meanings of the terms state and state-will, the individual must eventually bow to the more puissant will of the state, unless for some reason he is able to identify it with his own. The history of the identification of state with individual human will is the history of the great progressive movements of the world. Hebbel, however, has no idea of the clearly defined conception of political science, and his ''system'' defies analysis by scientific terminology.

It has been indicated that Hebbel regarded the ruler as vested with the ultimate sovereignty of the state, and as such as the most essential factor in state life. Just as the state per se is the symbolic representation of the Idea, so, in turn, the ruler is the symbolic manifestation of the highest characteristics of the state. When Hebbel, therefore, speaks of state-will and the right of the state, he means the right and the will which emanate from the ruler himself, and not from the collectivity of human wills as one might infer. If, with Hegel, the state-will was after all merely a manifestation of the universal will, which it postulated, with Hebbel this view has been necessarily perverted to the extent that it is the will of a single individual, the will of the ruler. This will, says Hebbel, is supreme, for it is the expression of state-will. The two are identical. In so far as this view is expressed in *Agnes Bernauer,* it resolves itself into the ruthless ownership of subjects which prospered under Darius and the Great Khan a great many years ago. It is not surprising to find this doctrine revived during the reactionary regime of a Metternich, but to assert that the individual who has the temerity to defy this will must inevitably go down in defeat before it, is an absurdity which even the most submissive political philosopher will hesitate to accept.

The result of this combat of individual wills, Hebbel's protests to the contrary, must depend upon the disposition of the collectivity of human wills in whom the ultimate sovereignty really lies. Is the ruler in a position to depend on this will, then the individual will go down in defeat, not before his will, to be sure, but before the real will of the state. But to the individual is reserved the same privilege of winning the support of the general will. In such a contingency, it is he who is triumphant.

It is apparent from this discussion of Hebbel's conception of the state, that whatever basis *Agnes Bernauer* had in political philosophy existed only in the imagination of the author or at best upon a mistaken conception of individual and of state. The real dramatic significance of these metaphysical abstractions is not difficult to find. True, the drama has turned out to be nothing more than a combat of individual wills, but the ethical law which still is undisposed of, stripped of its symbolic expression, looms up as a nineteenth century variant of the old Greek fatum, complete in its inexorable force like an all-consuming leviathan. And this was the character which Hebbel wished to ascribe to the state, not the fourteenth century creation of the drama, but the nineteenth century state which it was supposed to typify! Little wonder that this magnum opus was so coldly repudiated by the German people. If Hebbel in truth believed that he was reflecting in this drama the political tendencies of his time he was greatly deluding himself, showing at the same time a total misunderstanding of and lack of sympathy for the existing conditions. It is, however, possible that Hebbel may have been impelled to some extent by the change in his political affiliations which took place about this time. This leads us to the discussion of Hebbel's practical political activity.

The efforts of the author to find for Hebbel a niche in the political Hall of Fame are unfortunately misdirected. Hebbel's position in the political life of his time was an insignificant as his position in the realm of political philosophy. Granted that his poetics were "eminently political", they were scarcely of any great influence in shaping public opinion. Aside from this modest contribution to the struggles of the later forties and early fifties, Hebbel's share in the revolutionary movement seems to have been confined to reading the newspapers and being defeated for election to the Frankfort Parliament, a participation which was hardly of any great national significance. In fact, Hebbel's whole attitude toward both the great national political and social movements of the time were characterized by a fainthearted opportunism which contrasted greatly with his earlier populistic views. And so, it is difficult to find much to say in defense or even by way of comment on Hebbel's transfer of allegiance from Austria to Prussia. In the words of Treitschke it was "indicative of his political helplessness". Hebbel's tortuous and wavering course was certainly influenced by something more than the mere pleasure of exercising his talent as a political prophetaster. It will be remembered that about the time of his change in political affection, Hebbel's literary star was on the wane in Austria, and he had everything to gain by turning to Germany and to Prussia in particular. To us it is merely another instance of the poet's lack of political feeling which the author insists he possessed in great measure. This she tries to prove at the expense of the great Schiller. The superficial and patronizing way in which she remarks on Schiller's political thinking makes one wonder to what extent the author is acquainted with this illustrious predecessor of Hebbel. For every one familiar with the *Aesthetische Briefe* of Schiller would take issue with the author when she characterizes this poet as "skeptic and pusillanimous" in his political attitude. The singularly lucid and enthusiastic exposition in these letters of the functions of the state and its relation to the individual are not soon to be forgotten. In fact Schiller's conception of individual freedom shows an insight into fundamental political truth which was far in advance of his time. There is nothing in Hebbel which can compare with it.

As regards the attitude of Hebbel toward the social questions of the day, one is again obliged to wonder at the ingenuity of the author in avoiding the true facts and in inventing remarkable excuses by way of justification. Thus one wonders whether Hebbel's change from a radical socialist to a conservative between the years 1843 and 1848 was because he feared intellectual annihilation would result from the introduction of a communistic program, or whether it was the fact that his financial position took a decided turn for the better in the year 1846. At any rate this latter point is worth while considering in estimating the poet's socio-political views. And so we might go on at indefinite length in analyzing the fallacies of the present volume, which the author sometimes wittingly, sometimes unwittingly commits, in her enthusiasm for Hebbel. While it is true that the latter borrowed from Hegel both in subject matter and terminology, he chose what really constitutes the defect of the philosophy of state of his great prototype, and by this very fact betrayed his own weakness as a political thinker.

JULIUS GOEBEL, JR.

University of Illinois.

THE LATER GENESIS AND OTHER OLD ENGLISH AND OLD SAXON TEXTS RELATING TO THE FALL OF MAN—Edited by Fr. Klaeber. (Englische Textbibliothek herausgegeben von Dr. Johannes Hoops. Bd. XV) Heidelberg, Carl Winter, 1913.

The picturesque story of the disgrace of the rebel angels and the temptation and fall of Adam and Eve seems to have had a peculiar fascination for our Germanic ancestors. Revolt and disobedience were familiar motives in their secular poetry, and revenge, which prompted Satan to enter the Garden of Eden in the guise of a serpent, was held by them to be as much a duty as a passion. And so there runs through the narrative of the Fall of Man in the Anglo-Saxon paraphrase of the Book of *Genesis* a curious suggestion of sympathy for the rebel Lucifer, which gives the situation added dramatic interest. The difference between this narrative as a whole and the secular epic at its best is indeed very great. Yet despite its frequent diffuseness and uncertainty, the poem occasionally displays something of Miltonic grandeur and sonority, particularly in the speeches of the fallen angel. One who wishes to get an idea of the so-called Caedmonic poetry at its best can hardly do better than to read this portion of *Genesis*, comparing it with the paraphrase of *Exodus*, stiff with gorgeous and artificial adornment.

The little volume edited by Professor Klaeber presents, in convenient and inexpensive form, the whole of *Genesis B*, with the Old Saxon fragments by way of comparison, in the appropriate place, and 852-964 of *Genesis A*. There are also short extracts from the *Heliand* (1030-1049; 3588-3609), from *Christ and Satan* (410-421; 470-494), from *Guthlac* (791-843; 949-969), from *Phœnix* (393-423; 437-442), from *Christ* (1379-1418) and *Juliana* (494-505). The most significant passages relating to the Fall of Man are thus brought together within small compass. Variant readings and other textual information may be found at the foot of the page, and there are also brief annotations at the back of the book. The glossary covers only the Anglo-Saxon selections, and does not register, except in a few cases, the line-numbers of the words. There is a brief but well-selected bibliography, embodying the latest researches. As the editor says in his prefatory note, "the apparatus has purposely been kept within narrow limits." The general treatment is much the same as in Morsbach and Holthausen's *Alt- und Mittelenglische Texte*, with the brief but useful editions of *Beowulf*, *Elene*, *Emaré*, etc. The present volume might apparently have appeared in that series with equal propriety.

It is hardly necessary to say that the editorial work has been done with care and judgment. Professor Klaeber's wide knowledge of Anglo-Saxon idiom and sound critical sense give the brief annotations much value. Here and there one might wish some discussion of a difficult passage, as *Phœnix* 407b *tōþas idge*, in which the meaning of *idge* is merely queried in the glossary, and *tōþas* does not appear to be registered at all. This is the more regrettable as there is no detailed edition of *Phœnix*, as there is of *Christ*, for example. It would be unfair, however, to censure a text for brevity which aims chiefly at compactness, especially when the editor has contrived to suggest so much in small compass.

There is a very real need for such texts as this, as anyone who has guided a class through the minor specimens of Anglo-Saxon poetry can testify. And although designed primarily for students, such texts are of much use to the investigator. The smaller tools of scholarship are occasionally surprisingly convenient in hewing a way through the thickets of research.

WILLIAM WITHERLE LAWRENCE.

Columbia University.

THE THAT-*CLAUSE IN THE AUTHORIZED VERSION OF THE BIBLE*—By Hubert G. Shearin, Transylvania University Studies in English, I. Lexington, Ky., 1910. IV+85 pp.

In this monograph the author treats the subject under three main heads—the Substantive Clause, the Adjective Clause, and the Adverbial Clause. In his introduction he says, "The introductory conjunctional formulæ of the various *that*-clauses have for practical reasons been made the basis of the sub-divisions, so as to group like with like. However, any discrepancy between the form of the clause and its meaning is mitigated by the cross references." The following notices of the separate topics show that the formal classification has obscured the syntax in numerous cases where there are no cross references, and that certain apparently similar formulæ are really of different origin and function. The practical reasons for such a purely formal arrangement do not appear: convenience of reference could have been provided for by an index to the formulæ. The sub-divisions will here be considered separately. Those under the Substantive Clause are: Subject Clause, Object Clause, Clause of Specification, Predicate Clause, Appositive Clause, Absolute Clause, Omission of *That* in the Substantive Clause, *How That*-Clauses.

The statement (p. 4) that certain "*that*-clauses, though grammatically adjectival, may perhaps be considered as logical subjects—as in Gen. 45.8 So now it was not you that sent me hither—appears to involve a logical fallacy, as comparison with the original indicates.[1] It is not the *that*-clause that is logical subject, but the word that it limits, which is made the predicate for emphasis. The corresponding word in the original is grammatically the subject.

The observation (p. 5) that clauses like Gen. 27.20 How is it that thou hast found it so quickly . . . . .? and Acts 21.35 so it was that he was borne of the souldiers, verge upon the consecutive, is not substantiated. In the original of the first type no trace of result is visible, and none, so far as I can see, in the English. *It* refers, not to anything that produces a result, but to the succeeding *that*-clause as a fact. In the examples of the second type with *so* the English is equally free from idea of result: *so* is the very common Elizabethan adverb of pure manner, 'thus', not the derived

[1] The original will not always determine the syntax of the translation, but it often serves in doubtful cases to show the thought of the translators, and thus to help determine the syntax.

correlative *so,* and *it* as above refers to the substantive clause. The meaning is not "something [it] was such that [as a result] etc.", but "it was thus, namely, that etc." The Vulgate, Contigit ut portaretur, which is cited, lends only specious color to the consecutive theory. Even in old Latin the *ut*-clause of result had long become purely substantive after *contigit* and the like.[2]

The clauses after *than* (pp. 5 ff.) are likewise without consecutive relation, but are purely substantive. The occurrence of the substantivized infinitive in the originals quoted and in the English (Ex. 14.12 it had bene better for vs to serue the Egyptians, then that wee should die) points to the purely substantive construction. The Latin *ut* with the subjunctive (as in I. Sam. 27.1 melius est ut fugiam) lends no aid to the consecutive interpretation, for that probably never was consecutive.[3]

The two instances of *that*-clauses after *than,* Gen. 36.7, Isa. 28.20, which are described as adverbial, may possibly be constructed on the analogy of clauses like *so great (etc.) that,* and may therefore contain some consecutive force. The remaining examples of *than*-clauses with *that* omitted (like Ps. 40.5) are, however, probably not all *that*-clauses, but are of varying elliptical structure. Cf. Oxf. Dic. s. v. *than.*

Under Object Clause (p. 7) Lev. 13.8 if the Priest see, that behold, the scab spreadeth in the skin, is mentioned as noteworthy without assigned reason. It is noteworthy, it seems to me, as an interesting modern method of conceiving the object clause that points to the development of the conjunction *that* out of the demonstrative. Here the exclamatory demonstrative *behold* points vividly to the following fact in the *that*-clause just as the demonstrative *that* once did, and still may in such a sentence as "See that! the scab spreadeth in the skin!"

Sentences like Gen. 1.4 And God saw the light, that it was good, are explained as a "species of prolepsis" by which "the logical subject of the object clause is for emphasis brought forward into the main clause as object of the leading verb." The theory of prolepsis is here, I believe, only due to our modern grammatical conceptions by which we rationalize an older style of thought characteristic of English, especially of the popular idiom. It also occurs in the popular Hebrew and Greek originals, but less frequently. It illustrates the principle which Professor C. A. Smith calls "the short reach in English syntax". The sentence, *God saw the light, that it*

[2] See Bennett, *Syntax of Early Latin* (Boston, 1910), p. 299, b.
[3] See Bennett, p. 238.

was good, represents the normal psychological order of ideas— perception and judgment. The construction is constantly in use today in vivid language. Gen. 18.19 I know him, that hee will command his children, is more nearly equivalent to "I know this man: he will command his children," than it is to the more sophisticated "I know that this man will command his children." The earlier and more natural construction is often more appropriate: note the effectiveness of the following statement considered in the light of a situation bristling with human nature—Thou knowest the people, that they are set on mischiefe (Ex. 32.22). A shade of effectiveness—Aaron's throwing the responsibility off by appeal to Moses' experience with the Children of Israel—would be lost in the more complex form of expression.

II Sam. 14.11 hardly belongs in this group, for the *that*-clause is rather adverbial and final than substantive.

The sub-division of the Substantive Clause of Specification seems unjustified as a separate category. Many clauses belonging definitely to other categories may, like numerous infinitive constructions, be thought of as specifying the application of the governing clause, but it is better, and often just as obvious, to classify them in the proper historical categories. Substantive *that*-clauses depending on nouns like *commandment, confidence, hope, knowledge, oath, sentence,* and on adjectives like *confident, ignorant, sure, willing,* are simply extensions by analogy of object clauses after verbs of corresponding meaning. The same is true after such phrases as *make covenant, lift up the hand, take heed, make intercession, write letters, have need, call to record, give sign, show sign,* and so on. In a few instances with nouns like *cause, knowledge,* and adjectives like *sure, ignorant,* the early construction with *of* + *that*-clause probably assisted in the extension. With nouns like *joy* (cf. John 16.21), and with adjectives like *angry, ashamed, blessed, grieved,* and verbs like *care, marvel, praise, rejoice, thank, wonder,* etc. the *that*-clause is most easily explained as causal, so that these clauses would more properly be classed as adverbial.[4] This construction after certain expressions such as *have pleasure* (Ezek. 18.23) is often hard to distinguish from the object clause after similar verbs.[5] Wrongly assigned to this sub-division are: Ephes. 3.14-16 For this cause I bow my knees vnto the Father . . . . . That he would grant you. Here the *that*-clause

[4] Shearin fails to recognize at all this common Elizabethan causal clause with simple *that.*

[5] See my monograph in the Chaucer Society (Second Series, 44, 1909), pp. 68f., for a similar ambiguity in the use of the infinitive as complement or cause.

is not subordinate to *cause,* but is final after *bow etc.* Again, among the examples with *show (etc.) sign that* is placed Judges 20.38 there was an appointed signe . . . . . that they should make a great flame with smoke rise vp out of the citie. The author has apparently misunderstood the passage. After several repulses from Gibeah by the Benjamites, the Israelites manage to get liers in wait between themselves and the besieged city. They then feign another retreat, thus drawing the Benjamites off till the liers in wait, as agreed upon, fire the city. On seeing the smoke—the appointed sign—the Israelites turn and confound their enemies. The *that*-clause does not specify the application of *sign* or depend on it, but it is the sign, the clause being appositive.

I Kings 8.18 thou diddest well that it was in thine heart, belongs in a special category. See the Oxf. Dic. s. v. *that* conj. 1b, where this passage is quoted. The examples in the Oxf. Dic. point to the development of this construction by analogy from *that*-clauses in apposition to a single word, as in the example, Helmstan ða undæde ʒedyde ðæt he Æðeredes belt forstæl. The second example quoted would easily be transitional to the present construction.

Shearin's example from Ps. 50.16 what hast thou to doe, to declare my Statutes, or that thou shouldest take my Couenant in thy mouth? belongs with the group discussed by him on pp. 50-52 (See below, p. 161). The same is true of Ezek. 18.2, placed here by the author, though he places the parallel Isa. 3.15 in the other category.

The category of Specification is likewise inadequate to account for the clauses after interjections (pp. 25 ff.). The *that*-clause after words like *woe* and *alas* is probably different historically from that after optative interjections. The Oxf. Dic. assigns the former, in part at least, to the causal *that.* The Oxford offers no explanation of the second group, though it can hardly be doubted that they are extensions of the object clause after verbs of optative meaning.

The explanation of the development of *would God that* in the order *I would—I would to God—would to God—would God* (in which the "suppression of *to* renders *God* an apparent subject of *would*"), is directly opposed to the facts. The expression *would God that* appears to be equally old with *I would that,* and moreover in the former *God* is the real subject. Cf. Chaucer, *Book of the Duchess* 665: But god wolde I had ones or twyes etc., and D 1103 So wolde god myne herte wolde breste, "might God grant". The same construction is found in Old High German and is preserved in modern German with *Gott* still subject of the preterite subjunctive. I suggest that *would to God* is a cross between *would God* and *I would*, with *to* later inserted to rationalize the expression *I would God*. However this may be, it is of interest that in the Bible there is still a difference between *would God* and *I would*. In all the six cases of *would God* cited the thing wished for is conceived of as directly in the hands of God, death being usually referred to. On the other hand in the nine or ten instances of *I would* some ordinary wish is expressed without reference to divine intervention. In one case of *would to God* the wish refers to death, and in the others is general, as with *I would*.

In connection with the *that*-clause as Predicate, a distinction might appropriately have been made between such pure predicates as Eccl. 7.12 the excellencie of knowledge is, that wisedome giueth life, and those based on the analogy of the object clause, the subject being a noun implying action, as in Job 34.36 My desire is that Iob may bee tried vnto the end.

Among appositive *that*-clauses are included first some examples that the author regards as belonging equally well to the group of clauses of specification. Among them is Eccl. 7.10 What is the cause that the former dayes were better? This is certainly not appositive at all; it belongs rather to the group (see above, p. 149) analogically related to the object clause. The older construction, *cause of that* + clause, indicates the objective relation, as does the analogy with verbs of causing. Again, John 16.21 ioy that a man is borne, is probably not appositive, but the *that*-clause is a causal clause depending on *ioy*.[6]

Under what the author calls true appositives is quoted Gen. 34.15 in this will we consent vnto you : If ye will be as we be, that euery male of you be circumcised, with the implication that the *that*-clause is appositive to *this*. But it is the conditional clause, *If . . . . . be*, that is in apposition with *this*, and the *that*-clause is in apposition with *as we be*. John 16.4, included here, is an ordinary final clause. John 18.14 gaue counsell that, Rom. 4.13 the promise that, II Cor. 1.12 testimony that, Phil. 1.20 expectation and hope that, all belong to the group mentioned above (p. 149) as analogous to object clauses. Acts 3.18 is an object clause after *had shewed*. In II Cor. 12.8 the *that*-clause is object of *besought*, and *this thing* refers to the thorn in the flesh, so that the clause is not appositive.

Under the Clause Absolute are mentioned clauses that the

[6] For further discussion of the treatment of *that* causal see below, p. 164.

author calls grammatically absolute approaching the causal,
such as John 6.46 Not that any man hath seene the Father.
These clauses are, however, not absolute, but elliptical, and
they are of at least two kinds historically (cf. Oxf. Dic. s. v.
that conj. 2b), some of them going back to the causal *that*,
and others to the object clause after omitted verbs of saying
and the like. The distinction can be seen in the examples
quoted. In the first place, John 12.6 This he said, not that
he cared for the poore; but because hee was a thiefe, shows
the original of the first type in its unelliptical form, the *that*-
clause being causal and depending on *this he said;* this example belongs, therefore, not in this category, but among the
other causal clauses.[6] From this causal clause we may pass
easily to those in which the causal relation is dependent more
on what is implied than expressed, as in Acts 28.19 I was constrained to appeale vnto Cesar, not that I had ought to
accuse my nation of. The remaining examples that belong
here are of the second type—"I do not say that"—as in John
6.45f. Euery man therefore that hath heard, and hath learned
of the Father, commeth vnto me, not that any man hath seene
the father; so II Cor. 3.5, Phil. 4.11. Wrongly included here
are II Cor. 13.7, in which the *that*-clause is final; and Ezek.
23.40, which the author says is "absolute with merely additive
function." The *that*-clause is one of the accusations of
Aholah and Aholibah, being in apposition with *abominations*
in v. 36, and parallel with the other appositives in vv. 37, 38.

To the list of substantive clauses with omitted *that* (pp.
31-34, 49) should be added Num. 9.21 (quoted on p. 67, 4);
Gen. 8.13; Ex. 36.7; Gal. 4.15; I John 3.17; Rev. 2.2; 9.10;
22.9, which I have noted incidentally.

Shearin explains the *how that*-clause as a coalescence of
object *how*-clauses of manner with simple *that*-clauses. He
quotes four examples to show their similarity that could bring
about such a coalescence. Only one, however, is a combination
of a true clause of manner and a simple object *that*-clause,
as is clear from the Greek original and the Vulgate—Acts
9.27.[7] In two of the other three examples, Josh. 14.12 and II
Kings 19.25, *how* has already lost its force of manner, and the
clause is equivalent to a *that*-clause. I Cor. 15.3-5 how that
—that —that—that, is an example of the result of the "coalescence", not of its cause, which it is cited to illustrate.
The colorless use of *how that* is, however, probably not the
result of a coalescence of *how*-clauses and *that*-clauses, but

[6] For further discussion of the treatment of *that* causal see below,
p. 164.

[7] Shearin entirely obscures the force of this passage and its originals
by misquotation. See below, where it is correctly quoted.

is more probably due to the frequently occurring addition of
that to conjunctive words, as in *when that, if that,* etc. In
fact, in the above examples (excepting of course Acts 9.27)
that may be of the character of pro-conjunction in form,
though the sense of the first conjunction be weakened. This
is indicated in Kings by the marginal reading, *hast thou not
heard how I haue made it long agoe,* and *formed it of ancient
times?*

Whatever the genesis of the *how that*-clause from the *how*
clause, a more suggestive arrangement of material would have
been in the order of the gradual weakening of the modal force
of *how.* Acts 9.27, and declared vnto them how hee had seene
the Lord in the way, and that hee had spoken to him, and
how hee had preached boldly at Damascus ($\pi\tilde{\omega}\varsigma$—$\H{o}\tau\iota$—$\pi\tilde{\omega}\varsigma$;
quomodo—quia—quomodo), illustrates the *how*-clause with
its full force of manner, as the original and the Vulgate
show. Numerous ambiguous cases, in which the degree of
manner is doubtful, like Acts 23.30 And when it was tolde me,
how that the Iewes laid waite for the man, show the transition stage to those in which *how* has lost all its force of manner, as in Ex. 9.29 thou mayest know how that the earth is
the LORDS.

The so-called proleptical *how that*-clauses here treated are
subject to the same explanation I have given above (p. 149),
and this explanation applies to I Cor. 1.26, designated by
Shearin as unique.

The Adjective Clause is treated under the sub-divisions
That as Object of a Preposition, *That* as an Adverbial Accusative, *That* as a Compound Relative Pronoun, The Consecutive
Adjective Clause, The Final Adjective Clause, The Omission
of *That* in the Adjective Clause.

Under the Adjective Clause is treated the use of the relatives *that* and *which.* Shearin quotes Grainger,[8] who in turn
quotes Smith[9] regarding the greater "carrying power" of
which as compared with *that.* None of them, however, mention the reason for this greater carrying power—namely, that
in English *which* has higher stress than *that.* This is immediately connected with the predominance of *that* as a restrictive, and of *which* as an explanatory and progressive relative.
For in the use of the more highly stressed *which,* the relative
becomes by its emphasis separated to another phrase
group from that of its antecedent; whereas the low-stressed
that throws the emphasis on the phrase group containing the
antecedent, and is thus closely connected with it. When the

[8] James M. Grainger, *Studies in the Syntax of the King James Version,* University of North Carolina Press, 1907.

[9] C. Alphonso Smith, *Studies in Syntax,* Boston, 1906.

relative is omitted, the connection is closer still. Compare the following: "Here is a good book, which I brought with me to read;" "This is the book that I want;" "This is the book I want."

Stress and closeness of connection explain at least some of Smith's examples.[10] *And* (or *but*) in such cases always follows a logical pause, and in such a position the combination *and that*, both low-stressed, is difficult, the natural tendency being to give undue stress to *and;* while *and which* allows the normal stress relation. Besides this, in the majority of Smith's examples the first relative clause has a distinctly closer logical connection to its antecedent than has the second. Toller's sentence quoted, "There are other works than these just mentioned that have been connected with Alfred's name, but which for different reasons can hardly be considered to be of equal importance with them," is essentially equivalent to "There are other works connected with Alfred's name, but they can hardly etc." Of course it is natural that the relative most closely connected with its antecedent should usually come first, with the less restrictive one following.

When we come to the Bible instances, the closer connection of *that* to its antecedent accounts not only for most of the cases where *that* precedes *which*, but also where it follows. No absolute uniformity can of course be expected, as Grainger and Shearin emphasize; yet a comparison with the Hebrew and Greek originals makes it evident that in the great majority of instances a relative pronoun of the original is represented in English by *which*, while adjective clause relations of a more restrictive nature, such as the article+participle, the construct or the genitive relation, descriptive nouns, and the like, are usually represented in English by *that*, especially when it is desired to differentiate between the two relations. In the Greek of the New Testament a frequent construction for the looser relative connection is the noun or pronoun with post-positive article+participle (sometimes an appositive participle or noun), adding some characterization with more or less closeness of connection. This is regularly rendered by *which*. I have compared with the original all the *that's*, *who's*, and *which's* of the book of Revelation, and have found that of about 100 relative *that's*, 85 translate the article+participle, as ὁ κρατῶν = he that holdeth; 4 (restrictive) translate a relative pronoun; 12 (restrictive) translate the post-positive article+participle (or analogous construction); 1 (non-restrictive) a relative pronoun.

[10] I recognize the value of Smith's principle in certain cases; but I believe it is not the only one affecting the use of the two relatives.

It is sometimes difficult to distinguish between restrictive and non-restrictive *which*, but as nearly as I can determine, of about 130 *who's* and *which's* 34 restrictive and 24 non-restrictive represent relative pronouns; 30 restrictive and 23 non-restrictive represent the Greek post-positive article+participle (or analogous construction). Of about 20 exceptions several are the phrases *they which, them which, those which, those things which*, of more or less stereotyped nature, in many of which, however, *which* has the force of *qualis*. Many of the exceptions in the use of *which* and *that* can be accounted for by circumstances peculiar to each context,[11] but these figures establish the general rule that the use of *that* or *which* depends largely on the form of expression in the original. Note the following characteristic examples:—

Rom. 8.34 It is Christ that died, yea rather that is risen againe, who is euen at the right hand of God, who also maketh intercession for vs = Greek participle—participle—relative—relative; Rev. 2.1 he that holdeth the seuen starres in his right hand, who walketh in the midst = participle—post-positive participle; 2.14 them that holde the doctrine of Balaam, who taught Balac = participle—relative; 3.10 the houre of temptation, which shall come vpon all the world, to try them that dwell vpon the earth = post-positive participle—participle; 13.14 deceiueth them that dwel on the earth, by the meanes of those miracles which he had power to do . . ., saying to them that dwell on the earth, that they should make an Image to the beast, which had the wound = participle—relative—participle—relative; Mark 15.7 there was one named Barabbas, which lay bound with them that had made insurrection with him, who had committed murder = appositive participle—participle—relative. Josh. 24.17 he it is that brought vs vp and our fathers out of the land of Egypt, from the house of bondage, & which did those great signes = Hebrew participle—relative; Judges 4.2 Iabin king of Canaan: that reigned in Hazor, the captaine of whose host was Sisera, which dwelt in Harosheth. Here *that* introduces the closer connection, *which* the looser, preserving the difference of the Hebrew, which reads literally, "who reigned in Hazor; and the captaine of his host was Sisera,

[11] Note, for example, Luke 1.45 And blessed is she that beleeued, for there shalbe a performance of those things. Here the margin has, *or which beleeued, that there*. Here the change to *which* is obviously to avoid the repetition of *that* in different senses. In Rev. 3.2 strengthen the things which remaine, that are ready to die = adjective—relative, the use of *which* in the first clause throws the emphasis on the important part.

and he dwelt etc.'' Judg. 20.46 all which fell that day of
Beniamin were twentie and fiue thousand men that drew
the sword = article+participle—participle, the first relative
idea receiving in Hebrew more emphasis than the second, as
it does in English. Though both clauses are restrictive in
English, the high-stressed relative contains the important
idea: ''all those who fell were twenty-five thousand sol-
diers.''

The two examples quoted by Grainger of *which* restrictive
(p. 30), Gen. 6.2 and 11.6, both have relative pronouns in
the Hebrew.[12] Among the examples that Shearin gives to
illustrate the greater carrying power of *which, that* represents in the Hebrew and the Greek a closer connection than
which in the following cases: Deut. 30.7 on them that hate
thee, which persecuted thee; Eccles. 8.12 it shall be well with
them that feare God, which feare before him; II Cor. 10.18
not he that commendeth himselfe is approued, but whom the
Lord commendeth—all these translating the original construction participle—relative.[13] In Josh. 5.6 all the people
that were men of warre which came out of Egypt were
consumed, the translation represents noun of agent—participle (Vulgate: bellatores viri—qui egressus est), the same
differentiation being preserved between the relative ideas;
Josh. 24.33 a hill that pertained to Phinehas his son, which
was giuen him, = possessive genitive—relative; Lev. 15.12
(misprinted 7), and Josh. 17.16, quoted by Shearin to show
the greater carrying power of *which*, are irrelevant, for the
antecedent is repeated before the second relative.[14]

[12] In Gen. 6.2 they took them wiues, of all which they chose, *which*
shows some of its earlier force of *qualis*. This doubtless had some influence on the use of *which* in instances where we might expect *that*.
This use of *which* is still current. In a recent mathematical work I
noted a number of restrictive *which's* like the following: "Draw a line
which shall pass through A and B."

[13] It is of interest to note that the glossarist of the Lindisfarne
Gospels has taken a similar means of representing the close connection
indicated by the Latin present participle; namely, the use of the
asyndetic relative clause. See the article by Professor George O. Curme
in this *Journal* for April, 1912, p. 181.

[14] Grainger's view that *which* is used in Leviticus 15.12 because of its
separation [by the word *toucheth*] from its antecedent *he* can hardly be
maintained in view of the following passages from the immediate context: v. 4 whereon he lieth, that hath the issue; 6.9 what saddle so-
euer he rideth vpon, that hath the issue; 11 whomsoeuer hee toucheth
that hath the issue. More important here is the fact that every *that*-
clause is restrictive, as also in verses 7, 8, 10, and 13. In 12 the relative
of the Hebrew is rendered by *that* introducing a restrictive clause.
The use of *which* as the second relative in this verse may be due to
considerations of variety; at any rate it appears to be exceptional in
this context.

In II Cor. 12.6 aboue that which hee seeth me to be, or that [15] hee heareth of me, where the order of *that* and *which* is reversed, it is accounted for by the difference in the original (ὑπὲρ ὃ βλέπει με ἢ ἀκούει ἐξ ἐμοῦ), *that* by its low stress connecting the verbs *seeth* and *heareth* more closely than *which* connects its clause as a phrase group to the main clause; thus the effect of the original is secured. The case is similar in Gen. 24.7 The LORD God of Heauen which tooke mee from my fathers house, ... and which spake vnto me, and that sware vnto me. Here the obviously closer connection of the last two verbs with each other than with the first verb, is not expressed in the Hebrew or the Septuagint, but is indicated in the English and the Vulgate (qui locutus est mihi & juravit). So in I Kings 10.8 thy seruants, which stand continually before thee, and that heare thy wisedom, the English suggests the logical connection between *stand* and *heare,* not formally indicated in the Hebrew. The Vulgate, again, shows it: qui stant coram te semper & audiunt. In Isa. 51.10 and Jer. 27.8 *that* introduces the second of two closely parallel relative clauses, while the connection to the main clause is made by *which.* Compare v. 9, where, no such differentiation being needed, *that* is used. In Num. 14.36-37 *which* and *who* represent relatives in the Hebrew, and *that* represents a participle. In Lev. 4.18 And he shal put some of the blood vpon the hornes of the altar, which is before the LORD, that is in the Tabernacle,[15] where the Hebrew has parallel relatives, the English gives less emphasis to the last clause, in agreement with the Vulgate: quod est coram Domino in tabernaculo.[16] In I Kings 16.27 the *which*-clause is less restrictive than the *that*-clause, as is also indicated by the punctuation.

Even Gen. 37.6 and 10 by means of the use of *which* and *that* show more than a tendency to euphony and variety, which they are quoted to show. The Hebrew shows no distinction between the relatives, but in English there is a difference in the effect of the two: in Heare, I pray you, this

[15] Note also the separation of *that* from its antecedent. Cf. note 14.

[16] In a number of instances the form of the English, when different from the Hebrew or Greek, agrees with the Vulgate. Note, e. g., Rom. 8.28 where the Greek has participles in both cases, but the Vulgate has participle—qui = English *that*—who. Also Judg. 6.11, where the Hebrew has two relatives, but the Vulgate = quæ erat in Ephra & pertinebat, and the English = which was in Ophra, that pertained vnto Ioash. Cf. Rom. 10.5, 6, where, however, *which* has the force of *qualis.* Regarding the influence of the Vulgate on the translators, it should be remembered that it would often be unconscious, owing to their familiarity with it, probably more than with the Hebrew and Greek.

dréame whïch I haue dreamed, the relative clause is an emphasized separate statement = ''I have had a dream: hear it.'' In v. 10 What ïs this dréame that thou hast dreamed? the relative clause is more closely attached to the main, and so receives less separate emphasis: ''What is this dream of yours?'' [17]

In the classification of *that* as an adverbial accusative, it seems rather meaningless to classify according to the grammatical construction of the antecedent of *that;* e. g., nothing is contributed to the elucidation of the syntax of the *that*-clause by placing Deut. 31.14 thy dayes approach that thou must die, under *day* as subject, and 4.10 teach . . . the day that thou stoodst before the LORD, under *day* as object. The syntax and meaning of the clause is the same in both cases. A more significant arrangement would be to place together the examples showing the same relation of *that* to its antecedent; as, point of time or duration of time. Mark 6.21 And when a conuenient day was come, that Herod on his birth day made a supper, may be consecutive; on the other hand, I doubt whether John 12.23 The houre is come, that the Sonne of man should be glorified, is consecutive, as Shearin believes. The original points to a final clause as the basis of the construction, according to the Hebrew conception.[18] In the English, however, the clause has probably merely the force of an adjective clause limiting *hour*: ''the hour is come in which the son of man was to be (should be) glorified.'' Whatever final idea there is resides not in the adverbial nature of the *that*-clause, but in the force of *should.* [19]

---

[17] I do not attempt to say to what extent the nice distinctions between *that* and *which* are due to the translators of the Authorized Version and what to their predecessors. An exhaustive study of the use of the two relatives in connection with the originals would doubtless yield interesting results.

[18] See Winer's New Testament Grammar, and Burton's Moods and Tenses of New Testament Greek, on the passage.

[19] Cf. heading to John 13 discouereth to Iohn by a token that Iudas should betray him. So 13.1 and 16.32 in which *shall* shows the force of destiny and fairly represents the final force of the original. The *that*-clause as an adjective (not adverbial) element with final force is to be explained as denoting, not the purpose of the verb, but the end or application of the noun. This construction is related to the similar construction of the infinitive as an adjective modifier depending on the noun. *That*-clauses and infinitive phrases are interchangeable in this use. Cf. Time to go, with Time that he should go. See also Ex. 14.12, Ps. 50.16. Likewise in N. T. Greek the constructions are interchangeable. The three passages referred to above all have ἵνα-clauses. In Lk. 1.57, and I Peter 4.17 the Greek has dependent infinitive, with genitive inflection showing its immediate dependence

Why Shearin places here John 19.27 From that hour that, it is hard to see. The passage reads, from that houre that disciple tooke her vnto his owne home.

Under the heading *That* as a Compound Relative Shearin explains *that* as a contraction of *that that*. The present tendency with some scholars is to regard the single *that* as the original construction. The subject needs a larger collection of material and a fuller treatment than it has yet received. The Oxford Dictionary (s. v. *That* demonstrative and relative) appears to regard *that* relative with omitted antecedent as an earlier construction than *that* demonstrative with asyndetic relative clause, the earliest citation for the former being 888 where *that* refers to things and 1320 where *that* refers to persons; and for the latter 1523. Professor Curme, however, quotes Hwa is þæt þe slog? from Rushworth Matt. 26.28,[20] where þæt refers to a person. The Oxford editors admit that distinction between demonstrative and relative is difficult to make, as stress is uncertain, and in the earlier stages there was probably less variation between demonstrative and relative (s. v. *That,* demonstrative, introductory note). Moreover, there must be considered not only the earlier forms of *that,* but other inflected forms of the same pronoun. When these are all placed together the early occurrence of the demonstrative followed by asyndetic clause is much more evident. Professor Curme cites among others from O. E. the following examples:

Beow. 1397 gode þancode . . . . . þæs se man gespræc;
Gen. 1757 Lisse selle . . . . . þam þe wirðiað;
Rushworth Mark 9.23 alle mæhtiga ðæm gelefes.[21]

on the noun. Similar is Rev. 11.18. All three are rendered in English by *that*-clauses, as in the other cases. Note Tyndale's rendering of John 12.23: that the sonne of man must be glorified.

[20] *Journal of English and Germanic Philology,* Jan. 1912, p. 26. See Professor Curme's articles in the *Journal* of Jan. and April, 1912.

[21] See many other examples in Professor Curme's articles in the *Journal,* vols. X, p. 339; XI, pp. 26, 180. Surely he is right in rejecting the theory of attraction to explain the cases of these old demonstratives. I would suggest, however, that Professor Curme goes too far in interpreting most of these examples and many others throughout his articles as if the writers had no feeling of the relative force of these demonstrative forms. Many of them were doubtless felt as relative as early as the Beowulf, for changes of syntactical conceptions always long precede the corresponding formal changes, or, indeed, the form never changes but receives a new syntactical function. But the examples are equally significant as formal survivals of an earlier syntax. Moreover, the early conception of a relative force is not inconsistent with the survival of the demonstrative force in many later cases having the same origin. Among students of syntax the principle is even yet too little recognized that old constructions do

I incline to the view that the so-called compound relative *that* is a survival of the demonstrative *that* with following asyndetic relative clause ("'omitted relative'"). It is noteworthy that in Shearin's first group *that* is always neuter, and frequently still has considerable stress; e. g., Gen. 32.23 and sent ouer that hee had. Compare Gen. 39.6 And he left all that he had, in Ioseph's hand: and he knew not ought he had, saue the bread which he did eate, where *ought* occupies the same syntactical position as *that* in the previous example.[22] Compare also Gen. 12.18 What is this that thou hast done vnto me? with Gen. 26.10 What is this thou hast done vnto vs? Also note the present-day "What's that you have in your hand?" The demonstrative construction with asyndetic relative clause is still alive.

The nearness to the demonstrative construction is shown especially when a preposition precedes *that*, as in I Kings 10.15 Besides that he had of the merchant men; I Sam. 24.19 the LORD reward thee good, for that thou hast done vnto me this day; II Sam. 24.10 I haue sinned greatly in that I haue done; I Cor. 10.13 tempted aboue that you are able; John 16.19 enquire . . . of that I saide. It seems most natural to regard the demonstrative as the earlier construction in such cases and still formally surviving, in agreement with the history of *that* in other constructions, rather than to consider it a late development from a restressing of relative *that*.[23] The examples treated on p. 49 under The Omission of *That* probably therefore belong to this category. When, as in the example from Ex. 10.28 in that day thou seest my face, the

---

not usually die after giving birth to new ones. All chronological treatment of syntactical phenomena must take that into account. A tenth century example may be more modern than a twentieth century one.

[22] This passage is an excellent example of differentation in the rendering of the Hebrew relative clauses. The Hebrew is, somewhat literally, "And he left all which [was] to him in Joseph's hand; and he knew not anything with him except the bread which he ate." The first of the Hebrew relatives is the most restrictive, the second relative idea has no relative, and the third is least closely connected with the antecedent. With this the English corresponds exactly: *that*—no relative—*which*.

[23] Our modern feeling in this construction by which we rationalize *that* as a compound relative, is probably influenced by the use of relative *what* in sentences like "He found what he wanted," where *what* is felt as equal to *that which*, but probably originated in the indirect question, and the general relative *what*. The origin of *that* in an apparently similar use is probably different, and our assimilation of it to the *what*-construction obscures to our feeling in all but the most obvious cases the fact that *that* is at bottom demonstrative and followed by the asyndetic relative clause. I note that Schmidt in his Shakespeare Lexicon regards *that* in such cases as the demonstrative.

demonstrative precedes a noun, its nature is unmistakable.[24]

The second group of Compound Relatives (p. 47.2), like Neh. 5.2 For there were that said (cf. v. 3 Some there were that saide), are evidently a different construction, *that* being invariably a low-stressed relative with antecedent clearly implied in the substantive verb.

The Adverbial Clause is treated under the sub-divisions Consecutive Clause, Final Clause, Causal Clause, Temporal Clause, Conditional Clause, Clauses of Specification, *That* as a Pro-Conjunction, Omission of *That* in the Adverbial Clause.

Under the Consecutive Clause (pp. 50 ff.) the full list is referred to the appendix, and only the "more interesting cases" noted in detail. Among these, however, are indiscriminately placed examples that need classification. One group is separated—*that*-clauses of result dependent on questions, like Gen. 20.9 what haue I offended thee, that thou hast brought on me . . . a great sinne? In this class the *that*-clause is regarded as a consequence attributed to an implied answer to the question of the governing clause. Furthermore, the examples given by Shearin are of at least four different sorts. In one the *that*-clause contains a present or past indicative expressing an actual result of the fact implied in the protasis; as in Matt. 8.27 What maner of man is this, that euen the winds and the Sea obey him? John 9.2 who did sinne, this man, or his parents, that he was borne blinde?

In the second, the clause contains a future indicative of hypothetical result; as John 7.35 Whither will hee goe, that we shall not find him?

In the third, the clause contains a subjunctive, or its analytical equivalent, expressing hypothetical result; as Ex. 3.11 Who am I, that I should goe vnto Pharaoh?

Finally, the clause may have the form of hypothetical result, though by inference referring to a fact; as in Ruth 2.10 Why haue I found grace in thine eyes, that thou shouldest take knowledge of me? I Sam. 17.26 who is this vncircumcised Philistine, that he should defie the armies of the liuing God? So Ex. 9.17.

With clauses of the third and fourth class should also

[24] It is hard to see why Shearin offers a different explanation for I Sam. 11.9 To morrow by that time the sunne be hote, explaining *that* as a demonstrative with progressive relative force. It is not a progressive relative in the usual sense of that term (cf. Sweet's *English Grammar*, §218). This is obviously an old construction in English. Cf. Rushw. Luke 12.50 oðð ða hwil geended sie (=usque dum perficiatur), quoted by Curme in the *Journal* XI, 181.

Shearin (p. 47) places II Cor. 12.6 in this category, and also (p. 40) in that of the ordinary relative, without comment. It is undoubtedly the latter.

be classed in similarity of relation to the protasis, those, recorded elsewhere by Shearin, in which the interrogative governing clause is replaced by a negative statement, and the
that-clause is thought of as a consequence attributed hypo-
thetically to the thing that is denied in the protasis; as Deut.
30.12 It is not in Heauen, that thou shouldest say; Judg.
21.22 yee did not giue vnto them at this time, that you should
be guiltie; Isa. 53.2 there is no beautie that we should desire
him; so Gen. 40.15, Lev. 11.43.

These idiomatic consecutive clauses which are explained by
the fact implied in the governing clause are different in sense
from other ordinary result clauses, even when the latter are
hypothetical and depend on interrogative statements; e. g.,
Num. 14.13 wherefore hath the LORD brought vs vnto this
land, to fall by the sword, that our wiues, and our children
should be a pray? So Num. 20.4, Isa. 49.15, II Sam. 9.3.

Among these interrogative sentences Shearin includes several that do not belong here; two have only an external similarity—Gen. 31.26 What hast thou done, that thou hast
stollen away vnawares to me? Here the *that*-clause is not
consecutive but appositional with *what hast thou done*, the
meaning being, ''What did you mean by stealing away thus?''
The meaning is apparent if this is contrasted with I Sam.
20.1 What haue I done . . . that he seeketh my life? Parallel
is Judg. 8.1 Why hast thou serued vs thus, that thou calledst
vs not when thou wentest to fight? Job 41.17 is erroneously
classed among the interrogative clauses.

Several examples classed as consecutive clauses do not belong here; e. g., Ruth 2.7 so shee came, and hath continued
euen from the morning vntill now, that she taried a little
in the house. *That* in this case means 'when'; see the Oxf.
Dic. s. v. *That*, p. 254, 6b, where several examples are given,
among them two that closely parallel this: 1648 Until just
that we came ; 1780 till about half a year ago, that my ill
stars directed me. I have noted instances of this meaning
of *that* in Chaucer, Leg. Prol. A 54 Til on the morwe, that
hit is dayes light; and Milton, Comus 642 but little reckoning
made, Till now that this extremity compelled.[25] II Thess.

[25] It may be doubted whether the use of *now that* in the sense of
'since', 'seeing that', referred to in the Oxf. Dic. (Cf. *Now*, 12 b) is
parallel to this example. Here *that* carries the essential meaning,
while in *now that* = 'since' *that* is unnecessary, *now* formerly, and
sometimes even yet, being used alone, at first doubtless as a simple
adverb of time in a paratactic construction with the causal relation only
implied, as in "Now you are here: let us begin." *That* was apparently
added as it was in *when that, if that,* and the like. Cf. W. S. St. John
5.14 Nu þu eart hal geworden; ne synga þu.

2.6 And now yee know what withholdeth, that hee might bee reuealed in his time, is not consecutive but final, as the Greek shows and according to the idea suggested by the phrase *in his time,* which Shearin omits. The man of sin is withheld in order that he may not appear before his appointed time. II Peter 1.8 they make you that yee shall neither be barren, nor vnfruitful, is classed as consecutive, and this agrees with the classification of the Oxf. Dic. I believe, however, that this is wrong. It would give an unparalleled meaning to *make;* much more probably the *that-*clause is used after *make* just as the infinitive would be: "make you to be etc." Such interchange of the infinitive and *that-*clause is very common.[26] Cf. Job 21.3 suffer me that I may speake, with Gen. 31.7 God suffered him not to hurt me. That the clause is naturally a substantive clause in English is indicated by the omission of *that,* as in Chaucer, D 617 That made me I coude noght withdrawe.

After classing Gen. 36.7 For their riches were more than that they might dwell together, and similarly Isa. 28.20, as consecutive, the author adds, "Usually *that* is omitted in such sentences," and quotes a number of clauses with *than* that clearly are not consecutive at all, as can readily be seen by supplying the supposedly omitted *that;* as in Dan. 3.19 they should heat the furnace one seuen times more then [that] it was wont to be heat. In fact, the examples with *than* represent elliptical clauses of several syntactical varieties, depending on the nature of the protasis, as can be seen by a glance at the quotations in the Oxf. Dic. under *than.*

The clauses classed under *but that* introducing "a negative consecutive clause" need reclassification, for not all here included are of a consecutive nature. An examination of the Oxf. Dic. examples of *but (that)* clauses reveals the fact, not specifically stated, that *but* governs *that-*clauses (probably originally substantive clauses after the preposition *but*) of various sorts, in which *but* has the general sense of except or without, and the *that-*clause denotes result, accompanying circumstance, a contrary reason, etc., being sometimes negative and sometimes affirmative. For example, while Exodus 21.29 he hath not kept him in, but that he hath killed a man, clearly denotes negative result, "so that he hath not", the idea is different in Josh. 22.17, 18 Is the iniquitie of Peor too little for vs, from which we are not cleansed vntil this day . . . But that ye must turne away this

---

[26] The two constructions are sometimes mixed; see the two examples from Chaucer, in the Chauc. Soc. Pub. 2d Series, 44, 1909, p. 140. See Matt. 8.34, Mark 6.8, Ex. 14.12, Ps. 50.16.

day from following the Lord? Here *but* has the sense of
'without' before a substantive clause = "without your turning away'', which is not consecutive. Prov. 18.2 A foole hath
no delight in vnderstanding, but that his heart may dis-
couer itselfe, is neither consecutive nor negative. *But* is here
the coördinate conjunction, and the *that*-clause is analogous
to the object clause after *delight* and syntactically parallel
with *in vnderstanding*, Literally, the Hebrew reads, "no
delight in understanding, but in his heart's revealing itself''.
The same idea and syntax are found in Ezek. 33.11. In
Luke 17.1 *but that* means 'that not', but the clause is not
consecutive. Shearin is right in saying that Eph. 4.9 is
"probably substantive'', but it clearly is not consecutive.
The classification of such different examples together merely
because they contain a common phrase (formally), contributes nothing to the subject of syntax, and is hardly excused
in this case by the "assumption that the clause is absolute in
origin, *but* (*be+utan*) *that* being the syntactical equivalent
of *excepto eo, quod,*" for *but that* is by no means of the
same origin in all the cases cited. For Josh. 22.18 cf. Num.
16.13.

Under the Causal Clause Shearin says "Etymologically
considered, the *that*-clause is perhaps appositional to the
second (substantive) element in the compound *be + cause;*
historically, however, it is merely a survival of the added
relative common after all adverbial conjunctions etc.'' Here
there appears to be logical confusion; for what is the difference between etymologically and historically? An etymology
that does not reproduce the history of a syntactical phrase
is scarcely to be trusted. *That* introducing a clause in
apposition with *cause* in *be-cause* (as in Knight's Tale 2488
by the cause that they sholde ryse) is altogether different
in syntax from *that* added after conjunctions. Of course
after the appositional use had become stereotyped into the
expression *because that,* this phrase naturally came by analogy to be classed with *after that, before that,* etc., of different
origin. Indeed, this very phrase *because that,* may have
contributed to the development of *if that, when that,* etc.,
though the main source of these be the use of the prepositions
like *after, before,* etc., with *that* as pronominal object.

Under the introductory formula *seeing that,* indicating
the ground of thought or action, is wrongly recorded Gen.
28.8, 9 And Esau seeing that the daughters of Canaan pleased
not Isaac his father. Then went Esau vnto Ishmael. *Seeing
that* here is not the stereotyped formula meaning 'since',
'because', but the ordinary present participle of *see*. The

participle, it is true, may denote cause (just as it may also denote time, or other attendant circumstance), but the meaning is not "because the daughters of C. pleased not his father", but "because *he saw* that the daughters of C. pleased not his father." This is obvious in the English, and unmistakable in the Hebrew, where the construction is paratactic: "and E. saw . . . and E. went." In the English *seeing* limits the subject directly, but when it is used in the sense of 'because', it is detached from the subject and goes with the verb, as in Ezek. 21.4. Moreover, in this sense *seeing* corresponds to a causal particle or the equivalent in the original, and not to the verb *see*, as it does in Gen. 28.8.

All the examples of *knowing that* "with like function" are to be rejected on the ground that it is not a stereotyped phrase meaning 'because', but is simply the participle of the verb *know* in ordinary use in agreement with the subject and followed by a *that* object clause, corresponding in every instance to an inflected participle of the original. The fact that in many instances the participle is in itself syntactically causal does not affect the case: it does not mean 'because', but 'because I (he, etc.) know.'

One important category Shearin omits altogether—the causal clause introduced by simple *that*, which is common Elizabethan, as in Ps. 120.5 Woe is me, that I soiourne in Mesech. This category should include many examples that Shearin has called Substantive Clauses of Specification; as Gen. 45.5 bee not grieued, nor angry with your selues, that yee sold me hither; II Sam. 2.5 blessed be ye of the LORD, that ye haue shewed this kindnesse. So Job 19.3, II Chron. 29.36 (Sept. = διά), Isa. 63.5, Jer. 25.10, Lam. 5.16, Luke 9.21, 10.21, 11.38, Acts 4.2 (=διά), I Cor. 11.2, etc. etc.[27]

Under the Adverbial Clause of Specification is included the formula *in that*. It would have been well, however, to have referred to the original syntax here; namely, *in* (preposition) + *that* (demonstrative) + appositive substantive clause. Traces of this construction can still be seen in the varying meaning of *in*. In some cases *in* indicates the identity of the fact in the *that*-clause with the fact in the main clause; as in Matt. 26.12 in that she hath powred this ointment on my body, shee did it for my buriall. In other cases it indicates the ground or cause of the main action; as Rom. 8.3 what the law could not doe, in that it was weake through the flesh (ἐν ᾧ causal); Heb. 5.7 was heard, in that he feared (margin

---

[27] In some instances the syntax varies between causal *that*-clauses and what was perhaps one of their sources,—the object clause after verbs like *desire*, extended by analogy to verbs like *rejoice*, and to adjectives like *glad*, *angry*, etc.

for his pietie = ἀπὸ τῆς εὐλαβείας). The term *specification* is inadequate to describe the latter sort; they should have been included among causal clauses, or at least have had a cross-reference to that category.

In the same category of Specification, under the formula *now that* are classed examples that belong in different categories. In II Sam. 14.15 Now (νῦν, nunc) therefore that I am come . . . . . it is because the people haue made me afraid, *now* has its full force as a temporal adverb and is syntactically separate from *that*, which introduces a substantive clause in apposition with *it*. The *that*-clause has the same construction in Eph. 4.9 Now (δὲ, autem) that he ascended, what is it but that hee also descended, being in apposition with *it*, and *now* being merely the logical particle introducing a new point in argument (see Oxf. Dic. s. v. *Now*, 10). Only one example quoted, Ps. 41.8 and now that he lyeth, he shall rise vp no more, properly belongs here, but in this the formula *now that* does not denote specification but cause, and should accordingly have been classed with the rest of the causal clauses.

Under *That* as a Pro-conjunction the first example is very doubtful; Jer. 20.16, 17 let that man be as the cities which the LORD ouerthrew . . . . . Because he slew me not from the wombe: or that my mother might haue beene my graue. Here the substitution of *because* for the second *that* does not give the right sense. Whatever may be the sense of the original (cf. Rev. Vers.), the translators of the A. V. apparently regarded *or* . . . . . *graue* as alternatively parallel with *let* . . . . . *wombe*, so that the *that*-clause is a clause of wish,[28] like Wint. Tale I. ii. 12 that may blow No sneaping winds at home.[29]

Appendix IV contains the full list of references for consecutive *that*-clauses. In some cases it is difficult to distinguish between purpose clauses and clauses of conceived result. A large number of Shearin's examples, however, can hardly

[28] See also Oxf. Dic. s. v. *That*, conj. 2c.

[29] Shearin's explanation of the use of *that* as a pro-conjunction, which is far older than Elizabethan English, as due to a desire to avoid repetition, is hardly adequate, in view of the repetition of *that* itself. Several causes may have jointly contributed to its spread. In addition to those that have been suggested, one of the most natural is connected with *that* added to conjunctions. In such expressions as *before that* + clause, even after *before* became felt as a conjunction the *that*-clause would be felt as the unit depending on it. When several such units occurred in a series after one conjunction, they also would naturally be *that*-clauses introduced in succession by *that*.

The Oxf. Dic. gives no examples of this use of *that* between 1175 and 1489, though it occurs in Chaucer (e. g. B 4555, Troil. II. 766.)

be anything but final clauses, as the sense of the English and the originals show. E. g. I Cor. 1.28, 29 And base things . . . . . hath God chosen, yea and things which are not, to bring to nought things that are,[30] That no flesh should glory in his presence (=ὅπως μὴ καυχήσηται) ; 11.34 let him eate at home, that ye come not together vnto condemnation (=ἵνα μὴ συνέρχεσθε) ; so Ex. 28.32, 35, 43 ; 39.7, 23 ; Lev. 20.26 ; 21.23 ; Num. 32.9 ; Deut. 17.17 ; 21.23 ; Judg. 9.54 ; I Kings 2.15 ; 6.6 ; 18.44 ; Isa. 14.21 ; 48.9 ; 65.8 ; Lk. 4.42 ; 12.40 ; Rom. 11.8 (cf. 10) ; I Cor. 12.25 ; 16.2 ; Gal. 2.19 ; II Thess. 2.11 ; Tit. 3.7, 14 ; Heb. 11.5 ; I Pet. 2.9 ; Rev. 3.11 ; 7.1 ; 12.6 ; 18.4. If the thought in these examples be compared with that in the *so that*-clauses (App. V), the difference will be obvious. II Chron. 36.22 is marked doubtful. It contains two *that*-clauses, one final and one consecutive. Ezek. 1.1 is identical, but is cited without question as consecutive. Job. 9.32, 16.3, and John 3.1 belong to the group discussed by Shearin on pp. 50-52 (see p. 161 of this paper). Ezek. 20.32 is probably an appositive or a relative clause.

Among the references (App. V) for *so that* consecutive clauses are included three that are conditional, *so that* having the sense of 'provided that': I Kings 8.25 There shall not faile thee a man in my sight to sit on the Throne of Israel ; so that thy children take heede ; (margin = "*Heb. onely if*") ; the corresponding passage in II Chron. 6.16 There . . . . . Israel : yet so, that thy children take heede ; and Acts 20.24.

JOHN S. KENYON.

Butler College.

ESSAYS ON QUESTIONS CONNECTED WITH THE OLD ENGLISH POEM OF BEOWULF.—By Knut Stjerna, Ph. D., sometime Reader in Archæology in the University of Upsala. Translated and edited by John R. Clark Hall, M. A., Ph. D. (Viking Club Extra Series, Vol. III.) 1912. 4to. XXXV + 284 pp.

This is a novel kind of book. Countless treatises, great and small, in which the various *Beowulf* problems are attacked from the philological side, have been showered upon the world of scholars. There have also appeared a few minor studies of certain archeological features of the poem, not

[30] Observe in this passage the nice use of *which* and *that*, where the original makes no distinction. *Which* has more emphasis as a characterizing relative (qualis), the phrase being a striking statement, while in the following the stress drops in accord with the more normal conception. Note, too, that the alterations of word stress are natural.

to mention the cursory references scattered through some well-known handbooks. But here we find for the first time an exhaustive study of the complete Scandinavian archeological material combined with a systematic application of the knowledge thus gained to the elucidation of the *Beowulf* and its genesis. And it is a recognized specialist in Northern archeology that speaks to us in these pages. A brilliant scholar, in whom Montelius took an especial interest, for some time reader in archeology at the University of Upsala, Dr. Stjerna was prematurely called from his promising labors in the year 1909. But he left a notable record in the annals of a science in which Scandinavian scholars have gained an enviable reputation. During his short professional career he showed himself a wonderfully productive writer, a student of rare industry, learning, and a power of combination, which led him beyond the mere statement of facts to the working out of definite, fruitful conclusions. Those of his papers which relate to the *Beowulf* have now been brought together in this admirable English version, and it is safe to say that most of them have thus become really accessible for the first time, since previously they were more or less hidden away in a number of Swedish journals and two special publications dedicated to Montelius and Schück.

The scope of the investigations contained in this stately volume will appear from the titles of the individual essays. I. Helmets and Swords in Beowulf. II. Archæological Notes on Beowulf. III. Vendel and the Vendel Crow. IV. Swedes and Geats during the Migration Period. V. Scyld's Funeral Obsequies. VI. The Dragon's Hoard in Beowulf. VII. The Double Burial in Beowulf. VIII. Beowulf's Funeral Obsequies. Three of the papers, it will be seen, include studies of burial customs, two are concerned with important phases of early Scandinavian history, and the remaining three contain, generally speaking, a comparison of certain groups of archeological finds with their literary counterparts in the Old English poem. One hundred and twenty-seven excellent illustrations and two maps accompany the text.

In the first (and earliest) of the papers Stjerna examines carefully all the allusions to swords occurring in the *Beowulf* and then enumerates the archeological parallels, i. e. the remains or reproductions (on bronze plates) of some twenty helmets found in the North. Two of them, by the way, belong to England, viz. the well-known Benty Grange helmet and another one from Cheltenham. Some of the helmets are surmounted by complete boar images, others show only the upper part of the boar (the reduction being prompted by the desire to lighten the weight), and some are entirely without the ornament. A comparative study of this and similar characteristics enables the author to present the evolution of the helmet in five definite chronological series. The *Beowulf* terminology of the helmet points to the sixth and seventh centuries. More precisely, the poem deals with a still earlier period, when large boar images were worn, but its basic lays originated at a time when those images occurred in diminished form only or were entirely missing. Thus, the expression *swā hine fyrndagum / worhte wǣpna smiδ, wundrum tēode, / besette swīnlīcum* 1451 f. serves to set forth the actual historical conditions. By an analogous treatment of the evidence, the swords described in the *Beowulf* are shown to belong likewise to the period between (about) A. D. 550 and 650. Particular attention is paid to the 'ring sword', the hilt, and (in connection with the much discussed phrase *ātertānum fāh* 1459) the damascened blade.

Interesting discussions of various other archeological items, e. g. linked gold rings, diadems (*under gyldnum bēage* 1163), javelins (*eoferspreōtum* 1437), etc. are offered in the second paper. Even the 'good' *hafoc* of l. 2263 receives its share of consideration. By the discovery in one of the Vendel graves of the remains of an eagle-owl and a gerfalcon the fact has been established that falcons were tamed in Sweden as far back as the seventh century, probably for the chase. In England, on the other hand, trained hawks (or falcons) seem to have been unknown before the second third of the eighth century, see A. S. Cook, *The Date of the Ruthwell and Bewcastle Crosses* (1912), pp. 275 ff.

A definite thesis is propounded and—we need not hesitate to add—convincingly proved in the short article on 'Vendel and the Vendel Crow' (originally published in *Arkiv för Nordisk Filologi*), which has in fact already won the acceptance of some *Beowulf* scholars. Bugge had previously observed that the tradition of the fall of the Swedish king Ongenþēow in a battle with the Geats (Beow. 2924 ff., 2472 ff.) reappears in the *Ynglingatal* (*Ynglingasaga*, ch. 31), which mentions the slaying of King Óttarr (OE. Ōhthere) by two Jutish earls, and had moreover pointed out that in the latter version the thrilling incident had been erroneously transferred to Óttarr from his father Egill (answering to the Ongenþēow of the *Beowulf*). The scene of the battle is according to the *Beowulf* in Ongenþēow's own land, i. e. Sweden, but in the *Ynglingatal* is shifted to Vendel in Jutland. Now Stjerna rightly argues that the cruel nick-

name 'Vendel Crow' given to the dead king (who was likened
to a crow torn to pieces by eagles) cannot be a late literary
invention, but must have originated immediately after the
battle. As the king fell in his own land, the Vendel in question cannot be the large Jutish district of that name, but
must be the place called Vendel in Swedish Uppland. Vendel
is at present an insignificant church-village, some twenty
English miles north of Upsala, but being favorably located
for commercial traffic, it enjoyed a considerable importance
in the Middle Ages. There are exceptionally numerous ancient cemeteries near Vendel, the principal one of which dates
in its oldest parts from about A. D. 600 and was evidently the
burial place of a great chieftain's family. It may safely be
concluded that about the year 500 there existed a royal fort-
ress at Vendel, and that a noble family resided there.

A more comprehensive study of the relation between the
Geats and Swedes is contained in the illuminating chapter
on 'Swedes and Geats during the Migration Period'. The
migrations from Scandinavia to the South (of Europe) took
place between A. D. 300 and 550 (to give exact dates), and
resulted in a decided thinning of the population in southern
Scandinavia, as is proved by the remarkable decrease in the
number of graves. On the other hand, the southern European
kinsmen of the Scandinavians sent, in exchange for reinforce-
ments, large quantities of gold northwards. This importation
is traceable from about 400 A. D. and continued for a century
and a half. During that period there was a sharp contrast
between the Northern (Swedish) and the Southern (Geatish)
part. South of the great lakes there lived a relatively small,
wealthy, civilized population, whereas north of that boundary
line we find a people undiminished in numbers, much less
cultured, but energetic and aggressive. The natural result
was that the Northern people moved southwards and by dint
of superior force and numbers made themselves masters of
the land. ''The attack upon the South compelled them to
concentrate in Uppland, and from the sixth century inclusive
up to the end of the prehistoric period the dearth of finds
which had previously existed is followed by an over-abundant
wealth of them. The prototypes of the objects whose forms
now become the ruling ones in eastern and southern Scandinavia are however not found in Uppland only, but also in
Norrland. The lines of communication going through Uppland from north to south, along the rivers Temnare, Vendel
and Fyris, with the easternmost limits of the Mälar, become
thenceforward the most important, and here—at Vendel, Upsala, Ultuna, Håga, Tuna and Häggeby (Bjorkö)—the great-

est and most striking finds have been made, and the religious
and political headquarters grew up. This sudden increase in
wealth was the result of the victorious extension of the power
of the Swedes over the more southerly and richer borderlands,
and their great influence was gained at the expense of the
downfall of the independence of the Gauts. The overthrow of
the latter was thus the great event in which the movements of
the Migration period resulted in Scandinavia.'' (p. 72 f.)

To judge from the *Beowulf* and, indirectly, from the * Ynglingasaga*, the wars between the two tribes extended over a
considerable period and were evidently called forth by natural causes of a serious nature. Of the identity of the Beowulfian *Gēatas* and the *Gautar* Dr. Stjerna is fully convinced.
''It is difficult to conceive why the Swedes and (say) the
Jutes should attack each other time after time on lands so
widely separated. On the other hand it is quite natural that
the Swedes should attack and subjugate the rich and comparatively weakly-defended territory of the Gauts.'' (p. 89.)

Of the Geatish districts the island of Öland is considered
to have played an especially prominent part. It moreover
exhibits according to Stjerna the geographical features which
answer to the descriptions in the *Beowulf*. Thus the sea
mentioned in connection with the wars (ll. 2380, 2473) is
the Baltic, and even a direct allusion to the island is supposed
to be contained in the expression *ēaland*, 2334. That the encounters themselves happened ''on the water'' (p. 91), is,
of course, an entirely unwarranted inference.

It stands to reason that the *Beowulf* version is nearest to
historical truth. In course of time, the traditions became
confused, in particular 'Danified', and the place of the Geats
was taken by the Danes and Jutes, as may be seen from the
Ynglingasaga and—we may add—from the often quoted notice of Gregory of Tours, who represents Ch(l)ochilaic(h)us
as a king of the Danes.

One of the most admirable essays of the entire volume is
the one on 'Scyld's Funeral Obsequies' ('Sköld's Hädan-
färd'), which discusses the archeological and, incidentally,
the literary evidence bearing on the famous story of the
passing of Scyld. About the beginning of the third century
A. D. there was introduced (again) into the Northern countries the belief that the soul was released by death from the
body and lived a life free from martial or other activity,
together with other souls, in some distant place, a kingdom
of the dead. With this view was associated the idea (found in
many different countries) of a long journey by ship, boat,
horse, or sledge, according to the varying physical surround-

ings of the people. This idea of death, which was imported from the south, conflicted with the old view of warfare in the life to come. A compromise between the two conceptions appears in the great moor-finds of this time, which show the dead gathered into one heap in conformity with the Southern view, but at the same time provided with weapons in anticipation of continued fighting. The evolution of the sea-voyage idea is then traced through three successive stages evincing a progressive spiritualization. 'Scyld's Passing' is a pure specimen of the ship burial customs of the earliest type, which Stjerna ventures to assign to a period beginning about the close of the fourth and ending about the middle of the sixth century. Archaeology can of course produce no real parallel. But the remains of the Vendel boat-graves (representing the second stage) remind us in several details of the *Beowulf* account. That the incident of Scyld's sea burial is an original and significant element of the story and not merely an addition made for the sake of dignifying and embellishing the narrative, is rightly insisted upon by the author.

An examination of the last three papers—highly stimulating as they are—would unduly prolong this review. Suffice it to mention an interesting result reached in the chapter on 'Beowulf's Funeral Obsequies'. The combination of corpse-burning and grave-mounds, as it appears in the *Beowulf*, is paralleled by the finds in the eastern part of South Scandinavia only, i. e. in Öland. An exact counterpart of the Beowulfian mound (*Bīowulfes biorh*) is the royal barrow at Gamla Upsala, called Ödinshög; the two must have been contemporary. In this paper, by the way, and likewise in the one on 'The Dragon's Hoard' Stjerna goes too far in dwelling on (real or apparent) inconsistencies of the narrative and accounting for them by the assumption of an incomplete blending of duplicate lays.

The net result of Stjerna's investigations thus only briefly analyzed may be described as an emphatic confirmation of the Scandinavian character of our *Beowulf*. It is generally admitted today that the story material is largely derived from the North. But, if Stjerna be right in his interpretations and conclusions, much of the original "setting" also is retained in the Old English poem, or, in other words, the Scandinavian basic lays have left many more traces in the text of the *Beowulf* than conservative students hitherto dared to assume. With his characteristic precision the author occasionally draws a line of division between the original Scandinavian and the later English elements. "The Anglo-Saxon share of the *Beowulf* was first and foremost that of working up the original lays into a single poem; but besides this, certain parts of the poem exhibit Anglo-Saxon alteration of the original material. At first hand this is true of the description of the fight with the dragon, where archæological monuments of Scandinavian and Anglo-Saxon character are mentioned in turn, while as regards language a decided difference has been observed between this and those other parts of the poem which have not the stamp of the Anglo-Saxon mind.'' (p. 85.)

As may be seen from the last part of this quotation, Stjerna's philological views of the *Beowulf* must be taken with caution. He does not always look carefully enough at the text and the context, some of his interpretations are not quite up-to-date, and he is liable to overshoot the mark in drawing far-reaching conclusions from certain literal renderings unduly insisted upon. But even in those cases where we are bound to disagree with the author, the value of his wonderfully rich material in illustrating the 'life of the times' remains unimpaired.

Dr. Hall, the well-known author of one of the most helpful translations of *Beowulf,* has rendered us a genuine service in bringing out this book, especially as he did not content himself with rendering the Swedish essays into English, but assumed the function of a conscientious and skilful editor besides. In addition to a general Introduction setting forth the scope and importance of the treatises, he has introduced numerous critical footnotes of distinct value, in which he puts the reader on his guard against doubtful or erroneous statements of the text. He has also contributed an excellent 'Index of Things mentioned in the Poem of Beowulf', taken, with some alterations and additions, from his translation of the poem.   FR. KLAEBER.

The University of Minnesota.

DE MET HET PARTICIPIUM PRAETERITI OMSCHRE-VEN WERKWOORDSVORMEN IN'T NEDERLANDS door Dr. J. H. Kern. Verhandelingen der Koninklijke Akademie van Wetenschappen te Amsterdam. Afdeeling Letterkunde. Nieuwe Reeks. Deel XII No. 2. Amsterdam, Johannes Muller, 1912. Pp. V and 319.

This work treats of the historic development of the compound tense and voice forms that are made by the use of the past participle in connection with some auxiliary verb. It not only traces the history of form and meaning but also the history of the various theories that have been offered to explain these forms and their meaning. This treatise has a marked peculiarity. It does not put the author's own contributions in the foreground so that undue attention is attracted to them to the detriment of the general outline. The author modestly inserts the results of his own investigations at the proper place in the general development so that the orderly historical narrative is never interrupted and the view is never obscured.

This work is much more than it professes to be. The author modestly represents his treatise as a history of the Dutch forms. In fact it is a history of the Germanic development of active and passive tense forms. Not only the Scandinavian, German, English, Dutch, and Frisian forms have been treated, but the Dutch and Low German dialects have received careful attention, and the Romance languages, Russian, Sanskrit, Latin, and Greek have been skilfully introduced into the discussion. Professor Kern's official activity in Groningen in teaching English, Russian and Sanskrit has enlarged his vision and brought the breadth of view into this study that is usually so sadly lacking in treatises of this kind. This patient and valuable study of the different Dutch and Low German dialects has strengthened the present writer's faith in the value of dialect study in general and brought home to him in a rather painful way the fact that his own *Grammar of the German Language* would be a better book if he had paid a little more attention to the closely related Dutch dialects, which in a number of places throw bright light upon the German development. On the other hand, the writer feels that Professor Kern might possibly have profited a little if he had read the *Grammar of the German Language,* which in a place or two throws a little light upon the general question under consideration. Professor Kern has, like European scholars in general, not thought it worth while to read American publications, but he is thoroughly posted on everything that has appeared in Europe. It is interesting to note how even after his manuscript was closed he has worked into his treatise as best he could the fruits of the latest research. At the close among his "corrections" he comments favorably upon the recent valuable contribution of Professor Kurrelmeyer in "Zeitschrift für Deutsche Wortforschung" 12, 157 ff., and thus thru the instrumentality of a German periodical an American scholar comes to his own.

This treatise, one of the most valuable monographs the writer has ever read, ought to be in the possession of every Germanic scholar. Its 319 closely printed large pages are too crowded with facts to be reproduced briefly here. A few of the principal results are given here in the hope that they may stimulate to the reading of the original work or at least be of some assistance to the student of Germanic syntax.

In Germanic there were only two distinct tense forms, the present and the past. The former was used for both the present and the future. The first attempts to form compound tenses were made by associating the auxiliaries *werden* and *sein* with the past participles of transitives and mutative intransitives, i. e. intransitives that indicate a change of place or condition. Originally in all such compound tenses the past participle was merely a predicate adjective without the slightest temporal force: "das Dorf *ist* am Walde *gelegen*", "das Dorf *war* am Walde *gelegen*". The time was that indicated by the verb. Thus in the oldest period the tense was either present or past, for there were only two tenses. This is the situation after both *wairþan* and *wesan* in Gothic, the oldest Germanic language. This oldest condition is still occasionally preserved in modern German, as seen by these two examples.

The participle a little later acquired temporal force, as this new meaning was often naturally suggested by the situation: "er *ist gefallen*"; "er *war* gestorben, ehe ich ankam". The time is here no longer that indicated by the verb. We have here two new tenses—perfect and pluperfect. This was a very natural development, for it took place in a number of languages: "lapsus sum" "ich bin ausgelitten" "ik ben uitgegleden", etc. In the course of the Old High German period these compound forms acquired the following meanings. The past participle in connection with *sein* formed the perfect and pluperfect tenses, passive in force where the verb was transitive and active where it was intransitive: "er *ist gesehen*" (old perfect passive, which is still in use in North Germany and Holland), "er *war* gesehen" (old pluperfect passive); "er *ist gekommen*" (perfect active), "er *war gekommen*" (pluperfect active). The past participle in connection with *werden* formed the present and past tenses, passive in force where the verb was transitive and active where the verb was intransitive: "er *wird geschlagen*" (present passive), "er *ward geschlagen*" (past passive): "weorðeð . . . . . cumen" (old active present) (Gen. 2196) "will come", literally *becomes come*. At first the passive present with *werden* could only be formed where the participle had perfective force, i. e. represented the action as completed: " Das Haus *wird* jedes Jahr *angestrichen*" "The house is painted every year''. In the course of the O. H. G. period this form, which at first was only used to denote an act as a whole, as completed, and is called the actional passive, acquired in addition imperfect, progressive force: ''Das Haus *wird* jetzt *angestrichen*'' ''The house is now being painted.''

Of these forms the one made with *werden* and the participle of an intransitive verb, as in the example from Gen. 2196 given above, disappeared in the different languages. In O. H. G. and in O. E. alongside of the present and past passive forms with *werdan* there were also forms with *wesan* and *beon* in English and forms with *wesan* in German. Thus the participle with *wesan* was used to denote the present and past tenses and also the perfect and pluperfect. In the following centuries the German and English peoples tried to extricate themselves from this tangle and find a clearer expression for their thought. In German the forms with *wesan* gradually disappeared in the present and past wherever the reference was to an *act*, but remained where the idea of *state* was present:''Das Haus *wird* jedes Jahr *angestrichen*'' (actional) and ''Das Haus *wird* jetzt *angestrichen*'' (progressive), but ''Das Haus *ist angestrichen*'' (perfective form denoting a state). In accordance with the older usage, however, *sein* is still regularly used with actional force in the imperative and often also in the infinitive: ''Kusse Lieschen und die Kinder und *sei geküsst* von Deinem Theodor'' (*Fontane an seine Frau,* March 10, 1857). ''Er wollte nicht daran *erinnert sein*'' (Wildenbruch's *Die Alten und die Jungen*). The writer has given many examples in his ''Grammar'', (pp. 300-1). In general, however, the differentiation at this point in German became quite clear.

There remained, however, one difficulty—the perfective present and past had the same form as the actional perfect and pluperfect. In the thirteenth century the ambiguous *ist* and *war* of the old actional perfect and pluperfect were replaced by the perfect and pluperfect forms of *werden,* which was already in use as the auxiliary of the present and past tense, so that the same auxiliary might be used thruout the passive system: ''Das Haus *ist angestrichen worden*'' (actional perfect passive), etc. A corresponding perfective perfect and pluperfect were formed by the use of the perfect and pluperfect tenses of *sein*: ''Das Haus ist *angestrichen gewesen.*'' The old obscure actional forms still linger on in the colloquial language of North Germany and Holland. Es wird bestritten, dass ein japanischer Kreuzer *gesehen ist* (*Hamburger Nachrichten,* Jan. 14, 1905). Professor Kern on p. 38 warmly defends the older perfect and pluperfect forms here and brands the new Dutch forms with *worden* as a learned product introduced from Germany. The writer thinks Professor Kern is misled here by his enthusiastic love of natural expression as found in the language of the common people. Above *natural* expression is *more perfect* expression. Man has ever restlessly struggled to find a more accurate expression for his thought and feeling. Popular speech has always been a rich source of strength and vigor to all languages, but it is not the only source. The scholar has the same right that the humblest man or woman has, the right to fit his expression to his thought and feeling. Just like the common man he uses the means that are at his disposal. If the closely related German language suggests to the cultured Dutchman a clearer expression for his thought who can prove that in using it he is not contributing to the wealth of his mother tongue?

Unfortunately Englishmen did not work out of their difficulties at this point as successfuly as the South Germans. In the first place they lost *weorþan* entirely and thus lost the possibility of the differentiation found in German. We now use *to be* with the participle to express both the actional and the perfective present and past passive. English has, however, recently acquired a progressive present and past passive, for which German and Dutch have no distinctive form: *"The house is being painted"*. By the change of the old perfect and pluperfect *is* and *was* in the Middle English to *has been* and *had been*, the usual perfect and pluperfect forms of these words when used as independent verbs, we acquired clear perfect and pluperfect forms but unfortunately without any power to distinguish the actional and perfective idea: "The house has (or had) been painted", with either actional or perfective force according to the connection.

A little later than the earliest of the developments sketched above came the use of a transitive verb with *haben* or *eigan* (later entirely replaced by *haben*). In the first stage the participle was a predicative adjective, as in the case of the participle used with *werdan* and *wesan,* differing only in that it was an objective predicate, i. e. agreed with the object instead of the subject: "sie *eigun* mir *ginomanan* liabon druhtin minan" (Otfrid, 1.4.53) "they have taken my dear Savior from me", literally "possess him taken from me". The neuter adjective could always assume the uninflected form in the accusative: "ih *haben* iz funtan" (id). The meaning often naturally, as in the second example, suggested the association of the object with the participle rather than with the verb, and thus gradually the idea of a perfect and pluperfect tense became established with uninflected participle. This usage gradually spread to transitives without an object and to verbs that governed a genitive or dative, as there was in all these cases a close similarity of construction to that found in transitives.

The last step in the development was the extension of the use of *haben* to non-mutative intransitives, i. e. such as do not indicate a change of place or condition: "er *hat gearbeitet*", "er hat lange geirrt". Thus two groups of intransitives stood over against each other, the non-mutatives with *haben*, the mutatives with *sein*: "Der Schiffer *hat* (to denote an act) or *ist* (to denote a change of place) abgestossen". The non-mutatives assumed *haben* as they approached in meaning the transitives without an object, which had still earlier under the influence of transitives become associated with *haben*. Professor Hermann Paul's investigations led him to the conclusion that *haben* has imperfective or durative force, while *sein* has perfective meaning: "er *hat* lange gelitten", but "er *ist* in der Stadt *angekommen*," "er *ist* nach Hause *gefahren*", "er *ist erkrankt*", "er *ist gestorben*". Perfectives call attention, not to an act as a whole, but only to a point in the activity, the end, which may be either the final goal, as in "Er *ist* in der Stadt *angekommen*"—the effective perfective—or the beginning of something new, as in "Er *ist eingeschlafen, abgereist*" "He has fallen asleep, has departed", literally "He has gotten into sleeping, departing"— the ingressive perfective. Professor Kern has called attention to a serious error in Professor Paul's rule. We often use *haben* with intransitive perfectives, as in "Er *hat* laut *aufgelacht*" "He broke out into a loud laugh". His rule must be amended to: *Sein* is used with *mutative* intransitive perfectives.

Wherever there is a doubleness of conception South Germans are manifesting a growing fondness for *sein* to call attention to the mutative idea. Thus *haben* in "durch welche schulde die helde her *gevarn han*" (*Nibelungenlied*, Aventiure VI) "for what purpose the heroes have come here" has been replaced by *sein*. The M. H. G. poet calls attention to the linear perfective idea, i. e. the idea of a continuous movement until the goal is reached, while the modern South German feels the mutative idea as the more important. South German has had a marked influence upon the literary language at this point. Thus we now find quite commonly in the best authors such sentences as "Wir sind den ganzen Tag marschiert", altho the durative idea is prominent. The mutative idea has become associated with such verbs and *sein* is used even where there is no goal expressed. Hollanders here regularly give expression to the durative idea where it is prominent: "De soldaten *hebben* drie uur gemarzjeerd", but "Het leger *is* in een dag van A. naar B. gemarsjeerd". Also North Germans occasionally employ *haben* for the durative idea in accordance with the tendency in North German dialects: "So hat er lange Jahre neben seinem Hundefuhrwerk durch die Dörfer getrabt" (Frennsen's *Jörn Uhl*, chap. XI). North Germans generally resist South German usage in case of *beharren, beruhen, bestehen, hangen, hocken, liegen, schweben, sitzen, stecken, stehen*, etc.: "Viele Monate hatte er im Spital gelegen", where a South German regularly uses *war* as he does not think so much of the continuation in the lying position as of the ingressive linear idea of getting into a long-continuing prostration. The literary language of the North, however, follows this usage here in the case of *bleiben* and *sein*.

The latter verb did not originally belong here, and hence was once conjugated with *haben* in the North, but it has long been intimately associated with the mutative *werden* and in the South was influenced by it. Also in Dutch the auxiliary *hebben*, once almost exclusively in use here, has gradually yielded to *zijn* as auxiliary with *zijn*. Professor Kern does not positively state whether he regards this outcome as autochthonic development or the result of German influence. The writer thinks the latter probable, as this new usage, as far as he can see, developed, not in colloquial speech, but in the literary language, which has been subject to the influence of literary German. Of course the analogy of *worden* (=*werden*) facilitated the development. In both German and Dutch the verb *sein* "to be" has gradually been approaching the meaning of *werden*, differing however in that its meaning is ingressive linear, i. e. "to get into a long-continuing state", while *werden* indicates mere entrance into a state. When we translate: "Er ist lange im Gefängnis gewesen" by "He was in prison for a long time" we look at the thought from the English point of view. The German actually says: "He got into prison for a long period."

In contrast to their usual fondness for *haben* Hollanders and North Germans at one point use *sein* where South Germans employ *haben*, namely in case of *anfangen* and in Dutch also in case of *afnemen, toenemen, beginnen*: "Zijn krachten zijn weer toegenomen" = "seine Kräfte haben wieder zugenommen". Professor Kern does not call attention to this development in literary German. The writer gives two examples of this usage with *anfangen* in his "Grammar", p. 296. He has since found another: "Wie ich schon sagte, *ist* man erst in den letzten Jahren *angefangen,* von dem Kloster das zu retten und zu erhalten, was noch zu erreten und zu erhalten ist" (O. E. Kiesel in *Hamburger Nachrichten,* Feb. 13, 1905). This common Dutch and Low German construction is beginning to affect literary North German. This use of *sein* in a section of the country partial to *haben* is explained by the simple fact that these forms were originally passive: "Du hast natürlich nicht daran gedacht, dass gestern die Pfingstferein *angefangen sind*" (Frennsen's *"Die drei Getreuen,"* chap. II). Here *angefangen sind* is probably the perfect tense of a mutative intransitive, but it is also the common North German perfect passive and may possibly perform this function here as the subject of the verb is a thing, but such forms can only be interpreted as mutative intransitive perfects where the subject of the verb is a person, as in the sentence quoted above from the North German writer O. E. Kiesel. Thus both North and South Germany are contributing to the spread of *sein* and the mutative idea.

The English mind, on the other hand, began in the Middle English period to manifest a disregard for the mutative idea. Professor Kern gives no reason for this development. The present writer explains it by a desire for a clearer expression of the idea of tense. The colorless *has* was a more appropriate form for this purpose than *is,* which is too closely associated with present time to denote past time clearly: "he *has* often *come* too late", "he *has fallen* more than once", "he *has* often *gone* to town on stormy days". Thus English has developed more sharply than German and Dutch the idea of tense. Every verb in the language assumes the same form to denote the same tense.

GEORGE O. CURME.

Northwestern University.

AUS RUDOLF HILDEBRANDS NACHLASS

Die nachstehende kurze Characteristik Walthers und seiner Kunst
entstammt einem Collegienheft Hildebrands aus dem Jahre 1870, als er
zum erstenmale über seinen geliebten Dichter, den er wie Wenige
kannte, las. Sie wird hier nicht veröffentlicht, weil sie etwa viel neue
Erkenntnis brächte, sondern als Zeugnis dafür, wie einer unserer bedeutendsten Germanisten damals dem grossen Dichter nahe zu kommen
suchte. Wer freilich Hildebrand genauer kennt, der wird seine feinsinnige
Art auch hier entdecken. Wie beleuchtet z. B. nicht, heller als aller gelehrter Notizenkram vermöchte, der Vergleich mit der Empfindsamkeit
des 18. Jahrhunderts die versunkene Mode des mittelalterlichen Minne-
lebens. Denn mit Recht bemerkt Hildebrand in der Einleitung zu
seinen Vorlesungen über die Literaturgeschichte des 18. Jahrhunderts:
"Das Allerfernste wird uns nur verständlich, zugänglich, sehbar, soweit wir *es in Nahes übersetzen* können, soweit wir ein möglichst
deckendes Gegenstück dazu aus der Nähe, ja aus der Gegenwart haben,
sonst bleibt alle Wissenschaft gelehrter Kram, dem Form und Farbe
des Lebens, ein lebenspendender Mittelpunkt fehlen, ein Haufen gelehrter Notizen zum Anschwellen der Köpfe, nicht zur wahren Bereicherung des Menschen, der Nation, der Menschheit. An dem Nächsten
muss und *kann allein* die Wissenschaft den Blick schärfen, ihre Schule
machen, das *Leben* fassen lernen, um in der Ferne mit Sicherheit vor-
gehen zu können. Dass das nicht längst anerkannter Grundsatz aller
Wissenschaft ist, dass man noch dafür fechten muss, ist nur eine Nach-
wirkung des umgekehrten, verkehrten Weges, den die Bildung unseres
Volkes leider überhaupt einschlagen musste und den unsere gelehrten
Schulen leider noch immer hartnäckig festhalten."

Auch der deutsche Standpunkt, den Hildebrand auf Grund genauester
Kenntnis über den heimischen Ursprung der ältesten Lyrik und des
Spruches einnimmt, verdient Beachtung. Er hat damit im Wesentlichen
Recht behalten. Wie schade, dass er, den die Natur mit dem feinsten
musikalischen Sinn ausgestattet hatte, die Entdeckung der Melodien zu
einigen von Walthers Liedern nicht erleben durfte! Wie mir Professor J.
B. Beck, der Entzifferer der mittelalterlichen Notenschrift, auf Grund
eingehenden Studiums dieser Melodien mitteilt, ist Walthers Kreuzlied
ein Kunstwerk von unerreichter Höhe und lässt uns ahnen welche
Künstlerschaft der Dichter auch auf dem Gebiete der Musik besessen
haben muss. Zugleich versichert mir derselbe Gelehrte dass von einer
Entlehnung von Walthers Musik aus romanischen Vorbildern keine Rede
sein kann, sowenig wie bei den übrigen uns erhaltenen Minnesinger-
melodien. Sollte diese Tatsache nicht euch mitsprechen dürfen bei der
Entscheidung über den heimischen Ursprung des Minnesangs?

Wer Hildebrands geistvolle und fördernde Besprechung der ersten
Auflage von Wilmanns Waltherausgabe (*Neue Jahrbücher für Philologie
und Pädagogik* 1870 S. 73-83) und seine tiefgehende Erklärung einiger

Gedichte Walthers im 39. Bande der *Zeitschrift für deutsches Altertum*
kennt, der muss beklagen, dass es ihm über der aufreibenden Arbeit
an Grimms Wörterbuch nicht vergönnt war, selbst eine Ausgabe des
Dichters zu bieten, der ihm neben der Gudrun und dem Volkslied der
Höhepunkt unserer alten nationalen Poesie erschien. In Hildebrands
Bibliothek, die ich vor Jahren für die Stanford Universität erwerben
half, befindet sich ein Exemplar von Pfeiffers erster Waltherausgabe,
übersät mit Bemerkungen von Hildebrands Hand. Auf dem Vorsatz-
blatt hat er wehmütig eingetragen: "Dies Exemplar ist, aus dem Bande
gerissen, in Wien gewesen um Pfeiffern zur 2. Ausgabe zu dienen. Ich
schickte je 5 Bogen, die ich zu dem Zwecke früh vor der Schule [H.
war damals noch Gymnasiallehrer] durchging, alle Wochen eine Sendung
hin. Nach Pfeiffers Tode hab ich mirs von der Wittwe zurückerbeten
und neu binden lassen. Viel Mühe mit wenig Erfolg wieder einmal.
Pfeiffer hatte sich auf der Heidelberger Philologenversammlung 1865
meine Bemerkungen zu seinem Walther erbeten."

Auch Hildebrands Handexemplar von Wilmanns erster Ausgabe, das
mir die Familie gütigst zur Verfügung stellte, enthält eine Fülle fein-
sinniger Bemerkungen, von denen ich gelegentlich Einiges mitzuteilen
hoffe.

J. G.

ZU WALTHER VON DER VOGELWEIDE

Unsere genauere Kunde des lyrischen Dichtens, des Gesanges von Liedern, beginnt nicht vor der Mitte des 12. Jahrhunderts, um die Zeit als die Wirkung der Kreuzzüge nach
Deutschland herüberreichte. Manche nehmen schon da französischen Einfluss an, wie auch Wilmanns in der Einleitung
zu seiner Ausgabe von Walther von der Vogelweide (1869
S. 1) zu tun scheint, oder doch Einfluss des neumodischen
Rittertums. Aber der Kürenberger, die ältesten Lieder Diet-
mars von Eist und der Spervogel zeigen noch nichts fran-
zösisches, das sind rein deutsche Blüten, die einen glänzenden
Anfang machen zu einer Entwickelung, die eben abgerissen
oder doch abgelenkt wird durch den fremden Einfluss.[1]

Der trat ein vom Westen her um 1170 am Niederrhein mit
Heinrich von Veldeke, der doch mehr als Epiker wirkte, und
gleichzeitig am Mittelrhein oder südlicher mit Friedrich von
Hausen, der den höchsten politischen Kreisen angehörte, ein

[1] Dieser fremde Einfluss wird nun von W. Scherer einzig als unser
Heil gepriesen und Wilmanns in seinem Buche "Leben und Dichten
Walthers" tritt ihm nach! Man vergleiche was er auf S. 28 über Kürn-
bergers Kunst zu sagen hat, neben dem, was er auf S. 26 behauptet.

Begleiter Heinrichs VI. in Italien. Er fiel 1190 im Morgen-
lande.

Weiter Reinmar der Alte, wahrscheinlich aus Hagenau, der
uns zuerst die Ueberwindung des fremden Einflusses zeigt, die
doch sehr rasch eingetreten ist. Er ist der unmittelbare Vorgänger Walthers und ohne Zweifel in persöhnlicher Berührung
mit ihm gewesen. Auch er ist 1194 in Oestreich nachzuweisen
(Klagelied auf den Tod Leopolds VI., MF 167, 31 ff.).

Aber erst bei Walther von der Vogelweide ist die Ueberwindung des fremden Anstosses vollzogen, die neue oder junge
vollendete Form mit dem Inhalt einer bedeutenden Natur ausgefüllt. Er zuerst ist völlig Herr geworden über Vorbild und
Nachahmung, bei ihm steht Vollendetes vor uns, als wäre es
selbwahsen (αὐτοφυές). Natürlich in den Bedingungen seiner
Zeit, aber doch noch darüber hinaus.

Der Inhalt ist freilich anders als wir ihn für uns be-
friedigend, erfüllend finden würden, das Seelenleben gerade
im Liebesleben war damals ein anderes, als es wesentlich seit
Klopstock und Goethes Werther in unseren Bildungskreisen
ist: auf einer Seite kindlicher, einfacher, anspruchsloser, auf
der anderen unkindlich, übercultivirt, anspruchsvoller (bî-
ligen), einer Mode unterworfen [2] die mit ganzer Gewalt die
Seelen der Gebildeten beherrschte, wie es im 18. Jahrhundert
z. B. auch die Empfindsamkeit tat. Aber bei Walther gerade
erscheint diese Mode durch den weitgreifenden Gedanken ver-
arbeitet und zurecht gelegt, der *das Ganze* ins Auge fasst.

---

[2] Und doch bei Walther auch tiefste Innigkeit, wie z. B. im Folgenden (52, 35):

> möchte ich ir die sternen gar,
> mânen unde sunnen,
> zeigene hân gewunnen,
> daz waer ir, so ich iemer wol gevar.

oder auch kindlichste Empfänglichkeit, wie z. B. 115, 22:

> Als ich under wîlen zir gesitze,
> sô si mich mit ir reden lât,
> sô benimt si mir sô gar die witze,
> daz mir der lîp alumne gât.
> Swenne ich iezuo wunder rede kan,
> sihet si mich einest an,
> sô hân ichs vergezzen,
> was wolde ich dar gesezzen?

Es ist eine Theorie darauf gebaut, die in der Minne, wie sie
nun einmal war, den Grundstein oder Schlussstein zu einem
Gebäude der Gesellschaft sucht und erkennt.[3] Was daneben
das Volk[4] sang, das ahnen wir nur aus Spuren, wie Walthers
Lindenlied, es war wol den Liedern des Kürnbergers ähnlicher als denen Reinmars oder Walthers.

Aber in der Form offenbarte sich damals eine Vollendung,
wie nie wieder und wie heute nicht mehr möglich, ja uns
eigentlich unvorstellbar. Die deutsche Sprache erscheint hier
in ihrem Festkleide wie es ihre Natur nur immer möglich
macht oder mit sich bringt. Dieser kunstvolle Aufbau der
Strophen, deren letzter Kunstwert ohne die Weise nicht zu
ermessen ist, die Bildung der Gesätze nach verschiedener
Länge der Zeilen, nach manigfachster Stellung und Beziehung
der Reime aufeinander, diese Reinheit der Reime, dieser Aufbau von 3 oder 5 Strophen zu einem Ganzen—und das alles
nur vom *Ohr* zu fassen, nicht vom Auge wie wir es tun—das
alles setzt einen Kunstsinn bei den Sängern wie bei den
Hörern voraus, der für *uns* ein hoch über uns stehendes Ideal
ist.

Denn gesungen, gehört nur ward diese Liederdichtung,
noch nicht gelesen—auch das ein Zustand, den wir uns für
Kunstdichtung kaum vorstellen können. Und doch gibt es
auch für uns Ähnliches, dass wir einmal, zumal in den Jüng-
lingsjahren, ein Lied nur hörend, nur gesungen kennen
lernen, dass Wort und Weise so zu einem verwachsen an uns
und in uns kommen, dass es uns fast unmöglich ist sie auseinander zu reissen. Das Wort bringt uns von selbst die
Weise mit, die Weise das Wort, sobald wir an eins von beiden
nur denken. Wären das nur immer bessere Lieder als sie gewöhnlich sind!

So war denn auch Dichter, Sänger und Tonsetzer damals

---

[3] Wurde doch in Griechenland die Päderastie so philosophisch ethisch
zurechtgelegt.

[4] Neque enim secundum vestrates (die Deutschen) habet cantica
populus romanae linguae . . . . . dabat pro cantu lacrymas plebs
ignara canendi. Bericht von der Reise des heil. Bernhard, Januar 1147
bei Hoffmann, K. L. S. 40. Gerhoh von Reichersperg (+ 1169) im
Commentar zu den Psalmen freut sich des geistlichen Gesanges, maxime
in Teutonieis, *quorum lingua magis apta est concinnis canticis.*

eine Person, wie in allen natürlichen Zeiten. Das Entlehnen
einer Weise oder Strophe war verboten, wer sich dessen dennoch schuldig machte, hiess "doenediep".

Aber was auch Walther im Liede leistete—es kommt vor,
dass der einfache Inhalt mit der Form im Kleinen und Grossen so zu einem verwachsen ist, dass man eine Pflanze vor sich
zu sehen glaubt—seine *Sprüche* werden uns und wol in aller
Zukunft seine bedeutendste Leistung bleiben, wäre es auch
nur, weil die da behandelten Dinge uns teils noch näher, ja—
seit 1870—ganz nahe stehen, teils Menschliches behandeln,
das keiner Modeentwicklung unterworfen ist. In der Form
ist weniger Kunst als im Liede und wird es auch in der
Weise gewesen sein. Der Unterschied zwischen beiden Kunst-
gattungen wird jedoch nicht streng eingehalten, ja die Worte
"spruch" und "sanc" oder "lied" werden geradezu ver-
tauscht, ganz ähnlich wie "singen" und "sagen".

Der Spruch darf als ein ganz heimisches Gewächs [5] gelten,
und Walther, der sonst in der Mittelhochdeutschen höfischen
Dichtung im engeren Sinne als sein Vater erscheint und
reiche Nachfolge fand, muss doch darin Vorgänger gehabt
haben. Zum Glück ist uns deren einer, Spervogel, oder zwei,
da es wol zwei Spervögel gibt, erhalten aus der vorfranzösi-
schen Zeit. Ja es gab sogar eine Spervogelschule, der man
denn auch Walther in seinen Sprächen die Hand reichen sehen
kann.

Ueber Walthers Weltanschauung, seinen Dichterbegriff,
seine tiefe Auffassung der Minne, verschmolzen mit dem grossen Blick aufs Ganze, sein deutsches Herz, seinen Humor und
Spott, seinen heiligen Zorn und seine grosse politische Tätigkeit sollen die Lieder und Sprüche selbst zu uns reden.

[5] Dagegen Scherer, Deutsche Studien 1, 31: "die Gattung der Satire
auf allgemeine Zustände der Zeit übernahm Walther von den lateinisch
dichtenden Vaganten des 12. Jahrhunderts." Als hätte sie nicht Spervogel auch schon! Es muss doch fremden Ursprungs sein!

THE LANGUAGE OF FREYTAG'S "DIE AHNEN."

In the study of modern literature a great deal has been done during the past few years in presenting to us a clearer and more comprehensive view of literature as a whole, and in giving a more accurate and detailed description of a certain period and its characteristics. Much has been done too in the history of literature by the many excellent biographies of individual writers, as these often contain new and valuable criticisms of the best known works of the various authors. There seems, however, to be a large field for investigation into the peculiarities of an author's language and style, as they appear growing and developing through all his works, or as these peculiarities appear at some particular period of his life, or in some particular work. Such a study is to literature what a study of technique is to painting.

Heinrich von Kleist wrote on April 25, 1811, to Fouqué: ". . . . . Die Erscheinung, die am meisten bei der Betrachtung eines Kunstwerks rührt, dünkt mich, ist nicht das Werk selbst, sondern die Eigentümlichkeiten des Geistes, der es hervorbrachte, und der sich in unbewusster Freiheit und Lieblichkeit, darin entfaltet." However interesting or valuable a work may be to the general reading public, to the historian of literature and the literary critic the "Eigentümlichkeiten des Geistes" as they appear in the work, are of more importance than the finished product.[1] The peculiar characteristics of an author as they appear in his works differentiate him from the great mass of writers. As Buffon has said: "Le style, c'est l'homme."

We know that a certain writer created certain new expressions, or used them for the first time in literature. But how many did he so use, and how often? Are these expressions which have become permanent in literature? Are the peculiarities of an author those of his age, or did he employ certain peculiarities of language and style for a specific purpose? If so, with what success? Such a detailed study of the language and style of various authors should be of great value in giving

[1] Cf. Saintsbury—Essays in English Literature, 1780-1860. Introduction.

the necessary information for making comparison of various
styles, of outlining definitely an author's originality in vocabulary and style, and in analyzing his qualities as pioneer or
imitator. The following paper is a study of the peculiarities
in the language of Gustav Freytag's Die Ahnen.

Gustav Freytag (1816-1895) wrote his series of historical
novels, Die Ahnen, during the years 1872-1880. (Vol. I
Ingo und Ingraban, 1872; Vol. II Das Nest der Zaunkönige,
1874; Vol. III Die Brüder vom deutschen Hause, 1875; Vol.
IV Marcus König, 1876; Vol. V Die Geschwister, 1878: Vol.
VI Aus einer kleinen Stadt, 1880).[2] Externally the work is a
series of historical novels, each having a separate plot and
each plot dealing with a separate period. (Vol. I Part I—
357 A. D.; Part 2—724; Vol. II 1003; Vol. III 1226; Vol.
IV 1519; Vol. V 1647 and 1721; Vol. VI 1805). According
to Freytag's idea, however, the work is a history of the German people and their civilization, written in a series of chapters. Like Willibald Alexis, and especially like Scott, whom
our author looked upon as his master, Freytag thought of the
history of his people as a unit, and the various historical movements as manifestations of different characteristics of this
unified people. The idea of unity and continuity in the history of his people led him to write Die Ahnen.[3] The work
essays to portray the history of a single family, the various
members of which are bound together during succeeding generations by constantly recurring similarities in physiognomy,
character and fate.

In speaking of Die Ahnen in an explanatory note appended
to the final volume of the series, Freytag calls the series "a
symphony in whose eight parts, (Vol. I and Vol. V each contain two parts) a melodic theme is varied, carried on, and
interwoven with others, in such a manner that the several

[2] The editions of Die Ahnen from which quotations are made in this
study, are as follows: Vol. I. 38. Aufl. 1908; Vol. II. 31. 1907; Vol.
III. 26. 1908; Vol. IV. 21. 1906; Vol. V. 21. 1907; Vol. VI. 19.
1908. Published by Hirzel, Leipzig. A careful comparison of this
thirty-eighth edition of Vol. I. with a copy of the first edition shows
that absolutely no changes have been made.

[3] Cf. Meyer—Deutsche Literatur des 19. Jahrhunderts. S. 403.

parts united constitute a whole." This "melodic theme" means to Freytag continuity of life and its various interests. This continuity of life and its interests had been impressed upon Freytag while he was preparing the material for his "Bilder aus der deutschen Vergangenheit," which he used as basic studies for Die Ahnen.

The fact that Freytag portrays in this work German life of certain centuries or periods—many of which were far remote from his own—naturally led him to peculiarities of language and style which often become very marked. These peculiarities in language and style are often the local coloring by which the author portrays the age which he treats. Whether these are always used successfully and with the best taste will be considered later.

Foreign Words

The first topic treated in the study of Die Ahnen is the author's use of foreign words. This is not by any means the only work of Freytag where the attention of the reader is at once called to the use of foreign words. Hager in the Introduction to his edition of Aus dem Staat Friedrichs des Grossen [4] says: "As regards Dr. Freytag's style . . . . . there is only one feature in it to which exception might be taken, viz., to the frequent use of foreign words. There is no objection to words of foreign origin which passed at an early stage into the language of the people and thus shared in the changes by which Teutonic words have been affected . . . . . . There are, however, in the essay many words of foreign origin for which German has equivalents still in ordinary use, and for which there is therefore no necessity, even though long use may have made us familiar with many of them." In compiling a list of foreign words used by an author one must naturally ask, "What constitutes a foreign word in German?" A great many words now existing in the German language, and in current use, were once thoroughly foreign but have become so completely Germanized that they betray no trace of the foreign in accent, inflection or spelling. In making a list of the foreign words in Die Ahnen, the question as to whether

[4] D. C. Heath & Co. 1908.

a word is still foreign or has become thoroughly German is settled by adopting Heyse's Fremdwörterbuch as authority. If a word is listed in this book as a foreign word, then such authority is, for the purpose of this study, considered final. Naturally an absolute boundary line in this matter is hard to establish. A few words which have been counted in this list are quite thoroughly German, e. g. Bischof I, 342; brav V, 301; Form III, 350; Marsch V, 4; Null IV, 344; Post VI, 231; Prinz V, 377; Punkt V, 110; Sammet IV, 51; Sekt IV, 48, but inasmuch as they appear in Heyse, they are included in the complete list. Heyne's Deutsches Wörterbuch which does not regularly include foreign words contains each of the words mentioned above. Compound words containing a foreign element have also been included in this list, e. g. Abend-collation IV, 111; Acciseeinnehmer VI, 6. Many times a word occurring more than once [5] is spelled in two or more different ways, e. g. Alarm III, 232, Allarm IV, 367; Discretion V, 159, Diskretion VI, 25; Exerciren V, 275, exercieren VI, 297, Ex-erzierplatz VI, 187; Paradise III, 133, Paradiese III, 235. This change of spelling is especially noticeable in c and k before a consonant or before the vowels a, o, or u; in c and z before e or i; and -iren and -ieren. Many times a foreign word used for the second time will appear in a lengthened or short-ened form or otherwise changed. Sometimes the first occur-rence of the word shows the Germanized form while the next time it is in complete foreign dress, or vice versa: e. g. Adjes V, 102, Adieu V, 326; Candidat V, 175, Candidatus V, 422; Capitän V, 274, Capitain V, 276; Duellium IV, 101, Duell V, 285; Licentiat V, 100, Licentiatus V, 110; Ruin V, 155, Ruine IV, 73. Such change of spelling or form does not characterize a peculiar period or place or character, as e. g. in Vol. V, Candidat p. 175 and Candidatus p. 422 both occur in the nar-rative, and not in the mouth of any character; in Vol. V, p. 100 Hermann is described as "Licentiatus," ten pages later an "Licentiat."

In the complete list of words which was compiled (with the indication of the volume and page on which the word first

[5] In the figures indicating totals such varying forms of a word are counted as only one word.

occurs) no attempt was made to show how many times a particular word occurs. Many of these words occur a number of
times, especially in Vol. V, but only the first instance is
counted.

The complete list of foreign words contains 1344 words,
with the largest number coming from the French, the next
largest from the Latin. Words are also found from Greek,
Italian, Arabic, Polish and Russian. The complete list contains ninety-seven verbs in -i(e)ren. Freytag seems particularly fond of such verbs in Vol. V, dealing with the seventeenth and eighteenth centuries—a period in which one would
naturally expect to see strong French influence. Aside from
these verbs in -i(e)ren the words used are principally nouns,
abstract nouns in -tion being common.

Freytag has designedly omitted or used foreign words in
the various volumes to portray faithfully the linguistic characteristics of the period with which the volume deals. In
Vol. I which deals with the fourth century, there occur in
the first part "Ingo" only 10 foreign words, in the second
part "Ingraban" 26, making a total of only 36 in 514 pp. In
Vol. V which deals, as stated above, with the seventeenth
and eighteenth centuries, there occur 500 foreign words—
mostly from the French—in 436 pp. This reckoning—taking
account as it does of only the first occurrence of a foreign
word—hardly presents in its full meaning the great difference between Vol. I and Vol. V in this respect. An actual
count of every occurrence of a foreign word in Vol. V would
raise the number here given by some hundreds. Thus Freytag succeeded in giving to Vol. V the foreign French flavor
which so pervaded the literature of that age. In the matter
of his characters too, Freytag has taken care that foreign
words should be used principally by only such characters as
would naturally use them. Henner and the scholars e. g.
in Vol. III (Cf. p. 70) with their Latin training use many
of them, while in that same volume they are much more rare
in the speech of the common people.

Regarding the general use of foreign words in Die Ahnen
one may say positively that Freytag was not careful to avoid

the use of them. His use of words in his writings is careful and exact so that he is often quoted by lexicographers, but he many times uses a foreign word when a German word would have expressed the same idea. Many of the foreign words found here were not current in the decade during which Freytag wrote these novels. Two important reasons may be advanced for the use of many foreign words. First, Freytag was a trained student of Latin. He had studied the early history of the drama [6] and its development through the Middle Ages; he had given much time during his life to the study of historical records and chronicles.[7] In such documents he must naturally have become acquainted with a large number of foreign words of Latin origin. Secondly, the scenes described often call for foreign words. The author had lived a large part of his life near the Polish border and many of the scenes of the novels presented life as the writer had seen it in his youth. Such descriptions make many words, more or less foreign, not only natural but necessary. The Crusades, life in the East, descriptions of Eastern civilization called for a vocabulary that must needs be composed of words not of Teutonic origin.

Freytag is usually regarded as a purist in style. He seldom wrote without giving careful attention to the words which he employed. His style contains few mannerisms. Clearness is certainly one of its characteristics. If clearness could best be attained by the use of a foreign word, Freytag seldom hesitated to employ it. He uses foreign words in Die Ahnen with discrimination, as shown above, and often obtains through them a local coloring, a milieu, which no other expedient in the use of language could have produced for him. His use of foreign words in Die Ahnen is justifiable.

In order to give some idea of the kind of foreign words used here by Freytag a specimen list of ten words from Vol. II-VI is presented. As Vol. I, Part I contains only 10 different foreign words the complete list is given.

[6] Cf. Freytag's thesis: De initiis scenicae poesis apud Geranos. Berlin, 1838.

[7] Freytag's Bilder aus der deutschen Vergangenheit were written (1859-1867) just before Die Ahnen.

Vol. I. Bronze I, 249; Bussard 175; Metall 38; Noster-
pater 166; Protector 247; purpurrot 50, (two other compounds of purpur, Purpurzeichen 59, Purpurbild 59); Tra-
bant 81; Vers 81. Except in the case of Protector p. 247
no German word could exactly replace the ideas expressed
in these words. In the case of sixteen at least of the 26 different foreign words found in Vol. I, Part 2, no thoroughly German word could well be used.

Vol. II. Ambrosianum II, 114; Convent 48; Dekan 4;
Dialecktik 48; Dispens 197; Ductus 11; Gallerie 16; Grammatik 48; Hora 25; Kapsel 370.

Vol. III. Alarm III, 232; Asylrecht 218; Ceder 290;
Chevalier 196; Collier 196; Devoir 89; Elephant 263; Ka-
thedrale 349.

Vol. IV. Kreatur IV, 288; Mandat 151; memoriren 78;
Musikant 74; Obscurant 176; Prädicant 185; Procent 51;
protestiren 189; Recept 12; Scriptor 56.

Vol. V. Adoptiren V, 406; Affection 379; Alteration 425;
arrogant 256; Censur 258; Commandeur 418; Commilito 25;
Communication 323; dispensiren 384; Domestik 295; Gouver-
neur 387. As will be readily seen any one of these words
from Vol. V could be replaced by a thoroughly German word
with no loss of exactness in meaning. Of the 500 foreign
words in this volume less than one-fifth are words without
exact German equivalents.

Vol. VI. Française V, 169; illuminiren 5; Invalide 306;
Jubiläum 350; Kanoe 189; konservieren 361; konföderiren
292; Material 41; Modell 183; parliren 75.

The foreign phrases used throughout the volumes are not
numerous and show no particular tendency on the part of
the writer. The following table shows the number of such
phrases used in Die Ahnen, and the language from which
they come.

	I	II	III	IV	V	VI	Total
Latin	6	12	4	15	6	1	44
Greek	1						1
French			1		1		2
Italian			1				1
Spanish					1		1
	7	12	6	15	8	1	49

The Latin phrases form here about 90% of the total number. In Vol. I the six Latin phrases (two are only single words) are used by the priest, or in connection with church affairs. In Vol. II the Latin phrases come naturally to the mouth of monks because of their familiarity with the church ritual. In Vol. IV, which deals with the sixteenth century, the Latin phrases found are used principally by the "Magister," who, as an educated man and as an educator, would use them readily.

PROPER NAMES

The names which a writer gives to the characters of his novel are of no mean importance and call for most careful attention. By the mere naming of a character an author may ascribe to that person qualities of considerable significance in the development of the plot. Many writers of note have given great care to the details of this matter. In the "Literarisches Echo" Klaiber writes in an article entitled, "Die Namen im Roman": [8] "Da sind die Gesetze des Wohllauts und des Klangsinns, die in Betracht kommen. Da soll der Name dazu helfen, die Person zu charakterisieren . . . . Vom modernen Roman erwarten wir, dass auch die Nebenpersonen bis auf den Namen hinaus individualisiert sind. So wissen wir von Gustav Freytag, dass er das Addressbuch von Galizien durchstöberte, um für eine seiner Nebengestalten (Schmeie Tinkeles) in 'Soll und Haben' einen recht jüdisch-polnischen Namen zu finden. Auch andere Gestalten in 'Soll und Haben,' vor allem, Anton Wohlfahrt und Sabine Schröter, sind vom Dichter so getaucht, dass der Widerschein ihres Wesens in ihrem Namen aufleuchtet." In speaking of the choice of proper names for a work Meyer says: [9] "Zur Beurteilung der lautsymbolischen Feinheit von Schriftstellern dient besonders deren Namenwahl, d. h. die Wahl von Eigennamen für ihre Personen und Orte, und noch mehr ihre Namengebung, d. h. die Erfindung weiterer Namen in gleicher Absicht. . . . ., andere Virtuosen der Kunst, durch frei gewählte Namen die Atmosphäre, die ihre Helden umgibt, zu bestimmen sind, z. B. Gustav Freytag u. a."

[8] Literarisches Echo V, S. 1311-15. 1903.
[9] Meyer, R. M.—Deutsche Stylistik S. 29.

A consideration and comparison of the proper names which Freytag gives to the characters of the first seventy pages of Volumes I and VI will give an excellent idea of the distinct atmosphere which Freytag would create for his novels by means of proper names. That the events of Vol. I are supposed by the writer to have occurred in the year 357 A. D., and those of Vol. VI in 1805 is very clearly indicated in a general way by the names of the characters.

Vol. I. Answald p. 7, Irmfried 7, Bisino 7, Frida 11, Irmgard 11, Hildebrand 18, Hnodomar 19, Athanarich 19, Gundrun 21, Ingo 21, Ingbert 21, Siegfried 24, Theodulf 28, Isanbart 36, Aimo 50, Arnfried 50, Archimbald 51, Eggo 51, Bero 65, Albwin 66, Turibert 68.

Vol. VI. Baron Hille p. 10, Kapitän von Buskow 12, Henriette 28, Käthe 29, Bärbel 31, Liesel 31, (Mamsell) Jettchen 35, Katharine 39, (Herr) Beblow 45, Christian 50, Hans 54, (Herr) Hutzel 57, Kapitän Dessale 61, Meister Schilling 63, Steinmetz 64.

In using such names as those given from Vol. I, Freytag is always careful to give to a character a name which befits his office, or part in the plot. Many even of the minor characters bear names which well suit their words and actions. In Vol. I Answald is equivalent to God-prince,[10] Hildebrand, Battle sword, Gundrun, Battle enchantress, Ingbert, Nobledivine, Siegfried, Bringer of peace through victory, Theodulf, Folk-wolf—all of which represent quite exactly qualities of character, or the office of the individual in the plot. Sometimes a name has both a Germanized and a Latin form, as Pancraz IV, 63, Pancratius IV, 315; Gregor V, 391, Gregorius IV, 16. The double name, i. e. Christian name and surname, occurs for the first time in Bertram Schultheiss III, 88.

ARCHAISMS

In a series of novels like these, which portray the life of the people of earlier centuries one would naturally expect to find archaic language. It is one of the most effective means of

[10] Derivations and meanings here given are taken from Heintze, Albert—Die deutsche Familiennamen. 3. Aufl. Halle, 1908; and Letzner—Namenbuch. 2 Aufl. Leipzig, 1894.

putting the reader into the atmosphere of that earlier time. Archaic language is distinctly characteristic of these volumes, especially the first two.

On the question of Freytag's success in the use of archaic features in Die Ahnen critics have differed widely. Adolf Stern [11] writes regarding this work: "Ohne allzustarke Archaismen klingen die Geschichten aus der Zeit der Völkerwanderung und der ersten Verkündigung der christlichen Lehre auf deutschem Boden, der Empfindung und dem Ton unserer alten Dichtung nach." It seems much better, however, to agree with those who believe that Freytag has failed of the highest success in the use of archaic features here. Meyer [12] writes: ". . . . . besonders die Anfangsbände von Freytags Ahnen haben durch ihr (d. h. der Archaismen) Übermass sogar den Spott heraus gefordert . . . . ." Gottschall [13] believes: "Ingo (Vol. I) ist leider durch Archaismen entstellt." He calls the style "undeutsch" (p. 338). Such criticisms are too severe, though the archaic features in the earliest volumes attract the reader's attention to such an extent as to make the style appear labored, especially in the word order and the use of archaic words. Cf. "Ich trage Kunde, die das Herz der Männer bewegt, nicht weiss ich, ob sie Freude bereitet oder Trauer" (I, 19), and "Spende wegemüdem Mann den Trunk aus deinem Born" (I, 18). Freytag himself, in his Erinnerungen,[14] discusses carefully this use of archaic words and word order, stating that this style came to him naturally in the description of the life of the earlier periods.

The archaic features are here presented under four captions—(1) Archaic forms, (2) Archaic meanings, (3) Archaic constructions, (4) Obsolete or obsolescent words.

(1) Archaic Forms [15]

Verbs:—Many times the older forms of verbs occur where N. H. G. would use a more modern form, as bedräut I, 113,

---

[11] Stern, A.—Die deutsche Nationalliteratur S. 114. 5. Aufl. 1905.

[12] Meyer, R. M.—Deutsche Stylistik. S. 8.

[13] Gottschall—Deutsche Nationalliteratur des 19. Jhts. II, 432.

[14] G. Freytag—Erinnerungen. Leipzig, 1887. S. 363 ff.

[15] The list below quotes only a single example in most cases, though

beut I, 156, gebeut VI, 265, brimmend for brummend, ein brimmender Bär I, 52. Cf. M. H. G. and M. E. brimmen. däucht I, 71. Verb forms like lud, ward, frug etc, are not regarded as distinctly archaic features in Die Ahnen, as such forms are common in literature.

Nouns:—Vor Abends I, 10 for Vor Abend. Fels as dative in, auf steilem Fels III, 335. Rare as dative. Cf. Curme, Grammar p. 74. Gemahl for Gemahlin III, 60; das Ehegemahl for die Gemahlin III, 64. Gurt for later Gürtel I, 86; Leibgurt I, 337. Der Quell for later die Quelle I, 136. Wittfrau for Wittwe V, 257. The archaic Wittib does not occur. Plural of Jahr in same form as singular II, 30.

Adjectives:—Occasional weak endings where we should expect strong. Dies Wenige I, 332. Mehre always for mehrere. Cf. I, 199 et al. Peinvoll I, 256 for modern peinlich.

Adverbs:—Abseit I, 57 for abseits (Abseit, a seventeenth century form according to Grimm). Allerdinge II, 406 for allerdings. Niemalen IV, 284. Strack (biblical word) IV, 100 rare as adverb.

Numerals:—The numerals zwei, drei, and vier are frequently inflected throughout the plural. Cf. zweier Stiere III, 124; dreien Königen II, 361.

ARCHAIC MEANINGS [16]

Verbs:—Bessern for verbessern, ausbessern I, 117, 460, 504 et al; denken for zudenken, Wenn du mir . . . . . Übles gedacht hast I, 188. einen feindselig denken for gegen einen feindselig gesinnt sein II, 26. fahren used to express various motions and modes of travel whether by vehicle or otherwise . . . . . und doch fuhr die Keule zurück I, 38; wenn dein Zorn feindlich hinter mir fährt II, 192; obgleich du

---

many times a great many might be quoted. Nor does this list give one example of every archaic peculiarity noted. Of the complete list collected the following show the character of the archaisms.

[16] In connection with the discussion of the archaic meanings of words and the choice of special words, a very careful and painstaking list for Vol. II is given by Roedder and Handschin in their recent edition of "Das Nest der Zaunkönige" pp. 235-242. D. C. Heath & Co. 1912.

unbändig dahinfährst, for dich benimmst II, 34. In such cases Freytag follows the usage of O. H. G. and M. H. G. gesellen for zugesellen, dass der Fürst sich den Edlen meines Volkes geselle I, 55. künden for verkünden, auskünden. Ich will dem Fremden deine Botschaft künden I, 84-5. lodern for brennen. Usual form now is auflodern. Cf. I, 190 et al. löschen for auslöschen, ein Feuer aufgebrannt war, welches schwerlich durch klugen Rat gelöscht wurde I, 133. richten for aufrichten, errichten. Vor dem Saale des Königs war der Opferstein gerichtet I, 250. teilen for zuteilen, denn die Götter teilen dem Mann sein Schicksal nach seinen Gedanken I, 59. versteinen in the sense of abgrenzen I, 123. verweilen, transitive use for verhindern, Verweilt mich nicht IV, 388. ziehen for abziehen, Ich fand ihn auf der Strasse, zog die Mütze und ging stolz hinab IV, 134. An observation of the archaic features noted here shows that Freytag often used a simple verb to convey a number of shades of meaning which are now definitely designated by a prefix.

Nouns:—Fräulein, old use for kleine Frau. Wir merken auch, dass manche von ihnen Männlein sind, und andere Fräulein V, 107. Himmelsburg for Himmel II, 72. Landgenoss for Landsmann II, 334. Meinung for Gesinnung. Welche Meinung hat Graf Gerhard zu dir? II, 318. Mond for Monat I, 24. Mut for the English mood, disposition as in M. H. G. Ein schweres Geschick bereitet ein Gott, oder des Mannes trotziger Mut I, 20. Modern usage still retains this meaning in "zu Mute sein." Obstträger for Obstbaum II, 123. Werk for Taten II, 28. Wille for Absicht, der König naht . . . . . in feindlichem Willen, um den Raub zu rächen II, 349.

Adjectives:—der Gebundene for der Gefangene II, 393. hold for lieb II, 127. Schlecht for schlicht II, 28. tröstlich sein for trösten II, 316. übel for böse, schlimm II, 24. ungefüge for unschön II, 63. wert for lieb II, 24. wunderlich for erstaunlich II, 59.

A number of other more or less archaic features are found: ab und zu I, 242 as adverb of place; auf dass for the modern dass I, 244 et al.; wie lang ich lebe for seit ich lebe I, 217, etc.

Archaic Constructions

Freytag shows a tendency to use verbs with a case which they formerly governed (especially the genitive) instead of the modern accusative. The following are regularly found with the genitive: achten, begehren, denken, erinnern, freuen, geniessen, sich gewöhnen, harren, lachen, schonen, vergessen, walten, warten. Hängen and the preposition an with the dative for abhängen von occur in, So weit es an dem Willen der Nachbarn hängt I, 223. bitten with a direct object instead of um, Wer gewöhnt ist, fremdes Gewand zu bitten I, 28-9. sich neigen with dative for sich vor jemand verneigen I, 12. wehren for usual sich wehren I, 51.

Obsolete or Obsolescent Words

There occur here many obsolete or obsolescent words which give to the narrative an archaic tinge. Bändigen for hindern, fesseln II, 384; blinzen for blinzeln I, 190; ehelichen for heiraten V, 257; Born I, 18; Brautlauf for Hochzeit I, 169; Eidam for Schwiegersohn I, 168; Elend in its original meaning of "foreign land" I, 17; Gerstange, Cf. M. H. G. gêr; Met I, 26; Minne III, 15; Unhold for Teufel I, 425; Walstatt for Schlachtfeld I, 10 et al.; reisemüde I, 153; wegemüde I, 12; traun I, 76; weiland IV, 335; dreissig und ein I, 342. One might mention here the use of such epithets as langhaarig I, 314, pfeilschnell III, 190. Langhaarig is well applied to the early Germans but its use as a descriptive epithet may easily have been in imitation of Homer. Cf. Odyssey II, 7 et al. Pfeilschnell is also an Homeric epithet.

Aside from these specific archaic features there are more general ones which tend to give both style and content an archaic tone. These are most common in the earliest volumes. In some cases they seem artificial [17] though literary critics have recognized such means as legitimate when used with discretion. [18] The following list includes some of the most important: Description of customs characteristic of early German life, more or less definite reference to early German mythology, description of early German weapons (Cf. Keule,

[17] Lindau, H. Gustav Freytag. Leipzig, 1907. S. 194.
[18] Seiler, Fr. Gustav Freytag. Leipzig, 1898. S. 179 ff.

Gêr) ; the names of animals common to the period. Such features transplant the reader directly into the time of the narrative and are more effective than even archaic words or word order.

One might naturally conclude these observations on archaisms by stating that there are certain rather common archaic words and forms which do not appear at all in Die Ahnen. So is neither found as a relative, nor used for the conjunction wenn; denn is not used for als after comparatives, nor do da or its compounds occur with relative force. Obsolete preterit forms like sahe in the third singular are not found, and the uninflected neuter adjective is rare. Forms like jetzo, Wittib, dieweil, empfahen, jedwede, schier, do not occur.

Lieblingswörter

Though Freytag's style is characterized by few mannerisms, yet he does show in the work under discussion a marked fondness for particular words and particular kinds of words. These favorites appear so frequently that they become quite monotonous, as when versetzen is used in the sense of "answer," or "reply" two or three times on a single page. Cf. I. 125, 132, 133, 134, 139, 153, 154, 155, 158, 162, 165, 166, 167, 168, 171, 178, 180, 184, 186, 188, 192, 194, 195, 196. This is true of such verbs as kränken and drängen. The verb bergen occurs in Die Ahnen with great frequency and has a variety of meanings. Besides its use to convey the idea of concealing, hiding or covering, it is used in the sense of übertragen, unterbringen, einstecken, verbergen, verheimlichen etc.

The following list (without citing references or number of instances, or any details) gives some of the more striking of the favorite words and phrases.

Verbs :—Behaupten, bergen, drängen, kränken, spenden (used often where we might expect only geben, used also for schenken, erteilen, verschaffen), verderben, versetzen. Freytag often uses here a simple verb where we should most certainly expect a compound one, as e. g. (ab)fangen, (auf)-fordern, (er)greifen, (ver)handeln, (ein)laden, (er)lösen, (ver)mindern, (ver)wehren, (zurück)werfen where the prefix is regularly omitted in Die Ahnen.

Nouns:—Certain compound nouns are of remarkable frequency of occurrence. Compounds with Herr(en)- are numerous. Cf. Herrenaxt, -bank, -feind, -grund, -metall, -wunde, -zins etc. in which the element Herr(en)- seems to have little specific force; numerous compounds with Himmel-, with Hof-, with Holz-. Compounds with Mann(es)-, Menschen-, Männer- are especially striking. In Vol. I, for example, Männererde occurs twenty-nine times for "world," Menschenerde three times, while the word Welt occurs but seven times in the whole volume. These compounds of Männer- and Menschen- were without doubt used that the language might appear more like that used by the early Germans. Cf. O. H. G. mank(ch)unni for Menschengeschlecht; Gothic manasêþs, Welt. Cf. also the Icelandic compounds in maðr-.

Among the Lieblingswörter one may well mention certain adjectives. In this work the author shows great fondness for the power of the adjective.[19] Many adjectives (the form being compounded by the author in some cases) bear the brunt of the meaning of their phrases. Cf. aalgleich III, 17, esslustig III, 163, fadenscheinig I, 425, flachsköpfig I, 144, glückverheissend III, 207, gramdurchtfurcht III, 90 hemdsärmelig I, 144. The adjectives ansehnlich, vierschrötig and compounds in -selig are conspicuous because of their frequent use. For the same reason the following phrases (or slight variations of them) are noticeable: aufs neue, ins Freie, in gestrecktem Laufe, mit geflügelten Schritten, mit gefalteten Händen.

PHRASES

From early German times down to the present, combinations of two nouns (or sometimes other parts of speech), connected by und, have been common to the language. In many of these combinations the meaning of the individual words has been merged into the meaning of the phrase. Cf. German, Mann und Maus; English, Chick and child. Such phrases

---

[19] Cf. Meyer—Deutsche Stylistik S. 50. "Freytags Verwendung der Bildung neuer Beiwörter." Cf. also, Schönbach, A. S.—Gesammelte Aufsätze. S. 65.

are found in great abundance in Die Ahnen, and by their skilful use impart a thoroughly German flavor to a work, whose main object is to portray German civilization. In Vol. I ninety-nine different phrases of this nature have been noted, some of which occur as many as fourteen times. When used as a subject such a phrase sometimes has a singular verb. Cf. Frage und Antwort klang I, 151.

As the last feature of Freytag's use of words here we might mention that feature touched upon by Lindau [20] in his biography of Freytag: "Spruchweisheit und liederartige Form treten zumal an den wichtigen Stellen hervor." Throughout the volumes there are found pithy, proverbial sayings. These by their simplicity and directness are often suggestive of the older language, but they are in many cases only a favorite way in which Freytag casts his thought. Often these phrases could not be called more than "Gedanken-splitter" [21] as they have not become real proverbs. They express pithily and laconically what is proverbial in thought if not in form. A large number of these expressions pertain to animals and their habits, and to nature and natural phenomena. In the earliest volumes many are connected with fighting, hunting and such occupations as were common among the early Germans. Thus they give local coloring as well as conciseness to the thought. Cf. Wenn der Wolf tanzt, fliegen die Gänse auf den Baum und lachen I, 14; Edlen Sinn bindet nur Vertrauen I, 78 (Quoted by Lipperheide—Spruchwörterbuch, Berlin, 1907 p. 940b, as original in Die Ahnen); In der Not dient schnelle Tat I, 184 etc. A rather full list of these Sententious or Proverbial Sayings shows the following numbers: Vol. 1, 120; Vol. II, 80; Vol. III, 66; Vol. IV, 61; Vol. V, 36; Vol. VI, 12.

Pennsylvania State College.   HARRY T. COLLINGS.

NOTE. Since this article was written (1910) a German thesis has appeared, dealing in detail with a portion of the subject. Posern, A. Der altertümelnde Stil in den ersten drei Bänden von Gustav Freytags Ahnen. (Diss.) Greifswald. 1913. 8vo. 84 pp.

[20] Lindau, Hans. Gustav Freytag. Leipzig, 1907. S. 301.

[21] Cf. Sommer, Paul. Erläuterungen zu Gustav Freytags Die Ahnen. Leipzig, 1905.

MARGARET FULLER'S TRANSLATION AND CRITICISM OF GOETHE'S *TASSO*.

Few persons in America knew much of Goethe during the third and fourth decades of the last century, and a part of these—among them some of our most prominent writers—were awhile bitterly opposed to him. Goethe was accused of being irreligious and rather loose in his morals. None of the French writers, though introduced much earlier into this country, when the religious rigor was even stronger, ever suffered to such an extent from being misunderstood and misinterpreted. It is an interesting study to observe how Goethe gradually grew in the estimation of our best thinkers during this period, until they accorded him the place he now occupies among the world's greatest poets.

One of the first advocates of Goethe, and doubtless the strongest and most influential among them during this time, was Margaret Fuller. Few had ever understood Goethe as well or profited so much by a thorough and sympathetic study of his works as she. As a prominent member in a literary circle of young men and women with open minds, as editor of the *Dial* and leader in the ''Conversations'' which she held in Boston for five years she had ample opportunity to impress her thoughts of Goethe upon those who, along with her, were then the leaders of thought in New England. Her articles on Goethe and his works in the *Dial* (Boston, 1842), though tinged here and there by the rigorous spirit of the time and place, are certainly among the most carefully studied and appreciative criticisms written of him.

Only two years after Margaret Fuller commenced the study of German she began to translate for her friends and for publication, certain works from the original. From Goethe she translated *Tasso*, the first two volumes of Eckermann's *Conversations with Goethe* and a number of short poems, besides a considerable number of pages of quotations from other works, which she used in her criticisms.[1] The most important of these is her translation of *Tasso*. According to

[1] For a discussion of a number of the translations mentioned above, see Braun, *Margaret Fuller and Goethe*, New York, 1910, pp. 216-241.

a letter written to F. H. Hedge in November 1834, in which she expressed the hope that Hedge and Emerson would look over and help correct her manuscript, she must have translated this work the same year. (Higginson, *Margaret Fuller Ossoli,* Boston, 1884, p. 63). She failed, however, to find a publisher and it did not appear in print until 1860, when her brother Arthur B. Fuller included it, after her death, in a volume of her works entitled *Art, Literature and the Drama,* with a number of other papers by Margaret Fuller previously published (1846) under the title *Papers on Literature and Art.*

With what feelings Margaret Fuller translated this work is shown by a passage from her *Memoirs* (Vol. II, p. 105) "Beethoven! Tasso! It is well to think of you! What sufferings from baseness, from coldness! How rare and momentary were the flashes of joy, of confidence and tenderness in these noblest lives!"

That Margaret Fuller understood the deep significance of the play in relation to Goethe's life is certain. It is a portrayal of Goethe's own moods and innermost feelings, "for the poet is the only priest in the secrets of the heart." (*Dial,* Jan. 1842) "To me give a God to tell what I suffer" applies, she believed, as truly to Goethe's sufferings as to Tasso's into whose mouth he put these words. "You say there is no likeness between Goethe and Tasso. Never believe it; such pictures are not painted from observation merely. That deep coloring which fills them with light and life is given by dipping the brush in one's own life-blood." "The best criticism for the hearing of those that will hear is one of those matchless scenes in which Goethe represents the sudden breezes of eloquence, the fitful shadings of mood, and the exquisite sensitiveness to all influences that made the weakness and power of Tasso." (*Dial,* Boston, Jan. 1842, and *Life Without and Life Within,* Boston, 1859, pp. 28 f.)

"The central situation of Tasso," she notes in the introduction to her translation, "the manner in which his companions draw him out, and are in turn drawn out by him, the mingled generosity and worldliness of the realist Antonio, the mixture of taste, feeling, and unconscious selfishness in

Alphonso, the more delicate but not less decided painting of the two Leonoras, the gradual but irresistible force by which the catastrophe is drawn down upon us, concur to make this drama a model of art, that art which Goethe worshipped ever after he had exhaled his mental boyhood in *Werther* . . . . . It is, I believe, a novelty to see the mind of a poet analyzed and portrayed by another, who however, shared the inspiration only of his subject, saved from his weakness by that superb balance of character in which Goethe surpasses even Milton." (*Art, Literature and the Drama*—Boston, 1860, p. 356.)

"Goethe has described the position of the poetical mind in its prose relations . . . . . We see what he felt must be the result of entire abandonment to the highest nature. We see why he valued himself on being able to understand the Alphonsos, and meet as an equal the Antonios of everyday life . . . . . Goethe had not from nature that character of self-reliance and self-control in which he so long appeared to the world. It was wholly acquired and so highly valued because he was conscious of the opposite tendency. He was by nature as impetuous, though not as tender as Tasso, and the disadvantage at which this constantly placed him was keenly felt by a mind made to appreciate the subtlest harmonies in all relations. Therefore was it that when he at last cast anchor, he was so reluctant again to trust himself to wave and breeze." (*Life Without and Life Within*, Boston, 1859, pp. 28 f.)

In presenting her translation of this "very celebrated production of the first German writer," Margaret Fuller discusses and compares the two languages in question. With a fine perception and feeling for the distinction between them she writes of the high degree of perfection and the condensed power of expression attained by the German language, due to "the rapid growth of German literature and the concurrence of so many master spirits, all at once fashioning the language into a medium for the communication of their thoughts."

In the same connection she frankly calls attention to

the difficulties that may, as a result, beset any translator in rendering German verse into English. "There are difficulties attending the translation of German works into English which might baffle one much more skillful in the use of the latter than myself. A great variety of compound words enable the German writer to give a degree of precision and delicacy of shading to his expressions nearly impracticable with the terse, the dignified, but by no means flexible English idiom." (*Art, Literature and the Drama*, p. 355)

Margaret Fuller, however, "deemed," as Coleridge did in his translation of Schiller's *Wallenstein*, "the rendering of the spirit, on the whole more desirable than that of the letter." "The exact transmission of thought" seemed to her, the one important thing in a translation; "if grace and purity of style come of themselves," she writes, "it is so much gained. In translating I throw myself as entirely as possible into the mood of the writer, and make use of such expressions as would come naturally, if reading the work aloud in English. The style thus formed is at least a transcript of the feelings excited by the original." (Preface to translation of the *Correspondence of Fräulein Günderode and Bettine von Arnim*, Boston, 1861, p. VI.)

This rendering of the spirit rather than of the letter is the chief characteristic we feel in reading Margaret Fuller's translation. It has some of the merits of original composition, in fact, it reads like a piece of first hand work. The soliloquy of *Tasso* in scene 2 of Act II is an illustration.

Is it permitted thee to ope thine eyes
And look around—above thee? Did these pillars
Hear what she spake? They were the witnesses
How a descending goddess lifted me
Into a new, incomparable day.
What power, what wealth lie in this new traced circle!
My happiness outruns my wildest dream!
Let those born blind think what they will of colors,
To the cleared eye wakens a novel sense.
What courage, what presentiment! Drunk with joy,
I scarce can tread the indicated path,
And how shall I deserve the choicest gifts
Of earth and heaven? Patience, self-denial,

Must give me claim to confidence—they shall.
O how did I deserve that she should choose me!
What shall I do to justify her choice?
Yet that choice speaks my worth. Yes, I am worthy,
Since she could think me so. My soul is consecrate,
My princess, to thy words, thy looks. Whate'er
Thou wilt, ask of thy slave. In distant lands
I'll seek renown with peril of my life,
Or chant in every grove, thy charms and virtues.
Wholly possess the creature thou hast formed;
Each treasure of my soul is thine. I ne'er can
Express my vast devotion with the pen
In written words. Oh, could I but assist
The poet's by the painter's art! Did honey
Fall from my lips! Now never more shall I
Be lonely, sad, or weak. Thou wilt be with me.
Had I a squadron of the noblest men
To help me do thy bidding, some great deed
Should justify the boldness of a tongue
Which dared to ask her grace! I meant it not—
I meant not to speak now. But it is well;
I take as a free gift what I could never
Have claimed. This glorious future! This new youth!
Rise heart! O, tree of love! may genial showers
Call out a thousand branches towards heaven!
Unfold thy blossoms, swell thy golden fruit
Until the loved one's hand be stretched to cull it.

(Art, Literature and the Drama, pp. 387 f.)

If judged alone by Margaret Fuller's standard we must admit that the spirit is indeed well rendered. If judged, however, as a faithful rendition of the letter and meter, as well as of the spirit—the criterion by which any translation is sure to be judged finally—Margaret Fuller's exercise of too much freedom, or of her limitations, are at once evident. To arrive at a fair estimate of her translation in this stricter sense two representative passages have been chosen for comparison, the one subdued and descriptive, the other impassioned. Both are from the dialogue between Tasso and the princess in scene 4, Act V.

TASSO

Du warnest recht, ich hab' es schon bedacht.   (3140)
Verkleidet geh' ich hin, den armen Rock

Des Pilgers oder Schäfers zieh' ich an.
Ich schleiche durch die Stadt, wo die Bewegung
Der Tausende den einen leicht verbirgt.
Ich eile nach dem Ufer, finde dort   (3145)
Gleich einen Kahn mit willig guten Leuten,
Mit Bauern, die zum Markte kamen, nun
Nach Hause kehren, Leute von Sorrent;
Denn ich muss nach Sorrent hinüber eilen.
Dort wohnet meine Schwester, die mit mir   (3150)
Die Schmerzensfreude meiner Eltern war.
Im Schiffe bin ich still, und trete dann
Auch schweigend an das Land, ich gehe sacht
Den Pfad hinauf, und an dem Thore frag' ich
Wo wohnt Cornelia? Zeigt mir es an!   (3155)
Cornelia Sersale? Freundlich deutet
Mir eine Spinnerin die Strasse, sie
Bezeichnet mir das Haus, So steig ich weiter.
Die Kinder laufen nebenher und schauen
Das wilde Haar, den düstern Fremdling an.   (3160)
So komm' ich an die Schwelle. Offen steht
Die Thüre schon, so tret' ich in das Haus—

               I go disguised.
In the poor garb of shepherd or of pilgrim,
I easily shall thread the crowded streets
Of Naples unobserved. I seek the shore;
Then find a boat, manned by good, honest peasants,
Returning from the market to Sorrentium,
Where dwells my sister, who with me formed once
The painful joy of our lost parents. I speak not
While in the skiff, nor yet at disembarking;
I softly climb the path, and at the gate
I ask, "Where dwells Cornelia?" and a woman,
Spinning before her door, shows me her house.
The children flock to look upon the stranger,
With the disheveled locks and gloomy looks.
At last I reach the threshold—open stands
The door—I enter.

PRINCESS

Gar wenig ist's was wir von dir verlangen;
Und dennoch scheint es allzu viel zu sein.   (3235)
Du sollst dich selbst uns freundlich überlassen.
Wir wollen nichts von dir, was du nicht bist,
Wenn du nur erst dir mit dir selbst gefällst.
Du machst uns Freude, wenn du Freude hast,
Und du betrübst uns nur, wenn du sie fliehst;   (3240)

Und wenn du uns auch ungeduldig machst,
So ist es nur, dass wir dir helfen möchten
Und, leider! sehn, dass nicht zu helfen ist,
Wenn du nicht selbst des Freundes Hand ergreifst,
Die, sehnlich ausgestreckt, dich nicht erreicht.　　　(3245)

We ask but little from thee; yet that little
Has ever been too much: that thou wouldst trust us,
And to thyself be true! Couldst thou do this
Thou wouldst be happy, and we be happy in thee.
We must be gloomy when we see thee so;
Impatient when so oft we see thee need
The help we cannot give; when thou refusest
To seize the hand stretched out to thee in love.

TASSO

Du bist es selbst, wie du zum erstenmal,
Ein heil'ger Engel, mir entgegen kamst!
Verzeih' dem trüben Blick des Sterblichen,
Wenn er auf Augenblicke dich verkannt.
Er kennt dich wieder! Ganz eröffnet sich　　　(3250)
Die Seele, nur dich ewig zu verehren,
Es füllt sich ganz das Herz von Zärtlichkeit—
Sie ist's, sie steht vor mir. Welch ein Gefühl!
Ist es Verwirrung, was mich nach dir zieht?
Ist's Raserei? Ist's ein erhöhter Sinn,　　　(3255)
Der erst die höchste, reinste Wahrheit fasst?
Ja, es ist das Gefühl, das mich allein
Auf dieser Erde glücklich machen kann,
Das mich allein so elend werden liess,
Wenn ich ihm widerstand und aus dem Herzen　　　(3260)
Es bannen wollte. Diese Leidenschaft
Gedacht' ich zu bekämpfen, stritt und stritt
Mit meinem tiefsten Sein, zerstörte frech
Mein eignes Selbst, dem du so ganz gehörst—

Thou art the same who came to meet me first!
Angel of pity and of love, forgive
That my eye, clouded by the mists of earth,
Mistook thee for a moment. Now I know thee,
And open all my soul to adoration,
My heart to tenderness beyond all words.
Ah, what a feeling! What a strange confusion!
Is't madness which draws me thus towards thee?
Or is't an elevated sense of truth,
In its most lovely, earth-born form? I know not.
It is the feeling which alone can make me

Most blest if I may venture to indulge it,
Most miserable if I must repress it.
And I have striven with this passion—striven
With my profoundest self—have torn in pieces
The heart which beat with such devotion for thee.

PRINCESS

Wenn ich dich, Tasso, länger hören soll,   (3265)
So mässige die Glut, die mich erschreckt.

If thou wouldst have me listen longer, Tasso,
Avoid expressions which I must not hear.

TASSO

Beschränkt der Rand des Bechers einen Wein,
Der schäumend wallt und brausend überschwillt?
Mit jedem Wort erhöhest du mein Glück,
Mit jedem Worte glänzt dein Auge heller.   (3270)
Ich fühle mich im Innersten verändert,
Ich fühle mich von aller Not entladen,
Frei wie ein Gott, und alles dank' ich dir!
Unsägliche Gewalt, die mich beherrscht,
Entfliesset deinen Lippen; ja, du machst   (3275)
Mich ganz dir eigen. Nichts gehöret mehr
Von meinem ganzen Ich mir künftig an.
Es trübt mein Auge sich in Glück und Licht,
Es schwankt mein Sinn. Mich hält der Fuss nicht mehr.
Unwiderstehlich ziehst du mich zu dir,   (3280)
Und unaufhaltsam dringt mein Herz dir zu.
Du hast mich ganz auf ewig dir gewonnen,
So nimm denn auch mein ganzes Wesen hin!

And can the goblet's rim restrain the wine
Which foams above it? Every word of thine
Kindles my soul with fires unfelt before;
With each word beam thine eyes more clear and soft;
My soul dilates, each sorrow flies, I'm free,—
Free as a god,—and this I own to thee.
The power that fills me now thy lips have poured on me,
And I am wholly thine. Of all my being
No atom call I mine, apart from thee.
Ah I am blinded with excess of light!
My senses waver with excess of bliss!
I must approach. My heart throbs wildly towards thee;
I am all thine—receive me to thyself!

Again, as before, the spirit of Goethe's version is well preserved in the passages quoted. It is a "faithful transcript

of the feelings excited by the original'' but, as Margaret Fuller herself confesses, the beautiful finish of Goethe's style is
lost. (*Art, Literature and the Drama*, p. 356.) The meter is
not smooth, nor does one have to look far in her translation
to find shortened or lengthened lines.

In the passages quoted above seventy-three lines of the
original have been rendered by fifty-four, and in the whole
play Goethe's 3453 lines have been translated by 2600. This
reduction, as Margaret Fuller said, is partly due to the fact
that English words are, as a rule, shorter than German words.
A good example of this contraction is found in the translation of lines 3246-47, where one and one half lines, ''Du bist
es selbst, wie du zum erstenmal, ... mir entgegen
kamst'', are translated by one line, ''Thou art the same who
came to meet me first.'' In the same manner the two lines,
''Ich fühle mich im Innersten verändert, ich fühle mich von
aller Not entladen'' 3271 f. are somewhat freely translated by
part of one line, ''my soul dilates, each sorrow flies.'' Added to
this is the fact that the inflectional endings of the German in
the hands of a skillful writer help very materially in filling
up the line and smoothing out the meter.

In the present instance, however, as we shall see, the chief
factor in this decrease is Margaret Fuller's omission of many
of the minor details. A part of these she doubtless left out—
as she often left out parts in her translations of German prose
works—because she thought they added little to the development of the plot or thought, or to the interest of the reader.[2]
Granting that many of these passages could be spared without
seriously injuring the play, it must be admitted, however,
that it is often just these little details, frequently left out by
her, that lend picturesqueness and action to the narrative.

But not all of the omissions and changes made by the translator were deliberate. Margaret Fuller's abilities to translate
some of the German phrases which she encountered into the
''by no means flexible English idiom'' were at times severely
taxed. This she herself confesses in her introduction, already

[2] For examples of omissions in her prose works see her translations
of Eckermann's *Conversations with Goethe*—The whole discussion of the
Farbenlehre, wherever mentioned, is left out.

quoted, and the fact is all the clearer when we examine her translation more carefully.

Though a large majority of her lines are very fair translations in the stricter sense, especially those found in the first passage compared, yet the cases of a too free, often faulty translation, of omitted lines and insertions are common. The following are representative illustrations, as found throughout the entire work. In the original, line 3140, the sentence "Du warnest recht, ich hab' es schon bedacht" is omitted in the translation altogether, so is line 3149, "Denn ich muss nach Sorrent hinüber eilen." In lines 3155-3158 "Zeigt mir es an;" "Freundlich deutet mir . . . . . sie . . . . . die Strasse;" "So steig ich weiter," are all left out, as is also line 3237, "Wir wollen nichts von dir, was du nicht bist." In the six lines 3238-43, the wish that Tasso were only satisfied with himself (and his accomplishments) is translated by the request that he be true to himself. The thought "You cause us joy when you are joyful" is translated by "Couldst thou do this thou wouldst be happy and we be happy in thee," and "even if you make us impatient, we are so only because etc.," by "we must be impatient when etc." "Sehnlich" (3245) is translated by "in love." "Sie ist's, sie steht vor mir" (3253) is omitted. "Der erst die höchste, reinste Wahrheit fasst" (3256) is at most only partially translated by "in its most lovely earthborn form." "If I may venture to indulge it" is inserted after 3258. "So mässige die Glut, die mich erschreckt" (3266) is weakly rendered by "Avoid expressions which I must not hear." "With excess of bliss" is inserted after "es schwankt mein Sinn." (3279). "Mich hält der Fuss nicht mehr. Unwiderstehlich ziehst du mich zu dir" (3279-80) is translated by simply "I must approach;" and "Du hast mich ganz auf ewig dir gewonnen, so nimm denn auch mein ganzes Wesen hin." (3282-83) by the single line "I am all thine—receive me to thyself."

A large number of the changes noted are due, of course, to Margaret Fuller's custom of translating the general idea only. The omission of many of the minor details naturally follows. But often the changes are very clearly due to real difficulties in translating. It is interesting to note some of those which Margaret Fuller complained of in her introduction, quoted above, namely, those due to the difficulty of translating compound words from the German. Of the twenty-seven or more occurring in the passage quoted she successfully translates, directly or indirectly, at least twenty. Two or three others occur in expressions altogether omitted. "Verändert" (3271) and "entladen" (3272) are translated very freely, while such words as "unsäglich" (3274), "unwiderstehlich" (3280) and "unaufhaltsam" (3281) were real obstacles, though such compounds as "Schmerzenfreude" (3151), "verehren" (3251) and "widerstand" (3260) are translated successfully.

Nor can the translator easily rid herself of an objectionable phrase. "It is more difficult to polish a translation," Margaret Fuller writes, "than an original work, since we are denied the liberty of retrenching or adding where the ear and taste cannot be satisfied." (*Art, Literature and the Drama*, p. 356). A very difficult task always in translating is to find idioms in the language into which a work is to be translated that correspond in meaning and force to those of the original. When it is required in addition to keep the external form of the work intact, as in poetry, it is easy to understand why poetical translations are rarely successful except when done by another poet. Margaret Fuller, as is evident from her original verse, was not a poetess. She never made any pretensions in this direction, though she often set her thoughts down in verse. Many of these are hasty translations from the German, made for friends who had no knowledge of this language, and with whom she wished to share some of the enjoyment which she herself found in the poems translated. Her translation of *Tasso* may have been partly from the same motives—namely, that a larger circle might enjoy the same, not that she expected to produce a work of art—; for she writes after her apology for not doing the translation better: that though only a "hollow-sounding reed" is substituted for the "many-toned lyre on which the poet originally melodized his inspired conceptions," she believed "no setting could utterly mar the lustre of such a gem,'' or make the translation of this ''perfect work of art unwelcome to the meditative few, or even to the tasteful many.'' (*Art, Literature and the Drama,* p. 356).

Margaret Fuller was preëminently a literary critic, and as such she ranked among the best that our country ever produced. She was able to recognize a good piece of literature at first sight, sound its depth and meaning and reach an independent conclusion, which seldom needed revision. Much of her published verse, as T. W. Higginson has said, was never meant, or at least never prepared for publication. The latter was partly true of her translation of *Tasso*. There is no doubt that had she lived and published it herself she would have given it a final thorough revision and carefully smoothed out many of the rough places, just as she revised the few of her original verses which she printed now and then during her life-time.

FREDERICK A. BRAUN.

Princeton University.

JOHN OXENFORD AS TRANSLATOR.

In 1846, there was published in America the following book:
"The Auto-Biography of Goethe, Truth and Poetry; From
my Life," edited by Parke Godwin. (vol. 1, N. Y. Wiley &
Putnam, 161 Broadway). To this work was prefixed a preface by the editor, from which I quote:

"It is a little singular, with all that has been said about
Goethe, both in England and the United States, that no translation into English should have been made of the famous
Wahrheit und Dichtung, in which he gives such graphic accounts of himself and of his contemporaries. Several years
since there was what purported to be a translation published
in London; but this was a disgraceful imposture. Mrs. Aus-
tin speaks of it as the most flagrant piece of literary dishonesty on record, not without justice, and Mr. Carlyle refers
to it in much the same spirit. It was a poor copy of a
wretched French version, in which frequently twenty pages
of the original are omitted at a time, and hardly a sentence is
rendered with fidelity. Yet a great many people have read
the book, never suspecting but that they were reading a
translation from Goethe.

"The present attempt, therefore, has been undertaken by
the editor and some friends, to supply what may be considered
a great deficiency in English literature. They could not, of
course, aim at the grace and ease of style, which is one of the
finest characteristics of their author, but they have endeavored to be faithful to his meaning. Goethe is the hardest
of all Germans to translate, because he is such a consummate
master of *form,* which nothing but a genius equal to his own
could convey to another language . . . . .

"Goethe has taken his place, by pretty general consent, as
the First European Poet and Literary Man of the Nineteenth
Century. A book, then, in which he describes the process of
his peculiar development, and the way in which he regarded
the facts of existence and his own times, deserves to be read,
even through the imperfect medium of translation, by those
who can get no better. In the original, it is a masterpiece of
writing. It is a series of quiet but striking pictures, showing

the growth of the greatest of German minds, and at the same time the whole progress of German literature . . . . .

"The same persons have in preparation other works of Goethe, which will be published, if the success of this book should warrant the expense. His 'Annals or Day and Year Book', his 'Italian Journey', etc., and Dramas, will form part of the series."

The following year saw the appearance of vol. 2, containing the rest of the Autobiography. In this translation, Godwin was assisted by able collaborators; John Henry Hopkins, Jr., of Vermont translated Part 2; Chas. A. Dana, Part 3, and John S. Dwight, Part 4. Its great excellence was attested by the many favorable reviews in the leading American magazines.

U. S. Democ. R. 19:443-447, Dec. 1846. Washington & N. Y.; 20:14-21, Jan. 1847; 21:283-4, Sept. 1847. Amer. Whig R., N. Y., 5:539-540, May 1847. Graham's Amer. Mon. Mag., Phila., 31:156 Sept. 1847. Literary World, N. Y., 1:296-298 May 1847; 1:567 July 1847; 2:149-151 Sept. 18, 1847. Littell's Living Age, Bost. 13:568 Aug. 17, 1847. Southern Quar. R. Charleston, S. C., 11:441-467 Apr. 1847. Holden's Dollar Mag., N. Y. 2:499-500 1848.

Then in 1848, there appeared in London, a similar translation: "The Auto-Biography of Goethe, Truth and Poetry; From my own Life," translated from the German by John Oxenford. (13 books). This translation was the first volume of the series on Goethe's life and works, issued by the publisher, Henry G. Bohn, in his "Standard Literary," and it is very noticeable that he speedily followed the suggestions in the Preface to the American edition.

Preceding the translation, was an "Advertisement" which reads as follows:

"Before the following translation was commenced, the first Ten Books had already appeared in America. It was the intention of the Publisher to reprint these without alteration, but, on comparing them with the original, it was perceived that the American edition was not sufficiently faithful, and therefore the present was undertaken. The Translator, however, is bound to acknowledge, that he found many successful renderings in the work of his predecessor, and these he has engrafted without hesitation.

"The title 'Truth and Poetry' is adopted in common with the American translation, as the nearest rendering of *Dichtung und Wahrheit*, and preferable to 'Truth and Fiction,' which has sometimes been used. The poet, by the expression 'Dichtung,' did not mean that he invented incidents in the Auto-Biography, but merely that they were of a poetic or romantic character; 'Wahrheit' implies that they also possessed the truth of history. The 'Prose and Poetry of my Life' would, perhaps, convey to the English reader the exact meaning of the Author, although not literally his words."

The year following, Bohn published the remaining volumes (14-20), translated by the Rev. Alex. J. W. Morrison, M.A., a work which included the "Letters from Switzerland" and the "Travels in Italy." In the later editions, the credit of the translation of the entire autobiography is always given to John Oxenford.

In 1850, a second edition of the American translation was issued (2 vols. N. Y. Geo. P. Putnam, 155 Broadway), and in the Preface, the editor, Parke Godwin, quotes Oxenford's title-page and advertisement, and then discusses them in this wise:

"Now we quote this title-page and advertisement, in order to expose one of the most unblushing pieces of literary theft on record. Any person reading them would suppose, 1. That the English edition was a veritable new translation from the German; 2. That it had been made by John Oxenford, Esq.; 3. That the American version was not a faithful one; and 4. That the same version had merely been used occasionally to help Mr. Oxenford to 'many successful renderings' of the first ten books. But, in supposing so, the reader would be misled into just as many errors.

"The English is not a new translation at all, but a bold appropriation of the American version, which is proved by the fact, that whole pages of the two editions are precisely the same; that in other pages only slight verbal alterations have been made, such as 'felicity' for happiness; and 'progress' for advance, etc., etc.; that the very typographical errors of the American edition have been retained; that foot-notes added by the American translators are the same; and, finally, that the main difference between the two editions consists in the occasional reconstruction or transposition of a sentence, while the great body of the work, in tone, manner, and style, is entirely unchanged.

"Mr. John Oxenford, therefore, did not translate the English edition from the German; he simply appropriated the American edition; superadding to the wrong of the theft, the injustice of a false accusation. For he pronounces the American version 'not sufficiently faithful', meaning to convey thereby the idea that the translation is either incorrect or incomplete. But it is neither. Not a single line of the German original has been omitted, and it is believed that every sentence has been rendered with tolerable fidelity. It is very likely that the American translators may have, here and there, fallen into some verbal mistakes; for it is hardly possible to turn some thousand pages, particularly of so idiomatic and precise a writer as Goethe, out of one language into another, without a single error; but they confidently believe that they have committed no more errors than are usual with the best scholars in such cases. The translations of the different parts were first made by different individuals, and they were then carefully gone over by the editor, who compared each line with the original, and re-wrote many passages, to produce uniformity of style in the rendering.

"The 'many successful renderings,' then, of the first ten books, to which Mr. Oxenford refers, and under which phrase he attempts an adroit concealment of his fraud, comprise nearly the whole twenty books; that is, the entire work. It would have been more manly, to say the least of it, not to have made any allusion to the American edition at all, than to have noticed it in this uncandid and ungenerous manner."

Then Mr. Godwin quotes passages showing similarity in translation, even in poetry, and also that the English edition copied even the errors too; e. g. "that the Archduke Joseph would be crowned King of Rome" (see p. 13), although the American translators in the list of *errata*, appended to vol. 2, had said the translation should be "King of the Romans."

And he concludes his discussion thus: "But we will not pursue this matter any further. Our object is not so much to expose the dishonesty of John Oxenford, Esq., as it is to present the American public with one more proof of the necessity of an international copyright law. This translation occupied the time of several literary persons during the better part of a whole winter. It was printed and published by American publishers, at an expense of nearly two thousand dollars. But as both the translators and the publishers knew it was not likely to have an extensive sale in the American market, they confidently relied upon the English market for their remuneration. Yet the book had hardly appeared before a cheaper edition of it was issued in England, whereby the sale of the American edition was almost wholly cut off. Thus, the American translators have lost their time, and the American publishers their profits, for the want of that protection which the law extends to every kind of property except literary. What encouragement is there, in this state of things, for American scholars, or for the publishers of American books?

"As a mere question of international justice, it is perhaps right that American books should be reprinted in England, since we have reprinted English books. But in respect to the individuals whose labors are appropriated, this reciprocal free-booking, as Hood used to call it, operates as a signal wrong and calamity.

"We do not complain, we repeat, of the reprinting of our book in England, for that was to have been expected, in the present condition of the law, but we do complain that a bad name should have been given to it by the very party who surreptitiously published it as his own."

This second edition also received favorable reviews in the American Magazines. The "International Monthly Magazine of Literature, Science and Art" (N. Y. 1:194 Aug. 12, 1850) substantiates Godwin's Preface. "Mr. Godwin exposes one of the most scandalous pieces of literary imposition that we have ever read of. This translation with a few verbal alterations which mar its beauty and lessen its fidelity, has been reprinted in 'Bohn's Standard Library' in London as an original English version, in the making of which, 'the American was of occasional use,' etc. Mr. Godwin is one of our best German scholars, and his discourse last winter on the character and genius of Goethe, illustrated his thorough appreciation of the Shakespeare of the Continent, and that affectionate sympathy which is so necessary to the task of turning one language into another. There are very few books in modern literature more attractive or more instructive than this Autobiography of Goethe, for which we are indebted to him.''

In ''Harper's New Monthly Magazine'' (1:715 Oct. 1850) appeared this criticism: ''Truth and Poetry, from my own Life, or the Autobiography of Goethe, edited by Parke Godwin, is issued in a second edition by Geo. P. Putnam, with a preface, showing the plagiarisms which have been committed on it in a pretended English translation from the original by one John Oxenford. This enterprising person has made a bold appropriation of the American version, with only such changes as might serve the purpose of concealing the fraud. In addition to this felonious proceeding, he charges the translation to which he has helped himself so freely, with various inaccuracies, not only stealing the property, but giving it a bad name. The work of the American editor has thus found a singular, but effectual guarantee for its value, and is virtually pronounced to be a translation incapable of essential improvement. With the resources possessed by Mr. Godwin, in his own admirable command both of the German and of the English language and the aid of the rare scholarship in this department of Mr. Chas. A. Dana and Mr. John S. Dwight, to whom a part of the work was entrusted, he could not fail to produce a version which would leave little to be desired by the most fastidious critic. It is unnecessary to speak of the merits of the original, which is familiar to all who have the slightest tincture of German literature. As a history of the progress of literary culture in Germany, as well as of the rich development of Goethe's own mind, it is one of the most instructive, and at the same time, the most entertaining biographies in any language.''

The "Literary World" (N. Y. 7:132-133 Aug. 17, 1850 No. 185) also has a characteristic word to say about the translation. "It is a very cool thing for a man to find fault with what he borrows and doesn't intend to return; but to decry what one steals, and openly inform the victim of one's depradations that his wares are not quite up to expectation, is what might be considered as the Nova Zembla of impudence. The appropriations of the London translator (so-called) and his publication of the American version of Goethe's Autobiography, furnishes the proof that this degree of complacent piracy may sometimes be attained. Mr. Parke Godwin of this city, with the co-operation of some literary friends, translated the present work for Messrs. Wiley and Putnam's 'Library of Choice Reading,' in which the first edition made its appearance. It was a difficult and laborious undertaking, but the editor succeeded in presenting the Autobiography of Goethe to English and American readers in an accurate, careful and spirited version. The book itself is one of the most characteristic and powerful of the productions of its great author, and it only needed time and opportunity to become widely known and popular in the translation. The immediate circulation in this country of a work of this character could not, however, be expected to equal that of publications of more recent authorship and more immediate interest. The publishers here relied in part upon a favorable reception of the translation in England, to which it was eminently entitled.

"The way in which the book was bodily appropriated by the English publisher, and reprinted as an original English translation, and, at the same time, disparaged and decried so far as the New York edition was concerned, is a curious piece of effrontery of which we give the account entire as it appears in the Preface to the new American edition." Then follows the quotation of Godwin's entire Preface.

It is not my intention to make any accusations against John Oxenford. I shall simply cite corresponding extracts, taken at random, from each of the twenty books, and let the reader draw his own conclusions. In this citation, I use the American editions of 1846-7 and 1850, which are exactly alike in paging, and the English edition of 1872 in two volumes (Bell & Daldy), which, according to the prefaces is an exact reproduction of the works of 1848 and 1849.

GODWIN

Vol. I, part 1, bk. 1, p. 1.

On the 28th of August, 1749, at mid-day, as the clock struck twelve, I came into the world, at Frankfort-on-the-Maine. My horoscope was propitious; the sun stood in the sign of the Virgin, and had culminated for the day: Jupiter and Venus looked on with a friendly eye, and Mercury not adversely; while Saturn and Mars kept themselves indifferent; the Moon alone, just full, exerted her reflex power, all the more as she had then reached her planetary hour. She opposed herself, therefore, to my birth, which could not be accomplished until this hour was passed.

Bk. 2, p. 39.

Considering this impulse more closely, we may see in it a presumption similar to that with which the poet so authoritatively utters his improbabilities, and requires every one to recognize as real, whatever may in any way strike him, the inventor, as true.

Bk. 3, p. 73.

But even this sympathy in respect to art could not change my father's feelings nor bend his character. He permitted what he could not prevent, and so kept at a distance in inactivity, for the uncommon state of things around him was intolerable to him even in the veriest trifle.

OXENFORD

Vol. I, part 1, bk. 1, p. 1.

On the 28th of August, 1749, at mid-day, as the clock struck twelve, I came into the world, at Frankfort-on-the-Maine. My horoscope was propitious; the sun stood in the sign of the Virgin, and had culminated for the day: Jupiter and Venus looked on him with a friendly eye, and Mercury not adversely; while Saturn and Mars kept themselves indifferent; the Moon alone, just full, exerted the power of her reflection all the more, as she had then reached her planetary hour. She opposed herself, therefore, to my birth, which could not be accomplished until this hour was passed.

Bk. 2, p. 36.

Considering this impulse more closely, we may see in it that presumption with which the poet authoritatively utters the greatest improbabilities, and requires every one to recognize as real whatever may in any way seem to him, the inventor, as true.

Bk. 3, p. 66.

But even this sympathy in respect to art could not change my father's feelings nor bend his character. He permitted what he could not prevent, but kept at a distance in inactivity, and the uncommon state of things around him was intolerable to him, even in the veriest trifle.

Bk. 4, p. 115.

Our regards and interests are still fastened upon these regions. At last the founder of another race goes forth, who is able to stamp a distinct character upon his descendants, and by that means unite them for all time to come into a great and compact nation, inseparable under all changes of place or destiny.

Bk. 5, p. 159.

Scarcely had I set foot in the house when my father caused me to be called, and communicated to me that it was now quite certain that the Archduke Joseph would be elected and crowned King of Rome.

Part 2, bk. 6, p. 1.

Thus was I driven alternately to assist and retard my recovery, and a certain secret chagrin was now added to my other sensations: for I plainly perceived that I was watched, that they were loth to hand me any sealed paper without taking notice what effect it produced, whether I kept it secret, or laid it down openly, and other indications. I, therefore, conjectured that Pylades, or one of the cousins, or even Gretchen herself, might have attempted to write to me, either to give or to obtain information. In addition to my sorrow, I was now for the first time thoroughly soured, and had fresh opportunities for exercising my conjectures, and misleading myself by the strangest combinations.

Bk. 7, pp. 89-90.

And when I urged it upon him, he replied in his intelligent, serene

Bk. 4, p. 106.

But our regards, our interests, are still fastened to these regions. At last the founder of a race again goes from hence, and is so fortunate as to stamp a distinct character upon his descendants, and by that means to unite them for all time to come into a great nation, inseparable through all changes of place or destiny.

Bk. 5, p. 147.

Scarcely had I reached home than my father caused me to be called, and communicated to me that it was now quite certain that the Archduke Joseph would be elected and crowned King of Rome.

Part 2, bk. 6, p. 181.

Thus was I driven alternately to assist and to retard my recovery, and a certain secret chagrin was now added to my other sensations; for I plainly perceived that I was watched,—that they were loth to hand me any sealed paper without taking notice what effect it produced—whether I kept it secret—whether I laid it down open, and the like. I, therefore, conjectured that Pylades, or one of the cousins, or even Gretchen herself, might have attempted to write to me, either to give or to obtain information. In addition to my sorrow, I was now for the first time thoroughly cross, and had again fresh opportunities to exercise my conjectures, and to mislead myself into the strangest combinations.

Bk. 7, pp. 262-263.

And when I pressed him, he replied in his intelligent, cheerful manner: "If, in commenting on and explaining your friend, you will allow me to go on after his fashion, methinks he meant to say: that experience is nothing else than that one should experience what one does not wish to experience; which is what it amounts to for the most part, at least in this world."

Bk. 8, p. 99.

Now although from their situation, character, abilities, and opportunities, these amateurs and collectors inclined most to the Dutch school, yet while they practised their eyes on the endless merits of the North-western artists, a look of reverential longing was often turned towards the South-east.

Bk. 9, p. 165.

Now as one cannot deny to the whole mass a fine proportion of height and breadth, so also it maintains a somewhat uniform lightness in the details, by means of these buttresses and the narrow compartments between them.

Bk. 10, p. 220 *note.*

The general custom of the country villages in Protestant Germany on such interesting occasions.—*Trans.*

Vol. 2, part 3, bk. 11, p. 36.

It is highly remarkable, though not so commonly noticed, that at this time even the strong old rythmic artistic tragedy was threatened with a revolution, which was averted only by great talent and the power of tradition.

---

manner, "If you will allow me, while commenting on and completing your friend, to go on after his fashion, I think he meant to say, that experience is nothing else than that one experiences what one does not wish to experience; which is what it amounts to for the most part, at least in this world."

Bk. 8, p. 269.

Now although from their situation, mode of thought, abilities, and opportunities, these amateurs and collectors inclined more to the Dutch school, yet, while the eye was practised on the endless merits of the north-western artist, a look of reverential longing was always turned towards the southeast.

Bk. 9, p. 329.

Now as one cannot deny to the whole mass a fine proportion of height to breadth, so also in the details it maintains a somewhat uniform lightness by means of these pillars and the narrow compartments between them.

Bk. 10, p. 379 *note.*

The general custom of the country villages in Protestant Germany on such interesting occasions.—*American Note.*

Vol. 1, part 3, bk. 11, p. 423.

It is extremely remarkable, and has not been generally noticed, that at this time, even the old, severe, rythmical, artistical tragedy was threatened with a revolution, which could only be averted by great talents and the power of tradition.

Bk. 12, p. 71.

And shall that man not be immortal,
Who health and joys for us discovered,
Such as the horse swift in the race ne'er gave us;
Such as even the flying ball has not?

Bk. 12, p. 454.

"And should he not be immortal,
Who found for us health and joys,
Which the horse, though bold in his course, never gave,
And which even the ball is without?"

Bk. 13, p. 129.

It is always a misfortune to enter into new relations to which we are not accustomed. We are, often against our will, beguiled into a false sympathy. The incompleteness of such a position tortures us, but we see no means either of making it perfect or of escaping from it.

Bk. 13, p. 509.

It is always a misfortune to step into new relations to which one has not been inured; we are often against our will lured into a false sympathy, the incompleteness of such positions troubles us, and yet we see no means either of completing them or of removing them.

Bk. 14, p. 151-152.

The perseverance of an energetic character becomes the more worthy of respect when it is maintained throughout a life in the world and in affairs, and when a mode of dealing with current events, which to many might seem rough and arbitrary, employed at the right time, leads most surely to its end.

Vol. 2, bk. 14, p. 7-8.

In an energetic character this adherence to its own views becomes the more worthy of respect when it has been maintained throughout a life in the world and in affairs, and when a mode of dealing with current events, which to many might seem rough and arbitrary, being employed at the right time, has led surely to the desired end.

Bk. 15, p. 192.

Who will belong to himself alone,
Let him shut himself up in a cot of his own,
Company find in his children and wife,
Drink nothing but light new wine,
And never immoderately dine,
And nothing will hinder the course of his life.

Bk. 15, p. 45.

He who would serve himself alone,
Should have a cottage of his own.
Dwell with his children and his wife,
Regale himself with light new wine,
And on the cheapest viands dine;
Then nothing can disturb his life.

Part 4, bk. 16, p. 4.

Nature works after such eternal, necessary, divine laws, that the Deity himself could alter nothing in them. In this, all men are unconsciously agreed. Think only how a natural phenomenon, which should intimate any degree of understanding, reason, or will, would instantly astonish and terrify us.

Part 4, bk. 16, p. 65.

Nature works after such eternal, necessary, divine laws, that the Deity himself could alter nothing in them. In this belief, all men are unconsciously agreed. Think only how a natural phenomenon, which should intimate any degree of understanding, reason, or even of caprice, would instantly astonish and terrify us.

Bk. 17, p. 22.

    Heart, my heart, O, what hath changed thee?
        What doth weigh on thee so sore?
    What hath from thyself estranged thee,
        That I scarcely know thee more?
    Gone is all which thou held dearest,
    Gone the care which thou kept nearest
        Gone thy toils and after-bliss.
        Ah! how couldst thou come to this?

Bk. 17, p. 80.

    Heart, my heart, O, what hath changed thee?
        What doth weigh on thee so sore?
    What hath from myself estranged thee,
        That I scarcely know thee more?
    Gone is all which once seemed dearest,
    Gone the care which once was nearest,
        Gone thy toil and tranquil bliss,
        Ah! how couldst thou come to this?

Bk. 18, p. 51.

The wedding feast is in the house
Of mine host of the Golden Louse.

Bk. 18, p. 106.

The wedding feast is at the house
Of mine host of the Golden Louse.

Bk. 18, p. 67.

    If I, lovely Lili, had not loved *thee*,
        How I'd revel in a scene like this!
    And yet if I, Lili, did not love thee,
        Ah! what scene would yield me any bliss?

Bk. 18, p. 123.

    Dearest Lilli, if I did not love thee,
        I should revel in a scene like this!
    Yet, sweet Lilli, if I did not love thee,
        What were any bliss?

Bk. 19, p. 95.

Truly, lovers consider all that they have felt before only as preparation for their present bliss, only as the base on which the structure of their life can first be reared. Past attachments seem like spectres of the night, which glide away before the break of day.

Bk. 19, p. 149.

True, lovers consider all that they have felt before only as preparation for their present bliss, only as the foundation on which the structure of their future life is to be reared. Past attachments seem like spectres of the night, which glide away before the break of day.

Bk. 20, pp. 115-116.

"Child! child! no more! lashed as by invisible spirits, the sun-steeds of time rush onward with the light car of our destiny, and nothing remains to us but bravely and composedly to hold fast the reins, and now to the right, now to the left, here from a rock, there from a precipice, to avert the wheels. Whither he is going, who can tell? Scarcely can he remember whence he came!"

Bk. 20, p. 168.

Child! child! no more! The coursers of time, lashed, as it were, by invisible spirits, hurry on the light car of our destiny, and all that we can do is in cool self-possession to hold the reins with a firm hand, and to guide the wheels, now to the left, now to the right, avoiding a stone here, or a precipice there. Whither it is hurrying who can tell? and who, indeed, can remember the point from which it started?

In 1839, Margaret Fuller's translation of Eckermann's "Conversations with Goethe" was published in Boston as the fourth volume of Geo. Ripley's "Specimens of Foreign Literature" (414 pp. Hilliard, Gray & Co.). In her long preface, a very just characterization of Goethe, Margaret Fuller states that inasmuch as the two German volumes of 1836 would not make two English volumes of this special series, and yet were too much for one, she was obliged to omit in her translation some of the less important parts; e. g., Goethe's theory of colors, Eckermann's experiments and Goethe's remarks on them, Eckermann's brief account of his visit to Italy, a discussion of a novel by Goethe, as yet untranslated, and a few passages of a very local nature. But she adds: "I am aware that there is a just prejudice against paraphrastic or mutilated translations, and that, in this delicate process, I have laid myself open to much blame. But I have done it with such care, that I feel confident the substance of the work, and its essential features, will be found here, and hope, if so, that any who may be acquainted with the original, and regret omissions, will excuse them. These two rules have been observed, not to omit even such details as snuffing the candles and walking to the stove, (given by the good Eckermann with that truly German minuteness which, many years ago, so provoked the wit of Mr. Jeffrey,) when they seem needed to finish out the picture, either of German manners, or Goethe's relations to his friends or household. Neither has anything been omitted which would cast either light or shade on his character. I am sure that nothing has been softened or extenuated, and believe that Goethe's manners, temper, and opinions, wear here the same aspect that they do in the original.

"I have a confidence that the translation is, in the truest sense, faithful, and trust that those who find the form living and symmetrical, will not be inclined severely to censure some change in the cut or make of the garment in which it is arrayed."

This work was reviewed most favorably in the "New York Review" (5:233-4 July 1839) and in the "Boston Quarterly Review" (3:20-51 Jan. 1840).

Some years afterward, after the publication in 1848 of Eckermann's third volume of Conversations, there appeared in print a translation of the "Conversations of Goethe with Eckermann and Soret," by John Oxenford (2 vols. L. 1850 Smith, Elder & Co., 65, Cornhill). In his Preface, Oxenford writes: "Had I followed the order of German publication I should have placed the whole of the Supplementary volume after the contents of the first two; however, as the Conversations in that volume are not of a later date than the others (which, indeed, terminate with the death of Goethe), but merely supply gaps, I deemed it more conducive to the reader's convenience to re-arrange in chronological order the whole of the Conversations, as if the Supplement had not been published separately.

"Still, to preserve a distinction between the Conversations of the First Book and those of the Supplement, I have marked the latter with the abbreviation 'Sup.', adding an asterisk (thus, Sup.*) when a Conversation has been furnished, not by Eckermann, but by Soret.

"I feel bound to state that, while translating the First Book, I have had before me the translation by Mrs. Fuller, published in America. The great merit of this version I willingly acknowledge, though the frequent (?) omissions render it almost an abridgement. The contents of the Supplementary volume are now, I believe, published for the first time in the English language."

After the appearance of Oxenford's work, the "Monthly Literary Miscellany" (A Compendium of literary, philosophical and religious knowledge, edited by Daniel F. Quimby, Detroit, Mich. 1851 Beecher and Quimby) in an article entitled "Goethe's Opinion of Byron, Scott and Carlyle" (pp. 125-127) makes this very characteristic comment: "Mr. John Oxenford, who has shown remarkable capacities for appropriation, in the use he has made of William Peter, Parke Godwin, and others, in his various 'translations' from the German, has recently fallen in with Margaret Fuller d'Ossoli's version of the *Conversations of Goethe with Eckermann,* published many years ago by Mr. Ripley in his 'Specimens of Foreign Literature'; and the result is two volumes, embracing, with what Margaret Fuller translated, the great poet's conversations with Soret."

In order that the reader may gain an idea of these two translations of Eckermann's work of 1836, I append corresponding passages taken also at random from the record of every year.

FULLER	OXENFORD
Introduction, p. 5.	Introduction, vol. 1, p. 3.
Still I am far from imagining that the whole inner man of Goethe is here adequately portrayed. We may, with propriety, compare this extraordinary spirit and man to a many-sided diamond, which in each direction shines with a different light.	Still, I am far from imagining that the whole internal Goethe is here adequately portrayed. We may, with propriety, compare this extraordinary mind and man to a many-sided diamond, which in each direction shines with a different hue.

Page 10.

It has been said that animals are instructed by their very organization; and so may it be said of man, that he often, by some accidental action, is taught the higher powers which slumber within him. So something now happened to me which, though insignificant in itself, gave a new turn to my life, and is therefore stamped indelibly on my memory.

Pages 15 & 16.

It has been said that animals are instructed by their very organization; and so may it be said of man, that by something which he does quite accidentally, he is often taught the higher powers which slumber within him. Something of the sort happened to me, which, though insignificant in itself, gave a new turn to my life, and is therefore stamped indelibly on my memory.

P. 31, June 10, 1832.

I arrived here some days since, but did not see Goethe till today. He received me with great cordiality; and the impression he made on me during our interview was such, that I consider this day as the happiest of my life.

P. 53, June 10, 1823.

I arrived here a few days ago, but did not see Goethe till today. He received me with great cordiality; and the impression he made on me was such, that I consider this day as one of the happiest in my life.

P. 75, Jan. 27, 1824.

Goethe talked with me about the continuation of his memoirs, with which he is now busy. He observed, that this later period of his life would not be narrated with such minuteness as he had used in the *Dichtung und Wahrheit*.

P. 124, Jan. 27, 1824.

Goethe talked with me about the continuation of his memoirs, with which he is now busy. He observed, that this later period of his life would not be narrated with such minuteness as the youthful epoch of "Dichtung und Wahrheit."

P. 123, Dec. 9, 1825.

Goethe laughed at these last words. "Really," said he, "I would not have advised you to undertake 'Faust.' It is mad stuff, and quite beyond the customary range of feeling. But, since you have begun without asking my advice, we shall see how you will get through. Faust is so peculiar an individual, that few men can sympathize with the situation of his mind. And the character of Mephistophiles is, on account of the irony and ex-

P. 192, Dec. 9, 1825.

Goethe laughed at these last words. "Really," said he, "I would not have advised you to undertake 'Faust.' It is mad stuff, and goes quite beyond all ordinary feeling. But since you have done it of your own accord, without asking my advice, you will see how you will get through. Faust is so strange an individual, that only few can sympathize with his internal condition. Then the character of Mephistophiles is, on account of his extensive acquaintance with the world which it displays, not easily to be comprehended. But you will see what lights open upon you. 'Tasso' lies far nearer the common feelings of men, and all there is told with a minuteness of detail very favorable to an easy comprehension of it."

P. 170, Nov. 8, 1826.

Goethe spoke again of Lord Byron. "I have," said he, "just read once more his 'Deformed Transformed,' and admire his genius more than ever. His demon was suggested by Mephistophiles. It is, however, no imitation, but a new and original creation of great merit. There are no weak passages, not a place where you could put the head of a pin, where you do not find invention and thought. But for his hypochondriacal negative turn, he would have been as great as Shakespeare —as the ancients." I expressed surprise at such an assertion.

P. 188, Jan. 17, 1827.

We talked of Schiller's "Fiesco," which was acted last Saturday. "I saw it for the first time," said I, "and have been thinking whether those extremely rough scenes could not be softened; but I find very little could be done without spoiling the character of the whole."

P. 246, Oct. 3, 1828.

"Generally speaking, a man is quite sufficiently saddened by his own passions and destiny; he need

irony, and also because he is a living result of an extensive acquaintance with the world, also very difficult. But you will see what lights open upon you. 'Tasso,' on the other hand, lies far nearer the common feelings of mankind, and the elaboration of its form is favorable to an easy comprehension of it."

P. 294, Nov. 8, 1826.

Today, Goethe spoke again of Lord Byron with admiration. "I have," said he, "read once more his 'Deformed Transformed,' and must say, that to me his talent appears greater than ever. His devil was suggested by my Mephistophiles; but it is no imitation— it is thoroughly new and original, close, genuine, and spirited. There are no weak passages,—not a place where you could put the head of a pin, where you do not find invention and thought. Were it not for his hypochondriacal negative turn, he would be as great as Shakespeare and the ancients." I expressed surprise.

P. 327, Jan. 17, 1827.

We talked of Schiller's "Fiesco," which was acted last Saturday. "I saw it for the first time," said I, "and have been much occupied with thinking whether those extremely rough scenes could not be softened; but I find very little could be done to them without spoiling the character of the whole."

Vol. 2, p. 72, Oct. 3, 1828.

"Generally speaking, a man is quite sufficiently saddened by his own passions and destiny, and need not make himself more gloomy, by looking into the darkness of barbaric early days. He needs enlightening and cheering influences, and must therefore turn to those eras in art and literature, during which remarkable men could obtain that degree of culture which made them satisfied with themselves, and able to impart similar satisfaction to others."

not make himself more so, by the darkness of a barbaric past. He needs enlightening and cheering influences, and should therefore turn to those eras in art and literature, during which remarkable men obtained perfect culture, so that they were satisfied with themselves, and able to impart to others the blessings of their culture."

P. 278, Feb. 17, 1829.

"Lavater," said Goethe, "believed in Cagliostro and his wonders. When the impostor was unmasked, Lavater maintained— 'This is another; Cagliostro, who did the wonders, was a holy person.' "

P. 133, Feb. 17, 1829.

"Lavater," said Goethe, "believed in Cagliostro and his wonders. When the impostor was unmasked, Lavater maintained, 'This *is* another Cagliostro, the Cagliostro who did the wonders was a holy person.' "

P. 337, Feb. 10, 1830.

Dined with Goethe. He spoke with real gratification of the poem written by Riemer, for the festival of the 2d February.

"All," said Goethe, "which Riemer writes, is fit to be seen both by master and journeymen."

P. 227, Feb. 10, 1830.

Dined with Goethe. He spoke with real gratification of the poem written by Riemer, for the festival of the 2d February.

"All," added Goethe, "that Riemer does, is fit to be seen both by master and journeyman."

P. 359, Feb. 12, 1831.

"This," said Goethe, "is a most beautiful history, and one which I love better than any. It expresses the noble doctrine, that man, through faith and animated courage, may come off victor in the most dangerous enterprises, while he may be ruined by a momentary paroxysm of doubt."

P. 332, Feb. 12, 1831.

"This," said Goethe, "is one of the most beautiful legends, and one which I love better than any. It expresses the noble doctrine that man, through faith and hearty courage, will come off victor in the most difficult enterprises, while he may be ruined by the least paroxysm of doubt."

P. 411, Early in March, 1832.

"He is a very fine young man," said Goethe; "in his mien and manners the nobleman is seen at once. He can as little dissemble his descent as another man could his in-

P. 426, Early in March, 1832.

"He is a very fine young man," said Goethe; "in his mien and manners he has something by which the nobleman is seen at once. He could as little dissemble his de-

tellect; for both birth and intellect give their possessor a stamp
which no incognito can conceal.
Like beauty, these are powers
which one cannot approach without
some feeling of their high nature."

scent as any one could deny a
higher intellect; for birth and intellect both give to him who once
possesses them a stamp which no
incognito can conceal. Like beauty, these are powers which one cannot approach without feeling that
they are of a higher nature."

On page 13 of his bibliography, "Goethe in England and
America" (Ed. 2 L. 1909) Dr. Oswald states that the work
entitled "Tales from the German," translated by John Oxenford and C. A. Feiling (L. 1844 Chapman & Hall Large
8vo. XIV + 446 pp.) contains Goethe's tale "The New Paris" on pp. 306-316. I have not seen this particular English
edition, but the American reprint of Part 1. of these Tales
(N. Y. 1844 110 pp. Harper & Bros.) from an English edition
of Part 1. by Chapman & Hall, does not contain this tale.
The eight stories included are:

1. J. H. Musaeus—Libussa.
2. Schiller—The Criminal from Lost Honor.
3. Hauff { The Cold Heart
         { Nose the Dwarf (from Sheik Alexander and his Slaves.)
4. Immerman—Wonders in the Spessart (from Münchhausen)
5. C. F. van der Velde—Axel: A Tale of the Thirty Years' War.
6. E. T. W. Hoffman—The Sandman.
7. H. Kleist—Michael Kohlhaas.

Also in a review of the English edition, Part 1, in the "London Examiner" (pp. 661-2 Oct. 1844 reprinted in Littell's
Living Age 3:475-478 Dec. 21, 1844 No. 32) these eight tales
and their authors are named and briefly discussed, and the
article closes with these words: "We hope that notices of
these writers will be given when the collection is completed."
If this collection was later completed and if "The New Paris"
by Goethe was included in the list, it would be an interesting
study to compare Oxenford's translation of this particular
tale with Margaret Fuller's version in her article on "Goethe"
in the "Dial." July 1841 (Boston 2:141).

Margaret Fuller (Marchesa d' Ossoli) is well known
through a recent study by Dr. F. A. Braun, entitled "Margaret Fuller and Goethe", (N. Y. 1910 257 pp. H. Holt &

Co.) but perhaps a little biographical data about Parke Godwin, John Oxenford and the Rev. Alex. J. W. Morrison,
would not be amiss in this article.

Parke Godwin was born February 25, 1816, at Paterson,
N. J. His father was an officer in the War of 1812 and his
grandfather, a soldier in the Revolution. After graduating
from Princeton, in 1834, he was admitted to the bar in Ken-
tucky, but practised there only a very short time. From 1837
to 1853, excepting one year, he was on the editorial staff of
the "New York Evening Post", of which his father-in-law was
editor-in-chief. During the year 1843, he started a weekly
periodical, called "The Pathfinder" which was discontinued
after the issue of fifteen numbers. He also contributed many
articles to the "U. S. Democratic Review" and for a time edited "Putnam's Monthly Magaine." In these journals he advocated many political reforms that were subsequently
adopted in the constitution of New York. Under President
Polk, he was deputy-collector in the New York Custom House,
but later espoused the cause of the Republican party, although
he still continued to believe in free trade. Besides his journal-
istic work, Godwin found time to write or edit various works
on history, literature and politics. He died in New York
City, January 27, 1904, at the advanced age of eighty-seven
years.

Among his writings are the following:

1. History of France vol. 1. (Ancient Gaul) N. Y. 1830.
2. A popular View of the Doctrines of Fourier Ed. 2. N. Y. 1844.
3. Democracy, constructive and pacific N. Y. 1844.
4. Edited and translated Part 1. of Goethe's Autobiography. N. Y.
   vol. 1. 1846 vol. 2 1847. Ed. 2 1850.
5. Vala, a mythological tale N. Y. 1851.
6. Handbook of Universal Biography (Putnam's Home Cyclopedia)
   N. Y. 1852 New edition called Cyclopedia of Biography N. Y.
   1866.
7. Political Essays N. Y. 1856 (from Putnam's Mon. Mag.)
8. Out of the Past 2 vols. N. Y. 1870 (Essays from Putnam's Mon.
   Mag.)
9. Biography of William Cullen Bryant, with extracts from his
   private correspondence N. Y. 1883.
10. The First Settlers of Totawa (now Paterson, N. J.), an episode of
    Early History N. Y. 1892.

11. The Germans in America N. Y. 1893.
12. Edited Bryant's Works 6 vols. N. Y. 1883-1884.
13. Commemorative Addresses: Geo. W. Curtis, Edwin Booth, Louis Kossuth, John J. Audubon, Wm. C. Bryant N. Y. 1895.
14. Essays on John Jas. Audubon in Little Journeys to the Homes of American Authors N. Y. 1896 G. P. Putnam's Sons.
15. A New Study of the Sonnets of Shakespeare N. Y. 1900.
16. Translated Zschokke's Tales.
17. Translated Fouqué's Undine, and also Sistram and his Companions.

John Oxenford was born at Camberwell near London August 12, 1812. He was a self-educated man, and unaided by schools, learned the French, Italian, Spanish and German languages. Apprenticed to a solicitor, he studied law and was admitted to the bar, but soon he adopted a literary career. His first writings were on commerce and finance, but later he devoted himself entirely to literature. In 1835, he began writing for the stage, and until 1875, was a most prolific author of comedies, especially of farces, and of librettos for operas. The "Catalog of the British Museum" prints the titles of about forty plays, and the "Musical World" of March 10, 1877, records an incomplete list of sixty-eight dramas. His most noted farces, which by the way, are also his early ones of 1835, are "My Fellow-Clerk", "A Day Well Spent", and "Twice Killed", each of which had four editions and was translated into foreign languages.

Besides composing original plays, Oxenford was dramatic critic for the "London Times" for over a quarter of a century (from c. 1850). In regard to his critiques, Robin H. Legge writes in the "Dictionary of National Biography" (L. - 1892-1900 vol. 43 p. 13): "He was amiable to weakness, and the excessive kindliness of his disposition caused him to so err on the side of leniency as to render his opinion as a critic practically valueless. It was his own boast that 'none of those whom he censured ever went home disconsolate and despairing on account of anything he had written.' " [Cf. the "Advertisement" in his translation of Goethe's Autobiography (13 bks.) L. 1848]. He also wrote articles for the various magazines and to the "Penny Cyclopedia" contributed several biographical papers, notably one on Molière. His essay in the

"Westminster Review" April 1853 (New Series 3:388-407) entitled "Iconoclasm in Philosophy", based on Schopenhauer's writings, did much to create an interest in England in the works of the German philosopher, (see Art: Arthur Schopenhauer by Franz Hueffner in Fortn. R. 26: 773-792 Dec. 1876).

But it is especially as a translator that Oxenford's name is of interest to the student of German culture. Hence I shall append a list of his many translations. He died at Southwark, February 21, 1877, and was buried at Kensal Green.

Translations and Adaptations.

Spanish.

1. Calderón—La Vida es Sueno.

Italian.

Boiardo—Orlando innamorato (incomplete).

French.

1. Molière—Tartuffe.
2. Scribe & Legouvé—World of Fashion (Les Doigts de Fée) 1850.
3. C. Delavigne—Monastery of St. Just 1850.
4. J. M. Callery & M. Yvan—History of the Insurrection in China with supplementary chapter. 1853.
5. Illustrated Book of French Songs from the sixteenth to the nineteenth century 1855.
6. E. Cormon & M. Carré—Lara 1865.

German.

1. (With C. A. Feiling and Prof. Heimann) Edited J. G. Flügel—Comparative Dictionary of the German and English languages with additions and improvements 2 vols. Ed. 2 1838 (several editions).
6. Fr. C. W. Jacobs—Hellas, or the Home, History, Literature and Art of the Greeks 1855.
7. Kuno Fischer—Francis Bacon of Verulam 1857.
8. J. F. Kind—Der Freischütz 1866.
9. (With Dr. Franz Hueffner)—Selections from German opera texts for the Richard Wagner Festival in Albert Hall 1877.
10. Goethe—Die Wahlverwandtschaften (see Dict. of Nat'l. Biog. 43:13).

I wonder if Oxenford is the "Anon." who translated this novel for Bohn's "Standard Library" (see Preface to "Novels and Tales" L. 1854).

In regard to the life and works of the Rev. Alex. Jas. Wm. Morrison, A.M., Trinity College, Cambridge, all the biographies and encyclopedias are strangely silent. The only information I could obtain, was from the Catalog of the British Museum, where are stated the titles of his various original translations of German works, or revisions of translations, generally for Bohn's "Standard Library." I append a list of these translations. (See also Oswald, pp. 13-14-16).

1. Aug. H. Ritter—Hist. of Ancient Philosophy 4 vols. 1836-1846.
2. Hermann Ulrici—Shakespeare's Dramatic Art and his Relation to Calderón 1846.
3. Aug. W. Schlegel—Lectures on Dramatic Art and Literature 1846 (revised from John Black's translation in 1815).
4. A. Neander—General History of the Christian Religion and Church 1846 (revised from J. Torrey's translation).
5. Fr. Schlegel—Philosophy of Life and Philosophy of Language 1847.
6. Autobiography of Goethe (books 14-20), including the Letters from Switzerland and Travels in Italy 1849. Later Oxenford was given the credit of the entire Autobiography.
7. Schiller—Thirty Years' War 1851.
8. Schiller—Revolt of the United Netherlands (revised from Lieut. Edw. B. Eastwick's translation), also Trial of Counts Egmont and Horn and the Siege of Antwerp 1851. Cf. Geo. Moir's translations of the Thirty Years' War, Siege of Antwerp and the Trials of Counts Egmont and Horn Edinb. 1828 vols. 18 & 19 of Constable's Miscellany.
9. Heinrich E. F. Guerike—Manual of the Antiquities of the Church 1851.
10. Michael Baumgarten—Acts of the Apostles 1854 3 vols. (with the Rev. T. Meyer).
11. Gottlieb C. A. von Harless—System of Christian Ethics 1865.

In this study I have tried to state impartially the facts as I have found them in history and literature, and let the reader draw his own inferences. I have, however, a few questions yet unanswered, and I offer them to others for solution. Why is Parke Godwin's work entirely ignored by Doctor Oswald in his "Bibliography of Goethe", and by all editors of Goethe's complete works in translation? Why does the great "Dictionary of English Biography" (edited by Leslie Stephen and Sidney Lee, 63 vols. L. 1895-1900, 1st supplement in 3 vols. 1901; 2nd sup. in 3 vols. 1912, Smith, Elder & Co., 16 Waterloo Place) in an article by Robin H. Legge (vol. 43, p. 13) state that Oxenford's translation of the Autobiography was in *1846?* Why does the 1910-1911 edition of the "Encyclopedia

Britannica'' (29 vols. Camb., Eng. University Press) forbear even to mention Parke Godwin's name and repeat the same false date of *1846?* Why through all these years has John Oxenford always been lauded as *the* great translator of the Autobiography and of Eckermann, when the facts show that others deserve the credit?

''Mordre wil out; certes it is no nay,'' says Chaunteclere in Chaucer's ''Nonne Prest his Tale,'' and while I do not wish to disparage the service of John Oxenford in the diffusion of German culture, still it is time that justice should be done to Margaret Fuller and to Parke Godwin (also to his helpers, Hopkins, Dana and Dwight) as the *first great translators of Eckermann and of Dichtung und Wahrheit.*

EMMA GERTRUDE JAECK.

Converse College, S. C.

IBSEN'S *PEER GYNT* AND GOETHE'S *FAUST*.

That the great work of the great author of modern Norway presents more than chance analogies to the classic of modern Germany has not escaped notice. Both are dramatic poems in varied metre setting forth the career of an eminently national, but at the same time in only less degree universal figure. That the treatment of this figure is on the one hand synthetic and sympathetic, on the other analytic and relentless, has its inevitable basis in the widely differing natures of the two poets. In accordance with his deeply national tendency each author has drawn largely upon national legend and popular belief, not merely for his central character, but for much of his treatment as well. In these facts of general analogy there is however involved no necessary direct relationship between the two poems. Nor is it an easier matter here than elsewhere to demonstrate just how far Ibsen, who prided himself if ever author did upon "being himself" under all circumstances, may have fallen under Goethe's "influence", and just what the nature of his reaction to this influence as shown in his work was.

Doubtless the most striking and indubitable literary influence to be noted in Ibsen's life-work is found in his relation to that champion of the Norwegian woman's cause, Camilla Collett,[1] and the first manifestation of this relation is a peculiar but characteristic one. Camilla Collett's *Amtmandens Døtre* appeared in 1855. The thesis of this remarkable novel was that the type of "mariage de convenance" prevailing in a certain class of Norwegian society brought with it almost inevitably a sacrifice of woman's life-happiness. At the close of 1862 came Ibsen's *Kjærlighedens Komedie*, which deals satirically with love-matches on various stages of the way to matrimony and beyond and in a characteristically Ibsenesque dénouement places over against each other ideal love for love's sake which can find in the institution of marriage only its own destruction, and marriage for life-happiness, which had best be a marriage of reason. In this work Ibsen was not

[1] See Ibsen's admission, *Breve fra Henrik Ibsen*, II, 180 (Letter of 1889).

exactly contradicting Fru Collett, still less was he merely defending the "mariage de convenance"; he was putting the whole subject on a broader basis and introducing the element of absolute idealism, to which so much of his life-work and thought was devoted. In a spirit of conscious improvement upon the original that had so laid hold upon his mind he could not refrain from treating it to a bit of satire.[2]

The above relation is of great value in the way of an analogy for an understanding of the relation between Ibsen's shortly later work (1867) and its German prototype. That Ibsen actually knew Goethe's *Faust* when he wrote *Peer Gynt* and that it must have been vividly before his mind is sufficiently evidenced by a quotation from it.[3] The circumstances of the quotation are of such a sort as to perhaps reveal something of the author's attitude toward Goethe's work. Peer Gynt under the spell of the entirely physical charms of the dirty Arab girl, Anitra, says in delight as he gives her the jewel she demands:

> "Anitra! Evas naturlige datter!
> Magnetisk jeg drages, thi jeg er mand,
> og som der står hos en agtet forfatter:
> 'das ewig weibliche zieht uns an!' "

This last line contains the concluding words of the second part of Faust where they are from the lips of the "Chorus mysticus."[4] That these profound words are quoted by the worthless Peer under such peculiarly vulgar circumstances might almost seem an affront offered the great German poet. Of course it must be borne in mind that it is only Peer who is quoting them and that he is in the habit of quoting as scripture and otherwise a deal of miscellaneous matter, still the "agtet forfatter" is not exactly in the vein of Peer's usual quotations and one is doubtless justified in seeking Ibsen's "self" be-

[2] Cf. G. Brandes, *Det moderne Gjennembruds Mænd*, 2nd ed. (1891), 129 ff. (first edition dates from 1883).

[3] Cf. also his remarks on a Danish translation of *Faust*, Breve, II, 170, 185 (letters of 1888 and 1889); also J. Paulsen, *Samliv med Ibsen, Anden samling* (1913), 90, 170 ff.

[4] The fact that Ibsen has "an" for "hinan" of the original shows that he was quoting from memory (or was he purposely misquoting?).

hind it.[5] At the same time one should note that in a letter
to Björnson dated December 28, 1867, i. e., in the next month
after the appearance of *Peer Gynt*,[6] Ibsen alludes twice to
Goethe or his works. This is all the more remarkable as Ibsen
was not at all in the habit of spicing his letters with literary
allusions. In the first of these *Götz von Berlichingen* is cited
as a type of real poetry as distinguished from mere allegory.
In the second, advising Björnson to leave his own country,
Ibsen expresses his conviction that in Goethe's time the people
of Weimar probably formed his least appreciative public. Neither of these allusions savors in any way of a failure on the
part of Ibsen to appreciate the poetic greatness of Goethe, and
it is in fact not entirely the spirit of opposition to, still less
that of contempt for *Faust* that we shall find in *Peer Gynt*,
but rather again one of revision. This attitude applies particularly to the subject which through the most of his literary
career lay near Ibsen's heart, the woman-question. At
the close of *Faust* we are shown the spirit of the woman whose
life Faust had ruined leading his soul to ''higher spheres.''
At the close of Ibsen's poem Peer Gynt's soul seems similarly
to be saved through Solvejg's love (at least she herself is confident that such is the case, a confidence not necessarily shared
by the reader nor actually confirmed by the author) ; but this
outward similarity seems coupled with very essential difference in that Peer Gynt has done nothing whatever to deserve
salvation. He appears the exact antithesis of the striving and
aspiring Faust in that he has taken as guide of action and
motto of life the going round about difficulties and being self-
sufficient. Solvejg, who is first presented to us carrying a
psalm-book as Margarete is just coming from confession is,
unlike the latter, able by force of character and of purity to
repel the advances of her beloved, though herself endowed
with infinite devotion and in no respect deficient in the wom-
anly graces and virtues.[7]

    [5] In *Kjærlighedens Komedie* (Ibsen's *Samlede Værker, Mindeudgave*,
I, 327) the German poet is referred to as "geheimeråd Göthe"
    [6] *Breve fra Henrik Ibsen*, I, 164.
    [7] The similarity between Solvejg and Margarete is well brought out
by A. Ehrhard, *Henrik Ibsen et le théâtre contemporain* (Paris, 1892),

This fundamental relationship between the two poems other points of connection, in some cases more conspicuous, merely serve to confirm. Of the five acts the first three correspond to the first part of *Faust*, the other two to the second. In the first act the scene at the peasant-wedding in its presentation of popular life and gayety suggests the one "Vor dem Thor;"[8] in the second the scene with the three "sæter-jenter" corresponds in function with that in "Auerbachs Keller" (as forming a transition in its gross sensualism to the still grosser sensualism of the following) and those with the trolls in Dovre to the "Hexenküche" and "Walpurgisnacht."[9] Apart from the general likeness in the troll and witch-scenes several more particular points of agreement may be noted. The troll-princess in green has as steed a large swine suggested perhaps by the steed of Baubo in "Walpurgisnacht."[10] Among the troll-newspapers mentioned by the "Dovre-gubbe" at his reappearance in the fifth act is the "Bloksbergs-posten."[11] The really significant

---

165 f., the author noting further that each had a young sister of whom she was very fond and that Solvejg secures her information about Peer through his mother Aase, much as Margarete confided in Frau Marthe. This last point is of particular interest, as the contrast in character of the confidantes chosen by the two maidens serves to accentuate the point of difference in their own characters.

[8] Ehrhard (158 ff.) noted the relation between this wedding and the one in Björnson's *Synnøve Solbakken* (1857) and concluded further that Ibsen was satirizing Björnson's work; cf. also J. Paulsen, *Samliv med Ibsen, Anden Samling*, 132.

[9] The similarity of the troll-scenes to the "Hexenküche" and the "Walpurgisnacht" is noted by J. Collin, *Henrik Ibsen*, 307 (1910). Ibsen even introduces a "troldheks" with a ladle.

[10] Cf. Collin, *Henrik Ibsen*, 302 (1910). Her green garb as in fact much of the setting of the troll-scenes Ibsen owes of course to Asbjørnsen's *Norske Huldre-Eventyr og Folkesagn* (1845-48). It is noteworthy however that in a list of witches' steeds found in this work (3rd ed., 1870, p. 116) the swine is not mentioned.

[11] This fact in itself is of no great importance as the Blocksberg is sufficiently well known in Scandinavia. It is in fact mentioned in the *Huldre-Eventyr* (p. 308), but in the form Bloksbjerg. The idea of the troll-newspapers was doubtless suggested to Ibsen by the third act of Heiberg's *En Sjæl efter Døden*, where Mefistofeles treats the soul to a considerable discussion of the newspapers of hell. This act which satirizes Denmark as hell had obviously influenced Ibsen in no small degree in his thrusts at Norway as the troll-kingdom.

correspondence lies in the fact that Faust was taken to the "Hexenküche" to secure the magic potion which was to rejuvenate him and prepare him for his career as a sensualist; while there he was treated to a mirrored vision of a wondrously beautiful woman and was informed by Mephistopheles after having drunk the potion that he would soon see Helen in every woman. The troll-king also has a means of transformation, a simple operation on the eye in this case,[12] which in addition to the tail and the other accessories will finally make Peer over into a genuine troll and cause him to see his troll-bride no longer as an ugly troll, but as a beautiful woman. Peer refuses to submit to the operation not because he particularly objects to becoming a troll, but because he doesn't like to enter into a state from which he can not withdraw again. The "Bøjg" Ibsen has of course taken from the trolls of the *Huldre-Eventyr*, but the real significance he has given it as the power that bids Peer go round about and through which he is unable to force his way is not without relation to the "Erdgeist," which Faust conjures up only to have his intellectual aspirations dashed by the information that he cannot comprehend it. As Faust in his subsequent despair was about to take his own life, the Easter-song (introduced by the ringing of bells) saved him to the world. So Peer Gynt after his experience with the Bøjg is saved from death only by the ringing of bells and psalm-singing.[13] Ibsen lays emphasis on the fact that women (Solvejg and Peer's mother) are responsible for this bell-ringing. In both works the introduction of irrelevant contemporary satire is conspicuous in the troll and witch-scenes.[14]

In Ibsen's lengthy fourth act Peer Gynt after ripe experience

[12] The idea of this operation was suggested by Asbjørnsen; cf. Woerner, *Henrik Ibsen*, I, 233 f., where a convenient list of matter taken by Ibsen from Asbjørnsen (and Moe) is given.

[13] The ringing of church-bells as a means of dispelling trolls was of course available from Asbjørnsen's *Huldre-Eventyr*, where it is mentioned several times, and Peer had been saved from the other trolls shortly before by means of it.

[14] A "professortrold", "bispetrold", "folketrold" and "digtertrold" Ibsen left out in the poem as finally published (Cf. *Efterladte Skrifter*, II, 94 ff.)

is taken to the southward like Faust in the second part,[15] and possibly as a whimsical counterpart to the latter's union with the restored Helen (marriage of the North with the South) we are treated to Peer's amour with the Arab girl Anitra. Faust was deeply imbued with a desire for knowledge, a desire dashed by his meeting with the "Erdgeist". Peer after his humiliating experience with Anitra decides to devote himself to the intellectual, to investigate the past, with which end in view he wanders about Egypt with a note-book, only to fall in with a German of the significant name of Begriffenfeldt, the head of an insane asylum in Cairo, who has himself just gone crazy, and who takes Peer back to the asylum where he is crowned as "kejser." [16] As in the "Classische Walpurgisnacht" sphinxes among other creatures appear recalling the "Walpurgisnacht" of the North, so the Egyptian Sphinx and the column of Memnon recall to Peer the "Bøjg" and his experiences with the trolls in the Dovrefjeld.[17] Just before these Egyptian experiences a vision of Solvejg appears as had a vision of Gretchen to Faust in the "Walpurgisnacht," but what a contrast between the happy devoted Solvejg and the guilty Gretchen! It might seem far-fetched to connect the monkeys who in one scene molest Peer with the "Meerkater" and his family of the "Hexenküche," did not Ibsen himself expressly recall the troll-scene in the scene with the monkeys.[18] As Faust finally found eager occupation in the restoration of

[15] Somewhat further, it is true, to northern Africa. Greece does not however pass unmentioned, but that country Peer is inclined to avoid because of the war in progress there. Far from sympathizing with Greece he rather conceives the idea of loaning money to the stronger Turkey.

[16] In connection with this relationship J. Collin (*Henrik Ibsen*, p. 324) speaks of Peer as "der neue Wagner." Peer's ambition to become "kejser" seems to have been suggested to Ibsen by Schack's *Phantasterne* (1857; cf. Woerner, *Henrik Ibsen*, I, 258 ff. Woerner, strangely enough, denies a direct influence), which may well also be responsible for the introduction of the insane asylum.

[17] Cf. Collin, *op. cit.*, p. 324.

[18] Collin (pp. 319 f.) compares an episode from Holberg's *Niels Klim*, which appears indeed to have given Ibsen the idea of the adjustable tail and its ornamentation with colored bow (cf. already Woerner, *Henrik Ibsen*, I, 391. 1900).

land from the sea by means of dikes and drainage Peer Gynt
conceives temporarily the fantastic idea of letting the water
of the ocean into the low parts of the Sahara and thus gaining
land for cultivation and culture. That the last really suggested itself as a counterpart to the German feature is rather
confirmed, if confirmation were necessary, by lines discarded
by Ibsen in his published work,[19] in which he speaks of the
desert as "et Dødens Holland."

That in the fifth act the discussion as to the final disposition
of Peer's soul stands in some relation to *Faust* has long since
been noted. It may be said that in addition to the uncanny
fellow-passenger, who is not the devil, and the fantastic
button-moulder, who appears as a servant of the higher powers and whose occupation was suggested by circumstances of
Peer's early life,[20] the devil himself is actually introduced, and
much in the spirit of Goethe's Mephistopheles. There is considerable allusion to the horse's hoof as in *Faust*, and the devil
appears in response to Peer's need of confession disguised as
a pastor, as Mephistopheles among various disguises masquer-
aded on occasion for example as a teacher. For Ibsen's characterization of him as "den Magre" Collin [21] has called attention to the agreement with Goethe's conception of Mephistopheles. The idea of moulding the soul over again as unfit for
either heaven or hell shows *Faust* already modified by the
Danish works Paludan-Müller's *Adam Homo* (1841-48) and
Heiberg's *En Sjæl efter Døden* (1841), as is well known. The
former of these is an epic dealing with a (from any ideal point
of view) human failure, whose soul after death is placed on
trial and finally led by that of Alma, a woman once loved by

[19] *Efterladte Skrifter*, II, 104. That in Peer's idea of calling this
land "Gyntiana" and transplanting the Norwegian race thither there is
contained a satirical allusion to Ole Bull's colony "Oleana" in Pennsylvania (1852-57) has been noted; cf. *Efterladte Skrifter*, I, p.
LXXII. 1909.

[20] Oehlenschläger's *Aladdin* (1805) apparently suggested the idea of
moulding the soul over; cf. Collin, *Henrik Ibsen*, 338. Other features of
Peer Gynt recalling this work make it probable that Ibsen in satirizing
romanticism had it definitely in mind.

[21] *Henrik Ibsen*, 341.

him but forsaken, through a temporary purgatory.[22] The other is an "apocalyptic comedy" inspired in part at least by *Faust*. It deals in satirical vein with a soul that is turned out of heaven by St. Peter, of Elysium by Aristofanes; coming to hell it is instructed by Mefistofeles that hell-fire is only for sinners on a large scale, that for the great majority of humanity hell is simply a continuation of their philistine mundane existence.[23]

The above details appear to justify the conclusions: (1) that Ibsen in writing *Peer Gynt* had Goethe's Faust very vividly before his mind; (2) that he was consciously bent upon improving the woman's rôle in Goethe's poem; (3) that among the many things satirized in Ibsen's work the *Faust* does not escape without its share. This satire is not at all of the nature of an attack upon the German poet, though one cannot exactly agree with Mauthner that the relation is one of "Pietät" toward Goethe,[24] nor is there any reason to re-

[22] Ibsen's relation to Paludan-Müller is called by Ehrhard (p. 166) one of similarity in general inspiration which can hardly be explained as mere coincidence. Attention may be called to the fact that Adam recognizing Alma just before his death requests her to accuse him, to which she replies that he had been her joy through the many years, which is exactly duplicated at the close of *Peer Gynt* (cf. Woerner, *Henrik Ibsen*, I, 255-258 also 250. 1900). Both authors show similar fondness for bits from various languages, both making for example similar use of "Sic transit gloria mundi" (cf. Woerner *op. cit.* I, 391; see also in *Kjærlighedens Komedie* "Sic transit gloria amoris").

[23] The idea of a soul not being good enough for heaven nor bad enough for hell is of course no uncommon one (cf. Collin, *op. cit.* 338 f.) and has more recently found interesting expression for example in Kipling's *Tomlinson*. Brandes *Det moderne Gjennembruds Mænd*, 2nd ed., 86 f.) noted that it might have been suggested to Ibsen by Kierkegaard. One of the *Norske Folke-Eventyr* of Asbjørnsen and Moe (No. 21, 3rd ed., 1866, pp. 95 f.) tells of the smith who had difficulties in getting into either heaven or hell. This collection was used by Ibsen for *Peer Gynt* as well as were the *Huldre-Eventyr* (cf. Woerner, *Henrik Ibsen*, I, 234.).

[24] *Eine Faustiade von Henrik Ibsen* in *Deutsches Montagsblatt*, 1881, No. 9. This article has been accessible to me only in the citations of Halvorsen's *Norsk Forfatter-lexikon* III, 49. 1889, giving its general tendency. No less than three other of Ibsen's works have been compared by German commentators with Goethe's *Faust: Brand, Kejser og Galilæer* and *Når vi døde vågner*.

gard it as directed against Germany or the German people
through the medium of its representative, Faust.[25] It seems
rather inspired by flaws which Ibsen thought he detected in
the character of Goethe's hero, flaws which he wished to
make appear to correspond to the weaknesses of Peer Gynt:
egotistical selfishness, the avoidance of personal responsibility
and generally the lack of a sustained indomitable purpose,
the failure to be a personality as Ibsen at that time conceived
of personality.

A. LeRoy Andrews.

Cornell University.

[25] In a letter of 1873 (*Breve*, I, 277 f.) Ibsen took occasion to protest
against the accusation of having directed a poem against Germany.
In 1871 he had been obliged to defend himself against a petty accusation of the sort appearing in a German periodical (cf. *Breve*, I, 329 f.;
Efterladte Skrifter, I, 298 ff.). The satire of Germany or the Germans in "Von Eberkopf" is only parallel to that of England, France
and Sweden; in "Begriffenfeldt" is satirized not Germany, but the
Hegelian philosophy (cf. Collin, *op. cit.* 326 ff.).

DEQUINCEY'S LOVE OF MUSIC.

At its best, the prose style of Thomas DeQuincey is musical to the core. Other prose—all noble prose, indeed—is rhythmical, whether Arnold's, Macaulay's, or Pater's. But De-Quincey's in the Confessions of an Opium Eater, in some of his Autobiographical papers, in his Joan of Arc or the English Mail Coach, has more than rhythm; it has underneath a mellowness of tone wich suggests the depths of subliminal music, to borrow a psychological term, as if the very central thought were conceived in musical phrases, and were developed by means of harmony and counterpoint. It is a style consciously or unconsciously modulated, with development and progression strangely similar to musical composition.

Although such effects are present to the sensitive ear, their complete analysis will be admitted impossible. And yet, were one to make a guess at efficient cause, one might say that such style could flow only from a man to whom music was not merely an enjoyment, but a reality and a necessity; and one might well hark back to Milton with his organ-toned verse, which critics sometimes hold to be born of his love of music, and of organ music in particular. One might so guess, indeed, and with a tolerable feeling of security. Fortunately, however, such a supposition is based on tangible facts. In many places here and there throughout his works, DeQuincey drops a bit of information, a phrase, a reference which makes unmistakable in him a rare sensibility to music—a sensibility as he writes in his ''Recollections of Lamb''[1] ''rising above the common standard—viz., by the indispensableness of it to my daily comfort, the readiness with which I make any sacrifice to obtain a 'grand debauch' of this nature.'' So frequent are these passages and so definite are they in their information, that those who are not too sceptical may reasonably believe in the connection between his passion for music and his prose style.

As a boy, DeQuincey's opportunities to hear music at home could not have been many. The atmosphere of his mother's house, evangelical with all the severity of Hannah More, was

[1] *Collected Writings*, London, 1896, III, 45: cf. J. Hogg, *DeQuincey and his Friends*, p. 227.

hardly favorable. And yet he may have heard some music from a young woman for a time governess of his sister, a Miss Wesley,[2] niece of the great preacher, and a member of a family noted for musical talent. Outside, however, there was the music of the English church service. "I loved unspeakably the grand and varied system of chanting in the Romish and English churches," he writes in one of his autobiographic sketches.[3] "And, looking back at this day to the ineffable benefits which I derived from the church of my childhood, I count among the very greatest those which reached me through the various chants connected with the 'O, Jubilate,' the 'Magnificat,' the 'Te Deum,' the 'Benedicite,' etc." Now and then, too, he heard the larger choral works of Handel. He writes in the same essay—"Introduction to the World of Strife"[4]—that already at eleven, "with Handel I had long been familiar, for the famous chorus singers of Lancashire sang continually at churches the most effective parts from his chief oratorios." On rare occasions, also, there were visits to his guardian "B," in whose house before he was eleven years old, DeQuincey heard the children of the family sing "the old English glees and madrigals." "There first," he continues, "I heard the concertos of Corelli; but also, which far more profcundly affected me, a few selections from Jomelli and Cimarosa . . . . . But above all, a thing which to my dying day I could never forget, at the house of this guardian I heard sung a long canon of Cherubini's . . . . . It was sung by four male voices, and rose into a region of thrilling passion, such as my heart had always dimly craved and hungered after, but which now first interpreted itself, as a physical possibility, to my ear."

Yet, devoted as he was to music, his mother and guardians seem to have made no systematic attempts to have him study it. Indeed, the only knowledge of music which he claims as a child is that of chanting, gained as he half humourously says, from the son of another—a reverend—guardian, much older than himself, who "possessed a singular faculty of pro-

[2] *Works*, I, 135, n.
[3] *Works*, I, 73.
[4] *Works*, I, 109.

ducing a sort of organ accompaniment with one-half of his mouth, whilst he sang with the other half.''[5] Only considerably later did DeQuincey undertake to learn to play the piano, in that ill-fated year spent at the Manchester Grammar School in his middle ''teens.''[6] But this attempt soon fell through, and with it ended, so far as we can learn, any plan to acquire technical knowledge or understanding of music. Thenceforth, as previously, music was a ''necessity'' to him, but only as a passive listener, not as a student.

During the years at Oxford, and afterwards up to about 1815, when he made frequent visits to London, he was a constant attendant at the opera.[7] Now and then, indeed, he went to the opera in some of his opium debauches as a means of obtaining the most exquisite delight. In a striking passage of the Confessions[8a] which we shall have occasion to quote more than once, he tells of these experiences. ''The late Duke of Norfolk used to say, 'next Monday, wind and weather permitting, I purpose to be drunk;' and in like manner I used to fix beforehand how often within a given time, when, and with what accessory circumstances of festal joy, I would commit a debauch of opium. This was seldom more than once in three weeks, for at that time I could not have ventured to call every day (as afterwards I did) for a 'glass of laudanum negus, warm, and without sugar.' No; once in three weeks sufficed; and the time selected was either a Tuesday or a Saturday night, my reason for which was this :—Tuesday and Saturday were for many years the regular nights of performance at the King's Theater (or Opera House); and there it was in those times that Grassini sang; and her voice (the richest of contraltos) was delightful to me beyond all that I had ever heard; or ever shall hear.'' Yet she was not his only admiration. Madame Catalani, whom he met personally in Liverpool in 1807, he had heard ''repeatedly''[8b]—Madame

[5] *Works*, I, 73.
[6] *Works*, III, 270.
[7] *Works*, III, 389; Hogg, 55.
[8a] *Works*, III, 389.
[8b] *Works*, II, 233-4.

Catalani, "that marvel of women," "that mighty enchantress."

"Mingled with the old London operatic memories which always seemed to afford him such intense pleasure," writes Mr.
James Hogg [9] of DeQuincey's later years, "there appeared to
stand out clearer than all else the recollection of the chief
pieces played by every great violinist whom he had heard."
Concerts, then, also attracted him.

Of course, during the life at Grasmere in his lonely cottage,
and later when married there, the musical feasts must have
been rare indeed. Unless he traveled to London or Edinburgh, or some of the greater provincial cities—as, indeed,
he often did—opera, concert, or even good church music was
unattainable. He must content himself with the occasional
domestic music of the neighbors, or find enjoyment in the
mere whistling of a native postillion.

The removal to Edinburgh in 1828 seems hardly to have
made more music possible. Poverty, the struggle with ill
health and opium, afforded him small chance to take advantage
of the opportunities of even a provincial town. His increasing shyness in public, moreover, his shrinking from going anywhere among strangers, made his life more and more that of
a recluse. His growing daughters, however, were fortunately
musical; and we have an occasional account by friends of
pleasant evenings at Lasswade. "Music and laughter" [10] was
what DeQuincey promised visitors, a promise apparently delightfully fulfilled. "He exulted in the fervor of expression
and the musician-like touch and facility of execution with
which his youngest daughter, still under professional instruction, rendered Beethoven's Sonata Pathetica," etc.
writes Mr. Jacox; [11] and elsewhere,[12] "Fond as he was of music, he was not often in the room while his two younger
daughters played or sang during my stay; but he was a good
listener, for all that, in his 'den' down stairs, and would comment on his favorites among their pieces when he rejoined
us."

[9] Hogg, p. 185.

[10] Page, Life and Writings, I, 374.

[11] Hogg, p. 229, (The same Reminiscences by Jacox are in Japp's;
DeQ.'s Life and Writings, London, 1890. pp. 295 ff.)

[12] Hogg, p. 228.

Yet now and then, apparently, he went to a public concert hall during the last ten years of his life. In 1855 he planned to take his daughters to hear Mendelssohn's St. Paul,[13] and again to a concert given by Madame Pleyell.[14] Within the same years also, he heard with unspeakable joy, as Mr. Hogg[15] tells us, a concert by the Hungarian violinist, Remenyi.[16] Music was a necessity to him to the end; and in those last years he declared that "if ever again he visited London, it was his hope to frequent the opera."[17]

Such broadly are DeQuincey's musical experiences. From early childhood up to extreme old age, music was indeed to him a reality, a prepossession. Whenever he could hear music he did so, and always found in it the greatest joy. His taste, moreover, seems to have been catholic. He found the Italians singularly impressive—Corelli, Jomelli, Cimarosa, Pergolesi, Bellini; most of all Cherubini, whose canon already spoken of, was to him unspeakably thrilling.[18] He found joy in the Germans, too, if unappreciative for the most part of Mendelssohn, laughing at the music to Sophocles's Antigone, cold to the Songs without Words and the vocal duets, though manifestly interested in the St. Paul. Handel he knew early, and more than once mentions; Spohr he knew to some extent, and Weber.[19] But it is the music of Mozart and Beethoven[20] which awakened his chief enthusiasm—"the perfect music of Mozart and Beethoven," Don Giovanni, Fidelio, and the Sonata Pathetica.[21]

But he was not above more popular things. He writes of

[13] Page, II, 100.

[14] Page, II, 98.

[15] Hogg, 185.

[16] In 1856 (?) he says in one letter that the only time he stepped upon the street during three or four weeks was when he went out to hear Grisi sing. Page, Life, II, 113.

[17] Hogg, 227.

[18] Works, I, 109; Hogg, 228-9.

[19] Hogg, 228; Works, X, 381-383 f.; Page, II, 100.

[20] Hogg, 228; Works, I, 198.

[21] It is perhaps surprising that there are, on the whole, so few references to music and musicians in his works when one considers how much music meant to him.

getting "the loveliest of waltzes for Emily. Mrs. Lushington has played it for me a dozen times. It is a perfect dream of beauty."[22] "Nor would he tire," writes Mr. Jacox,[23] "of such time-tried strains as 'Time hath not thinned,' 'O lovely peace,' 'In chaste Susanna's praise,' 'Down the dark waters,' 'By limpid streams,' 'And will he not come again?' 'Birds blithely singing,' etc." But it is the undoubtedly great things which hold his memory and admiration; and the list of such pieces as he liked is on. the whole, even, at this day, excellent. Without thorough training in music, guided only by natural refinement and taste, he need never have been ashamed of his musical choice.

His taste was native; for as has been said, he was without technical training in music—a fact we gather from two circumstances:—first, nowhere does he mention any musical study except that one abortive attempt at the Manchester Grammar School; and second, in no passage in his voluminous writings does he show any precise knowledge of musical form or expression. There is much intelligent appreciation, much sensitive reaction and enjoyment; but of definite mention of the special problems of the composer and the performer, such as orchestration, development of theme, or technique of even his favorite violin—to no such questions is there any allusion. This fact might not be conclusive in itself, were it not for the first reason, in connection with the frequency with which he might have spoken of some such technical points; would, almost certainly have done so, had he had the necessary knowledge. And there is still another reason which makes it seem unlikely that he had technical knowledge. That is, the nature of the enjoyment which he derived from music. It is this nature of his enjoyment which is next before us, and which is curiously at one with what we should expect of the author of the Confessions.

There is in DeQuincey's attitude toward music almost always a certain excitement. Music in so far as it was a necessity of his nature, appealed strongly to his sensitiveness to artistic effects. Emotional in his appreciation of so much in

[22] Page, Life, I, 342.

[23] Hogg, 228.

life and literature, playing so boldly and so deliberately upon his sensations, he found in music an intense and irresistible pleasure. Less given to facing facts than to dreaming of them, or with subtle, logical progression of thought de-actualising them, he seems to have found in music an able assistant to supersensual flights. He was a man requiring few creature comforts but many luxuries, in so far as they were subjective and sensuous. And music opened for him a world of mind and feeling free from the realities of life which dealt with him so hardly. His mind ran to meet the occasion and rejoiced unrestrained in it.

In the passage already quoted in part, in which he plots an opium-musical debauch, we find what may fairly be considered the acme of his musical delight. "Thrilling was the pleasure with which almost always I heard this angelic Grassini.[24] Shivering with expectation I sat, when the time drew near for her golden epiphany; shivering I rose from my seat, incapable of rest, when that heavenly and harp-like voice sang its own victorious welcome in its prelusive threttanelo-threttanelo (θρεττᾰνελό-θρεττᾰνελό). The choruses were divine to hear; and when Grassini appeared in some interlude, as she often did, and poured forth her passionate soul as Andromache at the tomb of Hector, etc., I question whether any Turk, of all that ever entered the paradise of opium eaters, can have had half the pleasure I had." Fifty years later in sharp contrast to this exalted state in listening, due in some measure, of course, to opium, is the record, not less interesting perhaps from being that of a friend, of his enjoyment at that concert of Remenyi's. "I never saw DeQuincey exhibit such evidence of rapturous enjoyment," writes Mr. Hogg.[25] "He lay back for a long time in the dark corner (of the box) as if in a trance . . . . . For weeks that performance was a source of ever recurring pleasure. The exquisite nervous organization seemed to feed upon the recollection of the glorious sounds." And there is still another picture of the old DeQuincey listening to music; this, from an-

[24] Works, III, 389.
[25] p. 186.

other friend.[26] ''The young ladies played overtures and other
pieces on the piano, one of which DeQuincey particularly
praised, saying it soothed him like a delicious anodyne. Miss
Florence remarked that it was a poor compliment to the music
to say that it sent him to sleep. He explained to her, with
burlesque excess of particularity and politeness—the humor
of which he himself evidently enjoyed as keenly as the amused
auditors—that it was really the highest compliment he could
pay to it, for he meant that the music was giving him the greatest spiritual gratification, and being to him for the time the
highest good, as making him, usually so miserable, temporarily
happy; and therefore fulfilling its purpose, though not perhaps, in the ordinary way, or according to rule.''

In each case DeQuincey is rapt out of himself. In the first
he feels the excitement which makes it impossible to sit quiet
in the thrill of expectation and joy; in the second, the rapturous enjoyment which caused him to lie back as in a trance;
in the third, the music is to him a delicious anodyne—in
all these he shows himself utterly absorbed, utterly given up
to the intense delight which music had for him. Such absorption, moreover, must have been his habitual attitude. The
picture which he gives of his listening to Grassini shows himself in an abnormal state; but the normal state is undoubtedly found in this trance-like passivity of body. Surely this
was his attitude in early youth as well as in age, and a passage of the Confessions offers interesting confirmation.

As a boy he gave up his one attempt to acquire the art of
piano playing because he soon found, characteristically, that
practice of eight or even ten hours a day would be necessary
for any real efficiency; but chiefly because of this fact:—''Too
soon I became aware that to the deep voluptuous enjoyment
of music absolute passiveness in the hearer is absolutely
indispensable. Gain what skill you please, nevertheless activity, vigilance, anxiety, must always accompany an elaborate
effort of musical exertion; and so far is that from being recon-
cilable with the entrancement and lull essential to the true
fruition of music, that, even if you should suppose a vast

[26] J. R. Findlay, in Hogg, p. 133.

piece of mechanism capable of executing a whole oratorio, but requiring at intervals a co-operating impulse from the foot of the auditor, even that, even so much as an occasional touch of the foot would utterly undermine all your pleasure.'' [27] This is the same complete absorption in the sensuous effect— and yet not completely sensuous.

It was not mere sensuous pleasure which so held him. De-Quincey was at bottom intellectual. Even the joys of opium were in some measure intellectual. The intense vividness of his dreams, the overwhelming, almost painful, beauty of his visions charmed the intellectual man. Never for a moment could one compare his opium dreaming with that of a gross Chinese sailor. DeQuincey by delicacy of organism reached singular altitudes of intellectual delight. Hedonist he was, indeed; not sensualist. In this very love of music DeQuincey compares himself with Wordsworth and his sister in their love of nature—a comparison not to be disregarded in explaining his own feelings.[28] ''Music,'' he further says in another passage already quoted in part,[29] ''is an intellectual or a sensual pleasure according to the temperament of him who hears it . . . . . The mistake of most people is to suppose that it is by the ear they communicate with music, and therefore that they are purely passive to its effects. But this is not so; it is by the reaction of the mind upon the notices of the ear (the matter coming by the senses, the form from the mind) that the pleasure is constructed; and therefore it is that people of equally good ear differ so much in this point from one another. Now opium by increasing the activity of the mind, generally increases, of necessity, that particular mode of its activity by which we are able to construct out of the raw material of organic sound, an elaborate intellectual pleasure. But, says a friend, 'a succession of musical sounds is to me like a collection of Arabic characters; I can attach no ideas to them.' Ideas! my dear friend! there is no occasion for them; all that class of ideas which can be available in such a case has a language of representative feelings . . . . . it is

[27] Works, III, 270.
[28] Works, III, 45.
[29] Works, III, 390.

sufficient to say that a chorus, etc., of elaborate harmony displayed before me, as in a piece of arras work, the whole of my past life—not as recalled by an act of memory, but as if present and incarnated in the music; no longer painful to dwell upon, but the detail of its incidents removed, or blended in some hazy abstraction, and its passions exalted, spiritualised and sublimed.''

This long excerpt may be justified by its significance. The opium, it tells us, merely intensified for him the normal pleasures of music, by increasing the activity of his mind. And for him, the music called up with unusual vividness floods of remembrance, not distinctly as memories, but resolved into emotions transformed or heightened; incarnate in the music; all painful incidents softened by the incarnation; not ideas, but if one may say so, intellectual feelings, the direct appeal of sound to emotions through the medium of quickened association in the mind. Nowhere, probably, could one find an expression more admirable of the aim of music. But—and it is noteworthy—there is no word of the appreciation of the technical form of music; although one might well imagine in such moods of opiate elevation, mere matters of form were not likely to claim thought or feeling, perhaps could not. Yet in the after discussion of his enjoyment, one familiar with musical technique could hardly fail to ascribe some of his pleasure to some such knowledge.

As one might expect of a man who found such joy in the stimulated emotional and intellectual activity of music, the more impassioned moments have for him the greatest appeal. He rejoices in all sorts, indeed. He finds pleasure even in the jew's harp, when well played; [30] in the improvisations of the ventriloquist. He declares them on occasion ''capable of wooing St. Cecelia to listen.'' But it is the full turbulent music which gives him most pleasure. To this he constantly refers: —to the ''impassioned music of the highest class—the impassioned music of the serious opera;'' the music composed by Beethoven as an opening for Bürger's Lenore, ''the running idea of which is the triumphal return of a crusading host,

[30] Works, II, 353 f.

decorated with laurels and with palms within the gates of their native city" with all its "tumultuous festivity;" [31] the "terrific" chorus of Spohr's St. Paul; Handel's Hail-stone chorus; the "orchestral crash which bursts upon the ear;" the music of Mozart and Beethoven, arising "by the confluence of the mighty and terrific discords with the subtle concords." These are the effects which thrill him, which linger longest in his memory, and recur most often in his writings.

It is rarely that we know so closely the attitude of a man of letters toward music, and understand so completely his enjoyment and appreciation. Partly, no doubt, this is due to the fact that there are few men of letters to whom the art has so overwhelming an appeal; partly, of course, because there are few so capable of subtle self analysis and delicate phrasing of mood and feeling. But whatever the reason, we must accept the "necessity" of music for his happiness. His was a sensitive nature, abnormal in its physico-aesthetic intensity and need. He found in music a stimulant to emotional, intellectual, and imaginative activity. Sensual he was not, as I have said; but his craving for music was a demand through beauty of sound for enhanced and quickened life, an enlarged and elevated state of being.

Music for him, then, was innate. As a child he heard with unforgettable thrill a canon of Cherubini, just as he heard the playing of Remenyi with rapturous enjoyment sixty years later. No training is responsible for it, no knowledge. Music as an art spoke directly to him; and, interestingly, found in his intellectual make-up, a corresponding mode of thought and feeling. Like music, DeQuincey's expression of himself in his most characteristic style unfolds broadly, slowly, with subtle involutions, repetitions, modulations, variations. It has, beside underlying music, musical form. Whether his style takes on musical correspondence because of his love of music; or whether he loves music because of a peculiar mental structure predisposing him to expression in a style strangely musical in form, I do not pretend to say. The correspondence, however, is there—and the lurking melody.

[31] Works, I, 198.

How far this correspondence was known to DeQuincey himself is difficult to tell; and yet there is a passage descriptive of musical expression, near the beginning of his well-known essay on Style,[32] both eloquent and pertinent. He is discussing the obtuseness of the English to musical art. In the course of his remarks he speaks of the limitations of the mere tune as compared with "the most elaborate music of Mozart" —"A song, an air, a tune—that is, a short succession of notes revolving rapidly upon itself—how could that, by possibility, offer a field of compass sufficient for the development of great musical effects? The preparation pregnant with the future; the remote correspondence; the questions, as it were, which to a deep musical sense are asked in one passage and answered in another; the iteration and ingemination of a given effect, moving through subtle variations that sometimes disguise the theme, sometimes fitfully reveal it, sometimes throw it out tumultuously to the blaze of daylight; these and ten thousand forms of self-conflicting musical passion,—what room could they find, what opening, what utterance, in so limited a field as an air or song?" Primarily a description of the movement of great musical compositions, is it not secondarily a perfect description of his own full style, contrasted with the simple rythms of ordinary prose? And is not this secondary application highly suggestive and easy to make after examining the musical experiences and devotion of DeQuincey? Certainly, to one who is not too sceptical as to the affinity of style and taste, there is a vital connection between this love of music and the elaborate prose of the great prose harmonist.[33]

HORACE AINSWORTH EATON.

Syracuse University.

[32] Works, X, 136.

[33] Page, II, 243, points out briefly this same correspondence between taste and style.

STUART AND JACOBITE LYRICS.

The hundred-odd years of conflict between the English Stuarts and their various opponents occasioned a large number of comparatively neglected songs and ballads,—eulogy, satire, and historical narrative. The first two classes I shall not discuss in this paper, nor shall I treat in any way the numerous retrospective songs which appeared after political Jacobitism had degenerated into a sentimental love of the white rose. I shall confine myself to notes on the contemporary, historical ballads written by the partisans of the Stuarts, and shall attempt to include every such ballad that has reference to the two rebellions known as the Fifteen and the Forty-Five.[1]

These historical ballads are numerous, and covering in their inaccurate but rather interesting fashion the entire period from 1640 to 1745, record most of the events occasioned by the hostility towards the Stuarts. There are a few accounts of early battles in the Civil War, and several on Montrose and his campaigns. The Popish Plot, Rye House Plot, and Monmouth's rebellion, which disturbed the reigns of Charles II and his brother, are recorded in so many ballads that examples may be found in practically all collections of political verse. The revolution of 1688, prolific of satire, was so disastrous to the Stuarts that their supporters found little incentive to chronicle its events. The most interesting songs are Whig accounts of the Irish campaign. Claverhouse, James II's well-hated lieutenant, appears as the hero of one of the most spirited Jacobite songs that has been preserved, "The Battle of Killiecrankie." In addition to this, there are songs recording other events in his career,—the affair at Pentland Hills, and the two clashes so well known to all readers of *Old Mortality*, at Loudon Hill and Bothwell Bridge. The first Jacobite rising, the Fifteen, despite the fact that its end was

[1] It should be remembered that there is a large body of songs and ballads on the opposite side of the question, but with these I am not concerned. Nor shall I discuss the comparatively well-known work of men like Dryden, Suckling, and Cleveland. I am concerned primarily with the waifs and estrays of royalist verse, the street songs which may be found scattered through such collections as the *Roxburghe Ballads*, but which have never been examined as a whole.

inglorious, occasioned a few ballads of importance. Thirty years later came the Forty-five, when for a few months the songs and ballads appeared as fast as in 1660. And then, following Culloden, the Jacobites laid down their pens, for there was no longer a cause to support.

A.

FROM 1640 TO 1689

Loyalist accounts of battles fought in England during the Civil War are few. Professor Firth has published four in the third volume of the *Scottish Historical Review*,[2] which illustrate the eagerness of the King's men to make capital out of unimportant victories. "The Tribe off Banburye," in the *Percy Folio MS.*[3] and three ballads in *Rump Songs*,[4] afterwards reprinted in various places, may be added to this list, and passed without comment. The one good song reminiscent of this period that I have been able to discover is "Lesley's March to Longmaston Moor," first printed in the *Tea Table Miscellany*.[5] The song is well known, and need not be printed here. A word concerning its authorship, however, is in point. Ramsay marked it as an "old song," but gave no indication of the source from which he had secured it. Modern editors have not been able to say more than that this characterization may be accepted with hesitation. If Ramsay wrote it, however, it is surprising that he left it so comparatively "unpolished." [6]

Incidents in Montrose's career are chronicled in six songs which it is fair to call contemporary. "Bonny John Seton," a popular ballad,[7] neutral in its attitude, pictures Montrose

[2] Pages 262 f. These are really ballads on the "Bishops' War", which preceded the Civil War.

[3] II, 39.

[4] "The Battle of Worcester", 153; "Upon Routing the Scots Army", 248; and "The Scotch War", 228.

[5] The note in the *Minstrelsy*, II, 201, is incorrect in giving the *Evergreen* as the first place of publication.

[6] Allan Cunningham rewrote "Lesley's March" for his own *Songs of Scotland*, and entirely missed the point of the satire. See Vol. II, 141.

[7] *Child*, IV, 51; no. 198.

as leader of the Covenanters, opposed at the Bridge of Dee by the Royalists under Johnston. The ballad is easily accessible, and offers no perplexities to any one who will read Professor Child's introduction. It should be noted in this connection that Montrose appears in one version of the "Bonnie House o Airlie,"[8] a ballad most prolific of traditional versions and imitations. The allusion to Montrose will be found in the *D* text.

The next event in Montrose's career noted in the ballads is the battle of Auldearn, in which he defeated Sir John Hurry, 4 May, 1645. The record is found, badly confused, in "The Haughs of Cromdale."[9] It is interesting chiefly because it is pronouncedly loyalist in tone.

For a description of one of Montrose's victories written in a slightly less pedestrian fashion, one can do no better than read "The Battle of Alford."[10] The climactic stanza runs as follows:—

> "They hunted us and dunted us,
>   They drave us here and there,
> Until three hundred of our men
>   Lay gasping in their lair",—

no weak tribute to Montrose's clansmen.

The last two contemporary songs on Montrose which I have been able to find record his disastrous defeat at Philiphaugh, 13 September, 1645, and his final surprise and capture at Corbiesdale, after his return from the continent in 1650. Both songs are easily accessible, the former, "The Battle of Philiphaugh," in Child's *Ballads,* and the second, "The Gallant Grahams," in the same editor's *Ballads (British Poets).*[11] It is perhaps worth while noting that in the account of Philiphaugh, which is pronouncedly anti-Stuart, the Marquis is accorded the title "The Great Montrose." I quote the concluding stanza:—

[8] Ibid. IV, 54; no. 199.

[9] See the note in *Child (British Poets)*, VII, 234.

[10] Ibid., p. 238. This ballad records the death of Lord George Gordon, Montrose's lieutenant.

[11] *Child,* IV, 77; no. 202; and *Child (British Poets)*, VII, 137, respectively.

"Now let us a' for Lesley pray,
And his brave company,
For they hae vanquishd great Montrose,
Our cruel enemy."

The song on the affair at Corbiesdale was written some time after the Restoration, but it is fired by an animus against the
Whigs which ten years had not sufficed to cool. It may fairly
be called a contemporary production.[12]

Songs on the Restoration, which followed the execution of
Montrose after ten years, I purposely omit. They are numerous, uninteresting, and fairly well known. Their historical
value, moreover, is slight. They are chiefly eulogies of Charles
II. Between this event and the so-called discovery of the Popish Plot, in 1678, there are few songs that concern us here.
It was a period productive of satire, a period in which party
feeling ran high, but not a period in which many events demanded chronicling in the ballads. Even the songs on the
Popish Plot are apt to be more satirical than historical. There
are a good many of these stall ballads dealing with Oates's
conspiracy,[13] and they evidence in impressive manner the
widespread excitement which prevailed. But since specimens,
at least, are easily accessible, and there is nothing new in
either the forms or the temper of the songs, illustration does
not seem necessary.

Shortly after Shaftesbury's flight to Holland a plot was
set on foot to assassinate the king and his brother James at
the Rye House farm, which they were to pass on their way
home from a Newmarket visit. The plot miscarried, the
conspirators were betrayed, and several, including some of
high station, executed. As in the case of the Popish Plot,
there is a good deal of contemporary literature reflecting the
temper of the times.[14] Three stanzas from "The Whigs Ex-
posed" are rather more interesting than the average because of

[12] Sir William Aytoun's "The Execution of Montrose" is the best
tribute to the Marquis that has yet appeared. It is, of course, retrospective.

[13] Hogg preserves several which seem to be genuine; consult also
the *Rox. Bal.* IV, 121 f., V, 597 f.

[14] See *Rox. Bal.* V, *passim*, for representative accounts.

their echoes of the civil war, and the references to Monmouth
and Shaftesbury, the Whig leaders:—

> "Now the plotters and plots are confounded,
>   And all their designs are made known,
> Which smelt so strong of the Roundhead,
>   And treason of forty-one;
> And all the pious intentions,
>   For property, liberty, laws,
> Are found to be only inventions
>   To bring in their Good Old Cause.
>
> "By their delicate bill of exclusion,
>   So hotly pursued by the rabble,
> They hoped to have made such confusion
>   As never was seen at old Babel:
> Then Shaftesbury's brave city boys
>   And Monmouth's country relations,
> Were ready to second the noise
>   And send it throughout the three nations.
>
> *   *   *   *   *
>
> "The murder of father and king
>   And extinguishing all the right line
> Was a good and a godly thing
>   And worthy the Whig's design.
> The hanging of prelate and peer
>   And putting the guards to the sword,
> And fleying and slashing lord-mayors,
>   Was to do the work of the Lord." [15]

Two years after the Rye House plot, James, Duke of York,
succeeded to the throne. In the same year Charles's illegiti-
mate son, James, Duke of Monmouth, returned from his quasi-
exile on the continent, proclaimed himself king, and raised the
standard of rebellion. Despite a personal popularity which
had for some time been a cause of alarm to his uncle, Monmouth found himself attended by but few followers. When
his poorly organized force met the royal troops at Sedgemoor,
the battle was short and decisive. Monmouth himself fled,
was found hiding in a field of grain, taken to London, and
promptly executed. Then came Jeffreys and the "bloody
assizes."

[15] *Hogg*, I, 339. It is perhaps unnecessary to point out that the
events of the last stanza never actually occurred.

The suppression of the rebellion brought joy to Tories and Catholics alike, and ballads recounting the events of the three weeks flooded the country.[16] Then as Lord Jeffreys and his atrocities became notorious, a large number of songs reviling him and his methods swelled the total to an almost unbelievable extent. The accounts of the rebellion are not unlike the song from which I have just quoted; the latter, though in some instances published only after the Revolution of 1688, are interesting because of their presentation of the case from the opposite point of view. I quote two stanzas from ''Jefferey's Villainies Discovered'':—

> "Then next to the West he hurried with speed,
> To murther poor men, a very good deed!
> He made many honest men's hearts for to bleed.
>   Sing hey, brave Chancellour! Oh fine Chancellour!
>   Delicate Chancellour, Oh!

> "The prisoners to plead to his Lordship did cry,
> But still he made answer, and thus did reply,
> 'We'll hang you up first, and then after we'll try'!
>   Sing hey!" etc.[17]

The Revolution of 1688 did not offer loyalists many opportunities for chronicling victories, although naturally the advent of William and Mary provoked an outburst of vituperative satire which increased in bitterness as the hopelessness of the Stuart cause became apparent. A few historical songs appeared, however, one of which is rather interesting because it is a frank imitation of an older popular ballad. ''The Belgic Boar,'' a ''new song to the old tune of Chevy Chase,''[18] was written after James's exile, but near enough the events it records to be called contemporary. It is the best illustration I have found of a popular ballad forced bodily into the service of the Stuarts. I quote the first three stanzas to show the method used:—

[16] See *Rox. Bal.* V, 608-739.

[17] *Rox. Bal.* V, 721.

[18] On "Chevy Chase" and its history, see "Geschichte der Ballade Chevy Chase", by Karl Messler, Berlin, 1911.

"God prosper long our noble King,
   Our hopes and wishes all;
A fatal landing late there did
   In Devonshire befall.

"To drive our Monarch from his throne,
   Prince *Naso* took his way;
The babe may rue that's newly born
   The landing at Torbay.

"The stubborn Tarquin, void of grace,
   A vow to Hell does make
To force his father abdicate,
   And then his crown to take".[19]

The only song on the so-called "Reading skirmish" that I have found, is a Whig production, easily accessible.[20] A single ballad, "England's Joyful Welcome to her King,"[21] also accessible, records James's temporary return to Whitehall in the latter part of December, 1688, and illustrates the avidity with which the loyalists made political capital out of relatively unimportant events. The famous resolution of abdication is ridiculed best, perhaps, in an easily accessible song in Wilkins's *Political Poetry*.[22] Records of the Irish campaign are many,[23] but I have been able to find only one written by a Jacobite. This is a song of three stanzas, "King James's Welcome to Ireland,"[24] supposed to have been sung before the King at his entry into Dublin, 24 March, 1689.

Long before the Battle of the Boyne was fought and won, John Graham of Claverhouse, first Viscount Dundee, had gained an unenviable notoriety in Scotland. The portrait of "Bloody Clavers" painted by Sir Walter Scott in *Old Mortality* is so widely known that the book has become a sort of *locus classicus* for information concerning the able and generally hated loyalist commander. The contemporary songs offer no evidence concerning the fairness of Scott's characterization. Neutrality seems to have been undreamed of; the

[19] *Rox. Bal.* III, 437.
[20] *Child (British Poets)*, VII, 243.
[21] *Rox. Bal.* VII, 710.
[22] Vol. II, 7.
[23] See the *Percy Society*, Vol. I, part 3.
[24] Ibid. 29.

traditional ballads are strongly anti-Stuart, reflecting the temper of the Presbyterian Covenanters; to offset these are a few songs equally bitter against the Cameronians, and loud in praise of Dundee.

If we except "The Battle of Pentland Hills,"[25] in which Claverhouse's troopers are merely mentioned as "the gallant Grahams," the earliest song on Claverhouse is the traditional ballad "Loudon Hill," or "Drumclog."[26] This easily accessible version is a Whig account of the affair, and is included here only for the sake of making the picture more complete. The immediate result of the success of Robert Hamilton and his followers at Loudon Hill was the summoning of Monmouth and his army from across the border. The resulting battle at Bothwell Bridge occasioned several accounts which seem to be contemporary. Of these the best known is the traditional "Bothwell Bridge."[27] This too is strongly anti-Stuart in temper. Equally bitter is a Whig chap-book, "Bothwell Lines", with which, in the Harvard College library, is bound up a "Description of the Rebels in Scotland in Anno 1679."[28] The forty-eight eight-line stanzas are for the most part uninteresting; I quote three from the section which recounts the two battles:

> "At Lowdon Hill, as I hear say
> They set themselves in battil ray,
> And solemnly did swear and say
> 　　They would not be remiss
> To fight the battles of the Lord;
> They did consent with one accord
> All who does suffer for the Lord
> 　　Shall have eternal bliss.

[25] *Minstrelsy*, II, 244. See on this same affair "The Covenanters' Army at Rullion Green", Maidment's *Pasquils*, 232.

[26] *Child*, IV, 105; no. 205. A curious account of the murder of Archbishop Sharpe, which occasioned the battle at Loudon Hill, may be found in *Rox. Bal.* IV, 150.

[27] *Child*, IV, 108; no. 206.

[28] *Scottish Poetry, Welsh Poetry*, H. C. L. 15476.17. The volume is a miscellaneous collection of chap-books.

> "Now June the two and twenty day,
> At Bothwell Bridge began the play,
> At the first fire they fled away
>   As sheep out of the fold.
> Great things they promised to do,
> The which they solemnly did vow;
> But when the push they were put to,
>   Their courage waxed cold.

> "Our Cannoneer gave such a blast,
> That put them all in such agast,
> Which made the first of them be last,
>   The swiftest led the Van.
> Fled from the Bridge, their great support,
> Like cowardly cullions left their Fort,
> To see the flight it was good sport,
>   So couchingly they ran." [29]

Another loyalist account of the same general sort, but more spirited, is "The Battell of Bodwell-Bridge." I quote the two best stanzas:

> "The good Earle of Athole and gallant Montrose
> They pulled the Whigs Piriweegs over their nose,
> Then Captains and Chieftains did sleep in their hose,
>   When they came to the Battel of Bodwell.

> "The good Captain Clavers, with his good dragoons,
> He scattered the Whigs through the south country bounds,
> He gave them many sore deadly wounds,
>   When they came to the Battel of Bodwell." [30]

The best song on Bothwell Bridge is, I believe, the work of James Hogg, and may be found in his collected works.[31]

Claverhouse's last victory, won at Killiecrankie Pass in 1689, cost him his life. The battle is celebrated in the most spirited, and if one may judge by the number of times it has been reprinted, the most popular of all the earlier Jacobite lyrics. Practically every collection of Scottish poetry contains the verses, beginning,

> "Clavers and his Highlandmen
>   Came down upon the raw, man."

[29] This is from no. VIII, part II.
[30] *Fugitive Scottish Poetry*, ed. David Laing; Edinburgh, 1853. Number XXXV.
[31] Five vols., Glasgow, 1838-1840; see I, 284.

Further quotation is unnecessary. The song remains anonymous, despite the attempts of editors to find an author. Burns's account of Killiecrankie, "Where hae ye Been Sae Braw, Lad?" is probably founded on an older song, which has unfortunately disappeared.[32] Professor Firth has recently printed a contemporary ballad on Claverhouse in the *Scottish Historical Review* for July, 1911. Other contemporary accounts of his campaigns I have not been able to find.

B.

"THE FIFTEEN"

Between Killiecrankie, in 1689, and the outbreak of the first Jacobite rebellion in 1715, there appeared few historical ballads which come within the limits of this study. The satirists were never busier than during the early part of this period, and part of their work, such as the songs on the Union, and on Bishop Sacheverell's sermon, has a distinctly historical value. But for the ballads whose chief purpose was to chronicle events, we have to wait until 1715.

In this year the Jacobites made two feeble and unfortunate attempts to restore James Stuart to the throne. The Earl of Mar, expecting aid from France, raised the standard in September, and called on the Highlanders to support him. Two months later the drawn battle of Sheriffmuir virtually put an end to the rising. James did not reach his army till after the battle, and then his despondency only added to the demoralization. In the course of the winter he and Mar escaped to France, leaving the army to the mercy of Argyle and the English. This mismanaged affair, usually known as the "northern half," was no more unsuccessful than the southern. William Mackintosh, Thomas Forster, and the Earl of Derwentwater[33] led a small force into Northumberland, hoping

[32] See the *Centenary Burns*, III, 81; also *Child (British Poets)*, VII, 153.

[33] Forster held the Pretender's commission as General, and was the leader of the five hundred English Jacobites. Mackintosh brought over a thousand Highlanders, in chief part from the clan Mackintosh. Forster, as commander, surrendered "at discretion" to a force of hardly a thousand men, in spite of the protests of Mackintosh and others.

that the English Jacobites would rise. In this they were disappointed, however, and after a brief campaign the rebels surrendered at Preston, on the same day that Sheriffmuir was being fought.

Three ballads which seem approximately contemporary with the Fifteen, record the events of the northern half in a fashion that has won them long-enduring popularity. In practically any collection of Scottish verse one may find them,— "The Chevalier's Muster Roll," "Up and War Them A', Willie," and "Sherifmuir." The earliest texts I have been able to find are the versions printed in Herd's first collection, the 1769 *Scots Songs*.[34] Since that time they have been reprinted with additions and emendations to suit the whims of various editors.

Three other songs on the same campaign, less widely known, but apparently written not long after the event, should be mentioned in passing. "The Marquis of Huntley's Retreat"[35] is "a song made by some of the Grants . . . . . in obloquy of . . . . . the Gordons,"[36] and offers nothing of interest. "Aikendrum," first printed, I believe, by Hogg,[37] is even more unintelligible than he realized. Perhaps it is the Shepherd's own coinage. The third is the only song on

---

[34] *"The Ancient and Modern Scots Songs, Heroic Ballads"*, etc. [David Herd], Edinburgh, 1769. Herd did not tell where he found his songs, but I am inclined to believe they are approximately contemporary. "The Chevalier's Muster Roll" is not the sort of a song that would have been written after the rebellion had ended. There is a note in the *Museum*, IV, 220*, indicating that a version of "Up and Waur them A', Willie" had appeared in 1752, in *The Charmer*, a collection to which I have not had access. The third, "Sheriffmuir", is generally attributed to the Rev. Murdoch M'Lennan, (1701-1783). If he was the author, and the Editors of the *Centenary Burns* accept the ascription without question, (III, 357), the song was probably written before the Forty-five had taken place. An added reason for thinking these songs to be contemporary, is the fact that in 1769, when Herd published them, the Jacobite "revival" had not begun.

[35] The oldest text seems to be in Maidment's *A New Book of Old Ballads*, from which place Professor Child copied it for his *Ballads*, (*British Poets*), VII, 267.

[36] *Hogg*, II, 255.

[37] Ibid. II, 22. See the notes, p. 258.

the Fifteen containing a direct reference to King James's part
in the rising that I have been able to find. It is printed in
Peter Buchan's *Gleanings*,[38] and may very well be genuine;
I quote six of the stanzas :—

> "Here begins the guid New Year,
>   My mantle, my mantle,
> Guid bless us a' that 's present here,
>   My mantle 's on the green hay. (refrain *passim*.)
>
> *   *   *   *   *
>
> "King James is land't at Peterhead,
> Ane honor great to us indeed.
>
> *   *   *   *   *
>
> "He slept a' night in our good town
> Upon a guid saft bed o' down.
>
> "In the morning when he raise
> The Marischal's baillie brush'd his claithes.
>
> *   *   *   *   *
>
> "He's come to set auld Scotland free
> From curs'd Hanover's tyranny.
> "Them that does not wish him well,
>   My mantle, my mantle,
> May highland clans wi' German steel
>   Lay their mantles on the green hay."

In the little group of songs dealing with the southern invasion, James Radcliffe, third Earl of Derwentwater, is the
central figure. A stall ballad "On the First Rebellion"[39] was
not necessarily written after the Forty-five, despite the title
in Ritson's collection. The name may have been changed to fit
the exigencies of the occasion. It does not seem like a retrospective song, though it is possible that the execution of the
younger Derwentwater, in 1746, in fulfillment of the sentence
passed in 1716, recalled the fate of the elder brother, and
gave the necessary inspiration to the balladist.

Much more interesting is the traditional ballad, "Lord Derwentwater."[40] Derwentwater is the central figure; the only

[38] Page 149. *Gleanings of Scotch, English, and Irish scarce old
Ballads, chiefly tragical and historical*, Peterhead, 1825.

[39] *Northern Garland*, ed. Ritson, London, 1810; "The Northumberland
Garland", 85. Hogg prints a version of this as "An excellent New
Song on the Rebellion", *Hogg*, II, 102.

[40] *Child*, IV, 115; no. 208.

reference to the Stuarts or their claim occurs in the tenth stanza. After describing Derwentwater's summons to court, his will, and briefly, the ride to London, the account continues :—

> "When they came into fair London town
> Into the courtiers' hall,
> The lords and knichts in fair London town
> Did him a traitor call.

> "'A traitor! a traitor!' says my lord,
> 'A traitor! how can that be,
> An it was na for the keeping of five thousand men
> To fight for King Jamie?'"[41]

It is the last of the popular ballads with which we shall be concerned.

Derwentwater was executed in February, 1716. A good many songs have been written lamenting his fate, but few of them are contemporary. A formal poem in the *Towneley MS.*, "On the Executions in — 1716,"[42] is interesting solely because of its unquestionable authenticity. Hogg's "O Beautiful Brittania"[43] is undoubtedly a contemporary song, written soon after the rising, but thoroughly pedestrian. "By Carnousie's Auld Wa's" and "When the King Comes O'er the Water," both popular, are without much doubt spurious.[44]

After the utter collapse of the Fifteen, the Jacobites tried to get help from Charles XII, then finishing a disastrous reign as King of Sweden. Two songs of questionable antiquity refer more or less directly to this plan, but offer nothing of special interest.[45]

Hogg, and various editors since his time, printed other

[41] Ibid. IV, 117, ᴀ Text.

[42] Page 93.

[43] *Hogg*, I, 141.

[44] The former was not printed till 1861, in Mackay's *Jacobite Songs and Ballads of Scotland,* and is a worked over version of Burns's "There'll Never be Peace Till Jamie Comes Hame." The second seems to have been first printed by Hogg, (I, 45,) to whom I charge responsibility for the song and the legend that it was written by Lady Keith.

[45] The first is "Weel May We A' Be", *Museum*, IV, 167; the second, "Here's A Health to the Valiant Swede", which I have not found printed earlier than *Hogg*, II, 44.

songs on the Fifteen which have passed current. A few of these, notably "Will Ye Go to Sheriffmuir?" [46] and "The Auld Stuarts Back Again," [47] one dislikes to give up, for they are good songs. But I can find no evidence that they deserve to be included in this class of contemporary documents, and not a little that they are retrospective. [48]

This list of genuine Relics of the first rebellion is not long enough to warrant many generalizations, but one fact seems of sufficient importance to be noted. Loyalty to the Stuarts is all but entirely absent. Clan feeling and sympathy for Derwentwater underly the best ballads, but it is only occasionally that such sentiments appear as might have been expected from a nation in arms to support the exiled house. Hogg and his friends filled their retrospective songs with a sentimental sort of loyalty which has been accepted as indicative of the attitude of the highlanders and other Jacobites in the army. But in the contemporary songs this is conspicuously absent, a fact that seems to confirm the opinion that even by 1715 distrust of the Stuarts, or at least indifference to their fate, had become much more general than Mar and his unfortunate associates realized.

C.

"THE FORTY-FIVE"

Thirty years after James Stuart made his first attempt to regain the throne, his son Charles Edward led the clans in the last Jacobite rebellion. Charles landed in Scotland as his father's representative, and in all proclamations, manifestoes, and orders, signed himself simply "Prince Regent." In fact, however, he was the heart and soul of the rising. Without his personal appeal to Cameron of Lochiel, the first chieftain in arms, it is doubtful whether the loyalists could have gathered

[46] *Hogg*, I, 149.

[47] Ibid. I, 122.

[48] Hogg seems to have been the first man to discover them, a fact in itself enough to create suspicion. Moreover, they are unlike the undoubtedly contemporary songs which have survived, and exactly of a piece with the work which the Shepherd and his friends were doing in the early part of the nineteenth century.

a single regiment. During the march into England, and even more noticeably during the retreat, the Prince proved an able leader. Throughout his stay in Great Britain his personal popularity did far more to make the Forty-five, for a time at least, a formidable rebellion, than any claim his father may have had to the English throne.

Partly because of this genuine popularity of the Prince, and partly because the early successes of the Jacobites gave great encouragement to their ballad makers, the number of songs on the Forty-five is surprisingly large. If several formal addresses, and an ode or two be included, there are, I believe, some thirty contemporary songs or poems on the rising. Many written by Hogg, Allan Cunningham, and others, and printed as genuine relics, are, with those of doubtful age, left out of consideration.

Of these, the earliest, in point of time, are eight songs or poems written apparently before the battle of Prestonpans, indicative of the state of mind of the Loyalists at the very outbreak of the rebellion.[49] Without exception they are uninteresting, and nearly as fulsome as the poetry addressed to Charles II in 1660. I quote three stanzas from the *Towneley MS.*, as the best illustration of this class:—

> "To all loyal subjects glad tidings I bring;
> Come let us be merry and joyfully sing,
> And drink a health round to the son of our King
> The royal and charming bright Laddy,
>
> "Who now is arrived on our Scottish shore
> Demanding his own, & asking no more
> But to banish the usurping son of a w——e
> Who possesses the right of our Laddy.

>   *   *   *   *   **

[49] "June 10, 1745", in the 1745 *Edinburgh Collection,* 14; "On the Tenth of June", *Towneley MS.* 106; "To All Loyal Subjects", Ibid. 79; "The Gracious Declaration", *Hogg,* II, 302; "My Laddie", (of uncertain age), ibid. I, 115; "The Clans are Coming", *Ritson,* II, 85; "He Comes, the Hero Comes", *Hogg,* II, 82; "Britons who Dare to Claim", ibid. II, 52, or *Towneley MS. 77.*

"Let Jehovah have glory, the King have the crown;
O Heaven, assist him! (he wants but his own)
To pull usurpation and tyranny down,
And prosper the cause of our Laddy." [50]

Two popular and spirited songs which ostensibly belong to the same class I am sure are retrospective: "The Athol Gathering," [51] and "Wha Wadna Fight for Charlie." [52] Burns's "The White Cockade," first published in the *Museum*,[53] is an adaptation of "The Ranting Roving Lad," printed in Herd's 1776 collection, p. 179, not, as the editors of the *Centenary Burns* state,[54] in Herd's 1769 collection. It is barely possible that in the older song more is meant than meets the ear, and that it is a veiled Jacobitism. On the face of it, however, it is simply a love song.

The first actual battle in the Forty-five took place at Prestonpans, 22 September, 1745, after the Prince had occupied the town of Edinburgh. The result is familiar to all readers of *Waverley*. One charge of the Highlanders drove Cope's regulars from the field in a panic, and left Charles virtually master of Scotland. Contemporary record of the victory exists in the shape of some eleven songs or poems, a few of which are widely known. Some, on the other hand, may be dismissed with a mention of their titles in the note.[55] Better than these is "A Song Made in the Year 1745," which I have found only in the *Towneley MS.*[56] It is a chronicle of events from the landing of the Prince till after Prestonpans, written by

[50] Page 79.
[51] *Hogg*, II, 97. This I credit to the Shepherd himself.
[52] Ibid. 100.
[53] No. 272.
[54] III, 353.
[55] In this list are "Hail Happy Scotland", *Towneley MS*. 118 and 190; "On the Signal Victory at Gladsmuir", 1745 *Edinburgh Collection*, 17; "Ode to C. P. R. after the Battle of Gladsmuir", ibid. 18; "Now Charles Asserts his Father's Rights", *Hogg*, II, 159; and "General Cope's Travels", Mackay's *Jacobite Songs*, 240. William Hamilton of Bangour, a Jacobite who suffered temporary exile for his loyalty, wrote soon after the battle an "Ode on Prestonpans", and sometime later "A Soliloquy", both of which may be found in his collected works, Edinburgh, 1850.
[56] Page 56.

some one who drew freely from the older ''Up and War Them A', Willie'' and who also furnished Adam Skirving with a few hints for ''Prestonpans.''

Skirving's two ballads on this battle, ''Johnnie Cope'' and ''Prestonpans'', are among the best that the Jacobites ever wrote. The former seems to have been reprinted more often than any I have found, and occurs not infrequently outside of strictly Scottish collections. Skirving, ''although a Jacobite, and apparently a spectator of the battle, ... seems to have taken no other part in the rising than by singing ballads about it.'' [57] But he wrote ballads which are better than even ''Killiecrankie'' or ''Sheriffmuir.'' [58] The second of his two productions was printed, according to Professor Child, ''shortly after the battle as a broadside.'' [59] Like the first, it is easily accessible.

One more ballad on Prestonpans completes the list. ''The Mayor of Carlisle,'' printed by Hogg in a slightly improved form,[60] is inferior to Skirving's work in almost every respect, but should be noted because it is the only surely contemporary ballad I have been able to find containing a reference to the capture of Carlisle by the Jacobites.[61] In other respects it is unimportant.

After taking Carlisle the Prince's army marched south, finally reaching Derby, where, 5 December, 1745, they began the retreat into Scotland. There are few contemporary Jacobite accounts of the rest of the campaign. *Arms and the*

---

[57] D. N. B. LII, 358.

[58] The best text of "Johnnie Cope" seems to be the one printed in *Ritson*, II, 84, as a "variation". Hogg prints this as his "second set", II, 113. Burns furnished a version to the *Museum*, no. 234, beginning
    "Sir John Cope trode the North right far".

[59] *Child (British Poets)*, VII, 167. In "Arms and the Man", London, 1746, occurs an account of the rising interesting because it is surprisingly lenient towards the Highlanders. Hogg's version of this, II, 140, has been worked over by some hand.

[60] *Hogg*, II, 134. A better text may be found in *Ritson*, II, 90.

[61] Carlisle was subsequently retaken after the Prince had left it on his retreat into Scotland, and many of its defenders executed. Among these was Col. Francis Towneley, leader of a small band of English Jacobites, whose French commission did not save him.

Man, and its *Sequel,* both London documents,[62] tell of General
Hawley's defeat at Falkirk, 17 January, 1746, and of a skirmish in which the Prince's rear-guard under Lord George
Murray worsted a detachment of royal dragoons at Clifton.
Hogg prints two songs on Falkirk, ''The Battle of Falkirk,'' [63]
and ''The Highlandmen Came Down the Hill,'' [64] which are
surely retrospective, possibly his own work.

On the sixteenth of April, 1746, the Duke of Cumberland
won the battle of Culloden, and put an end to the Forty-five.
I have not found a single contemporary loyalist account of
this disaster. Plenty of songs were written sixty years later,
but none, apparently, at the time.[65]

After Culloden, and largely as a result of the rigorous
measures which the government took to prevent any future
rising, there appeared a number of songs attacking the
''Bloody Duke,'' or lamenting the execution of the Scottish
Lords, and a few pledging loyalty to the cause and urging a
third attempt.

The songs of the first class are uninteresting, despite their
undoubted sincerity.[66] Two songs in Hogg's *Relics,* ''The
Battle of Val'' [67] and ''Up and Rin Awa', Willie,''[68] do not
seem to have been written till some time after the affair.
Burns's ''I Hae Been at Crookieden,'' first published in the
Museum,[69] is said by the editors of the *Centenary* to be
''founded on an old Jacobite rhyme,'' [70] but no traces of it

[62] See note 59.

[63] *Hogg*, II, 136.

[64] Ibid. II, 138.

[65] The song ''Red Clan-Ronald's Men'', *Jacobite Minstrelsy*, p. 302,
is pretty surely retrospective.

[66] See for example, the two ''epitaphs'', *Hogg*, II, 375; ''Thou Butcher
of the Northern Clime'', *Towneley*, 78; ''Towneleys Ghost,'' ibid., facsimile
frontispiece, a rather good song, reminiscent in the first stanza of
David Mallett's ''William and Margaret.'' This is misprinted by Hogg
as ''Towley's Ghost.''

[67] *Hogg*, II, 196.

[68] Ibid. II, 177.

[69] No. 332.

[70] Op. Cit. III, 374.

are discoverable today.[71] "Cumberland and Murray's Descent into Hell," the most popular of all these attacks on the Duke, is the work of Allan Cunningham.[72]

As would be expected, the executions and banishments occasioned many laments for the victims. Several in the *Towneley MS.*[73] are obviously sincere, but otherwise negligible. The *Roxburghe Ballads* offer two, "Lady Kilmarnock's Lament,"[74] and "Lady Balmerino's Lament."[75] Shenstone's "Jemmy Dawson" is fairly well known, and may with some hesitation be included in the same class. Hogg preserves two which seem to date from approximately the end of the rising: "To All that Virtue's Holy Ties Can Boast,"[76] a formal attack on Murray of Broughton, who turned state's evidence, and "The Highlander's Lament."[77] Smollett's "Tears of Scotland," one of his earliest publications, is more widely known than it deserves to be. Ritson has a probably contemporary lament beginning "Let Mournful Britons now Deplore,"[78] most inappropriately set to the tune of "The Campbells are Coming." Only one song seems worthy of quotation here, and that chiefly for the reason that it does not seem to have been printed. On page 815 of the "original Buchan MS.,"[79] Harvard College library no. 25241.10, marked "N. P.,"— not published,—occurs "The Earl of Kilmarnock's Lament."

[71] Possibly a song in *The Bards of Bon Accord*, p. 192, represents the older version used by Burns. It does not seem likely, however.

[72] Using this song, with Burns's "I hae Been at Crookieden", and the anonymous "Though Geordie Reigns in James's Stead", someone concocted "Geordie Sits in Charlie's Chair", obviously retrospective.

[73] See "Verses on Lord Balmerino", p. 9; "To the Same Pretended Duke", p. 84; "If you the Paths of Honor Trod", p. 45; and others, *passim*.

[74] Op. Cit. VIII, 309.

[75] Ibid. VIII, 310. See "The Wandering Blackbird", Ibid. 311.

[76] In couplets; *Hogg*, II, 372.

[77] This second is of questionable age. It first appeared in the *Museum*, no. 588. *Hogg*, II, 170.

[78] *Ritson*, II, 92.

[79] "A volume entirely in Buchan's writing 'which contains all [the ballads] that Buchan ever collected except some "high kilted" ones in another volume'". (*Child*, V, 398).

It is probably retrospective; perhaps the work of James
Rankine :—

> "Hey my Eppie
> How my Eppie
> Sae lang's she'll think ere she see me now;
> In strong prison I ly,
> Has no power to fly,
> An' I'll never return to my Eppie, I trow.
>
> "Farewell to my Eppie
> My wish be wi' Eppie,
> Too soon will my Eppie receive my adieu;
> My sentence is past
> The morn is my last,
> An' I'll never won hame to my Eppie, I trow.
>
> "O Eppie my dearest
> O Eppie my fairest,
> Sae mony sweet nights I hae spent wi' you;
> Now cauld is my hands,
> Sleet in iron bands
> I'll never mair stretch them, dear Eppie, to you.
>   —Farewell, etc.
>
> "The charge is prepared,
> The lawyers are met,
> The judges have raised a terrible show;
> I gang undismayed,
> My life is a debt,
> A debt of demands, sae take what I owe.
>
> "Wi' the trumpet's loud sounding
> The city 's rebounding,
> Us that 's poor pannels to our sentence maun bow;
> An' the morn 's the knell
> O' our sepulchre's bell,
> 'Twill be a sad start to our Eppie, I trow.
>
> "But though I maun die
> I boldly defy,
> My faes for to say that my crime I do rue;
> Nor needs my proud kin
> Be ashamed of my sin,
> But sad will the heart of my Eppie be, now.
>
> "Good angels be keeping
> Her while she is sleeping,
> Cause fate may present my sad fate to her view;

And when I am dead
Support her widow'd head,
For sad will the heart of my Eppie be now.
—Farewell, etc."

Still more recent than these laments are a few songs written some time after Culloden, pledging loyalty to the cause,
and describing the condition of the Jacobites.[80] Hogg preserves a few of uncertain date,[81] and at least one, of some
value, which may possibly, as the gloss to the title indicates, be
a production of 1746. The title is interesting, and indicates
the general tone of the poem:—

"A ballad for those whose honour is sound,
Who cannot be named, and must not be found."

I quote the last stanza:—

"A health to those fam'd Gladsmuir gained,
And circled Derby's cross;
Who won Falkirk, and boldly strain'd
To win Culloden moss.
Health to all those who'll do't again,
And no just cause decline.
May Charles soon vanquish, and James reign,
As they did lang syne."[82]

Some time before 1769,—for the song is published in Herd's
collection of that year,—Dougal Graham, bellman of Glasgow,
wrote what may fairly be called the last contemporary Jacobite lyric, "Turnimspike." It is a *resumé* of the state of
affairs in Scotland after Culloden, a humourous ballad put
into the mouth of a Highlander. It has been popular ever
since Herd printed it, and is easily accessible.[83] After this

[80] Five in the *Towneley MS.* deserve passing mention. They are:
"The Loyal Resolutions", p. 20; "England's Prayer", p. 87; "The
Patriot", p. 117; (these three in couplets); "A Litany for the Year
1750", p. 108; and "From Caledonia's Loyal Lands", pp. 1 and 55.

[81] "Come Let us be Jovial", *Hogg*, II, 71, and "Be Valiant Still",
ibid. 89, are puzzling. "An Yon be He", ibid. 77, is made over from
a set in the *Museum,* and does not appear, even in its new dress, to
be a Jacobite lyric at all.

[82] *Hogg*, II, 169.

[83] *Hogg*, II, 109.

the "Poetry of the Jacobites" becomes merely "Jacobite Poetry," and that is another story.[84]

FRANKLYN BLISS SNYDER.

Northwestern University.

[84] The following works are cited by the abbreviations under which each is listed here:—

1745 Ed. Coll. "Collection of all Poems upon Charles, Prince of Wales." Edinburgh, 1745.

Child. "The English and Scottish Popular Ballads." Edited by F. J. Child; five vols., Boston, 1882-1898.

Child (British Poets). "English and Scottish Ballads." Selected and edited by F. J. Child; eight vols., Boston, 1857-1859.

Hogg. "The Jacobite Relics of Scotland." James Hogg; two vols., Edinburgh, 1819, 1821.

Jacobite Minstrelsy. "Jacobite Minstrelsy, with notes illustrative of the text," etc. [Edited Robert Malcolm?]; Glasgow, 1829.

Minstrelsy. Sir Walter Scott's *Minstrelsy of the Scottish Border.*" Edited by T. F. Henderson; four vols., Edinburgh, 1902.

Museum. "The Scots Musical Museum." James Johnson; six vols., Edinburgh, [1787-1803.] Edited in four vols. by William Stenhouse, Edinburgh, 1853.

Pasquils. "A Book of Scottish Pasquils. 1568-1715." [James Maidment]; Edinburgh, 1868.

Ritson. "Scotish Song." [Joseph Ritson]; two vols., London, 1794.

Rox. Bal. "The Roxburghe Ballads", with notes, vols. I-III by W. Chappell; vols. IV-IX edited by J. W. Ebsworth; London, 1871-1897.

Rump Songs. "An Exact Collection of Ye Choicest Poems & Songs, Relating to the late times, & continued by the most eminent witts, from Ao 1630 to 1661." London, 1662.

Towneley MS. "The Towneley Jacobite MS.; English Jacobite Ballads, Songs, and Satires." Edited A. B. Grosart, 1877. Privately printed.

Wilkins. "Political Ballads of the Seventeenth and Eighteenth Centuries." Annotated by W. Walker Wilkins; two vols., London, 1860.

THE USE OF COMIC MATERIAL IN THE TRAGEDY OF SHAKESPEARE AND HIS CONTEMPORARIES.

It is one of the commonplaces of criticism that the drama of Shakespeare's time is characterized by the commingling of serious and comic material in a manner peculiarly its own. And a widely prevalent opinion treats Shakespeare himself as representing this romantic mixture almost in its extreme form. Dr. Johnson's statement may be taken as typical, that all Shakespeare's plays are "an interchange of seriousness and merriment," and that "in tragedy he is always struggling after some occasion to be comic."[1] To this intermingling of comic and serious details the critics of the 17th and 18th centuries gave the name "tragi-comedy," confusing it with the quite different practice of mingling two plots of contrasting characteristics, or the still different one of bringing an apparently tragic situation to a happy conclusion. Often it is hard to say just which type of romantic fault is in question. Whetstone (Preface to *Promos and Cassandra*, 1578) objects to those who "make a clown companion with a king;"[2] Milton (Preface to *Samson Agonistes*, 1671) condemns the "error of intermixing comic stuff with tragic sadness and gravity, or introducing trivial and vulgar persons;" Rymer (*Tragedies of the Last Age*, 1678) alludes severely to the "drolls" who "make a sort of interlude" in Elizabethan tragedy;[3] Dryden (Preface to *The Spanish Friar*, 1681) speaks of tragedies that are "lightened with a course of mirth;"[4] Addison (*Spectator*, No. 40, 1711) describes under the term "tragi-comedy" the kind of play which is "a motley piece of mirth and sorrow;" and Hawkesworth (Prologue to the rewritten *Oronooko*, 1759) charges Southerne with having "joined the buskin and the sock" and stained "with ribald mirth . . . . . the sacred page" of tragedy.[5] Obvious-

---

[1] Preface to Shakespeare; *Works*, ed. 1801, ii, 87, 88.

[2] *Elizabethan Critical Essays* (ed. Gregory Smith), i, 59.

[3] *Critical Essays of the 17th Century*, ed. Spingarn, ii, 206.

[4] *Essays*, ed. W. P. Ker, i, 249.

[5] For other comments on the same subject, see Lounsbury's *Shakespeare as a Dramatic Artist*, pp. 142-158.

ly these various critics had in mind dramas of quite different kinds, such as—at one extreme—those predominatingly tragic but containing perhaps a single comic interlude, and—at the other—those in which a serious and a comic plot are intertwined.

Despite the numerous attacks directed against such usages in earlier periods, and corresponding apologies in our own time, there has been very little effort to examine the Elizabethan practice, or even that of Shakespeare, with a view to ascertaining without prejudice just how far the mingling of tragic and comic scenes really went, and what it may be thought to have signified in the art of the dramatists concerned. It is the object of this paper to ask these questions, and to make some attempt to answer them by examining the practice of Shakespeare in relation to that of his contemporaries.

It should be made clear at the outset that our study cannot take into account by any means all the elements of wit and humor which were introduced into tragedy in the period studied. To attempt any census or analysis of these, as they flash momentarily in dialogue, would be venturesome indeed. Only those passages are to be considered which are clearly the result of an intention to awaken laughter in the audience; and such passages usually involve something of the ridiculous in action as well as in speech. When scenes of this character are duly enumerated in the tragedies of Elizabethan times, they are seen to fall into certain fairly distinguishable classes.

1. Perhaps most characteristic, and certainly earliest in development, was what may be called the clown interlude. We can easily trace the origins of this in familiar scenes in the mysteries and other early serious popular plays, where the desire for variety was satisfied by farcical sub-action carried on by personages of low life.[6] As soon as popular tragedy emerges on the Elizabethan stage, scenes set for a clown—sometimes called simply ''clown,'' sometimes by name—appear; we may

[6] The notable examples, of course, are the *Noah* and *Secunda Pastorum* of the Wakefield cycle. For discussion of the comic elements here, see Professor Gayley's essay in *Representative English Comedies*, i, p. xxviii.

take as typical the scene between Wagner and the Clown in
Marlowe's *Faustus*.[7]   When these clowns are identified as
individuals with a normal environment, they are commonly
country boors or servants of rural origin, but it seems impossible to draw the line between the true clown of this character and the servant of more sophisticated sort.[8]   For the London public of Shakespeare's time the servant-class seems to
have proved amusing almost without limit; why this is true,
—why, for that matter, house-servants in England seem to
this day to afford those whom they serve rather more fun
than in most other familiar countries,—let the wise explain.
It is clear enough to any reader of Elizabethan drama that
when the servants appear comedy may be looked for, no less
in tragedy than elsewhere.   Some representative scenes may
be cited as exemplifying the indefinable passing over of the
pure clown interlude, accomplished by a character recognized
clearly as "clown," into the servant-interlude where some
realistic humor of character is availed of to give the same sort
of variety with rather less interruption of the main action.
In *The Spanish Tragedy*, Act III, occurs an interlude scene
(v) in which a servant-boy soliloquizes amusingly; while in
the following scene (vi) Pedringano, servant to Bel-Imperia,
indulges in comic by-play with the hangman.   In *Arden of
Feversham* (II, ii), Michael, Arden's servant, at the opening
of a scene fraught with the most serious import, entertains
his auditors with a comic love-letter to his mistress Susan;
and again, in the first scene of Act IV, indulges in horse-
play and head-cracking with his rival the painter.   In Part
Two of *Tamburlaine* a bit of comic prose concludes the first
scene of Act IV, where Calyphas indulges in ribald dialogue
with his servant Perdicas.   In *Faustus*, besides the clown-
scene already mentioned, we have the scenes in the inn-yard
where Ralph and Robin make merry and engage together in

---

[7] Scene iv.

[8] For the connection of "clown" with a definite social class, compare
the line from a Robin Hood ballad: "Both gentleman, yeoman, and
clown." And for the disputed etymology of the word, as well as for
a general discussion of the clown on the stage, see J. Thümmel, *Ueber
Shakespeare's Clowns, Jahrbuch*, xi, 78.

the conjuring of Mephistopheles. In *The Jew of Malta,* Ithamore, Barabas's slave, adds comic touches to the villainy of
the action in several scenes of Act IV, and in the last of them
Barabas himself condescends to take an amusing part. In
Marston's *Antonio's Revenge* the servant Nutriche provides
two or three comic scenes, in this case rather more closely interwoven with the main plot than commonly. Finally we
may note the interesting group of servant interludes in Heywood's *A Woman Killed with Kindness,* which are less purely
clownish and more realistically human than almost any of the
period except the Nurse scenes in *Romeo and Juliet.* Heywood, in other words, caught the notion of making his comic
figures blend with the tragic action through their loyal concern with it.[9]

2. One may distinguish from these interlude scenes a
few instances where a character of the clown type, or a substitute type, develops into such importance as to reappear in
a number of scenes at intervals, and to form a kind of secondary motif or even under-plot for the play. Of this the
earliest instance is the anonymous *Locrine,* where there is
interwoven with the stately scenes of the chronicle a series of
appearances of Strumbo the cobbler (whose companions are
significantly called "clowns" in the list of *dramatis personae*); at length, in the second scene of Act IV, the Strumbo

[9] Notice especially the figure of Jenkin, in II, iii, IV, iii, and V, iii.
Before leaving these servant clowns it may be pleasant to recall how
M. Maeterlinck has experimented with the Elizabethan practice, to
vary the usual monotone of his poetic tragedies, in one scene of
Pelléas and Mélisande (V, i). While the princess is dying, upstairs,
the old cook in the kitchen discourses in precisely the irrelevant humor
of the ancient interlude: "Mais oui, mais oui; c'est moi qui les ai
trouvés. Le portier dit que c'est lui qui les a vus le premier; mais
c'est moi qui l'ai réveillé. Il dormait sur le ventre et ne voulait pas se
lever. Et maintenant il vient dire: C'est moi qui les ai vus le premier.
Est-ce que c'est juste? Voyez-vous, je m'étais brûlée en allumant une
lampe pour descendre à la cave. Qu'est-ce que j'allais donc faire à
la cave? Je ne peux plus me rappeler. Enfin, je me lève à cinq
heures; il ne faisait pas encore très clair; je me dis, je vais traverser la
cour, et puis, je vais ouvrir la porte. Bien; je descends l'escalier sur
la pointe des pieds et j'ouvre la porte comme si c'était une porte
ordinaire. Mon Dieu! Mon Dieu! Qu'est-ce que je vois!"

motif is fused with that of the tragic action. The comic appearances of Mephistopheles in *Faustus* might be regarded as a development of the same character, as indeed might the Ithamore scenes in *The Jew of Malta* and one or two other examples already discussed. The Snuff scenes of *The Atheist's Tragedy* represent a late appearance of a similar sort; and so—with the primitive clown fashion now entirely laid aside—do the Calianax scenes of *The Maid's Tragedy*. But the most striking example of a tragedy in which the clown scenes rise to equal importance with those of tragic import is Heywood's *The Rape of Lucrece*. Here there is not only a clown, so-called, who appears in some half-dozen interludes, but in addition there is a comic singer, Valerius, whose ribald songs are related to the classic story in inverse proportion to their importance in popular interest. The abandon with which the dramatist permits the climax of the action, the dishonor of Lucrece, actually to be related in one of these comic ditties, is perhaps the nadir of the Elizabethan refusal to keep tragedy and comedy asunder.

3. Another stage of development of comic sub-action is the appearance of humorous or witty dialogue on the part, not of clownish servants or other supernumeraries, but of the principal, or at least the respectable, actors,—those whose social position puts them near the head of the list of persons. This sort of thing appears but slightly in the tragedy of the Shakespearean period, though Mephistopheles might be classed here, and Tamburlaine and Barabas on one or two occasions.[10] Tourneur's *The Atheist's Tragedy* is perhaps the earliest play to exhibit this kind of comic dialogue conspicu-

[10] Brome, in a well-known passage in *The Antipodes*, in which the extemporaneous talk of clown actors is reprobated, suggests that in the earlier period it was understood that the fooling would be largely left to the players' wit:

> Yes, in the dayes of Tarlton and Kempe,
> Before the stage was purg'd from barabarisme,
> And brought to the perfection it now shines with,
> Then fooles and jesters spent their wits, because
> The poets were wise enough to save their owne
> For profitabler uses.

(II, ii.)

ously,—in connection, here, with the more clownish type.
Beaumont and Fletcher used it effectively, beginning with
The Maid's Tragedy and *Cupid's Revenge,* with a noticeable
preference for wit over humor, and an atmosphere of satiric
disillusion which is suggestive—like so much of their work—
of the mixed plays of the Restoration period; this mood being
rather more inharmonious with the tragic spirit than the
broadest humor of earlier days. But the blending of serious
and comic in the chief characters and scenes is most striking
in the two great tragedies of Webster's. In *The White Devil,*
Flamineo may be said to embody in himself the spirit of this
strange blend, which finds its most daring expression at the
moment when he is near death. "Whither shall I go now?
. . . . . To find Alexander the Great cobbling shoes,
Pompey tagging points, and Julius Caesar making hair but-
tons!" . . . . . "I have caught an everlasting cold. I
have lost my voice most irrecoverably." In *The Duchess of
Malfy* there is no such representative character, but even more
of the effect of medley,—medley which we are sure expresses
not merely a stage practice, but the dramatist's view of human
life.

4. A final development of comic action in tragedy is represented in no play strictly of the Shakespearean period:
namely, the type in which two plots of approximately equal
importance, one tragic and the other comic, are intertwined.
At the very end, apparently, of the period of Shakespeare's
work,[11] this type is exhibited in Marston's *The Insatiate
Countess.* Here a broadly comic underplot not merely inter-
weaves itself with the serious portion of the "tragedy," but
actually supersedes the latter and controls the final scene.
In reaching this point we have attained the development of
the comic interlude into the true "tragi-comedy."

These being the types of comic by-play which are to be
looked for in the tragedy of our period, it remains to inquire to what extent they pervade that tragedy. We shall
exclude, for the time being, the tragedies of Shakespeare, in
order to compare his practice more readily with that of his
predecessors and contemporaries. Aside from his plays, the

[11] Schelling puts its date of composition as 1610-1613.

number of extant tragedies from the time of *Gorboduc* to 1611 or thereabouts is close to fifty. From these it will be proper to exclude, for our purposes, plays which distinctly follow the type of chronicle-history, such as *The True Tragedy of Richard III* and *The Tragedy of Thomas Woodstock*, except where, as in *Locrine*, the innovation of comic material is found. In general, of course, the comic interlude is not characteristic of chronicle-history. We may also throw out the whole group of tragedies generally called Senecan, including, besides *Gorboduc, Jocasta, The Misfortunes of Arthur*, and their like, the dramas of Daniel, Fulke Greville, and Sir William Alexander, and the translations of Garnier; for in these Senecan and closet dramas comic interlude or by-play was undreamed of. This done, there remain about thirty tragedies of our fifty; and these, as luck will have it, may be divided into three groups of not dissimilar size. The first is made up of plays which are practically without comic scenes; it includes Peele's *David and Bethsabe* and *The Battle of Alcazar;* the anonymous *A Warning for Fair Women;* Marston's *Sophonisba;* Jonson's *Sejanus* and *Catiline;* Chapman's *Revenge of Bussy* and *Tragedy of Biron;* and Barnes's *The Devil's Charter.*[12] (Most of these tragedies, it will be noticed, date from some time after 1600.) The second group is formed of the plays in which comic material appears in a few isolated scenes—sometimes in one only, sometimes in three or four,—varying from momentary comic dialogue to a succession of interludes like those already cited from *A Woman Killed with Kindness.* The tragedies of this character are: Kyd's *The Spanish Tragedy* (III, v and vi);[13] *Arden of Feversham* (II, ii; IV, i and ii); *Tamburlaine*, Pt. 2 (III, v;

[12] In *A Warning for Fair Women* there are two scenes where lowly *genre* characters are introduced, with momentary comic effects if the actors chose to avail themselves of the opportunity,—the scenes of Barnes and Beane and of John and Joan (Simpson's *School of Shakespeare*, vol. ii, pp. 275, 291.) The same question may be raised regarding *The Devil's Charter,* where the ruffians Frescobaldi and Baglioni (III, ii and V, i) exhibit a grim humor which may or may not have been emphasized on the stage.

[13] For convenience of reference, I note roughly the scenes enumerated for this classification. Obviously no two readers would be likely

IV, i) ; *The Jew of Malta* (IV, II, iii, iv, and vi) ; *Lust's Dominion* (III, v; IV, v) ; Chapman's *Bussy d'Ambois* (I, ii) ; Heywood's *A Woman Killed with Kindness* (I, ii; II, iii; IV, iii; V, iii) ; Tourneur's *The Revenger's Tragedy* (II, i) ; [14] Beaumont and Fletcher's *Cupid's Revenge* (I, i; II, i; III, i; IV, i (?)). The third group consists of the plays in which comic elements are introduced repeatedly, or to an extent sufficient to suggest a mixed type of drama; namely: *Locrine* (I, ii; II, ii and iii; III, iii; IV, ii) ; Kyd's *Soliman and Perseda* (I, iii and iv; II, ii; III, ii; IV, ii; V, iii) ; Marlowe's *Faustus* (Scenes iv, vii, viii, ix, xi) ; Marston's *Antonio's Revenge* (I, ii; II, i; III, ii; IV, i; V, i) ; Chettle's *Hoffman* (Acts I, II, III, *passim*) ; Heywood's *The Rape of Lucrece* (*passim*) ; Tourneur's *The Atheist's Tragedy* (I, iii; II, i, vi; IV, i, iii, iv, v; V, i) ; Beaumont and Fletcher's *The Maid's Tragedy* (I, ii; II, i; III, i, ii; IV, ii; V, ii) ; Marston's *The Insatiate Countess* (I, i; II, i; III, i, iii; IV, iv; V, ii) ; Webster's *The White Devil* (I, ii; II, i; III, i; V, i, iii, iv, vi) ; *The Duchess of Malfy* (I, i; II, i, ii; III, ii, iii; IV, ii; [15] V, ii).

With this analysis of the practice of his contemporaries in mind, let us now turn to the tragedies of Shakespeare. In *Romeo and Juliet,* perhaps his earliest tragedy, there appears at once a strikingly large amount of comic material. The play opens with a roystering servants' scene, while conventional house-servants furnish comic interlude briefly at the opening of I, v and IV, ii. Further there is a servant called "the clown" who furnishes a typical clown interlude in I, ii ("I am sent to find those persons whose names are here writ,

to agree in all the details of such a choice, and I cannot hope to have avoided overlooking some scenes which may deserve mention quite as much as those indicated.

[14] In addition to the comic dialogue of this scene one may note the bitter humor of Vendice, *passim*.

[15] This is the madmen's scene, and represents a different type of comic effect from any that has been discussed; different, also, from any other in the period, but analogous to the Ophelia scene in *Hamlet* (IV, v). In this case laughter and pain are not so much contrasted as awakened simultaneously. Cf. Mr. John Corbin's *The Elizabethan Hamlet*.

and can never find what names the writing person hath here writ''); and another servant, named Peter, who makes a presumably comic appearance for brief moments in II, iv and v, and presents an important interlude scene at the conclusion of Act IV.[16]   Besides this wealth of by-play of the old-fashioned clownish character, we have in the personage of the Nurse a *genre* character providing comedy of manners in immediate connection with the action (see especially I, iii; II, iv and v).[17]   And lastly, in the character of Mercutio the dramatist introduces comic dialogue of the gentler sort, on the part of one of the personages who is socially, if not dramatically, important.   One might almost conceive Shakespeare as resolving, in this his first original tragedy, to outdo his contemporaries in using freely and effectively every sort of contrast and blend which the different types of comic material made possible.   But closer consideration brings out the fact that the use of this material in *Romeo and Juliet* is distinguishable for one important circumstance from practically all the tragedies which we have analyzed hitherto.   This is the fact that the comic by-play is largely massed at the beginning of the play, diminishing rapidly in the third act, and being entirely wanting in the last.   Mercutio dies, with a jest on his lips, in the first scene of Act III; the further appearances of the nurse lose their comic exuberance; and were it not for the two servant interludes which flank the seeming death of Juliet in IV, v (where we may perhaps suppose it is necessary that we should be kept back from a wholly tragic mood till the real woes to come have ripened), the entire second half of the play would be almost purely serious.   This plunge from the abundant merriment of the earlier scenes to the rapidly deepening gloom of the later ones produces a very characteristic effect; one might name it *comi-tragedy.*

[16] This interlude is distinct from all others in having no connection with the action to serve as *raison d'être,* and being therefore obviously made *ad hoc.*   It is further interesting from the fact that the stage-direction in Q2 gives evidence that the part was taken by Will Kemp, a leading comedian of the period.   Of him more hereafter.

[17] In Thümmel's article, cited above, the nurse is treated as a true clown; but other matters than her sex render this doubtful.

It need hardly be said that there is no other tragedy of Shakespeare's like *Romeo and Juliet* in respect either to the character or the arrangement of the comic details. For some time following he seems to have written no more tragedies, and when he turned again to the form he treated it, on the whole, with pervasive seriousness. The comic interlude, however, was by no means abandoned. It reappears in various forms; characteristically as a single interruption of the main action, by a clownish personage who does not appear elsewhere. In *Hamlet*, while there is an abundance of comic matter (to certain aspects of which we must return later), a single clown-scene appears in the last act, the grave-diggers being named "clowns" in the text. In *Othello* the clown is also explicitly named; he appears at the opening of Act III, parrying jests with the musicians much after the fashion of Peter in *Romeo and Juliet*.[18] In *Macbeth* the clown is the humorous Porter (II, iii), whose jests suspend the action at so critical a moment.[19] In *Antony and Cleopatra* he is again called "clown," but has now a function of some importance, as the countryman who brings Cleopatra the "worm of Nilus" (V, ii),—one of the most engaging of these minor humorists. In *Coriolanus* a purely comic interlude cannot be found, but we have the relic of it, so to say, sobered by the present temper of the dramatist, in an old-fashioned house-servants' scene in IV, v.[20] From this list three tragedies have been omitted: *Julius Caesar*, *King Lear*, and *Timon*. In the last-named a fool takes the place of the clown, appearing in the

[18] He has no part to play in the action, and Professor Bradley calls him a "poor" clown, adding: "We hardly attend to him and quickly forget him; I believe most readers of Shakespeare, if asked whether there is a clown in *Othello*, would answer No." (*Shakespearean Tragedy*, p. 177.)

[19] On this scene see the various comments cited in the *New Variorum*, pp. 144-146, particularly the important remarks of Hales (from his *Notes and Essays*); and Bradley, pp. 395-397. Bradley's remarks serve to explain why in an earlier passage (p. 311) he had said, in effect, that there is no clown-interlude in *Macbeth*; yet as he admits that the groundlings probably "roared with laughter" at the porter's remarks, the statement can hardly be justified.

[20] For other partly comic scenes in *Coriolanus*, see *infra*.

usual single interlude scene (II, ii). In *Lear,* where the same
innovation is practiced, the importance of the fool demands
that he be reserved for separate discussion. In *Julius Caesar*
there are comedy clowns at the very opening of the play, in
the persons of the carpenter and the cobbler; and it is quite
likely that this cobbler, a witty fellow in repartee, was
thought of as the clown of the piece. If we seek an interlude
scene, however, we must find it in IV, iii, where the cynic
poet interrupts the generals. In the mere text the comedy of
this passage is slight enough, but if we recall that Shakespeare had found the bad poet described in Plutarch as one
who "took upon him to counterfeit a philosopher . . . .
. with a certain bedlam and frantic motion," which caused
Cassius to fall "a-laughing," it may seem not impossible that
he was treated on the stage with some of the buffoonery of the
clownish interlude.[21]

The significance of all this lies in the fact, which apparently has never been remarked, that Shakespeare made a practice,
in the principal period of his dramatic work, of avoiding the
repeated comic interludes of many of his predecessors and
contemporaries, introducing, nevertheless, a single clown
scene as a concession to the popular tradition—and perhaps
to the demands of his company that its leading comedian
should be furnished a part.[22] Sometimes this clown scene

[21] *Titus Andronicus* has been passed over for obvious reasons. If
included, however, it fits in precisely with the prevailing Shakespearean
practice; there is a single clown interlude in IV, iii ("Enter Clown, with
a basket," etc.).

[22] In this connection the name of Will Kemp is recalled, since he is
known to have played the part of Peter in *Romeo and Juliet,* and to have
been for considerable periods the leading clown of Shakespeare's company. To him also has been conjecturally assigned the first grave-
digger's part in *Hamlet* (first, perhaps, by Chalmers); Collier, on the
other hand, since Kemp appears to have been acting in 1602 with another company, believed that Shakespeare was casting a slur upon him
in the lines, "Let those that play your clowns speak no more than is
set down for them," etc. (*Memoirs of the Principal Actors,* etc., p.
89. And see, to the same effect, Brinsley Nicholson on "Kemp and
Hamlet," Transactions N. S. S., 1880, p. 57.) If he was the William
Kemp whose burial record Chalmers found under date of Nov. 2,
1603, we cannot assume that he appeared to interrupt the serious

was quite apart from the action of the play, as in *Romeo and Juliet* and *Othello;* more often Shakespeare preferred to interweave it effectively with the materials of tragedy, as notably in *Hamlet* and *Antony and Cleopatra.* *Macbeth* might form an intermediate type: the porter scene could be excised without affecting the action, yet despite Coleridge's objection few critics would call it gratuitous.

King Lear presents a case by itself. Here Shakespeare not only, as has been remarked, varied from the common practice by bringing a court fool into tragedy, but actually made him one of the important characters in the play. He proves, of course, not wholly a comic personage; on his first appearance (I, iv) he is called "a bitter fool," it is soon evident that he is to be emotionally concerned with the fate of the king, and his position in the second and third acts (II, iv; III, ii, iv, vi) becomes increasingly that of a tragic sufferer, though we must no doubt suppose that his sallies provided amusement also. After Act III he disappears. This fool has been made the subject of no little critical interpretation, and it is not to the present purpose to attempt any more.[23] But it is perti-

course of any of the tragedies subsequent to *Hamlet;* but if he survived that year, as is quite possible, he may have played the clown in *Othello* and the porter in *Macbeth.* Looking backward again, it is almost certain that he was in Shakespeare's company when *Julius Caesar* was produced, for he is known to have played Dogberry about that time in *Much Ado.* He may, then, have played the cobbler citizen, or the bad poet of the tent scene—if, as has been suggested, that scene was more clownish than the text reveals,—or both. All this is idle conjecture; but the fact that such a personage as Kemp was an important feature of the playing company, and that for him and his kind interludes in tragedies were deliberately made (as appears to have been the case with the Peter scene in *Romeo and Juliet*), is so far from idle that it is fundamental for the study of our subject. (For accounts of Kemp, besides Collier's partly untrustworthy article, see Dyce's edition of Kemp's *Nine Days' Wonder,* Camden Society, 1840; an unsigned article in the *Jahrbuch,* XXII, 255; and of course the *Dict. Nat. Biog.*)

[23] I cannot resist quoting Professor Bradley's fine comment: "One can almost imagine that Shakespeare, going home from an evening at the Mermaid, where he had listened to Jonson fulminating against fools in general and perhaps criticising the clown in *Twelfth Night* in

nent to remark that we have here the supreme instance of the transfiguration of the old comic interlude and its complete blending with the serious action—not only the action, but the emotional character—of tragedy. The result is an extraordinary emotional complex, which is partly expressed by the term tragic pathos, but which is too intricate, not to say chaotic, for analysis. It is the acme of "Gothic" art.

The comic material in the tragedies is not, of course, altogether covered by the clownish interlude scenes that have been enumerated. Besides these, in the first place, there are the momentary flashes of wit or humor that play over the dialogue, and cannot, as has been said, be listed for any such purpose as ours. Again, there are certain moments of comic action, evidently designed to stir up general laughter, but distinct from the interlude scenes in their brevity or their closer connection with the main tragic action; the drunkenness of Cassio in *Othello* (II, iii), the duping of Roderigo in the same play (end of Act II, and IV, ii),[24] the drunkenness of Lepidus in *Antony and Cleopatra* (II, vii), the dialogue of Cleopatra's attendants in the same play (I, ii), the grim humor of the populace in *Julius Caesar* (III, iii) and *Coriolanus* (II, iii), the bluff talk of the watchmen in the latter play (V, ii), the childish wit of Lady Macduff's little son in *Macbeth* (IV, ii) and the single speech—at once more humorous and more pathetic— of little Marcius in *Coriolanus* (V, iii) ;—these nearly, but doubtless not wholly, exhaust the list.[25]

particular, had said to himself: 'Come, my friends, I will show you once for all that the mischief is in you, and not in the fool or the audience. I will have a fool in the most tragic of my tragedies. He shall not play a little part. . . . . . Instead of amusing the king's idle hours, he shall stand by him in the very tempest and whirlwind of passion. Before I have done you shall confess, between laughter and tears, that he is of the very essence of life.'" (*Shakespearean Tragedy*, p. 311.)

[24] The description of Roderigo among the *dramatis personae* as "a gulled gentleman" marks his intentionally comic function.

[25] Except for *Timon*, whose satiric character makes it very difficult to distinguish what is comic from what is serious. For instance, the scene of the feast of warm water (III, vi),—is it comedy or tragedy? Neither, one might say; or both. The satiric mood also looms large in

To summarize what we have found: of Shakespeare's tragedies the earliest contains some ten or a dozen partly comic scenes; in the others there are altogether some twenty to twenty-five—of course no two readers would agree in the count,—an average of a little less than three each. Of these scenes one in each tragedy, *Lear* excepted, partakes of the nature of the old clown interlude; in *Lear* the clown, now become a fool, is developed to an important and partly serious character. The other comic scenes are of very various kinds. Three tragedies, *Julius Caesar, Othello,* and *Macbeth,* are free from outstanding comic details except for the single interlude scene,[26] though showing secondary moments of amusing by-play. Two tragedies have comic scenes in the first act; seven in the second; three in the third; four in the fourth; and three in the fifth.[27] There is none in which the

Coriolanus, and even in *Antony and Cleopatra,* greatly diminishing the full tragic effect (again the term comi-tragedy might be used), and making it possible for Professor Bradley to speak of *Macbeth* as "the last of the pure tragedies." Here also should be mentioned *Troilus and Cressida,* which is perhaps quite as tragic as *Timon.* This play, it will be remembered, the editors of the folio seemingly knew not how to classify; it is like a familiar type of modern drama in which the end is a dissonance, with neither comic nor tragic resolution. The end of the action is the death of Hector, but the last word (probably not Shakespeare's, to be sure) is a mocking laugh.

[26] This statement I believe would be accepted by most readers of *Othello;* yet since it was written I have seen *Othello* well performed, and was struck not only by the comic "relief" furnished by Roderigo the gull, but also by the amusement which the audience found in the witty sallies of Iago, notwithstanding the terrible import of that to which they were leading.

[27] *Romeo and Juliet* is still excluded from these figures. Professor Bradley, while justly observing that comic passages occur "most frequently in the early or middle part of the play," emphasizes their use in the fourth—or early in the fifth—act as a means of preventing the "drag" which threatens the five-act tragedy at this point. (*Shakespearean Tragedy,* p. 61.) This suggests an aspect of our subject which is not touched on in this paper, viz., the relation of the comic underscene to dramatic technique. An interesting example is the remark, made first I cannot now say by whom, that the porter scene in *Macbeth* was devised to provide time for Macbeth to wash his hands and change his clothing.

comic material tends to rise to the position of an underplot, nor any, indeed, which can be thought to give warrant for Dr. Johnson's saying that in tragedy Shakespeare "is always struggling after some occasion to be comic."

In the foregoing summary only the graveyard scene in *Hamlet* was included. Yet it is clear that a considerable portion of *Hamlet*, not readily placed in any of the groups thus far noted, is yet marked by distinctive comic effects. So far from being of the nature of interlude, this element is involved in the personality of Hamlet himself, and we are reminded that in this play we have the unique example of a Shakespearean tragedy whose hero is to some extent a comic part.[28] In Hamlet's dialogues with those whom he despises—with Polonius, Rosencrantz and Guildenstern, and Osric—is some of the most brilliant intellectual comedy to be found in Shakespeare. To explain or interpret the presence of this matter in the greatest of the tragedies is not here to be attempted. It must suffice to observe that it tends to make of the drama what might be called an intellectual complex, as compared with what was called an emotional complex in the case of *King Lear,* and that the dominant effect is now that of tragic *irony* as compared with the impression of tragic pathos.

Nor can we fail to note the interesting part played by insanity, real or feigned, in the creation of these complexes. That mental derangement was a recognized source of amusement in the Elizabethan period has been abundantly shown;[29] yet this is not to deny that it can ever have failed of its power to awaken pity and terror. Whether Professor Wendell and Mr. Corbin are right in their emphasis on the comic side of this element in *Lear* and *Hamlet* has been questioned, and cannot be argued here; but certainly, except for readers who reject altogether the possibility of such a dissonance of humor and pathos, the presence of comic material in the mad scenes, as in those which Webster probably derived from them,[30]

[28] Compare Furnivall's remark that "Hamlet himself does the main work of Lear's fool." (Transactions N. S. S., 1880, p. 65.)

[29] See Wendell's *William Shakespeare* and Corbin's *The Elizabethan Hamlet.*

[30] See the note on *The Duchess of Malfy, supra,* and Stoll's *John Webster,* pp. 142-144.

must be viewed as important for a full understanding of our theme. In *King Lear* the matter is of unique importance, because of the extraordinary combination of the real madness of the king, the partial madness of the fool, and the feigned madness of Edgar. Readers so disposed may well inquire which of these scenes are chiefly instrumental in effecting what has been called tragic irony, and which tragic pathos. Certainly in the feigned madness of Hamlet the former is outstanding, and in the real madness of Lear the latter. The audience is likely to laugh in both cases;[31] but the difference might be expressed in some such fashion as by saying that to laugh at *Hamlet* it is necessary to understand, to laugh at *Lear* it is necessary not to understand.

This last phase of our subject suggests a concluding inquiry, which is here to be raised rather than answered. How true is the statement commonly made, that the presence of comic detail in tragedy is for the purpose of *relief?* Relief in the literal sense of contrast—about that there can be little doubt.[32]

[31] A modern audience by no means so much, certainly, as an Elizabethan, but at times, as any observer may discover. Professor George P. Baker seems to question this, at any rate so far as *Hamlet* is concerned, in his recent introduction to that play in the Tudor Shakespeare, saying that if "Shakespeare meant the pretended madness to be comic, ... then in scenes profoundly moving and rich in the finest psychology he worked for a laughter that must largely break the very emotional spell he seems to be seeking to create." (pp. xv, xvi.) But this is to beg the central question—whether there is not an "emotional spell" to which serious and comic elements both contribute. Somewhat different is Professor Bradley's suggestion, in this case with regard to the porter scene in *Macbeth*, that Shakespeare intended the groundlings to roar with laughter, and at the same time "despised [them] if they laughed." This might seem a too supralapsarian Calvinism, to represent the poet as creating sinners in order to damn them; yet when we consider the problem of the relation of Shakespeare's majestic powers of idealization to his business as a purveyor of drama to the commonalty, it no doubt contains an aspect of the truth.

[32] Compare Dryden's defense of the practice, in the person of Neander: "Why should he imagine the soul of man more heavy than his senses? Does not the eye pass from an unpleasant object to a pleasant in a much shorter time than is required to this? and does not the unpleasantness of the first commend the beauty of the latter? The old rule of logic might have convinced him, that contraries, when placed near, set off each other." (*Essays,* ed. Ker, i, 70.)

But of the prevalent view that the main function of such scenes is to relax the tension of tragic feeling,[33] one may raise some question. The standard example for this view is the porter scene in *Macbeth*, but so important a witness as Professor Bradley tells us that this does not make him smile.[34] In general, we have found that in Shakespeare's practice the interlude scenes are most used in the tragedies which are least strongly moving to horror and despair. In *Othello*, where the need of ''relief'' is perhaps greatest, such interruptions are comparatively few. In *Lear* the quasi-comic details are fairly abundant, as we have seen, but they must be regarded as intensifying the tragic emotions rather than as softening them. The same thing is true of the most daring comic material in *Hamlet*. There is matter here for careful analysis, which psychology may in time accomplish for us.[35] Meantime it may be suspected, in view of what we have seen, that the most significant aspect of the use of the comic in tragedy is not that which is due essentially to the love of variety and contrast (important as that is in the more primitive types), but rather that which seeks to portray a mental or emotional state more complex and more dramatically moving than the purer and simpler states to which the drama of the classical school commonly confines itself. Lessing, in attacking the ''comi-tragic or tragi-comic drama. . . . .

[33] Cf. Thümmel, for instance: "Je schärfer und beängstigender der pragmatischer Verlauf im Trauerspiel sich zuspitzt, um so unabweislicher stellt sich beim Zuschauer das Bedürfniss nach Milderung der peinlichen Situation ein. Diese Milderung kann immerhin und wird am sichersten durch eine episodische Scene komischer Farbung herbeigeführt werden," etc.—*Jahrbuch* XI, 83.

[34] "The moment is too terrific. . . . . [The porter's remarks] are not comic enough to allow one to forget for a moment what has preceded and what must follow." (*Shakespearean Tragedy*, p. 395.)

[35] Volkelt, in his admirable *Æsthetik des Tragischen*, does not feel that he can go into the subject, except for the suggestive observation that "Dichtungen wie Shakespeare's *Lear* . . . . . bezeugen dass komische Szenen mit dem Tragischen nicht nur, wie in den mittelälterlichen Mysterien äusserlich zusammengestellt werden können, sondern dass zwischen dem Humor und dem Tragischen innere Zusammengehörigkeit sinnvolle und tiefgehende Bezogenheit stattfindet." (Page 393.)

. of Gothic invention,'' maintained that it is no defense to claim that it imitates the variety of nature; because, said he, while it may imitate the nature of phenomena, it disregards the nature of emotions, which it is the function of art to help us to unify.[36] The answer would seem to be that—at any rate in the highest specimens of the ''Gothic'' method—the object is not so much to depict the confusion of exterior nature as the confusion of the soul at moments when tragic and comic seem to form one indivisible experience.

RAYMOND MACDONALD ALDEN.

University of Illinois.

[36] *Dramaturgie*, LXX. "Alles, was wir in der Natur von einem Gegenstande oder einer Verbindung verschiedener Gegenstände, es sei der Zeit oder der Raume nach, in unsern Gedanken absondern oder absondern zu können wünschen, sondert sie [die Kunst] wirklich ab, und gewährt uns diesen Gegenstand oder diese Verbindung verschiedener Gegenstände so lauter und bündig, als es nur immer die Empfindung, die sie erregen sollen, verstattet. . . . . Es muss uns notwendig ekeln, in der Kunst das wiederzufinden, was wir aus der Natur wegwünschten."

SOME NOTES ON HENRY GLAPTHORNE'S *WIT IN A CONSTABLE*.

I. Textual

Recently I purchased a copy of the first edition of Henry Glapthorne's comedy, *Wit in a Constable,* in which numerous corrections and notes had been entered in a contemporary hand. The accuracy of these corrections and notes, and the general care shown in entering them, lead me to believe that they were made by some one who was familiar with the lines, and also possibly with the stage representation, of the play. The title-page states that the comedy was written in 1639, the first edition appeared in 1640; the manuscript entries, therefore, might have been made while the play was still being performed, or at least while its performance was still fresh in memory. It is not likely that the corrections were made by the author, but it is certain that they were made by some one who was especially interested in the play.

Since these corrections may prove of value to the student of Glapthorne, I give them below in full. For the convenience of those who do not have access to the first edition, I have prefixed page and line reference to Pearson's reprint of the play, 1874.

P. 165, l. 1. After "The Prologue" is added: "Spoken by the Constable"; p. 167, l. 17. After *"Nel"* is inserted "& Lucy."; p. 170, l. 8. "Metaphosickes" [?] is altered to "Metaphysickes"; p. 172, l. 5. "l-ve" [?] is altered to "live"; p. 173, l. 19. After "purpose" is inserted a period; p. 175, l. 5. After "fashions" is inserted a period; p. 175, l. 16. After "of it" the comma is changed into a period; p. 177, l. 26. The catchword *"Thoro"* prefixed to this line is cancelled; p. 177, l. 29. "you none here" is altered to "you've none here"; p. 184. The stage direction "Enter Holdfast, Brave, Tristram" is altered to "Enter Holdfast Bravely drest & Tristram"; p. 185, ll. 30-31. "he had him a schollar" is altered to "he had bred him a schollar"; p. 187. In the stage direction after *"Enter Thoroug."* is inserted: "drest like Holdfast as a scholler"; p. 188. In the stage direction "Gray" is altered to "Grace"; p. 189, ll. 31-2. A hyphen is inserted after "new" and before "Found"; p. 190, l. 20. Adds the stage direction: "Ent: Val & Tim:"; p. 190, l. 26. Adds the stage direction:

"Ex: Covet Thor"; p. 191, l. 20. After "neighbor" a comma
is inserted; p. 191, l. 34. "An heire long" is altered to "An
heire loom." [The correction has been silently made in the
Pearson edition.]; p. 192, l. 8. A double hyphen is inserted
between "thred" and "bare"; p. 192, l. 18. "get me 'hem"
is altered to "get me 'hence"; p. 193, l. 30. Adds the stage
direction: "Ex: Val: Tim:"; p. 198, ll. 31-2. "now wert for
the statute, That Bigamy" is altered to: "now wert not for
the statute Thats 'gainst Bigamy." [In the Pearson edition,
the text is silently changed to: "now wert not for the statute
'Gainst Bigamy."]; p. 199, l. 9. "Nay, come forward Land
lord Spoild else" is altered to: "Nay, come forward Land
lord, all's spoild else"; p. 202, l. 28. "Coy as a Voteresse below their suiters" is altered to "Coy as a Voteresse before
their suiters"; p. 205, l. 11. "I his behalfe" is altered to "On
his behalfe"; p. 205, l. 23. Adds the stage direction "Ex-
eunt"; p. 205, l. 28. "that she should heare" is altered to
"but that she should heare"; p. 207, l. 16. After "Company"
is inserted: "ent: Grace Val."; p. 207, l. 21. "that house" is
altered to "the house"; p. 209, l. 8. "and daughter and" is
altered to "and daughter are"; p. 209, l. 12. "I was your
Neice" is altered to "she was your Neice"; p. 211, l. 6.
"Freewit" is altered to "Thorowgood," and from this point
to the end of the play the alteration is painstakingly made
every time the name "Freewit" occurs; p. 212, l. 16. "Poore
wretched" is altered to "Poore wretch"; p. 213, l. 23. "azure
notes" is altered to "azure noses"; p. 215, l. 1. "As tis the
city fashion to a woman." After "to" a word is inserted
which seems to be "haue." [The line, however, needs only a
comma after "fashion" to make good sense and metre.];
p. 216, l. 18. "J ckdawes." The missing "a" is inserted;
p. 217, l. 18. "here's your Mr." is altered to "here's your
Man;" p. 217, l. 20. "Enter Grimes, Busie" is altered to
"Enter Busie & Tristram," and from this point on "Grimes"
is carefully altered to "Tristram"; p. 229, l. 1. To the stage
direction *"Int."* is added: "a sedan & passes ouer"; pp.
236, 240. The name "Freewit" in the stage directions is
cancelled.

A comparison of the first edition of the play with Pearson's reprint, shows that the text of the latter is thoroughly
untrustworthy. The editor carelessly omits words; and, whenever he thinks the text faulty, suppresses or introduces words
without the slightest notice to the reader. In punctuation,
capitalization, and line division, too, the reprint is chaotic.

At times the editor attempts to modernize the punctuation and capitalization, and to divide the lines according to the metre; at other times, he leaves the text as it is in the original. Thus the reprint is neither a faithful reproduction of the first edition, nor a consistent revision and modernization.

I cannot record here even the more important errors in the reprint. But I wish to suggest emendations for some of the passages which the labor of the half-hearted editor failed to better.

P. 175, l. 22. "whose these" read "who're these"; p. 180, l. 6. "some stale Hay, or Matron." For "Hay" read "Hag"; p. 182, l. 27. "Or shewing" read "On shewing"; p. 198, l. 11. "gentlewoman" read "gentlemen"; p. 199, l. 1. "them" read "them's"; p. 199, l. 11. "As is" read "As in"; p. 201, l. 3. "there" read "there's"; p. 205, l. 11. "this" read "his"; p. 207, l. 13. "*Cov.*" read "*Tim.*" p. 208, l. 12. "intention" read "intrusion"; p. 223, l. 14. The question, "How's that?" is run in as a part of Busie's speech. It should be attributed to Valentine; *i. e.*:

Free. Is this truth?
Val. How's that?
Bus. Upon the faith, sir, of a man in office.

p. 226, l. 2. "verilies" read "verilie"; p. 227, l. 16. "To buy the cheese" read "To buy thee cheese"; p. 227, l. 17. "they" read "they've"; p. 229, l. 20. "share like this money" read "share alike this money"; p. 231, l. 5. "bulke" read "hulke."

II. Miscellaneous

I. We know absolutely nothing of Glapthorne's early life. Yet from his various dedications and his poems, we conclude that he came of a good family; [1] and from the erudition of his plays and the excellence of his Latin verses, that he received a liberal education. From the fact that Alexander Gill, head-master of St. Paul's School, prefixed some commendatory verses to *Albertus Wallenstein*, it has been inferred that Glapthorne received his elementary training at St. Paul's.

Wit in a Constable, it seems to me, furnishes evidence that its author received a university training at Cambridge. The opening scene represents in a satirical vein the

---

[1] He dedicates *White-Hall* to "My noble Friend and Gossip, Captaine **Richard Lovelace**."

life of a Cambridge scholar; and throughout the play the university is frequently referred to. The following passage is especially significant: "But shall we have such wenches As are at Cambridge, hansom as peg Larkin?"[2] Perhaps this same Cambridge lass is referred to in a poem entitled *On the Banishment of Cambridge Lasses*, printed in Huth's *Inedited Poetical Miscellanies*. The first lass there referred to is named Peg:

> Thy damask cheek, my Peg, which nature made
> Of purest tinctures, such as never fade.

II. In the original edition, after Act III, Throughgood is called Freewit, and Tristram is called Grimes. From this fact Fleay concluded that *Wit in a Constable* was an older play revised by Glapthorne, and that the revision extended no further than through Act III. But the play gives no evidence of being an old play reworked by a new hand; indeed, it gives every evidence of having been throughout the product of Glapthorne. Yet the alterations in the names of the chief characters certainly point to a revision. Perhaps the play had been written by Glapthorne at Cambridge, and was later, in London, prepared for the public actors. It undoubtedly shows many traces of Cambridge, and throughout smells of the university.

III. But Fleay failed to observe all the peculiarities in the names given to the characters of the play. For example, Thoroughgood appears as the suitor in Glapthorne's *The Lady Mother*, and Freewit appears as the suitor in *The Hollander*; in *Wit in a Constable* the suitor is called Throughgood in the first three acts, and is called Freewit in the last two acts. An examination of these plays reveals other striking parallelisms in characters. The more important of these I summarize below.

1. Thoroughgood in *Wit in a Constable* is suitor to Clare; in Acts IV and V, he is called Freewit. Thoroughgood in *The Lady Mother* is suitor to Lady Marlowe. Freewit in *The Hollander* is suitor to Lady Knowworth.

2. Tristram in *Wit in a Constable* is servant to Jeremy

[2] Page 173, ll. 31-2.

Holdfast; in Acts IV and V, he is called Grimes. Grimes in *The Lady Mother* is servant to Bonville.

3. Clara in *Wit in a Constable* is a young lady beloved by Thoroughgood. Clariana in *The Lady Mother* is a young lady beloved by Thurston.

4. Sir Gefferie Holdfast in *Wit in a Constable* is a rich, miserly knight who has a very foolish son. Sir Gefferie [Holdfast? cf. p. 113; "And tis as hard to wrest a penny from him as from a bawd"] in *The Lady Mother* is a rich and miserly knight who has a very foolish nephew.

5. Maudlin is the name of a servant girl in both *The Lady Mother* and *Wit in a Constable*.

6. Timothy appears in *Wit in a Constable* as a foolish knight, and in *The Lady Mother* as a clever servant.

These repetitions of names are, to be sure, striking; yet even more striking are the repetitions of the characters themselves; without much change they are made to act in different plots. The explanation of this I must leave to someone who is more interested in Glapthorne than I.

IV. It has not been observed that in the play Glapthorne satirizes Thomas Heywood. On page 171 he makes Tristram say to the foolish Holdfast:

> You may arrive to be the City Poet,
> And send the little moysture of your braine
> To grace a Lord Maiors festivall with showes,
> Alluding to his trade, or to the company
> Of which he's free.

This is an obvious reference to Heywood and to his Lord Mayor's show of 1639, *Londini Status Pecatus,* which was performed at "the Charge and Expense . . . of the Right Worshipfull Society of Drapers," on the occasion of the "Initiation of the Right Honourable Henry Garway into the Majoralty of the Famous and farre Renowned City of London." Garway was free of the Company of Drapers, and to this fact Heywood frequently alludes. He celebrates the greatness of the Company of Drapers, and gives a list of the lord mayors who have been members of that organization. Moreover, he puts into the separate "shows" themselves

distinct allusions to the mayor's trade; note, for example,
the following:

> The Fleece of Aries Trumpets to eternity
>
> The Draper's Honour, due to that Fraternity.

Throughout the play Glapthorne satirizes the Drapers, and
incidentally Heywood's laudation of them. For example,
on page 210:

> Though I'me a Citizen, and by my charter
>
> Am not allowed much wit, as being free
>
> Oth Linnen-drapers, and a man in office.

It is interesting in this connection to observe that Peter
Hausted also refers satirically to Heywood's work as City
Poet: [3]

So may rare Pageants grace the Lord Mayor's show . . .

And Heywood sing your acts in lofty verse.

JOSEPH QUINCY ADAMS, JR.

Cornell University.

---

[3] *A Satire against Separatists,* 1648. Heywood seems to have been
made City Poet about 1630. He is said to have written "all the known
pageants for Lord Mayor's Day, between 1630 and 1640, when they
ceased for some years to be exhibited."

"SPENSER'S EARLIEST TRANSLATIONS"

The question, first raised by Koeppel,[1] as to the authenticity of the translations from Bellay and Petrarch in Vander Noodt's "Theatre of Worldlings" (1569), has been answered again recently by Mr. L. S. Friedland in the "Journal of English and Germanic Philology" for July, 1913. Since the matter has been so brought up afresh, I should like to offer a few further remarks confirmatory.

In the first place, it may be observed that while Ponsonby certainly leaves the impression of his assuming responsibility for the make-up of the "Complaints," he also leaves us puzzled. It is odd, for instance, that he should have by himself "got into his hands" just these particular "smale poemes"—and no others—which proved to have unity, "being all complaints and meditations of the worlds vanitie, verie grave and profitable." It is also difficult to see by what process of inference the excellent Printer concludes that "sundrie others, namelie, *Ecclesiastes* and *Canticum Canticorum* translated, *A senights Slumber, The Hell of Lovers*, his *Purgatorie*, being all dedicated to ladies, so as it may seeme he ment them all to one volume." Why should Ponsonby think Spenser meant just these poems for a separate volume? Nearly all, if not all, the "Complaints" were also dedicated to ladies. And, on the other hand, any translation of "Ecclesiastes" would seem of necessity to be one more of the "complaints and meditations of the worlds vanitie, verie grave and profitable." The fact is, Ponsonby's rôle reminds one strongly of that of "E. K." in the "Calender," to wit, one of very *wise* ignorance. We can hardly doubt, I think, that the poet, certainly in London when the "Complaints" were "entered," was behind his publisher, and—as before with "E. K."—using him as at once a spokesman and a "blind."[2] And Spenser may have had the same reasons as before in preferring to shift, at any rate for the time being, responsibility for the publication. He *may* have feared the consequences of reissuing the already suppressed "Mother

[1] Ueber die Echtheit der Edmund Spenser zugeschriebenen "Visions of Petrarch" u. "Visions of Bellay". Eng. Stud. XV (1891).

[2] Cf. J. B. Fletcher: Spenser and "E. K." Mod. Lang. Notes, June, 1900.

Hubberds Tale,'' or he may have merely desired to await a
favorable verdict on his new venture before acknowledging it,
or he may even—aspiring courtier as he was—be affecting the
disdain of aristocratic authors for making their accomplishments property of the common herd.

There is another matter making, I think, for the arrangement of the volume by Spenser himself. The three series of
''visions''—''Visions of the Worlds Vanitie,'' ''The Visions
of Bellay,'' ''The Visions of Petrarch''—follow without separate title-page ''Muiopotmos.'' This has a title-page, and is
inscribed to Elizabeth, Lady Carey. In Sonnet I of the
''Visions of the Worlds Vanitie,'' Spenser says of his visions—

> Such as they were (faire Ladie) take in worth,
> That when time serves, may bring things better forth.

And in the last sonnet of the Petrarchan series—and of the
volume—Spenser adds to the original envoy, translated as a
quatrain in 1569, this apostrophe:

> And ye, faire Ladie, in whose bounteous brest
> All heavenly grace and vertue shrined is,
> When ye these rythmes doo read, and vew the rest,
> Loath this base world, and thinke of heavens blis:
> And though ye be the fairest of Gods creatures,
> Yet thinke, that death shall spoyle your goodly features.

Apart from their position as following ''Muiopotmos'' in the
volume, these words conform very well to the tone and
promise of the dedication to Lady Carey. For as the last
words in the volume, they apply equally to the ''Visions'' and
to the whole volume, so by ''fortunate'' ambiguity fulfilling
his declaration of being ''absolutely vowed to [her] services,''
and in so far justifying Nash's assertion two years later in
''Christ's Tears over Jerusalem'' that ''Maister Spenser in
all his writings he prizeth [her].'' [3] Moreover, the emphasis

    [3] Cf. P. W. Long: Spenser and Lady Carey. Modern Language
Rev., April 1908. In the epistle dedicating *Mother Hubberds Tale* to
Lady Compton, Spenser says that he would present to her "these
my idle labours; which having long sithens composed in the raw conceipt of my youth, I lately amongst other papers lighted upon, and
was by others, which liked the same, mooved to set them foorth."
There follows without separate title-page the *Ruines of Rome;* then

upon her bounty, superlative beauty and *grace* fits Spenser's tributes elsewhere to Lady Carey.[4] If Mr. Long is at all right in interpreting the exceedingly ardent dedication of "Muiopotmos," together with the uniquely prominent dedicatory-sonnet in the first instalment of "The Fairie Queene," as effectively a declaration of platonic service—another aristocratic pose of the poet—there would be a special fitness in Spenser's setting a climax to his praise in his revamped "Visions of Petrarch": they would imply Lady Carey to be his "Laura." Furthermore, a motive would thus be given for his working over of the early translations, and a reason for the omission of the four Apocalyptic "sonets." It would be manifestly indecorous in praise of milady to enlist the Scarlet Woman on her ugly Beast.

In theme and *genre,* a goodly number of the "Complaints" actually grew out of the early translations. The "Visions of the Worlds Vanitie" are manifestly suggested by the "Visions" from the "Theatre;" "The Ruines of Time" by "The Ruines of Rome." The motif of "Virgils Gnat" is the inverse of that of the "Visions of the Worlds Vanitie." The fortunes of the great are in the former made, in the latter marred, by the small. And again, "Muiopotmos" is in idea and form

---

comes the title-page of *Muiopotmos,* followed by that poem and the *Visions.* One would naturally expect the *Ruines of Rome* to be grouped with the *Visions of Bellay,* the two together making one poem. It would look as if the poet were distributing these minor pieces for good measure, as it were, to his main gift. Hence the phrase "this smal poëme" in the epistle dedicatory of Muiopotmos need not, as Mr. Buck thinks (*Pub. Mod. Lang. Assoc.* xxiii, p. 92), preclude the "Lady" of the *Visions* being the dedicatee of *Muiopotmos.* Similarly, Ponsonby dedicates to Sir Robart Needham the volume of 1595, entitled *Amoretti and Epithalamion,* but containing as well certain epigrams; yet in his epistle he mentions "these sweete conceited sonnets" only.

Furthermore the declaration to Lady Compton would seem to admit responsibility for the publication of the volume of *Complaints.* The letter could hardly apply to any original "uttering" of the poem, for its author speaks of having "long sithens composed [it] in the raw conceipt of my youth," and but "lately" having "lighted upon" it.

[4] Cf. Long, *op. cit.* Mr. Long (p. 259, note 1) assumes without argument that the "faire Ladie" of the "Visions" is Lady Carey.

obviously related to "Virgils Gnat." Such developments of themselves give a certain importance to those sub-freshman exercises.

As has been before pointed out,[3] phrases and images thus early struck off lingered in Spenser's memory to be used anew later. I might cite two additional instances. Ll. 265-282 of "The Teares of the Muses" clearly echo Sonnet X of the "Visions of Bellay," as do stanzas four and five of the fourth canto of the first book of the "Faerie Queene" Sonet II of the same. Again, in "Faerie Queene," I, v, 49, there is allusion to

The antique ruins of the Romanes fall.

J. B. Fletcher.

Columbia University.

[3] Cf. Friedland, op. cit., p. 459, note 20.

REVIEWS AND NOTES

AN INTRODUCTION TO THE STUDY OF OLD HIGH GERMAN. By Lionel Armitage. Oxford: Clarendon Press. 1911. 8vo. pp. 264. I map.

This product of English scholarship is not as devoid of genuine merit as the scant attention bestowed upon it by American philologists would imply. In fact, its appearance in the same year that saw the publication of the third and fourth edition of Braune's Althochdeutsche Grammatik—which has already been reviewed elsewhere in this periodical, XI, 269 ff. —is on the whole fraught with as much significance to English-speaking students of Germanic philology as that justly appreciated classic authority.

Extensive comparison between the two works is precluded by the difference of motives that lay behind their making. The task Braune set himself was the faithful portrayal of the historical development of the High German dialect between the eighth and eleventh centuries, with especial emphasis, however, on the literary monuments of the ninth century. It is due to these delimitations that, on the one hand, the various glosses are not systematically enough drawn upon for reference and, on the other, the grammatical treatment is restricted to specifically Old High German phenomena and, in comparatively rare instances, to corroborating Gothic evidences. In a word, his treatise is one of the facts observed, not of comments and annotations as well.

As against this, Armitage's book contains much more than its title promises. It is an introduction not only to Old High German but to the study of Germanic philology by way of that dialect, based on scientific and historical principles, agreeably—as the preface states—to the previous training of the English student. Regarded from these linguistic and pedagogical viewpoints alone, the new work deserves more consideration than it seems thus far to have received.—The author presents his subject-matter in two parts. Part One treats of the bibliography, orthography and pronunciation of OHG. and contains a highly commendable feature in the inclusion of paradigmatic material. Chapter I. of Part Two represents the Indo-European element *par excellence*, in that it furnishes phonetic definitions and a detailed account of the First Sound-shift, Verner's law and the various combinative sound-changes that form the necessary presuppositions of OHG. linguistic study. Chapters II. and III. trace Pre-Germanic consonantism into its later equivalents, including

such characteristic changes as the High German Sound-shift
and Notker's law of Initial Consonants. Both Chapter III.
and the following one, which gives a corresponding discussion
of vowel developments, are summed up in convenient tabular
reviews.   Three other divisions are devoted one each to the
Verbal system, the Nominal and Pronominal system, and to
Numerals and Adverbs. The book concludes with a service-
able table of OHG. verbs and an index verborum.

The benefits that the student might derive from this arrangement are, however, to a slight extent minimized by dis-
advantages of one sort or another. A few considerations that
occurred to the present reviewer in the course of reading may
be set down at this point.

(a)   There are to be found in the book certain errors of
misstatement that militate to just such a degree against its
accuracy. Thus, on p. 9 the Germanic languages are misrep-
resented as having *possessed* a fixed accent. This, of course, is
incorrect: the *acquisition* of a fixed accent of the dynamic
character is just one of the few peculiarities that differentiate
Germanic from her sister dialects.   A short account here of
Indo-European stress would not have been amiss.   Again, on
p. 39 the formulation of Verner's law as "when initial unless
in unaccented syllable, prefix or second part of a noun compound or immediately preceded by the accent in IG. the voiceless spirants are retained, but in all other cases these voiceless spirants become voiced" will be admitted to be scientifically accurate, but certainly obscure and cumbersome as well.

(b)   Evidences of inconclusiveness force themselves upon
the reader's attention that impair the serviceableness of the
portions affected. On p. 11 and 231 the bibliographical matter is devoid of the customary information as to edition, date
and place.   This circumstance renders it worthless for working purposes, especially as it is designed for the guidance of
beginners.   The survey, too, of the OHG. literary remains
on p. 11 is not sufficiently illuminating.   One does not wish
for an extended *catalogue raisonné* of the various MSS. such
as is given, for instance, in Bülbring's Altenglisches
Elementarbuch, but it is reasonable to expect a few words
of extraneous comment as well as an acceptable dating appended to each.   On p. 28 Armitage states that the order of
the stages of the First Sound-shift was as there adopted. No
explanation for this is given; and yet the beginner might well
wish to know upon what reasons this dictum is based. Helpful
references are sometimes omitted, as when on p. 177 the discussion of the confusion of case-forms neglects to cite Brugmann's Grundriss II. or allude to the convenient little Über-

sichtstabellen of Wood. The classification of *swerien* [*s(w)uor, s(w)uorum, gi-sworan*] among the graded verbs of the fourth class on p. 223 and also on p. 161 among those of the sixth is ill-advised. For the rest, the reviewer fails to find a satisfactory treatment of Umlaut-phenomena.

Beyond such limits the contents of the book is not amenable to criticism. The author frankly avoids putting forth any theories of his own, but aims solely at an attractive presentation of the material culled from other sources. Indo-European students will therefore find no innovation in Armitage's work, save a hopeful tendency away from the current hybrid terminology toward a consistent English nomenclature. Vocalic and Consonant declension is surely more accurate than the meaningless Strong and Weak; similarly Graded and Non-graded—the term Vowel-gradation is familiar—are more descriptive of the two classes of verbs.[1] However, as far as the main intention of the book is concerned, viz. to locate and localize for the English-speaking student OHG. in all its Indo-European bearings, it seems to be defeated in part by the fact that the author attempts to be exhaustive within a comparatively small compass. Armitage's Introduction is clearly not elementary in the sense of Sweet's Primer or even some of Wright's Historical Grammars; its superabundance of information, whilst gratifying in the thorogoing handling of such parts as Grimm's law and the Second-shift, must be disconcerting to the beginner before whom it is placed as a practical handbook.

None of the foregoing remarks, however, should be interpreted as detracting from the general value of the work. It may not, because of some decisive defects, be fitting as a beginner's book, but taken intrinsically and in its totality, it makes an impression that is quite favorable—especially since it represents, in the English tongue, the first extensive comparative treatment of Old High German—and bespeaks its usefulness as a book of reference in any philological library.

Undoubtedly there was room for a work of this kind. The real desideratum, however, in the Old High German field is, at present, not the multiplication of grammatical manuals. Good work is necessary in at least two other directions: the one is more pedagogical, the other purely philological. By the pedagogical I mean the complete absence of paleographical apparatus to bring the student of OHG. in closer, first-hand

---

[1] It is questionable, at the same time, whether "Lengthening of Consonants" to render *Consonantendehung* is more expressive to English-speaking students than the term "Gemination" found in Wright and elsewhere.

contact with the linguistic monuments of the period, to visualise before him in a form more vivid than the often unsympathetic text of the printed book ever can, the *ensemble* of the literature under his consideration. Some attempt should be made thus to provide for a less expensive collection of specimens and reproductions than is, for instance, the excellent Facsimile-Mappe of Frau Magda Enneccerus (Die ältesten deutschen Sprachdenkmäler, Frankfurt, 1897.), perhaps in a student-edition of more accessibility. A face-to-face arrangement of alternate text and facsimile in a book like Braune's or Mansion's Lesebuch—the latter has wisely prefaced two sample pages of the Hildebrandslied—has also for some time seemed desirable to the writer of these lines. That the philological interpretation of ancient texts should really go hand in hand with such illustrative work, requires no brief at this place. It only needs to be emphasized that, for purposes of serious philology, reproductive material of this kind would be the highest possible stimulant to our University men to pursue their studies more intensively, not to speak of the probable excursions prompted by the collateral use of the MS. texts into the realms of MS. preparation and its various cultural aspects.

The other urgent need is, of course, an all-embracing syntax of Old High German. The worker in this field, particularly the student, when it comes to moot points of syntax, is at the mercy of his imagination. The existing sources of information are severally unsatisfactory. Wilmanns' Grammatik is not specifically OHG., nor Erdmann-Mensing's Grundzüge der deutschen Syntax. Erdmann's great work on Otfrid is, again, restricted to that writer alone. The fourth volume of Grimm, rich in inspiration, is yet invalidated in much of its abundant material by the evidence of investigations since the date of its publication. Placed side by side with Streitberg's 95 pages of Gothic syntax, Mansion's 9 pages of OHG. matter in the same series are insignificant and superficial. In this respect Old High German is quite as deficient as is Anglo-Saxon. There exist quite a few helpful treatises of the type of Delbrück's Synkretismus and multitudes of dissertations devoted to the marked peculiarities of the various monuments,[2] but all this is a closed field to the beginner and in a great many instances beyond the reach even of the more advanced student. The bridging over of the remaining

[2] It is needless to add that there is a sufficiently large room for important corrections and new viewpoints. The reviewer's recent monograph on "The Dative of Agency; a Chapter of Indo-European Case-syntax" might be referred to as one example of what may yet be done in a broad way for the amplification of our knowledge as to the case-functions of the Germanic dialects.

lacunae and the speedy codification of all the syntactic material in OHG. is, in the writer's opinion, one of the most pressing needs of present-day Germanic philology.

ALEXANDER GREEN.

University of Illinois.

ERNST LAHNSTEIN, ETHIK UND MYSTIK IN HEBBELS WELTANSCHAUUNG; (Bruns, Friedrich, Friedrich Hebbel und Otto Ludwig. Ein Vergleich ihrer Ansichten über das Drama; Lewin, Dr. Ludwig, Friedrich Hebbel. Beitrag zu einem Psychogramm) sämtlich: Berlin-Steglitz, 1913.

Drei Hebbel-Schriften, alle aus demselben Verlage und 1913 erschienen! Und das ist nicht etwa alles, was das Jahr auf diesem Gebiete gezeitigt hat. Schon das ganze letzte Jahrzehnt ist in der Tat ein gesegnetes für die Hebbel-Literatur gewesen. Hebbel-Schriften sind wie Pilze aus der Erde emporgeschossen, und während dieser Hochflut ist bisher wenig erschienen, was nicht im Tone unbedingter Huldigung dahinfliesst. Doch alle sind Bausteine zu dem Ruhmestempel, den man Hebbel errichtet. Dabei ist aber wohl die Frage am Platze, ob dieser Hebbel-Enthusiasmus ein ganz gesunder ist, ob die plötzlich erkannte Bedeutung Hebbels dieser Begeisterung auch wirklich entspricht. Diese intensive Hebbel-Forschung hat manches Nachteilige; besonders hat sie zahlreiche Wiederholungen dessen zutage gefördert, was für diesen eigenartigen Dichter charakteristisch ist, und der Gewinn an wirklich Neuem ist in vielen Fällen nur gering. Auch die vorliegenden Monographien haben mehr Wert durch das "Wie" als durch das "Was" des Gebotenen. Das Thema von Lahnsteins kleiner Schrift: "Ethik und Mystik in Hebbels Weltanschauung" ist vielleicht das schwierigste von obigen dreien, doch der Verfasser ist demselben gerecht geworden. Er schildert in sehr ansprechender Weise die mystischen Elemente in Hebbels Wesen und deren Anteil an der Entwicklung seiner Weltanschauung. Als läuternden Faktor bezeichnet er die ethischen Kräfte, die in Hebbels Natur schlummerten, aber erst ziemlich spät zum Durchbruch kamen. Der Umstand, dass sich Lahnstein bereits eingehend mit Hebbels Frühzeit beschäftigt hat, ist ihm sehr zustatten gekommen. Er geht davon aus, dass der Dichter, wie Hebbel selbst erklärte, unbedingt den Menschen voraussetzt. Er zeigt uns den niederdrückenden Einfluss, den Hebbels Jugenderfahrungen auf ihn ausübten, und den Konflikt, in welchen der mächtige Lebensdrang, dem die unerbittliche Not der Ver-

hältnisse gegenüberstand, den Dichter stürzte. Vergeblich
ringt er um einen Ausgleich; erst die vollständig gefestigte
und abgeklärte Lebensanschauung des reifen Mannes bringt
ihm die Erlösung. Richtig und wichtig ist Lahnsteins Ausspruch, dass Hebbels Weltanschauung nicht etwa schon zu
Beginn seiner Schaffenszeit wie aus einem Guss fertig da-
stand. In dem Ringen um das Problem der Willensfreiheit
war er zwar schon sehr früh zu der Ueberzeugung von der
dualistischen Form alles Seines gekommen, aber es gelang
ihm nicht sobald, sich mit dieser Erkenntnis, wenn wir seine
Anschauung als solche bezeichnen dürfen, persönlich abzu-
finden. Erst durch das Erwachen des Gewissens und die all-
mähliche sittliche Entwicklung Hebbels, findet Lahnstein, ist
er schliesslich zu einem gewissen seelischen Gleichgewicht gekommen. Interessant ist, dass dieser Sieg mit dem entschei-
denden Umschwung in Hebbels äusseren Umständen zeitlich
zusammenfällt. Hebbel gab sich schliesslich zufrieden mit
der Ueberzeugung, dass sich die Kultur der Menschheit mit
sittlicher Notwendigkeit in stetig aufsteigender Linie entwickeln muss, dass deshalb die ''Idee'' nie untergehen kann,
der Einzelne sich aber freiwillig den Anforderungen dieser
Entwicklung unterordnen, ja sogar opfern muss. Doch ist
nicht zu übersehen, dass wir hier nicht mit einer Tatsache
der Erkenntnis, sondern mit einer Ueberzeugung zu tun
haben. Der wahre Dichter ist allerdings nach Hebbel der
gottbegnadigte Seher, dem sich der Sinn des Lebens unfehlbar erschliesst. Lahnstein betont sehr stark den Wert von
Hebbels historischer Anschauungsweise. Bei der Beurteilung
dieses Punktes ist aber in Betracht zu ziehen, dass die Ueberzeugung von der sittlichen Notwendigkeit alles Geschehens
der geschichtlichen Erkenntnis vorausging. Im Grunde genommen ist diese letztere also nichts als eine Art Leichenbe-
fund, der schon bevor der Beschauung feststand, da diese darauf zielte, die sittliche Notwendigkeit der historischen Entwicklung zu erweisen. Hebbels Weltanschauung ist nicht
auf Vernunftschlüssen erbaut; sie beruht vielmehr vorwiegend auf Ueberzeugungen, die mystischen Ursprungs sind.
Ethische Erwägungen brachten mit der Zeit Klarheit und
Harmonie in das Ganze, so dass man es sehr wohl als eine
praktisch anwendbare Lebensanschauung bezeichnen darf.
Ein wichtiger und permanenter Bestandteil der Anschauung
Hebbels ist der Glaube an die Berechtigung des Individuums
mit all seiner Eigenart. Der Einzelne kann sogar sein eignes
Glück und gleichzeitig den Nutzen der Gesamtheit nur da-
durch fördern, indem er diejenige Kraft voll und ganz ent-

wickelt, die in ihm die bedeutendste ist. Doch der Mensch-
heit, der in ihr waltenden "Idee" gegenüber, ist er rechtlos
und dieser Widerspruch findet eine Lösung nur durch den
Tod. "Von einem einseitig mystischen Naturalismus ist
Hebbel ausgegangen von der Zeit an, da er die Bibel und
Schiller hinter sich gelassen hatte; der ethische Idealismus ist
sein letztes Wort, in ihm haben Ethik und Mystik dauernd ihr
Gleichgewicht gefunden . . . . . Durch sein trotziges
Ringen um Gott hat aber der Dichter den Weg zu einer festen
Ethik nicht gefunden, den Mittler hat er stolz verschmäht
und der Vater ist ihm stumm geblieben."

Wirklich Neues hat Bruns ebensowenig zutage gefördert als
Lahnstein. Doch seine Zusammenstellung ist insofern von
praktischem Wert, als sie sowohl die Gegensätze als auch das
Aehnliche in Hebbels und Ludwigs Ansichten über das Drama
klar vor Augen stellt. Ludwig war Kleinstädter, einsam,
bestrebt sich zu bilden; Hebbel liebte das Getriebe der Gross-
stadt, er war eine Herrennatur und suchte auf andre ein-
zuwirken, bestrebt, sie unter seinen Willen zu zwingen, denn
er fühlte sich als Meister. Ludwig geht der historische Sinu
ab, der bei Hebbel stark entwickelt ist. Ersterer geht von
dem Stoffe, letzterer von der Idee aus. Doch vor allem stehen
die beiden Dichter in Bezug auf ihre Weltanschauung in
schroffem Gegensatz zu einander. Bruns beruft sich zwar auf
Hebbels eignen Ausspruch, dass dessen Weltanschauung schon
in seiner Jugend vollständig war. Hebbel täuschte sich aber
hier wohl selbst. Lahnstein sucht darzutun, wie oben gesagt,
dass sich Hebbels Weltanschauung sehr allmählich entwickelt
hat, und m. E. hat er vollkommen recht. Doch bleibt un-
bestritten, dass Hebbels Weltanschauung in ihrer jeweiligen
Gestalt stets den Mittelpunkt seines künstlerischen Schaffens
bildete. Hebbels Ansichten sind zur Genüge bekannt. Ludwigs Weltanschauung "ist in ihren wesentlichen Grundzügen
die überliefert jüdisch-christliche: ein grosser gerechter Gott,
der Mensch schwach, er sündigt, Gott straft." Selbstredend
ist der Schuldbegriff der beiden Dichter ein ganz verschiedener. Für Hebbel ist der Schuld immer nur relativ und liegt
im Willen des Individuums an sich; für Ludwig liegt die
Schuld in der Richtung des Willens und ist gleichbedeutend
mit Sünde. Er findet, die Idee der Tragödie ist "der notwendige Zusammenhang von Schuld und Strafe." Oft tadelt
er die ungerechte Verteilung von Schuld und Strafe in dem
einen oder anderen Drama. Dementsprechend findet Hebbel
in der Moira der Alten einen ihm wesenverwandten Zug,
während Ludwig die Weltanschauung der antiken Tragödie

entschieden ablehnt, ja sogar als unmoralisch und irreligiös
bezeichnet. Wie zu erwarten stellen Hebbel und Ludwig
beide Sophokles am höchsten unter den Alten. Hebbel findet
in der griechischen Tragödie Einheit zwischen Form und Inhalt und er stellt in dieser Hinsicht die Griechen höher als
Shakespeare, den er historisch zu verstehen sucht. Anders
Ludwig: für ihn ist Shakespeare der grösste Dramatiker aller
Zeiten und Länder, und von seinen Werken abstrahiert er,
wie bekannt, die Gesetze des Dramas überhaupt; die griechische Tragödie lässt er nur gelten als ein Produkt ihrer Zeit,
durch die Weltanschauung der Alten bedingt. Hebbel ist der
Meinung, ''dass aus dem Stil der Griechen und dem Stil
Shakespeares durchaus ein Mittleres gewonnen werden muss'',
stimmt aber mit Ludwig überein, dass Shakespeare nicht die
Natur, sondern höhere Wirklichkeit darstellt. Auch ist
Goethe für beide der grösste unter den Dichtern der Neuzeit,
doch in der Bewertung seines Schaffens weichen sie wieder
weit von einander ab. Ludwig tadelt das Versöhnliche seines
Wesens, was ihn veranlasste, der echten herben Tragik soviel
wie möglich aus dem Wege zu gehen, und dass er seine
Helden zu entschuldigen sucht. Goethe und Schiller sind
Ludwig beide zu passiv in ihrem Verhalten gegen ihr eignes
Zeitalter. ''Shakespeare ist der Spiegel seines Jahrhunderts,
Schiller und Goethe sind ihres Jahrhunderts Spiegelbilder.''
Unter den Werken Schillers schätzt Ludwig ''Die Räuber''
und ''Kabale und Liebe'' am höchsten ein. In Hebbels Augen
stieg Schiller nach vorübergehender Abkehr fortwährend,
eine Tatsache, die noch nicht genügend Beachtung gefunden
hat, auch verehrte er in ihm den ethischen Lehrer, während
Ludwig behauptet, Schiller untergrabe gesund praktische
Lebensweisheit und Ethik. Sehr zutreffend ist, was Ludwig
über die Beziehungen zwischen Drama und Bühne, zwischen
Dichter und Schauspieler, und den Anteil des Zuschauers an
der vollkommenen Verwirklichung der künstlerischen Absicht
zu sagen hat. Von dem Drama im eigentlichen Sinne gelten
Ludwigs Ausführungen ganz entschieden, wenn auch dem
Lesedrama darum seine Berechtigung nicht abzusprechen ist.
Bruns hat m. E. Ludwigs diesbezügliche Aussprüche nicht
genügend gewürdigt. Hebbel und Ludwig stimmen im Princip überein, dass das Gemeine, das Elend des Alltags, kein
passender Stoff für das Drama ist. Der Gegensatz in ihren
beiderseitigen Weltanschauung machte ein persönliches Verhältnis zwischen Hebbel und Ludwig unmöglich. Hebbel be-
trachtete obendrein Ludwig als seinen Schüler und Neben-
buhler und konnte sein Urteil über ihn nie ganz von einer

gewissen persönlichen Verbitterung frei machen. Bruns hat recht, wenn er sagt, dass Ludwigs Kritik nirgends persönlich ist, dass er die Dramen Hebbels lediglich auf Grund seines eignen künstlerischen Standpunktes abfällig beurteilte, abfällig beurteilen musste. Im grossen ganzen ist die Darstellung Bruns unparteiisch. Er glaubt, "die grosse Kunst der Zukunft kann nur erreicht werden auf dem Wege, den sie (Hebbel und Ludwig) beschritten haben: dem Wesen ihres Volkes und den Aufgaben ihrer Zeit getreu und doch sich erhebend aus den Trivialitäten des Alltags zu den grossen ewigen Werten. Besonders Hebbel könnte hier der Wegweiser werden zu dem grossen Drama der Zukunft." Eine wirklich grosse Kunst dürfte vielleicht ihre eignen Wege gehen!

Dr. Ludwig Lewins Beitrag zu einem Psychogramm Hebbels weist neue Wege auf dem Gebiete der Biographie. Es ist aber etwas zweifelhaft, ob die Schrift "auch für den gebildeten Laien mit Nutzen und Genuss lesbar" ist, wie auf dem Umschlage versichert wird. Wenn auch auf "völlig neuer psychologischer Grundlage" aufgebaut, bringt doch auch diese Monographie eigentlich nichts Neues. Die Darstellungsmethode an sich ist aber wegen ihrer Uebersichtlichkeit eine wertvolle Neuerung. Für viele dürfte allerdings gerade das angewandte Verfahren etwas Abstossendes haben. Man kann sich anfänglich der Empfindung nicht erwehren, dass man nicht ein Menschenleben, sondern ein Skelett vor sich hat. Leib und Seele des Dichters, seine körperlichen und geistigen Funktionen, sind hier sorgfältig seziert und schematisiert worden. Eine oberflächliche Durchsicht des Registers genügt, um klar zu machen, dass die verschiedenen Punkte mit äusserster Kürze behandelt worden sind. Die Darstellung macht denn auch mehr oder minder einen steckbriefartigen Eindruck. Als Beispiel die folgende Stelle:

"Welcher Verkehrston herrscht im Hause? Friedfertig, zuweilen zänkisch, bei Anwesenheit des Vaters gedrückt. 'Dumpfe, erstickende Gespräche über die Schwierigkeit, Brot herbeizuschaffen, dürften wohl bevorzugte Themata gewesen sein.'" Wer indessen mit Hebbels Leben und Werken einigermassen vertraut ist, für den ergeben diese aktenmässigen Schilderungen ein klares, scharf umrissenes Bild. Allerdings ist dabei in Betracht zu ziehen, dass in diesem Falle wenige Worte oder Sätze eine Fülle von Vorstellungen und Erinnerungen auslösen, und dass dem Leser das Bild dadurch konkret wird. Ob das Resultat auch nur annähernd das gleiche sein dürfte, falls der Leser Hebbel

und seine Werke nicht kennt, lasse ich dahingestellt. Stellenweise versagt die Methode überhaupt, besonders in dem Abschnitt "Verkehr", mit Beginn der Wiener Periode (41 ff.).
Einzelne Ausführungen Lewins sind stark anfechtbar, so
z. B. ist es nicht erwiesen oder auch nur wahrscheinlich, dass
Hebbel Friese war; die Dithmarschen sind jedenfalls vorwiegend sächsischen Stammes. Auch dürfte Hebbels Um-
gangssprache, besondre Anlässe ausgenommen, bis zu seiner
Uebersiedlung nach Hamburg wohl niederdeutsch gewesen
sein (19). Unter "Nachruhm" erwähnt der Verfasser, dass
in Wien eine Strasse nach Hebbel benannt worden ist. Da
Lewin "in Berlin geboren und ansässig" ist, überrascht es
um so mehr, dass ihm die Hebbelstrasse im benachbarten
Charlottenburg entgangen ist. Es ist gern möglich, dass
auch noch anderwärts Oertlichkeiten nach den Dichter benannt worden sind. Doch das sind Kleinigkeiten. Im grossen
ganzen ist diese Schrift ein recht nützlicher Beitrag zur
Hebbel Literatur. Sie ermöglicht einen klaren Ueberblick
und selbständige Beurteilung, da der Verfasser ganz hinter
den Stoff zurücktritt.

JOSEF WIEHR.

Smith College.

ALTISLÄNDISCHES ELEMENTARBUCH von Andreas
   Heusler. Zugleich zweite Auflage des Altisländischen
   Elementarbuches von Bernhard Kahle. Heidelberg 1913,
   Carl Winter's Universitätsbuchhandlung. pp. XII, 264.
   (*Germanische Bibliothek* herausg. von Wilh. Streitberg.
   1. Sammlung germanischer Elementar-u. Handbücher.
   1. Reihe: Grammatiken. 3. Band.)

Heusler's *Altisländisches Elementarbuch* (1913) appears as
the second edition of Bernh. Kahle's Altisländisches Elementarbuch (1896), though the author has given the material
in the latter a most thoroughgoing revision in his own style
and has added much from his own knowledge of the present
status of the questions and from his own experience as a
University teacher and lecturer in Old Norse. Save for the
general outline, one may frankly say that the book is new.

For all of the main parts of the volume Heusler has followed his own plans. In the chapter on Phonology (as also
in that on Forms) rarely occurring and doubtful forms have
been excluded. A laudable practice is adhered to in the
chapter on Forms, in giving the Gothic word by the side of
the Icelandic, thus stressing the historical aspect in the study
of Forms also. There has always been a tendency, as the
author justly points out, to treat only Phonology historically,

while declension and conjugation are dismissed by description. The student who has had Gothic will welcome a book like Heusler's which constantly refers him to a Germanic dialect already learned.

To the third part, on Syntax, Heusler devotes four times the space given to it by Kahle, and it is here that we get the ripe fruits of the author's admirably clear and appreciative studies in Old Norse literature, especially Old Norse prose. A large number of examples with German translations illustrate the points in this more appreciative than coldly categoristic study of prose-syntax. Heusler succeeds here in giving what after all must be the ideal of any syntax study: the *spirit* of the sentence.

Five prose selections (pp. 212-240), a vocabulary, and a short list of *corrigenda* conclude the volume which is at once a scholarly and an appreciative contribution to the study of Old Norse.

HERMANN ALMSTEDT.

University of Missouri.

DR. LEONARD HETTICH: DER FÜNFFÜSSIGE JAMBUS IN DEN DRAMEN GOETHES. Ein Beitrag zur Geschichte und Methodik der Verslehre. (Beitr. z. N. Litgesch. N. F. Heft IV) Heidelberg 1913 8°. VIII, 271 S.

Wie Hettich in dem ersten Abschnitt seiner Untersuchung ausführt, forderte der Weimarer Stil Goethes eine "Rythmische Deklamation" nach dem Principe "Erst schön, dann wahr"; und dies Princip finden wir, wie wir im Laufe der Untersuchung sehen, in Goethes Blankvers wieder. Weniger von Bedeutung für die Gestaltung seines Verses war für Goethe die Beschäftigung mit metrisch-theoretischen Studien, während ein Einfluss des Endecasyllabo und des Blankverses Shakespeares nach Hettichs Ansicht sicher ist. Fragen müsste man hier doch auch, meine ich, ob die Vorliebe für einen starken Schnitt nach den ersten beiden Hebungen nicht ausserdem noch durch den Alexandriner bestärkt sein kann, wie ich in Goethes Jugendproduktion annehmen zu müssen glaubte, wo oft beide Metra gemischt werden.

Von den "zu langen und zu kurzen Versen" wird ausgeschieden, was als künstlerische Absicht angesprochen werden darf, sodass tabellarisch die Reihenfolge der Werke, was Reinheit des Fünffüssers betrifft, sich folgendermassen darstellt: Nat. Tochter (1799-1803), Tankred (1801), Tasso (1788-9),

Iphigenie (1786), Romeo (1812), Mahomet (1800). "In den drei Hauptdramen nimmt also das Gefühl für den Rythmus des fünfhebigen Verses immer mehr zu. Die Singspiele Erwin und Elmire, die chronologisch zwischen Iphigenie und Tasso fallen, ordnen sich auch prozentual vollkommen ein. Von den Übersetzungen steht Tankred der ungefähr gleichzeitigen 'Natürlichen Tochter' noch am nächsten, während Mahomet eine auffällige Unsicherheit im Rythmus zeigt, wohl weil er das erstere der beiden aus dem Französischen übernommenen Stücke ist. Mehr als zehn Jahre später folgt Romeo, der mit ungefähr 3 Prozent zwischen Iphigenie und Mahomet stünde, wenn er nicht noch viele andere metrische Freiheiten aufwiese. Die Prologe und Theaterreden sind natürlich freier gebaut." (p. 49). Ich kann nicht sagen, dass diese Schlussfolgerung für mich überzeugend ist, dazu sind die Prozentualunterschiede, die ausser in Romeo und Mahomet ein Schwanken von nicht einmal 1% aufweisen, zu gering. Statistik kann für mich in solchen Dingen keinen Ausschlag geben, es sei denn durch überwältigende Zahlen. Wertvoller wäre eine eingehendere Charakteristik der einzelnen Stücke. In der Natürlichen Tochter erwarten wir dem Inhalte und dem ganzen Stile des Stückes nach, was wir finden. Aber warum unterscheiden sich Tankred und Mahomet so stark? Sollte da nicht die Art der Nachdichtung Aufschluss geben können? Und wie weit geht tatsächlich die Einwirkung von Shakespeares Vers im Romeo? Was Iphigenie betrifft, so bin ich geneigt anzunehmen, dass Goethe verschiedentlich, unter dem Einfluss griechischer Chorgesänge ganz unwillkürlich in Rythmen verfiel wie der Dreier 689: "Voll Müh und eitel Stückwerk", der in dem schweren Ausgang "Stückwerk" (ohne dass man den Vers deshalb unbedingt vierhebig lesen müsste) die Reminiszenz deutlich zu verraten scheint. Auch die Verse 1053 und 1081 scheinen mir vielleicht zuerst unbewusst und dann absichtlich stehen geblieben zu sein, während 877 später (leider) ausgefüllt wurde. Bei 2174, dem wortkargen "Lebt wohl" des Thoas, giebt Hettich die Absicht selbst zu. Für meine Vermutung antiker Einwirkung spricht indess deutlich die Bezierung auf Klytaimnestras Aufhetzung der Eumeniden in Äschylus' Drama (Vers 94 ff.), die wir in Iph. 1055/6 finden:

[Lasst nicht den Muttermorder entfliehn!
Verfolgt den Verbrecher. Euch ist ed geweiht!]

Bei den Vierern, die in ganzen Komplexen stehen, ist natürlich die Beziehung noch viel klarer.

Während Hettich im Tasso die Dipodien V. 3300 und 3416

"sehr wirkungsvoll und ganz dem Inhalte angepasst" findet,
meint er, 3402 würde "gewissermassen dadurch entschuldigt,
dass Antonio Tasso unterbricht. Auffällig ist allerdings, dass
Goethe den Vers nicht auf zwei Personen verteilt hat, sondern
Antonio einen neuen Vers beginnen lässt." Ist es aber nun
nicht ungeheuer bezeichnend für das schmerzliche Einhalten
Tassos und den robusten Trost Antonios, der "nicht ohne
Rührung" geblieben ist wenn wir lesen:

> ich werde diese Stimme
> Nicht mehr vernehmen, diesem Blicke nicht,
> Nicht mehr begegnen—
>
> Antonio   Lass eines Mannes Stimme dich erinnern,
> Der neben dir nicht ohne Rührung steht!

Mahomet zeigt 68 Sechser und unter diesen 11, die direkt
Alexandrinerstruktur aufweisen; ebenso und sehr charakteristisch für diese Bearbeitung, zeigt Romeo eine Menge Sechser
mit halbierender Fuge, die noch dazu als Reimpaare oder
wenigstens Teile eines Reimpaares verwendet werden. Verteilung eines Verses auf mehrere Personen kommt in allen
Stücken verschwindend wenig vor, und auch dann noch liebt
Goethe die Ganzheit des Verses durch Versendpause zu betonen. Fehlende Senkung findet Hettich nur einmal (Tasso
1189) und Doppelsenkung fast in allen Fällen nur orthogra-
phisch in Wörten wie: breitere, andere, furchtbaren, kräftige,
tüchtigern etc.

Stumpfen Versausgang bevorzugt Goethe mit ca. 60%.
"Stumpfe und Klingende Verse wechseln ohne Zwang rein
nach den Gesetzen des Wohlklangs, und zwar so, dass im allgemeinen grössere Versgruppen mit gleichen Ausgängen ver-
mieden werden. Kommen dennoch hier und da mehrere
gleiche Versausgänge nach einander vor, so scheinen sie nur
selten in gewollter Beziehung zum Inhalt zu stehen. (Vgl.
Fries, Zföst. Gym. 57 (1906) Heft 12; Koch, beide Programme.) Fries meint: Bei Stellen, die eine iterative, gleich-
mässige Tätigkeit, oft mit Detailmalerei, schildern, liebt
Goethe tonverwandte Reihen von zwillingshaft gleichen,
weiblich abschliessenden Versen abzuwickeln, die jene Gleich-
mässigkeit versmalerisch veranschaulichen . . . . . All
das findet er in Tasso 3198-3212 . . . . . Ob man aus
solchen immerhin doch vereinzelten Fällen auf eine allgemeine
Tendenz des Dichters schliessen kann, bezweifle ich. Für eine
Gesammtdarstellung ist ein solch episodisches Vorkommen
von wenig Wert." (Hettich p. 68/9) Zugegeben, dass die
Friessche Ausdeutung des Falles nicht gerade sehr glücklich
ist, so scheint mir sein Verfahren doch durchaus am Platze.
Was heisst das: allgemeine Tendenz? Schliesslich machen

doch die Einzelfälle die allgemeine Tendenz aus, und ein
reicher Dichter, der bald durch dieses, bald durch jenes
Mittel charakterisiert und nicht starr immer denselben Kunst-
griff anwendet (wie etwa Grillparzer in der Verwendung von
freien Versen und Fünffüssern in seiner Medea, müsste dann
in der ''Gesammtdarstellung'' als armer erscheinen. Diese
Einzelfälle wären, wenn man ihnen eine bewusste oder unbe-
wusste Kunstabsicht nachweisen könnte, sicher wertvoller
als andere, hier und da doch verhältnismässig wenig über-
zeugende Prozentrechnungen.

Und mir scheint nun in der Tat, dass hier Absicht vorhand-
en ist, wie wir an Beispielen nachprüfen können, die Hettich
trotz allem fleissig zusammengestellt hat. Tasso 2483 ff., 2722
ff., 3323. sind äusserst charakteristisch für Tassos Wesen und
erinnern—auch das ist wertvoll—an einen gleichen Gebrauch
in Goethes Prosa in Werther und in seinen Strassburger
Briefen, wo die Anapher mit ''wenn'' oder ''wie'' in Er-
regung häufig auftritt. Die Kunstabsicht in den Versen 3198
muss Hettich selbst zugeben. Das allerdings muss man, glaube
ich, festhalten: stumpfer oder klingender Ausgang in stellen-
weiser Häufung charakterisiert an sich noch nicht, erst in
Verbindung mit Hoch- oder Tiefschluss, mit Enjambement
oder Fugenvertiefung wird er bald dies, bald jenes ausdrück-
en können. Man vergleiche dazu die angeführten Beispiele
oder auch die folgenden aus Iphigenie:

V. 656   Orest klagt über den ihm anhaftenden Fluch,
           Leid zu bringen: 7 verse, klingender Aus-
           gang mit fallender Melodiekurve ohne En-
           jambement, (Klagekurve).
V. 10   Iphigenies Klage, ganz ähnlich, 6 verse.
V. 2129   dagegen, flehend hoffnungsvoll: häufiges En-
           jambement mit Versnachschlag. Die Melodie
           kurve kommt erst im folgenden Verse zu
           Ende oder ein Vers ist dem andern in seiner
           Melodie übergeordnet (2138 wiederholt die
           Kurve von 2137, nur höher wegen der
           Steigerung, 2139 noch höher als 2138).
V. 1341   die langausholenden Perioden von 3 oder 4
           verknüpften Zeilen schildern die Freude des
           von Fluche befreiten Orest.

Stumpfen Ausgang dagegen finden wir in den knappen,
ehernen, schicksalsschweren Versen der Genealogie Iphigenies (330), in den trotzigen Worten Thoas' (463).

Absicht liegt möglicherweise auch vor, wenn, wie Hettich
beobachtet, Goethe bei geschlossenen, längeren Reden dem

letzten Vers das vom vorhergehenden verschiedene Versge-
schlecht giebt, ebenso, wenn bei stichomythischen Partieen die
Ausgänge wechseln. (Nat. Tochter 425-7, 1817-24; Tasso 1384
ff., wo Antonio in stumpfen, Tasso in klingenden Versen
spricht—in denen übrigens 5 mal i-Assonanz vorkommt.)

Hettich wirft im fünften Abschnitt (Metrische Drückung
und Erhebung) die Frage auf, ob die grosse Anzahl der
"Trochäen" im Tasso wohl durch Moritz' Theorie der Unter-
mischung der Jamben mit Spondeen, Daktylen etc. hervor-
gerufen sei. Er glaubt nicht, dass das Ethos in allen Fällen
der Grund für schwebende Betonung sei. Ist es nicht vielleicht möglich, dass die deutsche Sprache gar nicht so überaus
geeignet für jambisches Metrum ist, wie man oft anzunehmen
neigt, sondern dass durch Inversion, Relativpronomen, Conjunction etc. ein Compromiss verlangt wird, den eben
schwebende Betonung darstellt? Ausserdem glaube ich, dass
Hettich unter schwebender Betonung viele Fälle registriert,
wo tatsächlich nur ein Höherliegen der Senkung zu bemerken
ist wie in folgenden Beispielen:

Iph. 2074 Rasch Abgeschiednen; Faust 3222 Kalt Staunenden; Claudine 1401 Wohl ausgedachte. Hier kann tatsächlich das erste Wort gar keinen Akzent beanspruchen, obwohl es durch seine Höhenlage ein gewisses Gewicht hat.

Wie die Tabellen für Schwebende Betonung zeigen, finden
wir sie am häufigsten im Versanfang und am stärksten beim
Verb. Sobald aber Reim auftritt, steht das Verb nicht mehr
an erster Stelle (Prolog z. Eröffn. d. Berl. Theat.). Hat das
nicht etwa direkte Beziehung zum Zurückgehen des Enjamb-
ements zu gleicher Zeit? Solche Wechselbeziehungen sollten
noch einmal untersucht werden.

Die nächsten Abschnitte über falsche Wortbetonung enthalten nicht viel Wichtiges. Ich glaube fast, Goethe war von
der Theorie zu sehr beeinflusst, wenn er ein "Zusammen-
knicken des Schauspielers" bei Versen wahrgenommen haben
will wie etwa diesem: Des stolzen Hofs erniedrigende Gnade.

Was hier in den unbedeutenden Silben verloren geht, wird
eben in den stark gedehnten, malenden übrigen gewonnen.
"Dem Strandenden" würde ich eher wegen seiner Kakophonie
peinlich empfinden; und was Worte wie: "unkenntlich",
"unsterblich", "vollkommen" anbetrifft, so sind sie eben von
Natur in Jamben zu schwebender Betonung bestimmt.

Reihenbrechung, Enjambement definiert Hettig als "das
Hinwegsetzen des Rythmus über die Gruppe der fünf Jamben,
d. h. als Nichtrespektierung der graphisch festgehaltenen
Verszeile auch als rythmisches Versganze. Dieser Fall tritt

ein, wenn die Pause am Versende kleiner wird als eine im
Versinnern, und infolge dessen ein Teil des Verses rythmisch
enger mit dem folgenden oder vorausgehenden Verse zu-
sammenhängt als mit dem andern Teil des gleichen Verses.''
Ich habe bereits früher einmal (Euphor. XVII, p. 588) meine
konservativere Ansicht darüber geäussert, konservativer insofern, als ich behaupte: der 5 füssige Vers kann und muss
trotzalledem bewahrt werden. Eigene Erfahrung beim Rezi-
tieren solcher Verse sowie beim Vorbereiten von Studenten
für Aufführungen haben mich in dieser Überzeugung immer
mehr bestärkt. Schwere Fälle von Brechung haben fast
immer ihren Grund in der beabsichtigen Hervorhebung der
letzten Silbe der Reihe. Wir sollten demnach nicht von End-
pausenabschwächung sprechen, da es darauf eigentlich nicht
ankommt, sondern von Dehnung der letzten Silbe, die genau
dieselbe Wirkung hat, als ob die Endpause vorhanden wäre.
Trotz des hohen Prozentsatzes von Brechungen bei Goethe
(ca. 30% ohne deutliche chronologische Entwicklung für oder
wider) bleibt der Vers demnach doch intakt. Es würde sich
sicherlich lohnen, einmal zu untersuchen, in wie vielen Fällen
bei Goethe die Brechung wirklich dem Zweck der Dehnung
der letzten Silbe dient und in wie vielen Fällen Spannungs-
pause beabsichtigt ist, gegen solche Fälle, in denen keine
künstlerische Absicht angenommen werden kann. Ausserdem
scheint mir, dass epische Partieen Brechung bevorzugen, lyrische sie vermeiden; die Beispiele, die Hettich (p. 133/4)
anführt, sprechen durchaus für meine Ansicht.

Sehr hübsche, malende Wirkung von Brechung stellt dann
der Verfasser zusammen auf Seite 148 ff. und zwar mit grossem Geschick, sodass man in der Tat wünschen möchte, er hätte
sich gegen diese Art interpretierender Betrachtung nicht im
allgemeinen ablehnend verhalten. Hier einige Beispiele:

Iph. 394 Viel Taten des verworrnen Sinnes deckt/Die Nacht mit
schweren Fittichen
Claud. 973 Es schwebt die Nacht/Mit allen ihren Schauern um uns
her
Erwin 156 Hoch und höher/Die Nacht sich über unsern Klagen
wölbte
Iph. 678 drangen wie die Sterne/Rings um uns her unzählig aus der
Nacht
Tasso 2121 und alles rings/umher verschwindet ihm
Nat. Toch. 1325 Weit/Verbreitet euch ihr . . . . .
Tasso 1133 Welch neuer Kreis/Entdeckt sich meinem Auge
Nat. Toch. 1978 Fern am Rande/Des nachtumgebenen Ozeans

Ganz entschieden muss bei solchen Untersuchungen auf
das Ethos geachtet werden. Es scheint mir, dass Hettich da
oft fehlt und Pausen oder Fugenschnitte ansetzt, wo nur bei

ruhigem, diskutierenden Vortrage solche möglich wären. Man
nehme zum Beispiel Vers 16 der Iphigenie:

> Ihm zehrt der Gram
> Das nächste Glück vor seinen Lippen weg

Eine mittelmässige Pause (No. 3 nach einer glücklichen Ab-
stufung Hettichs) wäre dort möglich, wenn es darauf ankäme,
uns zu sagen, dass es der Gram und nichts anderes ist, der
ihm das Glück wegzehre; die Kurve machte dann einen stark-
en Sprung aufwärts in ''Gram'' und fiele auf ''das'' wieder
stark zurück. In Wirklichkeit aber drängt ein intensiv ge-
spanntes Gefühl über die Zeile hinaus mit ungebrochner
Kurve und langem fallend-klagenden Gleitton in ''Gram''.
Ein Gegenbeispiel wäre Tasso 294 ff., wo tatsächlich das dis-
kutierende Ethos Pausen verlangt:

> Vaterland
> Und Welt muss auf ihn wirken. Ruhm und Tadel
> Muss er ertragen lernen. Sich und andre
> Wird er bezwungen recht zu kennen. Ihn
> Wiegt nicht die Einsamkeit mehr schmeichelnd ein.

Bei diesem Beispiel stellt dann der letzte Vers mit seiner
fugenlosen Fünfjambenform die Ruhe wieder her, wie das
Goethes Gewohnheit ist (Siehe Hettich p. 143).

Die Tabelle über Goethes Gebrauch der Fugen zeigt, dass
die orchestischen Einschnitte (entweder x′ x′ oder x′ x′ x′)
alle andern überwiegen, ihnen zunächst kommen die Schnitte
nach x′ x′ x′ oder x′ x′ x′ x′. Chronologisch ist kaum
eine Entwicklung festzustellen, aber sobald der Reim auftritt,
wie im Berliner Prolog, steigt die Prozentzahl sofort von ca.
35-40c/o auf 60c/o (also im umgekehrten Verhältnis zu Enjambement und schwebender Betonung!).

Allgemeine Sentenzen ziehen die orchestische Fuge durchaus vor, wie Hettich sehr treffend beobachtet (p. 170). Es
leuchtet ein warum: die ersten beiden Hebungen schlagen
das Thema an, die übrigen führen es aus:

Tasso 59   Ein edler Mensch/zieht edle Menschen an
Iph. 147   Man tadelt den,/der seine Taten wägt
Erwin 250   Es fehlt der Mensch/und darum hat er Freunde

Nach Zitelmanns Methode wird in einem Abschnitt über
akzentuelle Gliederung der höhere Rythmus untersucht:
Nachtaktverse überwiegen, dann folgt Zwischentakt und endlich Vortakt. Sehr gut sind Goethes Änderungen um einer
bessern Gliederung willen nachgewiesen, und eine ''Zusam-
menfassung'' giebt klaren Überblick über erhaltene Resultate.
Prinzipieller Gründe wegen muss ich hier zu einigen Beispielen meine abweichende Lesung anführen:

Nausikaa 23   Was rufen mich | für Stimmen ‖ aus dem Schläf

Diese Notierung scheint mir falsch. Odysseus weiss, er hat geschlafen, und der Zuschauer weiss es auch. "Schlaf" darf daher nicht akzentuiert werden, "Stimmen", das fragende, bekommt die ganze Kraft des Akzentes, und die Fuge muss hinter "mich" oder sogar hinter "für" verschoben werden.

In Vers 25 sollte "ahmt" den Hauptakzent haben, weil es genug Umspannungsvermögen erzeugen muss um auf "nach" vorzudeuten:

oder áhmt der frische Wind,
Durch's hohe Rohr des Flusses sich bewegend,
Zu meiner Qual die Menschenstimmen nach.

Vers 31: O, | dass sie freundlich mir | und zarten Herzens
Dem Vielgeplagten ‖ doch begegnen möchten

wie Hettich teilt, würde bedeuten: Sie sollen ihm doch *begegnen;* macht man die Fuge dagegen *nach* "doch", so bedeutet es: sie sollen ihm *freundlich* begegnen.

Nat. Tocht. 426 O möcht ich (Tag auf Táge) so erlében!

Hettichs Gliederung und Akzentuierung scheint mir hier wieder einmal ohne Rücksicht aufs Ethos, prosaisch. Mit starkem Gefühl würde sich der Vers für mich so darstellen:

O mòcht ich Tág | auf Táge sò erlèben

Nausikaa 46 Erprobte Männer | in Gefahr | und Mühe

Die Fuge vor "und" ist steigernd, das sollte es aber hier nicht sein, bei einfacher Aneinanderreihung tritt der Schnitt immer nach "und" ein.

Scheint es auch oft so, als wäre nach dieser Seite hin der Willkür ein weites Feld gelassen, und als könnte der eine den oder jenen Vers so "empfinden", der andere so, es kommt trotz alledem auf die richtige Interpretation an, die in gleicher Weise Sinn und Ethos der Stelle genau beachten muss. Prinzipielle Untersuchungen experimenteller Art täten uns sehr not!

Der vierte Teil der Arbeit, Euphonisches und Melodisches behandelnd, giebt vor allem einen Überblick über die Sievers-Rutzschen Theorieen ohne viel Eignes hinzuzutun (was dem Verfasser durchaus nicht zur Last gelegt werden soll). Es ist vorläufig, wenn man nicht selbst mit Sievers oder Rutz gearbeitet hat, schwer, sich auf diesem Gebiete zurecht zu finden, da viele von den früheren Veröffentlichungen veraltet oder in der Terminologie irreleitend sind, so meine eigenen Ausführungen in meiner Untersuchung über Goethes Knittelvers (Leipzig 1909).

Ein letzter Abschnitt endlich orientiert über Hiatus und Synkopierung.

Wenn wir somit überschauen, was in dem Buche Hettichs geleistet ist, so möchten wir vielleicht anfangs geneigt sein, mit dem Verfasser zu fragen, ob die Resultate "als nicht im Verhältnis stehend erscheinen zu der Unsumme von Zeit und statistischer Arbeit, die sie erforderten." Das wäre indessen durchaus ungerecht; zurückblickend unterschätzt der Schwimmer meist die zurückgelegte Strecke, und man darf von einer Untersuchung von über 15000 Versen verschiedenster Werke keine völlig ausschöpfende und abschliessende Arbeit verlangen. Der Verfasser hat mit ungeheurem Fleiss, mit Umsicht und guter methodischer Schulung und endlich mit ausserordentlicher Belesenheit in der einschlägigen Litteratur eine feste Grundmauer aufgebaut und das statistische Gerüst geschlagen. Seine Nachfolger werden bei weitem leichtere Arbeit haben. Was nunmehr getan werden muss ist dies: Die einzelnen Werke müssen in ihrer besondern Eigenheit eingehender charakterisiert, die Darstellungsmittel müssen in ihren Wechselbeziehungen verglichen und Goethes Vers muss—ein Anfang dazu ist schon von Hettich gemacht—in die Entwicklung der Form im allgemeinen und die Reihe der übrigen Dramatiker eingeordnet werden. Eine Arbeit wie die vorliegende bedeutet einen guten Schritt vorwärts auf dem Wege.

ERNST FEISE.

University of Wisconsin.

NEWPORT, CLARA PRICE: WOMAN IN THE THOUGHT AND WORK OF FRIEDRICH HEBBEL. A Thesis submitted for the Degree of Doctor of Philosophy. The University of Wisconsin. Madison, Wis. 1912.

Dr. Newport approached her subject from the standpoint of the scholar and of the woman, and was, therefore able to see some of the Hebbel problems from a new and interesting angle. A brief Introduction traces succinctly the changes which have taken place since 1800 in the position of women in the world and hence in literature. Hebbel's works, both in prose and verse, prove that he passed through a similar evolution in his attitude towards women—an evolution which kept pace exactly with his own inner development and was influenced by the varying fortunes of his life and the women with whom he came in contact.

During the Wesselburen period, as the autobiography and the lyrics show, woman was to him the dream-maiden, the creature all soul, all loveliness, "to be adored rather than desired." True love often culminated in death, marriage was usually looked upon as a profanation (pp. 13 ff.). The women who entered his life during the Hamburg and Munich period—mainly Elise, Emma Schroeder, Josepha Schwartz—changed the picture. The predominating trait of all three, as seen from the letters and diaries, was their complete subjugation to the powerful masculine personality, with whom they had no means of coping on equal terms, and who repaid their worship with passion not unmixed with contempt. Hebbel's mental attitude at this time is best reflected in ''Judith'' and ''Genoveva''. The latter is the ideal: submissive, saintly, beautiful, and noble. She does not by entering the sphere of action go beyond the legitimate limit of her sex, (p. 71); Judith, though inspired by the Deity, has stepped beyond woman's permissible bounds, by attempting initiative action. Mirza serves as the mouthpiece of Hebbel's condemnation of Judith's deed. He himself had stated that Judith was aimed against the emancipation of women. In other words, Genoveva is held up to women as a model, Judith as a warning (p. 69). Later Dr. Newport points out that Mariamne, whom she calls ''the new Judith'' implies a complete reversal in Hebbel's attitude (p. 95). ''Maria Magdalena'' marks a step beyond Judith, for here Hebbel arraigns society for its use of woman. ''Judith is a criticism of woman, and 'Maria Magdalena' of society'' (p. 80). In the last period, when Christina Enghaus had made him acquainted with a new type of woman, one who could love without exhausting her entire personality in the sex function, he took a further step: the admission that woman has a right to protection against attacks on her individuality (p. 81), we might add even when these attacks are made in the name of love. Mariamne is the culmination of this development. ''Here for the first time in his work, we have a real tragic heroine treated sympathetically'' (p. 95). Judith has been rendered unfit for life by breaking through ''woman's sphere'' of passivity; Genoveva, the saint, was martyred for the good of the world without being given a chance of resistance; Clara was ''pushed out of life''; but Mariamne left life when life was bereft of inner dignity (p. 96). Illuminating is the author's parallelism between Judith and Mariamne, Clara and Eugenie, Genoveva and Agnes, showing that Hebbel went back to the same type of dramatic heroine, but from a new point of view.

In the process of tracing this evolution Dr. N. gives some acute analysis of dramatic characters. Her sympathetic depiction of Judith (p. 60) contains an original bit of criticism upon the passage in which Judith describes the humiliating events of her marriage night to Mirza. "Such a scene would be forever locked in the secret recesses of a woman's nature . . . . . In madness or delirium she might reveal her secret, but never to explain her refusal of another man . . . . . She would guard such a secret with her very life." (p. 60). Here a woman knows that Hebbel was psychologically at fault. The entire delineation of Genoveva with its touch of humor is fascinating. (p. 69). In the discussion of 'Gyges und sein Ring" the author shows the evolution from "Diamant" and "Rubin" in the attempt at creating a symbolic drama, in which the fairy tale and reality should blend to afford a deeper insight into the mysteries of the human soul. (p. 113). A comparison of "the lovely, dreamy heroines" of these plays with similar figures of the Maeterlinck drama might have afforded new insight here. Elucidating is the footnote in which the delicate question of the unveiling is treated. Dr. N. takes the position that the unveiling is not to be interpreted in the "old brutal sense", and adduces good evidence for her argument from the emphasis which Hebbel laid on Rhodope's eastern origin "making her more of an oriental than even the Lydians" and on her almost morbid delicacy. She sums up: "Kandaules sins against his wife by venturing to decide against her will what is fitting for her, and it remains a sin, even though his view is more reasonable than hers." (p. 113). This plausible interpretation sets Rhodope next to Nora.

A number of minor characters which usually go unnoticed are well treated and throw new light on Hebbel's power of depicting dramatically. Dr. N. shows that Margareta in "Genoveva" is the only woman in the play who undergoes a dramatic conflict; Alexandra and Salome, far from being merely vixens or foils for Mariamne, are shown to be truly tragic characters with a great deal of justification on their side; the mother of Clara, Frigga, Marfa, and Marina are carefully studied.

Dr. N. further contributes to the understanding of Hebbel by calling attention to the stress which the dramatist lays on the inherent antagonism often found between the sexes, an antagonism that is frequently intensified rather than diminished by passion, as in the case of Golo, Judith, Herod, Brunhild (pp. 32, 55, 121). Now that Strindberg has come into prominence, this stress on Hebbel's part seems particularly interesting. A study of Hebbel as a predecessor of Strindberg as well as of Ibsen might be well worth while.

With so much that is new and helpful to be welcomed it

may perhaps without cavil be suggested that the study before
us would have gained in value and accessibility, had the bulk
not been unduly increased by lengthy analyses of those works
of Hebbel which furnished virtually no material for this
study, and of the many male characters which have no bearing upon the subject under discussion. In the Introduction,
Kleist's heroines are rather summarily disposed of as on the
same plane with Schiller's from the point of view of modernity. Kleist was—probably quite unconsciously—one of the
first innovators in this direction. His Natalie and Marquise
von O. exhibit at least traces of that conscious assertion of
the dignity of the individual which shows itself both in
questioning the social order and in initiative action, and
which marks the parting of the ways of the old conception
of woman and the modern. Though it may seem a far cry from
Natalie to Nora, yet Kleist must rank as one of the first of the
moderns. We look forward with anticipation to the author's
promised study of the women of Kleist and of Ibsen, and
suggest that illuminating sidelights might be obtained by comparisons with those of Maeterlinck and of Strindberg.

HENRIETTA BECKER VON KLENZE.

FRIEDRICH GUNDOLPH, SHAKESPEARE UND DER
DEUTSCHE GEIST—George Bondi, Berlin, 1911. VIII
+ 360 pp.

During the last few years a movement has sprung up in
Germany toward more vital literary criticism than was possible when scholars aimed to make of this discipline a pure
science. New insights into the nature of art have aroused
and fostered new ideals of scholarship. For some time artists
as well as critics and writers on aesthetics have laid emphasis
upon the fact that 'something experienced'—an *Erlebnis*—is
the great generative principle of art; and they have felt that
the value of art lies in its ability to arouse such 'experiencing'
in those who react upon it, such 'experiencing' being valuable
indeed, because it liberates vital forces and thus gives that
heightened sense of 'life-feeling' which is cherished as the
summum bonum. This being the *rationale* of art and its
effect upon others, one has come to feel that the office of the
critic lies in determining and interpreting the artist's concrete
'experience', which found expression in the particular work
of art, in the light of the larger 'experience' or manner of re-
acting upon life and the material of living, which was dom-

inantly characteristic of him, and which underlies and suffuses all his separate art-productions. By disengaging and describing this 'experience' the critic produces in his reader a more vivid sense of it than would otherwise have been probable; and he thus aids that liberation of vital processes, with the consequent heightening of life-feeling, which is indeed one of the great functions of art.

It is obvious that the chief process involved in the critic's task is that of *Einfuehlung* or sympathetic identification of himself with the artist and his work. The critic holds in abeyance his personal subjectivity and aims at truthful objective analysis; yet he knows that purely objective criticism is as impossible as it is undesirable. For it has been recognized that an artist's work—being, as it were, a universe in itself, infinitely suggestive in the complexity of its component parts and characteristics—is capable of freeing widely differing sets of life-forces in different people and in different ages: only that being apprehended at any one time which is recognized because it aids the self-unfoldment of those who react upon the work of art. The critic's reaction having thus itself been an 'experience'—the nature of which was determined by his personality and his needs as determined in their turn by the character and needs of his age and people—a certain amount of subjectivity in his work is unavoidable. The more completely he is a typical, focalized embodiment of the chief forces and tendencies of his age, the greater and more vital will be his criticism. He will be an active power in promoting the cultural growth of his people.

A study, through successive periods, of the critical reactions upon a single artist—if he is a great artist and if the 'reactors' upon his work are of typical importance and of dominating influence—undoubtedly furnishes an interesting and valuable contribution to the story of a country's cultural growth. The process which must underlie such historic criticism is again, and in a heightened degree, that of *Einfuehlung*: *Einfuehlung* into all the possible phases of the artist's work, and likewise into the 'experiences' of the various critics.

Such a history of criticism has lately been given to the German world in Gundolph's *Shakespeare und der deutsche Geist*. Not only is the subject of the investigation—Shakespeare—one of the transcendent artists of the world, but, moreover, the critics whose reactions are analyzed are for the most part the great typical poets who have shaped German literature and German mental life. Having studied all earlier reactions upon Shakespeare, Gundolph ends by giving his own reaction—his own reaction as determined by the mental structure and the needs of the German people of today.

Stimulated by Nietzsche's vindication of the mere process of life, and influenced, also, by Bergson's dynamic interpretation of its ceaseless flow, Gundolph feels that what the world and Germany in particular need today, is the "will and the power to endure reality", that is, the power to endure concrete life in its sovereign brutality, with all its throes as well as joys. This reality, this teeming brutal reality, as well as the power to endure it, he finds in Shakespeare: Shakespeare seems to him the "humanly embodied *creativeness* of life itself", the symbol of that tireless vital impulse which rejoices in its inexhaustible flow of concrete creations without any thought of ulterior purpose.

Approaching the study of the influence exerted by Shakespeare in Germany with this view dominant in his consciousness, Gundolph says that Shakespeare is the most important and the most easily intelligible symbol of the process by which this *creativeness* was won for German poetry, and he interprets the story of Shakespeare's influence in Germany as the story of the reawakening and gradual development of the creative life-powers which seemed to have been lost during the ascendency of rationalism. He shows how the various followers and proclaimers of Shakespeare, themselves symbolic precipitates of forces active at their time, discovered and opened up province after province of mental life; each one finding in Shakespeare just that quality, just that soul-value, that 'experience', which his own particular 'experience' or manner of apprehending life needed and demanded. The nature of each of these *influences* or tributaries into the great stream of German mental life is carefully formulated.

Gundolph shows first how Germany in the seventeenth century—during the age of disintegration which culminated in the Thirty Years' War—received from the English comedians a Shakespeare shorn of his great qualities: the mere crude material of a number of plays transformed into melodrama, horse-play, and blood-and-thunder. After a consideration of Gottsched horrified, who could see in Shakespeare only absolute lawlessness, Gundolph says that Lessing, having recognized in Shakespeare's plays the same tragic power or quality which he had found in the Greeks, admired and proclaimed in him the supreme "intelligence" the possession of which, he says, makes it possible for the genius of every race and of every age to recognize essential laws, in this case, the fundamental, eternal laws of tragedy and the tragic. Next

Gundolph shows how, on the other hand, Gerstenberg, Wieland—who translated Shakespeare—, Herder, young Goethe, and the poets of the Storm and Stress period, discovered, step by step, Shakespeare's sensuousness, his magical atmosphere, and above all his vigorous frank language and inexhaustibly fertile creative power; and he shows how coming to him hungry for mere life, and knowing him chiefly through Wieland's prose translation, they extolled in him the same chaotic formlessness which they saw, or joyously thought they saw, in unsubdued triumphant nature. Young Goethe is seen to have found in Shakespeare's plots illustrations of the fateful conflict between the will of the individual and the will of society; and to have learned to appreciate through him the tragic dualism inherent in the very nature of passion. The later Goethe, however, after the Romanticists' glorification of the fleeting manifoldness and fluidity which they found in Shakespeare, discovered and exalted in him, more and more, his plastic power, form, and control. Schiller, the preacher of moral idealism, in his turn exalted Shakespeare because his world seemed to be pervaded by transcendent moral law and justice, thus reflecting perfectly the divine world-order. Schiller's interpretation Gundolph regrets, and calls attention to its harmful influence on later critics and dramatists.

Novalis, Tieck, Friedrich Schlegel, Wilhelm Schlegel, all interpreted Shakespeare, who, after having at different stages in the past been proclaimed inexhaustible creator, profound analyst of character, portrayer of passion, painter of nature, and moral teacher, was now exalted as consummate artist by these prophets who believed that conscious and intelligent artistic creation—inasmuch as it is the analogue of that divine artistic activity which creates the universe—is the sovereign activity of human life. These romantic critics show the harmonious synthesis of the rationalistic and the emotionalistic interpretations of Shakespeare; and August Wilhelm Schlegel's translation thus represents a climax in the history of Shakespeare's influence in Germany.

But Gundolph feels that the work of interpretation has not yet been completed. He says that Wilhelm Schlegel was, after all, still under the influence of Goethe and the idealistic philosophy of his time; that he therefore saw in Shakespeare's characters the typical element, the universal embodied in the individual; that he read into him the ideals of the good and true and beautiful; that he rounded outlines and softened harsh movements; and that he appreciated neither Shake-

speare's frank supermoral realism nor his robust acceptance
of mere elemental life in its brutal actuality.

To Gundolph himself, permeated as he is by the new life-
feeling of which Nietzsche is the great exponent, Shakespeare
seems a symbol of the superconscious, supermoral vital impulse which wills life unwearyingly; and Shakespeare's work
seems the symbol of sovereign concrete reality "beyond good
and evil." Therefore, finding in him the power to endure and
to present the depths and heights of reality, its brutality, its
concrete 'individualness', he thinks that the time is now ripe
for a new interpretation of Shakespeare, and for a new translation. This translation he himself is making.

Thus the story of Shakespeare's influence in Germany is
seen to form an important chapter in the story of the development of German mental life, and in the history of
German civilization. At the same time it has typical value.
A similar investigation of Shakespeare's influence in England
would be both interesting and valuable. In many ways the
judgments in this book, and the whole argument, are strongly
colored by Gundolph's Nietzschean outlook upon life; yet
though one may sometimes disagree, as e. g. in the case of
his onesided and petty criticism of Schiller, one is always stimulated; moreover, the treatise contains many excellent and
suggestive appreciations of Shakespeare's work; thus the book
is one which should in every way command the interest of
the English-speaking public. It is a masterpiece of historic
criticism, competent, vital, original.

LOUISE MALLINKRODT KUEFFNER.

Vassar College.

NEUE FAUSTLITERATUR.

Die deutsche Faustforschung der letzten Jahre hat sich,
soweit sie mir fruchtbar und fördernd erscheint, vorzüglich
mit dem Problem der Entstehung der Dichtung beschäftigt.
Sie hat, um nachschaffend das Geheimnis zu ergründen,
tiefer als bisher geschehen war, in die Werkstatt des Dichters
einzudringen versucht und hier in der wunderbaren Ver-
schlingung der magisch-theosophischen Mystik mit Herders
gärender Geisteswelt die beiden Grundmächte erkannt, die
den dichterischen Schöpfungsprocess heimlich bestimmten.
Der Untersuchung dieser beiden Grundmächte sind denn auch
die Schriften gewidmet, die hier besprochen werden sollen.
Da ich glaube in meinem Faustcommentar (New York, Henry

Holt & Co., 1907) den ersten Versuch gemacht zu haben, die Doppelwelt, die die Weltanschauung des jungen Goethe umfasste, genauer zu prüfen, so sind mir zunächst vielleicht einige persönliche Bemerkungen erlaubt.

Als ich vor ungefähr zehn Jahren an die Ausarbeitung meiner Faustausgabe schritt, war mir längst klar geworden, dass sich mit der überlebten philosophischen Erklärungsweise eben so wenig anfangen lasse wie mit der landläufigen Mikrologie der sogenannten Faustphilologie. Denn wie jene hinter der Miene des Tiefsinns die hölzernste Vorstellung von Dichtung und dichterischen Schaffen barg, so versteckte sich hinter dieser bei aller gefeierten Vollendung der 'Methode' eine Unfähigkeit künstlerischen Nachfühlens und Nachschaffens, für die es eine Einsicht in den Dichtungsprocess überhaupt nicht gab. Und nicht weniger war ich überzeugt, dass gerade von dieser Einsicht d. h. von dem divinatorischen Tiefblick in die Dichterseele und ihr fühlendes Sinnen und webendes Träumen die höchste Leistung des Interpreten abhängt: hinzudringen zu dem Punkte aus dem das Kunstwerk gequollen ist, das es von hier aus nachschaffend zu verstehen gilt.

Da fiel mir eines Tages die reiche Sammlung alchemistischer Werke eines befreundeten, frühverstorbenen Chemikers in die Hände. Die Neugier, selbst einmal in die seltsame Welt zu blicken, die den wissenschaftlichen Freund interessiert hatte, liess mich mehrere der Werke vornehmen, und es dauerte nicht lange bis ich mich gefesselt fühlte. Nicht nur von dem Anklang mancher Wendungen und Ausdrücke an bekannte Fauststellen, sondern vor Allem von dem mystisch-poetischen Hauch der Weltauffassung, die hinter diesen krausen Dingen stand und unzählige Geister jahrhundertelang in ihrem Bann gehalten hatte. Erst jetzt trat mir lebendig vor die Augen wie eng die Alchemie mit der Astrologie verknüft war, und wie beide von dem Gedanken der natürlichen Magie zusammengehalten wurden. Einmal in diesen Zauberkreis getreten, empfand ich es wie einen inneren Zwang ihn ganz und nach allen Seiten hin zu durchmessen, und zu erfahren, wie Alchemie, Astrologie, und Theurgie 'eins im andern lebt und alles sich zum Ganzen webt.' Ich lebte nach was der junge Goethe in seiner Frankfurter Dachstube erlebt haben musste, als er diese Welt mit der religiösen Inbrunst des rettungsuchenden Totkranken ergriff, und die Umrisse der Faustdichtung zuerst dem 'trüben Blick' schauernd aufgedämmert sein mögen. Noch klingen ja diese tiefen mystisch religiösen Erfahrungen der jungen Dichterseele,

wenn auch gedämpft, in dem ausführlichen Bericht von Dichtung und Wahrheit nach. Und in dem Kapitel über Johann
Baptist Porta in seiner Geschichte der Farbenlehre weiss
Goethe noch auf der Höhe des Mannesalters der Bedeutung
der natürlichen Magie für die Entwickelung der Naturwissen-
schaften gerecht zu werden und vor Allem die ihr zu Grunde
liegende Geistesstimmung zu würdigen: das erwartungs-
volle, hoffende, gläubige Verhalten dem Geheimnis gegenüber,
das Vorahnen zukünftiger Möglichkeiten, das seiner eigenen
Geistesrichtung so viel eher entsprach als Zweifelsucht, Un-
glaube und die negierende, erkältende Manier der Neueren.

Ich habe in der Einleitung zu meiner Faustausgabe versucht, die noch ungeschriebene Geschichte der mystich-theo-
sophischen Weltanschauung wenigstens nach ihren Umrissen
darzustehen: ihre Entstehung im Neuplatonismus, besonders
bei Plotin, ihre Wiedergeburt und Ueubegründung im Zeitalter der Renaissance, ihr Fortleben in der Theosophie des
17. Jahrhunderts und ihr schliessliches Eindringen in die
Kreise des Pietismus, in denen sie Goethe zum innersten Erlebnis ward. Ich könnte heute, nach eingehender Beschäftigung mit der Vorgeschichte der Royal Society of England und
dem Einfluss deutscher Mystik, namentlich Weigels und
Böhmes auf das Geistesleben Englands, dieser Skizze noch
hinzufügen, dass auch die Anfänge der experimentellen Na-
turforschung und der rein mechanistischen Weltauffassung
noch von der Hülle der Theosophie umschlossen sind. Fast
alle Begründer der Royal Society sind dieser Weltanschauung offen oder geheim noch zugetan.

Es war vorauszusehen, dass mein Versuch das Problem der
Entstehung von Goethes Faust auf diesem Wege der Lösung
näher zu führen, der landläufigen deutschen Kritik nicht bequem sein würde. Noch ist es ja nicht so lange her, dass es
Herrn Wagner beim blossen Worte Mystik um Herz und Busen
bange wurde. Etwas papiernen Einfluss von Swedenburg
auf die bekannte Stelle im ersten Monologe Fausts hätte er
mit Erlaubnis Erich Schmidts wol noch zaghaft zugegeben.
Aber in die dunklen Regionen zu dringen, allwo die wolbe-
kannte Schaar haust, die dem Menschen tausendfältige Gefahr von allen Enden her bereitet, wie hätte der Aengstliche
es wagen dürfen? Dazu kam, dass er kein Englisch versteht,
und mein Commentar war in dieser geheimnisvollen Sprache
geschrieben. Mit Recht hat kürzlich Hermann Collitz im
Vorwort zu seiner trefflichen Sammlung *Hesperia* über die
Nichbeachtung der Leistungen amerikanischer Wissenschaft
in Deutschland sich beklagt. Nach meinen eigenen Erfahrungen verbirgt sich hinter dem hochmütigen Totschweigen

unserer Leistungen gar häufig nur eine sträfliche Unkenntnis des Englischen.

Zum Glück haben jedoch Totschweigen und Philisterkritik den Fortschritt der Wissenschaft noch nicht aufgehalten. Konrad Burdachs geistvolle und tiefdringende Studie 'Faust und Moses' (1912), die, ohne meinen Faustcommentar zu kennen, den mystisch-theosophischen Einwirkungen auf Goethe eine ähnliche Bedeutung zuschreibt, wie ich, ist in diesen Blättern schon eingehend besprochen worden. Noch schlagendere Bestätigung der Resultate meiner Versuche brachte indessen ein Buch, das schon ein Jahr vor Burdachs Studie erschienen war. So überraschend war die Uebereinstimmung gewisser Ausführungen in Agnes Bartscherers Schrift *Paracelsus, Paracelsisten und Goethes Faust*,[1] dass ich mich an die Verfasserin brieflich um Auskunft wandte, ob ihr meine Faustausgabe, die in ihrem Literaturverzeichnis fehlte, bekannt gewesen sei. Sie antwortete mir darauf, was sie seitdem auch in der *Germanisch-Romanischen Monatsschrift*, 1913 S. 723 ff. wiederholt hat: dass ihr nur mein Aufsatz 'Die Quelle zur Erdgeistscene im Faust' (*Journal of Engl. and Germ. Phil.* IX, 1 ff.), auf den sie W. Wilmanns seinerzeit hinwies, nicht aber meine Faustausgabe zugänzlich gewesen sei.

Fasse ich die Hauptpunkte zusammen, in denen A. Bartscherer mit mir zusammen trifft, so ist es zunächst die Erkenntnis, dass die Magie, der Faust, des Kopf- und Wortwissens müde, sich ergibt, nicht die *magia illicita* d. h. also die Zauberei und Teufelsbeschwörung, sondern die *magia naturalis* ist. Das war ja und ist noch der Grundfehler der bisherigen Faustforschung, dass sie, dem Volksbuch und Puppenspiel folgend, Faust sofort zum Teufelsbeschwörer machte und darum für die Vision des Makrokosmus, wie die Erscheinung des Erdgeistes, ja schliesslich sogar für die wirkliche Beschwörung des bösen Geistes aus der Pudelgestalt keine genügende Erklärung fand. Wol hatte schon Kuno Fischer auf den Unterschied zwischen Magie und Zauberei hingewiesen—ein Unterschied, den weder F. Th. Vischer noch W. Scherer, mit dessen veralteten exegetischen Kunststückchen Frl. Bartscherer auf S. 10 sich unnötig auseinandersetzt, gesehen hatte—aber auch er machte von seiner Einsicht für die Auslegung keinen Gebrauch.

Mit Recht weist die Verfasserin ferner darauf hin, dass es in Goethes ursprünglichem Plan gelegen haben muss, den halb schuldigen, halb unschuldigen Uebergang Fausts vom Magus und Theurgen zum Teufelsbeschwörer vorzuführen

---

[1] Dortmund, 1911.

und damit seinen Helden unter das Gesetz der Entwickelung
zu stellen. Wie der Dichter dabei an Wellings Warnung an-
knüpfte, wonach die bösen Geister der Luft sich dem
Menschen leicht in verstellter Gestalt gesellen, ihn aus einer
Verführung in die andere treiben, 'bis endlich die voll-
kommene Zauberei und der gänzliche Abfall durch das Ab-
schwören gezeuget, so dann die letzte Scena der Opera ist,'
hat die Verfasserin ebenfalls bemerkt.

Ob Goethe den Unterschied zwischen den beiden Arten der
Magie gekannt habe, ist sonach eine überflüssige Frage. Es
geht nicht nur aus Fausts Worten:

> Ob mir durch Geistes Kraft und Mund
> Nicht manch Geheimnis würde kund,
>
> Dass ich erkenne, was die Welt
> Im Innersten zusammenhält,
> Schau alle Wirkungskraft und Samen
> Und tu nicht mehr in Worten kramen,

womit er das Wesen der Magia naturalis ausspricht, sondern
auch aus dem weiteren Verlauf der Scene hervor. Denn wer
sich in der Literatur der natürlichen Magie näher umgesehen
hat, der weiss, dass ihre Bekenner die Erscheinung und
Berufung von Geistern—natürlich von guten—für möglich
und erlaubt hielten. Wenn Frl. Bartscherer in ihrem einseitigen Bestreben Goethes Kenntnis der Magie und Theurgie
allein auf Paracelsus zu beschränken, besonderes Gewicht
darauf legt, dass dieser in seiner *Philosophia occulta* lehre,
die wahre Magie gebrauche Ceremonien, Conjurationes, Con-
secrationes u. s. w. nicht, so hat sie übersehen, dass derselbe
Paracelsus in seiner *Astronomia magna* (Frankfurt 1571
S. 28 ff.) dem wahren Magus die Macht zuschreibt, die Flagae
d. h. die Geister, 'die des Menschen Heimlichkeit wissen,' zu
zwingen ihm ihre Geheimnisse zu offenbaren. Und in demselben Werke (S. 44) erklärt er, dass 'Wörter und Charac-
teres' d. h. also Beschwörungsformeln und Zeichen, wie Faust
sie gebraucht, Kraft besitzen und dem Magus zu Gebote
stehen.

Wie die Bedeutung der Magia naturalis, so hat die Verfasserin auch die Wichtigkeit der Astrologie und Alchemie
für die frühe Faustdichtung richtig erkannt. Hatte doch
Agrippa von Nettesheim, *De incertitudine* p. 161 (1643)
schon längst betont: 'Magia cum Astrologia sic conjuncta
atque cognata est, ut, qui magiam sine astrologia profiteatur
is nihil agat, sed tota aberret via.' Mit welcher Kunst es
Goethe verstanden hat, von dieser engen Verwandtschaft für
den Aufbau der Scene Gebrauch zu machen, tritt bei Frl.
Bartscherer freilich nicht klar genug zu Tage.

Der angehende Magier Faust wendet sich dem Manuscript des Astrologen Nostradamus darum zu, weil er auf dem Wege der Astrologie zum Verkehr mit den Geistern kommen will. Es handelt sich in der betreffenden Fauststelle vor Allem um Begriff und Bedeutung der 'Seelenkraft.' Ich glaube in meinem Commentar wie in dem erwähnten Aufsatz über die Quelle zur Erdgeistscene über jeden Zweifel festgestellt zu haben, dass es die *vis imaginationis* ist d. h. das Geistesvermögen der Phantasie das nach neuplatonischer Anschauung, besonders aber nach der Lehre des Jamblichus, das Mittel ist, durch das die Geister mit dem Menschen verkehren. Kein besserer Beweis aber für die Richtigkeit meiner Auffassung als das wunderbare Bild, das in Fausts Phantasie sofort beim Anblick des Makrokosmoszeichens aufsteigt. Denn ein grossartiges Phantasiebild und nicht etwa eine Geistererscheinung ist es, was Faust vor diesem Zeichen erlebt. Und er kann es erleben Kraft der geheimnisvollen Wirkung der 'heiligen Zeichen'—divina synthemata oder symbola nennt sie Jamblichus—in denen die Geister ihr Ebenbild erkennen und durch die sie darum, ohne menschliches Zutun, der Phantasie des Theurgen sich kundgeben.

Auch hier hat Frl. Bartscherer mit ihrer Annahme, dass Paracelsus den Gebrauch von Zeichen und Beschwörungen nicht zulasse, sich das tiefere Verständnis verbaut. Daher ist ihr denn die ausserordentliche Bedeutung, die das Wort (λόγος, verbum, nomen, sermo ist der technische Ausdruck dafür) in der Magie, der natürlichen, wie in der Zauberei hat, verschlossen geblieben. Ich müsste hier meinen Commentar ausschreiben, wollte ich diese Bedeutung des 'Wortes' mit Stellen belegen und zeigen, dass sie dem jungen Goethe unmöglich kann entgangen sein.

Schliesslich stimmen Frl. Bartscheres Ausführungen über die Alchemie in Goethes Faust vielfach mit meinen Ergebnissen überein. Ich halte diesen Abschnitt für den wertvollsten ihrer Schrift, wenn es mir auch scheinen will, als habe die Verfasserin hier ebenfalls manches Wichtige übersehen. Zunächst die volle Bedeutung der Tatsache, dass Goethe den Vater Fausts einführt und zwar als Alchemisten und Quacksalber. Zweierlei hat der Dichter damit beabsichtigt. Wie der Blick auf die Herkunft und die Jugendzeit Fausts uns zeigt, in welcher Luft Goethe ihn aufwachsen lässt—es ist der paracelsisch gefärbte mystisch-theosophische Pietismus der Klettenbergschen Kreise—so wird gerade die Erinnerung an diese dumpfe Jungendzeit, die Faust nun, nach der Enttäuschung durch den Erdgeist, ein Meer törichter, ja verbrecherischer Irrtümer erscheint, zum stärk-

sten Motiv innerlich den Uebergang zur Teufelsbeschwörung
vorzubereiten und schliesslich zu vollziehen, wovor Welling
den Magus warnte. Nicht umsonst hat der Dichter gerade
hier, wo Faust die 'Geister der Luft' anruft und wo Wagner
vor der 'wolbekannten Schaar' warnt, sich an Wellings Werk
angelehnt. Damit aber steht wol über allem Zweifel fest,
dass wenigstens dieser Teil der Scene 'Vor dem Tor' mit zu
des Dichters frühen Conceptionen gehörte und dass er bei
ihrer schliesslichen Ausarbeitung viel altes Material benutzt
haben muss.

Dies führt mich zu einer allgemeinen Bemerkung. Ich
halte Frl. Bartscherers Methode zum Beweis ihrer These auch
spät entstandene Fauststellen heranzuziehen, für verfehlt.
Es lassen sich in Goethes Verhältnis zur magisch-theosophischen Mystik deutlich zwei Perioden unterscheiden. Ich
möchte die erste die Periode des naiven Erlebnisses und die
zweite die der gelehrten Vermittelung nennen. Die erste
reicht bis in die Zeit der italienischen Reise und hat in der
Hexenküche wie in der Scene 'Wald und Höhle,' wo die er-
sehnte Henosis der Theurgie erreicht scheint, ihre letzten
Ausläufer. Die zweite Periode beginnt mit der Wiederaufnahme der Dichtung unter Schillers Einfluss und schliesst
die Arbeit am 2. Teil in sich. Was sich aus dieser Scheidung
für die Entstehungsfrage und die Faustkritik überhaupt ergibt, habe ich in meinem Commentar zu zeigen versucht.
Dass Goethe auch in seiner ersten Periode die magisch mys-
tiche Literatur durchforscht habe, versteht sich nach seinem
eigenen Zeugnis von selbst. Aber ein anderes ist die Lektüre, auch die ausgebreitetste, des gläubigen Jüngers der
Magia naturalis, und ein anderes das bewusste Studium des
reifen Mannes, der sich auf diese Weise in die versunkene,
ahnungsvolle Jugendwelt zurückversetzen will.

Ich glaube, dass sich Frl. Bartscherer Goethes frühes Schaffen am Faust viel zu büchermässig gelehrt, zu schulmeister-
haft auf historische Treue berechnet vorstellt (s. z. B. S. 17).
Sie vergisst darüber die Tradition der magischen Mystik, in
der die Literatur, die Goethe damals bewältigte, noch in
einem Masse lebendig war wie wir heute kaum mehr ahnen.
Für den Kenner der Zeit ist es darum gerade zu ausge-
schlossen, dass Goethe einzig auf Paracelsus und die von
ihm abhängigen Schriftsteller sich beschränkt und in jenem
das Urbild zu seinem Faust gefunden haben solle. Nicht
nur Morhofs *Polyhistor*, sondern vor Allem Arnolds *Kirchen
und Ketzergeschichte*, diese weitblickende historische Apologie
der magisch-mystischen Weltanschauung durch einen ihrer

Bekenner, mussten dem jungen Dichter die Vertreter und
Zeugen der grossen Bewegung und deren Literatur als gegenwärtig und weiterwirkend nahe bringen.

Damit hängt noch ein Weiteres zusammen, das Frl. Bartscherer wol andeutet (S. 111), aber in seiner ganzen Tragweite kaum überschaut hat. Ich meine die innige Verwandtschaft zwischen den seelischen Grundlagen der Magie und
der Genieperiode. In meiner Faustausgabe habe ich bereits
darauf hingewiessen, wie der junge Goethe bei Agrippa, Paracelsus und Böhme Anschauungen vom Wesen und den Kräften
des Menschen gefunden hatte, für die ihm Herders Lehre
vom Genie wie eine neue Bestätigung scheinen musste. Hier
wie dort der Nachdruck auf die Phantasie, die göttliche
Schöpferkraft, die im erregten Gefühl, im 'Herzen' ihren
Sitz hat, hier wie dort die Verachtung der Schulwissens, das
Vertrauen auf die 'Eingebung', das Streben nach intuitiver,
absoluter Erkenntnis und das titanische Ringen nach Ver-
göttlichung des Menschen. Nicht von ungefähr sahen die
orthodoxen Feinde Böhmes in ihm schon im 17. Jahrhundert
einen Prometheus und Titanen, und nicht umsonst spotteten
die Gegner des Geniewesens über die Stürmer und Dränger,
'die Jakob Böhme für ein Genie erklärten und keine neue
Wahrheit mehr bewiesen, sondern *fühlten*.' Es ist für mich
keine Frage, dass die eigentlichen Keime und Wurzeln der
Geniebewegung, besonders aber des Begriffs vom Ueber-
menschen in der magisch-theosophischen Mystik zu suchen
sind, und nur so wird uns auch verständlich, wie sich in
Goethes ältester Faustdichtung diese Mystik und Herdersches
Geniewesen so innig verschmelzen konnten.

Fasse ich mein Urteil über Frl. Bartscherers Buch zusammen, so halte ich es, von gewissen Schiefheiten und Mis-
griffen, die sich aus der einseitigen These und der von dieser
bestimmten Methode ergeben, für einen wertvollen Beitrag
zur Entstehungsgeschichte von Goethes Faust. Was auch
rückständige Kritiker über das Werk sagen mögen: es hat
der Faustforschung nun auch in Deutschland ein neues Feld
erschlossen, auf dem die Verfasserin hoffentlich bald recht
viele Mitarbeiter finden wird.

Nach dem bisher Dargelegten wird man es verstehen, wenn
ich in Günther Jacobys tiefdringender Studie 'Herder als
Faust,'[2] trotz ihres scharf geprägten Titels, die wertvollste
Ergänzung zu Frl. Bartscherers Schrift erblicke. Da das
viel umstrittene Buch im letzten Hefte des Journals eingehend besprochen wurde, so kann ich mich hier auf einige
Bemerkungen beschränken.

[2] Leipzig 1911.

Zunächst möchte ich meine Verwunderung nicht zurückhalten über die beklagenswerte Unkenntnis Herders und den wahren Character seines Verhältnisses zu Goethe, welche die Kritik von Jacobys Buch vielfach zu Tage gefördert hat. Denn um diesem Buche völlig gerecht zu werden bedarf es nicht nur der grössten Vertrautheit mit Herders Geisteswelt, sondern auch der genauen Einsicht in die Art wie Goethe andere bedeutende Zeitgenossen der Reihe nach lebendig auf sich wirken liess: Klopstock, Wieland und zuletzt, ja neben Herder am tiefsten, Schiller, seinen grössten Mitbewerber. Die Zeugnisse, die hierfür in dem Briefwechsel zwischen Goethe und Schiller vorliegen, sind ganz besonders lehrreich, Goethes einzige Fähigkeit aufnehmender Hingabe und innerer Umbildung zu begreifen. Er gibt sich Schiller sozusagen in die Hand, will von diesem aus seinen Grenzen hinausgetrieben werden, lässt sich von ihm zum 'Wollen lernen' und zum Vaterländischen mahnen und nimmt sogar selber 'philosophisches Denken' in Schillers Sinne an. Noch lange nach dessen Tode lässt sich beobachten, wie er in Schillers Geist spricht und denkt.

Der so im reifsten Mannesalter sich nach anderer Geistesrichtung 'umzuarten' suchte, wie muss er in bildsamster Jugendzeit Herder umfasst und in sich aufgenommen haben, den geistgewaltigen Verkünder eines ganz neuen Lebens! [a] Und wie selbstverständlich ist es, dass sich die Grundanschauungen der Beiden auf Jahrzehnte hin decken! Als ob die Grossen jener Zeit nicht schliesslich alle an der Verwirklichung *eines* grossen Programmes gearbeitet hätten!

Dass es sich in Jacobys Buch um den bis heute wichtigsten Beitrag handelt, das einzige Verhältnis zwischen Goethe und Herder zu ergründen, die Abhängigkeit des jüngeren vom älteren Freunde zu bestimmen und ihr Zusammendenken zu verfolgen, scheinen die meisten seiner Kritiker übersehen zu haben. Keiner aber scheint mir bedacht zu haben, dass gerade dann, wenn man Jacobys These, Herder = Faust, ablehnt, immer noch ein höchst bedeutendes und schwieriges Problem zu lösen übrig bleibt.

Mit erstaunlicher Belesenheit und feinem Spürsinn hat Jacoby die Zeugnisse des Zusammendenken der Beiden, soweit die geistige Welt der Faustdichtung in Betracht kommt, in seinem Buche vorgelegt und zu zeigen versucht, dass eine Uebereinstimmung wie eine Abhängigkeit Goethes von Herder auch in den Teilen der Dichtung stattfindet, die nach meiner Ueberzeugung in den oben besprochenen, magisch-theosoph-

[a] Vergl. meinen Aufsatz 'Herder und Goethe', *Goethe-Jahrbuch* XXV, 156 ff.

ischen Erlebnissen Goethes wurzeln. Habe ich damit Recht, dann bleibt eben immer noch die Aufgabe zu lösen, wie so Vieles im Faust an Aehnliches bei Herder anklingen kann, zumal Jacoby es selbst als 'lächerliche Zumutung' abweist, 'sich vorstellen zu sollen, Goethe habe den Faust aus den einzelnen Schriften Herders zusammengestoppelt' (S. 371).

Ich glaube, dass die Lösung des Problems in der Tatsache zu suchen ist, dass auch Herder tief aus dem Geiste der Mystik getrunken hatte, und dass die vielen Zusammenstimmungen und Anklänge zuletzt aus gleicher Quelle geflossen sind. Noch fehlt uns ja eine gründliche Untersuchung über den Anteil, den die Mystik an der Grundverfassung des Herderschen Geistes, des vielseitigen, allumfassenden hatte. Was ihn, den Schüler Hamanns, zu ihr hingezogen hatte, mag eine Stelle aus einem Briefe an Lavater wenigstens andeuten: 'Ich habe durch keinen unsere Bibel lieber bekommen als durch Kinder und Narren d. i. Mystiker und Philosophen. Die Mystiker sind auch Philosophen nach ihrer Art, anders nicht zu betrachten (sie entwickeln und räsoniren aus ihrer *Natur* und *Empfindung*), und im Ganzen zieh ich sie den Wolffianern weit vor. Bei diesen wird alles Maschine, bei jenen doch alles *Leben und Empfindung*. Nur ihr Licht brennt im Rauch.'

Mit Recht weist Jacoby in dem wichtigsten Kapitel seines Buches (Das Gefühl und die Lehre Herders vom Menschen) auf die centrale Bedeutung hin, die gerade die Begriffe 'Leben' und 'Gefühl' für den jungen Herder hatten. Begriffe, die er an Goethe weiter gab, wie sie ihm selbst gewiss einst an der Mystik aufgegangen sein mochten. In dieser wurzelt auch das neue Erkenntnisverfahren Herders,[4] das er Goethe mitteilt: die Identificirung des Ich mit der Aussenwelt, 'die Synthese von Welt und Geist,' für die er anstatt 'denken' und 'erkennen' die von der Mystik geprägten Ausdrücke 'geniessen', 'fühlen' und 'schmecken' gebraucht.

Wie vertraut Herder mit der Vorstellungswelt und Sprache der Mystik, der Alchemie, des Neuplatonismus, etc. war, zeigen zahlreiche Stellen, die Jacoby in seinem Buche zu anderen Zwecken beibringt. Ganz aus dem Geiste der Mystik stammt schliesslich was Jacoby die Selbstvergottung Herders nennt. Es ist die Henosis des Neuplatonismus, die, aus ähnlichen seelischen Voraussetzungen geboren, bei den Mystikern aller Zeiten wiederkehrt.

Ist es nicht schwer zu verstehen wie sich bei gleicher seelischen Grundstimmung, bei gleicher geistigen Befruchtung

[4] Vergl. *Goethe-Jahrbuch* XXV, 160 ff.

und innerster Erfahrung ähnliche Gefühle und Gedanken in
beiden Geistern entwickeln konnten, so zeigt sich doch auch
ein bedeutender Unterschied in der Art wie das aus mystisch-
theosophischer Anschauung Gewonnene oder Gewachsene bei
beiden zum Ausdruck kommt. Während es bei Herder zum
Schlüssel wird zur tiefsten und umfassendsten Erkenntnis
der Welt, der Kunst und der Geschichte, drängt und formt
es sich in Goethes schöpferischem Dichtergeist zu lebendigen
Gestalten. Gewiss, auch in Herders Gedichten weben in Halb-
dunkel Geister aus der Welt der Magie, aber sie erscheinen
ihm nur in der Ferne, in Träumen oder nächtlichen Visionen,
und seine geringere Dichterkraft hat es nicht vermocht sie zu
zwingen, dass sie sich ihm völlig enthüllen und ihre
Geheimnisse offenbaren.

Und doch glaube ich, dass Herder der Faustgestalt Goethes
wesentliche Züge gegeben hat. An dem geistesmächtigen
Freunde ist dem jungen Dichter wol zuerst die innige Verwandtschaft zwischen Magus und Genie aufgeblitzt und zum
klaren Bewusstsein geworden, was er bisher nur dunkel ge-
ahnt hatte. Jetzt erst ward es ihm möglich der Sagengestalt
des Magiers den Geist der neuen Botschaft des Mannes ein-
zuhauchen, als dessen 'Apostel' er, trotz zeitweiser Verstimmung und vorübergehender Entfremdung, bis tief in die Weimarer Zeit hinein sich fühlte.

JULIUS GOEBEL.

SPENSER'S SHEPHERD'S CALENDER IN RELATION
   TO CONTEMPORARY AFFAIRS, by James Jackson
   Higginson, Ph. D. New York. The Columbia University
   Press, 1912. Pp. xii + 364.

After the scathing but just [1] notice of the *Athenaeum* (1912,
p. 755), one approaches Mr. Higginson's dissertation in a
spirit of extenuation. It certainly shows praiseworthy industry in research (see p. 220, n. 52), and sometimes achieves
(as in the cases of Palinode and the relation of the alleged
Areopagus to the *Shepherds' Calender*) contributions to
Spenser scholarship of distinct value. The fundamental objection is one from which Columbia dissertations are almost
uniformly free—the publication of argumentative matter,
which should be threshed out in journals, in the semi-
expository form of a book which is likely to be referred to as
expository. Nor need this topic have been so treated: the

---

[1] Unjust, however, in suggesting that Mr. Higginson wholly fails to
allow for Spenser's indebtedness to Marot, Mantuan, and others.

author is over anxious to provide solutions made to order for almost every problem.[2] Were his conclusions usually sound, as they are clearly in the cases of Rosalind, Sidney, and the myth concerning Lancashire—cases in which he makes no constructive argument—his suggestions would invite further research. Unfortunately, however, his logic is, almost throughout, a tissue of probabilities and plausibilities. ''For my part I believe'' (p. 180) and variants (pp. 137, 187, 197, 203) constitute the burden of almost every conclusion. This is commendable modesty; but scholarship is not an act of faith. It is unconscious irony to say (p. 231): ''But I will leave guessing to others;'' and later (p. 313), in dealing with the same topic, to offer what one styles ''a mere surmise.''

The reviewer is at first tempted to arraign Mr. Higginson's immediate supervisors. And certainly his failure to know that Spenser was Rochester's secretary (see p. 130)—an oversight through which his whole account of Spenser's ecclesiastical position becomes discredited—must be laid at their desks.[3] More fundamentally, however, there occur errors of a type which should have been earlier eliminated by elementary training in composition. I do not refer to lapses such as *diverse* for *divers* (p. 2, last line), *expect* for *surmise* (p. 5, l. 3), or the punctuation of p. 4, l. 6; p. 15, l. 10; p. 16, l. 2, *etc.*, or the construction of p. 175, last line—all of which may be as accidental as *mariage* (p. 58, l. 23). There is often an apparent deficiency in logic and sense of evidence. Examples are the repeated citation of opinion as having strong evidential value (p. 153, n.; p. 280), and appeals to persons ''entitled to speak with authority.'' Of similar force is the observation (p. 198): ''The name Thomalin . . . . . must have been unknown to English writers before the Calender appeared, for none of his editors have cited parallels.''

No less disconcerting is Mr. Higginson's maladjustment in structure. The first thirty-eight pages constitute a detached historical resumé of facts which need to be cited and are therefore often repeated in the subsequent argument. There

[2] P. 90: "I think that an explanation is demanded by the circumstances, and I therefore am prepared to advance one . . . . ." P. 185: "As an absolute identification seems impossible, I merely offer the opinion that . . . . ." P. 289: "Any work upon the *Calender* would be incomplete without some speculative discussion of it, and this I now propose to give." No small portion of the book is of this tentative character, pernicious in its risk that suggestions here be printed elsewhere as established facts.

[3] The information was accessible in such inconspicuous sources as the *Athenæum*, the London *Times*, and the publications of the British Academy (1908).

is also, as in the cases of Rosalind and Lancashire, a vast deal of unnecessary reprinting. Moreover, Part II should precede Part I, since its identification of the interlocutors and of the persons of whom they speak, as well as the determination of Spenser's position and interests, logically forms a basis for interpretation of the purport of his eclogues. This would have obviated frequent distracting references to premises subsequently submitted to examination.

It is perhaps too much to demand that professors shall train graduate students in fundamentals of composition; yet one does expect insistence on the use of superior rather than inferior texts. Mr. Higginson quotes[4] throughout from the Globe edition or from Herford's, neglecting both Dodge's careful text and the edition of E. de Sélincourt, which stands in a class by itself as the most scholarly. One expects also accuracy of observation. But Mr. Higginson's argument repeatedly depends on the statement (pp. 43, 188) that "In Spenser's ecclesiastical eclogues a shepherd who has a flock is meant to represent a clergyman." Unhappily we read (July, 145-7) :—

"But nothing such thilk shephearde was,
   Whom *Ida* hyll dyd beare,
   That left hys flocke, to fetche a lasse . . . . ."
Priest of Venus Paris may have been, but no clergyman.

Similarly,[5] Mr. Higginson is undecided (p. 178) whether Cuddie in October is or is not the same person as in the other eclogues. He overlooks E. K.'s gloss (October, l. 1), which says: "In the eyght Aeglogue the same person was brought in." At another point (p. 129) he misunderstands Grosart's theory of Lowder=Lloyd. Grosart—not absurd in this instance —realizes that Spenser is apologizing for Lowder as for one who had done wrong merely because he had been deceitfully misinformed. Again, in rehandling the identification of Rosalind, where he shows unimpeachably (pp. 218-221) that an entry in Lord North's book of household charges does not

---

[4] Compare with p. 125 the September eclogue, l. 144. Again, the line July 22 should not be read *dogges* (see p. 174). In the 1579 quarto the text and E. K. alike have *dogge*.

[5] Among minor points: (1) the dedicatory sonnets were affixed, not prefixed, to the *Faerie Queene* (p. 244, l. 3); (2) As to Virgil's first eclogue (p. 296, n. 38) he should consult Renaissance interpretations, not those of modern scholiasts; (3) I did not "follow" J. W. Hales' hint (p. 216), but discovered it a year after completing my argument; (4) Spenser did not depart from London on August 12, 1580 (p. 333), but arrived with his patron in Dublin on that day.

prove that Thomas North was in 1578-9 a widower,[6] he does not observe that the conclusion remains unaffected. At best it was a surmise: Mr. Higginson in no way precludes the possibility that the surmise was correct. He is incomprehensible in urging (p. 226, n. 70) that the theory under discussion "depends upon the passionate love of the poet for his lady." If so, the author at least was unaware of it, and meant to indicate that self-interest dictated the poet's addresses.

Turning to an examination of Mr. Higginson's contentions, one finds his chief theses to be that (1) Spenser (p. 39) "was an ardent, thorough-going Puritan" and "the February, May, July, and September eclogues . . . . . reflect a spirit of opposition to the policy of Elizabeth and Burghley;" (2) "Spenser's association with Leicester and Sidney was short-lived" (p. 337), was lost because of his satire in *Mother Hubberds Tale*, and was not the source of his appointment as secretary to Lord Grey. Incidentally Mr. Higginson presents scholia on the bearing of the eclogues and identifications of the personages involved.

A review dealing with each point would manifestly become insupportable. In general, however, regarding the contention that Spenser was a Puritan, we have to note that the headmaster of Spenser's college—and examiner at the Merchant Taylors School—throughout his course sufficiently approved of Spenser to choose him as his secretary; that this headmaster, admittedly high church (pp. 130, 327), was made Bishop of Rochester, therefore court bishop—a place "always occupied during Elizabeth's reign by Anglo-Catholic High Churchmen" (p. 130); that this headmaster had been chaplain of Grindal, whom Elizabeth and Burleigh thought safe enough to appoint Archbishop of Canterbury; and, finally, that Spenser praises both these men in these very eclogues,—praises them as pastors, and cites their views as sound. Apart from this, his alleged opposition to the Queen is hardly borne out by the ostentatious and self-interested praise of her in a song in the April eclogue. Again, his alleged Puritanism and alleged opposition to Burleigh are hardly consistent, since Burleigh appointed as his private chaplain and tutor of his son Walter Travers, who was, with Cartwright, a chief leader of the Puritan movement. Few, judging by temperament, would pronounce Spenser—lover of pageants—a Puritan, and Burleigh

[6] Spenser's possible rustic use of *widow* = *widower* is not invalidated by its non-appearance in church registers, when E. D. D. and Oxf. E. D. show its existence before 1579 and its subsequent wide use.

—scorner of the muses—not. Harvey, too, Spenser's intimate friend, by his correspondence with Young shows himself in close affiliation with this high churchman.

That Spenser while secretary to Rochester—as he was in 1578—should have written a covert satire on the Anglican clergy is inherently implausible. That the eclogues under discussion were then written is clear from frequent allusions in them to Kent. Nor can the year be in doubt; for Spenser, alluding [7] to Grindal's confinement (July, e. 216), describes him as "long ypent." Grindal's punishment dated from June 1577. Under such circumstances the satire against Catholics to which E. K. repeatedly draws attention is natural, and the more so in that Grindal's chief services had been against Catholics in the north.

For any other course it is difficult to supply Spenser with a motive. He was not a churchman; his environment and the two eclogues on religion in his source, the school book Mantuan, sufficiently account for his inclusion of this element in the *Calender*. So far as we know, Mr. Higginson rightly contends, he had not come under the influence of Leicester. Nor is it easy to see what effect he could have hoped for. With his praise of the Queen and her high churchmen, with his commentator's directing attention to the Catholics, (see pp. 45, 46, 72, 112) Spenser's hits could not have told. When Spenser chooses to direct a shaft, as at Burleigh in *The Ruines of Time* and the *Faerie Queene* (IV, Prologue), his aim is palpable, unmistakable; and tradition here assigns a plausible reason—that Burleigh, as Lord Treasurer, had withheld and diminished Spenser's pension. But any antagonism preceding Spenser's complimentary sonnet to him in 1589-90 is to be assumed only from a conjectural interpretation of *Mother Hubberds Tale*, published in 1591, and therefore perhaps made over in those parts which may be read as an attack on Burleigh.[8] In the *Calender* no one before Mr. Higginson—so far as we have record—detected such satire.

What sort of evidence, then, does Mr. Higginson advance? He says regarding his theory of the February eclogue (p. 70): "It is not susceptible of absolute proof;" regarding the May eclogue (p. 99): "That it satisfies the contents of the fable and that no lack of motive for the satire existed is all that may be safely claimed;" regarding the July eclogue—but here

[7] The allusion is not a basis to the poem, but is prompted by Mantuan's allusion to Pollux in his eighth eclogue, as was the allusion to Paris by Mantuan, 7.27-8.

[8] See also "The Date of Spenser's Earlier Hymns", *Eng. Stud.*, Jan. 1914.

there is no considerable point; regarding the September eclogue—but this is at once discredited by ignorance that Roffy is the Bishop of Rochester. Yet, for example, consider the February eclogue. Grant that E. K. lies in his throat when he says: "This Aeglogue is rather morall and generall, then bent to any secrete or particular purpose." Mr. Higginson's interpretation requires that the Briar as well as the Oak be reckoned a "tree of state" (p. 48), which E. K. explains as "taller trees, fitte for timber." That there is a particular allegory he assumes (p. 46) from the Briar's description of his own—

"Colours meete to clothe a mayden Queene." According to Mr. Higginson's comment, "The reference to Queen Elizabeth is, of course, unmistakable." Such is the cornerstone of his argument. But the simile is of frequent occurrence in Spenser: once where it is directly applied *as a simile* to Elizabeth (April eclogue); twice at least (*Teares of the Muses* 309, *Epithalamion* 158) where it cannot apply to her.

The foregoing is, I believe, a fair example. Mr. Higginson's individual interpretations may ultimately have to be dealt with seriatim; for the present it is sufficient to note that they are not proved and are inherently not plausible.

Turning to Part II, one carries away a much more favorable impression. The writer here rests on more solid ground, especially where his argument is negative as in the cases of E. K., Rosalind,[9] Lancashire, Sidney,[10] and the Areopagus. On the other hand, he is elsewhere seldom content to leave a problem without some suggested solution, however far sought. One case in point is Diggon Davie. His travel abroad and Hobbinol's offer of shelter send Mr. Higginson afield. They but parallel once more Mantuan's Candidus in his ninth eclogue, who—to use Turberville's 1567 translation—

> "from native home
> A wight exilde in forreine lond
> and strangie Realme dost rome . . . . ."

Faustulus, like Hobbinol, invites him,—

> "To my poore house to come,
> of fellowship do so."

Another case in point is Piers, whom Mr. Higginson identifies as Thomas Preston. He observes (p. 187): "Preston may have been called 'Pres' for short, a word which is close

[9] It is not merely the anagram, however, which forbids identifying "the widow's daughter" as Lady Carey or Mary Sidney. Of both the parents were living. Nor could either be styled "a private personage unknowne."

[10] See also "Spenser and Sidney", *Anglia*, July 1914.

to Piers in both spelling and sound." He disregards (p. 185)
Dr. John Piers, the immediate predecessor of Young as
Bishop of Rochester. Yet this cleric's known learning, liber-
ality, and personal rectitude—conjoined with his work in
1573 in abolishing popish practices in Salisbury—make him
entirely suitable as a foil for Palinode. Piers is, by the way,
unlike Preston, the keeper of a flock (July, 173).

The book closes—apart from an appendix on Mr. Green-
law's theory, which I leave to him—with a discussion of
Spenser's passing from service under Leicester to a secretary-
ship under Grey. This again is partly vitiated (pp. 320,
330) by the author's ignorance that Harvey intends Rochester
in speaking 9 May, 1580, of "a goodly Kentishe *Garden* of
your old Lords." Since this former lord must have been the
"Southern Shepherd"—my Lord Bishop of Rochester—the
allusion proves nothing as to Spenser's service with Leicester.
Otherwise, the account, though not established as proved, is
at least as plausible as any hitherto presented.

                                             PERCY W. LONG.

Harvard University.

THE LEGEND OF LONGINUS IN ECCLESIASTICAL
    TRADITION AND IN ENGLISH LITERATURE,
    AND ITS CONNECTION WITH THE GRAIL, by Rose
    J. Peebles. Bryn Mawr, 1911. vi + 221 pp. (*Bryn Mawr
    College Monographs*, Vol. IX.)

The passage in the account of the crucifixion in Matthew
(XXVII, 54): "*Centurio autem, et qui cum eo erant, custodientes Jesum, viso terrae motu et his quae fiebant, timuerunt
valde, dicentes: Vere filius Dei erat iste*", and the passage in
John (XIX, 34): "*Sed unus militum lancea latus Domini per-
foravit et continuo exivit sanguis et aqua,*" gave rise to a widespread legend in the Middle Ages. In the *Acta Pilati* (fifth
century) both the soldier and the centurion are given the
name Longinus. In the *Martyrology of St. Jerome* of the same
or the following century, the entry occurs under the
fifteenth of March: *In Cappadocia S. Longini Martyris.* In
the eighth and ninth century martyrologies, all these various
scraps of tradition are attributed to the soldier. He is called
Longinus, and is represented as converted by the miracles
of the crucifixion, and suffering martyrdom in Cappadocia.
By the accretion of a stock episode, the judge who condemns
the saint is stricken blind, but is subsequently converted and

miraculously healed. The typical form of the legend in this stage is as follows:

Id. Martii: In Cappadocia passio sancti Longini martyris: de quo in libello martyrii ejus narratur quod aliquando militans sub centurione Romano, in passione Domini latus ejus cum lancea in cruce aperiret, et viso terrae motu et signis quae fiebant, crediderit in Christum, poenitentiam agens de operibus suis pristinis: postea monachus factus per triginta et quatuor annos Christo militavit, multos convertens ad fidem Dei; ad extremum vero martyrizavit in Cappadocia sub Octavio praeside, quem, propter infidelitatem suam divino judicio percussum corporea caecitate, post martyrium suum illuminavit (pp. 1-15).[1]

The Bollandists print an elaborated version of this legend of the soldier, and also a life of the centurion. The latter also is called Longinus, and is said to have suffered martyrdom in Cappadocia. The account is followed by a story of a miracle wrought by the head of the dead saint: a woman is cured of blindness, and her son is brought to heaven (pp. 16-21).

Already in a ninth century miniature showing Longinus piercing the side of Christ, a zig-zag line of red, drawn from the side of the Saviour where the spear point rests, to the eyes of Longinus, suggests that he was blind, and that his sight was miraculously restored. In later manuscripts Longinus is represented as kneeling to the left of the cross and pointing to his eye, while he pierces the Saviour's side with a spear. In literature Dr. Peebles finds no mention of the blindness of Longinus previous to the twelfth century, at which time a great number of passages in devotional works and in romances attest the general currency of the tradition (pp. 44-55; cf. p. 21).[2]

[1] It is not surprising that the centurion and the soldier were gradually identified. In one gospel the one, in another the other insignificant figure is introduced just after the final moment of agony. Someone—his identity mattered little—pierced the side of the Saviour. Someone—equally indifferent except in this one action—was suddenly stricken with a sense of the great sacrilege. The passage in Matthew, *centurio autem, et qui cum eo erant, custodientes Jesum*, would lead to the association of the soldier in John with *qui cum eo erant, custodientes Jesum*. A similar confusion of personages is seen in the folk ballads which identify the woman "which was a sinner" (Luke vii, 37), Mary Magdalen, and Mary the sister of Martha and Lazarus. Cf. G. Doncieux, *Le Romancéro populaire* (Paris, 1904), p. 154; C. Chabaneau, *Sainte Marie-Madeleine dans la Litt. provençale*, Appendix III, *Revue des langues romanes*, 1887.

[2] Dr. Peebles is probably right in believing that the tradition of Longinus' blindness is based on the idea of spiritual blindness implied

Dr. Peebles gives a brief account of allusions to the lance of Longinus as a relic and in the liturgy. In the latter it appears for the first time in the *Mass of St. Chrysostom* (7th century). The priest, taking the sacred bread in his left hand and the holy spear in his right, pierces the wafer five times, and then cuts it crosswise. Finally, piercing the right side with the lance, he says: *Et unus militum lancea latus ejus aperuit et statim exivit sanguis et aqua* [3] (pp. 56-71).

In the final chapters of the book, Dr. Peebles examines the theories that have been propounded in regard to the relation of the lance of Longinus to the Baldr myth and to the Grail lance. She points out that Bugge's theory of the origin of the former in the Christian legend is weakened by the fact

---

in the act of piercing Jesus' side. His healing is the symbolical expression of his conversion. The early appearance of this idea in art and its late appearance in literature seem fitting when we consider its appropriateness for plastic representation. The lack of narrative details in the literary accounts point to the same conclusion.

One might fancy that the suggestion of passivity in *accipiens autem Longinus milites lanceam*, prefixed to the account of the piercing of the side in the *Acta Pilati*, had some influence in the development of the idea of Longinus' blindness. In the English translations the passive interpretation of the word is apparent from such phrases as, *A blynd Knyght, so thoght tham best. A spere thai gaf gud spede* and *and hym they made to put a spere to Jhesus syde.* (MSS. cited by Dr. Peebles, pp. 88, 89.) The trait is preserved in many of the English accounts. The story of the blindness and conversion of the judge, already associated with the Longinus story, may have aided the development.

Dr. Peebles brings together a number of examples to show that healing by blood is not uncommon in mediaeval tradition. There is another point, which she does not mention, that is characteristic of some of the examples cited. There is a close connection between the victim and the agent of the wound, between the person who receives the healing and the person who accomplishes it. In the incident cited from the *Seven Sages,* the king, blinded by heaven in punishment for the bad government of the sages, decapitates them and receives his sight. The authors of the blindness are the seven sages; it is by them that it is healed. St. Christopher blinds the judge who is causing his suffering. The judge anoints his eyes with the blood of the martyr and is cured. As we have seen above, the same story is found in the Longinus legend.

[3] Dr. A. C. L. Brown, in his review of Dr. Peebles' book, *Modern Language Notes* XXVIII, 21-26, objects (p. 23, n. 10): "Miss Peebles writes as if the slender knife of the Greek Eucharistic procession were, in the minds of mediaeval writers, identical with the spear of Longinus. . . . . . Pseudo-Germanus (of uncertain date) adds at the end of his account of the Mass, *Nam vice lanceae quae punxit Christum in cruce a Longino est haec lancea."* Dr. Brown fails to observe that the association is also distinctly indicated in the Mass of St. Chrysostom (c. 8th century): *Sacerdos autem ipsum* [*sanctum panem*] *in dextera pungens cum sancta lancea dicit.* Then the priest recites the passage from John describing the piercing of Jesus' side.

that our earliest evidence of the blindness of Longinus is in a manuscript of the ninth century, and that the absence of the trait from the ninth and tenth century martyrologies shows that even then it was not generally current (pp. 142-166).

Dr. Peebles emphasizes the similarities between the accounts of the lance of Longinus and the Grail lance. In a great many of the descriptions of the piercing of the Saviour's side, the writers dwell on the fact that the blood runs down from the point of the lance to the hilt, upon the hand of the bearer. For example,

Le sang et l'esve en fist ruceler;
Aval la lance commencza devaler,
Juqu'à ses poigns ne se voulst arester. (Roman d'Aquin, 195 ff.)

Longinus feels the blood on his hand, rubs his eyes, and is healed. In Cynewulf's *Christ* and in other poems, the wood of the cross is represented in a vision as bleeding (p. 188). In this characteristic the crucifixion relics are like the lance of the Grail, of which Crestien says:

S'en ist une goute de sanc
Del fer de la lance el somet,
Et, jusqu'à la main au varlet
Couloit cele goute vermelle. (*Perceval*, 4376 ff.)

The paradox of the destructive and healing character of the lance of Longinus is the paradox of the redemption. The death of Christ gives life to the world; the spear that wounded the Redeemer's side healed the sinner who struck the blow. A similar paradox is found in certain accounts of the Grail lance, which is represented as at the same time healing and destructive (*Parzival* IX, 489-490.)

The shining of the crucifixion relics is mentioned in various documents. The *Breviarius de Hierosolyma* (c. 7th century) says of the lance: *et lucet in nocte sicut sol in virtute diei.*[4]

Dr. Peebles emphasizes the fact that there is no strict line of demarcation between pagan and Christian characteristics. The lance of the crucifixion absorbed pagan attributes from many sources. The Christian feast days are compromises with pagan festivals. The Christian ceremonial adopted elements

[4] The date of the passage is uncertain. F. de Mély, *Exuviae sacrae constantinopolitanae*, Paris, 1904, p. 32, places it subsequent to the seventh century, on the ground that it is a comment on the clause preceding it, *et de ipsa facta est crux*, which is a borrowing from Arculf (670). As Dr. Peebles (p. 179) and de Mély (p. 32) both observe, the attribute of shining is frequently mentioned of mediaeval weapons, relics, etc. Dr. A. C. L. Brown overlooks this fact when he explains shining as characteristic of the Grail relics and traceable to a Celtic origin (*P. M. L. A.*, XXV, p. 32, *M. L. N.* XXVIII, 22).

of pagan ritual. The close relationship between agrarian mysteries and early Christian rites is recognized by investigators
of the origins of Christianity. The Grail rites described in
Crestien are, to be sure, different from the twelfth century
Christian ritual, but they are not so different from the ritual
of the earlier church. Dr. Peebles considers it possible that
the Grail romances preserve in a corrupt form the account of
a Christian ceremonial which had been rejected by the ortho-
dox before the time of our extant texts. She brings forward
an interesting piece of evidence to support this suggestion, a
letter from certain French bishops of the sixth century, con-
demning the practices of Irish priests who celebrate the mass
on portable altars carried from dwelling to dwelling, and
who are assisted by women in the administration of the Eucharist (pp. 166-217). A similar document dating from the
ninth century, cited by B. Fehr,[5] shows that three centuries
later these heterodox usages were still practised.

In spite of the many excellent qualities of the book,[6] one
wishes that Dr. Peebles had attempted a smaller field and
treated it with more critical detail.[7] Instead of being dismissed with the statement, ''It seems not impossible that the
lives of other martyrs contributed to the growing story,'' the
legends in question should have been examined.[8] The author
accepts dates without close inquiry as to their authenticity.[9]
She cites documents obviously related, without indicating the
relation or emphasizing the more important document.[10] She

[5] *Beiblatt zur Anglia* XXIV, p. 295, *Episcoporum ad Hludovicum im-
peratorem relatio* 829 c 52 M. G. H., Leg. sect. I, Cap. II, 42. Professor
Fehr also refers the reader to his edition of Aelfric's Pastoral letters I,
15, and III, 78, 79. We gather from his references to this edition in
another article (*Anglia, Beiblatt,* XXIV, p. 359, 360) that it has not
yet been published.

[6] Dr. Peebles' book has been favorably reviewed by B. Fehr, *Beiblatt
zur Anglia* XXIV, p. 291-295, and by others (*Archiv für das Studium
der neueren Sprachen* CXXVIII, 435-6; *Journal of Theological Studies*
XIII, 624). Dr. A. C. L. Brown (*Mod. Lang. Notes* XXVIII, 21-
26) attacks an exclusively Christian interpretation of the Grail rites,
and puts forward a plea for a 'Celtic or fusion theory.' Dr. Brown had
previously interpreted the Grail lance as of exclusively Celtic origin (*P.
M. L. A.* XXV, 1 ff.).

[7] Cf., e. g., R. Fawtier, *La Vie de Saint Samson, Bibliothèque de l'école
des hautes études,* No. 197, Paris, 1912.

[8] B. Fehr, *Anglia, Beiblatt,* XXIV, p. 292-293, has made some suggestions in this connection.

[9] E. g. p. 186, notes.

[10] E. g. pp. 32-35, legends of various martyrs by name Longinus; pp.
64-67, Mass of St. Chrysostom and Slavonic liturgy; p. 57, Arculf and
Bede.

makes no effort to group texts that present striking points in common, or even to call attention to such points. She might have noted, for example, the representation, both in art and in literature, of two distinct processes for the healing of Longinus: the one in which the blood is represented as gushing from the spear point into Longinus' eyes; and the other in which it runs down the spear on his hand and in which he is healed by rubbing his eyes. The division of material into *Longinus in the Apocrypha, The Testimony of the Fathers, The Martyrologies, Other Writers, Longinus in Art, Longinus in the Liturgy, Longinus in Charms, Longinus in English Literature* is artificial, and obscures the historical relations. The writer confines her critical remarks on the development of the legend to the chapter *The Legend of Longinus a Fictitious Narrative* (pp. 27-37), and limits them to a discussion of the name of Longinus and the tradition of his blindness. She gives a brief account of other martyrs of the same name. This is far from exhausting the problems raised by the material presented. The position of this chapter is, moreover, unfortunate. The criticism of the tradition of the blindness should not precede the documents which first give evidence of the tradition, the illustrations discussed in the chapter *Longinus in Art*. The diligent collection of a large number of allusions to Longinus from Middle English literature (pp. 80-142) is deserving of commendation.[11]

GERTRUDE SCHOEPPERLE.

University of Illinois.

[11] There are numerous misprints. The quotation on page 214 from W. Staerk, *Über den Ursprung der Grallegende,* Leipzig, 1903, p. 20, n. 2, is badly mutilated. The passage should read:

Es verlohnte sich, aus den Gralromanen die Züge zusammenzustellen, in denen sich der mittelalterliche Abendmahlsritus wiederspiegelt . . . . . Ich will hier nur auf zweierlei hinweisen: der mit dem Gral verbundene Speer—ursprünglich wohl eine selbständige Blutreliquie —erinnert an die "heilige Lanze" im Ritus der orientalischen Kirche, und der in einigen Gralromanen sich findende Zug, dass der kranke "Fischer-könig" aus dem Gral Blut mittels einer Röhre säugt, verrät Bekanntschaft mit der im Abendland vor der Durchführung der Kelchentziehung in Verfolg des Transsubstantiationsdogmas, also bis zum 12. Jahrhundert verbreiteten Sitte, den Wein mittels der *fistula eucharistica* zu geniessen.

Dr. Peebles is mistaken in introducing this passage at this point. The *tuiel* (Crestien 20160, *Elucidation* 275) by which the abundance of blood flowing from the lance is carried away from the Grail cup is one thing. The *roere* (Heinrich von dem Türlin, *Diu Crône*, 14761 ff.), which lies in the cup and through which the Grail King partakes of the blood, is another. Dr. Staerk is alluding to the second. Dr. Brown (*P. M. L. A.* XXV (1910), p. 24, cf. pp. 14, 15) is discussing the first.

THE ELIZABETHAN PLAYHOUSE AND OTHER STUDIES, by W. J. Lawrence. J. B. Lippincott Company, Philadelphia; Shakespeare Head Press, Stratford-upon-Avon. 1912. (8 vo, pp. xvi + 265, illus.)

Mr. Lawrence claims to have been "the pioneer" in the modern scientific study of "the physical conditions and stage conventionalisms of the Elizabethan playhouse." After readily granting this modest claim, we may add that he is at the present time one of the most expert investigators in this field, and that a volume from him presenting his mature opinions on a subject so important to the study of the Tudor-Stuart drama is heartily welcome.

In this volume, he has assembled ten papers which during the past decade he had published in various periodicals—the *Shakespeare-Jahrbuch, Englische Studien, Anglia, The Gentleman's Magazine*, etc. Yet he has taken care to revise, to amplify, and even in places to rewrite these papers, in order to keep them abreast with the notable progress recently made in this subject; and in addition, he has enriched the volume by the insertion of thirteen full-page illustrations, which, he states, "have been chosen as much for their rarity as their appositeness."

The first paper, entitled "The Evolution and Influence of the Elizabethan Playhouse," is, on the whole, the best general discussion of the subject that we have. The author accepts with too much faith, perhaps, the conjectures of Professor Wallace (*The Children of the Chapel at Blackfriars*); and virtually all his conclusions about the influence of the Blackfriars theatre on the evolution of the playhouse must be modified in view of the recent discoveries regarding the history of that building. For this, of course, Mr. Lawrence is in no way to blame. Luckily, before his book was off the press he was able to read in *The Daily Chronicle* Monsieur Feuillerat's brief announcement of those discoveries, and to add a supplementary paper, "New Facts About the Blackfriars," in which he corrects his earlier statements and rewrites the history of the private playhouses; and this supplementary paper is one of the most valuable in the book. Other papers elaborate special topics connected with the playhouse—"The Situation of the Lords' Room," "Title and Locality Boards," "Music and Song in the Elizabethan Theatre"; still other papers take up separate themes—"The Mounting of Carolan Masques," "Early French Players in England," "Did Thomas Shadwell Write an Opera on *The*

Tempest?'' and ''Who Wrote the Famous *Macbeth* Music?'' In this review, however, I shall confine myself to those papers dealing particularly with the Elizabethan playhouse.

On not a few matters of detail one may feel inclined to disagree with Mr. Lawrence. This, however, is somewhat hazardous, for the author does not always substantiate his assertions with a citation of evidence, so that it is hard to know when he is merely speculating, and when he could, if pressed to do so, advance the necessary proof. Nevertheless I shall call attention to some of his statements which seem to me to be questionable.

P. 6. Of the rear stage he says: ''Its employment was, to some extent, restricted by the remoteness and obscurity of its position, an inconvenience which almost invariably demanded the bringing in of lights at the commencement of all inner scenes.'' Mr. Lawrence has failed to observe that in the scenes to which he refers for proof of this statement, the torches, candles, or lanterns were brought in for the purpose not of illuminating the rear stage, but of indicating to the audience that the action took place at night. In the open playhouse, with the afternoon sun beating down on the platform, the rear stage would not be dark; and there is abundant evidence that at times much action took place in this restricted area.

P. 8. The well-known ''shadow'' which protected a part of the stage from the weather is thus described: ''A thatched (or possibly, tiled and leaded) half-roof, sloping down from the tiring-house, and known indifferently as 'the shadow,' or 'the heavens'.'' Was not this half-roof called ''the shadow,'' ''the shade,'' or ''the cover'' (see the Fortune contract), and was not the term ''the heavens'' applied rather to a hut which overhung a part of the lower stage, and through the floor of which gods and goddesses were lowered? Note Heywood's *Silver Age* II. i: ''Juno and Iris descend from the heavens''; *The Valiant Welshman* I. i: ''Fortune descends downe from heaven to the stage.'' The Hope contract is too vague to prove anything in this connection, but the ''heavens'' there referred to may well be a hut projecting over the stage. The following reference to the Fortune bears on this point: ''There shall also great inflammations of Lightning happen this year about the Fortune, in Golding Lane, if the players can get leave to act the tragedie of Doctor Faustus, in which tempest shall be seen shag-haired divils run roaring with squibs in their mouths, while drums make thunder in the tiring house, and the 12 *d.* hirelings make artificial light in her heavens."—*Crete Wonders Foretold.* The "shadow," it would seem, sloped from the "heavens" rather than from the tiring-house.

P. 9. Of the "turret" over the stage (which I would identify with the "heavens") Mr. Lawrence says: "Through its apertures stage ordnance were let off, a custom that led to the destructive fire at Shakespeare's Globe." The destructive fire here referred to is not in itself sufficient to prove this statement. In the various accounts of that catastrophe no indication is made of the location of the cannon; but distinct reference is made to a strong wind that was blowing, which might account for the landing of the "stoppage" in the thatched roof. I can recall no stage-direction that reads: "Ordnance shot off above," whereas the direction "Ordnance within" is not uncommon.

P. 9. "Not all, if any, of the rooms and galleries were provided with seats, although in most parts stools and cushions could be procured by paying extra." Surely there are abundant references to seats and benches in the galleries of the "penny-bench theatres." See the Fortune contract.

P. 11. "An extra charge [for admission to the galleries] was subsequently enforced, according to the locality, the fee being collected during the performance by 'gatherers'." The last clause appears doubtful. Would it not be simpler, and easier (not to say surer), to collect the extra fee at the time of entrance to the gallery? Some proof of Mr. Lawrence's statement is needed.

P. 13. "For the benefit of those who, through coming early, arrived dinnerless, eatables, and drinkables, including fruits, nuts and bottled beer, were vended in the theatre." Undue emphasis is put on those who arrived dinnerless. Such persons must have been comparatively few in number, and the "eatables and drinkables" were primarily intended for those

> Fellows that at ordinaries dare eat
> Their 18 *d.* thrice out before they rise
> And yet go hungry to a play.[1]

P. 14. "There was seldom any absolute certainty in the Bankside houses as to what would be performed." (Cf. also p. 50.) Some modification of this assertion is surely needed, or some conclusive proof. It is hardly in keeping with what we know of the dignity of the actors, or with their custom of posting bills throughout the city:

> Then hence, lewd nags, away
> Go read each post, view what is played to-day.

[1] *The Scornful Lady* IV. 2.

Note also the following custom referred to by Humphrey Moseley in his poem "The Stationer," prefixed to the First Folio of Beaumont and Fletcher:

> As after th' *Epilogue* there comes some one
> To tell the *Spectators* what shall next be shown.

The fact that a play was occasionally changed at the demand of an unruly audience led Mr. Lawrence, I suspect, into making too sweeping an assertion.

The statement that the Theatre and the Curtain were used not only for plays but also for bull and bear baiting, and that their stages, as a result, were removable, is open to grave doubt. Upon this assumption rests the theory that the oblique disposition of the stage doors was a contribution to the stage arrangement from the private playhouse of Blackfriars. The hypothesis is plausible, yet fails to take into consideration the fact that in the public playhouses the stage was constructed of wood, and hence could be easily modified. It is hard to say when the oblique doors came into use; and, moreover, the first Blackfriars seems merely to have continued the court usage of multiple setting.

The second paper deals with "The Situation of the Lords' Room." The theory that these rooms were over the stage held sway, I believe, before Mr. Lawrence wrote. The most original part of his essay is the suggestion that at some time before 1609 these rooms were degraded into a shameful resort for courtesans: "Dark and ill-placed, they could no longer have been let to spectators, but the cupidity of the players induced them to turn the deserted rooms into a licentious rendezvous for the lower middle classes . . . A mart for illicit love and bought kisses." This astonishing theory, not in keeping with what we know of the better actors of the time—for example, Shakespeare, Heminge, or Heywood,—is based solely on the well-known passage in Dekker's *The Gull's Hornbooke*: "I meane not into the Lords roome (which is now but the Stages Suburbs): No, those boxes, by the iniquity of custome, conspiracy of waiting women and Gentlemen-Ushers, that there sweat together, and the covetousnes of Sharers, are contemptibly thrust into the reare, and much new Satten is there dambd, by being smothred to death in darknesse." Accordingly, the gull is advised not to go near the Lords' Room.

Now, every student of Elizabethan literature knows that the term "suburbs" was often applied to that section of London which contained the houses of ill-fame. But this usage of the word was secondary, and it is not to be supposed that in the

passage quoted Dekker necessarily meant to imply that the
Lords' Rooms were "suburbs" in that odious sense. The
rest of the passage fails to carry out such an idea. Exactly
what is meant, to be sure, is not clear; but we may infer that
the Lords' Rooms at the time Dekker wrote had ceased to be
highly fashionable, and had been turned over to the servants of
fashionable people ("waiting women and Gentlemen Ush-
ers"), the natural successors. Furthermore, we may infer
that the rooms were much over crowded, and that because of
their location they gave poor opportunities for the gallant to
display his gorgeous apparel. Dekker, in his satirical vein,
would hardly have been so earnest in urging the gull not to
enter the Lords' Room, if it enjoyed the reputation that Mr.
Lawrence wants to give it.

Mr. Lawrence takes Professor Schelling to task for stum-
bling in his interpretation of the phrase "advance yourself
up to the Throne of the Stage," and shows that Dekker refers
to the stage as a whole (the throne of the playhouse), not to
an actual property throne on the stage. It may be proper,
therefore, to point out that Mr. Lawrence himself stumbles in
this passage. He says, by way of interpretation: "He [the
gull] has come in by the tiring-house door, having duly paid
the preliminary price of admission; more remains to be dis-
bursed for a stool. The same doorway leads to the Lords'
room." Now, to my mind, the passage shows clearly that the
gull entered by the regular door of admission, paid his penny
to the gatherer who stood there with the "box," and then
"advanced" through the playhouse *"up to"* the stage. Observe the passage itself: "Whether therefore the gatherers of
the publique or private Playhouse stand to receive the after-
noones rent, let our gallant, (having paid it) presently advance himself *up to* the Throne of the Stage." It is not likely
that regular gatherers stood at the tiring-house entrance to
accommodate the few who entered there. Besides, having entered the tiring-room, the gallant would be on the stage at
once, and could not well "advance himself up to the throne of
the stage."

On pages 95-6, Mr. Lawrence says of the tiring-room: "Its
identity with the 'upper stage' seems well assured." And
he proceeds to give what he is pleased to call "proof of the
position of the tiring-room." The proof, however, shows
nothing of the kind, for there is no reason why the hangings
through which the half-dressed players peeped "to see how the
house did fill" were not on the lower stage. Nor is this theory
in full harmony with the statement (p. 7): "At many of the

theatres, when not in dramatic use, the upper stage was occupied by the musicians and boy-singers.''

On many other points of minor importance one might feel inclined to question the statements of Mr. Lawrence. But the physical conditions of the early playhouses have not yet been exactly determined by careful research, and many details still remain in obscurity. Mr. Lawrence's book is valuable as a summing-up, and in the case of doubtful points, as an inspiration to further investigation.

It would be pleasant, in conclusion, to dwell on the many commendable features of the volume. I have space, however, to mention only two.

In the paper, ''New Facts about the Blackfriars,'' is presented an ingenious and plausible explanation of the term ''private'' as applied to certain playhouses. The author connects the word with the city ordinance of 1575, forbidding public performances within the city; ''Provydid allwaie that this Acte . . . shall not extend to anie plaies . . . in the pryvate hous, dwellinge, or lodginge, of anie nobleman, citizen or gentleman . . . without publique or common collection of money of the auditorie.'' This seems conclusive.

In the paper on ''Title and Locality Boards,'' and again in the final essay, Mr. Lawrence has done a valuable service by emphasizing the use of the multiple setting which long held sway at the court, and, at first, in the private, and to a less extent, in the public playhouses. The need of calling special attention to this fact is well proved by the clumsy attempts of modern editors to give exact locations to the scenes in our early plays. The disastrous results of such an attempt are to be observed in Mr. Bond's recent edition of the plays of John Lyly. As Mr. Lawrence remarks (p. 237): ''It is advisable that the student of Elizabethan drama should make himself thoroughly conversant with the distinguishing characteristics of the multiple scene and the conventionalisms its employment gave rise to, so that he may readily recognize a play constructed strictly on its principles, when he comes across it.''

JOSEPH QUINCY ADAMS, JR.

Cornell University.

DIE KAILYARD SCHOOL: EIN BEITRAG ZUR NEUEREN ENGLISCHEN LITERATURGESCHICHTE, von Dr. Fritz Loose. Berlin, Emil Eberling. 1912. Pp. 93.

The material which Dr. Loose has here brought forward in a formal thesis would have served much better for a magazine article, to the length of which it might be reduced by the omission of a good deal of padding. At least a third of the ninety-three pages are occupied by perfectly useless summaries of the plots of the stories treated and by extracts taken rather at random from contemporary book-reviews. For a magazine article, however, it must be added, there would be needed not only compression but a radical change of style, for the method of composition is dry and mechanical in the extreme, quite unrelieved by critical insight or originality, and with but a single flash of humor, perhaps unmeant: in answer to the charge that the Kailyard novelists have maligned their countrymen by bringing so much whisky into their stories, Dr. Loose protests: "Auch der Whisky spielt in den Werken der Kailyarders nur eine untergeordnete Rolle, wie jeder Leser zugeben muss. Er nimmt nur den Platz ein, den der Schnaps in jedem wohlgeordneten Haushalt der niederen Landbevölkerung einnimmt."!

However disappointing in execution, the study which Dr. Loose has made of the Kailyard School deals with a subject by no means lacking in interest. Until recent times the literary school has been a phenomenon far more familiar in France and even in Germany than in England. The most conspicuous example of it in English literature is, of course, the so-called Lake School, the term being applied to a group of writers who had hardly any single quality in common. But at present the tendency to cohere into groups seems distinctly on the increase. The group of Scottish writers for whom W. E. Henley in 1895 first suggested the name "Kailyard School" is by no means the only genuine school that has arisen during the last half-century, nor is it the most important. But it is one in which the common impulse and the common characteristics are especially manifest and well marked. It includes four or five writers whose work deserves to be remembered, and it produced about a dozen volumes of good short stories and three or four fairly good novels, all of which appeared between 1888, when Barrie initiated the movement with his *Auld Licht Idylls,* and 1900, when Barrie turned to the drama and the others ceased to produce significant work.

As his five chief representatives of the school, Dr. Loose selects Barrie, its founder and leader, "Ian Maclaren", Crockett, "Gabriel Setoun", and "Anne S. Swan." There can be no quarrel with the choice of the first three; but the work of "Gabriel Setoun" (Thomas Nicoll Hepburn) is distinctly of minor importance, and that of "Anne S. Swan" (Mrs. Burnett Smith) is certainly of no importance at all from the point of view of literature. In view of the inclusion of these it seems strange that David Storran Meldrum should have been entirely omitted, even from the list of lesser writers given on page 13. Meldrum's novels of Fifeshire are pronounced by one well-known critic [1] "to come nearer to Galt's ideal, as set forth in his *Annals,* than any of the works of his other successors, except the very best of Mrs. Oliphant's." Galt was, as Dr. Loose declares in a later section, the true father of the Kailyard School, and Meldrum certainly deserves at least mention among his literary descendants. Besides his five Kailyarders, Dr. Loose also discusses Douglas Brown, whose *House with the Green Shutters* (1901) he quite rightly classes apart, for it was written in intentional reaction against the school of Barrie and in the spirit of the English naturalists. Had Browne lived to follow up his fine first effort he might have founded a rival and perhaps truer school; as it was, the Kailyard never recovered from his brilliant attack.

The most satisfactory part of Dr. Loose's treatise is the section in which he analyzes the points of kinship in the body of work that he has selected. He has no difficulty in showing a remarkable agreement, without mere imitation of each other, in subject-matter, in spirit, in form and style, and especially in selection of scene and period. All the members of the school place their stories in Lowland Scotland, in the "landward" rather than the "burghal" portion, and among the conditions of a former generation rather than at the present day. They do their best work in the distinctively modern short-story form, not infrequently reducing it to a mere sketch, and they embroider upon it much the same brand of Scotch dialect, Scotch humor, and Scotch pathos. But their most characteristic mark is found in the way in which they all combine with the attempt at realistic portraiture of manners an idealizing spirit, which their enemies are prone to call sentimentality, and which leads them to ignore whatever is repellent or unpleasant. It is this that sets them sharply apart from the contemporary English school of Hardy, Phillpotts, and Quiller-Couch and from such isolated Scotch work as *The House with the Green Shutters.*

It is less easy to distinguish the work of the school from that of its Scotch predecessors. In his section on the relations of the Kailyarders to the older Scotch novelists Dr. Loose begins with Scott, who was the first to use Scotch peasantry in fiction in the *Antiquary* and *The Heart of Midlothian.* But he maintains that it was Scott's contemporary Galt who created

---

[1] William Wallace, "The Limits of Scottish Patriotism," *Fortnightly,* vol. 88 (1907), pp. 610-20. This striking article on writers of the school has escaped Dr. Loose's bibliography.

the novel of Scotch humble life, and traces the succession from Galt to Barrie through Moir, Miss Ferrier, Mrs. Oliphant, and George Macdonald. The omission of Stevenson's name is justified by the statement that his work is national, that of the Kailyarders parochial; but William Black, whose glowing tales of the North of Scotland did much to create the public that later welcomed the Kailyarders, might well have been added to his list at this point. In studying the relations of the Kailyard School to these earlier writers, Dr. Loose has analyzed so copiously the elements of their art which they took over that the reader begins to wonder what new thing they brought with them. This we are nowhere told. As a matter of fact, it is rather difficult to put one's finger on any single new feature in Kailyard fiction, although it is impossible to escape the conviction that it did constitute to some extent a new type. Perhaps the originality lay in a shifting of the balance of fictional elements, by which atmosphere or local color became foremost for the first time in Scotch fiction, the sole purpose and the chief attraction of the story. A minor innovation lay also in the introduction of the short story into the fiction of Scotch humble life.

The shortest and least satisfactory section of the treatise is that devoted to the circumstances favoring the rise of the school. Dr. Loose quite rightly regards the Kailyard School as merely a part of the greater movement of the last half-century which has been named in Germany the "Heimatkunst." But he makes the suprising statement that the "Heimatkunst" movement is confined to Germanic countries (among which he includes England and Scotland) because only in Germanic countries are the factors needed to produce it present. These necessary factors are, to quote his words, "in erster Linie eine tiefe Naturliebe, und daraus hervorgehend eine wahre Frömmigkeit, innige Liebe zur engeren Heimat, und das Gefühl der engsten Zusammengehörigheit untereinander." Surely it is only the writer's own "innige Liebe zur engeren Heimat" that leads him to suppose that these qualities are confined to his own race. In France, to take only the most conspicuous omission, the "Regionaliste" movement, associated with the names of Erckmann-Chatrian, Theuriet, Le Braz, Bazin, and others from every French province and almost every department, is closely parallel in its history and its ideals with contemporary "Heimatkunst" schools in Germany, England, and Scotland. Especially instructive for the English and Scotch movements is it to note how the seeds of French "Regionalisme" were planted in

Balzac's provincial novels, just as the school of Hardy in England derives from George Eliot and the Kailyarders from Scott. And perhaps the most notable results of the movement as a whole are to be found not in any of the large countries, in little sectional schools like the Kailyard and the various provincial groups of France and Germany, but in the literary revivals that have been going on in so many of the small nationalities and languages during the last fifty years,—Flemish and Provencal, Norse and Polish, Breton and Gaelic. The Germanic countries have only borne their part in the remarkable intensification of local, sectional, and racial spirit which has been a European tendency.

To answering the question what circumstances favored the rise of the "Heimatkunst" movement in the latter half of the last century Dr. Loose devotes but a half-dozen lines, stating merely that it was a reaction against over-civilization and a consequent delight in the portraiture of more primitive conditions. Undoubtedly the longing of *blasé* city folk for the "simple life", or rather for books about the "simple life", had its part in the development, just as in ancient Alexandria it helped to give rise to Greek pastoral poetry. But for the modern movement it might have been well to consider also the suggestive explanation offered by Kellner in his history of Victorian literature, that it is a paradoxical result of the rise of modern methods of transportation, by which there has been effected a greater mingling of races than ever before in the world's history. The uprooting of so many thousands from the homes of many generations, he tells us, has brought about a well-nigh universal spiritual strain and soreness, a dissatisfaction and longing which finds voice in the literature in question. In accordance with this explanation are the many signs that these intensely local books are written not so much for those who have stayed at home as for the expatriates; the popularity of the Kailyarders has been far greater in England and America, Dr. Loose assures us, than in Scotland. We can also see the reason for the bitter and pessimistic tone which sounds through the work of so many divisions of the "Heimatkunst" and allies it so often with the naturalistic movement; less so in the Scotch division perhaps than usual, but even there breaking out in the work of Douglas Brown at the close. It is all a literature of the disinherited; not so properly to be called "Heimatkunst" as "Heimwehkunst."

R. L. RAMSAY.

University of Missouri.

SEJANUS, by Ben Jonson, edited by W. D. Briggs. Boston, D. C. Heath and Company, 1911.

The edition of *Sejanus* by Prof. Briggs in the Belles-Lettres Series presents to us another of Jonson's plays with modern editing. The significance of Jonson's work for both the Renaissance and the classical period renders every new and careful edition of any of his plays very welcome, and Prof. Briggs's *Sejanus* is an accomplishment of broad scope, showing earnest workmanship.

The text is based on the Folio of 1616, with variant readings from the Quarto and from modern editors. Prof. Briggs's variations from the Folio in such matters as the use of certain letters, punctuation, and some points of form prevent the text from being so nearly a reprint as modern editions of Elizabethan works often are, but these changes do not in general affect the value of the edition even for the scholar. The annotation of the play is a matter of greater interest. Jonson himself has left us a mass of references to passages from historians and satirists which he used in building a play that was to represent with entire truth not only the salient events of Sejanus's career but also the social conditions of a corrupt Rome, with the ambition and the criminal indulgence of those in power, and the servility of their parasites and of the masses in general. To trace and verify these references and to publish in notes all the important passages among them was the task needed to furnish modern students material for an understanding of Jonson's workmanship. It is here that Prof. Briggs's scholarship reveals itself at the best. Not only has he followed up Jonson's own source notes but he has added a number which indicate still more fully the range of our dramatist's classical lore. It is now possible, without the extremely laborious task of tracing Jonson's references, to judge of his learning as shown in *Sejanus,* his devotion to the classics, his art and literary methods, his didactic purpose and serious outlook—in short, his place in the late Renaissance. Probably the classical passages reflected in the play have not all been found yet. Indeed, he would be a hardy editor who could hope to exhaust the classical borrowings of Jonson, even with the author's help. But the possibility of future discoveries does not make Prof. Briggs's annotation less admirable. If some objections might be mentioned, they are minor ones. Thus I feel that the note on Hugh Holland, who wrote complimentary verses on *Sejanus,* might be more significant if attention were called to the fact that Jonson wrote similar verses for Holland's *Pancharis* in 1603. But there is little opportunity to cavil at this part of the work.

The introduction dealing with Jonson as a writer of tragedy shows Prof. Briggs's intimate acquaintance with Jonson's ideals and his art. I must confess to some disappointment, however, in the general point of view chosen, that of Jonson's failure to measure up to our present ideals of great tragedy. *Sejanus* and *Catiline*, we must admit, are interesting to this generation chiefly as documents for the student of literary history. Why this is true, Prof. Briggs has adequately explained, but he has not accounted sufficiently, it seems to me, for the fact that Jonson's tragedies were read with appreciation by the scholarly and the cultured for two centuries. To my mind, for the present day student the key to an understanding of Jonson's art lies in the historical point of view. Jonson's tragedy must be approached primarily from the basis of ideals of tragedy in his day. To measure him by the rod of modern critical ideals seems beside the mark, so different were his aims. The scrupulous didacticism of his work Prof. Briggs has stressed as expressing a fundamental tenet of Elizabethan criticism. Further, seventeenth century humanists and classicists demanded rationality in literature, condemned imaginative and impressional art—which Jonson probably essayed in *The Spanish Tragedy* but would not father, as Prof. Briggs suggests. That Jonson, even toward the close of his career, was capable of a delicately romantic and highly imaginative art *The Sad Shepherd* proves beyond doubt. But he could hardly have made *Sejanus* less philosophical, less scientific, and retained his place as leader among literary men who insisted on the didactic and the rational. Moreover, with the humanists' insistence on decorum, even if Jonson had not developed his own rigid idea of humours, there would have been no place in the work of so genuine a humanist for the play of complex individuality which we consider essential in character portrayal and which Prof. Briggs demands of Jonson. Jonson bent the whole weight of his learning and his genius toward building up a type of drama that was close akin to satire. His early comedies he called "comical satires", but the finest specimens of his satirical dramas are his tragedies and *Volpone*, a comedy which, as Prof. Briggs points out, is essentially like *Sejanus*. It is as specimens of satiric poetry in which philosophy and reason are deliberately exalted above imagination and emotion that Jonson's plays are most significant for the later development of English literature. Prof. Briggs of course recognizes all of this. In fact, he points out that Renaissance tragedy shared the faults of Jonson's tragedy and that these faults rested on critical principles of the

day. I do not mean to imply, indeed, that Prof. Briggs's
treatment is entirely inconsistent with the historical treatment. My regret is merely that the historical point of view
has been obscured.

C. R. Baskervill.

University of Chicago.

THE COMMEDIA DELL'ARTE, A STUDY IN ITALIAN POPULAR COMEDY, BY WINIFRED SMITH. STUDIES IN ENGLISH AND COMPARATIVE LITERATURE. NEW YORK. THE COLUMBIA UNIVERSITY PRESS, 1912 IN 8°XV—290 PAGES.

The book is a timely one, since the 'Commedia dell'Arte'
has thus far had scant attention from English scholars, in
spite of its connection with English drama. The greater part
of the material is not new, having been drawn from the various Italian and French works, which treat the subject in more
detail. However, the chapter devoted to the 'Commedia
dell'Arte' influence in England, is an original contribution in
the main, and together with an appendix of English plays revealing Italian motifs, indicates fresh and thorough investigation on the writer's part. No little skill is shown in choosing and presenting the striking aspects of the 'Commedia
dell'Arte', so that a distinct impression of the genre may be
gained even by the least initiated. The treatment of the various character-types, the inclusion of effective extracts and of
summaries of the most important scenarios, all make for an
interesting exposition of the subject. It is perhaps to be
regretted that some one of the more important scenarios was
not included entire, so that the reader might realize fully
the slender basis upon which the actors worked. It is these
very illuminating chapters, however, which give the book its
somewhat too popular character, although that character is
suggested throughout by the style, which should perhaps be
more impersonal or more colourless, for so technical a subject.

The Table of Contents by no means does justice to the
amount of material in the book, yet it would be almost impossible to give adequate clues, because in almost any one
chapter, the mass of detail is too heterogeneous to be subordinated clearly to the subject in hand. The heaping-up
of comparatively extraneous information frequently destroys
the effectiveness of the argument involved, and confuses the
main line of thought, which is sufficiently interesting in itself
to be allowed clear passage.

A long chapter of the book is devoted to the discussion of theories of the origin of the 'Commedia dell'Arte'. Here the author has a new theory to propound:—namely that the 'Commedia dell'Arte' is a composite of popular and literary elements, the product of the sixteenth century Italian actor class, who as "mountebanks" of the previous generation played the 'Commedia' in embryo. In order to place this theory, Miss Smith feels it incumbent upon her to sweep aside all previous ones, instead of utilizing any of them as pre-requisite to her views. She apparently ignores the fact that the majority of scholars in this field have not been primarily concerned with sixteenth century influences upon the 'Commedia dell'Arte' but with proving that the dramatic tradition was continuous from the time of the Atellane farce through more fully developed Roman comedy; or by way of the strolling players to the 'Commedia dell'Arte'. Nor does she seem to realize that their emphasis upon similar characteristics in the Atellane farce and Roman comedy or in a mediaeval profane drama on the one hand and in those of the 'Commedia dell'Arte' on the other, is subsidiary to this general purpose. She does not, to be sure, actually discuss the existence of such a continuous dramatic activity, but she implies her disbelief in it by tracing the Commedia back only to the fifteenth century. Yet in accounting for familiar motifs and types of the 'Commedia dell'Arte' and in outlining them in the farce performances of the "Mountebanks", she inevitably does take an earlier dramatic art for granted, although she has already vitiated the theory by her earlier attitude towards it and its supporters. Her investigation of these mountebank representations has genuine interest, but it fails of its mark because she treats as hostile the very critics who should be of service to her, and in so doing, she confuses her argument.

In the treatment of the new material, that is, the 'Commedia' influence in England, it is noticeable that there is a manifest care not to lay too great emphasis on questionable evidence and that the conclusions drawn are very fully supported. Unfortunately, the same cannot be said of the work as a whole. In tracing the development of the 'Commedia dell'Arte', Miss Smith is tempted, when the number of facts accumulated by earlier investigators is insufficient for her needs, to bridge the gap with mere hypothesis, on which she founds a number of arguments,—a dangerous method for a subject in which every point is disputed.

The book, in spite of the shortcomings suggested, leaves the impression of wide reading, keen intelligence and of a power of restraint not always exercised. As an introduction to an unfamiliar field, it is distinctly valuable and will be found to be a convenient epitome of necessary information for untechnical study of the field it covers.

A few statements needing guarantee of further detail and some, clearly incorrect, should be noted:

(1) p. 9 "A Spanish desperado in the oldest known scenario"
(2) p. 10 "Some of Zanni's names point back to a remote antiquity"
(3) p. 11 "Such Pulcinelli are mentioned as long ago as 1363"
(4) p. 15 "The Commedia, at least in its beginnings, an amusement for men only"
(5) pp. 120, 125, No references or names are given for plays described.
(6) p. 219, note—"Campardon gives 1595 as the earliest date for the establishment of the Foires, but theatrical performances did not begin there till 1660."

The incorrect dates are

(1) p. 61—1565 for 1566—No authority given
See Scherillo, 'La Commedia dell'Arte' Chap. VI, p. 140
(2) p. 68, footnote—The date of Ariosto's "Cassaria" is cited as 1488 (no authority given)
See Commedie de L.Ariosto, Milano, Ed. Gonzogno 1883 —Prefazione (Olindo Guerrini) p. 8—1497.
c/ Prologue of 'Cassaria' in verse.
(3) p. 111, A play in which Vittoria figures as an actress, dated before 1578 because Vittoria left the Company of the Gelosi at that time.
No authority stated.
See D'Ancona, Origini del Teatro II p. 467 where an original document is cited to show that Vittoria was a member of the Company as late as 1585, but not in 1593.
(4) p. 116, footnote. Scenery in Rome as early as 1518 See Gardner, King of Court Poets, p. 329, Vasari VIII, 227, where it is claimed that it was used there before 1514.
(5) p. 151, Borromeo's modifying the prohibition of plays, 1580 for 1583.
No authority stated, but in discussing the question in another place, Miss Smith quotes Scherillo—(p. 62 note)
See Scherillo, Commedia dell'Arte Chap. VI, p. 156.
(6) On page 145, a quotation of six lines from Nichols, Progresses etc. of Queen Elizabeth, I, 304, shows several inaccuracies in transcription.

V. L. PARSONS.

Bryn Mawr College.

NOTES

We have received the third enlarged edition of Max Förster's useful pamphlet, Beowulf-Materialien.

One should not need a monograph to prove that Pater influenced Oscar Wilde. We have Wilde's word for it. To accept his testimony and obvious evidences of influence does not of course excuse us from the task of interpretation. Sherard in his Life of Wilde says:—"It pleased him to say that some single book which had come into his hands when he was a young man, had thus revolutionized his entire mentality; and he attributed to the influence of this book all the things that seemed to have been prompted in him by what was not common sense." If this cavalier judgment fails to satisfy the critical, that class will perhaps also be disappointed in Edward J. Bock's *Walter Pater's Einfluss auf Oscar Wilde* (Bonner Studien zur Englischen Philologie, Heft VIII). The study offers many parallels, which, though in some cases not without interest, as a whole prove little more than was generally known before about the two aesthetes, who enjoyed a similar heritage of culture and breathed a similar spiritual atmosphere.

Professor Cook's Sir Eglamour (Henry Holt and Company) is an inexpensive edition of Professor Schleich's text (Palaestra, No. 53). The book is furnished with a nine page introduction and with a generous number of marginal glosses. It should be useful in and out of Middle English courses.

John Manning Booker's *A Middle English Bibliography* is a chip from a German workshop. It had "its beginning in my doctor's dissertation;" and since "the compilation of this material ceased in the early summer of 1907," we may add that at the time of publication, 1913, it had not had its ending. The regret of the author that his work is not up-to-date will be shared by those who use it. A comparison of the Bibliography with others, say that in Körting's *Grundriss*, will reveal that even for 1907, the compilation of titles is far from adequate. Under the heading *The Folk and the Wolf*, for instance, we are referred only to Mätzner's *Altengl. Sprachpr.!*

Max Bellows' German Dictionary (Henry Holt and Company) follows the arrangement of John Bellows' "French and English Pocket Dictionary;" that is, the *Deutsch-Englisch* and the *English-German* vocabularies are so distributed throughout the book that pages are divided between the two or several pages of one glossary will be followed by several pages of the other. Moreover, the genders of nouns are distinguished by different types; the pronunciation of English words is often indicated phonetically in italic type; and there are various signs and symbols. Those who use the dictionary are "advised to devote some time and attention to a study of the pages inside the front cover and immediately after the Introduction, and thus grasp its peculiar features."

After an interval of more than twenty years Professor Viëtor has brought out his second edition of the Hamlet Parallel Texts (Marburg, 1913) in the Shakespeare Reprints series. In preparing this new edition he has collated the earlier text throughout with Grigg's facsimiles of the first and second quarto and with Halliwell's F. However, since these facsimiles were available for the first edition, the superiority of the second edition will be largely due to the careful comparison of its Folio Text with that of Lee's facsimile of the Duke of Devonshire's copy.

16. Allgemeiner Neuphilologentag zu Bremen

Das Programm für die in der Pfingstwoche (1.—4. Juni 1914) stattfindende Tagung des Allgemeinen Deutschen Neuphilologen-Verbandes ist soeben vom Vorstande zur Versendung gelangt. Einige Änderungen bleiben vorbehalten. Der wissenschaftliche Teil enthält eine grosse Zahl interessanter Vorträge, die von hervorragenden Männern des In- und Auslandes gehalten werden, und die hoffentlich nicht verfehlen werden, zahlreiche Fachgenossen zum Besuch der alten Hansestadt an der Weser zu veranlassen. Die Sitzungen finden in den weiten Räumen des Künstlervereins statt. Eingeleitet wird die Tagung durch eine Vorversammlung der Delegierten der verschiedenen neuphilologischen Vereine (Montag, 1. Juni, nachmittags 5 Uhr). Am Dienstag (2. Juni) vormittags 9 Uhr wird der Neuphilologentag durch den Vorsitzenden des Verbandes, Oberlehrer Dr. Gaertner (Bremen), eröffnet werden. Es schliesst sich daran die Festrede des Ehrenvorsitzenden, Geh. Rat Prof. Dr. Hoops (Heidelberg) über "Bremens Anteil an der neuphilologischen Forschung". In fünf allgemeinen Sitzungen (2.—4. Juni) werden folgende Vorträge gehalten werden: (1) Cloudesley Brereton, Divisional Inspector of the London County Council: English Education and its problems in 1914; (2) Prof. Henri Lichtenberger (Paris, Sorbonne): L'enseignement de l'allemand dans les Universités françaises; (3) Prof. Dr. Deutschbein (Halle): Shakespeare und die Renaissance; (4) Prof. Dr. O. Jespersen (Kopenhagen): Die Energetik der Sprache; (5) Prof. Dr. M. Förster (Leipzig): Prinzipielles über die Aussprache von Eigennamen im Englischen; (6) Prof. Dr. F. Strohmeyer (Berlin-Wilmersdorf): Zur stilistischen Vorbildung für die freien Arbeiten im Französischen; (7) Geh. Rat Prof. Dr. Morsbach (Göttingen): Universität und Schule mit besonderer Berücksichtigung der englischen Philologie; (8) Prof. Dr. Schneegans (Bonn): Welches sollten die Anforderungen des Staatsexamens für neuere Sprachen sein, und wäre eine Reform des heutigen Zustandes nicht dringend erforderlich? (9) Oberrealschuldirektor Dr. Wehrmann (Bochum): Die Ausbildung der Lehrer der neueren Sprachen; (10) Geh. Hofrat Prof. Dr. Varnhagen (Erlangen): Oskar Wilde und die Schule; (11) Privatdozent Dr. Friedmann (Leipzig): Die französische Literatur des 20. Jahrhunderts; (12) Oberlehrer Dr. Gaertner (Bremen): Über die bevorstehende Neuregelung der Stellung der fremdsprachlichen Assistenten in Frankreich; (13) Prof. Dr. Spies (Greifswald): Über den augenblicklichen Stand der englischen Syntaxforschung; (14) Oberlehrer Dr. Weyrauch (Elberfeld): Der Unterricht in den neueren Sprachen und die Sprachwissenschaft; (15) Oberlehrer Dr. Zeiger (Frankfurt a. M.): Mitteilungen über den Stand der Bestrebungen zur Vereinfachung und Vereinheitlichung der grammatischen Bezeichnungen.

Ausserdem werden am Mittwoch (3. Juni) nachmittags in der Aula der ehemaligen Hauptschule zwei Vorträge über Phonetik gehalten. Herr Daniel Jones (London) wird sprechen über "The Importance of Intonation in the Pronunciation of English and French", und Oberlehrer W. Doegen (Berlin) über die Bedeutung der experimentellen Phonetik für die Lehrer der neueren Sprachen (mit Lichtbildern und Demonstrationen), woran sich einen Lehrprobe mit Sprechmaschinen anschliessen wird.

Selbstverständlich ist auch eine Anzahl geselliger Veranstaltungen geplant, welche hoffentlich dazu beitragen werden, den Teilnehmern am Neuphilologentage den Aufenthalt in Bremen recht angenehm zu machen. Am Montag (1. Juni) findet ein Begrüssungsabend statt im grossen Saal der Union und am Dienstag Abend ein Festmahl im Künstlerverein. Für den Mittwoch (3. Juni) hat der Senat der Freien Hansestadt Bremen die Teilnehmer zu einem Ratskellerfest geladen. Am Donnerstag werden die Hafen- und Schiffahrtsanlagen des Norddeutschen Lloyd in Bremerhaven besichtigt, woran sich ein Essen schliesst, dargeboten vom Norddeutschen Lloyd. Nach der Ankunft in Bremen findet noch ein geselliges Beisammensein im Parkhause statt. Für die Teilnehmer ist folgendes zu beachten: Mitglied des Verbandes kann jeder Neuphilologe oder Freund der neueren Sprachen werden (auch Damen) gegen Entrichtung eines jährlichen Beitrages von 1 M. Zur Teilnahme an der Pfingsttagung ist eine Festkarte (10,05 M) zu lösen, die zum Besuch aller wissenschaftlichen und festlichen Veranstaltungen, sowie zum Empfang der Festschrift berechtigt. Für Familienangehörige der Mitglieder beträgt der Preis der Festkarte 6 M. Der Betrag ist möglichst bald an den Kassenwart, Herrn Oberlehrer Fischer, Bremen, Postscheckkonto Hamburg 6746, einzusenden, spätestens bis 18. Mai. Mit Rücksicht auf den zu Pfingsten stattfindenden Fremdenverkehr ist dringend zu raten, sich rechtzeitig eine Wohnung zu sichern. Die Besucher des Neuphilologentages werden gebeten, sich gleich nach der Ankunft behufs Eintragung in die Teilnehmerlisten und zur Entgegennahme der zu verteilenden Drucksachen u. s. w. beim Empfangsausschuss zu melden. Das Bureau befindet sich Pfingstmontag (1. Juni) von 10 Uhr früh bis 8 Uhr abends im Hauptbahnhof, an den anderen Tagen im Künstlerverein. Ein besonderer Damenausschuss ist bereit, den an der Tagung teilnehmenden Damen mit Rat beizustehen.

EINIGE MISSVERSTÄNDNISSE ÜBER "HERDER ALS FAUST"

Dem von mir veröffentlichten Werke "Herder als Faust" ist neben warmer Anerkennung ein solches Mass von Unverständnis entgegengebracht worden, dass ich mich entschlossen habe, zum besseren Verständnis der Sachlage, einige Erklärungen abzugeben.

Erstes Missverständniss: Goethe hat bei der Abfassung des Faust an Herder "gedacht".

Von Goethes "Gedanken" bei der Abfassung des Faust weiss ich gar nichts. Mein Buch ist keine Erforschung von Goethes Bewusstsein, während er den Faust schrieb, sondern eine Untersuchung der vollendet vor uns liegenden Dichtung. Ich habe nachgewiesen, dass in dem vollendeten Schauspiele Faust Herders Züge trägt. Wie weit sich Goethe dessen bewusst gewesen sei, das weiss ich nicht. Aus allgemeinen Erwägungen aber glaube ich, dass der Vorgang unbewusst gewesen ist. Darüber möchte ich mich näher erklären.

Zweites Missverständniss: Herder als Faust ist eine "psychologische Unmöglichkeit".

"Psychologische Unmöglichkeit" heisst Unverträglichkeit einer gewissen Psychologie mit gewissen Befunden. Eine solche Unverträglichkeit erklärt sich entweder daraus, dass diese Befunde, oder daraus, dass jene Psychologie "unmöglich" ist. Nun sind im vorliegenden Falle die Befunde Tatsachen und können als solche nicht "unmöglich" sein. Es dürfte deshalb das zweite Missverständniss daher rühren, dass einige Leser ihre eigene "unmögliche Psychologie" mit einer "psychologischen Unmöglichkeit" der Tatsachen verwechselt haben.

"Unmöglich" ist die Psychologie einer dichterischen Schöpferkraft aus dem Nichts. Menschliches Schaffen ist immer nur ein Umgestalten schon vorliegender geistiger Besitztümer. Für grosse Teile des Faust hat Goethe solche Besitztümer von Herder empfangen. Darin ist für eine richtige Psychologie nichts Wunderbares. Es ist das bekannte Verfahren unseres Seelenlebens, das wir wie bei Goethe, so bei allen Dichtern und, den veränderten Bedingungen entsprechend, auch bei den

Gelehrten, Musikern, Künstlern durch die Jahrhunderte beobachten können: nämlich dass ihr "Schaffen" nur ein Umschaffen ist. Man muss die dichterische Schöpferkraft nicht mit der Schöpfungsgeschichte aus dem Nichts in der Bibel verwechseln.

Die Unklarheit über die dichterische "Schöpferkraft" stammt aber nicht nur aus einer Verwechslung mit der biblischen Geschichte, sondern auch aus einer Verwechslung zwischen den Quellen des Dichters und seinem Bewusstsein von den Quellen. Der Dichter weiss gewöhnlich nicht, woher das stammt, was er schreibt. Es pflegt aus seinem Unterbewusstsein hervorzutauchen wie eine wirkliche Schöpfung aus dem Nichts. Tatsächlich aber ist es keine Schöpfung aus dem Nichts, sondern das Unterbewusstsein ist erfüllt mit einem Erinnerungsschatze, dessen Ursprung von dem Denker selbst zwar vergessen ist, der aber dennoch einstmals von ihm empfangen wurde. Freilich pflegt sich innerhalb des Unterbewusstseins der Erinnerungsschatz umzubilden, ja in dieser Umbildung besteht die Grösse des Menschen: darum bleibt aber ein solcher Erinnerungsschatz doch nichtsdestoweniger Erinnerungsschatz. Für wichtige Teile der goetheschen Faustdichtung weist nun "Herder als Faust" den Erinnerungsschatz bei Herder nach. Es scheint also auch Goethe " im unbewussten Momente" aus dem Erinnerungsschatze seines Unterbewusstseins "geschaffen" zu haben. Auch ihm galt aus diesem Erinnerungsschatze Alles "wie geschenkt". Und es war in der Tat geschenkt. Aber natürlich nicht aus dem Nichts sondern aus dem, was Goethe erworben hatte. Zur Zeit der Entstehung des Faust hatte Goethe nun seine Seelenbildung von Herder erworben. So dürfte es gekommen sein, dass hinter der Niederschrift des Faust, Goethe selbst vielleicht unbewusst, Herder als der Schenkende stand.

Aus der Verwechslung zwischen den Quellen des Dichters und seinem Bewusstsein stammt auch eine Ansicht, die ich selbst von Männern habe lesen müssen, von denen ich Besseres erwartet hätte: nämlich dass, wenn wir die Gedanken- und Sprachgemeinschaft zwischen Herder und Goethe Bruchteil für Bruchteil nachweisen, dann Goethe Bruchteil für Bruchteil aus Herder "abgeschrieben" habe. Das ist natürlich barer Unsinn.

Drittes Missverständniss: dass Herder Faust sei, ist eine "Hypothese".

Dieses Missverständniss scheint aus einer Unklarheit über das Wort "Hypothese" zu stammen. Denn sonst müsste ich annehmen, dass einige Leser den Sinn meines Buches gar nicht verstanden hätten. "Hypothesen" braucht man, wo etwas nicht unmittelbar erkannt werden kann, sondern aus der Beschaffenheit des Beweisstoffes erst mittelbar erschlossen werden muss. Eine Hypothese z. B. ist es, das Goethe durch Herder von Lessings Faustplan wusste. Das können wir nicht beweisen; wir können es nur wahrscheinlich machen. Der Satz: "Herder ist Faust" ist aber von ganz anderer Art. Er ist nicht mittelbar aus dem Beweisstoffe erschlossen, sondern er ist nur ein zusammenfassender Ausdruck dieses unmittelbaren Beweisstoffes selber. Solch ein zusammenfassender Ausdruck dessen, was unmittelbar vorliegt, ist keine "Hypothese".

Viertes Missverständniss: der Verfasser ist "verblendet".

Das ist an und für sich natürlich möglich. Die Entstehungsgeschichte meines Buches ist die, dass mir bei Forschungen über Herders Philosophie zunächst beiläufig auffiel, wie viel grösser an Zahl und Gewicht die Beziehungen Herders zu Goethes Faust sind, als unseren Goetheforschern bekannt ist. Ich richtete in der Folge auf dieses Nebenergebnis ein besonderes Augenmerk und legte meine Funde in dem Buche "Herder als Faust" dar. Der Vorgang ist hier also der, dass sich bei einer ursprünglich auf ganz anderen Wegen gehenden Forschung durch die eigentümliche Beschaffenheit des Stoffes von selbst ein Urteil herausbildete, das dann zu einem leitenden Gesichtspunkte in der ferneren Forschung wurde. Man kann auch dies ein "Vorurteil" nennen. Aber ursprünglich war dieses Vorurteil ein Nachurteil. Und auf *solchen* "Vorurteilen" ruht alle wissenschaftliche Forschung.

Trotzdem könnte ich natürlich irregeleitet sein. Dies brauchte nur im Einzelnen nachgewiesen zu werden. Bisher aber hat sich noch keine einzige gegen mich geltend gemachte und wirklich belegte Behauptung als stichaltig erwiesen. Im Gegenteil: was vorgebracht worden ist—die sorgfältige

Besprechung von Karl Alt ausgenommen*—zeugt teils von einer so mangelhaften Kenntnis der Herderforschung teils von so unaufmerksamen Lesen, dass ich über die bisherige Schwäche meiner Gegner erstaunt bin. Ich hatte geglaubt, ich würde mich verteidigen müssen. Statt dessen bin ich durch die Oberflächlichkeit der bisher vorgebrachten Einwürfe unwillkürlich statt in die Verteidigungs- in die Angriffsstellung gedrängt worden.

So hat sich der sonst so verdienstvolle ehrwürdige Hermann Baumgart im Kampfe gegen mich leider solche Blössen gegeben, dass ich gar nicht antworten konnte, ohne ihm schwere Wunden beizubringen.[1] So bezeichnet sich Theodor Matthias ausdrücklich als Herderforscher, veröffentlicht aber gegen meine richtigen Angaben die bedenkliche Behauptung, dass sich die für die Kenntnis Herders so wichtigen staatswirtschaftlichen Pläne im Reisetagebuche auf eine "Rückkehr an die Rigaer Ritterakademie" (!) bezögen.[2] Dr. Willy Brandl ist der Meinung, dass ich nicht imstande sei, wirkliche Gleichungen aufzustellen, bringt aber zum Beweise dessen Gleichungen vor, die ich gar nicht entdeckt sondern aus der längst bestehenden Faustforschung übernommen habe, und die von Forschern ersten Ranges wie Suphan, Erich Schmidt und Jacob Minor längst anerkannt sind.[3] Ähnlich zweifelt Georg Witkowski den Vergleich Herders zwischen der Geschichte und dem "Buche mit sieben Siegeln" als etwas erst von mir Beigebrachtes an[4] und weiss, wie auch aus seinen Faustanmerkungen hervorgeht,[5] offenbar nicht, dass diese Herderstelle zu dem ganz alten und allgemein anerkannten Rüstzeuge der Fausterklärung gehört, ich aber lediglich das Verdienst an ihr habe, noch innigere und beweiskräftigere Zusammenhänge nachgewiesen zu haben, als bisher bekannt waren. An anderer Stelle behauptet Georg Witkowski, as fehle bei

---

*Literaturblatt für Germanische und Romanische Philologie 1914.
[1] Königsberger Blätter 1912 No. 25.

[2] Zeitschrift für den deutschen Unterricht 1912. S. 568. Dazu die geradezu unglaubliche Antwort M.'s ebenda S. 831.

[3] Münchener "Allgemeine Zeitung" (27. September 1913) Sp. 632 f.

[4] Literarisches Echo 1912.

[5] Leipzig (bei Max Hesse) 1908. S. 209.

Herder die Kennzeichnung Mephistos als "Verderber",[6] gibt sich aber nicht die Mühe, die Herderstelle, über die er urteilt, aufzuschlagen. Er hätte dort gefunden, was er für fehlend erklärt, und wenn er nur eine Seite in meinem Werke weiter gelesen hätte, würde er es dort auch gefunden haben.[7] Theodor Matthias beschuldigt mich der Unsicherheit einer Gleichung zwischen Herder und Faust, übersieht aber, dass es sich an der in Frage stehenden Stelle um eine Gleichung zwischen Herder und Faust überhaupt nicht handelt.[8] A. Biese wirft mir Dinge vor, die ich nie geschrieben habe noch je geschrieben hätte, und führt dann gegen diese vermeintliche Ansicht von mir ein Wort Goethes an, das ich selbst gegen eben diese Ansicht angeführt habe.[8a] Morris schreibt: es träfe sich "unglücklich für meine These, dass ein grosser Teil des Urfaust in den zwei Jahren entstanden sei, während deren Goethe gegen Herder verstimmt war und ihm nicht einmal schrieb", vergisst aber im Eifer, dass gerade aus jener Zeit der berühmte, bekanntlich von Goethe geschriebene, begeisterte Brief an Schönborn vom Juni 1774 stammt: "Er (Herder) ist in die Tiefen seiner Empfindung hinabgestiegen" u. s. w.; vergisst das berühmte Selbstzeugnis, mit dem Goethe den Briefwechsel an Herder wiedereröffnet: "im Grund hab ich doch bisher für dich (Herder) fortgelebt".—Nicht glücklicher ist M. K. wenn er mir vorwirft, ich hätte "S. 343 den berühmten Vers Hallers vom Menschen als Mittelding zwischen Engel und Vieh, S. 285 eine bekannte Legende vom hl. Augustin" verwendt, wobei "doch die Gleichung Herder—Goethe nicht am Platze" sei;[9] dabei aber nicht merkt, dass in jedem der beiden Fälle der Vergleichungspunkt zwischen Herder und dem Faust an einer ganz anderen Stelle der Anführung liegt (!), die mit Augustin und Haller schlechterdings nichts zu tun hat.

Angesichts dieser Proben warne ich vor der allgemeinen Redewendung: der Verfasser des "Herder als

---

[6] Literarisches Echo 1912. Spalte 1566.

[7] S. 230.

[8] Zeitschrift für den deutschen Unterricht 1912. S. 567, dazu S. 830.

[8a] Monatschrift für höhere Schulen. Bd. 13, p. 34. Biese hat übrigens brieflich sein Versehen in vollem Umfang zurückgenommen.

[9] Literarisches Zentralblatt 1912 No. 9.

Faust'' müsse wohl ''verblendet'' sein. Hätte sich diese
Rede auf handgreifliche Tatsachen stützen können, so hätte
sie Wert. Sie hat sich aber selbst entwertet, indem sie an
allen Tatsachen zusammengebrochen ist, die sie für sich und
gegen mich geltend gemacht hat. Allgemeine Redensarten
gelten wie Wechselscheine nur dann, wenn der Unter-
schreibende zahlungsfähig ist. Im vorliegenden Falle gelten
sie also nicht. Denn bisher haben die Unterschreibenden an
jeder Stelle versagt, an der sie ihre Behauptungen zu er-
härten, d. h. bar zu bezahlen versuchten. Dagegen habe ich
selbst in meinem Buche Alles mit handgreiflichen Tatsachen
bar belegt und den Leser nirgends mit dem Wechselschein
blosser Redewendung vertröstet.

Zu solchen blossen Redewendungen gehört auch der von
Morris und Anderen wiederholte Gemeinplatz: die Über-
einstimmungen zwischen Herder und Faust erklärten sich
durch den allgemeinen Wortschatz der Stürmer und Dränger.
Ich habe in meinem Werke nachdrücklich darauf hingewiesen,
das auch diese Redensart nie bar bezahlt worden und ihre
Zahlungsfähigkeit zweifelhaft ist.[10] Unter diesen Umständen
bitte ich M. Morris, mich eines Besseren zu belehren.

Doch zurück zu der Redewendung: ich müsse wohl ''verblendet'' sein. Es ist wirklich nicht unbedingt notwendig, dass
die Beschäftigung mit einem wissenschaftlichen Gegenstande das Auge verblendet. Sie kann es auch schärfen—
und zwar über die Sehkraft der in diesem Gebiete Ungeübten
hinaus. Wir pflegen von einem Naturforscher nicht zu sagen,

---

[10] S. 6 f. meines Buches.—Karl Alt (Literaturblatt für Germanische
und Romanische Philologie 1914 Spalte 54) gibt zu, dass der herdersche
Sprachgebrauch im Faust den eigentlichen Stürmern und Drängern in
keinem wesentlichen Umfange zugehört, glaubt aber den Namen ''Sturm
und Drang'' im weitesten Sinne fassen zu dürfen, wobei er namentlich
Rousseau hervorhebt. Daran ist zweifellos richtig, dass Herders seelische
und philosophische Einstellung mit unter dem Einflusse der deutschen
Rousseaubegeisterung steht, wiewohl Herder selbst keineswegs ein unbedingter Rousseauschwärmer war. Das Wichtige jedoch ist, dass die
Gefühlslehre Herders wissenschaftlich über die rousseausche Gefühlslehre weit hinaus geht und dass die hierher gehörigen Übereinstim-
mungen zwischen Herder und Goethe, die ich in meinem Buche nachgewiesen habe, unmittelbar nicht auf Rousseaus sondern auf Herders
Sprach- und Gedankengebrauch zurückgehen.

er sei für den Gegenstand besonders ungeeignet, weil er sich so lange mit ihm beschäftigt habe. Im Gegenteil. So glaube ich, dass auch mein Auge durch die lange Beschäftigung mit dem Gegenstande nicht verblendet, sondern dank der damit zusammenhängenden reichen Erfahrung vielmehr eigentümlich geschärft sei. Und ich stütze diesen Glauben nicht auf blosse allgemeine Erwägungen, sondern auf Tatsachen. Denn wie aus den Beispielen von Baumgart, Willy Brandl, Witkowski, M. K. und Morris hervorgeht, hat mich mein Auge dort auf die richtige Fährte geleitet, wo diese der Untersuchung ferner stehenden Herren fehl gingen.

Es geht das aber auch aus anderen Beispielen hervor. Auf die richtige Fährte geleitet, wo diese der Untersuchung ferner ich nämlich an mehreren Stellen meines Buches auch Gleichungen aufgenommen, bei denen der beweisende Tatsachenstoff vorläufig noch nicht schlechthin schlüssig war, sondern nur Wahrscheinlichkeit für sich hatte. Ich hoffte dabei auf eine gewisse geistige Freigebigkeit bei meinen Lesern, die auch Wahrscheinlichkeiten zu schätzen wüssten. Diese Hoffnung hat mich bei Einzelnen meiner Leser getäuscht. Sie haben jene Stellen sofort wider mich auszunützen versucht: mit Eifer aber nicht mit Glück. Denn wo ich zur Zeit der Drucklegung zwingende Beweise noch nicht bringen konnte, da kann ich sie heute bringen und habe sie unter mürrischem Rückzug meiner Angreifer jedesmal erbracht: so in meiner Antwort an Baumgart,[11] an Dr. Willy Brandl [11a] und an Matthias,[12] und im Hinblick auf den Einwurf von Pernerstorfer und Morris betreffs der Jugenderinnerungen Herders[13] werde ich sie noch erbringen. Sogar Witkowskis vielverlangender Einwand:[14] die Teufelslitanei bei Herder genüge nicht; denn es fehle doch noch in ihr der Ausdruck "Fliegengott", kann befriedigt werden; denn wirklich gehört der "Fliegengott' statt des geläufigeren "Beelzebub" zu Herders

---

[11] Königsberger Blätter 1912 No. 25.

[11a] Von der Münchener Zeitung nicht veröffentlicht.

[12] Zeitschrift für den deutschen Unterricht 1912 S. 830 f.

[13] Wiener Arbeiterzeitung 1912 No. 201. Es handelt sich um Fausts Kindheitserinnerung in der Osternacht.

[14] Literarisches Echo 1912. Spalte 1566.

Wortschatz während jener frühen Zeit.[15] —Ausnahmslos hat es sich an allen solchen Stellen gezeigt, dass mein geübtes Auge nicht verblendet gewesen war und ''zu viel'' gesehen hatte, sondern das naturgemäss noch ungeübte Auge der der Untersuchung ferner stehenden Forscher nicht scharf genug gewesen war und ''zu wenig'' erkannt hatte.

Endlich: wäre ich wirklich ganz verblendet, so müsste mit mir zusammen eine grosse Zahl von Lesern und Forschungs- genossen auch ganz verblendet sein. Wenn die Übereinstim- mungen, die ich nachweise, nicht da wären, wie käme es dann, dass diese Männer dasselbe sehen, was ich sehe, und den Beweisstoff ''mustergültig'', ''overwhelming'', ''glänzend'', ''überzeugend'', ''überwältigend'' finden? Es müsste entweder sein, dass alle diese Männer solche Narren wären, wie ich, und etwas sähen, was gar nicht wirklich da ist; oder aber, dass die Gegner des Buches, was wirklich da ist, gar nicht sehen. Nun, ich glaube nicht, dass jene anderen Männer von der Kraft besessen sind, Gesichte aus dem Nichts zu erzeugen. Sie kamen gewiss nicht mit dem Vorurteile, dass Herder doch Faust sein möchte, an den Beweisstoff heran; nach ihrem eigenen Ge- ständnis vielmehr mit Zweifel. Sie sind aber trotz ihres an- fänglichen Zweifels durch die Beschaffenheit des Beweisstoffes selber überzeugt worden.— Anders verhält es sich mit Manchen meiner Gegner, die nach ihrem mehrfachen eige- nen Geständnis das Buch bereits verurteilt hatten, bevor sie es kannten. Solche Richter erwecken kein Vertrauen.

Es kann kein Zweifel sein, dass wir zuweilen nicht glauben, was wir nicht mögen, und dass unsere Endurteile durch unsere Vorurteile getrübt werden. Ich habe mich unter diesen Um- ständen des Lächelns nicht erwehren können, wenn mir, wie gesagt, meine Gegner im Eifer Gleichungen als meine eigenen Schrullen vorwarfen, die gar nicht von mir sondern von Männern wie Scherer, Hildebrand, Suphan, Erich Schmidt, Jacob Minor kamen und längst ein anerkanntes, aber diesen meinen Gegnern nicht bekanntes Rüstzeug der Faustforschung bilden. Dieses längst anerkannte Rüstzeug ist, wie der angedeutete Missgriff meiner Gegner wider Willen beweist, sachlich von meinem eigenen Rüstzeuge gar nicht zu unter-

[15] Herders Werke, herausgegeben von Suphan Bd. l. S. 275.

scheiden. Der einzige Unterschied ist, dass dank jahrelanger Herderforschung jener Beweisstoff jetzt durch mich um das Vielfache gewachsen ist, und dadurch nun ganz andere Folgerungen an den Tag treten. Das ist meinen Gegnern sehr unbequem. Daher möchten sie gerne zurücknehmen, was wir alle früher als Rüstzeug um so mehr anerkannt haben, als es damals von den grössten Forschern unserer Literaturgeschichte stammte. Allein, das geht jetzt nicht mehr an. Denn wenn wir bisher a gesagt haben, so können wir nicht plötzlich aufhören, a zu sagen, weil wir nicht gerne b sagen möchten.

Fünftes Missverständniss: Die späte Abfassungszeit gewisser Faustteile spricht gegen Herder als Faust.

Dass wir über die Abfassungszeit jener "gewissen" Faustteile so genauen Bescheid haben, ist mir unbekannt. Wir wissen über diese Fragen tatsächlich sehr wenig. Was wir wissen, ist, dass Goethe in bestimmten Jahren an bestimmten Teilen des Faust *"gearbeitet"* hat—und dem wird durch "Herder als Faust" durchaus nicht widersprochen. Wir wissen aber nicht, wann jene Teile *"entstanden"* sind. Es ist Goethes Gewohnheit, frühe Entwürfe spät in vollendete Gestalt zu bringen. Wenn er daher in den neunziger Jahren an gewissen Teilen des Faust "arbeitet," so heisst das keineswegs, dass diese Teile damals auch "entstanden" seien. Das ist eine blosse Vermutung. Und diese Vermutung wird dadurch erschüttert, dass ihr die Ergebnisse der Untersuchung "Herder als Faust" widersprechen. Aber manche Goetheverehrer sind mit ihren Denkgewohnheiten so tief in ihren Vermutungen eingewurzelt, dass sie lieber die Tatsachen zum Opfer bringen als die gewohnten Vermutungen. Die Tatsache ist: dass eine erdrückend grosse Zahl engster Beziehungen zwischen frühen Herderschriften und vermeintlich späten Teilen des Faust auf den Anfang der siebziger Jahre weist, d. h. auf die Ursprungszeit der Faustdichtung. Aber statt aus dem Vorhandensein dieser Beziehungen auf die Unrichtigkeit ihrer damit unvereinbaren Vermutungen zu schliessen, schliessen manche Goetheverehrer aus dem Vorhandensein ihrer Vermutungen auf eine Unrichtigkeit der Tatsachen. Ich fürchte, das heisst: den Wagen vor das Pferd spannen, und erinnert an den berüchtigten Hegelianer, der als ihm bewiesen wurde, dass die

Tatsachen nicht zur hegelschen Lehre stimmen, einfach antwortete: um so schlimmer für die Tatsachen. Damals haben
sich die Tatsachen vor der hegelschen Lehre nicht gebeugt,
sondern die hegelsche Lehre ist an den Tatsachen gescheitert.
Die Tatsachen werden sich auch vor unseren noch so lieb
gewordenen Vermutungen über die Abfassungszeit bestimmter
Faustteile nicht beugen, sondern wir werden uns entschliessen
müssen, jene Vermutungen nach den Tatsachen zu richten.[16]

Als ein besonders auffallendes Beispiel für das soeben genannte fehlerhafte Verfahren verweise ich hier wiederum auf
Georg Witkowski. Er wirft mir unter anderem vor, ich solle
bei der Stelle über die "Namen" des Mephisto, die mit
Herders Erläuterungen zum Neuen Testament zusammen-
hängt, "nicht berücksichtigen, dass diese Partie einer Zeit
entstammt, in der Goethe den Einfluss herderschen Denkens
längst überwunden hatte". In Wahrheit ist es Witkowski,
der nicht berücksichtigt, dass es an dieser Stelle die Tatsachen
sind, die gegen die Vermutung über ihre späte Abfassung
zeugen, nicht aber, wie Witkowski es wendet, die Vermutung,
die gegen die Tatsachen spräche. Als könne überhaupt jemals
eine Vermutung gegen Tatsachen sprechen, ohne sich damit
selbst zu richten: ganz abgesehen davon, dass Goethe niemals
"den Einfluss herderschen Denkens überwunden hatte".[17]
—Es ist aber auch aus anderen Gründen vergeblich, dass sich
Witkowski gegen den Zusammenhang jener Stelle mit Herders
Erläuterungen sträubt. Denn die unmittelbar folgende
Selbstkennzeichnung Mephistos und die unmittelbar vorange-

---

[16] Nichts ist langwieriger als der Kampf der Tatsachen gegen die
Überlieferung. Goethes "Seefahrt," so sagt die Überlieferung, sei gar
keine "Seefahrt", sondern beziehe sich "sinnbildlich" auf Goethes Abreise
von Frankfurt nach Weimar: eine Annahme, gegen die Alles und für
die so gut wie nichts spricht. Aber es ist nun einmal die Überlieferung.
Wenn ich daher an der Hand der Tatsachen zeige, dass das bisher un-
beachtete Gedicht Herders über seine wirkliche Seefahrt in vielen Einzelheiten eine Art Vorlage für das Goethesche Gedicht ist, so halten mir
Männer wie Matthias und Morris einfach die geliebte Überlieferung entgegen: jenes "Seefahrt" genannte Gedicht bedeutet "bekanntlich" keine
Seefahrt, sondern die Landfahrt Goethes von Frankfurt nach Weimar.—
Um so schlimmer für die dagegen sprechenden Tatsachen. Näheres
darüber findet man im nächsten Hefte des Euphorion.

[17] Literarisches Echo 1912. Spalte 1566.

hende Übersetzung des Johannesevangeliums stammen aus genau denselben Erläuterungen Herders wie Mephistos Namengebung. Das ist für die Übersetzung des Johannesevangeliums nach Vorgang von Bernhard Suphan, nicht erst von Erich Schmidt, wie Witkowski in seinen Faustanmerkungen angibt,[18] von der gesamten Goetheforschung und sogar von Witkowski selber längst anerkannt.[19] Wie will nun Witkowski den Einfluss der Erläuterungen Herders an dieser Stelle erklären, wenn doch ''diese Partie einer Zeit entstammt, in der Goethe den Einfluss herderschen Denkens längst überwunden hatte''? Witkowski setzt sich mit seinen eigenen Waffen matt.

An anderer Stelle wendet er genau dieselbe fehlerhafte Beweisführung an. Er behauptet: das himmlische Vorspiel des Faust stamme aus den neunziger Jahren und könne deshalb nicht mit Herders Hiobstudien in den siebziger Jahren zusammen hängen. Gut. Wie steht es dann aber mit der alten Beobachtung, dass das himmlische Vorspiel voll ist von Hinweisen auf die älteste Urkunde, die bekanntlich auch in die siebziger und nicht in die neunziger Jahre gehört? Alle, die die älteste Urkunde wirklich kennen, bestätigen das. Wie will nun Witkowski das erklären, wenn doch ''diese Partie einer Zeit entstammt, in der Goethe den Einfluss herderschen Denkens längst überwunden hatte''? Er setzt sich auch hier mit seiner eigenen Waffe matt.

Ich habe bei dieser Gelegenheit noch eine kleine Nebenabrechnung mit Witkowski und Morris zu halten. Beide führen in ihren Besprechungen die Leser von der Wirklichkeit ab, indem sie ihnen geringe, oft nebensächliche Bruchstücke der von mir erbrachten Beweise so darstellen, als seien sie der eigentliche Beweis. Das gilt zunächst von Witkowskis Darstellung der Beziehungen zwischen dem himmlischen Vorspiele und Herders Beschäftigung mit Hiob, die er so darstellt, als ob es sich hier nur um ganz allgemeine und daher nicht schlüssige Anklänge handele. Er weiss aus der Darstellung des Buches selbst ganz gut, dass hier ungezählte handgreifliche Einzelbeziehungen herüber-hinüberfliessen. Er müsste das

[18] A. a. O. S. 221.
[19] Ebenda.

wenigstens wissen, wenn er aufmerksam gelesen hätte. Noch
ausgiebiger bedient sich Morris dieses Verfahrens.

Doch zurück zu der Abfassungszeit angeblich später Faustteile. Die Lösung der Schwierigkeiten heisst da nicht: die
Tatsachen des Herder als Faust widersprechen unseren Vermutungen, also sind die Tatsachen falsch; sondern sie heisst:
unsere Vermutungen widersprechen jenen Tatsachen, also
sind unsere Vermutungen falsch. Der nun einmal vor-
handene Befund, von dem uns keine Macht der Welt
erlöst, nämlich dass die auf Herder weisenden Beziehungen
vermeintlich späterer Faustteile in eine frühe Zeit deuten,
muss wohl oder übel in Einklang gebracht werden mit
unseren Nachrichten von Goethes später Arbeit an jenen
Teilen. Ob man dabei nun meiner Annahme folgen will, dass
jene Teile früh entworfen, aber spät in dichterische Gestalt
gebracht sind, oder glauben will, dass Goethe diese Dinge so
lange im Gedächtnis behalten habe oder eine andere Erklärung
bringen will, wenn sie nur glaubhaft ist: das ist von gerin-
gerem Belang. Sobald die Tatsachen aufhören, ist für Vermutungen weiter Raum. Aber jene Tatsachen, an denen die
Lehre von der späten Abfassungszeit früher Faustteile scheitert, die lassen sich nicht wegschelten: sie sind da, und die
Faustforschung muss sich mit ihnen abfinden.

*Sechstes Missverständniss: die späte Abfassungszeit gewis-
ser Herderstellen spricht gegen Herder als Faust.*

Ein Gegenstück zu dem Vorwurf: ich hätte frühe Herderschriften auf späte Faustteile bezogen, bildet der andere Vorwurf: ich hätte späte Herderschriften auf frühe Faustteile
bezogen. Diese letztere Behauptung steht, in erfreulichem
Unterschiede von jener ersteren, wenigstens auf dem Tat-
sachenboden. Ich möchte dabei aber vor einem Missver-
ständnisse warnen.[20] Einer der schwerwiegendsten Beweis-
gründe der Untersuchung ''Herder als Faust'' liegt darin,
dass neun Zehntel aller Belege aus den Werken Herders just in
die Zeit der Faustentstehung gehören, während die späteren
Schriften Herders als Quelle für den Faust bis auf die
wenigen noch zu erwähnenden Ausnahmen ganz versagen. Es

---

[20] Vgl. zu dem Folgenden meine Antwort an Baumgart in den "Königsberger Blättern" vom Juni 1912 (No. 25).

ist das eine der auffallendsten und verblüffendsten Tatsachen des Beweisstoffes.

Was aber jene Ausnahmen betrifft, so sind sie als ein Anzeichen dafür zu fassen, dass Herder Bruchteile seines Sprachgutes aus den siebziger Jahren noch in den achtziger und neunziger Jahren verwendet. Der weitaus grösste Teil jener Ausführungn meines Buches, in denen spätere Herderstellen zur Sprache kommen, benützen diese nur, um einen von mir selbst für die siebziger Jahre schon nachgewiesenen faustischen Sprachgebrauch Herders bis in die achtziger und neunziger Jahre hinein zu verfolgen. Ich kann mich nicht entsinnen, späte Herderstellen je anders verwendet zu haben. Hätte ich es aber getan, so wäre auch das kein wissenschaftliches Verbrechen gewesen.

Darüber möchte ich mich näher erklären: der Hauptunterschied zwischen meiner Auffassung der Sachlage und der meiner Gegner liegt darin, dass diese voraussetzen, wenn Gedanke und Ausdruck des Faust in einer Herderschrift nachgewiesen werden, so müsse Goethe aus dieser Schrift abgeschrieben haben; während ich eine derartige Vorstellung für ein wunderliches Missverständniss halte. Es handelt sich überhaupt nicht um Herders Schriften und Goethes Faust, sondern um Herders Gedanken- und Wortschatz und Goethes Faust. An eine Abschrift des Faust aus Herders Werken zu denken ist barer Unsinn. Dagegen ist die weitgehendste Beeinflussung des Gedanken- und Wortschatzes Goethes durch Herder einfach eine Tatsache.

Demnach stellt sich die von meinen Gegnern angeregte Frage ganz anders. Spätere Schriften Herders bisweilen zum Vergleiche heran zu ziehen, verdient nicht den Vorwurf mangelhaften Verfahrens, sondern jener Vorwurf verdient den Tadel mangelhaften Nachdenkens. Nur dann hätte der Vorwurf nämlich einen Sinn, wenn Goethes Faust aus Herders Schriften unmittelbar herübergenommen wäre. Statt dessen bilden Herders Schriften, so weit sie der Abfassungszeit des Faust nahe stehen, lediglich für uns Spätgeborene eine Quelle, aus der wir uns den Gedanken- und Wortschatz Herders während dieser Zeitlage wiederherstellen können. Wir können uns für dieses Verfahren auf Goethe selbst berufen, der von dem Strassburger Winter mit Herder schreibt: "Was die Fülle dieser wenigen Wochen betrifft, welche wir zusammen lebten, kann ich wohl sagen, dass Alles, was Herder nachher allmählich ausgeführt hat, im Keime angedeutet ward". Ähnliche Ausführungen Goethes betonen dasselbe, und ihre Richtigkeit wird durch den nachweisbaren Entwicklungsgang des Gedanken- und Wortschatzes Herders bestätigt. Unter diesen Umständen ist es sachlich geboten, den *gesamten* Gedanken- und Wortschatz Herders namentlich in dem der Faustentstehung nahe liegenden Zeitraume heran zu ziehen. Wenn sich daher Gedanke und Ausdruck des Faust in Herders Schriften während der zweiten Hälfte der siebziger Jahre finden, so ist mit der hohen Wahrscheinlichkeit; wenn sie sich im Anfange der achtziger Jahre finden, noch mit der guten Möglichkeit zu rechnen, dass sie in Herders Gedanken- und Sprachschatz bereits in der ersten Hälfte der siebziger Jahre vorhanden waren. Und selbst, wenn sie einem der Faustentstehung ferner liegenden Zeitraume angehören würden, so wären solche Anklänge, falls sie gefunden würden, immer noch ein bedeutender Fingerzeig dafür, dass man nachzusuchen hätte, ob dieser Sprachgebrauch Herders vielleicht bis in die frühen siebziger Jahre zurück geht. Es ist nämlich eine unter den Herderforschern bekannte Tatsache, dass ein grosser Teil des herderschen Sprachgebrauches in den neunziger Jahren schon während der siebziger Jahre bei ihm vorhanden war. Daraus wäre der sonst schwer erklärbare hie und da zu findende Anklang später Herderworte an frühe Faustteile zu erklären. Das Wesen dieser Anklänge schliesst in den mir bekannten Fällen die umgekehrte Entstehung des Wortschatzes Herders aus dem Faust aus. Jedes vorschnelle Urteil, dass spätere Herderschriften unter keinen Umständen für frühe Fauststellen in Frage kämen, scheitert hier an den Tatsachen als eine der Allgemeinheiten, die zwar leicht auszusprechen sind, aber zusammen brechen, sobald man sie an der niemals so einfachen Wirklichkeit erproben will.

Das richtige Verfahren mit späteren Herderschriften in Fragen Herders als Faust ergibt sich lediglich aus einer eingehenden Fachkenntnis, namentlich einer Kenntnis des tatsächlichen Entwicklungsganges von Herders Gedanken- und Wortschatz. Gerade diese Fachkenntnis, die die einzige Bürgschaft für das wissenschaftlich richtige Verfahren bildet, lassen viele meiner Gegner vermissen. Statt dessen pochen sie mir gegenüber auf ihre "Methode".

> "Das preisen die Schüler aller Orten,
>   Sind aber keine Weber geworden".

Wahre "Methode" entwickelt sich erst an einem tiefen Einblicke in die Eigentümlichkeit des jeweiligen Wissenschaftsstoffes. Sie besteht darin, dass man die dort obwaltenden besonderen Verhältnisse genau kennen lernt, und zuweilen darin, dass man imstande ist das zu sehen, was sich dem oberflächlichen Leser verbirgt. Wem jene Fachkenntnis und diese Sehkraft fehlt, der bleibt trotz der schönsten "Methode" im Argen.

Siebentes Missverständniss: Ausser Herder hätten noch die anderen Faustquellen herangezogen werden sollen.

Diese Forderung ist nur von G. Witkowski aufgestellt worden. Aber Witkowski, dessen eigene Faustanmerkungen allenthalben die wichtigsten Quellen vermissen lassen, scheint bei der Aufstellung seiner Forderung die "anderen" Quellen hier ebenso wenig aufgeschlagen zu haben wie den Herder an der schon erwähnten Mephistophelesstelle. Sonst hätte er eine solche Forderung schwerlich gestellt. Denn er hätte dann gewusst, dass fast durchgängig bei dem für Herder in Frage kommenden Beweisstoffe die anderen Quellen gerade versagen. Dies Ergebnis steht auch auf der Witkowski offenbar unbekannten Seite 9 meines Buches.

Eine Ausnahmestellung bildet das mittelalterliche Zauberwesen, dessen Sonderstellung aber Witkowski nicht zum Bewusstsein gekommen zu sein scheint. Die Lösung ist hier, wie ich in "Herder als Faust" bereits hervorgehoben habe, noch nicht spruchreif. Wir müssen uns daher vorläufig damit begnügen, den Beweisstoff, der für eine Beeinflussung durch Herder spricht, aufzuzeigen. Dass daneben auch andere Quellen in Frage kommen, weiss jeder, der je eine Fausterklärung aufgeschlagen hat. Die Schwierigkeit der Sachlage mit Rücksicht auf das mittelalterliche Zauberwesen ist die, dass Herders Denken selbst, lange bevor er mit Goethe zusammentrifft, starke neuplatonische, mittelalterliche und mystische Einschläge zeigt. Unter diesen Umständen halte ich vorläufig an der von mir in "Herder als Faust" gegebenen Kennzeichnung der Sachlage fest: "In den wenigen Fällen, in denen Herder mit anderen Quellen zum Faust im Wettbewerb steht, wie namentlich im Falle des mittelalterlichen Zauber- und Geisterwesens: da legt sich die Vermutung nahe, dass Herder und Goethe, wo nicht aus derselben Quelle, so doch aus demselben Quellstrome schöpften".[21] Wir müssen hier wissenschaftliche Zurückhaltung üben, bis der Zusammenhang jener Beziehungen durch Einzeluntersuchung ausgemacht worden ist.

Aber Witkowski und Morris üben diese wissenschaftliche Zurückhaltung nicht. Beide erklären ohne Weiteres die verdienstvolle Arbeit der Agnes Bartscherer über den Einfluss des Paracelsus auf den Faust und meine Arbeit für unvereinbar. Morris kommt gar in einem Seiten langen Vergleich zwischen den beiden Büchern zu dem Ergebnis, Agnes Bartscherer müsse mich und ich sie "in einer seltsamen Verblendung befangen" sehen. Meines Teiles denke ich gar nicht daran. Der Einzige, den ich "in einer seltsamen Verblendung befangen" sehe, ist Max Morris. Agnes Bartscherer weist uns in die Richtung jenes gemeinsamen Quellstromes, an den auch ich glaube. Aus diesem Strome haben wahrscheinlich Herder wie Goethe geschöpft. Wer freilich bei dem äusserlichen Buchstaben stehen bleibt, wer wie Morris Sätze aus dem Zusammenhange reisst sie dann neben einander stellt, und auf diese Weise das Wesen der beiden Schriften vergleichen zu können glaubt, der hat

> "Die Teile in seiner Hand,
> Fehlt, leider! nur das geistige Band".

In Wahrheit besteht ein Zwiespalt nur zwischen Bruchstücken und Buchstaben beider Schriften. Ihr geistiges Verhältnis ist das einer wechselseitigen Ergänzung. Zudem ist die innere Zusammengehörigkeit zwischen neuplatonischen und herderschen Einflüssen im Faust längst von Julius Goebel betont und ausführlich dargelegt worden.[22] Witkowski und Morris

---

[21] Herder als Faust S. 9.

[22] Julius Goebel "Goethes Faust", New York (Holt) 1907, 2. A. 1909.

freilich scheinen Goebels Faustkommentar gar nicht zu kennen.

Achtes Missverständniss: Nicht Herder sondern Goethe ist Faust.

Durch dichterische Einfühlung ist jeder Dichter jede Gestalt jedes seiner Erzeugnisse. Er muss sie erleben können, um sie zu dichten. Dichterisch hat Goethe den Faust sicher erlebt und ist insofern allerdings selbst Faust. Dichterisch hat er aber auch alle anderen Gestalten seiner Werke erlebt: Goetz von Berlichingen, Iphigenie, Hermann und Dorothea. Trotzdem pflegen wir nicht zu sagen, dass Goethe Goetz, Iphigenie oder Hermann und Dorothea sei; und zwar deshalb, weil Goethe in seinem eigenen Leben diesen Gestalten nicht glich.

Verhält es sich mit dem Faust wirklich anders? Mir scheint dass man auch hier zwei Dinge scharf auseinander halten muss: eben die dichterische Einfühlung und die menschliche Gestalt, abgesehen von dem dichterischen Erlebnis. Dass Goethes dichterisches Erleben des Faust besonders innig gewesen sei, leuchtet mir durchaus ein. Aber eben so einleuchtend ist, dass Goethes menschliche Gestalt der Gestalt des Faust keineswegs glich: namentlich da nicht, wo Faust die Züge Herders trägt. In seinem dichterischen Erlebnis ist Goethe Faust. In Wirklichkeit ist Faust Herder. Herder erlebte die Erfahrungen des Faust wirklich, aber freilich nicht immer dichterisch. Umgekehrt erlebte Goethe die Erfahrungen des Faust dichterisch, aber freilich nicht wirklich. Das war möglich als eine Folge der eigenartigen seelischen Beziehungen des jungen Goethe zu Herder. Niemals hat es irgend jemand in Goethes Leben gegeben, in dessen Wesen er sich so eingelebt, um das Verständnis von dessen Wesen er so gekämpft hätte, wie um das Wesen Herders. "Ich lasse Sie nicht los. Ich lasse Sie nicht! Jacob rang mit dem Engel des Herrn. Und sollt' ich lahm darüber werden". Die Faustdichtung, vielleicht mehr als alle anderen Schriften des jungen Goethe, ist ein lautes Zeugnis dafür, dass Goethe damals nicht vergebens um das Wesen Herders gerungen hat. So tief war er damals in das Seelenleben Herders eingedrungen, dass uns heute, was Goethes Darstellung des *herderschen* Seelenlebens ist, als "selbsterlebt" erscheinen kann. Es ist in der Tat ein Selbsterlebnis: nämlich Goethes Weise, Herder zu erleben. Und doch ist dieses Erleben Herders bei dem jungen Goethe wiederum kein Selbsterlebnis. Denn Goethe selbst ist hier zwar der Erlebende, aber ist nicht der Erlebte. Der Erlebte ist Herder.—Allein diese Dinge kann man nicht durch schöne allgemeine Redewendungen sondern nur durch Tatsachen ausmachen.

Goethes Lebensgeschichte zeigt uns einen ganz anderen Menschen als Faust. Der verbitterte und vergrämte Faust im ersten Auftritte des Schauspiels ist nicht der lustige ''Frankforter Bub'', Herders ''Spatz'' und ''Specht'', der junge Goethe, den wir wirklich kennen. Dagegen wissen wir aus Herders eigenen Bekenntnissen, dass *ihn* allerdings diese Fauststimmung gerade zur Zeit seiner Freundschaft mit Goethe beherrschte.

Von faustischen Geistererlebnissen Goethes wissen wir nichts. Dagegen wissen wir von solchen ganz auffallend an Faust erinnernden Erlebnissen bei Herder, und wissen aus Herders Briefen, dass ihn diese Erlebnisse gerade in Strassburg aufs Neue beschäftigten.

Dafür dass Goethe Faust im Gespräche mit Wagner sei, haben wir nicht den mindesten Anhalt. Dagegen können wir zeigen, dass nicht nur sachlich sondern auch wörtlich Fausts Sprüche an Wagner die Sprüche Herders gegen die Aufklärung zur Zeit der Abfassung des Faust sind.

Die Vergottungserlebnisse, die im Faust als Fortsetzung der Erdgeisterscheinung nach dem Fortgange Wagners auftreten, gleichen aufs Haar den Vergottungserlebnissen, die bei Herder als Fortsetzung der Geistererscheinungen auftreten und jene niedergedrückte, dann wieder gewaltsam gesteigerte, das Erdenleben verneinende, ein höheres Leben fordernde Stimmung verraten, welche in dieser Form dem jungen Goethe fremd, dagegen Herders damalige Grundstimmung war.

Da Faust in der Osternacht an seine Jugend zurück denkt, denkt er nicht an Goethes Jugend noch auch an seine Knabenzeit ''im Allgemeinen'', wie Pernersdorfer und Morris verkünden. Diese Verkündigung ist bequem, entbehrt jedoch jeder sachlichen Unterlage und, was schlimmer ist, des tieferen Einblicks in den Sinn des Faust. Goethe beabsichtigte schwer-

lich in Fausts geheiligter Kindheitserinnerung einen Knaben
im Allgemeinen zu schildern, wie es deren Dutzende gibt, wie
"jeder kirchlich erzogene ordentliche Knabe" (!) ist, um
Morris's eigenen Ausdruck zu brauchen. Offenbar ist Morris
ausser Stande, das für jeden verständnisvollen Leser hier
selbstverständlich zu bemerken, dass das Kind der Vater des
Mannes ist ; dass sich in dem unbegreifflich holden Sehnen des
jungen Faust wie des jungen Herder die seelische Qual des
herangereiften bereits vorbereitet hatte. Morris sieht in diesen
tief angelegten zum Grossen geborenen Knaben nichts als
Durchschnittsjungen. Wir Anderen sehen mehr in ihnen.—
Diese Erinnerung geht nun auf Goethes eigene Kindheit nicht
zurück. Sie erinnert aber Strich für Strich an Herders Kinder-
zeit. Der erwachsene Faust trägt die Züge Herders ; und da in
dem Kinde Herder der spätere Mann schlummerte, ist auch die
Kindheitserinnerung des Faust Herders Kindheitserinnerung
geworden.[23]

Aber weiter. Faust als Übersetzer des Johannesevangeliums
verhält sich genau so wie Herder als Übersetzer des Johannesevangeliums. Eine Übersetzung des Johannesevangeliums
durch Goethe selber ist mir unbekannt. Das dann folgende
Gespräch des Faust zeigt diesen wiederum in jener äussersten,
weltverneinenden Verbitterung, die dem jungen Goethe in
dieser Form fremd, dagegen Herder damals eigen war, und
zwar nicht nur "im Allgemeinen" sondern in jeder einzelnen
Stufe des Gespräches sachlich und wörtlich.

Endlich der Aufriss des gesammten Schauspieles einschliesslich des zweiten Teiles erinnert so auffällig an Herders Lebens-
plan zur Zeit der Entstehung des Faust, dass auch hier
schwerlich von einem Zufall gesprochen werden kann. Dagegen wissen wir nichts von einem derartigen Lebensplane des
jungen Goethe.

Nach alledem ist, sobald man an die Tatsachen geht, Faust
zwar dichterisch von Goethe erlebt, ist aber nicht selbst Goethe :
nämlich nicht der Goethe, den wir aus seiner Lebensbeschrei-
bung, seinen Briefen und den Zeugnissen seiner Zeitgenossen

---

[23] In einem späteren Aufsatze werde ich, wie ich bereits früher
andeutete, weiteren Beweisstoff für Fausts und Herders Jugenderinnerungen bringen.

kennen. Dagegen trägt der Faust auf Schritt und Tritt tatsächlich herdersche Züge. Unter diesen Umständen ist das Wort: "Faust ist nicht Herder sondern Goethe" falsch. Das richtige Wort lautet: "Faust ist nicht Goethe sondern Herder". An diesem Punkte kann ich also weder sachlich noch im Ausdrucke irgend etwas nachgeben. Dagegen bin ich gerne erbötig, in anderer Beziehung Einräumungen zu machen. Mehrfach habe ich mich nämlich in meinem Buche des Ausdrucks bedient, dass an der in Betracht kommenden Stelle "Faust kein anderer als Herder" sei. Daraufhin redet mich Hermann Baumgart durch Goethes Sprachrohr folgendermassen an: "O du Esel, du einfältiger Bursche, du heilloser Kerl".[24] Ich bin gerne bereit, mir den auf diese Weise beanstandeten Ausdruck abzugewöhnen. Für andere Leser brauche ich nicht zu sagen, dass wenn ich mich jenes Ausdrucks in seinem allgemein verbreiteten volkstümlichen Sinne bediene und sage: Faust sei an vielen Stellen "kein anderer als Herder", ich damit nicht meine: Faust sei an allen Stellen "ausschliesslich Herder".

Eine solche Ausschliesslichkeit würde für mich gar keinen Sinn haben. Die Dichtung Goethes heisst nicht "Herder" sondern "Faust". Darum ist Faust auch da, wo er Herders Züge trägt, selbstverständlich nichtsdestoweniger Faust. Und insofern Goethes dichterisches Erlebnis in Frage kommt, ist er, wie wir gesehen haben, auch Goethe. Ich hoffe später noch einmal Gelegenheit zu dem Nachweis zu haben, dass Faust die Züge des Adam trägt als des urbildlichen Menschen nach Herders Ausdeutung. Und im Gretchenschauspiele wie in den Einzelheiten des zweiten Teiles mag man in der Faustgestalt zu finden suchen, wen man will.

Ich könnte also eine mir von Konrad Burdach im Briefwechsel vorgeschlagene Gleichung: Faust = Goethe + Herder + X + Y + ... N "gern unterschreiben (wiewohl ich für das + Zeichen in diesen Fragen nicht viel übrig habe) lieber als die im Druck von ihm abgegebene Entscheidung: "Auch Faust selbst ist nicht Herder, wie man neulich erweisen wollte, sondern Goethe".[25] Diese letztere Entschei-

[24] Königsberger Blätter 1912 No. 16.

[25] Sitzungsberichte der Königlichen Preussischen Akademie der Wissenschaften 1912. Bd. 35. S. 656.

dung halte ich für falsch, jene andere für richtig: nur dass
auch in ihr die Grössen Goethe, Herder, X. Y, ... N
beileibe nicht, wie es vielfach geschieht, als etwa gleichwertig
behandelt werden dürfen. Verglichen mit den Grössen Goethe
und Herder stellen X, Y bis N ganz geringe Werte dar. Sie
sind als Faustquellen blosses Druckwerk und alte Schmöcker.
Dagegen ist Goethe, der Dichter selbst und Herder, sein ver-
götterter Freund, unmittelbares schlagendes Leben in Goethes
Seele. Die grossen Werte in Burdachs Gleichung sind nicht
X Y Z oder N, sondern lediglich Herder und Goethe. Ich
habe nachgewiesen, dass abgesehen von Goethes dichter-
ischem Erlebnis Faust da nicht Goethe ist, wo er Herder ist.
Ob und inwieweit Faust im übrigen Schauspiele Goethes
eigene Züge trägt, darüber enthalte ich mich vorläufig des
Urteils.[26]

An dieser Stelle habe ich noch eines Einwurfs von Georg
Witkowski zu gedenken.[27] Herder, das scheint Witkowski zugeben zu wollen, sei zwar Faust im ersten Teile bis zum
Auftritt im Auerbachkeller und im Entwurfe des ganzen
Schauspiels einschliesslich des zweiten Teiles. Er sei aber nun
doch nicht Faust und mein ganzes Buch mit seiner Aufschrift
verfehlt, weil Herder nicht auch im Gretchenschauspiele und
in den Einzelausführungen des zweiten Teiles Faust sei (!).
Die Gedankenfolge dieses Einwurfes krankt an einer Unklarheit über die Bedeutung des Wortes: "als". Die Aufschrift
meines Buches heisst "Herder als Faust", und ich erinnere
Witkowski höflichst daran, dass im Deutschen das Wort "als"
die zeitweise Rollenübernahme das Einen durch den Anderen
ausdrückt. So heisst: "der Neffe als Onkel" nicht, dass
der Neffe überall Onkel sei, und der Onkel überall Neffe,
sondern dass die Rolle des Onkels zeitweise von dem
Neffen übernommen wird. Auch Herder als Faust heisst
nicht, dass Herder überall Faust und Faust überall Herder sei, sondern dass die Rolle des Faust zeitweise von
Herder übernommen wird. Diese Bedeutung des Wortes "als"
scheint sich Witkowski nicht klar gemacht zu haben.

[26] Einiges zu dieser Frage findet man in meinem Aufsatze über Konrad
Burdachs "Faust und Moses," Journal of English and Germanic Philology Bd. 12. S. 1 ff. (Januar 1913).

[27] Literarisches Echo 1912. Spalte 1567.

Neuntes Missverständniss: "*Herder als Faust*" *wider-*
spricht unseren Neigungen.

Hinter den meisten Angriffen gegen "Herder als Faust"
stehen zwei von manchen Lesern eingestandene, zwar
sehr natürliche aber nicht wissenschaftliche Triebfedern:
nämlich einmal das geistige Beharrungsvermögen, das den
Zusammenbruch liebgewordener Überlieferungen scheut, und
zum Anderen die Furcht vor einer etwa drohenden Herab-
minderung unserer Verehrung zu Goethe.

Beide Beweggründe sind sehr begreiflich. Man muss sich vor
Augen halten, dass die Faustforschung wie jedes Lehrgebäude
einen geschlossenen Zusammenhang von Erkenntnissen bildet,
und dass in diesen Erkenntnissen Tatsachen, Deutungen und
Annahmen schier unentwirrbar verflochten sind. Nun
schneien in dieses Geflecht die neu aufgedeckten Tatsachen des Herder als Faust hinein und erregen zunächst eine
arge Verwirrung. Manche längst gewohnte Überlieferungen
werden erschüttert und selbstverständlich von ihren Freunden
verteidigt. Aber wie es dann zu geschehen pflegt: die Ver-
teidiger vergessen, was an der Überlieferung Tatsache ist, was
lediglich Deutung und Annahme, und führen in Ermangelung
besserer Stützen die Letzteren ins Feld, als seien sie das
Erstere. Gegen solche Verteidigung ist die Untersuchung
"Herder als Faust" im Vorteil. Denn da sie sich fast
ausschliesslich auf Tatsachen aufbaut ohne Vermutungen, so
kann sie mit ihren Tatsachen die blossen Vermutungen und
Deutungen der verteidigten Überlieferung unschwer in Schach
halten. Ich habe das namentlich an dem Beispiele von Witkowski gezeigt; [28] ich hätte es aber auch fast Schritt für
Schritt an den Ausführungen von Max Morris zeigen können.

Im Übrigen habe ich nicht den mindesten Grund, die Angriffe
und Ausfälle meiner Gegner übel zu nehmen. In Fragen
Herders als Faust kann man nicht von heute auf morgen um-
denken. Es bedarf dazu geraumer Zeit, und ich habe viel
Zeit und Geduld.

Es kommt hinzu, dass Herder als Faust einer gerade erstarkenden und an sich sehr zu begrüssenden Tagesrichtung
nicht folgt, sondern Wege einschlägt, die, freilich ganz mit

[28] S. dieses Aufsatzes.

Unrecht, zu jener Tagesrichtung in Gegensatz gebracht werden. Meine Untersuchung verwendet statt des "philosophischen" Verfahrens das "philologische" nicht aus irgend welcher Abneigung gegen die Philosophie, der ich vielmehr mein Leben gewidmet habe, sondern in der Erkenntnis, dass im vorliegenden Falle nicht ein "philosophisches" sondern nur ein "philologisches" Verfahren weiter führt. Was für ein Verfahren eingeschlagen wird, das richtet sich nicht nach der Herzensneigung oder einer Tagesrichtung sondern einzig und allein nach der Sachlage. Es gibt eben, wie in allen Wissenschaften, so in der Literaturgeschichte mehrere Verfahrungsweisen neben einander, die sich wechselseitig ergänzen. Dies ist auch das Verhältnis zwischen dem "philologischen" und "philosophischen" Verfahren. Ohne jenes kann dieses gar nicht bestehen, und wie mich dünkt, lässt sich auch von Männern wie Hildebrand, Scherer, Suphan, Erich Schmidt und sogar aus meinem Buche "Herder als Faust" Manches für die Philosophie wie für das geistige Verfahren Goethes lernen.

Nichtsdestoweniger haben Einige meiner Gegner geglaubt, als Vertreter der Zunft gegen mich Misstrauen erregen zu sollen, indem sie zu verstehen gaben, als "Philosoph" sei ich in literarischer Forschung verdächtig. Das Unglück hat es jedoch gewollt, dass sich gerade diese Männer in ihren Besprechungen schlimme Blössen gaben und so selber bewiesen, dass die Stärke des Zunftbewusstseins nicht immer der Stärke des Wissens entspricht. Zudem erkläre ich für Leser, deren Vertrauen zu mir davon abhängt, dass ich seit dem Beginne meiner akademischen Lehrzeit "Philologie" und nicht nur deutsche studiert habe, dass ich mir schon 1903 auf Grund einer rein "philologischen" Arbeit die Lizentiatenwürde erwarb, dass ich bereits 1904 die Oberlehrerprüfung für deutsch in der Oberstufe bestand, dass ich dann zu meiner weiteren Ausbildung unter Erich Schmidt studierte, mit einer die Literaturgeschichte berührenden Arbeit zum Doktor promovierte und seit neun Jahren mit Herderforschungen beschäftigt bin. Lesern, die auf solche Dinge Wert legen, werden diese Angaben als Bürgschaft für meine fachwissenschaftliche Zuständigkeit genügen.

Die Neigung zu dem gegenwärtig erstarkenden "philosophischen" Verfahren in der Literaturgeschichte und die Abneigung gegen das "philologische" Verfahren ist von dem
Bewusstsein geleitet, dass durch die letztere Art der Forschung
dem Werke des Dichters weniger Ehrfurcht angetan werde als
durch die andere. Ich will zugeben, dass sogenannte "Würdi-
gungen" eine besonders günstige Gelegenheit zu Ehrfurchts-
bezeugungen geben. Ich will auch zugeben, dass eine oberflächliche Quellenuntersuchung ehrfurchtslos sein kann—
welche oberflächliche "Würdigung" wäre nicht ebenso ehrfurchtslos? !—Dagegen bestreite ich entschieden, dass die
Quellenforschung als solche und dass mein Buch "Herder als
Faust" einen Mangel an Ehrfurcht beweise. Ich kann nicht
dafür, dass mir unaufmerksame Leser andichten, ich er-
niedrige Goethes Faust zu einem "Zusammensetzspiel" (Dr.
Willy Brandl). Dem Geiste des Buches ist diese allzu oberflächliche Ausdeutung der Sachlage, die ich in meinem Buche
selber gebrandmarkt habe,[29] völlig fremd.

Einer wahren Goetheverehrung tut Herder als Faust nicht
den mindesten Abbruch. Der Grösse eines wirklich grossen
Mannes können Tatsachen überhaupt keinen Abbruch tun.
Und in meinen Augen ist Goethe wirklich gross, einer der
Grössten, die je gelebt haben. Mir ist er durch die Art seiner
Beziehungen mit Herder nicht kleiner sondern grösser geworden. Das liegt daran, dass ich diese Beziehungen sorgfältig
untersucht und ihre psychologische Tragweite durchdacht
habe. Nur wer sich dieser Sorgfalt überhoben glaubt, wird
zu einem anderen Ergebnis kommen.

Die Besorgnis, dass meine Untersuchung eine "Verleidung
der Freude an Goethe" (Matthias) und eine Störung des
natürlichen Beharrungsvermögens bedeuten könne, ist weniger
wissenschaftlich als menschlich, und das rein Menschliche an
ihr hat die allzu menschliche Folge gehabt, dass Manche unter
meinen Gegnern im Gegensatze zu dem vornehmen Tone
meines Buches dieses und mich selbst mit beleidigenden Schelt-
namen überhäuft haben. "Fratzenhaft", "Dilettantenwust",
"Esel, einfältiger Bursche, heilloser Kerl", "Gymnasiasten-
aufsatz", "einer der übelsten Auswüchse der Pseudophilo-

---

[29] S. 370 ff. meines Buches.

logie" und Ähnliches habe ich lesen dürfen; und ich darf hinzufügen, dass zwischen solcher persönlichen Schärfe und einer damit Hand in Hand gehenden sachlichen Schwäche der Angriffe ein eigentümliches Missverhältniss zu bestehen pflegte.

Alles begreifen heisst Alles verzeihen. Und in diesem Falle kann ich um so lieber und leichter verzeihen, als ich die sachliche Stärke bisher auf meiner Seite sehe. Noch ist der junge Herder unseren Goetheforschern ein wenig vertrautes Gebiet. Daher werden die Forschungen über die Bedeutung Herders für den Faust auch weiterhin einige Zeit brauchen, um sich durchzusetzen. Aber durchsetzen werden sie sich. Denn sie vertreten die einfachen Tatsachen; und den Tatsachen kann sich keine Wissenschaft auf die Dauer entziehen. Viele Mitforscher und Leser haben sich ihnen von Anbeginn nicht entzogen. Diesen Männern danke ich für ihre Ermutigung und ihren Beistand.

GÜNTHER JACOBY.

Greifswald.

DRAMATIC FASHIONS ILLUSTRATED IN SIX OLD PLAYS

From the end of the sixteenth century to the end of the eighteenth there were written in England six plays, all dealing with the same story. The plays are, the anonymous *A Knacke to Knowe a Knave*, Edward Ravenscroft's *King Edgar and Alfreda*, Thomas Rymer's *Edgar; or, the English Monarch*, Aaron Hill's *Elfrid*, the same writer's *Athelwold*, and William Mason's *Elfrida*.[1] The story is the old legend of the love of King Edgar for the fair Alfreda or Elfrid. The plays are of little intrinsic merit, but the various changes in the treatment of the same theme well illustrate the varying dramatic fashions during two centuries. To the student of dramatic theory and practice in England the modifications introduced in these successive plays are full of significance, and a study of them from this point of view may well be worth while.

In examining these plays it is necessary to have in mind the process of change in the formulation and application of English dramatic theories from the mid-Elizabethan era, when detached neo-classical rules were preached but not much practiced, to the Restoration period, when a partial and superficial neo-classicism was combined with the heroic type; to the early eighteenth century development of the sentimental domestic tragedy; to the practically contemporaneous vogue of neo-classical plays following French models; and to the time later in the century when there arose a group of plays which hark back directly, without the mediation of interpreting rules, to Grecian models. All of these schools of dramatic composition are represented, or approximately represented, by the series of plays mentioned above. The Elizabethan comedy represents the relative formlessness of the popular drama of the time. Ravenscroft's is a heroic play in the straight-jacket of superficial neo-classicism. *Edgar*, as will be seen, stands apart as an example of the strict application of neo-classical rules. Hill's first play belongs distinctly to the sentimental group. His *Athelwold* shows the influence of the

[1] Ward, English Dramatic Literature, II, 610, note, mentions these plays, but no one, as far as I am aware, has attempted a comparison of them.

"regular" tragedies of French authorship. And Mason's *Elfrida* is fairly typical of what may be termed the pseudo-Grecian method, in contradistinction to the neo-classic. The story on which these plays are based is old. Ward [2] points out that it is found in an old "Song of King Edgar, shewing how he was deceived of his Love".[3] He might have added that many of the old chronicles relate practically the same story.[4] It is worth summarizing here. The song relates that King Edgar,[5] a widower, having heard of the beauty of Estrild (Alfrid), daughter of Earl Orgstor of Devonshire, summoned a knight, Ethelwood, (Ethelwold, Athelwold) and sent him to see Estrild, and, if he found her beauty equalled report, to woo her for the king. The knight went to Devonshire, became himself enamoured of the maid, and planned to win her. So he returned to the king with the assurance that the girl's beauty was far less than had been reported, and that she was

"......far unmeet in everything
To match with such a noble king."

However, Ethelwood hinted that her riches would make her no bad match for himself. The king consented, and the knight wedded the lady. The king, after these events, continued to hear reports of Estrild's beauty, and concluded that he had been deceived. Therefore, not betraying his wrath, he told Ethelwood to prepare for a royal visit. The knight, dismayed, confessed to his wife his wretched deceit, and begged her to disguise her beauty by homely attire and repulsive behavior. She seemed to assent to the request, but when the king came, greeted him in her costliest robes, and returned his glances with interest. The king, seeing her beauty, was angered. Calling to the earl, he suggested that they go hunting; and during the hunt "with a shaft the earl was slain." And in time the king married the lady. The song concludes,

[2] Hist. Eng. Dram. Lit., II, 610, Note 2.

[3] Found in *Old Ballads*, Thos. Evans, 1777, Vol. I, p. 22; and in Publications of the Percy Society, Vol. XXX, p. 12.

[4] Gerard Langbaine, *An Account of the English Dramatic Poets*, 1691 edition, p. 434, points out some, but not all, of these.

[5] The Saxon king, reigning A. D. 959-975.

"Thus he that did the king deceive
Did by desert his death receive.
Then, to conclude and make an end,
Be true and faithful to thy friend.''

This is substantially the story found in the chronicles.
They add certain details about Edgar's reign which appear
in some of the later plays. For example, Holinshed and
Stow, not to mention the early chroniclers, such as Roger
de Hoveden and Matthew of Westminster, tell how Edgar had
eight captive kings row his barge on the river. Edgar's great
navy is referred to by most of the chroniclers; Holinshed re-
frains from mentioning any definite number of ships; Speed,
following Hoveden, puts it at 3600; Stow gives the same
number, but thinks 300 the more likely; Matthew of Westminster makes it 4800. Rymer, in the prologue to his play,
rates it at an even four thousand. Grafton and Holinshed
relate the story of the quarrel between "Kynadus", king
of Scotland, and Edgar, and several authorities vouch for
the presence of the Scottish king at the English court, an
incident of which Rymer makes use. These details, and the
love-story of Edgar, form the stuff out of which the plays
were fashioned.

In *A Knacke to Knowe a Knave*[6] the Edgar-Alfreda story
is practically the same as in the old song, save in the catastrophe. Edgar sends Ethelwald as his proxy to woo Alfreda,
and is deceived by his envoy, who marries the girl himself.
The king visits the traitor, and is determined to kill him,
when Dunstan, who in the play is related to Ethelwald, summons the devil, whereupon the king forgives the bishop's
relative. The time element of the story is unmodified, and
the various episodes are shown completely in action; the

[6] Dodsley's Old English Plays, Vol. VI. This play is not, of course,
representative of the fully developed Elizabethan technique. It was
printed in 1594. Henslowe (W. W. Greg. ed.) enters the play in
June, 1592. Greg (II, 156) in comment says the play was performed
as a new play June 10, 1592. The general crudity in design and
dialog, especially the utter absence of connection between the "morality"
portion of the play and the Edgar-Alfreda portion, save as both
are connected with the king, seem to be indications of an early date
of composition.

unities of time and place are broken with cheerful unconcern. There is not even unity of action in the play, for a wholly distinct set of incidents is introduced, dealing with the efforts of "Honesty" to reveal the knavery of the four sons of the "Bayliff of Hexam". These scenes and the Edgar-Alfreda scenes are jumbled confusedly, and on top of all there is added a farcical incident dealing with the mad men of "Goteham" and their petition to the king.

In dramatic technique the play is crude, and not representative of the best of its time. The writer, in the portion dealing with the Alfreda story, adheres closely to the original, and makes no attempt to adapt it to stage presentation. When he wants to add complexity to his plot, instead of increasing the intricacy of the main set of incidents he throws in a morality and a bit of farce. In these matters the play is decidedly below the standard of attainment in 1592. On the other hand, in its disregard of the neo-classical principles so strongly advocated by Elizabethan critics, it follows the general example of the plays of its time. For instance, it ignores the neo-classical insistence that there shall be no mingling of the serious and the comic in a play; here they alternate with great rapidity. Again, the rules of decorum forbid the inclusion of "low" characters in a serious play, but here king and clown rub elbows. The disregard of the unities has been noted. Theory and practice are widely separated during this era.

Ravenscroft's play [7] carries us forward almost a century.[8]

---

[7] It has been pointed out by Ward (III, 28) and Schelling (II, 232) that Massinger's *Great Duke of Florence* (licensed 1627) is but a thinly disguised treatment of the Edgar-Alfreda theme, with the names of the characters changed and the scene transferred to Italy. This play would furnish an example of the development of Elizabethan technique, and the changes are significant of changing dramatic fashions. But to include Massinger's play in this discussion would pave the way for the inclusion of other plays on the same general theme of lovers' envoys (in narrative poetry *Miles Standish* would belong in this class) and would consume more space than would be profitable. Therefore it seems best to limit ourselves to the six plays on the actual English story.

[8] Ravenscroft's play appeared in 1677. But it is a revised version of an earlier play by the same author. In the prolog the author says,
   "This Play at least Ten Years ago was writt;

It was acted in 1677[9] and was printed the same year. It probably appeared toward the end of the year, for its first and only advertisement in the Term Catalogues appears on the 28th of February, 1678.[10]

The lapse of time has brought about a decided change in dramatic methods, and whereas we see the Elizabethan playwright adhering closely to the story in the old song, and gaining variety of interest at the expense of utter loss of unity of action, we find Ravenscroft manipulating his material and adapting it to his purpose, if not with skill, at least with boldness. It is true that the antecedent action which is indicated follows the first part of the Edgar-Alfreda story with considerable fidelity, but the catastrophe is changed, and new characters and new incidents are freely introduced. Says Ravenscroft in his Preface, ''I have introduced new Persons to raise a Plott, and vary'd from the *Chronicle*, to better the Character of the King; Knowing that the Criticks in Poetry are more Censorious and Severe, than the Historians.'' This consciousness of critical standards, and this avowed effort to meet their demands, are significant of changes since the easy Elizabethan era.

Ravenscroft's play, like those coming after his, takes up the Edgar-Alfreda story at a point where it is already well advanced. The initial situation of the play shows departure from sources. Ethelwold does not remain at home, but is at court with his newly won Alfreda. Edgar, the king, is pro-

---

A time when th' Author had more Zeal than Witt;
But pondering on't he found it wou'd not do.''

That is, an old play has been remodeled to suit the taste of the times. For example, in regard to rime, so distinctly characteristic of the heroic drama, Ravenscroft writes that the playgoers are surfeited; consequently he has changed much of the dialog into blank verse. Likewise he feels the need of reaction from the excess of the heroic drama; so,

"We have no Rant, no Rapture, nor high flight,
The Poet makes us Men and Women all to Night.''

For all this, there *is* rant and exaggeration. But it is evident that the play was first written to conform to the heroic method, and was rewritten to agree with new standards, involving some of the dicta of neoclassicism.

[9] Genest, *An Account of the English Stage*, Vol. I, p. 201; Theatre Royal, 1677.

[10] Cf. Arber's Reprints of Term Catalogues, date cited.

vided with a queen, the daughter of a lord Ruthin, through whose machinations she has attained her position. For a time events move along as in the old story. Ethelwold reveals his treachery to Alfreda, who agrees to do her best to rescue him from his predicament. But, angered, she exerts herself to attract the king, who, noting her beauty, is furious at Ethelwold's deception. After various complications Alfreda and the king agree to meet that night. But Alfreda, who does not wish to go too far, warns the queen, who takes her place. Ethelwold, learning of the appointment but not of the substitution, plans to enter the bower and kill his guilty wife. He kills the queen, is himself killed, and the king is left free to marry Alfreda.[11]

In addition to the main plot minor episodes are introduced by means of new characters. Edgar is provided with a sister, Matilda, and Alfreda with a brother, Aldernald, a young admiral, who comes to court accompanied by Durzo, "a blunt Sea Captain." Aldernald is paired off with Matilda, while

[11] It is worthy of note that Ravenscroft and Rymer both depart from the chronicles to adopt virtually the same catastrophe. The practically simultaneous appearance of the two plays makes borrowing either way improbable, unless Rymer got hold of that early version which Ravenscroft speaks of, and this appears unlikely. A common source seems probable.

Ravenscroft in his Preface remarks "Several Forreign Authors have writ upon this part [i. e., the Edgar-Alfreda part] of the Story; some have disguis'd it under borrow'd Names, but all of 'em were at a loss when they came towards a conclusion, and have left it imperfect, fearing to blemish the Character of the King: I found it difficult, but hope I have succeeded so well as to make the last Act the best, and the Catastrophe in that point not blameable; the Husband receives his death from another hand, whence it appears just, yet accidental." This would seem to imply that Ravenscroft invented the catastrophe; but the word of a Restoration dramatist can never be taken as final on that score, and Rymer in his preface seems to point to an old source: "I must appeal from the late Epitomizers, who make Edgar point-blank guilty of Ethelwold's Death, without any sufficient ground from Antiquity." This last clause is puzzling. Had Rymer forgotten the old chronicles? However this may be, Rymer claims authority for *his* version, in "the Histories". Langbaine (1691 ed.) refers to "The Annals of Love" (no author stated), and "Ubaldino, Le Vite delle Donne Illustri" for sources, and these might throw some light on the matter; but they are not accessible to me.

Durzo falls in love with Hillaria, a lady of the court. Thus there are two minor strands of love-plottings, only slightly connected with the main plot by the blood-relationship of the characters. Complication is still gained somewhat at the expense of unity, but not by the introduction of such utterly foreign material as the Elizabethan playwright felt free to use.

The unities of time and place are strictly observed. The action all takes place at the court, and consumes one day. Some attention is paid to the principle of decorum—in regard to the characters which are suitable to tragedy, and to the qualities and traits these characters ought to manifest. That this was conscious is evinced in the portion of the Preface already quoted, in which Ravenscroft states that he has bettered the character of the king, to conform to critical standards. In general the participants in the action are of that rank which decorum insists must grace personages in tragedy; but the vulgar and rough Durzo would be condemned by the strict neo-classicist in one word: low. Moreover, another neo-classical canon is violated when because of the nature of the scenes in which Durzo takes part comedy is introduced into the tragedy. Finally, bloodshed and murder are permitted to occur on the stage, and the queen and Ethelwold die in the presence of the audience.

In a word, Ravenscroft's play shows an advance in technique over its Elizabethan forerunner; but on the other hand it is still considerably removed from those standards, some of which English dramatic critics had been setting up for a hundred years. There has been progress toward "regularity", especially in regard to the unities; but not complete attainment of it, even in externals. And in spirit the play is far from neo-classical, as will be seen when it is compared with Rymer's play. Yet in all this, *Edgar and Alfreda* is typical of its time.

When we turn to Rymer's *Edgar* [12] we come to a play distinctly not typical, but interesting as an illustration of what

[12] *Edgar* was licensed Sept. 13, 1677. The title page bears the date 1678. It was advertised in the Term Catalogues on November 26, 1677, so that it must have been ready for the public soon after that time. That is, it appeared about the same time as Ravenscroft's play. There is no evidence to show that Rymer's play was ever acted.

the English drama might have become had it ever yielded complete and thorough allegiance to the neo-classical rules. For in this play Rymer, a critic whole-heartedly supporting a most rigid Aristotelian formalism, applies his rules to creative work.

The plot, as in the case of Ravenscroft's, although based on the familiar story, departs from it in details, in order to gain unity of time and place, and intricacy of action. The scene is again placed at Edgar's court, to which Ethelwold has just brought his bride, Alfreda, or Alfrid, as Rymer calls her. In essentials the main plot, developed by original episodes, carries out the chronicle story, save in the *dénouement*, in which, much as in Ravenscroft's play, the queen is substituted for Alfrid in the bower, and Alfrid and Edgar are left free to marry.

Complication is gained by introducing new characters and new and sometimes irrelevant episodes. The love affairs of Edgar's sister and the deposed and disguised Lewis IV of France, and of the princess Gunilda of Denmark and Kenneth, the captive king of Scotland, their mutual jealousies and final happiness, form a sub-plot which, as in the preceding play, is practically unrelated to the main story. In addition to the situations thus furnished Rymer has included a masque, in which Neptune lays his trident at Edgar's feet, and a gorgeous scene in which the eight captive kings row the royal barge.

The modifications and changes which Rymer has introduced are significant of his dramatic standards. For example, Alfrid is made more obedient and devoted than she appears in the chronicles, presumably to the end that the successful outcome of her affairs may be deserved, and poetic justice safeguarded. The writer is mindful of the dictum that tragedy shall deal only with the affairs of illustrious personages, and the new characters are all of gentle birth and manners—no Durzo stains the pages of *Edgar*. The standard of probability, which Rymer so sternly preached, he has not forgotten in his treatment of the sub-plot. His pairs of lovers have already met, and it is not surprising that they finally come to terms during the ten hours of the play; whereas Ravenscroft's lovers meet and woo and agree to marry all within one short day. Finally, in the choice of a subject for a masque, Rymer, following his announced theories, is emphasizing patriotic ideas, in contradistinction to the bombastic mouthings of vaguely oriental potentates in the still popular heroic drama.

Rymer's rigid standards are apparent not only in his treatment of the sub-plot and new material, but also in his management of the play as a whole. The unities of time and place are strictly observed; the place is Edgar's court, and at the beginning of the play it is announced that "the time of the Representation [is] from Twelve at Noon to Ten at Night." On the other hand, unity of action, a principle rather slighted by neo-classical critics in their zeal for the other unities, is likewise slighted in this play. The principle of decorum, translated into the rules of court etiquette, is carefully followed. The illustrious characters, in their relations with each other, have the utmost regard for place and precedent.[13] Due heed is paid to the demands of poetic justice. Ethelwold's sins are visited upon his own head during the very progress of the play, and "nothing left to God Almighty and another World."[14]

Measured by the rules, the play is weakest on the score of probability. In spite of the previously noted indication of Rymer's attention to this standard, he has sometimes neglected it. For example, it seems improbable that within the ten hours of the play's duration news should be received, first that Scotland has rebelled, and secondly that the people have resumed their loyalty. Of course, this might be accounted for on the ground that the first message has been delayed; but it is not thus explained away in the play. Again, Ethelwold's action in bringing his wife to court, when he is highly

---

[13] Professor Lounsbury (in *Shakespeare as a Dramatic Artist*, p. 241) has pointed out that Rymer sins against his own precepts by permitting a woman to kill a man, though it is done decorously behind the scenes. But if Rymer's rule be consulted, it will be found to read that no woman is to "kill a man, except her quality gives her the advantage above him" (*Tragedies of the Last Age*, p. 117); and the woman who kills the man is the queen.

[14] *Tragedies of the Last Age*, p. 26.

interested in keeping her from the king's view, is, as Genest has pointed out [15], highly improbable. To be sure, Ravenscroft is guilty of a similar lapse, but he had not preached the doctrine of probability as Rymer had. In this respect, then, Rymer nods at times—although not always.

In general, however, the play is exceedingly "regular". The difference in spirit between a thoroughly neo-classical play and one possessing merely a few of the external characteristics of regularity will be apparent if Rymer's play be compared with Ravenscroft's. The emphasis in the one is quite unlike the emphasis in the other. In *Edgar* the love element is subordinated as much as possible to the tragic aspect of the story. Not the sentiment of love so much as the accompanying misunderstandings receive attention, in plot and in sub-plot alike. As much as possible "all the soft things, all the amours, the flowers and fleurets", to quote from Rymer's criticism, are banished. Furthermore, every possible opportunity is taken to emphasize the features of Edgar's reign which appeal to the patriotic feelings,[16] instead of leaving the love motif in unrelieved prominence. The patriotic element is entirely lacking in Ravenscroft's play, and the love, which is frankly emphasized, is for the most part either open or veiled sensual passion. One significant detail may be instanced which corroborates this view. In *Edgar* there is no scene in which the king makes his appointment with Alfrid to meet in the bower; in *King Edgar and Alfreda* the appointment is made in one scene and ratified in a second with marked emphasis. Rymer is consciously avoiding "gallantries". Ravenscroft is following the Fletcherian and Restoration tradition, which revels in such "gallantries". Rymer follows the neo-classic idea of restraint and austerity to the point of frigidity; Ravenscroft enjoys excess. The difference between Rymer's play and Ravenscroft's shows the difference between a play almost wholly in harmony with the rules, and one which superficially meets some of their requirements, but

[15] Vol. I, p. 223 ff.

[16] In the "Advertisement" inserted before the play, Rymer states definitely that he has "chiefly sought occasions to extoll the English Monarchy." His choice of title: *Edgar; or, the English Monarch*, was not haphazard.

really is only in part "regular." The comparison illustrates the difference between the so-called "regularity" of the plays of the seventies, and genuine compliance with the demands of Aristotelian formalism.

Aaron Hill's *Elfrid* brings us to 1710. The very title is an indication of a change in emphasis. The full title is *Elfrid: or, the Fair Inconstant.* That is, Elfrid is the central personage. With Rymer, Edgar had been the chief character. With Ravenscroft, Edgar and Alfreda divided attention. With Rymer, patriotic fervor is implied in the sub-title, *The English Monarch.* With Hill the attention is focused upon the love-theme.

In the plot of Hill's play there is a tendency to revert to the original story as found in the old song and in the chronicles. In these the catastrophe occurs at Ethelwold's home and nearby; so in *Elfrid* the scene is not at the royal court but at "Athelwold's House." Edgar's wife, with whom he had been furnished by Ravenscroft and Rymer, disappears. Elfrid is portrayed, not as submissive and loving, but as ambitious, and rebellious to her husband's plans of concealing her beauty from the king. Besides these reversions to the old story, Hill has introduced other changes. Athelwold is furnished with a friend, Ordgar; Elfrid with a sister, Ordelia. The love affairs of Ordgar and Ordelia form the sub-plot. Accompanying the king is Egbert, the villain, who aids the king in attaining his desires in regard to Elfrid because her husband, Athelwold, is a rival in the royal favor, and a rival whom Egbert actively desires to humble and remove.

The plot is simple. Besides the minor theme of the loves of Ordgar and Ordelia, there is the main story of the king's arrival; the attempt to pass Ordelia upon him as Elfrid, because Ordelia is less temptingly beautiful; the treachery of Elfrid in revealing herself to the king; the plotting of Egbert whereby the king sends Athelwold away upon royal business, so that Elfrid may be obtained; Ordgar's discovery of Egbert's complicity, and his murder of the villain; the return of the suspicious Athelwold in time to discover his wife's guilt; his murder of Elfrid; the king's murder of Athelwold, and his immediate repentance.

In this plot it is seen that poetic justice in the neo-classical sense of the term is swift. Egbert, the villain, is killed. The king, misled by Egbert, repents. Elfrid, who is here guilty, is killed. Athelwold, who was guilty of the original deceit, likewise atones for his treachery with his life. And he dies most piously, crying,

"Oh! Ordgar, let my sad example teach thee
Not to make Love thy Plea for Guilt!"

and calling upon his friend with his last breath,

"Farewell! and—if Ordelia shall be thine,
Bid her—remember Elfrid—Elfrid—oh!"

He is bound that, since he has to die, others shall profit from his death and from a study of the causes leading up to it. One rather regrets that his last thought is of Elfrid's sins and not of his own. However, although one may ridicule the manner of accomplishing the end, there can be no doubt but that Hill had the distinct purpose of emphasizing the moral lesson. The purpose is one of which Rymer would have distinctly approved; the emotional excess with which it is accomplished is hardly Rymerian.

In regard to the unities, the play is absolutely impeccable. The scene is in Athelwold's house and in the garden beside it. The time is proudly announced in the Preface to be "no more than the Play requires in its Representation". And the action is "one and entire". The comic is as strictly barred as in *Edgar* itself. Decorum is observed in the treatment of the king. Athelwold draws his sword against the royal person, but Elfrid opportunely saves him from any such breach of decorum as would be involved in thrusting at Majesty, by entering and thus transferring her husband's resentment to herself, so that he kills her instead of his royal master. To be sure, this is in turn a breach of the rule that a man must not draw his sword against a woman; but inasmuch as Athelwold is here acting as an agent of poetic justice, his action is excused by the more potent law. The violation of the rule prohibiting bloodshed on the stage is, however, open and inexcusable. Three murders are committed before the very eyes of the audience. In short, the play is externally "regular" save as it errs, where English plays so often err, in permitting scenes of violence on the stage.

But it is in the treatment of the love theme that Hill differs from both Ravenscroft and Rymer, and departs most widely from the demands of Aristotelian formalism. Love, in Hill's play, is not the external, impossibly exalted love of the heroic drama; it is not the Fletcherian passion exemplified to some degree in Ravenscroft's play; it is not the restrained and subordinated love of *Edgar;* it is a transport of emotion. Love is the very centre of the play. Ravenscroft had relieved the central love theme by lighter treatment of it in the sub-plot. Rymer had subordinated it to patriotism. Hill banishes everything which will overshadow it, and leaves it in unrelieved prominence. In the very opening scene Athelwold enlarges upon his love for Elfrid; when the news of the king's coming is brought, and the guilty husband reveals the deceit of which Elfrid was the victim, love is the excuse:

"Oh! think on all the Arts, that Love can use,
To gain the Object Lov'd!" [17]

Ordelia constantly preaches the power of love, in palliating Athelwold's crime. The king, when he learns of Athelwold's guilt, cries,

"O Love! thy Power is uncontroul'd indeed,
If it can make an honest Man a Villain."[18]

Near the close of the play Athelwold laments,

"I had been honest, had not Love seduc'd me!"[19]

And the king concludes the play with the lines,

"And oh! may this Example serve to prove,
He treads on dang'rous Ground, who walks on Love."

And this love which dominates the play is in some of the characters sensual, in some idealistic, in some marital, but always serious, passionate, and emotional. Hill's course in locating the action not at the royal court but at Athelwold's home is significant. The outward position of the characters does not interest him; their inner feelings are to form the subject of his play. The emphasis is upon the emotional throughout, and one can imagine the audience weeping in sentimental sympathy as Ordgar weeps over his dying friend.

[17] *Elfrid*, 1710 edition, p. 7.
[18] *Elfrid*, p. 23.
[19] Ibid., p. 43.

The play is typical of the change in dramatic fashions since the time of Ravenscroft. The neo-classical rules seemingly triumphed; in externals Hill's play is almost as ''regular'' as Rymer's own. But side by side with the tendency to admit the validity of the rules, there grew up an interest in the sentimental, the emotional, which affected much of English literature, and which so influenced the drama that plays superficially ''regular'' were in essence as much opposed to the neoclassic ideas of restraint and rule as could well be imagined. At the time when *Elfrid* appeared this sentimentalist influence was particularly noticeable in comedy, but it made itself felt in tragedy, too, culminating twenty years later in the domestic tragedy of Lillo. The peculiar significance of *Elfrid* lies in the distinct trend it shows toward this developing domestic tragedy. The characters are not, indeed, middle-class citizens, but their rank is of superficial import; and the background of domestic life, and the plot with its emotional stress and melodramatic excess, smack decidedly of the typical domestic tragedy.

It is all the more interesting, therefore, to see Hill, two decades later, at a time when domestic tragedy was culminating in *George Barnwell*, realign himself with a different school of dramatists. This he did in his *Athelwold* (1731).

Although *Athelwold* deals with the same material as *Elfrid*, it is not a revision of that play, but in reality a new one. The main theme is the same, but the point of view is changed, the scene is different, the characters, save for the three chief ones, are new, the incidents are new, and the whole effect is different.

The changed point of view is significant. Not the domestic aspect of love, but love in regal trappings, is what Hill now strives to portray. The scene is not a secluded residence, but the royal abode at Chester. Curiously enough, the episode of the eight rower-kings, used by Rymer, is here once more employed to aid in the impression of splendor and power that the royal presence should give.

This would seem to indicate a reversion to those neo-classical ideas which Rymer had voiced in his criticism and had followed in his play. Indeed *Athelwold* is fairly representative of the neo-classical plays of its own time. But in it neo-classicism is not so all-pervading as in *Edgar,* and, though more effective than in *Elfrid,* is still modified by traces of sentimentalism. Furthermore, this neo-classicism is to be attributed not so much to the influence of past English criticism as to the great vogue in England of contemporary French drama. *Athelwold* belongs to a rather numerous group of English plays of the time formed after French models.

This French influence seems especially clear in the case of Hill, who was himself a translator or adapter of some of Voltaire's plays. Thus, after having early flirted with the developing domestic tragedy in his *Elfrid,* Hill turned to French models and wrote *Athelwold* at the very time when domestic tragedy was to attain its most noteworthy development.

Hill's preface contains hints of his attitude. He refers slightingly to his early play as "an unprun'd Wilderness of Fancy," lacking judgment. He mentions respectfully the rules; but evidently they are not all-sufficient. Under their sway, "mysterious Dullness, and the dry Pride of Commentators" have injured the drama. This is not quite equivalent to Rymer's sublime faith in his rules. Knowing Hill's experience with French plays, one suspects that he regards example as rather more weighty than precept.

Of course, many of the rules are followed, just as they are in the French models. The characters are all royal or illustrious. Due regard is paid to decorum, that is, to court etiquette. Athelwold will not for a moment draw his sword against his royal master. The unities of time and place are observed, though not so much stressed as in the earlier play. And, especially significant, there is no bloodshed on the stage. French example here accomplishes what English precept has failed to effect.

But Hill, though following neo-classical models, does not entirely escape from his earlier habit of sentimentality. Undue and unmotivated emotionalism manifests itself at times. Athelwold wavers between mistresses in an impossible but sentimental manner. Ethelinda, whom Athelwold has deceived and deserted, makes repeated and mawkish advances toward reconciliation, in a way to rejoice all lovers of tears.

Edgar, originally a monarch of force and decision, betrays a quick sensitiveness and a delicacy that hint of the eighteenth century "man of feeling".

In a word, the play, while in externals it conforms to French neo-classical models, and while it is a departure from the tendency toward the domestic tragedy shown in *Elfrid,* falls short of the Rymerian standard of genuine "regularity".

As an example of Hill's growth in the management of dramatic material, *Athelwold* is enlightening. Hill evidently desired greater complexity than he had given *Elfrid;* but he had sufficiently mastered technique not to seek this complexity through adding a distinct group of unrelated characters and incidents, as his forerunners had done, but rather through introducing two or three new characters and then binding closely their fortunes with those of the main characters. The main story is of course the usual one of Athelwold's deception of Edgar and marriage of Elfrid. But there are added to these characters Leolyn, who is a deposed prince of Wales, Oswald, a minister of state, and Ethelinda, Oswald's niece. And their fortunes are bound up with those of the chief characters. Under promise of marriage Ethelinda has yielded to the solicitations of Athelwold, and her despair on learning of his marriage to Elfrid materially affects the outcome of the play. Leolyn loves Ethelinda, and his hot resentment against Athelwold involves him in the main action. And Oswald, already jealous of Athelwold, is brought into the main stream of events by the measures he naturally takes upon learning of his niece's wrongs. In managing the additional complication and in binding the various episodes firmly to the main story Hill shows distinct ability. The example of the French drama may be responsible for his increased deftness of workmanship; although it cannot be said that this French deftness was widely copied in England.

However, although in plot coherence *Athelwold* cannot be considered thoroughly typical, it does offer in its pale reflection of neo-classicism and in its traces of sentimentality an example of the group of English plays of its era which owe their inspiration and much of their form to the contemporary drama of the French neo-classicists.

A number of mid-eighteenth century plays hark back not to French but to Greek models. Of these Mason's *Elfrida* is a somewhat extreme representative. Not originally written for the stage,[20] it follows some of the conventions of the Greek drama to a degree rather beyond that possible to other more practical playwrights whose work belongs in this group. Yet it will serve to illustrate the tendencies of its companion plays, which themselves were less thoroughly adapted to stage presentation than even the poorer plays of England's great dramatic period.

Forming a preface are five "Letters" dated "Pembroke Hall, 1751", which analyze and defend the distinguishing features of the play. They throw light upon Mason's standards and aims. He announces that he will follow Greek models. But he is not seeking "to give an exact copy of the ancient drama". He will only "pursue the ancient method so far as it is probable a Greek Poet, were he alive, would now do"— which leaves considerable room for variation from classical models. The unities are prescribed by "good sense" as well as by antiquity, hence they are observed. But to meet the demand of the times, ancient precepts are ignored in the choice of a theme, and "a story was chosen, in which the tender, rather than the noble passions were predominant, and in which even love had the principal share". Again a certain deviation is noted: the characters "as nearly approach private ones, as tragic dignity would permit". The emotions are to be aroused "rather from the impulse of common humanity, than the distresses of royalty and the fate of kingdoms". That is, Mason is consciously deviating from his chosen models and he defends his deviations on the plea that modern conditions demand them. It is to be noted that the changes are in the direction of the practices of domestic tragedy, which was still influential in English drama. The third and fourth letters defend the introduction of the chorus in the usual way: it is conducive to the

[20] It first appeared in print in 1752. It was altered for the stage by Colman in 1772, and by Mason himself in 1779. The original version is the one used here. The others offer no essential variations. In them some flowery passages are missing, and the play is divided into five acts. However, the songs of the chorus afford sufficient indication of division in the 1752 version.

preservation of the unities and affords opportunity for conveying moral reflections. The other letters discuss various neo-classical doctrines of less significance. To sum up: the important features of the introductory letters are, on the one hand the announcement that Greek models are to be followed, and in particular that the Greek idea of the chorus is to be introduced; and on the other hand the intimation that the author is to depart from classical precedent by using romantic love as a main theme, and by portraying the private life rather than the public activities of his characters. From all this one is led to expect that Mason's play will conform neither to Greek practice nor to rigid neo-classical precept. So far as Greek models are to have any influence at all, they will affect form rather than spirit.

The play fulfills these expectations. The chorus is ever present, and plays its part, somewhat incongruously, it must be noted, in so English a story. But through it Mason gains what he desired to gain: "poetic" ornamentation, and a clear presentation of the moral to be drawn from the various events of the plot.

Furthermore, the play is rigidly simple. The characters are few in number. The old story is followed more closely than in any of the preceding plays, and there is absolutely no sub-plot. Even the earliest play of the group dealing with the Edgar story had sought some relief from the simplicity of the main plot, and the rest of the plays had gained complexity through the introduction of new characters and new interests, but Mason discards all such measures, and presents the main events without any accessories, comic or serious. The story as found in the old song is followed save in two not very important respects: Elfrida's father is the means of uncovering Athelwold's guilt to the king, Elfrida being an unwilling instrument; and at the very end, Elfrida gives no hope that she will eventually marry the king. The changes both result in making Elfrida a more sympathetic character—a result which it was desirable to attain, since around her the tragedy was built. Simplicity, and the employment of the chorus; these characteristics, and the accompanying introduction of somewhat conventional "odes", show what Mason

meant by following Greek models. They distinguish the play
from its predecessors.

In addition, it possesses certain neo-classical characteristics
already familiar. The comic is barred. No murder is committed on the stage. The unities are strictly observed. Decorum in the sense of etiquette is never forgotten. Poetic
justice is wrought, and is driven home by the chorus. In one
of the choral odes it is proclaimed that heavenly defense will be
lacking ''if guilt, if fraud, has stained your mind''.[21] Then
Athelwold, the perpetrator of the fraud, is killed, and ''Semi-
chorus'' sings,[22]

> ''As Truth directs
> So only shall we act. This day has shewn
> What dire effects await its violation.''

And Elfrida's father, Orgar, also in accordance with the demands of poetic justice, is successful as long as he seeks to
frustrate Athelwold's villainy, but frustrated in turn when
he would give play to his own ambition and make his daughter
a queen against the demands of propriety.

These features are neo-classic. On the other hand, there are
present, as the introduction has led us to expect, elements of
still a different nature. The characters in the main are shown,
not in their royal or noble capacity, but as human beings. The
emotions stressed are intimate and personal. As in Hill's first
play, the fact that the scene is not at the royal court but at
Athelwold's home is significant of the different emphasis.
Patriotism is incidental. The emphasis is upon the private and
the personal. The fact that love designedly forms the main
theme of the play is a second characteristic which may be regarded as a concession to the dramatic tastes of the time. But
the emotionalism of love is not so exaggerated as it was in
Hill's first play. There is not so much soft sentiment. The
ideals of domestic tragedy, while still powerful enough to influence this professed follower of Greek models, have somewhat
lost their first force.

Mason's play, then, seems influenced in form by its Greek
models; it possesses many of the conventional neo-classical

[21] 1752 ed., p. 50.

[22] Ibid., p. 76.

characteristics; and it also shows distinct traces of the impress of domestic tragedy.   And in all this it is not untypical of its group.

In the series of plays we have now considered neo-classicism has played an important part.   Yet, although there has been much that is neo-classical in form, there has been little really classical in essence.   The triumph of neo-classicism has been barren, and the way is clear for the operation of new forces. From 1590 to 1750 there has been a growth in technique, a growth in the sense of form, an increase in "regularity"; but a loss in spontaneity, and a loss in the power to win an audience.   *A Knacke to Know a Knave* must have appealed to its audience; *Elfrida* left its beholders cold.

GEORGE B. DUTTON.

Williams College.

SPENSER'S FOWRE HYMNES

In the green period of his youth, a student at Cambridge or fresh from its halls, wrapt in the sweet spell of Ficino, of Benivieni, of Castiglione, Spenser composed two hymns in honour of love and beauty. Many years later, in sobered middle life, he wrote two other hymns, of heavenly love and beauty, and, with abundant apology for the "lewdness" of the earlier hymns, published the four.

These four hymns have recently been interpreted by a brilliant American scholar[1] as the culminating expression of that doctrine of romantic love which so fascinated the neo-Platonic mystics, the first two hymns describing the earlier stages in the progress of the ideal lover toward the attainment of perfect love and beauty, and the last two hymns completing the interpretation.

It is the purpose of this essay to put forth the view that, while the earlier hymns are in complete accord with this neo-Platonic theory of love, the later hymns are based upon Calvinistic doctrines that are squarely opposed to it and that admit of no compromise.

According to Castiglione, who gives the clearest and most direct explanation of the neo-Platonic doctrine, reducing to a clear prose statement a theory of love that appears elusive and half-veiled in the poetry, there are six stages in the history of the ideal lover, marking his progress from the moment when, a woe-begone mortal, he feels the promptings of love at the sight of a beautiful face to the time when, kindled by the most sacred fire of true divine love, without veil or cloud, the soul views the wide sea of pure divine beauty, and receives it unto herself.

First of all, the lover beholds a beautiful woman and loves her. Then, to alleviate the distress of separation he impresses her fair image upon his mind. Straightway, however, his imagination idealizes the face and she appears to his mind fairer than she really is. In the second stage it is this idealized face that the lover loves. But, once bent on the

---

[1] Professor J. B. Fletcher, A Study in Renaissance Mysticism: Spenser's 'Fowre Hymnes,' P. M. L. A. (19.) 452.

26: 452-73

quest of beauty, the true lover knows no stay. So anon, stimulated by this idealized image of his lady, he comes to form an image of a face which is, as it were, the sum of all loveliness, a combination of selected charms. In the language of Castiglione: "Besides these blessings (of beholding the idealized face) the lover will find another much greater still, if he will employ this love as a step to mount to one much higher; which he will succeed in doing if he continually considers within himself how narrow a restraint it is to be always occupied in contemplating the beauty of one body only; and therefore, in order to escape such close bonds as these, in his thought he will little by little add so many ornaments, that by heaping all beauties together he will form a universal concept, and will reduce the multitude of these beauties to the unity of that single beauty which is spread over human nature at large. In this way he will no longer contemplate the particular beauty of one woman, but the universal beauty which adorns all bodies".[2]

When the lover becomes fully aware that this concept of universal beauty is primarily the product of his own mind, he realizes that beauty must be an inherent part of the soul, and, the passion for beauty growing apace with each fresh activity of the spirit therein, he now joyously contemplates beauty as he finds it within himself, quite unembarrassed by any remembrance of the senses. So long as he had before him the image of a woman, even though it embodied the universal beauty of womanhood, he could not discern beauty with complete clearness, because the phantom bearing some resemblance to the substance, the shadow of the senses rested thereon. But now the veil of sense is entirely dissipated in the rays of the pure sun of beauty. Again in the words of Castiglione: "Then the soul . . . . . devoted to the contemplation of her own substance, as if awakened from deepest sleep, opens those eyes which all possess but few use, and sees in herself a ray of that light which is the true image of the angelic beauty communicated to her."[3] This contemplation of beauty within the soul is, then, the fourth rung of the ladder which leads from

[2]Fourth book of the Courtier, 67, tr. by L. E. Opdycke.

[3] Ibid., p. 304.

love of physical beauty ''to the lofty mansion where dwells the heavenly, lovely and true beauty which lies in the inmost secret recesses of God.''

Now the same impulse which hitherto inclined the lover to universalize the beauty of woman, impells him to universalize that abstract beauty which he discovers within himself, and he feels out after and discovers that encircling, all-inclusive beauty of which he had before recognized but partial and subordinate manifestations. No longer does the soul contemplate beauty in her own particular intellect, but she looks forth, enraptured and ravished by its splendor, upon the vast sea of universal beauty.

The beauty of a particular woman, the idealized beauty of the same, the universal beauty of woman, beauty an inherent part of the human spirit, beauty all-encircling, identical with divine love, wisdom, goodness. Such is the progression.

Last stage of all, the soul, burning with the sacred fire of true love and yearning to unite herself with so great beauty, actually becomes identified therewith, incorporate in the life of God.

Such a doctrine, presupposing an inborn excellence in humanity, accepting the senses and even exalting them as aids to the spirit and recognizing a natural progression in the attainment of the divine life, such a doctrine is strictly Catholic. It could only have been formulated in a society permeated with Catholic thought and feeling.

This attitude towards the natural man marks the fundamental difference between the Catholic discipline and the Calvinistic. While the Calvinist regards the natural and the spiritual as irreconcilably opposed, and permits the one to exist only at the expense of the other, the Catholic accepts both the natural and the spiritual as gifts of God, though because it is temporary and its pleasure of a lower order, he recognizes that the one gift is less precious than the other. The Catholic appreciates that the senses may, and often do, suffer corruption, but while aware that the senses are thus of the earth, earthy, he also appreciates that they assist one heavenward, inasmuch as they offer a language wherewith God can make his thoughts partially known to man, and are an indispensable medium in the earlier stages of man's spiritual development. Hence the physical element is present in every appeal that the Church makes to man. Harmonious colours, sweet sound and fragrant odours suggest to the imagination, through the senses, the inscrutable glories of the Unseen. The holy eucharist itself, the very heart of Catholicism, is a mystical blending of the natural and the supernatural, wherein God takes advantage of physical means to impart his saving health to a needy humanity. The Catholic must perforce regard the senses with favour, since they thus establish a channel of intercourse between God and man.

While the Catholic thus recognizes no sharp line of cleavage between the senses and the spirit, and passes easily from the realm of the one to the realm of the other, he believes that the body, with the shadow of earth resting upon it, must gradually be consumed by the encroaching fire of the spirit. Therefore the normal development of a life is the gradual metamorphosis of the natural into the spiritual, the spirit of God suffusing itself through the natural, purifying it from all earthly dross, and transforming it into the divine likeness.

To the Catholic the human spirit is not a sorry weed, but a sun-inclined flower, and to the neo-Platonic Catholics the sight of a beautiful woman was the natural foundation for a religious transformation. How far removed from Calvinism! Calvinism, that held the natural man to be altogether vile and sinful; Calvinism, armed with its scourge, that would drive out the senses and cleanse the house, that God might enter in.

A man, and of all men a poet, is hard put to it when he must choose between the things that he loves; when he must give up the one that he lose not the other. A dream of a fair lady, a walk with her through sun-suffused meadows and woodlands of kindly shade, the sight of a city whose loveliness invites the soul and draws it on so sweetly that it forgets that the fair lady has faded from his side, a welcome entry within the city gates. This was the dream that Calvinism asked the poet Spenser to renounce. To be sure it promised entry to the same fair city, but by how different a road! A road that led by a sorrow-crowned hill and through the valley of remorse. Which would the poet choose? The four hymns give the answer.

In the "Hymne in Honour of Love", the first of the four, the attraction of beauty for the lover and the effect of the passion of love upon him are explained. While the lower animals multiply through lust, man is prompted by divine inspiration, and he therefore seeks beauty, which is heavenly in origin:

> But man that breathes a more immortal mynd,
> Not for lusts sake, but for eternitie,
> Seeks to enlarge his lasting progenie:
> For, having yet in his deducted spright
> Some sparks remaining of the heavenly fyre,
> He is enlumined with that goodly light,
> Unto like goodly semblant to aspyre;
> Therefore in choice of love he doth desyre
> That seemes on earth most heavenly to embrace,
> That same is Beautie, borne of heavenly race.

> For sure of all that in this mortall frame
> Contained is, nought more divine doth seem,
> Or that resembleth more the immortall flame
> Of heavenly light, than Beauties glorious beame.

The attractive power of beauty being so great, Love, the imperious boy, shoots his arrow from the lady's eyes and causes great suffering to the lover, but only to test the lover's loyalty and worth. Lust cannot stand this test, but true love can. For the sincere lover,

> Such is the powre of that sweet passion,
> That it all sordid baseness doth expell,
> And the refyned mynd doth newly fashion
> Unto a fairer forme, which now doth dwell
> In his high thought, that would it selfe excell,
> Which he beholding still with constant sight,
> Admires the mirrour of so heavenly light,

> Whose image printing in his deepest wit,
> He thereon feeds his hungrie fantasy.

We are thus found to be in the familiar atmosphere of the neo-Platonic doctrine of love, though only the first two stages of the progression are given: the attraction of a fair face for the lover, and his idealization of its beauty.

In the "Hymne in Honour of Beautie", in addition to these first two, the third and fourth stages are presented. After explaining that love is ordained in heaven, and that the sincere

lover consequently does not love the first pretty woman that
he sees, the lover's advancement in the appreciation of beauty
is thus explained:

> But they, which love indeede, looke otherwise,
> With pure regard and spotlesse true intent,
> Drawing out of the object of their eyes
> A more refyned forme, which they present
> Unto their mind, voide of all blemishment;
> Which it reducing to her first perfection,
> Beholdeth free from fleshes frayle infection.
>
> And then conforming it unto the light,
> Which in it selfe it hath remaining still,
> Of that first Sunne, yet sparkling in his sight,
> Thereof he fashions in his higher skill
> An heavenly beautie to his fancies will;
> And, it embracing in his mind entyre,
> The mirrour of his owne thought doth admyre.

As in the preceding hymn, there is first the beautiful face
and then the idealization of it. But not content to stop here,
the mind of the lover now discovers the universal type, the
pure idea, of which the beauty of any particular woman is but
a porch lamp, and then, quickened to a partial remembrance of
that divine beauty which it had erstwhile known in heaven,
the eager mind turns its eyes inward and admires the vision of
heavenly beauty thus at length discovered within itself. With
this stage, the second hymn concludes.

So much is Spenser an exponent of the neo-Plantonic doctrines in this hymn that he does not hesitate to say that beauty
in woman is brought from heaven by the soul, and that, being
an immortal thing, it is absolutely incapable of corruption.
However much the flesh may be defiled, beauty is ever intact
and resides beyond the reach of taint.

Had Spenser remained satisfied with his neo-Platonism,
when he returned to the theme of the hymns in later life he
would simply have completed the exposition so well begun
and have described the conduct of the soul as it gained a
larger and larger understanding of the beauty which is God,
and, crowning stage of all, its rhapsodic union with the divine
life. As a matter of fact, he turns his back upon all that he
had so feelingly expounded in the first two hymns, repeatedly
disclaims any faith in earthly love as an aid to soul develop-

ment and expounds a new sequence of stages, based upon Calvinistic dogma, for the heaven-bent progress of the soul.

In the "Hymne of Heavenly Love" is shown the surpassing
love of Christ, the great Lord of Love, in his merciful redemption of mankind, and the reciprocal beatific growth in
love of the man who gives himself wholly to the love of Christ
is portrayed. One must fully and freely give himself to Christ,
love him with all his heart and soul and mind, completely renounce all other loves. If one does so, a consuming passion for
Christ will take possession of the soul, entirely absorbing one's
life, leaving room for delight in no earthly thing. One will
never wish to turn his eyes from a sight so sweet and amiable.
If one thus experiences this passion for Christ, the vision of
the man-Christ will be replaced by the vision of the God-Christ,
the "Idee" of Christ:

> Then shall thy ravisht soule inspired bee
> With heavenly thought farre above humane skil,
> And thy bright radiant eyes shall plainly see
> The Idee of his pure glorie present still
> Before thy face, that all thy spirit shall fill
> With sweete enragement of celestial love,
> Kindled through sight of those faire things above.

Just as in the neo-Platonic system the lover, after idealizing
the beauty of the one he loves, comes to perceive the perfect
type of beauty in woman, as it were the model resident in the
thought of God, or, as Plato would have it, the *Idea* of feminine beauty, so if the love of Christ, who became a man and
died for mankind, takes possession of the life, one will come to
see his full perfection, will replace the picture of Christ moving among men and dying on the cross, with the vision of
Christ as one with God; will see Christ as he essentially is,
see him as God sees him. Then will the soul be filled with the
divine love and will experience that felicity which is vouchsafed to those who enter into this mystic relation with God.

The approach to God through Christ, as explained in this
hymn, not only does not grow out of the experience of earthly
love, but is absolutely antagonistic to it. Calvinistic theology
is not imposed upon a superstructure of neo-Platonism; one
does not advance from love of woman and adoration of her
beauty to the love of Christ and adoration of God. The natural

man is totally corrupt until he experiences the redemptive love of Christ; the human heart is wholly of flint, until touched and softened by remorse; the human mind totally abased, "moyled in durty pleasures", until uplifted by Christ's "soveraine mercie." In the language of Calvin, until renewed by the grace of Christ "man . . . . . is but rottenness and a worm, abominable and vain, drinking in 'iniquity like water'." [4] There is no room in such a theology for the partial salvation of man through earthly love. Salvation is wholly of Christ, and an unsaved man is lost in sin, miserable, utterly debased. Scant room here for the engaging fancy that Christ takes over the half blown flower that some maiden has been tending. Love of woman is merely one of those loves

with which the world doth blind
Weake fancies, and stirre up affections base.

It is a "mad fit", which only fools call love, and when the heat expires nothing but ashes remains. For Spenser, to love a woman is no longer to find God. Distrust of so-called beauty and stern asceticism replace the pleasing fancy of the Italian mystic (Ficino).

The "Hymne of Heavenly Love" thus sets forth how the soul may advance through love to mystic union with God as Christ, the redeemer of the world. The "Hymne of Heavenly Beautie" explains how the soul may advance through contemplation of God's handiwork to mystic union with Sapientia; Sapientia, which may signify the Holy Spirit, as ingeniously and brilliantly maintained by Professor Fletcher, or which may stand for Christ as the Logos, the mind of God, as distinguished from the Christ of the third hymn, the redemptive love of God. Two avenues of approach to God are thus open; one, through the loving mercy of Christ, the other, through mystic contemplation.

In the "Hymne of Heavenly Beautie" the poet first suggests that one who would enter into the mysteries of intellectual beauty begin with observing the admirable beauty of the earth, then the beauty of the air, and then the beauty of the sky, all sown with glistering stars and ruled by the sun and moon, as it were the king and queen of day and night. Looking upon these let one appreciate that

[4] Institutes, 3. 12. 5.

> farre above these heavens which here we see,
> Be others farre exceeding these in light,
> Not bounded, not corrupt, as these same bee,
> But infinite in largenes and in hight,
> Unmoving, uncorrupt, and spotlesse bright,
> That need no Sunne t' illuminate their spheres,
> But their own native light farre passing theirs.

But because the eye cannot visualize splendor so far surpassing anything the earthly eye can behold, one must try to form some conception of the majestic beauty of God through reflecting upon the goodness of God as revealed in his handiwork:

> The meanes, therefore, which unto us is lent
> Him to behold, is on his workes to looke,
> Which he hath made in beauty excellent,
> And in the same, as in a brasen booke,
> To reade enregistered in every nooke
> His goodnesse, which his beautie doth declare;
> For all thats good is beautifull and faire.

Thus mounting upon wings of contemplation, humbled with fear and reverence, let the soul approach the awful splendor of the majesty of God, where he sits upon the throne of truth, built upon eternity, from which proceed pure and bright beams, which encompass his presence with glorious light, while

> in his bosom Sapience doth sit,
> The soveraine dearling of the Deity,
> Clad like a Queene in royall robes.

Whosoever is allowed to look thereon, bereft of sense, and transported with delight, experiences the ecstatic bliss of heaven.

This is that supreme experience which the neo-Platonic mystics felt to be the ultimate reward of the true lover. But though Spenser has acknowledged it to be the fruits of the contemplation of God's handiwork, the poet is careful not to make any mention of beauty in woman as a part of that handiwork. When he enumerates those works they are all the wonders of external nature, on the one hand, and God's truth, love, wisdom, bliss, grace, judgment, mercy and might, on the other. Indeed the beauty of woman is actually a painful and mortifying memory as mundane and misleading as love of ostentation or riches:

ᴴ ᴰ

    And that faire lampe, which useth to inflame
    The hearts of men with self-consuming fyre
    Thenceforth seems fowle, and full of sinfull blame:
    And all that pomp to which proud minds aspyre
    By name of honor, and so much desyre,
    Seemes to them baseness, and all riches drosse,
    And all mirth sadnesse, and all lucre losse.

It is a false beauty that misleads "with flattering bait" and leads one to "pursue vain deceitful shadows."

How great the contrast between this attitude toward woman's beauty and that of Castiglione, who, in the moment of ecstasy, could still hark back to beauty in woman as that which inspired the soul to seek for the beauty which is God; Castiglione, who, in that moment, saw things celestial and terrestrial held by one common bond, and in beauty "the sweetest bond of the universe": "Thou art father of true pleasure, of grace, of peace, of gentleness and goodwill, enemy to rustic savagery and sloth—in short, the beginning and the end of every good. And since thou delightest to inhabit the flower of beautiful bodies and beautiful souls, and thence sometimes to display thyself a little to the eyes and minds of those who are worthy to behold thee, methinks that now thy abode is here amongst us".[5]

In thus recognizing the contemplation of nature as an avenue of approach to the Divine, Spenser is in complete accord with the doctrines of Calvin. The metalic sharpness and hardness of Calvin's legalistic thinking is in marked contrast to the hymns, suffused with mysticism as they are, but the doctrinal basis is the same. It would almost seem that Spenser had turned fresh from the "Institutes" when he penned the stanzas which speak of God's universal revelation of himself in nature:

    These unto all he daily doth display,
    And shew himselfe in the image of his grace,
    As in a looking-glasse, through which he may
    Be seene of all his creatures vile and base,
    That are unable else to see his face,
    His glorious face! which glistereth else so bright,
    That the Angels selves cannot endure the sight.

[5] Ibid., p. 306.

The meanes, therefore, which unto us is lent
Him to behold, is on his workes to looke,
Which he hath made in beauty excellent,
And in the same as in a brasen booke,
To read enregistered in every nooke
His goodnesse, which his beautie doth declare,
For all that's good is beautifull and faire.

Compare with these stanzas the following sentences from Calvin's chapter on the revelation of God in the creation and continued government of the world: "His essence, indeed, is incomprehensible, utterly transcending all human thought; but on each of his workes his glory is engraved in characters so bright, so distinct, and so illustrious, that none, however dull and illiterate, can plead ignorance as their excuse".[6]

"It is impossible to contemplate the vast and beautiful fabric as it extends around, without being overwhelmed by the immense weight of glory. Hence the author of the Epistle to the Hebrews elegantly describes the visible worlds as images of the invisible (Heb. XI. 3), the elegant structure of the world serving us as a kind of mirror, in which we may behold God, though otherwise invisible".[7] "Hence it is obvious, that in seeking God, the most direct path and the fittest method is, not to attempt with presumptive curiosity to pry into his essence, which is rather to be adored than minutely discussed, but to contemplate him in his works, by which he draws near, becomes familiar, and in a manner communicates himself to us . . . . . As Augustine expresses it, (in Psalm CXI. v), since we are unable to comprehend Him, and are, as it were, overpowered by his greatness, our proper course is to contemplate his works, and so refresh ourselves with his goodness".[8]

Spenser is also in accord with Calvin in believing that, though God's glory is thus displayed in nature to all humanity, only the elect are able to profit by it. Spenser says that only those who are chosen of God's grace may behold his Beloved, Sapience, and that she will bestow her riches only on those who are worthy to receive them, and again and again in the book from which quotations have already been

[6] Ibid., 5, 1; tr. by Henry Beveridge.
[7] Ibid.
[8] Ibid., 9.

made Calvin affirms that any opinion which man can form in heavenly mysteries is the parent of error, that no sooner do we obtain some slight knowledge of deity, than we pass by the true God, and set up in his stead the dream and phantom of our own brain: "In vain for us, therefore, does Creation exhibit so many bright lamps lighted up to show forth the glory of its Author. Though they beam upon us from every quarter, they are altogether insufficient of themselves to lead us into the right path. Some sparks, undoubtedly, they do throw out; but these are quenched before they can give forth a brighter effulgence. Wherefore, the apostle, in the very place where he says that the worlds are the images of invisible things, adds that it is by faith we understand that they were framed by the word of God (Heb. XI. 3), thereby intimating that the invisible Godhead is indeed represented by such displays, but we have no eyes to perceive it until they are enlightened through faith by internal revelation from God".[9]

Spenser's distinction between God's revelation of himself in external nature and his revelation in the treatment of mankind, is Calvin's distinction between works of the first class and works of the second class. From the first class of works, those in accordance with the ordinary course of nature, may be learned the omnipotence and eternity of God; from the second class, those above the ordinary course of nature, the goodness, justice and mercy, the providence, power and wisdom of God.[10] Calvin's exposition of these different kinds of revelation is compressed by the poet into the following stanza:

> Cease then, my tongue! and lend unto my mind
> Leave to bethinke how great that beautie is,
> Whose utmost path so beautiful I fynd;
> How much more those essential parts of his,
> His truth, his love, his wisdome, and his blis,
> His grace, his doome, his mercy, and his might,
> By which he lends us of himselfe a sight!

[9]Ibid., 14.
[10]Ibid., 6-8.

The indebtedness of the last two hymns to Platonic and neo-Platonic writings is, to be sure, very great; hardly a stanza that is not reminiscent of Plato, of Ficino, of Benivieni, or of Bruno. But these Platonic and neo-Platonic origins are construed to the satisfaction of Calvinism and disciplined to its creed. For example, it is highly significant that though the passage in which Spenser argues that to enjoy heavenly beauty one must begin by observing the beauties of the lower world, is based upon Plato, Spenser confines himself to the beauties of external nature, while Plato speaks of the beauties of humanity, the fair forms, which lead one to contemplate the fair minds which they contain, the fair minds which lead on to the contemplation of the products of the mind, and so from stage to stage.

This interpretation of the hymns is exactly in accord with the language of the dedication, in which the poet speaks disparagingly of the first two hymns and professes to offer the last two as a corrective: "Having in the greene times of my youth, composed these former two Hymnes in the praise of Love and Beautie, and feeling that the same too much pleased those of like age and disposition, while being too vehemently caried with that kind of affection, do rather sucke out poyson to their strong passion, than honey to their honest delight, I was moved by the one of you two most excellent Ladies, to call in the same. But, being unable so to doe, by reason that many copies thereof were formerly scattered abroad, I resolved at least to amend, and, by way of retraction, to reforme them, making, instead of these two Hymnes of earthly or naturall love and beautie, two other of heavenly and celestiall." If Spenser still honestly looked upon beauty in woman as a natural introduction to the most exalted experience of the soul, this dedication is certainly a fine bit of insincerity.

Nor does the theory that the two later hymns represent the more advanced stages in the neo-Platonic progression find support in the "Faerie Queene". The "Faerie Queene" presents the ideals of chivalry as modified to conform to a court society, and its indebtedness to Castiglione is abundantly evident, but if, on the one hand, it avoids that deliberate self-

seeking which at times mars the consistency of "The Courtier" and impairs it as a Christian document, it avoids, on the
other, the transcendentalism of Bembo. The knights of the
"Faerie Queene" do not gain knowledge of the mysteries
of divine beauty and love at the expense of the gentle ladies
who first inducted them into the noble passion. In the economy of the "Faerie Queene" neither sex is sacrificed for
the spiritual advancement of the other; man must realize
himself through the inspiration of woman's love, and woman
herself through the inspiration of man's. The ideal society
is that in which men who are "wise, warlike, personable,
courteous and kind" [11] love women who are courteous, kind,
gracious and modest, and whose beauty is enhanced by the
flower of chastity, transplanted from heavenly gardens; [12]
chastity, which crowns the heads of ladies with coronals
such as the angels wear [13] and which causes their praise to
be hymned by saints in heaven. [14] Moreover, though love
leads the base to sloth as well as to sensuality, the noble it
prompts to high and worthy activity, suffering no idleness,

> For love does alwaies bring forth bounteous deeds
> And in each gentle heart desire of honor breeds. [15]

This mutual dependence of men and women is the basis
of the allegory of love in the "Faerie Queene". Marinell,
gently nurtured in purity and shielded from the society of
woman, is not a normal man until his indifference is supplanted by love of Florimell; Florimell, preëminent in chastity, virtue and beauty, [16] is yet a forlorn figure, assailed as
she is by the rough love of the loutish youth, by the violent
rapine love of the fisher, by the subtle, insinuating love of
Porteus, and too timid and fearful to tell friend from foe, [17]
—a pathetic figure until she finds safe harbor in the protect-

[11] III. 4. 5.

[12] III. 5. 51-55.

[13] III. 5. 53.

[14] III. 8. 42.

[15] II. 1. 49.

[16] III. 5.

[17] III. 4.

ing love of the self-reliant Marinell. And, to pass by the minor characters, Britomart and Artegall, around whom the love allegory is built and to whom the other characters serve as foils, find in each other that affection which satisfies the heart and that stability and sense of values that hold one to high and assured achievement. Spenser is careful to make it clear that for both Artegall and Britomart the love of the other was the one thing needful for full self-realization. Britomart is an ideal expression of the renaissance woman, feminine in affection, masculine in judgment and in strength of will. She possesses the delicacy of Florimell, without her timidity; the strength of Radigund, without her boldness and bourgeois vulgarity; the chastity and elevation of Belphoebe, without her austerity and aloofness; the charm of Amoret, without the ardency, all too apparent, that was ever arousing passion in men. Britomart is a character of beautiful balance. Yet it is the love of Artegall that gives focus to her character. Similarly, Artegall, the acknowledged superior of other knights, has not complete mastery of himself until Britomart becomes enthroned in his life; before this he is unable to withstand the fascination and the intrigues of Radigund; after it, he cannot be tempted by the superior charms of Duessa; before this he is inconstant in the pursuit of his quest, the relief of Irenee; after it, he

> Went on his way; ne ever howre did cease
> Till he redeemed had that Lady thrall.

"The Faerie Queene", in short, shows the equal worth of men and women and their mutual dependence. Love inspires men to brave deeds and large endeavor, and women to acts of gentleness and deeds of mercy. Through love they find themselves socially. The "Faerie Queene" lays emphasis upon the life of action, and the life of contemplation is not made an end in itself, but rather contemplation serves to make the life dynamic.

Though the "Faerie Queene", then, is a noble presentation of courtly ideals, it does not support the neo-Platonic theory that love leads the lover away from and beyond the beloved.

Is it not reasonable to conclude that Spenser had come to feel that, beautiful as the theory of the neo-Platonists might be, it was but a dream, not to be seriously entertained by the Christian, and that the "Hymne of Heavenly Love" and the "Hymne of Heavenly Beautie" record this conviction.

FREDERICK MORGAN PADELFORD,

University of Washington.

QUEEN ANNE AND QUEEN ALCESTIS.

Chaucer's Prologue to the *Legend of Good Women* has long had its riddles requiring solution. The question most discussed recently has been that of the allegorical interpretation of Chaucer's fervid worship of the daisy and of his devotion to the mythical heroine, Queen Alcestis. In 1890 Ten Brink advanced the theory that both the daisy and Alcestis were intended to represent Queen Anne. This view was generally accepted until Professor Lowes challenged it in 1904.[1] Since that time the question of the identification of Queen Anne with Alcestis and the daisy has been much discussed and argued pro and con.[2] When we read version B[3] for internal testimony, we are indeed somewhat bewildered with the array of evidence that can be gathered on both sides of the case. It is almost paradoxical, as the following summary of some of the arguments will show. We shall first review the arguments for identification, and then those against it. Our final purpose is to offer a solution which attempts to reconcile to each other the conflicting groups of arguments.[4]

First of all on the side of identification, we have conclusive proof that Queen Anne was in Chaucer's mind when he wrote the Prologue. Lines 496-7 tell us that the *Legend of Good Women* was to be presented to her in her palace at Shene. Secondly there is described in the Prologue a queen, much like Queen Anne, although she bears the name of the

[1] *Publications of the Modern Lang. Ass. of America*, XIX, 593 ff.

[2] Compare the argument of Professor Tatlock in *The Development and Chronology of Chaucer's Works*, pp. 102 ff; of Professor Kittredge in *Modern Philology*, VI, 435 ff; and of Professor Moore in *Modern Language Review*, VII, 488 ff.

[3] In this article, I approach the question of identification from the standpoint of version B, since the priority of that version over version A, thanks to Professor Lowes and Professor Tatlock, seems to be generally accepted. All references, therefore, will be to version B, unless otherwise stated.

[4] In what follows, I am indebted to Professor Root for certain suggestions, arising from work in a graduate class conducted by him.

mythical heroine Alcestis. She is young, beautiful, merciful, and an exemplary wife. These are all characteristics of the living Queen. In the next place Alcestis in the Prologue is identified with the daisy, just as ladies then living, were identified with that flower in the *marguerite* poems of Chaucer's distinguished French contemporaries, Machault, Froissart, and Deschamps.[1] To be identified with the daisy was the kind of honor which would be particularly pleasing to Queen Anne. She was young and presumably a lover of fashion. Symbolism by flowers was one of the fads of the time, as is attested by the prevalence of the flower and leaf *balades*. An introduction of a *marguerite* poem into the English court by Chaucer, one of the court poets,[2] would attract general attention. In a poem, presented to her, perhaps written at her express command, if we may believe Lydgate,[3] Queen Anne might well expect to receive the chief honor. Everyone, who had intelligent interest in such matters, would be asking who the flower was, for we need not suppose that the fourteenth century Englishman was less likely to make conjectures than we are today.

The view that Queen Anne was meant to be identified with the daisy gains additional confirmation in an examination of lines 84-96, the lines which Mr. Lowes shows to have

---

[1] One of the achievements of Mr. Lowes in the article above cited is to elucidate the prevalence of these poems.

[2] See the article by Mr. Kittredge on "Chaucer and some of his Friends" in *Modern Philology*, I, 1-18; and also Mr. Tatlock's presentation of Chaucer's connection with the court, in *Chaucer Chronology, op. cit.*, pp. 108-9. The mere facts that Chaucer wrote the *Parlement of Foules* to celebrate the betrothal of Richard and Anne, and that the *Legend* is to be presented to the Queen, go a long way toward indicating the relations of Chaucer, as a poet, with the royal family.

[3] Cf. the Prologue to the *Fall of Princes*.

"This poet wrote, at the request of the quene,
A Legende, of perfite holynesse." etc.

For references, in which the value of this allusion has been discussed, see Mr. Tatlock's *Chronology, op. cit.*, p. 111-2. If this be only a conjecture of Lydgate, based on internal evidence from the Prologue, it is none the less interesting as the conjecture of an Englishman almost contemporary with Chaucer.

been borrowed from the *Filostrato* of Boccaccio.[1]　The latter
wrote the passage in honor of a living lady.　But Chaucer
uses it to honor a lady through the medium of the flower.
He refers with almost passionate fervor to the daisy as his
light, the mistress of his wits, the guide who leads him in
this dark world, his lady sovereign, his earthly god.　It
would seem absurd for Chaucer to lavish such extravagant
homage upon the pale figure of a long forgotten mythical
heroine, like Alcestis.　Chaucer, staid and forty-five, would
become a visionary, a chaser after moonbeams.　Moreover we
must not disregard the transition which later leads to the
dream.　Alcestis has not been introduced as yet.　She is
distinctly a figure of the dream.　We should hardly expect
Chaucer to make Alcestis the guiding star of his life here
in the waking day in the field.

After reading this passage, if we go on in the poem, we
find another, which not only tends to confirm the impression
of Queen Anne's identification with the daisy, but also in-
duces the belief that Queen Anne is to be identified with
the lady of the dream as well.　The dream has begun, and
a lady has been led in by the god of Love.　She is not
mentioned here by name.　Chaucer merely alludes to her
as ''a quene'' (213).　The specific name Alcestis is not introduced until much later in the poem.　Chaucer thus describes the effect made on his dazzled eyes.　He says, ''If men
were to seek over the earth, they could not find a creature
one-half so beautiful as she.''　(241-6)　Now Queen Anne
was not only on the earth, but, what is more, she was in
Chaucer's mind, for he dedicates the poem to her.　This
would seem a sorry compliment to Queen Anne, when she
came to read it, if Alcestis and Alcestis alone is meant.

These words are scarcely out of Chaucer's mouth, before
he is moved to express the same sentiment in the form of a
balade.　(249-269)　The burden of his song is, that the
approaching lady is fairer than all other fair and peerless
ladies.　She may disdain them all.　No name has been mentioned.　Yet Chaucer seems not to doubt who the lady is.

[1] See the article of Mr. Lowes above cited, pp. 618-626.

It is "his lady" as we learn from the refrain thrice repeated. And so we are inclined to identify her with the lady praised through the daisy in the working day in the field.

More tributes to the lady follow the *balade*. Among them we find this line:

I prey to God that ever falle hir faire! (277)

This line strikes us queerly.   To judge from the meaning, it is a prayer made for one who is to be subject to future dangers, who is to live the hazardous life of earth.   It is not a natural note to arise spontaneously [1] in the mind of a poet, when speaking solely of Alcestis, whose earthly troubles may now be considered to have passed, seeing that she lives with Cupid in the "Paradys" of the blessed.   (564)   Chaucer certainly cannot profess to be anxious about her welfare.   And so behind this line, we think we see a prayer for the future health and prosperity of the living Queen.

Let us now consider the arguments which militate against identification.   They are short but apparently decisive, especially that contained in the following lines, found when we approach the close of the poem:

And whan this book is maad, yive hit the quene

On my behalfe, at Eltham, or at Shene. (496-7)

These words are spoken by Alcestis.   Now if Alcestis *is* Queen Anne, we realize the absurdity of the situation.   It is as if Alcestis should say "on my behalf give the book to myself", nonsense for which we cannot easily give an explanation.

This presentation ordered by Alcestis is followed up a few lines later with a vivid allusion to the descent of Alcestis into hell.   (513-16)   Again if Queen Anne is Alcestis, it certainly is not a pleasing picture which associates her with so gruesome an event.   Rather than believe Chaucer so tactless, so entirely without discrimination, we would almost entirely discard the identification.

[1] See A 180, where the name Alcestis is specifically mentioned. An idea, which had arisen spontaneously out of the conditions under which B was written, might well remain in A, revised under different conditions. The inferences, to which a single line of this kind might lead, could easily escape Chaucer's notice in a working over of the Prologue.

Then over and above these facts, when we conclude the Prologue, we are left with this inquiry in our minds: How would Chaucer have told the story of Alcestis among the number of the legends, if it were encumbered with the allegorical trappings which connected it with the name of Queen Anne? It would have been embarrassing to attempt to carry on the allegorical interpretation throughout the rather dismal events of the life of Alcestis. But Chaucer, once having identified the two queens, would have found it a delicate matter to disentangle Alcestis from the double identity. So the conclusion is that the identity never existed, for originally he certainly intended to incorporate the tale in the *Legend*.[1]

When we recall all that has been said above, it will be seen that a fairly good case can be made either for or against identification. There is only one path out of the maze, and that is to make the explanation as shifting, as self-adjustable, as the identification itself seems to be. And after all the problems of the Prologue are not the problems of mathematics. If Alcestis=the daisy, and Queen Anne=the daisy, it is not necessary to assume that Queen Anne=Alcestis=the daisy, for ever one, and inseparable.

It will be noted that the arguments, based on internal evidence, *for* identification come almost entirely in the early part of the poem; the arguments against it, in the latter part. We have reached by a deduction from the distribution of the passages on which the arguments above are based, from the scattered allusions to the daisy throughout the poem and from considerations soon to be enlarged upon, the following conclusions. Till the beginning of the dream, Chaucer's worship of the daisy in the field does honor to Queen Anne and Queen Anne alone. Then from the beginning of the dream (210) until the first mention of Alcestis by name is a neutral zone, where Queen Anne, Alcestis and the daisy merge one into the other by an almost indefinable and dreamlike process. We feel the residual in-

[1] The three arguments above discussed are all urged against identification by Mr. Kittredge in his article in *Modern Philology*, VI, 435 ff.

fluence of Queen Anne from the first two hundred and ten lines and the forecasting of the influence of Alcestis to come. In the last one hundred and fifty lines of the Prologue, Alcestis stands practically alone. Queen Anne enters only in so far as the daisy enters and that is only to a very small extent. During the course of the poem, the prominence of Queen Anne and the daisy gradually diminishes to the vanishing point, whereas the prominence of Alcestis correspondingly increases.

A solution for such an interpretation of the Prologue is not to be found by emphasizing the study of it as a type of allegory. It is entirely possible to conceive that Chaucer was not deeply interested in allegory for its own sake but that he was using it rather as a tool for accomplishing two definite purposes which he had in mind, the first to compliment Queen Anne, the second to introduce the *Legend*. For these two purposes Chaucer had on hand two types of allegory; for the first purpose he had the machinery of the *marguerite* poems wherein ladies were complimented through the medium of the daisy, for the second, he had the conventional dream allegory wherein he was enabled to unfold the graceful fiction of the "good Alceste" who enjoins upon him the task of writing his poem. It was his business, after he had decided upon the two themes of the Prologue, to couple them together as smoothly as possible. If he could so unite them that the one would lend aid in heightening the effect of the other, so much the better. If he could make anything out of the fact that both Anne and Alcestis were good and beautiful queens, well and good; he would take whatever advantages accidentally happened to arise. And so well has Chaucer succeeded in blending his two *motifs,* that one is hardly aware that the earlier part of the poem, and the prolonged adoration of the daisy through almost two hundred lines is really irrelevant in the sense that it contributes nothing essential to the introduction of the *Legend of Good Women.* It now becomes our purpose to find more exactly the respective parts which Queen Anne and Queen Alcestis play in the Prologue.

We take a step toward the truth, if we can realize that all which pertains to the daisy relates primarily to Queen Anne. The Prologue is to be read with the thought in mind that Queen Anne *is* the daisy. When Alcestis first appears in the dream, she looks *like* a daisy. (214-25) She wears daisies in her crown. Her hair is covered with a fret of red gold above which the white crown rises. She is clad in a garb of green. Why? Merely to suggest the flower which Chaucer worships and to honor it further. When Alcestis and the god of love first accost Chaucer, he is still kneeling over the real daisy; (308-321) the living Alcestis stands above him. Cupid fiercely rebukes Chaucer, the scoffer at love, for profaning the flower with his presence. Cupid alludes emphatically to the daisy as ''myn owne flour''. From Cupid's point of view, depending on his knowledge of events soon to be disclosed, the allusion may be to Alcestis, but Chaucer and the reader have no reason for differentiating the flower over which he is now kneeling from the one originally introduced. Indeed it is almost as if Chaucer and Cupid had a misunderstanding as to whom the flower really did represent. When Cupid says what business have you near my flower, Chaucer, evidently seeing no reason why he should not be near it, replies with some spirit: '' 'And, why, sir,' quod I, 'and hit lyke yow?' ''

Then we pass on in the poem. Any classical learning that we may happen to have receives somewhat of a shock. The god of Love, incidentally to explaining who the lady really is, casually drops the remark that she, Alcestis, had once been turned into a daisy (512). He does not explain the why nor the wherefore of this transformation, nor does he explain how, once having been turned into a daisy, she was there, a living queen. The only explanation for these surprising mysteries is to be found, it would appear, in an old book that lies in Chaucer's chest. That old book has never been discovered. Nowhere in the whole range of classical or mediaeval literature has evidence ever been found that Alcestis underwent such a transformation.[1] So

[1] See Professor Neilson's *Origins and Sources of the Court of Love,* p. 145.

far as can be discovered, it was Chaucer's imagination which produced it. And why? The invention suggested itself to Chaucer as another bond between the two queens and another sweeping compliment to Queen Anne. But it is only here at the very end of the poem that Alcestis is identified with the daisy in the literal sense that Queen Anne is identified with it.

We may consider farther the lines where Chaucer a moment later recognizes Alcestis:

> Now knowe I hir! And is this good Alceste,
> The dayesye, and myn owne hertes reste? (518-19)

The transitional word between "Alceste" and "myn owne hertes reste" is to be noted. Why was Alcestis Chaucer's own heart's rest? Not particularly because she was Alcestis, but because she was a daisy, and the daisy represents Queen Anne.

We said a little while ago that there was a neutral zone in the middle of the Prologue, where the two Queens are blended. Let us look more carefully at the method of this blending. We recall Chaucer's enthusiastic praise of the approaching queen, before the mention of her name. It has often been argued that Chaucer purposely reserved the mention of the name Alcestis until very late in the Prologue, so that meantime he could leave the impression that he was praising Queen Anne. But it would be a very poor compliment to her majesty, if the lady praised turned out after all not to be she, but some one else. Suppose, however, that Chaucer intends to picture *himself* as at first mistaken in the identity of Alcestis. It would be a distinct compliment to Queen Anne to be mistaken for so glorious a lady as Chaucer describes in Alcestis. In this case all the praise showered on Alcestis, applies equally to her. There is evidence to support this view, that Chaucer pictures in the dream that he was thus mistaken. In presenting this view, we shall not think of the Prologue as a dream allegory essentially. We shall suppose, for example, that Chaucer did not bring in the belated recognition *motif*, blindly and because he thought no dream allegory would be complete

without one. We shall consider that the allegory afforded
him material, in his hands more or less molten, so that he
could shape it for his own purposes.

Let us examine first the *balade* wherein is found the outburst of praise of the approaching queen. It runs, somewhat as follows ''hide your tresses, Absolom. Ester, lay
down your meekness. Isould and Helen, hide your beauty;
for *my lady* comes that all this may bedim''. Chaucer says
''my lady'', as to him, in his enthusiasm for her beauty, it
can be only one person, the lady of his own adoration.
Really, as later becomes apparent, he was mistaken. It
was Alcestis who approached. But he does not realize this
until events begin to develop. Then the recognition gradually dawns on him. In line 432 he for the first time hears
the name Alcestis. She speaks of herself as ''Alceste, why-
lom quene of Trace''. He is puzzled. The first time he has
an opportunity to speak to her thereafter, he takes advantage of the opportunity to explain that he does not know
who she is. After thanking her for her intercession in his
interest with the God of Love, he says:

> And yeve me grace so long for to live,
> That I may knowe *soothly* what ye be,
> That han me holpe and put in this degree.   (459-61)

After Chaucer has finished, Alcestis replies in a speech
which concludes with the injunction for Chaucer to present
the book that he is to write to Queen Anne at Shene. Then
the God of Love, at this allusion begins to smile:

> 'Wostow', quod he, 'wher this be wyf or mayde,
> Or quene, or countesse, or of what degree,
> That hath so litel penance yiven thee.'   (499-501)

Chaucer, now, stoutly insists that he knows nothing about
her. Cupid explains to his satisfaction. Finally Cupid, in
his parting words, calls Chaucer's attention to the fact that
he had neglected to put the name of ''Alceste'' in the
balade. (537-41) Chaucer had indeed forgotten her. In
a list of noble heroines of old, Alcestis should have been
named along with Ester, Isould, Helen, and the rest. Cupid's
rebuke shows clearly that in his mind, at least, the ''my

lady'' of the refrain meant not Alcestis but some unnamed
lady of Chaucer's devotion. In this rebuke of Chaucer by
the God of Love, we see Chaucer, the literary craftsman,
using a device to stress the idea that he, in his dream, had
thought the lady upon her first approach Queen Anne.[1]
It is to the extent just described, we believe, that Chaucer
has blended the two Queens. Whether we accept the explanation as the true one, depends on whether we can think
of the Prologue as a record of human feeling, involving the
pride of the young queen of twenty and Chaucer's ability
to comply gracefully with her wishes, or whether we think
of it as an elaborate example of the dream allegory, wherein
little weight may be attached to what is actually said and
done.

BERNARD L. JEFFERSON.

Princeton University.

[1] It is true that the belated recognition occurs also in version A,
and there Chaucer's failure to know who the lady is, might be considered even more surprising than in B, because in A her name has
been mentioned from the very first. There is never any doubt in A,
therefore, but that the lady is Alcestis. Mr. Moore, in a footnote
to his article in the *Modern Language Review*, VII, p. 489, has urged
this point to prove that the belated recognition of Alcestis in B has no
bearing whatever on Queen Anne. But let us consider for the moment,
with Mr. Tatlock, that version A is a revised form of the Prologue,
wherein all allusions to Queen Anne are removed on account of the
intense grief of Richard II at her death. According to this view
Chaucer goes back and substitutes "Alceste" in the places where
"my lady" previously appeared. Let us suppose, then, that in this
process of revision he finally comes to the lines in B where he has
described himself as learning who she really is. (507-576) He finds
himself confronted with a difficulty. It is the very explanation of
her identity by the god of Love which has enabled Chaucer in B to
introduce the connecting link between Alcestis and the daisy. It is
here that Chaucer has explained that Alcestis herself had been turned
into the daisy. And this link is necessary to make plausible his introduction of the daisy *motif* in the first part of the Prologue. Rather
than invent a new device for connection, he is willing to let an inconsistency stand in the revised form. Here it may be said that Mr.
Tatlock's explanation for the revision of the Prologue accounts most
admirably for the changes made in A.

REVIEWS AND NOTES

GERTRUDE SCHOEPPERLE, TRISTAN AND ISOLT,
a study of the sources of the romance, Frankfurt a/M.
and London, 1913, 2 vols. XV + 590 pp.

Miss Schoepperle's *Tristan* recommends itself to the reader
by two admirable qualities: the clarity of the exposition and
the soberness of the judgments expressed. In the present
instance this fact is doubly valuable. As is well-known
Arthurian literature abounds in pitfalls for the unwary, and
the Tristan story in particular, owing to its subjective nature,
lends itself readily to discussions that are often more interesting than profitable, at least from the point of view of scholarship. It was no easy task to follow the conflicting views of
Paris, Bédier and Golther, and yet not lose sight of the theory
of development which a fresh study of the facts appeared to
warrant. Other explanations of the *Tristan* may in time
prove to be nearer the truth, we ourselves still prefer that
of Bédier in many respects, but certainly no explanation thus
far produced is more exhaustive in detail or more diligently
set forth.

The study is divided into seven parts, as follows: 1. an
introduction, which also serves as a kind of summary since
the views of other scholars are not only criticized but corrected
in accordance with the author's own results; 2. an outline
of the Eilhart version—and we may say at once that Miss
Schoepperle regards this version as closest to the original
estoire, mentioned by various authors as their source; 3. a
defense of the written source thus established; 4. the courtly
(*courtois*) nature of the latter, and its date; 5. the popular
traits in it and its narrative technique; 6. an examination
of the *estoire* for traces of Celtic tradition; and 7. the conclusion. There are five appendices dealing with various aspects of Miss Schoepperle's theme, such as the abduction-
motif in other forms, the problem of the second Isolt, the
evidence of tragic love tales in Old Irish, etc. A general index
and an index of names facilitate the use of the volumes for
reference. A noteworthy trait of the publication is the attractive dress in which it appears; for this, however, a
European and not an American publisher is responsible.

According to Miss Schoepperle the Tristan story is essentially of French origin; that is, the written source mentioned
by Béroul is a French work. Herein she agrees with Bédier.
But "its nucleus is a Celtic elopement story"; herein she
agrees with Paris, at least in the view that the theme is Celtic.
Yet Eilhart, and not Thomas, or a combination of the two,
comes closest to representing this *estoire,* as Béroul calls it.

Thus the latter is not, as Bédier ingeniously argued, the work of a great poet producing at one stroke a masterpiece, nor is it "the archetype from which proceed all the extant versions of the Tristan story, and all those that ever existed" (Bédier, II, 313). It is the source only of the Béroul-Eilhart version, of Thomas, and of the *Folie Tristan* of the Berne version. Miss Schoepperle would "hesitate to call it the source of the continuation of Béroul, or of the Prose Romance." In fact, these latter versions, she thinks, perhaps go back to an earlier redaction prior to the *estoire*. In other words, she favors Foerster's theory of an Ur-Urtristan, without, however, using this cumbersome name and without referring to Foerster otherwise than in a note (p. 183).

In considering now her points in detail, her theory of the *estoire* hinges on two important considerations: 1. the effect or duration of the love potion in the various versions; 2. the degree of *courtois* interpretation which we can ascribe to Eilhart's source. In both respects it seems to us that she forces her argument, not as so many have done in neglecting or underrating the value of the texts, but in giving them an importance not always justified by their late and probably secondary condition. One may err fully as often in assuming "quod non est in actis non est in mundo" as in assuming the opposite.

Thus Miss Schoepperle argues that since in Béroul and Eilhart the return of the lovers from the forest is dependent on the disappearance or diminution of the effect of the potion, this conception precedes that of Thomas, the Prose Romance and the continuation of Béroul, in which versions the potion is either operative throughout or at least no mention is made of a term to its influence. But as Miss Schoepperle herself admits, the duration of the potion's influence is consistent with the fatality of the love theme itself. Or as Golther well expresses it: "Der Liebestrank verknüpft alle Ereignisse zum Schicksalsroman." In the Old Irish elopement stories to which Miss Schoepperle traces the "nucleus" of her story we find the same idea expressed in the form of a *geis* or a "love-spot." Thus Diarmaid is under a *geis* to go with Grainne, who has caught a glimpse of the love-spot in his cheek. So, too, Naisi resists Deirdre, the wife of Conchobar, until she put a *geis* on him. One might cite also the "clew" or "ball of thread" in the *Imrama*, the *don* in Crestien's *Erec*, Vivien's *cerne* in the *Merlin*, etc. In all these cases the bond coexists with the symbol. Therefore if Tristan, try as he will, cannot break with Isolt, the probable reason—it seems to us—is that in the original story the love potion lost none of its power until the hero's death.

To allow, as Miss Schoepperle would, that such may have
been the case in the version preceding the *estoire* but not in
the *estoire* itself, is equivalent to saying that Thomas unconsciously reverted to the primitive form of the tale, and that
hardly seems probable. So that granting that Bédier had
exaggerated the formal excellence of the *estoire*, his theory is
nevertheless justifiable that in regard to the potion Thomas,
and not Béroul-Eilhart, represents the *estoire*.

As for the second question, Miss Schoepperle in her desire for certainty again seems to strain a point. "The
series of incidents", she says, "from the return from the forest
to the death of Tristan must have been composed under the
influence of the courtly literature which came into vogue
during the time of Eleanor." This may be true. But the
natural conclusion is that the series in question is late and
probably did not belong to the *estoire* in its original form.

In the first place, the continuation of Béroul does not give
the same series. Secondly, Golther argues plausibly that
both the continuation and the Béroul proper (Miss Schoepperle does not solve their relationship) go back to "eine und
dieselbe einheitliche Vorlage, nämlich den Urtristan [our
estoire]." Thirdly, the ambiguous oath is not in Eilhart.
Fourthly, Miss Schoepperle herself grants that "the early
part of the poem implies the condemnation of adultery,
whereas in the narrative that follows the return from the
forest the fundamental conception is courtly and unmoral."
Since the shift in attitude is clear, the point at issue is where
did the change occur. Miss Schoepperle, who is committed to
the weakening of the love potion, says in the *estoire*. We
should prefer to say in Eilhart's and Béroul's source, based
on the *estoire*.

This preference has various advantages in its favor. It
would explain the epic traces in Béroul's composition and
style.[1] It permits us to regard the *estoire* not necessarily as
a well-balanced, finished literary product but at least as having
an essential unity of its own (Bédier II, 175, 179), in harmony with the first part of Béroul and Eilhart. This unity
does not imply the "condemnation of adultery" as such. Nor
is that at all necessary: in the *Historia regum Brittaniae*
(1135) Arthur himself is the product of an adulterous marriage, and other cases can easily be cited. The unity consists
rather in the fact that Tristan is Mark's closest kin, his
sister's son, and, yet is fated to love Mark's wife: herein lies
the human tragedy of the situation. This tragedy, we take it,
was the theme of the *estoire*, as indeed it is the theme of the
Diarmaid and Grainne, where Diarmaid is the nephew of

[1] Cf. Muret, pp. LXVI ff.

Finn. Had the *estoire* been written contemporaneously with Thomas and the second part of Eilhart's source, it seems to us improbable that this trait would have persisted, as it does in Béroul, in all its poignant vigor.[2]

Another advantage of thus siding with Bédier is that Thomas' statement as to the veracity of his source need not be arbitrarily rejected, as Miss Schoepperle is compelled to do. For Thomas adheres to the pathetic interest in Mark even after the return of the lovers: thus Mark, more than anyone else, rejoices in Isolt's acquittal by oath and by the ordeal of fire; when the lovers are banished again (this banishment Thomas interprets idyllically) it is Mark who, conscious that he has wronged them, shields Isolt's face with a glove; and when finally Mark's hopes are shattered in the garden scene his wavering nature craves witnesses, who when they arrive, arrive too late, for Tristan has fled and the king stands confounded. Thus, in the constant interplay of affection and suspicion Mark's attitude in Thomas is consistent throughout—an attitude, we believe, which reflects the *données* of the source, where the family tie was of the strongest, and where the "péripéties sont subordonnées au développement des caractères une fois posé des personnages" (Bédier, II, 175). Cf. Béroul, 2170:[3] "Dex! tant m' amast mes oncles chiers, Se tant ne fus[s]e a lui mesfet!"

Finally, Thomas and MS. 103 of the Prose Romance appear to us closer to the *estoire* in the incident of the second Isolt's lie as to the sail. Her motive there is jealousy. Eilhart, even if Miss Schoepperle be right (p. 96) in thinking he believed the second Isolt jealous although not desiring Tristan's death, actually gives no explanation of her motive. It is "hazardous"—to use a favorite word of Miss Schoepperle's —to assume that the *estoire* was similarly vague or sophisticated.

In making these strictures on Miss Schoepperle's work we do not wish to detract from our admiration of it. To treat the Tristan story adequately would require an intimate knowledge, linguistic and literary, of a vast body of literature. Where Miss Schoepperle is at her best is on the Celtic side of the problem: in the quantity of parallels she has gathered in this field her study is without a rival. We now know

[2] Compare Crestien's *Cligés*, where the uncle is no longer a friend but a usurper who has sought to take the nephew's legal inheritance. Thomas occupies a middle position: Tristan is still Mark's sister's son but the interest in his tragic guilt is replaced by the scholastic concept of the ideal struggle between the hero's *volonté* and his *désir*. In the Prose Romance Mark is an abject villain. The significance of this I hope to elaborate shortly. Thomas does not depart from the setting; he simply enlarges it.

[3] See *Modern Philology* IX (1912) 312.

that the Tristan "theme" is Celtic; of that fact there can be no doubt. Where her work will doubtless need revision is in the field of Old French. For example, the late date (shortly before the last decades of 1100) assigned the *estoire* will hardly win many adherents: tone, language, concepts and treatment would all indicate the approximate date given by Bédier. To speak of the "moral *insouciance*" of such a masterpiece as *Flamenca* is somewhat naïve; and the remarks on p. 177 as to the second Isolt appear likewise ill-advised.

As to matters of detail, we may note the following: p. 37 "Gawain's plan" should be compared to similar incidents in *Erec, Ivain* and *Perceval,* cf. *Mod. Phil.* IX (1912), 294, note; p. 77, note, far from not daring "to efface the love potion entirely" Thomas represents its influence as lasting; p. 83 Bédier's "sub-source y" seems to us probable; p. 108 in view of the historical Bledhericus can Breri be dismissed as a "pleasant literary fraud"?; p. 114 on Bernart de Ventadour and Eleanor see further Jeanroy, Rom. XXXVI (1907), 116 ff. and F. Bergert, *Beihefte* 46 (1913), 12; on the Italian (and Spanish) *Tristan* see the interesting study of G. T. Northup, *Romanic Review* III (1912), 194 ff.; p. 132 the *Chevalier du* [not *au*] *Perroquet* was edited in 1896 by Heuckenkamp, its real title is *Chevalier du Papegau;* p. 143 the "Bastun" in *Chievrefoil* might be compared to the primitive "message-stick", cf. A. W. Howitt, *Native Tribes of South-East Australia,* 678-710; p. 151 on *Lanval* and the group of associated "lais" see now T. P. Cross, *Kittredge Anniversary Papers,* 1913, pp. 377 ff.; p. 157 on the proverb "qui m'aime il aime mon chien" see J. Ulrich, *ZfS.* XXIV (1902), 29, 197; p. 178 on the "broken-couplet" see F. M. Warren, *Modern Philology* IV (1906), 662; contrary to Miss Schoepperle we believe (with Paris and Golther) that *Cligés* is subsequent to Thomas; p. 215 on the "sleeping arrangements" in Irish and Old French see *Elliott-Studies,* 19-51; p. 254 on *Camille* as a type of beauty see *Enéas,* 3980 ff. and Faral, *Rom.* XL (1911), 183 ff.; p. 277 on Matriarchy in Arthurian romance see *Mod. Phil.* IX (1912), 291-322 and Farnsworth, *Uncle and Nephew in the Chansons de geste,* 1913, pp. 217 ff.; p. 299 on the "Tobiasnächte" see W. Hertz's translation of *Parzival* and K. Schmidt, *Jus Primae Noctis,* 1881, *passim;* p. 299, note, Gargeolain may belong to the same "wort-sippe" as Gurgalon, Garlan, Garlagon, etc., cf. *PMLA.* XXIV (1909), 408; p. 452 Miss Schoepperle mistakes Crestien's purpose in *Cligés* (only in the *Charrete,* the *San* [*s*] of which Mary of Champagne gave him, does he fail to uphold conjugal love); cf. *Cligés,* 2304: "Par mariage et par enor Vos antraconpaigniez ansamble. Einsi porra, si

con moi sanble, Vostre amors longuemant durer;'' p. 454 on
the 12th century ''evolution'' of the Tristan situation see
F. M. Warren, *MLN.* XIII (1898), 339-351 and Paris'
favorable comment in the *J. d. S.* 1902; p. 473 no mention is
made in the two volumes of La Chèvre (*li Kièvres*); Miss
Schoepperle speaks of the *pastourelle* but makes no reference to Golther's interesting hypothesis that La Chèvre is
Robert de Reims (p. 75); we heartily agree that Crestien
is not the author of the *estoire*, see Bédier II, 308 note, for
reasons.

In conclusion, let us say that Miss Schoepperle's work is
sure to rank among the notable contributions to the study of
Arthurian literature.

WM. A. NITZE.
Chicago.

VOWEL ALLITERATION IN THE OLD GERMANIC
LANGUAGES.

By E. Classen, M. A. Manchester University Press, 1913.

The University of Manchester, in whose Germanic series
the above slender volume is the first publication, is to be
congratulated if the standard here set can be maintained in
the succeeding numbers. The neatness and attractiveness of
the dark green binding and the excellent type and paper
awaken a certain favorable expectation as to the contents
which in this case is certainly not disappointed.

In masterly fashion and with exemplary clearness and
brevity the author, who is described as Assistant Lecturer in
English Language and Literature, discusses one of the moot
questions of Germanic alliterative poetry, takes his own
modest but decided stand on it, and backs up his argument
with an imposing and (to the reviewer) convincing array of
investigations whose results are painstakingly tabulated and
summarized.

The form of such a book as this is almost as important as
its matter; and in this respect too Mr. Classen shows admirable taste and judgment. In his Introduction he discusses the whole problem; Part I is devoted to a careful
consideration of the three principal attempts at its solution,
of which two are rejected and the third supported by general
argument; Part II consists of the results of Mr. Classen's
own special investigation undertaken to test the validity of
the theory he accepts, concluding with a statistical summary.
Thus those who wish to get the special contributions of Mr.

Classen, without working through the whole treatise, can do so by reading the introduction, the third section of Part I, and the final summary.

It has long been felt by scholars that the freedom with which different vowels alliterate in the old Germanic poetry was anomalous, in view of the rigidness of the rule regarding consonant alliteration. To explain this anomaly, three principal theories have been advanced. The glottal stop theory assumed that every accented initial vowel was preceded by the glottal stop, as in modern German, and that it was the glottal stop which alliterated, so that the vowel sound was negligible. The objections which lead Mr. Classen to reject this theory are that there is no evidence of the existence of a glottal catch in old Germanic tongues, and that so important a sound would surely have been given a symbol. Some of the argumentation here is not wholly free from speciousness, and indeed Mr. Classen's best service consists not in his refutations of the old theories, but in his own positive contribution to the subject. He finds not many objections to the sonority theory, according to which vowels have in common a greater sonorousness of sound and hence could resemble each other regardless of their individual quality. To this Mr. Classen dissents: it is not true, he claims, that *i* is more like *a* than for example *p* is like *b*; on the contrary, the two vowels are never confused, the two consonants not infrequently interchanged. He is on more congenial ground in his consideration of the third theory, which claims that originally vowels as well as consonants had to be identical for the alliteration. But two circumstances combined to break down this identity. In the first place, vowel sounds are more subject to change than consonantal sounds, and consequently words which originally could alliterate would in the course of time represent false rhymes. Secondly, just as the two accents of the first half-line could have either identical or different consonants, so they could have identical or different vowels; lines with different vowels would help to break down the rule. To these might be added a third consideration, the relative scarcity of words with initial vowels: thus in the vocabulary of the Heliand there are but four words with initial *i* capable of alliterating.

To the third theory the principal objection is the outstanding fact that a large proportion of the vowel alliteration is wholly haphazard. Mr. Classen's reply is that it is not as haphazard as it seems, and devotes Part II to a detailed study of vowel alliteration in order to ascertain the actual facts. For this purpose lines with vowel alliteration are grouped into four classes: I, lines with text-identical vowels; II, lines with approximately identical text vowels; III, lines with vowels which become identical if traced back into the older language; IV, lines with different vowels which remain different when traced. The importance of group III lies in the fact that, as we know, certain lines or even groups of lines became traditional and were used by poets widely separated in time; hence the evidence of this group is weightiest in the Edda, so much of which was transmitted in purely oral fashion, less weighty however in the Heliand and Beowulf.

Mr. Classen's investigations deal with minor monuments, Beowulf entire, part of the Heliand, and four books of the Edda, and his results show that "under the most favourable interpretation of the material, the percentage of lines with originally identical or approximately identical vowels is in every case above 58, and reaches 82.6 in the Vǫlundarkviþa, 74 in the Heliand, and 75.2 in Beowulf". Under the most unfavorable interpretation, the lowest percentage is 38, the highest 57. Even this would be sufficient, I think, to substantiate Mr. Classen's claim of great probability for the theory he supports, and he may be congratulated on having virtually settled a question of no little importance for the theory of the old Germanic alliterative verse.

B. Q. Morgan.

University of Wisconsin.

GENEVIVE BIANQUIS, CAROLINE de GÜNDERODE.
   Ouvrage accompagné de lettres inédites.   Paris 1910.
   Félix Alcan xi 508 pp 8mo Francs 10-

In her book on Günderode, which was accepted as doctor's thesis by the University of Paris, Mlle. G. Bianquis gives us a thorough, intelligent and sympathetic study of the life and work of this "tragic Muse of German romanticism", whose touching figure has exercised its potent charm on many a writer ever since that fateful July evening of 1806 when she put an end to her striving and suffering by stabbing herself to death with a dagger.

The "First Part" treats of Günderode's life and gathers together into a complete picture the various studies which have appeared on the subject from 1878 when Schwartz,

Günderode's first biographer, published his long article in
Ersch und Gruber's Encyklopädie I Section Teil 89, to
1903 when Euphorion vol. X brought R. Steig's then latest
contribution to Günderode. Of the three chapters the first
(Années d'Enfance et de Jeunesse. Savigny) is based on
Schwartz, the second (Caroline et Bettina. Clément Brentano) mainly on Bettine's "Günderode", the third and last
(Creuzer) on Rohde's "Fr. Creuzer und K. von Günderode".
From this, however, it must not be inferred that Mlle.
Bianquis' work is merely that of a compiler, which in itself would be welcome. She has made a distinct advance
over her predecessors by the critical use of Geiger's publications as well as of the searching inquiries which W.
Öhlke has made into the authentic value of Bettine's two
books bearing on our subject "Goethe's Correspondence with
a Child" and "Günderode", (which latter work was translated by our Margaret Fuller). And to the understanding
of the last chapter she has brought a renewed study of
Creuzer's Correspondence with Günderode, of which we are
given a complete edition in the "Pièces annexes".

In passing I wish to point out the fact that in this book
on Günderode written by one of her own sex, Creuzer fares
better and, we may say, receives more equitable treatment
than in the two essays based on Rohde's publication, which
were written by two of the author's compatriots of the
"sterner sex", M. Cherbuliez in the Revue des Deux Mon-
des février 1895 and T. de Wyzewa Écrivains Étrangers
2nd Serie 1897.

For the Second Part, "L'Oeuvre littéraire", where Dr.
Bianquis had practically no predecessor except Büsing in
his Berlin thesis 1903, ("Die Reihenfolge der Gedichte K. von
Günderode"), she has done excellent work not only by showing in detail how all the writings of the poet are truly part
of a great confession, but by tracing the literary influences
which are reflected in the ideas and the content of her
literary productions. She establishes the fact that Günderode owes her inspiration to the older Romanticists, especially to Novalis and Schleiermacher, and in general to the
theoreticians and philosophers of that school rather than
to its poets. Thence a certain conquering note, a fine assurance and confidence, which prevails in the products of the
calmest years between the early idyl, her love for Savigny,
and the final drama, the tragedy of her love for Creuzer.
Then follows a period whose watchword is renunciation without apathy and finally that of an attitude of fatalism and
pessimism which pervade the last collection where the influence of Schelling and Creuzer's symbolism is predominant.

"Melete" is truly "the lyric testament of a poet, the last tribute of her tenderness, admiration and gratitude to her master and friend whose thoughts she had so profoundly and thoroughly made her own".

In the fourth chapter, On Style, the author traces the different currents clearly perceivable in Günderode's work, first Ossian and the oriental world, and later the Romanticists to whom the poet is indebted for the symbolic use of flowers, of ocean and river, and of night. Metrically, we are shown, Günderode was content with the established standards of classical usage and has not undergone the emancipating influence of romanticism. The faults of versification, so frequent in earlier works, are rarer in "Melete".

To the question why so very little of the work of Günderode has survived Dr. Bianquis gives this answer: that the fact is to be accounted for not so much by such unhappy circumstances as the suppression of her last and in many respects most perfect production, "Melete", but by more serious causes the most important of which is the frequent imperfection of form. It is true that "whenever she allows her heart to speak and her own voice to make itself heard she touches us most deeply and is the most simply great" but "her finest poem and her most pathetic drama is her life and death with all that it reveals of human weakness, human tenderness, romantic passion and unshaken fidelity to a dream that was but too precious to her".

Turning now from the book as a whole to the details I wish to speak first of a number of points in the third chapter of Part I, in which I cannot agree with the author. "A remnant of religious respect for the Christian marriage" (p. 63), plays *no* part in Creuzer's resolution to give up his plan of a divorce from his wife. He does not make any mention of such scruples, but on the contrary asserts quite emphatically: "Du siehest, Savigny hält die Scheidung für unrecht, weil Sophie (his wife) sie nicht aus freiem Antriebe gewollt habe. Dass es *nicht unrecht* sei, ist meine volle Überzeugung, und in dieser Überzeugung habe ich gehandelt". (Letter to Leonhard Creuzer, 20. Nov. 1805.)

If we are to believe Dr. Bianquis (p. 69), "Creuzer at first admires the zeal with which Günderode takes up the study of Latin and by way of encouraging her to persist writes her short notes in Latin which she answers in the same language. But soon, as Günderode pursues this study with increasing enthusiasm Creuzer becomes alarmed and gently makes fun of it. He undertakes to show her that women who have known Latin have always been singularly unhappy,

Alessandra of Florence, Cecca, Olympia Morata serving him
as examples''. But as a matter of fact the reference to
these learned but unfortunate dames occurs in a letter of
Feb. 6. 1806, while all the Latin passages in their correspondence belong to a later period, May 1806. Creuzer, therefore, is at first against Günderode's study of Latin but later
encourages it with persistent sympathy.

Against Dr. Bianquis' assertion (p. 72) that Creuzer suggests to his ''Friend'' the idea of a ''new poetry, at the
same time mystical and possessing a plastic beauty'', we
have the explicit statement of Creuzer: Deine Poesie ist
mystisch.....eben darum ist sie *nicht plastisch*. (Feb. 20.
1806).

To hold Creuzer's teachings even in part responsible for
Günderode's readiness to die because he discussed the bacchic
doctrine that death is more blessed than life Jan. 23, 1806
(see Bianquis p. 75) is hardly fair, for can we not trace
these moods of pessimism and misanthropy in Günderode's
life as far back as 1799, and hasn't she thought of starving
herself to death as early as the spring of 1805, when Creuzer refers her emphatically to the teachings of *her* Pythagoras
whose central doctrine of practical wisdom is a dietetics of
body and life, which makes us *obey* Nature and yet stand
above life? (March 21, 1805). (Preisendanz, see below).

Seckendorf's name appears as early as Nov. 1805 (see
again Preisendanz) and again March 13, 1806 as a possible
suitor for the hand of Günderode. It is therefore not correct to speak of Creuzer as being suddenly jealous of this
man who happens to pass through Frankfort, only a few
days before Günderode's suicide. (p. 81). There can be
no doubt that Creuzer hoped for some time that by Günderode's marriage to Seckendorf all entanglements could be
solved; he discusses, in fact, quite seriously—in cold blood,
if you please—in Nov. 1805, the possibility of this marriage
and in June 23, 1806 (Preisendanz) he again says: ''Wenn
ich Dein Verhältniss zu Seckendorf zu würdigen bemüht war,
und ihm Gerechtigkeit widerfahren liess—insofern ich dachte,
es sei wirklich etwas dabei, was zu einem für Dich natürlichen
und schönen Ziel führen könnte,—'' I hold no brief for
Creuzer, this Romantiker im Schlafrock und Pantoffeln, as
I should like to term him, but the points in which I differ
from the author, and which are backed by good testimony
cast a more favorable light upon the poor distracted lover
whose passion could never rise to heroic heights.

With regard to Part II, the following remarks suggest
themselves. The word of praise which Goethe is believed to

have had for Günderode's Gedichte und Phantasien (p. 90) is identical with the review in the Jenaische Litteraturzeitung, which Günderode sent to Creuzer, who on his part read it to Clemens and Sophie Brentano and Savigny. And this review Steig has shown *not* to be from the pen of Goethe.

Page 138 reference should have been made to that extraordinary letter of Clemens Brentano which justly scandalized Günderode. For in this letter which is given on p. 47-48, we must see the inspiration of the speech of Egestis in the second act of Nicator.

Passing over the somewhat slighting treatment which Schiller's influence receives—a poet for whom Günderode had a preference which Savigny would not forgive, as we are told on p. 126—, I should like to raise this question: Why is only the literary influence of Novalis given to explain the poet's "nostalgie de la nuit" and her love of the soft light of evening when we have the physiological fact of her weak eyes which forced her to spend many dreary hours in a darkened room and made her write her letters on green paper? It is certainly a most significant fact that one of the few original concepts which Dr. Bianquis can point out in Günderode's poetry is found in these lines:

Sie schliessen blinzelnd ihre kleinen Augen,
Geblendet von der Sonne hellem Schein. (p. 209. n.).

I come now to that part of Dr. Bianquis' book which it ought to have been a special pleasure to announce and review, her edition of Creuzer's correspondence with Günderode, covering pp. 247-492.

The author was quite right in thinking that such an undertaking must be welcomed both for its biographical and psychological interest, as her own numerous references to it in the chapter "Creuzer" prove, and because it acquaints us with the literary life of Heidelberg, then one of the strongholds of the younger romanticists, besides offering a "document humain" of the first order for the life in a small struggling German university town in the beginning of the nineteenth century.

In 1896 Rohde could hold with some show of reason that the unabridged reprint of the correspondence was not warranted, but with the greatly increased interest in the Romanticists things have changed and today such an edition is necessary. To see that Rohde was mistaken we need only to recall the remark of Steig who in reviewing Rohde's excellent book finds that the correspondence betrays a very slight interest in what the circle of men and women, in which the lovers moved, was aspiring to and achieving intellectually. This was a—pardonable—misconception, but due solely to the fact that Rohde had been content to give selections only. The complete edition tells quite a different story and shows us that the two lovers were not so exclusively centered in themselves as to lack a sympathetic understanding of the work done by others. For here we find under date of June 6, 1805, the reference to the "Wunderhorn" collection of old German folk-songs, which Steig so sadly misses, and we are also given an explanation for Creuzer's not knowing more about it—"his information comes from his book-seller. Clemens he hardly ever sees". Again under the 15. of the same month we read: "Die Brentano war sehr krank. . . . .Lange war ich nicht dort. Zuweilen treff ich Clemens und Arnim—called "der Volkspoet" in Oktober 1805—am dritten Ort", immediately followed by Abends. Die beiden waren wieder bei mir. "Sie sassen lange—zu lange. (For he had no chance to read a letter he had just received from Caroline). Ich musste aushalten, obwohl ich unempfänglich war für Arnims heitere Scherze". Then there are references to Clemens's Ponce de Leon, to "Mereau's" plan of translating Fiametta of Boccaccio, to her work on several old stories and to the fact that she has completed a poetic tale of a minnesinger, which Clemens owns in ms., and a tragedy of an old poet Gryphius (Cardenio and Celinde), both of which Creuzer judged well done. Finally we learn that Clemens and his wife were asked to contribute to the "Studien".

The question now arises: Has Dr. Bianquis given us such an edition of the letters as we had a right to expect? The answer must be an emphatic No, and the proof is that Karl Preisendanz's edition (see below) has in the meantime shown us how such a task should be performed.

The edition of the correspondence was clearly an afterthought on the part of the author for—and here I must touch upon the most serious criticism to be made on the monograph—her references in the main part of the book are with a very few exceptions not to her own appended edition but to Rohde and the "lettres inédites".

We can grant the author that it would have been useless pedantry to indicate what in her edition is new or differs from the text as edited by Rohde. But it is against the most elementary rules of scholarly procedure to refer to selections and incomplete extracts when the complete text is available—available within the covers of the same book!

To illustrate: On page 25, n. 5 two quotations from letters are given, not according to the edition which appears in the

Pièces annexes, but to Rohde's book; similarly on p. 33, n.1 we are referred to: Rohde et lettres inédites, and again p. 53, n. 2: Rohde p. 10(should be 13) et lettres inédites. This is most trying, of course, throughout the third chapter, "Creuzer", where e. g. page 55, n. 1 we read: Rohde p. 50-51 et surtout les morceaux inédites de cette lettre. We are expected therefore first to turn to Rohde and then to Dr. Bianquis' text, the only guidance being that the letter is one dated Sonnabends and written after June 11, 1805. It is found to be the letter xxxv page 342, and the proper reference would have been: letter xxxv or letter of Sonnabends (29. juni) or most simply p. 342 ff.

The whole matter is aggravated—and this indeed caps the climax—by the fact that Dr. Bianquis when finally deciding upon the publication of the whole set of Creuzer's letters has assigned *new* dates to a considerable number of letters: so e.g. the one referred to on page 59, n. 1 as of December 3, 1804, appears in the edition under date of December 9, another referred to ibid, n. 2, as of June 15, 1805 appears in the edition under date of June 29, another is mentioned p. 137, n. 2, as of Feb. 20, 1806, the edition gives it under Nov. 20, 1804, and so in fifteen other cases!!

So much for the availability of the text for purposes of reference in the monograph.

It would perhaps be unfair not to mention the fact that Dr. Bianquis labored under the great disadvantage of having to prepare the final form of the edition and to supervise the printing of her book in Montreal, far away from the ready supply of books, but that explains the serious defects of her work without excusing them. She should, in all circumstances, have brought the references to the correspondence up to date—or, printing her thesis as originally presented, should have left the publication of the material now offered in the *Pièces annexes* to a later date. "Weniger wäre mehr gewesen!"

What other strictures are called for with regard to the edition of the correspondence I can pass over as it is my pleasant duty to conclude with a few remarks on *Karl Preisendanz's* book: *Die Liebe der Günderode.* München, 1912. xix, 338.

Here we have not only a truly critical edition of Creuzer's correspondence with Günderode, but also a number of letters from Creuzer to his cousin Leonhard, to Frau von Hayden, notes of Creuzer's wife to Günderode and several other documents, which all help to shed light on this tragic and sad love story. The innumerable misreadings of Dr. Bianquis are corrected, many letters redated, references correctly ex-

plained, also some letters which exist only in copy inserted:
in short everything is done to make the edition a standard
and final one.

MAX F. BLAU.

Princeton University, Feb. 13, 1914.

DAS WERK WILHELM RAABES VON HEINRICH SPIERO.

Im Xenien Verlag zu Leipzig 1913. Preis geh 3, geb. 4 M.

In seinem neuesten Werke hat Spiero wieder ein Gebiet
betreten auf dem er schon früher edle Früchte gezeitigt:
das der Raabe-Forschung. Nicht als ob er auf diesem Gebiete
überall selbständig vorgegangen, der Raabe-Wissenschaft
neue Wege und Ziele gewiesen hätte. Spieros Buch traf
ausgezeichnete Vorgänger. Otto Gerbers schönes Werk:
Wilhelm Raabe. Eine Würdigung seiner Dichtung, Leipzig,
1907, obwohl hier und da an Schematismus und pedantischer
Trockenheit leidend und in manchen seiner Folgerungen verfehlt und überholt, ist in seiner tiefschürfenden Gedanken-
analyse noch immer eine ergiebige Fundgrube für den, der
sich ernstlich mit Raabe beschäftigen will. Was aber Ger-
ber fehlte: das tiefe Einfühlen in Raabes Eigenart, das feine
Gehör für die Untertöne einer vergeistigten Gedankenkunst
die, um bis in ihre feinsten Verästelungen hinein verstanden
zu werden, eine gleiche Welt- und Lebensanschauung unbedingt voraussetzt, ersetzt Wilhelm Brandes Buch: Wilhelm
Raabe. Sieben Kapitel zum Verständnis und zur Würdigung
des Dichters. Zweite Auflage, Wolfenbüttel, 1906, bei weitem.
Ein vertrauter Freund Raabes, selbst schaffender Künstler,
war es Brandes in jahrlangem körperlichem und geistigem
Zusammenleben mit dem Dichter vergönnt, Blicke in dessen
Seele zu tun, die uns deutlich erscheinen lassen, wie sehr
der Mensch in Raabe den Künstler bedingt, wie unauflöslich
in seinem dichterischen Schaffen beide Naturen ineinander-
fliessen. So bietet denn auch Brandes Buch eine Menge
scharfbeobachteter charakteristischer Einzelzüge, die sich zu
einem grandiosen Gesamtbilde der dichterischen Persönlichkeit Raabes verdichten und uns aufs Intimste mit der Werkstatt des Künstlers Raabe bekannt machen. Ausschliesslich
mit den Jugendwerken Raabes beschäftigt sich Hermann
Anders Krügers Buch: Der junge Raabe. Im Xenien Verlag. Leipzig, 1911, eine recht fleissige Arbeit. So werden
''die Chronik der Sperlingsgasse'', ''die Kinder von Finken-

rode'', ''der Frühling'' und die kleineren Erstlingswerke
Raabes zum Gegenstande eindringlicher, analytisch — ver-
gleichender Studien gemacht. Besonders gilt dies vom
''Frühling'', dessen erste Fassung vom Jahre 1857 mit der
zweiten, vom Verfasser auf Drängen des Verlegers verball-
hornten Bearbeitung, die 1872 erschien, gegenübergestellt
wird, wobei Krüger zu dem Ergebnis gelangt, dass der erste
''Frühling'' an Frische, Technik und sicherer Linienfüh-
rung der zweiten Fassung durchaus vorzuziehen sei. Auch
sonst bringt Krügers Buch viel Interessantes wie auch der
Raabe-Forschung Wertvolles: z. B. eine Bibliographie der
Werke Raabes wie auch die Raabe-Literatur, die ja in den
''Mitteilungen der Gasellschaft der Freunde Wilhelm Raabes''
von Hans Martin Schultz weiter fortgeführt wird. An Einzel-
untersuchungen mögen dann noch die Arbeiten Marie Speyers
über Raabes ''Hollunderblüte'' in ''Deutsche Quellen und
Studien'', Regensburg, 1908, und Wilhelm Junges: ''Wilhelm
Raabe''. Studien über Form und Inhalt seiner Werke, im
IX. Heft der Schriften der literarhistorischen Gesellschaft
Bonn, 1910, erwähnt werden.

Julian Schmidt hat einmal — ich glaube in der deutschen
Rundschau—von Dickens gesagt, dass man an diesem Dichter
''nur mit dem Hute in der Hand'' Kritik üben dürfe. Er
hätte das ebensogut von Raabe oder irgend einem anderen
Grossen sagen können. Jeder für edles Menschentum und
echte Grösse empfängliche Geist wird dieser vornehmen Auffassung einer Kritik beipflichten müssen deren Bestimmung es
ist, den Anfeindungen solcher Leute die Spitze abzubrechen,
die sich kraft ihrer Stellung und angeblichen Fähigkeit berufen fühlen, ihren oft kleinen und verkümmerten Mas-
stab Dichtern anzulegen, deren ins Riesenhafte sich herauf-
reckende Gestalt jeder kleinlichen Kritikasterei einfach spot-
tet. Ist es an und für sich schon eine missliche Sache, das
Genie in das Prokrustesbett schematischer a priori Ideen zu
sperren, seine künstlerische Eigenart zum Gegenstande oft
so fruchtloser Erörterungen zu machen, so müssen solche
Versuche besonders da versagen, wo man einem solchen —
wie man es bei Raabe so oft getan und noch tut — mit allerlei zufälligen Entgleisungen der Sprache und des Stils oder
dem Vorwurfe der Verletzung der künstlerischen Syntese
kommen will, Einwände, die auf den innern Kern seines
Wesens absolut keinen Einfluss haben, nichts destoweniger
aber von ''berufenen'' Kritikern als schwere künstlerische
Defekte dargestellt werden. In Raabes Falle ist es nun von
Junge überzeugend nachgewiesen worden, dass der Dichter
an mehr als einer Stelle solche von der Kritik gerügten

"Stilwidrigkeiten" bewusst als Stimmungsmittel gebraucht.
Geben wir übrigens ruhig zu, dass Raabes Komposition oft
recht fahrig ist, dass er im "Heiligen Born" wie in "Nach dem
grossen Kriege" und in andern seiner "Kinderbücher", mit
welchem Name der Dichter seine Erstlingswerke kurz und
ungerecht abfertigte, den Stoff durch allerlei romantische Zu-
taten interessant und etwas theatralisch aufzuputzen sucht.
Näheres darüber möge man ja in Hans Martin Elsters ausge-
zeichneter Studie: "Das Romanhafte bei Wilhelm Raabe" im
Raabe-Kalender 1913 nachlesen. Raabes Kunst sprang eben
nicht wie Pallas Athene fertig aus dem Haupt des Zeus hervor. Der starke Most musste gären, damit später der edle
Wein desto herrlicher die Geister erquicke. Bezeichnend für
das lesende Publikum ist es ja, dass "Die Chronik der Sperlingsgasse" und "der Hungerpastor" noch immer die stärkste
Auflageziffer aller Werke Raabes aufweisen. Raabes Kunst
aber auf Grund der offenbaren Mängel der genannten und
anderer Erstlingswerke einfach in Bausch und Bogen das Urteil zu sprechen, ist ebenso einseitig wie ungerecht. Schon
"Die Leute aus dem Walde" zeigen deutlich, wie Raabe über
die Fehler seiner Jugenderzeugnisse hinaus wächst. Wie es
auch Spiero S. 63 ausdrücklich hervorhebt, dass hier Raabe
einen völlig realistischen Stil gewonnen, "Schärfe der Beobachtung, Treue bis ins Kleine, Fülle des Lebens und der Anschauung, Zurückdrängung romantischer Schweifereien und
tendenziöser Einflechtungen gehörten dazu und wurden im
weiteren Aufzug des Werkes immer stärkere Kennzeichen des
reifenden Stils" —
Etwas eigentümlich aber berührt es wenn ein so hervor-
ragender Literarhistoriker wie R. M. Meyer dem Dichter
Mangel an nationalem Gefühl vorwirft, eine Behauptung, die
nur aus einer ganz oberflächlichen Bekanntschaft mit Raabe
hervorgegangen sein kann und jeder tatsächlichen Begründung
entbehrt. Ich verweise auf die sattsam bekannte Stelle S. 497
der "deutschen Literatur des neunzehnten Jahrhunderts"
"Als alles daniederlag in Deutschland, da schloss er sich, wie
Heine es von sich selbst sagt, als des deutschen Volkes guter
Narr mit ihm ins Gefängnis ein, tröstete es, verwies es auf
die unverlierbaren Güter, mahnte es, sich treu zu bleiben.
Als dann aber die Ketten sprangen und ein unerhörter Sieg
deutscher Tatkraft die Welt überraschte, da war Raabe fast
so unzufrieden wie französische Ideologen, Michelet, Renan,
die es der Nation von Träumern übelnahmen, dass sie erwacht
war". — Trotz häufiger Widerlegung nun — Raabe selbst
sprach sich spöttisch gegen diese Unterstellung seines Patriotismus aus, so z. B. in einem Briefe an Rob. Lange, den der

Raabe-Kalender 1912 mitteilt,—hält Meyer auch in der vierten
Auflage seines Buches an seiner Behauptung fest. Die
glänzendste Widerlegung nun dieses Vorwurfs der "Reichsver-
drossenheit" bietet der Aufsatz Max Adlers: "Hastenbeck, ein
Zeugnis von Raabes Patriotismus" im Raabe-Kalender 1913.
Mit Recht weist Adler darauf hin, dass ein Mann, der als
einer der ersten die Bedeutung Bismarcks erkannt, der seiner
preussenfreundlichen Stellung wegen in den sechziger Jahren
in Stuttgart persönlichen Anfeindungen ausgesetzt war, dass
man von einem solchen Patrioten unmöglich glauben könne,
er habe der neuen Grösse des geeinten Reiches verständnislos
gegenübergestanden und sich mit missvergnügtem Zuschauen
begnügt.

Derselben Überzeugung gibt auch Spiero in seinem Buche
beredten Ausdruck, nur dass er dem Deutschtum Raabes noch
eine tiefere Bedeutung beimisst. Schon das Titelblatt mit
dem Raabe-Spruch aus dem Akten des Vogelsangs gibt uns
darüber hinreichend Aufschlus: "Der Menschheit-Dasein
auf der Erde baut sich immer von neuem auf, doch nicht von
dem äussersten Umkreis her, sondern stets aus der Mitte".
Diese Wahrheit auf ein einzelnes Volk angewandt will wohl
folgendes sagen: Es sind die inneren ethischen Werke, der
Menschheit unveräusserliches Teil die ihre vorwärtsschreiten-
de Entwicklung bedingen, und was einem an Äusserlichkeiten
hängenden, vom Strome des Materialismus fortgerissenen
Volke niemals gelingen wird, das erfüllt sich in herrlichster
Weise der Rasse, der ein gesunder, auf ethischer Grundlage
ruhender und alles Dekadente von sich abstossende National-
charakter als höchstes aller Erdengüter erscheint. Spiero hat
es denn auch, seinem hier angedeuteten Programme gemäss,
aufs glänzendste verstanden, den ethischen, weltumfassenden
und wiederum echt-völkischen Charakter der Werke Raabes
an der Hand ihrer sorgfältigen Analyse überzeugend dar-
zustellen. Besonders hell lässt Spiero den Patriotismus
Raabes aus dem Chaos romantischer Stimmung und Situationen in "Nach dem grossen Kriege" hervorleuchten. Hier
ist Raabe ganz der glühende Patriot, der begeisterte Worte
findet wo es gilt die matten Seelen wachzurütteln zum Bau
am deutschen Reich: "Ans Werk, ans Werk, mit Herz und
Hand zu bauen das Haus, das Vaterland!" Diesem Patriotismus Raabes fehlt bei aller Gegenständlichkeit auch das
Prophetische nicht. "Zuversicht auf künftige Geschicke
durchtränkt das ganze Werk". Und so schaut Fritz Wolken-
jäger mitten in der Zeit der Demagogenriecherei des Fürsten
Metternich dem frohen Tage entgegen der die Ketten brechen und die Freiheit bringen wird, an dem die Schlacht

auf dem Westerfelde geschlagen und "der eine und ungeteilte
Heerschild am blühenden Birnbaum hängt, und ein Purpur-
mantel feil ist um einen Zwillich und ein gutes Schwert".
Dieser grosszügige Optimismus Raabes sollte dann später bei
Sedan herrlich in Erfüllung gehen. Und von der Grösse und
Macht seines Vaterlandes überzeugt, ist es ihm ebenso gewiss,
dass die deutsche Eiche "noch durch die Jahrtausende in Herr-
lichkeit und Pracht grünen und blühen, und alle Völker unter
ihrem Schatten versammeln" wird. Von "der Chronik der
Sperlingsgasse" bis "Hastenbeck", dem letzten vollendeten
Werke Raabes, fliesst ein mächtiger Strom nationalen Em-
pfindens, dessen Breite und Tiefe Spiero überall überzeugend
nachweist, wie auch erst kürzlich Otto Elsters Aufsatz "Die
Freiheitskriege in den Werken Wilhelm Raabes" im Raabe-
Kalender 1914. Mit Vorliebe wendet sich der Dichter historischen Ereignissen zu die so recht dazu geeignet sind, deutsche Treue, Glaubensmut und Tapferkeit auf die Probe zu
stellen und ihren bleibenden Wert zu beweisen. Näheres darüber möge man besonders in dem vorhin erwähnten Aufsatze Otto Elsters nachlesen, ich möchte hier nur an den
todesmutigen Kampf der Stadt Magdeburg gegen den Kur-
fürsten Moritz von Sachsen im Jahre 1550 erinnern, dem
Raabe in "Unseres Herrgotts Kanzlei" ein ewiges Denkmal
gesetzt hat. In diesem Werke, sagt Spiero S. 53 "bricht das
keusche, kräftige, und wie selbstverständliche nationale Gefühl Raabes schon mit der ganz reifen Aussprache späterer
Jahre hervor". Durch das "Odfeld" rauscht der Flügel-
schlag der grossen friederizianischen Zeit und mitten in den
Zeiten alter deutscher Bundesmisere, alter deutscher Kleinstaaterei findet Raabe im "Eulenpfingsten" das feine Wort
"Es ist doch der höchste Genuss auf Erden, deutsch zu ver-
stehn" S. 116. Der vereinten Beweisführung Spieros und
Elsters gegenüber bricht R. M. Myers Behauptung, dass
Raabe seine Deutschen nur "als die Stillen, als die Demüti-
gen" liebe, "gerade so, wie Wolfgang Menzels feuriger
Patriotismus sie um Gotteswillen nicht haben wollte" wie
ein Kartenhaus zusammen. Allerdings: billiger Hurrah-
patriotismus mit allen seinen byzanthinischen Begleiterschei-
nungen ist Raabe fremd, und seine Helden wissen ihrem deutschen Empfinden auch ohne viel Säbelrasseln Ausdruck zu
geben. Wie es auch Spiero S. 146 kurz und treffend präci-
siert: "Das Echte und Bleibende wird nicht von denen geleistet die die grossen Reden halten, sondern von denen, die
still ihre Pflicht tun". Sie wirken mehr durch stille Grösse,
die den billigen Schein des Heroismus leicht entbehren kann
und eben dadurch desto wirkungsvoller in die Erscheinung

tritt. Ich möchte hier besonders auf den Magister Noah Buchius im "Odfeld" als Typus eines solchen raabischen Helden hindeuten. Und als sein Gegenstück der junge tapfere Thedel von Münchhausen den der Klosterzucht entlaufenen Scholar, der an der Spitze seiner Reiter lachend in den Tod jagt. Jeder Zoll ein Held! Und als Raabe an sein letztes Buch ging, da gab er ihm als Motto das Wort des Freiherrn von Stein: "Ich habe nur ein Vaterland, das heisst Deutschland". Fein führt Spiero S. 49 und 50 auch aus, wie innerlich Raabe das Wort "Deutsch" auffasste und mit welch scharfem Blick und unbestechlichen Urteil er die Schäden "Das armselige Schwammgeschlecht am Baume Gottes" erkennt und beurteilt, "die Saugschwämme, die Herrenpilze die Speitäubinge, die Judasohren, die Bovisten, die am Marke der Eiche zehren". Gross will Raabe seine Deutschen, gross im Handeln und Denken, nicht "zur trüben Resignation erziehen" wie uns einer seiner Kritiker glauben machen will, sondern ihnen vorwärts helfen auf dem Wege äusserer und innerer Entwicklung.

Engherziger Partikularismus wie verbissener Chauvinismus sind Raabe gleich fremd. Die deutsche Volksseele als solche hat nie einen wärmeren Befürworter gefunden; die deutsche Politik aber, die Regierung vom grünen Tisch, ist nicht immer nach seinem Geschmack und er scheut sich keineswegs, die ätzende Lauge seines Spottes über Personen und Zustände zu ergiessen, die ihm eine Gefahr für deutschvölkische Ideale bedeuten. Auch hier ist es Spiero gelungen, das Wesentlichste herauszuheben und so das Gesamtbild des Deutschen Raabe nach allen Seiten hin abrundend zu gestalten. So weist er S. 107 auf eine Stelle im "Dräumling" hin, wo Raabe die nach dem französischen Kriege eingetretenen Gründer- und Schwindeljahre von der hohen Warte eines ernsten Mahners betrachet, und ihrer Zeit im Bilde eines Syrupfasses, das auf der Strasse geplatzt und um das sich Alt und Jung mit allerlei Schöpfapparaten begierig ansammelt, ironisch-kritisch das Urteil spricht: "Es hatte fast den Anschein, als sollte dies der grösste Gewinn sein, den das geeinigte Vaterland aus seinem grossen Erfolge in der Weltgeschichte hervorholen sollte". Mit welch eisigem Hohne wird nicht die erbärmliche Kleinstaaterei nach dem grossen Völkerfrühling von 1813 in "Abu Telfan" verspottet, der in "Gutmanns Reisen" gemässigtere Formen annimmt um in den "Gänsen von Bützow" gänzlich in Parodie umzuschlagen. Das von Spiero angeführte Motto des "Odfeld", das Raabe einem alten Holzmindener Zeitungsblatt entnahm, bedarf keines Kommentars: "So ist es

also das Schicksal Deutschlands immer gewesen, dass seine
Bewohner, durch das Gefühl der Tapferkeit hingerissen an
allen Kriegen teil nahmen; oder, dass es selbst der Schau-
platz blutiger Auftritte war. Dass, wenn über die Grenzen
am Orinoko Zwist entstand, er in Deutschland musste ausgemacht, Kanada auf unserm Boden erobert werden''. Die
innere Zerrissenheit Deutschlands jener Zeit, die Raabe bitter beklagt, treibt seine Söhne in die Fremde, wenn sie nicht
gar von vergnügungssüchtigen, geldbedürftigen Fürsten einfach dorthin verkauft werden um dort für andere Nationen
ihr Blut zu verspritzen. Man denke nur an die hessischen
Regimenter im amerikanischen Befreiungskriege. So klagt
denn auch der alte müde Reiter in ''Lorenz Scheibenhart''
''Wahrlich, das ist die leidige Not! Ihr möget gegen den
Feind anreiten, wo ihr wollt in der Welt, ihr treffet immer
gegenüber einen, der euch euren Schwertschlag oder Pistolen-
schuss mit einem deutschen Fluche zurückgibt. Mag es sein
in Welschland, Polakien oder im amerikanischen Reich,
deutsche Fäuste trommeln immer überall aufeinander soweit
die Sonne leuchtet, soweit die Nacht dunkel ist. (Halb Mähr,
halb mehr, S. 152).

Die Frage, ob Raabe die durch Siebenzig erlangte Grösse
Deutschlands richtig einzuschätzen gewusst, ist für den echten Raabe-Freund und -Kenner überhaupt nicht debatier-
bar. Ihre summarische Beurteilung aber, wie sie R. M.
Meyer gibt ist eines Forschers durchaus unwürdig. Eine
solche Methode kritischer Arbeit, ohne ihr übrigens auch
nur den Schein einer Berechtigung geben zu wollen, mag
hier und da einmal bei kleinen Geistern das Rechte treffen:
ihre Anwendung einem Schriftsteller und Philosophen wie
Raabe gegenüber ist einfach absurd und kann nicht scharf
genug verurteilt werden. Wagt sich ein Kritiker an Raabe,
so tue er es ''mit dem Hute in der Hand''. Und überhaupt:
Wem das Organ für diesen im besten Sinne deutschen
Dichter überhaupt fehlt, überlasse dieses Amt lieber einem
Raabe-Verehrer, der dann, wie Spiero, es wohl vorziehen mag,
sich mit der Rolle eines staunenden Bewunderers zu begnügen. Denn dazu muss jede ernstliche Beschäftigung
mit Raabe werden, bleibt sie nicht an Äusserlichkeiten haften, sondern dringt durch die oft rauhe Schale raabischer
Kunst zum vollen reichen Gemüt des Dichters hindurch,
das der Welt Wunder und Schönheit in seinen Tiefen birgt,
zur warmen echten Menschenliebe, die wie bei Dickens, den
Grundton seines Schaffens bildet.

Was den Dichtungen Raabes nun ihren besondern Wert
gibt: Das Abtun alles Äusserlichen, Hand in Hand mit tief-

ster Verinnerlichung, sucht auch Spiero in ihrer Besprechung zu erreichen. Wie ernst er seinen Beruff auffasst und wie hohe Fordenungen er an sich selbst stellt, mag hier in seinen eigenen Worten gesagt sein: "Zucht und Versenkung erfordert dieses Lebenswerk, Abwendung vom blossen Schein und-Lauschen auf die Innenstimmen, es erfordert Einfühlen in andre und nicht blosses Drauflosschreiten nur für sich, es fordert Verinnerlichung statt Veräusserlichung, und es lehrt, immer wieder in die Gassen, aber auch immer wieder über sie hinaus und hinauf und nach den Sternen sehen (S. 176). Diesen hier niedergelegten kritischen Grundsätzen ist auch Spiero bei der Besprechung des Lebenswerkes Raabes durchweg treu geblieben. Kein Haften an Äusserlichkeiten, keine langatmigen Stil-Untersuchungen mit deren Resultaten so mancher Kritiker glaubt, den Künstler Raabe vernichten zu können. Mit sicherer Hand greift Spiero hinein in den sprudelnden Quell raabischer Poesie, und was er aus seinen Tiefen heraufholt, ist reines gediegenes Gold. Und wo seine Fechterklinge durch die Lüfte blitzt, da stürzt manche alte Theorie, die schon lange ihr Leben von einem Buche ins andre gefristet hatte. So die Märe von der Beeinflussung Raabes durch Jean Paul, dem "innigen Wechselverhältnis beider Dichter", dem ja auch R. M. Meyer und selbst Adolf Stern im Raabe-Kapitel des ersten Bandes seiner "Studien zur Literatur der Gegenwart" das Wort redet, Raabe selbst wehrte sich gegen diese Zusammenstellung (Fritz Hartmann: Wilhelm Raabe, wie er war und wie er dachte S. 14) wie denn auch der Verfasser dieser Schrift S. 15 betont, dass Raabes Stil, "weit entfernt von hesperisch-titanischer Krausheit", seinen eigenen, "individuellen Rhytmus, seine persönliche Klang- und Gedankennote" habe. Noch treffender spricht sich Spiero S. 36 über diesen Punkt aus: "Die beste Probe für die Verschiedenheit ja den Gegensatz beider ist dies: Bei Jean Paul kann man fast überall das Episodenwerk glatt überschlagen, und verliert von der eigentlichen Handlung des Werks nichts, wenn einem auch manche dichterisch wertvolle Stelle dabei verloren geht; in Raabes Chronik darf man nichts auslassen, weil mit bewusster Kraft alles ineinandergefügt ist, dass am Ende jeder Stein und jedes Steinchen nötig waren, um den ganzen Bau in seiner Fülle und seiner Einheit erscheinen zu lassen".—
Auch gegen die landläufige Auffassung des "Pessimisten" Raabe spricht sich Spiero in klarer und überzeugender Weise aus. Besonders S. 73-98 bei der Besprechung der Trilogie. "Frei durchgehen" war das Lieblingswort Raabes, wie es auch zum Motto vieler seiner Helden geworden ist die, wie der Ritter von Glaubigern im "Schüdderump" zwar oft äus-

serlich der "Kanaille" unterliegen, innerlich aber Sieger bleiben. Denn der Wert eines raabischen Helden hängt nicht
davon ab, ob er im Kampfe mit der Welt siegt oder untergeht.
Und "frei durchgehn" können nur die, die das Leben mit
allen seinen Wechselfällen willkommen heissen und sich zur
rechten Zeit zu bescheiden wissen. Sustine et abstine! Wie
mancher und manche Edle und Feine bei Raabe drückt sich
nicht im Kampfe gegen "die kalte mitleidslose Welt" die
Ehrenkrone selbst aufs Haupt. Mit Recht weist darum auch
Spiero auf die berühmte Stelle im 16. Kapitel in "Abu Telfan" hin, "das hohe Lied des Lebens" wie Heinrich Goebel
diese wundervollen Worte bezeichnet. "Wohl dem, der seines Menschentumes Macht, Kraft und Herrlichkeit kennt und
fühlt durch alle Adern und Fiebern des Leibes und der
Seele! Wohl dem, der stark genug ist, sich nicht zu über-
heben, und ruhig genug, um zu jeder Stunde dem Nichts in
die leeren Augenhöhlen blicken zu können. Wohl dem vor
allen, ... welchem der ungeheure Lobgesang der Schöpfung
an keiner Stelle und zu keiner Stunde ein sinnloses oder gar
widerliches Rauschen ist, und der aus jeder Not und jeder
Verdunkelung die Hand ausstrecken kann mit dem Schrei:
ich lebe, denn das Ganze lebt über mir und um mich!''—So
spricht kein Pessimist, kein müder Nirvana-Sucher, wie denn
auch Spiero S. 86 ausdrücklich betont, dass Raabe keinen
seiner Helden durch Selbstmord aus dem Leben scheiden lässt,
so nahe auch die Veranlassung dazu manchmal gelegen haben
mag. Gleich weit entfernt vom oberflächlichem Optimismus
wie buddhistischer Daseinsflucht stellt er seine Helden mitten
in den Lebenskampf und lässt sie, im Vertrauen auf ihr Herz,
den Streit mit den dunklen Mächten selbst ausfechten. Allerdings, und das sei hier noch einmal ausdrücklich erwähnt:
Raabes Lebensanschauung bis in ihre feinsten Verästelungen
verfolgen und erkennen zu wollen ist eine feine Kunst, der
nur diejenigen völlig Meister werden, die der Dichter gelehrt hat "auf jene Glocke zu hören, die über alle Schellen
klingt''.
Durchgeistigter Optimismus und echtes bodenständiges
Deutschtum: das sind die beiden Pole um die das schöpfe-
rische Leben Raabes kreist. Und prächtig ist es Spiero
gelungen, diese grossen Momente bei Raabe plastisch hervorzuheben. Doch damit ist der Inhalt seines Buches noch lange nicht erschöpft. So werden im ersten Kapitel, gleichsam
als Präludium zur eigentlichen Besprechung der Werke des
Dichters, vorzüglich durchgeführte Verbindungslinien gezogen: vom sterbenden Klassizismus durch die Romantik und
Tendenzdichtung hindurch bis zu den Anfängen volkstüm-

licher Realistik bei Gotthelf, Alexis und Zimmermann, zum
Ideal der Lebenstreue, das dann durch Raabe seine Krönung
erlebte. Auch bringt das erste Kapitel eine kurze Biographie
Raabes, dessen Leben in Hermann Andres Krügers Buch,
"Der junge Raabe" ja ausführlicher nachzulesen ist, wie denn
überhaupt die biographischen Notizen Spieros und Krügers
kaum mehr als Vorarbeiten zur grossen Raabe-Biographie,
gelten können, die der berufenste Interpret des Dichters,
Wilhelm Brandes, im Auftrage der Familie vorbereitet. Dem
Einleitungskapitel folgen dann vier weitere Kapitel, eine
Besprechung des eigentlichen Lebenswerkes Raabes die, an
scharfsinniger Analyse und seelischer Vertiefung gleich wertvoll, das reiche Geistesleben des Dichters vor uns ausbreiten
und dessen Hauptmoment ich schon besprochen habe. Doch
möchte ich noch einiges nachzuholen suchen.

Spiero ist meines Wissens nach der Erste, der auf den grossen Fortschritt raabischer Kompositions- und Konzentrierungs-
kunst in "Drei Federn" hinweist, nachdem dieses Buch bis jetzt
bei der Kritik sowohl wie beim lesenden Publikum und selbst
in den Kreisen der Raabe-Freunde wenig Beachtung gefunden. Raabes völlige Verzichtleistung auf das "Requisitenkäst-
chen der Romantik" in diesem Buche, die straffe gradlinige
Handlung und vertiefte psychologische Kunst, die besonders
in der von Spiero S. 68-71 bezeichneten Szene zwischen
August Sonntag und dem Kriminalkommissar auf dem Elb-
dampfer zur vollen Geltung kommt, werden zweifellos diesem
so lange vernachlässigten Meisterwerke Raabes erneute Aufmerksamkeit sichern. Und das Wort der Antigone, in das
nach Spiero "Drei Federn" so herrlich ausklingt: nicht mit-
zuhassen, mitzulieben bin ich da, "durchzittert auch" als Leit-
motiv Raabes grosse Trilogie, vom "Hungerpastor" durch
"Abu Telfan" bis zum "Schüdderump", dem grössten Ro-
mane aller Zeiten. In diesen Meisterwerken der Stuttgarter
Zeit erhebt sich Raabe auf die überragenden Höhen seiner
Kunst, und das in ihnen lebende faustische Ringen um die
letzten Geheimnisse des Werdens und Vergehens, stempelt
ihn zu einem Tragiker von grandioser Gestaltungskraft. Und
mit vollendeter Kunst feinster Einfühlung hat uns Spiero
S. 72-98 die Schätze des fruchtbaren Schaffens jener Periode
erschlossen: Der mit den finsteren Lebensmächten ringende
Hunger Hans Unwirsch nach Licht und Erkenntnis; die in der
Katzenmühle wohnende "Frau von der Geduld" zu der die
Schritte aller im Mälstrome des Lebens Gescheiterten führen;
die sterbende, äusserlich unterliegende, aber innerlich siegen-
de Antonie in den Armen des Herrn von Glaubigern "des
grössten Ritters aller Zeiten", die vergebens an die Tür ihrer

Freundin im Armenhaus zu Krodebeck klopfende "alte Hexe"
Jane Warwolf, ".....fünfzig Jahre, sechzig Jahre, und auf
solche Weise vorbei! Tür zu und Fenster zu, und alles vorbei, alles vorbei, als nie etwas gewesen"—. Und am Schlusse
seiner Besprechung wendet sich Spiero S. 98 noch einmal
gegen die, so in der Trilologie, und besonders im Schüdderump das pessimistische Glaubensbekenntnis des Dichters
sehen wollen "nicht der Pessimismus, sondern jene Weltanschauung, die mit glanzlosem Idealismus die Menschheit weiter führt, die das Leben erst wirklich leben lehrt — sie spricht
aus dieser Reihe von Meisterwerken, die Raabe auf der
Höhe seines Lebens abschloss".

Im Schlusskapitel fasst dann Spiero noch einmal die
menschliche und dichterische Persönlichkeit Raabes klar und
übersichtlich zusammen. Seine reiche Bildung, die er aus
allen Quellen gezogen "ganz unaufdringlich, als etwas Ver-
arbeitetes und Zugehöriges, nicht als aufgepfropfter Putz, redet sie aus seinen Werken" S. 158. Auch widerholt hier Spiero
was schon Brandes viel ausführlicher über den Humor Raabes
gesagt hat; dass dieser sich in seinen Höhepunkten durchaus mit Vischers Definierung des "freien Humors" decke,
dem freien Schweben über die Ereignisse des Lebens. Recht
hat auch Spiero, wenn er Raabes Humor nur als einen Bestandteil "tragisch-grosser Gestaltungskraft" ansieht, wie
denn überhaupt die meisten Raabe-Kritiker über dem Idylliker
Raabe den Tragiker fast ganz vergessen, der sich in der
Wucht geschilderter Lebensschicksale dem grossen Hebbel getrost zur Seite stellen kann. Auch Raabes Deutschtum wird
noch einmal in kurzen Sätzen fein charakterisiert. Und zuletzt seine Liebe zu den Kindern und sein Mitleiden mit der
Kreatur "die ihren Schmerz aussteht und stirbt und es nicht
mit Worten aussagen kann, wie ihr dabei zumute ist". Und
dies tiefe Mitgefühl Raabes für die Schwachen und Wehr-
losen ruft uns einen andern grossen Geist in die Erinnerung,
dem das gleiche Gefühl die Feder in die Hand drückte:
Charles Dickens.

Ich möchte Spieros Buch besonders denen empfehlen, die
die Notwendigkeit eines bewährten Führers in die Gedankenwelt Raabes empfinden: den Anfängern. Es bietet aber auch
den schon tiefer in Raabe eingedrungenen Lesern eine reiche
Fundgrube fruchtbarer Anregungen und eine Quelle unver-
siegbaren Genusses. Man spürt es dem Autor an, dass ihm
die Liebe zu Raabe die Feder führte, dass das Bild des einzigen Menschen gross und mächtig vor seiner Seele stand. So
hat sich denn auch sein Buch aus einfachen Rahmen hinaus
zu einer gewaltigen Apotheose des Dichters entwickelt von

dem Spiero sagt, dass er "wie kein anderer neuerer Dichter geschaffen und berufen sei, sein Volk noch in weite künftige Geschicke hineinzuleiten".

EMIL DOERNENBURG.

Ohio University.

DR. KURT REICHELT, RICHARD WAGNER UND DIE ENGLISCHE LITERATUR. Leipzig, 1912. Xenien Verlag. 8°, 179pp.

Since the publication of Muncker's admirable biographical sketch in 1891, there has been an ever-increasing tendency to treat Wagner from the literary-historical standpoint. Numerous valuable and sane contributions to Wagner literature have been made by the "Literarhistoriker" Golther and Koch; among these, Volume I of Koch's Wagner biography is especially to be commended for its presentation of Wagner in connection with contemporaneous literary and cultural movements. On the whole, these studies have been of a more general character, not based on close, literary-historical or philological investigation of a narrowly circumscribed theme. Lately, however, especially under the direction of Golther and Koch, monographs have been appearing which aim to treat Wagner's relationship to various literatures or individuals in accordance with the objective methods of modern research. The day of blind fury in attack and of equally blind adulation in defence and propaganda is fortunately past—or nearly past. Wagner has become an historical character. In place of the countless subjectively colored books on the Bayreuth master which poured forth uninterruptedly into the glutted market, we may, in the future, hope for less production but more objective treatment.

Subjects such as "Wagner and the Greek drama"; "Wagner and E. T. A. Hoffmann", "Wagner and English Literature" are typical of what may be expected in the more serious discussion of Wagner as undertaken by the literary-historian. The obvious inadequacy of all such investigation lies in the fact that no comprehensive treatment of the musician Wagner is attempted. Without his music, Wagner is but half the man, perhaps less than half. In the unprecedented combination of dramatist and musician, the creator of 'Tristan' and the 'Mastersingers' is surely worthy of being classed with the greatest geniuses of German history. Without his music to complete the expression of his dramatic works, Wagner would not rank with a Goethe or a Schiller. The literary-historian,

dealing only with Wagner's literary production, yet realizing
that he is dealing with a supreme genius, is prone to forget
that this lofty position of his hero is not due to his poetry
alone, and is easily led to exaggerate the value of Wagner's
poetical output. The influences of Greek tragedy, of Hoffmann, of English literature were, to be sure, potent in the
stimulation of Wagner's musical as well as his literary genius,
but the real, the whole Wagner cannot be explained by showing the indebtedness of passages on the printed page to earlier literature or even by demonstrating the remarkable
dramatic structure of a Tannhäuser as compared with its un-
connected sources. Nevertheless such investigations are indispensable in determining the genesis and development of
the various works and are helpful contributions to the complete understanding of the tone-dramatist Wagner.

In his monograph on "Richard Wagner und die englische
Literatur", an expansion of his Breslau dissertation, Reichelt
attempts to trace Wagner's acquaintanceship with English
literature from his early youth, "when he learned English in
order to read Shakespeare", to his old age, to discuss Wagner's attitude at different periods of his life towards England's greatest dramatist, and to show the nature of Wagner's
art by comparing his works with their English sources.

Chapter I, the most interesting of the seven, gives an admirable short general survey of Wagner's acquaintanceship
with English literature, largely based on Wagner's own accounts. Here, to be sure, Reichelt occasionally attempts to
deduce too much from a simple statement. Like most great
Germans, Wagner, too, went to school to Shakespeare, and
wrote in his autobiography that he had "made a metrical
translation of Romeo's monolog". From this statement,
Reichelt infers that the boy Richard made use of one of the
prose translations rather than the Schlegel-Tieck translations
which he certainly used later. Or "was it possible that in
boyish arrogance, self-confidence and bold creative fervor, he
believed himself capable of a more perfect metrical translation"? Neither of these alternatives is called for. Like
any young fellow of literary bent, Richard admired the passage and thought he would try his hand at it.

Chapter II discusses Wagner's relationship to Shakespeare.
Throughout his life Wagner considered Shakespeare "the
mightiest poet of all time" and in every new stage of his own
development he felt bound to propound and answer the question as to what position he should assume in reference to the
personality and genius of the English dramatist. Being artist
rather than philosopher, Wagner was prone to err in his theo-

ries, if not in his productive work, and his explanations of Shakespeare's genius are interesting rather than valid. Reichelt justly criticizes Wagner's contention that Shakespeare's genius is to be explained only or chiefly from his talent as an improvising mime, and that his drama has remained free from any influence of "der antikisierenden Renaissance". On the other hand Wagner was right in demanding that Shakespeare be judged only by his own measuring rod and not by that of ancient tragedy, while not in the least assuming that Shakespeare himself should be the model for slavish imitation throughout all future time. Faulty again is Wagner's theory that the drama originated in the novel. According to Reichelt, Wagner's study of Shakespeare may be divided into two periods; the first 1849-1851, in which Wagner was occupied with the question as to the origin of the Shakespearean drama; the second, about twenty years later, when he was attempting to define its character. In neither of these periods are Wagner's conclusions wholly reliable.

In the two following chapters detailed comparisons of Wagner's 'Liebesverbot' with Shakespeare's 'Measure for Measure' and Wagner's 'Rienzi' with Bulwer's novel are given. Reichelt rightly emphasizes the fact that the 'Liebesverbot', which Wagnerites are prone to pass over lightly, is just as necessary in Wagner's development as "die Räuber" in that of Schiller. The treatment of 'Rienzi', while comprehensive, is not altogether satisfactory. As Golther suggests in his review, D. Lit. Ztg. Oct. 12, 1912, Reichelt might well have profited by a study of Reuss's excellent article on Rienzi in the Bayreuther Blätter, Vol. XII, p. 150.

The concluding chapters on "English influences in 'Leubald', 'Hochzeit', 'Feen', und 'Holländer', on "Second Sight", and on "Wagner and Thomas Carlyle" are short, fragmentary and unconvincing. On the whole, Reichelt's monograph contains much valuable material and is an interesting contribution to Wagner literature; nevertheless it can hardly be considered the last word on the subject and leaves the impression that the author was not yet fully master of his theme or fully acquainted with the literature. A number of minor errors in the orthography or use of English words and names indicate also that Reichelt was not fully conversant with the language. Yet in his chapter on Rienzi he cites regularly the English edition, although Wagner himself made use of Bärmann's translation. An alphabetically arranged bibliography and an index would have been welcome additions to Reichelt's monograph.

PAUL R. POPE.

Cornell University.

KULTUR, AUSBREITUNG UND HERKUNFT DER INDO-
GERMANEN von Sigmund Feist. Mit 36 Textabbildungen
und 5 Tafeln. Berlin, Weidmannsche Buchhandlung, 1913.
M. 13 (unbound).

Feist's book is scarcely to be described as a new attempt
to determine the location and characteristics of the people
who spoke primitive Indo-European; it seeks rather to give a
popular summary of the various facts relating to this question
and gives comparatively little space to theorizing from these
facts. In such theorizing as he allows himself Feist places the
Primitive Indo-European community in Central Asia, leaving
the reader free choice of a more exact location within this
vast territory (pp. 518 ff., especially 527). As to the physical
and cultural description he is even less dogmatic; again and
again he foregoes the choice between a number of possibilities;
thus, about the family (p. 115), the dwelling (p. 139), flora
(p. 196), metals (p. 198), weapons (pp. 216, 219), and so on.
Those who are acquainted with the cock-sure statements which
most writers on this subject affect, often only to withdraw
them a few years later in favor of contrary but equally confident and equally unproved assertions, will thank Feist for
this attitude. Indeed, he who looks for scientific certainty will
wish that the author had come even nearer to accepting
Wundt's dictum (*Völkerpsychologie*, I, 2, p. 612, quoted by
Feist, p. V. f.): "Alle Annahmen über die primitive Kultur
der Indogermanen sind ins Gebiet der wissenschaftlichen
Mythenbildung zu verweisen, und nicht viel anders wird man
über die mannigfachen Versuche denken können, die Urheimat
dieser Völkerfamilie auszufinden."[1]
The case is perhaps not quite so desperate, but, whatever
the future may bring, this sentence does fairly well describe
the present state of the problem. By the name "Primitive
Indo-European" we designate the uniform language or dialect
which must have been spoken at the moment before the setting
in of the first of those dialectal differentiations which have resulted in the multiplicity of languages of our family. Our
reconstructions of forms of this language are, to some extent,
only symbolic; whatever their significance, though, so much is
certain: they apply only to the last moment of uniformity
before the first dialect-cleavage that has left any record. After
that point in time we can no longer speak of Primitive Indo-
European, but must speak of pre-Greek, pre-Germanic, and
so on; even such groupings as pre-Balto-Slavic (instead of

[1] In his third edition (p. 658 ff.) Wundt expresses himself more
mildly but no less decisively.

pre-Baltic and pre-Slavic) or pre-Italo-Celtic (instead of pre-Italic and pre-Celtic) have been seriously questioned. The grouping into a *centum*-dialect and a *satem*-dialect also has been severely attacked and is probably unfounded,—as Feist, I am glad to see, agrees (p. 445 ff.).

Now, in the days before writing, rapid travel, and all the rest, a language as uniform as that postulated by our reconstructions could have been spoken only in a very small community,—at most by a few thousand souls. And although the oldest actual records of Indo-European language may not go safely back of the year 1000 B. C., yet it is impossible to say how ancient the time may be when the uniform Primitive Indo-European language was spoken; the earliest differentiation which is to be compensated in our reconstructions may lie millenia upon millenia back of the Indo-European names in the records of Boghazköi and Tel-el-Amarna. In short, the people who spoke that speech which we call by the ponderous name of Primitive Indo-European was a small community, indefinitely far back in pre-history. It existed without those improvements in civilization which bring about the wider numeric expansion of speech-communities. Its speech may have been related to that of other similar communities whose dialects have since died out or been changed beyond recognition. At any rate, it was one tribe among many others, struggling and also wandering over the earth, much like the tribes of North America,—one tribe, whose speech has since displaced that of hundreds or even thousands of others. All this, be it noted, follows directly from the linguistic data,—that is, from the postulated uniformity of speech, to which we must adhere, no matter how far back in time we must go to find it.

Feist, by the way, like most writers on his subject, sometimes ignores this postulate,—upon which, of course, the whole discussion is primarily based and by which alone it is made possible. He likes to speak of a larger community divided into groups so as to admit of several possibilities of civilization (cf. especially, e. g. pp. 97, 115, 211).

The task, then, of him who would tell us of the "Culture, Spread, and Derivation of the Indo-Europeans" is only to outline the facts which come into question as possibly relating to these things; more one cannot do. These facts fall under the heads of linguistics, pre-history, ethnology, and anthropology. The linguistic facts are definite, but, as we do not know where, when, and by whom the language in question was spoken, the other three subjects can be dealt with only by acquainting the reader with the vast range of possibilities,—one might almost say, by giving an outline of these three sciences. Feist

has at his command considerable bibliography and is well
learned, but his arrangement of the discussion is not good;
it is highly uneven and often confusing. Thus part of the
discussion of somatic types inserts itself suddenly (p. 83)
into that of ceramics; the transition to matters anthropologic
could have been made at a dozen points and should have been
placed more carefully. The anthropologic part of the book
is generally weak; Boas' work on change of somatic features
with change of environment is not mentioned. Ethnology also
is slighted; a perfunctory reference to Wundt's *Elemente der
Völkerpsychologie* (p. 24, in lieu of a treatment of totémism
and related phenomena) is seen to deserve this adjective when
the totally inadequate description of early beliefs and world-
view contains such a statement as this (p. 333): "Der Geist
oder Gott wird in bestimmten Bäumen lokalisiert, dort verehrt
und schlieszlich mit dem Baume identifiziert." Pre-history
fares best of all and is well illustrated, but even here the
discussion lacks coherence. Feist deserves credit, however,
for not in this connection overestimating etymologic data.

The linguistic part also is inadequate. On pages 42 ff.
Feist makes the old, hopeless attempt to give the facts of Indo-
European comparative linguistics in a nutshell, a thing which
can't be done and would interest no one if it could. As is
usual in such cases, phonology, which alone lends itself to summaries, disproportionately outweighs morphology and syntax,—which, by the way, receive no interpretation throughout
the whole book, although they tell us more about the Primitive
Indo-European people than all other sources together. And,
as is also not uncommon, brevity here means inaccuracy. Thus,
p. 49, we hear that the P. IE. labiovelars appear in Celtic
throughout as labials, and on p. 51 we are told that French
and Swedish have no fixed word-accent, that musical word-
accent like that of Swedish exists in German Rhenish dialects
("oder in der Kindersprache", adds Feist), and on the same
page the "free" word-accent ("free" here needs definition,
of course, for the layman) of Russian, Servian, Lithuanian,
and Modern Greek is cited as if to prove that the word-
accent of P. IE. was musical; though these are the only mis-
statments, this confused paragraph would mislead the lay
reader on other points as well, if he read it. On p. 313 we are
suddenly given two Lithuanian strophes in the original "um
den Wohlklang dieser altertümlichen idg. Sprache zu zeigen",
—although not the slightest indication of pronunciation is
given, even the accent-marks being left off. Of other languages
Basque for some reason receives on pages 360 ff. a description
of almost Saycean quality, but that is not altogether Feist's

fault. As a linguist Feist ought to use the term "Semitic" as a linguistic concept, but he is not doing this when he calls the Masai Semitic; they have been called so because some of their legends sound like Old Testament stories.

The most interesting parts of the book are—the passages which deal with the more newly found Asiatic IE. languages, and those (32 f., 480 ff., 510 ff.,—especially 483) in which Feist presents his own theory (cf., PBB. 36, 350 f.), according to which Germanic is simply Celtic speech in the mouths of a population that previously spoke a non-Indo-European language; the Germanic sound-shift and other features of Germanic sound-history are the alterations which Celtic suffered in the mouths of this population, and about one-third of the Germanic vocabulary is retained from the earlier non-Indo-European language.[2] Needless to say that this theory in its specific form has little to support it, and in general it is likely that Germanic represents a decidedly normal development from P. IE. and Celtic rather that of an IE. language imposed on a people of other tongue.—For the most part, however, the book is not interestingly written; Feist's style is not brilliant and his presentation is inconvenient. In spite of the praiseworthy abstention from dogmatism Feist's book will not take a place beside Schrader's foundation-work and Hirt's fascinating exposition. Publisher and printer deserve high credit for the appearance of the volume.

LEONARD BLOOMFIELD.

University of Illinois.

[2] This whole theory has been abandoned by Feist in his recent pamphlet *Indogermanen und Germanen* (Halle, 1914), in which he discusses most ably and, for the most part, convincingly, a number of problems which he could only touch upon in the larger work, owing to the limited space allowed to him by the publishers.—[Editor.]

AARON HILL. POET, DRAMATIST, PROJECTOR. By Dorothy Brewster, Ph.D. New York. Columbia University Press. 1913.

This recent volume of the Columbia University Studies in English and Comparative Literature brings to light a mislaid author. With the single exception of Southey, Aaron Hill affords the most monumental example of a vanished reputation. His name stood in the headlines of his own age, but in the footnotes of posterity. Like the author of "Wat Tyler," Hill was undoubtedly the most moral man of letters of his time, for Richardson's long-skirted morality occasionally tripped the wearer. For founding a colony in America, Hill entertained an abortive scheme, which differed from Pantisocracy only in being more practical, and like Southey, too, he

meditated tremendous epics (witness the eight books of "Gide-
on".) But his personality was greater than his works. We
may forgive a man who devoted the greater part of his time
to the "study of history, criticism, geography, physic, commerce, agriculture, war, law, chemistry, and natural philosophy" if he failed to be also a great poet. The single example
of Hill's verse currently known, the familiar lyric beginning

> "Tender-handed stroke a nettle,
>   And it stings you for your pains,"

startles our admiration more by its bold use of "nutmeg-
graters" in an age that shrank from the mention of a hoop,
than by its purely poetic qualities. Too versatile to achieve
great distinction, Hill was too energetic not to make his presence widely felt. As traveller, tutor, secretary, poet, translator, historian, dramatist, stage manager, opera librettist,
critic and essayist, teacher of dramatic art, and commercial
projector he was constantly active. But in spite of his mani-
fold claims to notice, in spite of his connection with Peter-
borough, with Handel, with Fielding, with Voltaire, Hill has
never been given more adequate attention than the few pages
in "Cibber's Lives" or the summary paragraphs by Leslie
Stephen in the "Dictionary of National Biography." Critics
have generally emphasized only one of his varied powers, his
power to bore; but the injustice of their verdict is made apparent by Hill's latest and definitive biography. Dr. Brewster
has rendered valuable service to students of the eighteenth
century by collecting the many scattered memorials of Hill
in compact and accessible form; she has rendered a service to
humanity by making the volume readable.

One of the surprises in store for those not versed in Hillian
scholarship is the account of Aaron's adventurous boyhood.
Nothing could be more unexpected than for a school-mate of
placid Johnny Gay to complete his education by a voyage to
Constantinople, but Hill with the help of a romantic grand-
mother accomplished the journey, and with a tutor provided
by his kinsman Lord Paget, then ambassador to the Porte,
spent more than a year rambling through Greece, the islands
of the Aegean, the Holy Land, and Egypt. He quoted Musaeus
to the memory of Hero and Leander, found the tomb of Hector, tried sponge diving at Samos, and met with a thrilling
adventure in the catacombs near Memphis. In his love for
out of the way travels and even more in his ardent, inquisitive,
and sentimental temperament he often reminds us of the romantic tourist of a century later. But by the use which he
made of his Oriental experiences Hill showed himself a true
denizen of the age of reason. Instead of a "Childe Harold"

or a "Bride of Abydos" he gave to the world "A full and just Account of the Present State of the Ottoman Empire in all its Branches" (to quote only the first phrases,) wherein his interesting adventures occur only as illustrations of various prosy facts. Curiously enough, however, Hill in a poem called "The Northern Star" anticipated Byron in prophesying the liberation of Greece from Turkish rule.

The restless, sanguine disposition already manifested in his boyish travels remained characteristic of the man through life. His inquisitive mind caught the spirit of speculation then rife in Europe; he was always enquiring, experimenting, scheming. Of the long list of his projects from beech-nut oil to English wine the only one of direct interest to the literary investigator is the commercial venture which in 1709 established Hill as stage manager of Drury Lane. For the next forty years he was intimately connected with almost every phase of the drama, but his chief claims to distinction in the field are two. As director of the opera Hill was responsible for engaging Handel to write his first composition in England, and for making "Rinaldo" a distinct operatic triumph. Second, he introduced Voltaire to the English stage. "Zara" (*Zaire*) and "Alzira" (*Alzire*) were produced in 1736 with infinite success, while Garrick in 1749 was finally persuaded to undertake "Mérope". But though Hill's services to the opera and the drama were immediately important, neither entitles him to especial distinction. His appearance in each case was fortuitous rather than inevitable. Handel was already invited to England before "Rinaldo" was thought of, and Voltaire would have been known to the English public without Hill, though the latter would probably have fared ill without his original. Hill's own "Elfrid", or "Athelwold" as it was eventually called, was less than mildly successful. But in the occasional dramatic criticisms of "The Plain Dealer" and "The Prompter" Hill rendered a real though secondary service to the stage.

Outside the theatre Hill was known chiefly as the friend of minor authors. He was among the earliest to recognize Mallet, Mitchel, and Thomson. Savage's pathetic story was first made public in the columns of "The Plain Dealer", where Young and Dennis also received warm praise. Like Poliarchus and the Matchless Orinda, "Hillarius" and Clio (the Mira of Thomson's "Winter") formed the center of a mutual admiration society composed of aspiring and penurious writers such as Dyer, Bond, and Mrs. Haywood. To all Hill dispensed patronage, friendly criticism, and even financial aid, and they in turn rewarded him in grateful song. No demand upon him could awaken his resentment, no enraptured compliment his sense of the absurd. His connections with many *literati* bred not a single quarrel—except his celebrated passage-at-arms with Pope.

The accurate and complete statement of Hill's relations with Pope and with Richardson is perhaps the most valuable part of Miss Brewster's work. She has corrected and supplemented Mr. Courthope's discussion of the well-known misunderstanding between Hill and Pope over the diving contest in the "Dunciad," a dispute in which solidity triumphed over superior but shifty wit, so that Mr. Pope was obliged to do penance by reading and rereading "Caesar" for the injured "swan of Thames." The later and indirect bickerings between Pope in "The Grub Street Journal" and Hill in "The Plain Dealer" are recorded for the first time in the present account. Of the equally important correspondence between Hill and the author of "Pamela," their complaints and their medicines, their compliments and their criticisms, of the diffident novelist's desire for corrections which he inevitably rejected, and of Hill's vain attempt to abridge "Clarissa," the last chapter gives an amusing summary. In the light of new material there presented the character of Richardson becomes particularly vivid.

The reader cannot fail, too, to catch something of the biographer's respect for Aaron Hill, an original, generous, vigorous soul placed in a shallow, pretentious, and self-interested society, though he may find himself wondering, as he emerges from the book, whether its chief interest is not due more to the fine discrimination and abundant humor of the biographer than to the character or achievements of the subject. As a presentation of the facts of Hill's life, Miss Brewster's monograph can hardly be improved. If there is any criticism to be made, it is that the author's modesty has held her too closely to the Bergsonian dictum that the highest achievement of science is to refine facts from the coloring of theory. It is hard to avoid a suspicion that Miss Brewster's opinions would prove more valuable than the details of her hero's undertakings. What after all was the significance of Hill's life and work? Did his "Ottoman Empire" play a part analogous to that of the Oriental Tale in popularizing the vogue of the mysterious East? Was he the first to tap the spring of Gaelic lays later the source of MacPherson's inspiration? How far was Hill an advocate of enthusiasm, a romantic born out of his time and stifled in an age of prose? We cannot quarrel with the excellence of Miss Brewster's scholarly work, but we cannot altogether escape a regret that her systematic and pains-

taking study should be devoted to that admirable, though distinctly minor person, A. Hill, Esq.

G. F. WHICHER.

University of Illinois.

THE INFINITIVE IN ANGLO-SAXON. By Morgan Call-
away, Jr. Professor of English in the University of Texas.
Washington, D. C. Published by the Carnegie Institution of
Washington (Publication No. 169). 1913.

Professor Callaway is to be warmly congratulated on contributing the most valuable investigation which has yet been
made in the field of Anglo-Saxon syntax. His work may be
commended without reservation for all the qualities which render a piece of special research like this permanently useful.
He has treated his subject with such absolute thoroughness
as seemingly to leave nothing for the most painstaking gleaner
who may come behind. The vast and perplexing mass of
facts by which the student of the infinitive is usually bewildered has been marshalled by him in orderly and logical
array. Every passage in the entire body of Anglo-Saxon literature in which an infinitive occurs has been scanned, analyzed,
measured, and compared from every possible angle with the object of settling the meaning of the passage and thereby determining its classification or of throwing light on the origins
of the construction. Professor Callaway has weighed scru-
pulously and acknowledged generously the views of all earlier
investigators, but he has also thought independently, and as a
result of it all he has succeeded in clarifying a number of
questions the solution of which has hitherto seemed almost
hopeless. Conspicuous among Professor Callaway's new results is the discrimination between the uses of the infinitive
with and without *to* and the determination of the extent of
Latin influence on the various uses of the infinitive, results
which were made possible only by a judicious avoidance of
broad generalizations and adherence to a system of minute
discrimination.

The plan of the work, briefly, is as follows. The first thirteen
chapters are devoted to a detailed description and analysis of
the various uses arranged according to their function. Chapters I-III deal with the noun uses—subject, object, apposition,
etc.; Chapters IV-IX with the predicate uses—after auxiliary
verbs, verbs of motion and rest, *wuton*, and *beon*, and with accusative or dative subjects; Chapters X-XII with the adverbial uses, and Chapter XIII with the adjectival use. In

each chapter active and passive infinitives are treated separately. The fourteenth is the most important single chapter, containing as it does the discussion of the origin of the constructions described in the first thirteen. Chapter XV, under the title "Some Substitutes for the Infinitive in Anglo-Saxon", treats of the change from infinitive to present participle after verbs of motion and of the substitution of the present participle in the construction of the accusative with infinitive. In Chapter XVI the writer seeks to confirm all his findings with regard to the uses of the infinitive in Anglo-Saxon by a careful examination of the status of these constructions in the other Germanic languages. It takes a separate chapter of ten solidly printed large octavo pages to sum up the results of the investigation in the most compendious form. There are also very useful Appendices. Appendix A gives a list of all the occurrences of the infinitive, classified primarily as in the general treatment, the instances in each class being given with the finite verbs, alphabetically arranged, of the passages in which they occur. Appendix D is a chart showing the number of times that all the constructions are found, in poetry, in prose, and in each individual work. Appendix B is a bibliography, and Appendix C has a detailed comment on the article *to* in the New English Dictionary.

It must be evident from this bare description with what system and what minuteness, altogether above praise, the work has been done. And yet one is sometimes impelled to ask whether Professor Callaway has not carried his virtues to an extreme degree of refinement. In analyzing the factors which determine whether the infinitive is inflected or uninflected, he lays much stress on the distance which separates the infinitive from the governing word or phrase and sometimes attaches more significance to slight variations of position than is easily apparent. And in supporting his view that the form of the objective infinitive is in the greatest measure determined by the governing power of the verb on which it depends, the infinitive without *to* being characteristic of verbs with accusative regimen and the form with *to* after verbs with dative or genitive regimen, he is forced to seek evidence in distinctions which were effaced before the historical period of Anglo-Saxon. The writer's method of splitting hairs is even more notable in his discussion of Latin influence. He is not content with putting the question separately in connection with every special use of the infinitive, or even in connection with every homogeneous group of words with which it happens to be employed. For example it is not enough only to determine whether Latin has influenced the use of the infinitive as predicate to a noun in the objective case, or more narrowly, whether it has affected this construction after verbs of mental perception, but we must further restrict ourselves to an examination of the verbs of seeing and even scrutinize each particular verb of seeing. We may then discover that although the construction is native after *seon,* it is due to Latin influence after *sceawian* (see p. 206). This does not seem to us to make sufficient allowance for the operation of analogy in the extension of a usage admittedly indigenous, and it results in attributing more influence to Latin models than is absolutely necessary. But we are free to say that this criticism is purely theoretical, for there is no individual conclusion in the work from which it is safe to dissent. Professor Callaway always has probability at least on his side.

With particular eagerness do I wish to express my agreement with Professor Callaway on a point in regard to which he unjustly takes me to task. On pages 211 and 229 he cites passages from my dissertation on the Accusative with Infinitive which seem to attribute the origin of that construction in part to an earlier use of the accusative with the ''present participle'' as predicate. To such a view Professor Callaway reasonably objects, and he has little difficulty in disposing of it and in proving that the use of a present participle with an accusative is considerably later than the similar use of the infinitive. I repeat that I am entirely in accord with this view and that all the material in my dissertation tends to confirm it. I have given no example of the use of the present participle before the late Anglo-Saxon period and my citations become fairly common in early Middle English. The misunderstanding is due to Professor Callaway's inferring *present participle* where I wrote *participle* meaning only *past participle.* I must plead guilty to a failure to make myself clear. I wrote (p. 66) that ''an adjective, adverb, participle, or prepositional phrase'', used with predicative force after a noun in the accusative case, ''is a very important factor in the development of the construction of the accusative with infinitive in English'', and (p. 110) that ''after verbs of declaration the early language, in its original literature, shows only the faintest beginnings of the construction in the form of an accusative followed by a predicate noun, adjective, or participle.'' The passages which I cited in illustration, aside from those which contained adjectives or nouns, were those containing *past* participles, such as ''þa he *hit* geare wiste synnihte *bescald,* susle *geinnod, geondfolen* fyre ond færcyle'', ''Ne wat ic *mec beworhtne* wulle flysum'', ''Mine *stige* ongit *gestaþelode*'', ''Selfe forstodon his *word onwended*'', and others.

There were none with present participles. Nor can I see
what there was in my footnote referring to Dr. Grimberg's
opinion which should have led Professor Callaway to think
that I endorsed it. I make this elaborate explanation not
merely to vindicate my agreement with Professor Callaway
in regard to the present participle, but to point out that he
unduly ignores the importance of such passages as I have cited
in contributing to the development of the accusative with infinitive. A reviewer who cannot find anything else to disagree
with may be permitted so much.

All students should join the author in thanking the Carnegie Institution for the handsome form in which the work
has been printed. With such an auxiliary to call upon, no
person need despair who has anything of scientific value to
put before the world.

JACOB ZEITLIN.

University of Illinois.

THE GREEK ROMANCES IN ELIZABETHAN FICTION.
S. L. Wolff. Columbia University Press, 1912. $2.00.

In Wolff's dissertation evidences of assiduity are everywhere. Much actual contribution to knowledge is nowhere
present—and what little new material is scattered in this
volume of 482 pages has to a distinct extent appeared in two
articles, one on *Robert Greene and the Italian Renaissance*
(*Englische Studien*, XXXVII, pp. 321-374), the other on *A
Source of Euphues* (*Modern Philology*, VII, pp. 577-585).
The pseudo-scholarliness of Wolff's work may best be seen by
an analysis of its content. One-half of the book is devoted
to a discussion of the Greek romances themselves; and one-
half of this space is given up to summaries. Of the second
half of the book, the influence of the Greek romances upon Nash
and Lodge is comprised in two pages, upon Lyly in thirteen,
upon Greene in ninety-one, upon Sidney in one hundred and
four; of the material upon Sidney forty-five pages are a summary of the *Arcadia*. That the summaries are well-done would
assuredly be no defense for allowing them such vast proportions in a "contribution to knowledge."

But if the summaries are to be found in a half-dozen other
works, one might at least expect that in a book which can
scarcely command any audience other than busy fellow-
researchists, the one hundred and twenty-six pages on the
nature of Greek romance should present more than stereotyped facts known to every lecturer upon fiction—that the
plot of the Greek romance emphasizes the relation of love and

adventure; that the love is purely physical though chaste and capable of endurance; that the characters are cowardly and dissimulating in general; that Achilles Tatius introduces in *Clitophon and Leucippe* coarse comic relief; that the setting is vague, save for a peculiar fondness for digressive accounts of animals, pictures, etc.; that stage terms are employed, as well as highly artificial oxymoron, antithesis, and homeophony; that, finally, the narrative of the *Theagines and Chariclea*, after plunging *in medias res*, advances and retrogresses at once, with dubious employment of suspense, whereas the relation of the *Clitophon and Leucippe* and of the *Daphnis and Chloe* is of the type called "straightforward." Most of these matters were alluded to by Amyot in 1547, by Sorel in 1627, by Scudéry in 1641—not to mention their to my mind final treatment by Rohde in *Der Griechische Roman*. New to a certain extent, of course, are Wolff's emphasis on the hieratic tone of the *Theagines and Chariclea* and his consequent distinction between the conflict of Providence and Fortune in this romance as against the rule of Fortune almost alone in *Clitophon and Leucippe* and of Eros and Fortune in *Daphnis and Chloe*. Had this material constituted the text of some dozen pages and all the remainder of the discussion been rapidly given in a half-dozen more, the author's volume would thus far be valuable to the specialist. As for the innumerable citations proving points no one would possibly contest, many might have been relegated to footnotes, many more omitted.[1]

---

[1] If the reader think this judgment harsh, let him consider that Wolff has used so much illustrative material that he has fallen into yet another difficulty; instances of self-contradiction abound. Thus, on p. 132 we read: "the 'love-interest' is nowhere based upon a sufficiently exalted conception of love, or upon a sufficiently sound 'psychology', or upon a sufficiently profound understanding of human character, to be in itself ennobled;" on p. 155 we read of Melitta in *Clitophon and Leucippe*: "for once, his analysis is entirely appropriate, perfectly measured, and quite free from superficial rhetoric." Of yet another scene in the same work we are told: "The change of Melitta's mood, so clearly and truthfully portrayed; the impassioned eloquence and power of her pleadings; the real pathos of the situation; make the scene a masterpiece of serious, nay, almost tragic, characterization." Again, on p. 139 we learn: "Daphnis is utterly incapable of courage;" but on p. 190 his courage is ably analyzed. Finally, for any one who will read carefully may note other instances for himself, we observe on p. 132: "How this episode, so suggestive of later fiction, got into *Clitophon and Leucippe*, I cannot attempt to say. It is connected with the main plot by only the slenderest of threads, and the main action is in any case wholly unaffected by the chivalrous (*sic*) character of Callisthenes's love;" to this statement comes a direct contradiction on p. 201: "This novella is bound to the main plot by a single thread, but a very strong one: the abduction of Calligone renders impossible her marriage to Clitophon as planned, and permits the

That in the second half of Wolff's thesis there is some new material has already been stated. The discussion starts with the influence of Greek romance upon Lyly, discusses its effect upon Sidney, Greene, and Nash, and finishes with its relation to Lodge. Thereafter come three appendices, one upon the resemblances of Amyot's and Day's versions of *Daphnis and Chloe*—this appendix being of much interest to investigators of fiction; one upon the relations of the Old and the New Arcadia; one upon Burton's translation of *Clitophon and Leucippe*.

Perhaps the most serious censure of the second half of Wolff's dissertation lies in its limitation of the field of investigation. If every parallelism of incident, characterization, setting, and style in Elizabethan fiction and Greek romance is to be attributed to borrowing—and such is Wolff's attitude—, then every possible source of influence must be minutely scanned. Yet in the table of translations of Greek romance given on pages eight to ten, there is no mention of the Spanish versions—even though Underhill has devoted a "Columbia University Study in Literature" to *Spanish Literature in the England of the Tudors;* the very possible effect of the *Clareo y Florisea* (Sp. 1552; Fr. 1554; Eng. 1575) is never considered; above all, the influence of Boccaccio's *Fiammetta,* which reached Spain in 1492, France in 1534, and England in 1587, is totally ignored. The significance of these omissions for Wolff's argument may best be shown by remarking that, if no Greek romance had been known in England, either the *Clareo y Florisea* or the *Fiammetta* would have furnished, one the typical Greek plot, the other the typical Greek psychology to Elizabethan authors.[2] And, even, were there omissions of no importance, what of the failure to evaluate the influence of the Italian *novellieri* other than Boccaccio? Of the *Amadis*

---

successful prosecution of his love-affair with Leucippe." I repeat that, were most of this illustrative material properly condensed into notes, Wolff's meaning would be much clearer.

Incidentally, I personally should be inclined to question the attribution of the general structure of the *Theagines and Chariclea* to the struggle between Providence and Fortune; is not the constant quest of the author for contrasts between hope-arousing and dismay-inspiring adventures to be taken into consideration? Similarly, I doubt the statement that Clitophon and Leucippe had no cause to flee. In the first place, the midnight scene in Leucippe's bed-room would make most lovers want to flee; in the second place, given Leucippe's shameless advances, Clitophon could scarcely fail to attempt the midnight adventure. (cf. Wolff, p. 148.)

[2] I am not claiming influence for these works. I merely insist that an investigator should have considered them. Spanish novels, too, like the *Clareo y Florisea*, were in England; and Book V of the *Amadis de Gaula* shows Greek influence.

itself? In particular, of the *Diana Enamorada*, which Sidney so certainly knew, and whence, I suspect, comes more than one portion of the *Arcadia*? Surely, without proving the failure of influence from these sources, parallelisms are most hazardous.

There is yet other objection, however, to be urged against the pages and pages of parallelisms which constitute the greater part of Wolff's "borrowings in Elizabethan fiction." Nor do I wish to complain that a reader is tempted to cry out: "Had Lyly, Greene, and Sidney no imaginations? Were they masters of the *verba ipsissima* of leaf after leaf of the Greek romances?" My criticism is, I hope, more scholarly than that. What I am wary of is Wolff's clever presentation of assumption, which is not fact, and then the transference of this assumption to the world of fact. This is best seen in relation to the *Euphues*. The first fourth of the *Euphues* is paralleled to the opening scenes of the *Tito et Gisippo* of Boccaccio,[3] the *Tito et Gisippo* is then traced back to the *Athis et Prophilias*, the *Athis et Prophilias* is then assumed to be taken from a "lost" Greek romance.[4] With Sidney, Wolff is on much surer ground. He gratefully acknowledges that without Mr. Dobell's discovery of the MSS. of the old Arcadia, the most significant portion of his tracing of influence from Heliodorus would be impossible. For, after admission that both as regards characterization and humor Sidney owes little to Greek influence, and that as regards setting Sidney has his own manner,[5] Wolff elaborates upon the entire remodeling of the first version of the *Arcadia* in accordance with the structure of the *Theagines and Chariclea;* the old *Arcadia* was, it seems, chronological in order and fairly free from episodes, whereas the *New Arcadia* began, as every one knows, with a shipwreck; employed constant suspense both in the concealment of the oracle and in the insistent use of episode and reverting narrative; laid emphasis upon the contest of Providence and Fortune; introduced a vow of chastity before the elopement; and

---

[3] In the parallelism between Boccaccio and Lyly it should not be overlooked that Wolff ignores that Tito and Gisippo were friends from earliest youth, that the soliloquies of Tito and Euphues are startlingly different, and that in Boccaccio much time elapses before Tito reveals to Gisippo his love for Gisippo's betrothed. Why should Lyly have so stupidly ruined Boccaccio's admirable motivation?

[4] Some parallelisms of style are hinted at (p. 256).

[5] "The only characters directly traceable to Greek Romance are Gynecia (and) Andromena" (p. 329). "Strangely enough, too, the storm which brought about the Princes' first shipwreck does not owe anything specific to either Heliodorus or Achilles Tatius; nor does the exquisite description of the river Ladon—a lovely bit of landscape apparently Sidney's own" (p. 335).

developed greatly the device of "pathetic optics" wherever possible.[6] In the *Arcadia*, too, the influence of Achilles Tatius is to be reckoned with. The famous execution scenes, a number of names, the references to events in terms of the theater, the use of antithesis and oxymoron, the employment of oratory —these are with some plausibility attributed to the influence of the author of *Clitophon and Leucippe*—though it should be suggested that Sidney's style surely owes something to that diction of Montemôr's *Diana*, so curiously called *baxo estilo*, and that the *Amadis* was a treasure-house constantly rifled for all types of eloquence. What to say of Wolff's treatment of Greene furnishes a difficult problem. On the whole, were I not distrustful of Wolff's entire parallelistic method and use of assumption, I should be inclined to accept such a statement as this (p. 445): "Thus in compounding *Menaphon* Greene took something from Warner; more from Sidney, and, through him, from Greek romance; and most from Greek romance direct." In general, also, one may agree with this (p. 456): "It (borrowing) begins with mere transcripts from Achilles Tatius in *Arbasto, Morando,* and *Carde of Fancie*— a stage of immaturity and superficiality, which, in the main, borrows non-structural ornament. *Philomela*, which seems to fall in immediately after this group, shows Greene taking less from Achilles Tatius (only the trial at the end), and more from Heliodorus, chiefly by way of incident,—not yet by way of structure. The influence of the Greek romances reaches its height in *Pandosto*, which takes a little from Achilles Tatius, but now gets structure as well as matter from the solid Heliodorus, together with incident and ornament from the decorative Longus. The influence degenerates at once in Menaphon . . . . . flickers up for a moment in his half-realistic, half-autobiographical *Groatsworth*." It may, indeed, be well, to close this review of a book, often very cleverly worded, but always provocative of distrust of the "special pleader", by showing how little is left to other source-hunters in connection with Greene, if Wolff's account be accurate. *Via* Boccaccio's vanished sources come the first and second tales in *Perimedes* and the story of *Fabius and Terentia* in *Tullies Love*. The influence of *Clitophon and Leucippe* is seen in Greene's "Tychomania", through which Fortune is not only mentioned innumerable times, but is invoked to move the plot needfully or needlessly; in the framework of *Arbasto*, in

---

[6] I question entirely the statement (p. 338): "Pamela's description of Musidorus on horseback.....is a palpable imitation of the description of Theagenes riding in the pomp at Delphi." Sidney's recognition of his digressions is traced—and rightly, I think—to similar passages in the *Theagines and Chariclea*.

Clinias's invective against women in the *Carde of Fancie,* in
the painting of Europa in *Morando;* in the use of such names
as Lewcippa, Clerophontes, Thersander, Melytta; in the rhetoric, the characterization by soliloquy or antithetical analysis,
the homeophony of style. The influence of the *Theagines and
Chariclea* is seen in its mention three times (*Mamilia,* II, 6, 7,
91; *Alcida* (IX, 80); in Fortune becoming inventor of theatrical situations and in the Eros motive; in the entire plot
of *Menaphon*—the oracle, the shipwreck, the establishment of
chastity by public trial, the pathetic optics; in the *dénouement*
of the *Carde of Fancie,* of *Tullies Love,* and of *Philomela;*
and in many "most certainly borrowed" incidents. The influence of *Daphnis and Chloe* is seen in the use of the pastoral
as an harmonious element in the solution of a longer story;
in the ridicule of shepherd life; in the management by Love
and Fortune of the *Menaphon;* in the general tone and many
of the incidents of both *Menaphon and Dorastus and Fawnia.*
Que diable allait-il dans cette galère? May not one ask this
question of the shade of poor Greene?[7]

University of Minnesota. ARTHUR J. TIEJE.

[7] Lodge mentions Heliodorus twice (*Forbonius and Prisceria,* I,
53, 54; *Robert of Normandy,* II, 52). Nashe is uninfluenced.

LORD BYRON AS A SATIRIST IN VERSE. By Claude
M. Fuess, Ph.D. Columbia University Studies in English
and Comparative Literature, Columbia University Press,
1912. $1.25.

BYRONIANA UND ANDERES AUS DEM ENGLISCHEN
SEMINAR IN ERLANGEN. ERLANGEN, 1912.

Dr. Fuess's thesis is a contribution to our knowledge
of two much neglected fields of English literature. Satire,
particularly later English satire, receives almost as little attention from investigators as from readers, and Lord Byron,
though the subject of hundreds of articles and books, has
never been given the scholarly consideration that has fallen
to the lot of most of his great contemporaries.

The book begins with a rapid survey of English satire
from 1660 to 1809 and then proceeds to a chronological survey of Byron's poetry. It is concerned principally with
the study of the influences at work upon Byron's satires. Dr.
Fuess shows very clearly and in detail what students
have in a general way surmised,—that Byron's early satires
were modelled rather closely upon the work of Pope,
Churchill, Gifford, etc., while the later, freer ones, written
during his residence in Italy, were extensively influenced

by the poets of that country. The value of the dissertation does not lie in new discoveries or startling conclusions but in the examination for the first time of all Byron's poetry exclusively as satire and in the study of the influences upon it. Yet the book is not without new facts. It is shown, for example, that *Beppo,* though suggested by Frere's *The Monks and the Giants* derives not a little from Frere's own source, the Italians. Dr. Fuess makes clear that Byron was familiar with Italian poetry similar to *The Monks and the Giants* before that work appeared; yet it may be that he states his case somewhat too strongly and gives "Whistlecraft" less than his due. The most important fact to be gained from the book is the extent of the influence of Giambattista Casti (1721-1804) upon *Beppo, Juan,* and *The Vision.* Churton Collins pointed out Byron's indebtedness to Casti's *Novelle* and Dr. Fuess, following this clue, discovered that *Gli Animali Parlanti* and *Il Poema Tartaro* of the same author may have had almost as great an influence. If we have found an important new source for the style and tone of *Beppo* and *Don Juan,* it is a matter of considerable importance. Dr. Fuess's readers would be in a much better position to pass judgment on this matter if they were given in an appendix a number of consecutive pages of translations from each of the important Italian poets discussed. Many persons who will be drawn to the book will not have access to Casti's work. It may be suspected, furthermore, that the differences between the early and late satires were not due exclusively to Casti, Pulci, and the rest but in part to the difference between Byron the Oxford student and Byron the man of the world. All readers would be glad if Dr. Fuess had distinguished the humorous element in the later work from the satirical.

This general chapter on *The Italian Influence* is the most valuable in the book. It must be confessed that the later chapters which examine *Don Juan* and *The Vision of Judgment* as satires are disappointing. What Dr. Fuess has to say on these poems does not reach the heart of the matter or measure up to the greatness of the pieces he is considering. This may be ungenerous criticism, for it would be an unusual graduate student who could handle adequately these problems; yet one cannot but wish that the author had waited a few years before publishing. One would, like, for example, an analysis of what makes *The Vision of Judgment* the   great work it is. One would like an adequate discussion of the elements that entered into Byron's satiric spirit. Did he laugh at himself lest others should laugh at him? How far are his sneers pose, how far misanthropy, and how far the disgust and loathing which usually follow excesses? It is to be hoped that Dr. Fuess will some day extend the scope of his work so as to include Byron's letters and perhaps his conversations and will then consider questions such as these.

It is surprising that Tennant's *Anster Fair* (1812) is not mentioned as a possible influence. It is a burlesque written in what Dr. Fuess likes to call "the octave" though the last line of the stanza is an alexandrine. Lines like the following certainly recall *Don Juan.*

Yet with her teeth held now and then a-picking,
Her stomach to refresh, the breast-bone of a chicken.

The core of *Byroniana* is a fifty-page catalog of the Byron collection of the English seminar in Erlangen. This is apparently one of the best if not the best in Germany and, as the catalog is brought down to 1911, is a useful supplement to older bibliographies. Preceding this are seven seminar papers which discuss the text of *Manfred,* the continuations of *Don Juan,* early Swedish, Russian and Greek references to Byron in poetry, and seven new letters by him, one of which is of considerable interest.

RAYMOND D. HAVENS.
University of Rochester.

NOTES

Useful additions to the rapidly increasing number of modernized and translated mediaeval texts are made in Professor Martha Hale Shackford's Legends and Satires from Mediaeval Literature (Ginn and Co., $1.25). The selections cover a wide range of material: Debate, Vision, Saints' Lives, Pious Tales, Allegory, Bestiary, Lapidary, Homily, Satire, Lay; and they have been judiciously made. We may question the wisdom of using a sixteenth century version of Phillis and Flora and we regret that the interesting description of a lay which prefaces the English Sir Orfeo in two out of three MSS. has been omitted from Professor Shackford's reprint of this poem. On the other hand she has done well to print the simple Middle English text of the Orfeo. A brief introduction in which the matter published is brought into general relation with the work of Chaucer and notes of a descriptive and bibliographical character contribute to the value of an uncommonly useful book. The frontispiece is a reproduction from Fra Angelico's *Last Judgment*.

The Minor Poems of Joseph Beaumont (Houghton Mifflin Company, 1914, $5.00) is a painstaking edition by Miss Eloise Robinson of a unique manuscript owned by Professor Palmer. "The manuscript contains 177 poems; of these thirty were published in the 1749 edition with large omissions, here mentioned in the textual notes." From this quotation it will be seen that Miss Robinson's volume is one of considerable importance in bringing to light poems not in the editions and in setting right the text of a number that are improperly printed there. Besides, she has written a critical and carefully documented life of the poet and a competent estimate of his poetry. The parallels to Beaumont's verses which Miss Robinson finds in contemporary poetry and to which several pages of her introduction are devoted, are interesting, however they may be interpreted in individual cases. The frontispiece of the volume is a portrait of Beaumont. We wish to congratulate the publishers upon the beautiful pages with their clear type and wide margins and indeed upon the general format of the book.

In Rudolf Fischer's *Quellen zu König Lear* (A. Marcus u. E. Webers Verlag, Bonn, 1914) we have the first of the series *Shakespeares Quellen* published under the auspices of the *Deutsche Shakespeare=Gesellschaft*, with Professor Brandl as editor-in-chief. Apart from a brief introduction to the series by the general editor, the volume contains nothing in the way of editorial comment or annotation, unless we except a schematic *übersicht* of the relations of the sources. Each one of the six "Quellen" is accompanied page by page with a German translation, in some cases the translation of Simrock revised by Fischer. It should be added that the series inaugurated by Professor Fischer's book undertakes to supply the deficiencies of the Collier-Hazlitt Shakespeare's Library.

The *College Chaucer*, (Yale University Press, New Haven, 1913, $1.50 net), edited by Professor MacCracken, though not a complete edition, presents more of the poetry of Chaucer than can easily be read in the class-room in the course of a year. The typography of the book is incomparably better than what the complete Chaucers furnish and there is a glossary, which besides definition and etymologies supplies much information that is ordinarily to be found in notes. The appendix dealing with Pronunciation, Language, Notes on Special Usage, etc., is brief.

In his *Phonetic Spelling, A proposed universal Alphabet for the rendering of English, French, German and all other forms of speech,* (Cambridge: at the University Press, 1913), Sir Harry Johnston represents his phonetic alphabet as a combination of the best features of the work of Volney, Lepsius, Norris, Barth, Koelle, Sweet, Meinhof and the International Phonetic Association with a few original ideas of his own. Hoping that the nations of the world will soon desire to adopt a universal phonetic alphabet he lays great stress upon the practical side of his system, which uses only such symbols as could be easily employed in writing with the hand. He recommends for English that a standard pronunciation be established by an authoritative representative committee recruited from all parts of the English speaking territory. This standard pronunciation should then be spelled phonetically by means of this new alphabet.

**VERLAG DER WIEDMANNSCHEN BUCHHAND-
LUNG IN BERLIN.**

Soeben erschienen:

Vom Mittelalter
zur Reformation

Forschungen zur Geschichte der deutschen Bildung

Im Auftrage der Königl. Preussischen Akademie der
Wissenschaften herausgegeben von

Konrad Burdach

Zweiter Band

Briefwechsel des Cola di Rienzo

Herausgegeben von

Konrad Burdach und Paul Piur

Dritter Teil. **Kritischer Text, Lesarten und Anmerkungen.**
Mit 3 Faksimilebeilagen. Gr. 8°. (XXIII u. 471 S.)
Geh. 16 M.

Vierter Teil. **Anhang.** Urkundliche Quellen zur Geschichte
Rienzos. Oraculum Angelicum Cyrilli und Kommentar
des Pseudojoachim. Gr. 8°. (XVI u. 354 S.) Geh
12 M.

Die vorliegenden beiden Teile bieten den erhaltenen Bestand aller
von Rienzo und an ihn ergangenen Briefe, sowie aller seine Person betreffenden gleichzeitigen urkundlichen Quellen in kritischer Herstellung
und eine Übersicht der zu Grunde liegenden handschriftlichen Überlieferung.

Die vorangehenden Teile folgen später.

THE DEVELOPMENT OF MODERN GROUPSTRESS
IN GERMAN AND ENGLISH

In a modern syntactical group the last member has the stress : die Màcht des Feúers, the pòwer of fíre, die jùnge Fráu. In oldest Germanic the stress rested upon the first member. This older stress is still often preserved in compounds : die Feúersmàcht, die Júngfràu. For years the writer has struggled to penetrate into the mystery that surrounds this change of stress. He believes he has discovered the forces at work in this development and now desires to present here his evidence.

The fact that the older stress survives in compounds suggests that there is a relation between group and compound. Thus also modern compounds have modern group-stress, as in "Mùttergóttes" (image of the Virgin Mary). As a basis of this study serve the oldest German and English compounds, i. e. such as have for their first component a mere stem, as in "hórd-bùrh" (treasure-castle). The development of these compounds has been traced from the earliest period to the time when the compound form is replaced by a group of words that stand in a syntactical relation to each other. Thus Old English "haér-lòcc", "stán-brỳcg" have been replaced by "lòck of háir" and "stòne brídge". In more modern compounds, the so-called spurious or improper compounds, there is an evident syntactical relation of the components, as in "Fraúenhànd". Here the first component is a genitive. There must have originally been a syntactical relation between the components of *all* compounds, even the oldest, for the oldest have later in many cases been dissolved into a group with a clear designation of the syntactical relations, as "lòck of háir", the modern form of older "haèrlócc". In case of Old English "stán-brỳcg" the accent has shifted upon the second component, "stòne brídge", as according to our modern conception we construe "stone" as an adjective and give it the weak accent that an adjective assumes in our modern groupstress. Thus our ancestors who were nearer to the source of the language than we are, ascribed syntactical values to the components of the old compounds and gave a formal expression to this interpretation by syntactical form or by appropriate stress.

The fact that a very large number of the oldest compounds have been replaced by a syntactical group seems to indicate clearly that these old formations were not *compounds* at all, but were *groups* or *phrases*. The non-inflection of the first member of these old groups indicates that in the oldest period of the language nouns and adjectives were not inflected. The thought was expressed by the mere juxtaposition of the words. These old groups survived in the later order of things because they had assumed a peculiar meaning which could not be expressed by the newer system of inflection. They were felt, however, as groups, not as compounds. The idea of a compound had not yet developed out of these groups. As long as they were felt as groups they were left undisturbed, for they were clearly differentiated from the new groups by the non-inflection of the first member.

Great confusion arose, however, when these old groups began to develop into compounds and thus ceased to be groups. Some of the old groups had become compounds, some remained groups, but both had a heavy stress on the first element, and thus *group* could not be distinguished from *compound*. The confusion was increased by the development of a large number of new compounds out of the new groups with inflection in the first member, as in Fráuenhànd, Gótteshaùs, etc. Thus in the old groups and the newer groups there was no way to distinguish compound from group.

In English there arose a strong desire to bring law and order into this chaotic condition by distinguishing sharply between group and compound. The old formations were left undisturbed where they had developed into compounds, but were dissolved into groups where the group-idea prevailed: "hoúse-wàrming" (festivity), but "wàrming the hoúse"; "wóol-gàthering" (idle reverie), but "gàthering wóol"; "múckràking", but "ràking múck"; etc. Likewise "shóp-lifting", "glóbetròtting", "haírsplìtting", etc. Likewise words with specialized meanings, as "wóol-gròwing", "shéep-sheàring", etc. The natural impulse to differentiate the meaning here is strong in English, but much stronger is the feeling for the modern group-form. Thus in most cases old groups with specialized meaning are dissolved into modern groups wherever the idea of group becomes pronounced. Thus we usually say "He is busy with sheàring shéep", rather than "with shéep-sheàring". We reserve "shéep-sheàring" for the specialized idea of a trade.

German, on the other hand, has remained wonderfully conservative and often preserves the old group-formation where the group-idea is even clearly present: "Wegen einer *Kópfverlètzung* bleibt er zu Hause". Here the old form has been retained although the group-idea is pronounced. In English we must say: "on account of injuring his head". German also can often dissolve the old form into a modern group: "die Verlètzung des Kópfes". In such cases there is usually a slight differentiation between the old group-form and the new group-form. This gives German very often a peculiarly rich differentiation not found in English. In German also, however, the modern group-form *must* be assumed when any ambiguity might arise. This is especially liable to happen in groups with a genitive as the first member, whenever there is before the genitive an article that belongs to the last member, as in "die heilige góttes òffenunge" (Schönbach's "Altdeutsche Predigten", III. 27, 37). We now prefer to say "die heilige Offenbàrung Góttes", as we desire to indicate clearly that "Gottes" is a subjective genitive to distinguish it from the "Gottes" that enters into firm compounds, such as "Gótteshàus", where both components blend into one word to form one idea. The frequent ambiguity here has led to the entire disappearance of this construction as a modern group. It only survives as a compound, as in "Gótteshàus", or as a "groupword", as in Hérzensergièssung.

In the modern group, as in "die Offenbàrung Góttes", the stressed modifying element is usually placed *after* the governing noun to distinguish it from the compound which regularly has its stressed modifying component *before* the governing noun. The writer in his "Development of the Analytical Genitive in Germanic" (*Modern Philology*, vol. 11) has described other forces that led to the placing of the modifying element after the governing noun. In all these cases the trans-

fer of the strongly stressed modifying element to a place after
the governing noun changed the position of the group-stress.
The accent now rested upon the last member of the group.
This establishment here of the group-stress upon the last member helped solve other problems. Adjectives and often also
genitives remained in their old historic position before the
governing noun. Group could now be distinguished from compound by leaving to the compound its old stress upon the first
member and by giving to the group the modern group-stress
upon the last member: ''des Königs Sée'', but ''Königssèe''
(city); ''die jùng (later always junge) Fráu'', but ''die Júng-
fraù''.

The chronology of the development is most easily fixed in
English where the movement was strongest and most clearly
marked by formal change. The development is traced by the
gradual transfer of adverbial and objective modifiers to a
position after the governing word. These strongly stressed
modifiers brought with them their strong stress and in course
of Middle English established firmly a new group-stress with
the accent upon the last syllable. In English the old group-
stress upon the first syllable was entirely destroyed except in
case of real compounds like ''hoúse-wàrming'' and old groups
with specialized meaning like ''shéep sheàring''. Other old
groups were entirely destroyed. As we shall see below this was
quite different in German. Thus it is quite evident that the
chief force at work in the dissolution of old groups in English
was the strong feeling for modern group-stress.

In German, on the other hand, there is still a vivid feeling
for the old group-stress upon the first element. It exists in
countless cases: ''er will *Feúer màchen*''; ''er hat *Feúer
gemàcht*''. Thus it is only natural that with the strong support of this common group-stress in such old groups with
verbal elements it should be preserved in other old groups
containing verbal elements: ''Kópfverlètzung''; ''Blútver-
gìessen''; ''Blútverlùst''; ''Haúsdurchsùchung'', etc. The
strong stress upon the first member of these old groups gave
a distinct shade of meaning to the first member and made
natural the retention here of the old stress. This led to the
development of a new stress—a logical stress upon the first

member in contradistinction to the new, more mechanical group-stress upon the last member, which merely serves to mark the unity of the group, as in "diese Verlètzung des Kópfes". In the prehistoric period, where the stress was always upon the first member, logical stress could only be distinguished by a stronger stress. The old stress upon the first member survives as a logical stress and differentiates the old groups from modern groups. There is here in German amazing wealth. There are thousands of examples. As the construction is so common we can study it carefully. It can be clearly seen that these old formations are still groups, not compounds, as in case of "Ábendmàhl" (the *Lord's Supper*), "Júnggesèll" (bachelor), "Júngfràu", etc., where both members have fused into one, to form one idea. As the force of the individual members in compounds are no longer felt, they may suffer a loss of form, as in "Junker" (=junger Herr), "Jungfer" (=junge Frau), etc. In the old groups, however, the force of each member is distinctly felt. The writer desires to introduce a new name for these old groups and proposes the term "group-word". They are written as one word but are in fact a group.

The old group-words are constantly developing into compounds, as illustrated above, but the line of division between the older and the younger class cannot be accurately drawn. In a large number of words, as in "Hérzverfèttung", "Hérzlähmung", etc., the parts are blended into a certain unity, but the old group-idea is still so strong that the syntactical relations can still be felt. Thus "Herz" is subject in the first example and object in the second. Although new compounds are constantly forming in German from the old group-words it must not be inferred that feeling for the older "group-words" is weakening. In such old "group-words" as "Kópfzàhlung" and "báum= und búschumgèben" (Spielhagen) we see a bit of prehistoric life that is very interesting. Here "Kopf", "baum" and "busch" are evidently plurals, but there is no plural form. The mere juxtaposition suggests the plural idea. These are modern formations, but along the line of older expression. Their fine shades of thought and their forceful terseness show that older life need not always be wantonly destroyed, but may be retained and become the source of new power.

We have three stages of group-development: (1) Kópfverlètzung; (2) Tágeslìcht (the members originally written apart, but in this word-order and with this stress); (3) Verlètzung des Kópfes, Lìcht des Táges. The formations of the first stage are the oldest. We call them "old group-words". Those of the second stage are younger. We call them "younger group-words". Those of the third stage we call "modern groups". To these three classes of group-formations correspond the following three classes of compounds: (1) Ábendmàhl, hóusewàrming, etc., "old compounds"; (2) Gótteshàus, Júngfràu, géntlemàn, etc., "younger compounds"; (3) Muttergóttes (image of the Virgin Mary), der Hòhepríester, zùfríeden, ìnstéad, "modern compounds". The writer recommends these terms instead of those now in use.

A more detailed account of the dissolution of Old English group-words into modern groups will appear soon in "Anglia" under the heading "The Gerund in Old English".

Northwestern University.   G. O. CURME.

GERMANIC ETYMOLOGIES

1. OE. *acan* 'ake', MLG. *eken, ecken*, 'eitern', *ek, ak* 'Eiter, eiterndes Geschwür, bes. Finger geschwür', EFries. *äk (e), ek* 'ein kleines, bösartiges, sehr schmerzhaftes Eiter-geschwür', etc., probably come from the primary meaning 'swell'. Compare Lett. *ûga* 'Beere, Blatter, Pocke', Lith. *ûga* 'Beere, Kirsche', OBulg. *(j)agoda* 'Frucht', Czech *jahoda* 'Beere', earlier also 'Wange', etc. Here also belong Goth. *akran* 'Frucht', OSwed. *akarn*, OE. *æcern* 'acorn', etc. (cf. Lidén, *IF.* XVIII, 503 ff).

2. OE. *āc* 'oak', *āc-melo* 'acorn', ON. *eik*, OHG. *eih*, OS. *ēk* 'Eiche' are from Germ. **aik-* 'acorn: acorn-tree, oak', whence the demin. OHG. *eichila*, MDu. *eikel, ekel* 'Eichel', etc. That the 'acorn' was not named from the 'oak', but the 'oak' from the 'acorn' is probable from Gr. βάλανος 'an acorn or any such fruit: the trees which bear these fruits'. Hence the IE. **aig-* or **əig-* of the above would mean 'swelling, bunch, lump' or 'projection, point'. These meanings would fit in Gr. αἰγίς 'a yellow kernel in the pith of the pine; a speck in the eye; (boss, umbo) shield, aegis', αἰγανέη (point, Spitze) 'spear, javelin', αἰγίλωψ 'a kind of oak with sweet fruit', perhaps also in the sense 'a kind of oats; an ulcer in the eye', though differently explained by Boisacg, *Dict. Ét.* 21.

The meaning assumed as underlying these words could have developed from the meaning in Skt. *ējati* 'rührt sich, bewegt sich'.

Or possibly an IE. **aig-* 'swell' may have existed, with which we may compare (whether related or not) various other bases **aix-* (or **əix-*) with the ablaut **oix-* (or **ōix-*). Compare Nos. 3-8.

3. ON. *eigin* 'eben hervorgesprossener Saatkeim': Gr. αἴχλοι· αἰ γωνίαι τοῦ βέλους *Hes.*, αἰχμή 'the point of a spear; spear, dart, arrow; scepter', OIr. *āel* 'fuscina, tridens', Lith. *ëszmas* 'Bratspiess', OPruss. *aysmis* id. (cf. Boisacg, *Dict. Ét.* 24 with lit.). Or the ON. and Gr. words may have IE. *q*: OPruss. *ayculo* 'Nadel' (Fick III⁴, 2). Or finally ON. *eigin*, Gr. αἰχμή, together with OE. *ig(i)l*, OHG. *īgil* 'Igel' may have IE. *gh*: ChS. *igla* 'Nadel', LRuss, *ihlá* 'Nähnadel;

Dorn, Stachel', Serb.-Cr. *iglica* 'kleine Nadel, Sprosse', etc. (id. ibid.; Berneker, *Et.Wb.* 423).

4. OE. *āte* 'oat', Norw. *eitel* 'Drüse, Knoten, Knospe', ON. *eitell* 'Drüse, Knorren am Baum', NIcel. *eitill* 'gland', MHG. *eizel* 'kleines eiternades Geschwür', *eiz* 'Geschwür, Eiterbeule', *eiter*, OHG. *eitar* 'Gift', etc.: Gr. οἶδος 'swelling, tumor', οἶδμα 'swell of the sea, wave, billow' οἰδέω, 'swell, swell up; be tumultuous', οἴδησις 'a swelling up, fermenting', Arm. *ait* 'Wange', *aitnum* 'schwelle', Lat. *aemidus* 'tumidus' (if for *aedmidus, cf. Walde, *Et. Wb.*[2] 15 with lit.).

5. Goth. *aiz* 'Erz, Geld', ON. *eir* 'brass, copper, bronze', OE. *ār* 'brass, copper', NE. *ore*, OHG. *ēr* 'Erz, Eisen', etc., Lat. *aes* 'ore, brass, bronze', Skt. *áyaḥ* 'Erz, Eisen' (cf. Walde, *Et. Wb.*[2] 17 with lit.), IE. *ạies or *ǝịes* 'lump, mass (of metal)'. Compare No. 6.

6. OE. *īs* 'ice', ON. *íss*, OHG. *īs* 'Eis', etc., may be from **īso-* 'chunk, lump': ChSl. *isto* 'testiculus', OBulg. *istesa* pl. 'Nieren', ON. *eista* 'testicle': MLG. *īs-bēn* 'Hüftbein, Eisbein', MDu. *ijs-*, *īse-been* 'hip bone; os sacrum'. For meaning compare Czech *kra* 'Klumpen; Eisscholle', Russ. *ikra* 'Eisscholle'; *ikrá* 'Wade'.

7. OE. *ād* 'heap; funeral pile; fire, flame', OHG. *eit* 'Glut, Scheiterhaufen', Gr. αἴθω 'flame', Lat. *aestus* 'waving, billowy motion: fire, glow; swell, surge', Ir. *āed* 'Feuer', Welsh *aidd* 'Eifer, Hitze', etc.: ON. *ið* 'restless motion', *iða* 'eddy, whirlpool', *iða* 'move to and fro, fidget', Skt. *ēdhate*, 'wächst, gedeiht, wird gross' (author, *Color-Names* 50).

8. OE. *ǣlan* 'burn, burn up; kindle, light', *ǣled* 'fire, firebrand', ON. *eldr* 'fire': Welsh *ilio* 'gären', *iliad* 'Gärung', Swab. *illen* 'Beule', OFries. *ili* 'Schwiele', OE. *ile* 'callosity; sole of the foot', Lat. *īlia* 'flank', Wz. **il-* etwa 'schwellen', Walde, *Et. Wb.*[2] 378.

9. OE. *āfor* 'harsh (to taste); fierce, vehement', OHG. *aipar*, *eiber* 'acerbus, amarus, horridus': early NHG. *yfer* 'Eifersucht', NHG. *Eifer* (Weigand, I,[5] 412) Gr. αἶψα 'quick with speed', αἰψηρός 'quick, speedy, sudden', αἴφνης 'on a sudden', αἰπός 'steep, lofty', αἰπύς 'headlong, sudden; high and steep; fierce (anger); painful, difficult'. According to others

the Gr. words have IE. *q* (cf. Boisacg, *Dict. Ét.* 31 with lit.).

10. NE. dial. *awvish, hawfish, haufish* 'slightly unwell, out of sorts; reluctant, undecided' is explained by Wright, *Dial. Dict.*, as being probably for *halfish*. This is altogether improbable. It is rather the same as *offish* 'inclined to keep aloof, distant in manner, reserved' (*Cent. Dict.* V, 4093). Colloquially *offish* is also used in the sense of slightly ailing, 'off one's feed'. This expression, though used primarily of animals, is more often applied to men.

For the formation of *offish* from *off* compare *uppish* 'proud, arrogant, airy, self-assertive, assuming' from *up*.

11. OHG. *fehōn, gifehōn* 'verzehren, essen', *farfehōn* 'hinwegraffen, vernichten', OS. *farfehon* 'verzehren' belong to the IE. root **pek-* 'pluck, tear' just as *verzehren* is related to *tear, zerren*, etc. Compare Lith. *pèszti* 'pflücken, rupfen', Gr. πέκω 'comb, card; pull, pluck out; shear', etc.

To the same root I refer OHG. *gifehan* 'sich freuen', primarily 'geniessen', Goth. *faginōn* 'sich freuen', etc. Cf. *Mod. Phil.* II, 473.

12. Goth. *gatils* 'εὔκαιρος, passend; εὔθετος εἰς, geschickt zu' (*in* with acc.), *ga-gatilōn* 'zusammen fügen' are probably not derivatives of *til* 'Gelegenheit', but of a Germ. root **gat-* 'join, fit; fitting, proper'. Compare OE. *geatolic* 'adorned, splendid' and OBulg. *godŭ* 'ὥρα, Zeit; καιρός, rechte Zeit', *vŭ godŭ* 'εὔκαίρως': (Goth. *gatilaba* id.), *vŭ godë byti* 'passend sein, gefallen', *u-goda* 'Wohlgefallen', *u-goditi* 'gefallen', etc. (cf. Berneker, *Et. Wb.* 316 ff): MHG. *ergetzen* 'vergüten, erfreuen' (author, *Zfvgl Sprf.* XLV, 69).

These imply an IE. root **ghad-* as well as **ghadh-*: OFris. *gada* 'vereinigen', MLG. *gaden* 'passen, gefallen, sich gatten', Goth. *gadiliggs* 'Vetter', *gōþs* 'gut', etc.

13. ON. *geð* 'Sinn, Mut, Charakter, Wohlgefallen, Zuneigung', NIcel. 'mood, temper, disposition; mind; spirits; liking', Norw. *gjed* 'mind; mood; eagerness, eager desire; a wanton person' represent Germ. **gadja-*, which may better be separated from Gr. πόθος 'a longing, yearning, fond desire or regret'. For this may be compared with Lith. *bādas* 'Hungersnot, Hunger', Skt. *bādhatē* 'drängt, drückt' (Uhlen-

beck, *Et. Wb.*² 26), and Germ. **gadja-* is from pre-Germ.
*ghadhio- rather than **gᵘhodhio-*.

Compare Russ.-ChSl. *u-goda* 'Wohlgefallen', *goditi* 'gefallen', Russ. dial. *godít* 'zögern, warten; zielen', Bulg. *godŭ*
'schaue worauf, sorge wofür, bereite vor; suche eine Gelegenheit; verlobe mich', Pol. *godzic* 'unterhandeln, mieten, dingen;
aussöhnen; auf jemd. eindringen; trachten wonach', *godza*
'Lust, Wunsch', etc.: MLG. *gaden* 'passen, gefallen, sich
gatten,' No. 12.

14. OE. *gor* 'dung, dirt', NE. *gore* 'thick or clotted blood',
dial. *gore, gor* 'dirt, mire, slime', *gurr* 'mud, dirt', *vb.* 'defile,
soil with mud, do dirty work', ON. *gor* 'the half digested fod-
der in the inwards of animals', NIcel. *gor* 'cud; chyme', Swed.
gorr, går 'pus; contents of the stomach', Norw. *gor* 'mud,
slime; chyme', OHG. *gor* 'Mist, Dünger', NHG. Swiss *gur*
'frischer Kot des Rindviehs', MLG. *gore* 'Mistpfütze', MDu.
gore, goor 'filth, slime; fishroe; mire, marsh', *goor* 'filthy',
etc., Germ. **gura-* 'wet, moisture, slime', etc.

These words are referred in Fick III⁴, 128 f. to a Germ.
root *ger-* '(warm sein) gähren'. Cf. Schade, *Wb.*², 341 f.;
Franck, *Et. Wb.*² 201. But the words that may properly
be referred to a Germ. **ger-* 'gähren' differ in meaning from
Germ. **gura-* of the above, though, no doubt, the various
derivatives of these two bases as well as others from the root
*jes- 'gähren' were more or less confused.

Germ. **gura-* 'wet, moisture, slime', etc. may come from
pre-Germ. **ĝhu-ro*, root **ĝheu-* 'giessen': Gr. χῡμός 'juice,
liquid; taste', whence late Lat. *chȳmus* 'the fluid of the
stomach', NE. *chyme* (:NIcel, *gor* 'chyme'), Gr. χῡλός 'juice,
moisture; juice drawn out by digestion, chyle; flavor, taste';
Goth. *giutan* 'giessen'; ON. *giósa* 'gush forth', Norw. *gysja*
'slime, mud; wind with rain or snow', *gyrja* 'slime, mud; wet
weather'; *gor* 'slime, mud; chyme', *gora* 'eat gluttonously',
gurma 'make muddy; eat continuously, munch', *gyrma* 'sedi-
ment, dregs; slime, mud; cloudiness', etc.

15. MLG. *gore* 'Gährung und der sich dabei entwickelnde
starke Geruch', MDu. *gore, geure* 'fragrance, odor', *goren*
'emit odor', Du. *geur* 'Duft, Wohlgeruch', *geuren* 'duften;
prunken' may represent Germ. **gur-* in the above or **guz-,*

geus-; early Du. *guysen* 'effluere cum murmure seu strepitu', ON. *giósa* 'spout, gush out', *gusa* 'gush, spurt out', Norw. *gusa* 'blow gently', *gosa* 'breeze, gust; babble', *gose* 'stream of air or vapor', *gøysa* 'bubble, effervesce; babble', *gøysen* 'boastful', etc., root **ĝheu-* also in Norw. *gūva, gjūva* 'rauchen, dampfen', Dan. *gyve* 'dampfen, rauchen, stinken', ON., NIcel. *gufa* 'steam, vapor', *gufa* 'steam, reek', *gubba* 'vomit', Norw. *gauva* 'rauchen; gähren, aufbrausen, schäumen', *gubba* 'dampfen', EFris. *gubbeln* 'brodeln, brausen'. Compare the following.

16. MLG. *gole* 'Sumpf, feuchte Niederung, mit Weiden oder schlechtem Holze bewachsen': (Gr. χῡλός 'juice, moisture'), ON., NIcel. *gola* 'gentle breeze', Shetl. *gol* 'blast', *gula* 'wind', *gola* 'wind, blast; bad weather with heavy wind', Norw. *gol, gul, gola, gula* 'breeze, wind', *gule* 'gust of wind', *gula* 'blow', *gaula* id., *gaul* 'gust of wind; breeze, wind'.

17. OHG. *cheibo*, MHG. *keibe* 'Leichnam, Aas; Viehseuche; Mensch, der den Galgen verdient', NHG. Als. *keib* 'Aas; schlechtes Pferd, magere Kuh; Schuft, Schelm (grobes Schimpfwort)', Loth. *keib* 'Schelm, Schuft; Sonderling', MHG. *keibic* 'pestilens', Als. *keibig* 'in Folge von schlechter Behandlung struppig; elend, schlecht', *verkeiben* 'verhunzen, verderben; verleumden; verschwenden', etc., may be referred to ON. *keifr* 'schief, krumm', Norw. *keiv* id., *keiva* 'make crooked; sway', *keiva* 'left hand', Swed. dial. *kēva* id., LG. *kippen* 'wanken, schwanken, umwerfen', etc.

The primary meaning is therefore 'sway, bend; droop, give way, perish', etc. So we may further compare Lett. *ǧibt, ǧeibt* 'ohnmächtig, schwindelig werden', *gaiba* 'Faslerin, Törin', and also *gibt* 'sich bücken' (cf. Trautmann, *KZ.* XLII, 372).

The following, which according to Berneker, *Et. Wb.* 373, belong to a Slav. base **gyb-, *gub-,* may in part represent a root **geib(h)-*: Serb. *is-po-gíbati* 'umkommen, fallen (von einer Menge)', *gïnuti* 'zugrundegehen, dahinschwinden', *põgībao* 'Verderben', Slav. *gíniti* 'dahinschwinden', *iz-gíbati* 'verschwinden', Pol. *ginąć* 'verloren gehen, verschwinden': OBulg. *gybati* 'zugrunde gehen, verderben', *prě-gybati* 'beugen', etc.

18. NE. *cozy* 'snug, comfortable, warm, social', *sb.* 'a kind of padded covering or cap put over a teapot to keep the tea warm', *coze* 'be snug, comfortable, or cozy, cuddle', *coze* 'anything snug, comfortable, or cozy; a cozy conversation' (in this sense probably influenced by Fr. *causerie*), Scotch *cosh* 'neat, snug, quiet, comfortable', and also ME. *cosche*, NE. dial. *cosh* 'a cottage, hovel' belong to a Germ. base **keus-* 'curve, bend; bend down, cuddle, snuggle; bend out, swell': ON. *kióss* 'Höhlung, Bucht', ESwed. dial. *kusa* 'inner corner of the eye; blister, eruption', *kusa* 'swell, cause to puff up', Norw. dial. *kūsa* 'bunch of flowers, cluster of trees', *kos, kosa* 'heap, pile', *kysja* 'mass, heap', *kause* 'a little pompous person', *kausen* 'pompous, important', *køysa* 'a heavy, clumsy thing or person'.

These and other related words have a wide variety of meaning, but they can all be combined under the primary meaning 'bend down, in, out'. Compare the following.

19. OS. *kūsko* adv. 'mit Anstand', MLG. *kūsch* 'keusch', MDu. *cuusch*, Du. *kuisch* 'reinlich, sittsam, keusch', OHG. *kūski* 'sobrius, pudicus, honestus, modestus', *kūsko* 'caste, honeste, sobrie, parce', MHG. *kiusche* 'keusch, rein, unschuldig, sittsam, schamhaft; mässig im Essen u. Trinken; ruhig, sanftmütig', NHG. *keusch* 'chaste, pure, modest', Tirol. 'zart, zierlich, hübsch', Bav.-Austr. 'dünn, fein, zart, schwächlich' (ch. Kluge, *Et. Wb.* s. v.), Steir. 'schlank, schmächtig, schwach, zart, dünn, fein, leicht verletzbar' (Unger-Khull 385).

These words are explained in Kluge, *Et. Wb.*, and Weigand[5] as meaning primarily 'rein'. But how could such meanings as 'schlank, schmächtig, schwach, dünn, zart, fein', etc., come from 'rein'? The primary meaning was rather 'bending, yielding, retiring', hence 'modest, chaste; gentle; delicate, dainty; weak, soft', etc.

Compare Scotch *cosh* 'neat, snug, quiet, comfortable', NE. *cozy* 'snug, comfortable, warm', etc. (No. 18), Norw. dial. *kusa* 'bend down', root **gŭ-, *geu-*: MHG. *kūme* 'dünn, schwach, gebrechlich', OHG. *chūmīg* 'schwach, kraftlos', OE. *cȳme, cȳmlic* 'zierlich, lieblich', NE. *comely* 'handsome, graceful' (which has been crossed with meanings belonging to *become*).

20. ESwed. dial. *krasa* 'grabbing hand or fist', *krasa* 'card, grab, gather' belong to the Germ. root **kras-* 'draw together,

press, clutch', etc. Norw. dial. *krasa* 'press, crush; cluster, form in clusters', *krase* 'bunch, cluster; a scraggly tree or limb with crooked twigs', to which are related OBulg. *groznŭ grozdŭ*, Russ. *grozdŭ* 'Büschel, Traube, Weintraube', etc., root, **ger-* in Gr. ἀγείρω 'gather' etc. (author, *Zfvgl-Sprachf.* XLV, 63). To the same enlarged root **geres-* belong also the following words, which correspond in meaning with the above: OBulg. *grŭstĭ*, Russ. *gorst'* 'handful, hollow hand' (Brugmann, *Grdr.* I,[2] 453, 572), Gr. ἀγοστός 'hand' (*ἀγορστός, Solmsen, *Beitr. z. gr. Wtf.* I, 1 ff., 17).

21. ON. *loppa* 'big, clumsy hand', NIcel. *loppa* 'paw, hand', are from Germ. **lumpōn-* 'lump', and related to the following: ON., NIcel. *loppinn* 'with hands benumbed with cold', Norw. *loppen* 'benumbed, stiff in the fingers with cold', Wfal. *lumpen* 'plump, gross; matt, steif von Kälte', EFris. *lump* 'lumpig, plump, dick; klotzig, grob', *lump(e)* 'Lumpe', Du. *lomp* 'Lappen, Lumpen, Klumpen', NE. *lump* 'Klumpen', Norw. *lopputt* 'uneven, lumpy', *lepputt* id., NE. *limp* 'schlaff herabhängend', *vb.* 'hinken', etc. For other related words cf. Walde, *Et. Wb.*[2] 431, Fick III,[4] 363.

22. NE. *pit* 'hole, cavity, depression', OE. *pytt* 'pit; grave; pond; pustule' represent two distinct words: Lat. *puteus* 'well, pit' and a Germ. **putja-*: OE. *pyttan* 'dig, prod', *pyttede* 'pitted, marked with hollows (of sword)', *potian* 'but, gore; prog, prod', NE. dial. *pote* 'push, kick; plait; creep about listlessly or moodily, poke', NE. *put* 'place, deposit; (Sc.) cast, throw', Norw. *pota* 'stick, bore, poke; dig in the ground; knit in a certain manner (in this sense also *poda*); stop, stuff, cram', Swed. *påta* 'stochern, wühlen', etc.: OE. *pūnian* 'pound (in mortar)', ME. *pounen*, NE. *pound*, etc. Cf. *IE. a^x* 50 f.

23. OE. *gerāwende* 'dividing, cutting', occurring once in a gloss, may be compared with WFlem, *reeuwen* 'bederven, schenden, zwaarlijk beschadigen', 'gâter, abîmer', *op-reeuwen* 'verwoesten, schenden en scheuren', 'ravager', and referred to Germ. **raigw-*: OE. *rāw, rǣw* 'row', MHG. *rīhe, rīge*, OHG. *rīga* 'Reihe, Linie', Skt. *rēkhā* 'Riss, Strick, Linie, Streifen, Reihe', *rikháti* 'ritzt', Lith. *rëkiu* 'schneide (Brot); pflüge zum ersten Mal', etc. (Cf. Zupitza, *Germ. Gutt.* 67 f. with lit.).

Here also belong the following: Du. dial. Hageland. *rije*
'pflügen' (Tuerlinchx 526), WFlem. *inrien, -rijden* 'met den
ploeg inrooien, inakkeren', 'plow in', *omrien* 'die bovenkorst
van eenen akker met den ploeg scheuren en breken, ombeeren,
slooven', 'déchaumer', *oprien* 'diep omploegen om te zaaien of
to planten, opeeren': (Lith. *rēkiu* pflüge zum ersten Mal),
rien 'wühlen', 'van mollen die onder de oppervlakte van den
grond zich eene pijp wroeten; eene prikkeling in de neus ver-
wekken, sprek. van goed levendig bier' (De Bo-Samyn 406,
667, 694, 813; Schuermans 540).

The forms with *d* are due to false association with *rien,
rijden* 'ride'.

24. OE. *ropp* 'intestine, colon', ME. *rop* (pl. *roppes*)
'intestines', MDu. *rop, roppe* 'entrails of an animal, fish-
entrails' are, so far as I know, unexplained. They probably
belong to MDu., MLG. *roppen* 'rupfen', MHG. *ropfen, rupfen* 'rupfen, zausen, zupfen, pflücken', Goth. *raupjan* 'rupfen', etc. For meanings compare NE. *pluck* 'a pull, tug: the
heart, liver, and lungs or lights of a sheep, ox, or other animal
used as butchers' meat'.

25. Goth. *skōhs* 'Schuh', ON. *skór*, OE. *scōh*, OHG. *scuoh*,
etc. represent a Germ. **skōha-*, the primary meaning of which
was probably 'clump, clog'. This primary meaning is indicated by MHG. *schuoch-bein* 'Wade', i. e. 'bulge-leg'. Compare ON. *skógr* (clump) 'wood; bush', OE. *scaga* 'copse',
ON., NIcel. *skaga* 'jut out, project', *skagi* 'cape, headland,
promontory', Norw. dial. *skaa* 'schief', MHG. *schœhe*
'schielend'.

These may be related to OBulg. *skokŭ* 'Sprung', *skočiti*
'springen', MHG. *schehen* 'eilen', etc. (Cf. Zupitza, *Gutt.*
154). This brings us to the connection made by Uhlenbeck,
Et. Wb.², 134: Goth. *skōhs* etc.: OHG. *scehan*, OBulg. *skokŭ*,
etc.

These may be referred to a root **skhĕk-*, with which compare **skheng-* in Skt. *khañjati* 'hinkt', Gr. σκάζω 'limp', ON.
skakka, skekkia, 'schief machen', *skakkr* 'hinkend, schief',
Dan. *skank* 'lahm': OE. *scanca* 'shank, leg', MHG. *schenkel,
schinke* 'Schenkel, Schinken', etc. (author, *IF.* XVIII, 27).

26. MHG. *schedel* 'Schädel; Trockenmass', early NHG.
also *hirn-scheitel*, MDu. *schedel, scheel* 'lid; eyelid; skull',
Du. *schedel* 'cover, lid, bowl', MLG. *schedel* 'Büchse, Dose',
schidele 'Behältnis, Kiste' point to a primary meaning 'something round' and may be referred to OHG. *sceida* 'Schwert-
scheide', OS. *skēðia*, OE. *scǣþ*, ON. *skeiðer* 'sheath', Swed.
skida 'Scheide; Schote, Hülse'.

With these compare OIr. *scíath*, Welsh *ysgwyd*, OBret, *scoit*
'shield', OBulg. *štitĭ* id., and perhaps Lat. *scūtum* 'shield'
(cf. Fick II,[4] 309), primarily 'disk, Scheibe': OIr. *scíath*
'shoulderblade', Welsh *ysgwyd* 'humerus'.

27. OE. *wearte* 'wart', ON. *varta*, OHG. *warza* 'Warze',
etc., represent pre-Germ. *$uordon$-, -$\bar{a}$- 'swelling', with which
we may compare Slav. *$verd\breve{u}$ 'Geschwür' in Pol. *wrzod*,
Czech *vřed*, ChSl. *vrĕdŭ*, Russ. *véredŭ*, etc. These are referred by Mikkola, *Urslav. Gram.* 94, to Lat. *varus* 'blotch,
pimple', Lith. *vìras*, Ir. *ferb* 'Finne', but without mentioning
the Germ. words. For other related Germ. words cf. *MLN.*
XXIX, 72.

FRANCIS A. WOOD.

University of Chicago.

DAS SCHALLANALYTISCHE VERHÄLTNIS VON GOTTFRIEDS VIERZEILERN ZU DEN ERZÄHLENDEN PARTIEN DES "TRISTAN."

Sievers konstatiert in seinem Aufsatz "Zu Wernhers Marienliedern" [1] p. 13 ff. einen prinzipiellen rhythmisch-melodischen Gegensatz zwischen den Vierzeilern in Gottfrieds "Tristan" und den gewöhnlichen Reimpaaren des Gedichts. Die knappe Schallanalyse, die er mit den damals noch wenig ausgebildeten Mitteln seiner neuen Kritik an zwei entsprechenden Belegpartien anstellte, ist immerhin ausreichend, diesen Gegensatz erkennbar zu machen. Worum es sich für mich also allein handelt, ist die Auffassung der Differenz. Sievers glaubt, es verhalte sich damit *genau so* wie in Schillers "Glocke" mit dem rhythmisch-melodischen Gegensatz zwischen den Strophen, die sich auf den Glockenguss beziehen und den betrachtenden Strophen. Da die Neudrucke in den "Rhythmischmelodischen Studien" Umarbeitungen prinzipiell ausschliessen, ist es leider unmöglich zu sagen, ob Sievers an seinem Standpunkt noch jetzt festhalten würde. Ich jedenfalls gewann, anders als er, bei unbefangenem Lesen des Tristan den Eindruck, als stellten die Vierzeiler nur eine besondere Unterart der gewöhnlichen Gottfriedischen Verse dar, deren von diesen abweichende Rhythmik und Melodik sich bei den gegebenen Umständen erst sekundär im Dichter ergeben musste; bei Schiller dagegen—das wird man zugeben—haben wir ganz generell absolut und bewusstermassen verschieden gebaute Verse vor uns, worüber also für unsre Zwecke keine Untersuchung weiter nötig ist. Zur Erhärtung meiner Ansicht über Gottfried lege ich nun die folgenden Untersuchungen vor. Dass eine befriedigende Lösung der Aufgabe, die ich mir gestellt, auch zur Klärung unsres prinzipiellen Standpunkts mittelalterlicher Rhythmik und Melodik gegenüber ihr Teil beitragen würde, gedenke ich am Schlusse zu zeigen.

Worauf es Sievers bei der ganzen Erörterung offenbar besonders ankommt, ist die Verdeutlichung des Unterschieds

---

[1] Zuerst erschienen in der "Festgabe für Hildebrand" 1894, wiederabgedruckt in Sievers' "Rhythmisch-Melodischen Studien", Heidelberg, 1912 (wonach ich zitiere).

von dipodischem und podischem Versbau (vgl. a. a. o. p. 15).
Nach ihm sind also Gottfrieds Vierzeiler in Dipodien geschrieben (doch vgl. die Einschränkung p. 15, zweite Hälfte),
wogegen die gewöhnlichen Reimpaare in dem a. a. o. p. 13
unten gegebenen Sinne podisch gebunden wären. Mir scheint
es wesentlich, dass man die Untersuchung von der Behandlung
der wirklich erzählenden Partien des Gedichts ausgehen lässt,
die des Erzählers natürlichste Art der Versifizierung doch
jedenfalls darbieten; ich wähle daher den Anfang des eigentlichen Epos, v. 243 ff.

Es kann kein Zweifel sein, dass die eben zitierte Sievers'-
sche Charakterisierung der Reimpaarverse als podisch auch
hier im grossen Ganzen ihre Geltung hat: in v. 243 haben wir
nur eine rhythmisch ausgezeichnete Hebung *(-nî-)*, ebenso in
v. 244 *(kint)*, v. 251 *(fröu-)*, v. 258 *(al)* usw.; in v. 247
dagegen zwei *(-bür-* und *kün-)*, ebenso in v. 248 *(lan-* und
für-), sowie in den vv. 254-257 (wo die Notierung wohl klar
ist); in v. 249 schliesslich tritt nur die letzte der vier Hebungen zurück; die nun bis v. 259 noch übrigen Verse sind
dagegen rhythmisch rein monopodisch, d. h. ihre Hebungen
sind unter sich gleichwertig (v. 245, 246, 250, 252, 253, 259).
Wir haben also bereits in diesem kurzen Abschnitt eine überaus grosse Mannigfaltigkeit der Betonungsformen, und Stich-
proben würden leichtlich deren Anwesenheit über das ganze
Gedicht hin ergeben. Gleichwohl ist eins wohl allen diesen
Versen gemeinsam: man wird die Druckabstufungen der Hebungen nie zu stark ausprägen dürfen, wenn anders der
leichte Plauderton des Gottfriedischen Stils nicht ohne weiteres verloren gehen soll.

Nun fragt es sich aber doch, ob das immer so der Fall ist.
Schon bei den vv. 247-48, 254-57 kann man wohl eine deut-
lichere Kontrastierung zwischen ''stärker'' and ''schwächer''
eintreten lassen, noch eher bei v. 271 oder v. 365; man muss
es aber m. E. unbedingt bei Versen wie 320-21, wenn der
Hörer richtig auffassen soll. Man mag einwenden, der Unterschied sei eben nur graduell; wir werden aber noch sehen, ob
er nicht ganz ebenso gross ist wie der zwischen gewöhnlichen
Reimpaaren und Vierzeilern überhaupt! Wenn wir, die Tat-

sache zunächst zugegeben, nämlich untersuchen, was diese
Dipodien verursacht hat, so finden wir in den angeführten
Beispielen, und zumal in v. 320-21, stets irgend eine Sinnes-
kontrastierung, eine Pointierung, ein Wortspiel. In der Natur
der Sache liegt es dann in der deutschen Sprache, dass je
ein Wort, bzw. seine Tonsilbe, auf beiden Seiten der Gegen-
überstellung einen starken Nachdruck auf sich zieht, die je
übrig bleibende Hebung also rhythmisch zurücktritt—: die
Dipodie ist fertig, wenigstens eine äusserliche. Lässt sich
zeigen, dass die Dipodien der Vierzeiler auf gleiche Weise
entstanden sind, so ist der prinzipielle Gegensatz zwischen
ihnen und Gottfrieds Reimpaarvers in der Hauptsache be-
seitigt.

Vergleichen wir nun also speziell Tristan, v. 1-44. Sievers
setzt für diese Verse (a. a. o. p. 15, zweite Hälfte) ''eine
etwas gekünstelte Abart des alten [dipodischen] Verses'' an,
jedenfalls also doch Dipodien, wozu auch seine Notierungen
p. 13 stimmen. Es kann aber kaum ein Zweifel sein, dass
wir in v. 2, 4, 16, 24, 29, 42 ganz solche rhythmischen Mono-
podien vor uns haben, wie z. B. in v. 245-46. Es zeigt sich
nun, dass gerade diese Verse aus den Kontrastierungen, die
hier allemal eine ganze Strophe durchlaufen, zwar nicht dem
Wortmaterial, wohl aber dem Sinne nach herausfallen: in
der ersten Strophe besteht ein innerer Gegensatz schlechterdings nur zwischen v. 1 und v. 3, während v. 2 und v. 4
nur nähere Zusätze zu gewissen Wörtern in jenen bringen,
die für den Satz wohl, nicht aber für die Pointe nötig sind;
v. 16 gibt eine zwar gut passende, aber keineswegs mehr
notwendige Einschränkung zum vorhergehenden Verse, und
wiederum ohne jeden inneren Gegensatz; ähnlich liesse sich
die mangelnde Dipodisierung der übrigen genannten Verse
erklären. Wir haben also nicht nur Dipodien in Gottfrieds
Reimpaarversen gefunden, sondern finden nun auch Mono-
podien unter seinen Vierzeilern! Daraus geht hervor: erst-
lich, Gottfried schreibt podisch, oder gar monopodisch, wo
er einfach erzählt oder beiläufig erklärt; er wird dagegen
sofort dipodisch, wo er begrifflich zu kontrastieren, zu poin-
tieren hat.

Sievers führt nun noch mehr Unterschiede zwischen dem Vierzeilervers und den Reimpaarvers an: zunächst hält er das Tempo bei jenen für schneller als im Erzählervers. Seine Ausführungen dazu p. 16 sind zwar im Prinzip sicher richtig, aber nur, insoweit nicht etwas Drittes noch störend einwirkt, und das scheint mir in Gottfrieds Vierzeilern das deutlich ausgeprägte deiktische Element in der Tat zu tun, so dass die beiden resp. Tempi hier zusammenfallen dürften. Ausserdem will mir hier das Argument nicht einleuchten, in den Senkungen ständen "nur sprachlich ganz unbetonte Silben" (a. a. o. p. 13): wie sollten dann die "schwebenden Betonungen" in v. 17, 21 (zweimal), 24(?), 25, 33, 37, 40, 41 verstanden werden?, wo doch ein schnelleres Tempo unfehlbar zu "versetzten Betonungen" und damit zu völliger Ruinierung der Versmelodie führen müsste. Mir will darum fast scheinen, Sievers habe bei seinen Ausführungen p. 16 weniger an Gottfried als etwa an den streng und ursprünglich dipodischen Wolfram von Eschenbach gedacht, für den alles dort Gesagte genau stimmen würde.

Sehen wir uns nun nämlich die Gottfriedischen Dipodien noch einmal näher an. Sievers sagt selbst, worauf schon hingewiesen wurde (a. a. o. p. 15, Mitte), in Gottfrieds Vierzeilern, die "schon eine etwas gekünstelte Abart des alten Verses darstellen", trete die Verbindung zweier Füsse zu einer höhern Einheit, eben der Dipodie, "nicht so klar hervor wie anderwärts"; und mit Recht. Das nämlich ist der einschneidende Unterschied zwischen diesen Dipodien und z. B. denen bei Wolfram: die Gottfriedischen Dipodien sind weder in den Reimpaaren noch hier als ein Residuum oder eine Wiederaufnahme älterer Technik aufzufassen, ja sie sind nicht einmal aus einem primären rhythmischen Erlebnis entstanden zu denken. Vielmehr ist, in den Vierzeilern wie sonst, Gottfrieds Erlebnis *virtuell* nur podisch, und erst seine Spielerei mit Worten und Begriffen, die hier in den meisten Versen je zwei Tonsilben stark nachdrücklich herauspresst, verursacht den Anschein eines Dipodisierens. Das aber ist keine Frage, dass dabei das gedankliche Element im Dichter eher vorhanden war als die Rhythmisierung davon, dass der

dipodische Rhythmus hier also als etwas Sekundäres und daher
"Gekünsteltes" zu fassen ist. Man mag einwenden, auch in den
erzählenden Partien müsse doch Gottfried wissen was er schreiben wolle, ehe er wirklich schreibe; gewiss, er kennt seinen Stoff,
aber hier nicht nach Begriffen geordnet, sondern nach Phanta-
sie-Vorstellungen, und während sich beim Überwiegen des Be-
grifflichen unabweislich das begriffliche Element den Rhythmus unterwirft, schieben sich hier die andrängenden sprach-
lichen Äquivalente der Phantasievorstellungen ganz simultan
in das rhythmisch-melodische Schema des Schaffenden ein,
wobei natürlich der Dichter bei mehreren sich darbietenden
und dem Sinne nach gleich brauchbaren Worten dasjenige
auswählen wird, das sich seiner Rhythmik und Melodik am
besten einfügt (vgl. Sievers, a.a.o. p. 16, zweite Hälfte). Das
Erlebnis als solches ist aber auch bei Gottfried virtuell ein-
heitlich.

Damit wäre ein Sachverhalt festgestellt, der sich von dem
in Schillers "Glocke" prinzipiell doch erheblich unterscheidet,
und es ist ersichtlich, dass man auch nur *illustrando* jenen
Vergleich lieber nicht wiederholen sollte, denn er ist geeignet,
unsre Vorstellungen vom innern Schaffen unserer mittelalterlichen Dichter zu verwirren. Dazu sei nun dieses bemerkt, wodurch die ganze Untersuchung, bei mir begreif-
licherweise nichts so fern gelegen als eine Art Polemik gegen
meinen verehrten Lehrer, vielleicht erst einigen Wert erhält.

Sievers hat von vornherein seine epochemachenden Ent-
deckungen als Hilfsmittel zur philologischen Kritik verwandt.
Es fragt sich, ob ein Gelehrter, dessen spezielles Arbeitsgebiet die moderne Literatur wäre, so leicht die gleiche kühne
Folgerung gezogen hätte. Bei manchen Dichtern auch unsrer
Zeit hört man zwar die Autorschaft oft unschwer heraus,
z. B. bei Heines Vierzeilern. Derselbe Heine aber hat die
"Nordseebilder" geschrieben—in freien Rhythmen. Auf
die unendliche Mannigfaltigkeit Goethes in gedachter Beziehung braucht man nur hinzuweisen. Es wird nun behauptet, für das Mittelalter, d. h. das *deutsche* Mittelalter,
läge die Sache anders. Was berechtigt uns zu solcher Annahme? Sievers (a. a. o. pp. 17, 71, 96 und 97) konsta-

tiert nur die Tatsache auf Grund experimenteller Nachprüfung und hält den Umstand für "höchst merkwürdig" und "an sich in keiner Weise theoretisch notwendig." Dem gegenüber möchte ich darauf hinweisen, dass es doch wohl nötig ist, die Entwicklung des rhythmisch-melodischen Erlebnisses in der deutschen Dichtung ganz genau so in den Gang unsrer allgemeinen inneren Kulturentwicklung einzubeziehen wie etwa die Entwicklung des Erlebnisses in Ornamentik und Malerei. Ebensowenig wie wir einen Rembrandt im XII. Jh. erwarten können, ebensowenig einen Dichter von der rhythmisch-melodischen Ausdrucksfülle moderner Zeiten,—was natürlich nur als Vergleich, nicht als Beweis gemeint ist. Gerade das Gegenbeispiel der provenzalischen Dichtung des Mittelalters, das Sievers p. 71 anführt, erläutert meinen Gesichtspunkt, denn die Provence, alter Boden des *imperium Romanum* in der Antike, war Deutschland damals kulturell überhaupt um Jahrhunderte voraus. Diese Sachlage dürfte uns also auch wohl die grosse Einförmigkeit erklären, die die Schallanalyse für unsre mittelhochdeutschen Dichter ergibt, und die uns berechtigt, schallanalytische Kriterien auch zur Textkritik zu verwenden.

Doch ist ersichtlich, dass Beispiele wie Gottfrieds, wenn auch, wie Sievers konstatiert, "eine grosse Seltenheit" (a. a. o. p. 17), alle so gewonnenen Ergebnisse stark in Frage stellen könnten. Als Hauptgewinn meiner Arbeit würde ich also ansehen gezeigt zu haben, dass sich bei sorgfältiger Anwendung der neuen Methoden Schwierigkeiten gedachter Art sehr wohl und zwanglos beseitigen lassen, so dass wir hoffen können, auch das grösste rhythmisch-melodische Problem unsres Mittelalters, Walther von der Vogelweide, noch zu lösen.

H. W. NORDMEYER.

Ohio State University.

THE ANALYTIC AGENT IN GERMANIC

1. In the morphological classification of languages, as distinct from their geneological aspect, the concept of Analysis has with the lapse of time undergone a thoroughgoing modification. From being regarded as a highly regrettable organic degeneration, this gradual discarding of the older inflectional accretions in favor of single word-forms qualified by a series of prepositions and auxiliaries, is now considered by every advanced philologist to have been a decided progress in language. This much must however even now be emphasized: the analytic process is not to be thought of as a providential blessing in disguise. That quality of free and easy combination of short linguistic units which sets modern English, for instance, at a radical variance with the frequently unwieldy vocables of the classical tongues, would never have evolved from the older synthetic prototypes, had not time and place both been propitious and necessary for such alteration. Call Analysis an 'economy of expression' or a 'law of specialization,' [1] it is simply a species of linguistic struggle for existence, a natural tendency to secure greater ease and precision in discourse and document.

2. A single glance at the declensional apparatus of Old English will bring home the ineffectiveness of a system where there is not only an absence of that rigid application of a given suffix to a given idea which characterizes Latin in the large, but even the possibility exists of a definite case-function being expressed at the same moment by various conflicting devices. In Latin itself declension by the modification of final syllables proved in time equally wanting, and this not alone for the commonly assigned grounds of phonetic corruption and analogic instinct, but rather because the available case-forms were too few in number to express all the relations natural to the human mind,—a feat, it will be recalled, which even Indo-Iranian with eight cases failed of performing. For the resulting incongruities Language offered that spontaneous tendency toward its combined ideal of least resistance and greatest efficiency, which we call Anal-

[1] Bréal, *Essai de Sémantique*, Chap. I.

ysis. More specifically, in the field of noun-accidence prepositions were resorted to in place of the confused case-terminations, and self-sufficient constants substituted for dependent variables.

3. Nor is there need to conjure up a mental picture of a mad scurry on the part of devoted linguists, at the very end of their synthetic resources, to discover new devices that might replace case-forms destroyed through popular ignorance. The history of Latin demonstrates that analysis is possible at the very period a language is enjoying the Golden Age of its literature and that, when the terminations are finally set aside altogether, it is for the reason that they had long outgrown their serviceability. So that if in expressions like *ad Rōmam* and *dē Rōmā*, GREGORY OF TOURS felt the full force resident in the prepositions, it is no wonder that he did not keep the endings distinct, nor that he often joined *cum* to the accusative and *per* to the ablative.[2] In the Germanic dialects such a natural reduction of the original case-forms, followed at first by the customary amalgamation of case-functions, and then by the employment of prepositions, must have occurred sometime during the period antedating their literatures, for in the latter the predominant mode of denoting syntactic relations is the analytic. At the side of modal and material instrumentals, for example, which persist longest in use, we find in the earliest documents prepositional locutions of all kinds displacing synthetic equivalents. The preposition thus becomes a pivotal point in the further development of these dialects.

4. The Agent, i. e. the person functioning as the logical subject of passive expressions, seems to have been one of the first categories in Germanic to require the elucidative services of prepositions. Altogether there are but spare remnants in WULFILA, the BEOWULF and the EDDIC poems of that prepositionless form of agency which, judging by the testimony of related Indo-European languages, must have been characteristic of the older stages of the Germanic dialects. But even these remnants furnish a sufficient and con-

---

[2] Bonnet. *Le Latin de Gregoire de Tours*, Paris, 1890, p. 521 ff.

clusive evidence. A few examples are given here: GOTHIC
—*Mt.* 6, 16, *ei gasaihvaindau mannam fastandans* ὅπως φανῶσιν
τοῖς ἀνθρώποις νηστεύοντες; *Rom.* 7, 10 *bigitana warþ mis anabusns
χαì εὑρέθη μοι ἡ ἐντόλη; Mk.* 10, 12 *jah liugada anþaramma
χαì γαμηθῇ ἄλλῳ.* ANGLO-SAXON, with suitable emendations offered or adopted,—BEOW. l. 12 *þǣm eafera wæs
æfter cenned geong in geardum,* 1068 *Finnes eaferum hæleð
Healf-Dena feallan scolde,* 2957 *þā wæs ǣht boden Sweona
lēodum, segn Higelāce;* CÆDMON, *Gen.* 1765 *fromcynne
folde weorðeð þine gefylled; Sat.* 558 *þā wæs on eorðan ēce
drihten folgad folcum; Dan.* 92 *metode gecorene,* 150 *se wæs
drihtne gecoren.* OLD NORSE—EDDA, *Vm.* 25, 2 *vas
Nǫrvi borin, HH.* II 8, 6 *því vas . . . . . mér litt steikt
etit, Ghv.* 10, 2 *vask þrimr verum vegin at húsi, Hm.* 7, 2
ofnar vǫlundum, and numerous examples in the prose and
poetic literature before the preposition *af* finally obtained
full sway. For OLD HIGH GERMAN, besides OTFR. 1,
5, 23 *thū scalt beran einan . . . . . fatere giboranan
ebanēwigan,* only few parallels can be drawn upon with any
degree of confidence, cf. §37 ff.

5. These and similar instances, the character of whose
datival forms had not before been deciphered with satisfaction
—the general opinion held of them being that they all were,
in and for themselves, a mere subtype of the dative of personal
interest, despite the fact that there were found certain well-defined examples which even on the closest scrutiny refused to reveal a connotation of '*commodi vel incommodi*'—the writer collected and discussed elsewhere.[3] As will be seen by reference
to the pages cited, an attempt was made there to define and
delimit the nature of this hitherto neglected functional type
of the Germanic dative and to locate its provenience on the
basis of such cognate languages as Indo-Iranian, Balto-Slavic,
Latin and Greek; accordingly a distinction was drawn in
theory and practice between the real dative of agency that
could reasonably be traced back to a former dative of interest
and what with due regard to the syncretistic peculiarities of

[3] *The Dative of Agency. A chapter of Indo-European case-syntax.*
Columbia diss. 1913, pp. 81-113.

the Germanic Dative, was termed the dative-instrumental of agency and derived from an original instrumental case expressive of association. The purpose of the present pages is to form a pendant to the larger discussion in the treatment of the later analytic substitutes for these synthetic agents in Germanic.[4]

6. It will not be entirely useless in view of current misconceptions one still encounters in manuals, to preface this account of the exchange of prepositional phrases for the unaided case-forms, with a few words concerning the prepositions themselves. Originally they were merely adverbs, designed to clear up the meaning of the verb through some special explanatory circumstance. The case-form which in later times, after the change of the adverb into a preposition, came to be correlated with the latter, was then as yet actually referred to the predicate and received its fixation directly from its relation to this predicate. Subsequently, by dint of the constant juxtaposition in this triverbal combination, the adverb was placed by the side of the noun—became adnominal—in order to make the force of the substantive itself clearer. Its adverbial quality thus dwindled down in the same proportion as linguistic consciousness came to regard a given function as fully expressible by a given case-form associated with a certain adverb. But this means that the adverb is no longer solely an element that strengthens but one that also determines, 'governs' the case-form. Withal there is a parallel process taking its origin from the whilom close connection existing between verb and noun, in that the same preposition may 'govern' any of the various forms that used to depend on the general meaning of the verb,—witness Greek, where it is often the case that determines the sense of the preposition.

7. That many of the Indo-European languages present the use of prepositional phrases to express agency, is to be expected as a direct product of the analytic tendencies distinguishing them. But, although we are permitted to associate

---

[4] With regard to the method of presentation, the citation in any particular case of but a few instances is intended to convey the writer's satisfaction that such instances are typical enough to need no amplification.

the prepositionless locutions with the older or synthetic stages
of a language, age is merely a relative term. Thus already in
AVESTAN, we find an auctorial preposition like *hača*, which
takes the ablative, originally for the denotation of spatial
origin, acting to all intents like Latin *ab*, as *V.* 19, 6 *barəθryāt
hača zāviši* 'a matre vocatus sum'.[5] LATIN *ab c. ablativo*
goes back to the earliest times. LITHUANIAN *nů* 'from'
with genitive, as in *mótina nů kůdikio mylimà* 'the mother beloved of her child' is again of modern date and may even be a
Germanism, '*von*', imported by bilingual Germans.[6] The corresponding Greek preposition, ὑπό *c. gen.* is Homeric and even
varies with ὑπό *c. dat.* as Π 490 ὑπὸ Πατρόκλῳ κτεινόμενος,—a
dative which has locatival antecedents. On the other hand,
modern English, with a highly analytic character, has not yet
lost all the earmarks of synthesis, cf. the co-existence of the
inflected genitive with the *of*-phrase of possession.

8. The genuine Indo-European dative noun-case does not
seem to have originally been connected with any preposition.
The so-called 'dative' case-forms therefore in Germanic which
we find combined with them must be referred to the locatival,
instrumental or ablatival constituents of said 'dative',—what
is functionally so termed being nothing but an instrumental in
the plural[7] and partly locative, partly instrumental in the singular.[8] (The only Germanic prepositions to be connected
with the real dative force are Pregermanic **nǣhw[ō]*, Got.
nēhv[a], Ags. *nēah*, OHG. *nāh*, and **to*, the latter of which
must have attained its directive force in the dialects themselves
and thus become attached to the dative as the natural case
of reference.) The following is the list of the authorship
prepositions considered in this light, Gothic, Anglo-Saxon,
Old Norse, Old High German and Old Saxon being drawn
upon for illustration:

    (a) PREPOSITIONS OF REST—**bi*, **at*, **in;*

---

[5] Reichelt, *Awestisches Elementarbuch*, p. 276.
[6] Kurschat, *Gramm. d. lit. Sprache*, p. 393.
[7] Streitberg, *Urger. Gramm.* p. 232.
[8] Dieter, *Laut- und Formenlehre*, p. 537.

(b) PREPOSITIONS OF MOTION,

    (1) separation—**fram, *af, *fon(a), *uz;*

    (2) accompaniment—**miði, *wiþ;*

    (3) direction—**þurh, *to.*

9. A schematic survey of the uses of these particles brings out the fact that GOTHIC employs the prepositions *fram, af, us* and *þairh,* ANGLO-SAXON and ENGLISH *þurh, fram, of, be, æt, with* and *to,* OLD NORSE, regularly *af,* HIGH GERMAN *fon(a),* (OS. *fan[a]*), *duruh* and even *mit.* Of these dialects, Anglo-Saxon and English lend themselves best to the study of auctorial relations, for the reason that, while in Ags., as we have seen, we are still fortunate to find purely inflectional means used for our purpose, the later course of the language is exceptionally rich and varied in the choice of suitable prepositions antedating the modern *by.* The idea of agency itself, as relating to persons, is rare in BEOWULF; passive expressions are frequent enough, but the terseness of the poetic style seems easily able to dispense with such defining elements as agency offers. One important circumstance, however, must be noted, viz. that none of the authorship examples found are of the variety of prepositional locutions; it is only after CÆDMON, notably beginning with CYNEWULF, that the tendency is entirely toward the analytical. So in *Elene,* a typical poem, all personal agency is expressed by *þurh c. acc.,* which in CÆDMON is not yet used in such a sense. Example, *El.* 775, *sē-ðe on rōde wæs ond þurh Marian in middangeard ācenned weard in cildes hād,*—which should illuminate *Beow.* 12, or *El.* 1058 *þurh gāstes gife gecorenne,* which stands in a similar relation to the dative-instrumental in CÆDMON'S *Dan.* 92, cf. §4. This use of *þurh,* certainly a derivative of its function of denoting the intermediate person—the sole one to-day—is at this time distinct as yet from the latter, and expresses the person immediately operative, in the same manner as *by* to-day introduces the logical bearer of the passive action.

10. The persistent force of this preposition carries it in this function well up to Old English. It is a fascinating but also a very intangible pursuit to observe how later Anglo-Saxon—sometimes termed Half-Saxon or Old English—and

Middle English present simultaneously several prepositions
of radically different basic connotation to render this one idea
of agency. Thus, although as late as *Town M.* 282 we find
this dede thrughe God is done, the competition of *fram* dates
back to much earlier times. In BEOWULF, to be sure, *fram*
has only a local signification, as l. 110 *mancynne fram.* Socin's
emendative insertion of *fram* in l. 1068 *Finnes eaferum hæleð
Healf-Dena feallan scolde,* whilst of interest in that the editor
felt the need of some more forceful expression, is out of
question not only because the bare dative-instrumental already
denotes the desired logical subject, but because it would add
to BEOWULF the sole *fram* in the sense of the personal
agent, when diligent search fails to discover it in CÆDMON
and but rarely in CYNEWULF. Thus I cannot consider as
satisfactory the only adducible examples in the latter's *Elene,*
for l. 701 is simple means and 1141 purely locative, 190 *swā
fram Siluestre lærde wæron,* auctorial in intent, permits the
locative force to be still distinctly felt, cf. German 'von
seiten'. There are altogether six other instances in Ags.
poetry, to wit CYNEWULF's *Crist* 1617 *scyle from his
Scyppende āscyred weorðan; Soul and Body* 46 *ic wæs gæst
on þē from gode sended,* is really locatival; BOET. *Metra*
20, 245 *swā him lȳfed wæs from þām ælmihtigan; Psalms*
67, 23 *from þām þine gangas wæron gesewene; ibid.* 113, 23
wesað gē fram gode geblētsade; Pater Noster, 3, 87 *þē fram
wīfe and fram were wurdon ācenned* [9]—which I would, again,
recommend as an aid to the interpretation of Beow. l. 12
þām and 1357 *him.*

11. *Fram,* in turn, receives already in Old English a com-
petitor in *of.* In ÆLFRED, to be sure, *fram* is yet the
rule, as *Be.* 3, 14 *he wæs fram eallum monnum lufad,* 477, 31
Albanus ic eom geciged fram minum yldrum,[10] but *of,* even
as exception, is quite often in evidence, so that there is laid

[9] Cf. pp. 2 and 21, Wullen, *Der synt. Gebrauch der Präpositionen
fram, under, ofer, þurh in d. ags. Poesie.* I. *fram, under.* Diss. Kiel,
1908.

[10] Cf. Harstrick, *Untersuchungen über die Präp. bei Alfred.* Diss.
Kiel, 1890, p. 13.

the beginning of an even fluctuation between the two prepositions. Witness in ÆLFRED himself, *O.* 154, 28 *seo burg wæs getimbred of Læcedemonium*, but *O.* 164, 10 *sio wæs getimbred from Elisan þæm wifmen*, with no perceptible degree of difference. The usage of ÆLFRIC and of the BLICKLING HOMILIES of the 10th century is similar,[11] *Bl. H.* 187, 20 *forþon þu ær gecoren wære fram gode* 'electus es a Domino', cf. CÆDMON, *Dan.* 92 for pure dative-instrumental; ÆLFRIC II, 4, 48 *he wæs gecnyssed fram sumum geþancum*, 'pulsatus est a quibusdam cogitationibus', but *Bl. H.* 233, 26 *ic geseo þæt þas broþor synd geswencede of ðisse sæwe hreonesse.* Only in one instance can we establish a fast demarcation, viz. with verbs of begetting, in that ÆLFRED and ÆLFRIC prefer *of* to the *from* of BL. HOM. So. *Bl. H.* 93, 28 *þæt hi næfre næron acennede from fæder ne from meder*, but ÆLFRED, *Be.* 586, 12 *of Fæder acennedne* and ÆLFRIC I, 10, 2 *hū ure hælend crist acenned wæs of þæm halgan mædenne marian.* It will not be amiss to remember that auctorial *þurh* is at this time still 'constructional', *Bl. H.* 9, 5 *heofonrices duru sceal þurh þe ontened béon.*

12. Certainly less frequently used in Old English than *fram, of*[12] begins to gain ground on the other preposition in SAXON CHRONICLE *E, F* and the interpolations of *A*,[13] so that by CHAUCER and onward *from* falls back exclusively to its original locative signification, as II. 83 *from Pluto sent, at requeste of Saturne; Cov. Myst.* 185 *I am sent fro God;* SHAKSPERE, 3 *Hy* 6, 2, 1 *he was lately sent from your kind aunt.* As a result partly of this restrictive change, we observe *of* gaining the foreground and becoming the predominating auctorial preposition of Middle English, e. g. *Rich. C. de L.* 2596 *he was aspyyd (warnyd) off a spye,* CHAUCER, II.

[11] Cf. Fischer, *Der synt. Gebrauch der Partikeln of und from in Ælfric's Heiligenleben und in den Blickling Homilien,* Diss. Leipzig, 1908.

[12] Reference may be made here to Jacobsen, *Der synt. Gebrauch der präp. for, geond, of und ymb in d. ae. Poesie,* Diss. Kiel, 1908.

[13] Cf. Bødtker, *Critical Contributions to Eng. Syntax,* I. Christiania, 1908, p. 6.

226 *I wolde not of him corretted be*, MAUN. 5 *she was buryed of the aungels.*

13. *By*, the preposition that gained the final upper hand, is rarely found in *ME.;* on the other hand, in *MnE. be* seems to be the regularly employed particle, whilst *of* appears but infrequently. In the *Cov. Myst.* we find both 'his sowle of develis is al to-torn' and 'alle thyng xal be wrowth be me'; MAUNDEV. 15 'that cytee was destroyed by hem of Grece'; CHAUCER, VI. 310 'by the, lady, y-maked is the pes bitwix angelis and man'. The conquest of *by* over *of* and the ever-recurrent *þurh* is well known. What is not so generally dis-seminated, however, is that *by* had two other competitors arrayed against it, namely ME. *with* and ME. *to*. A continu-ant of the OE. *mid* after the latter merged into *wið– *well before CHAUCER, as there is no single instance of *mid* in his works—*with* assumes the force of agency in Middle Eng-lish, as CHAUCER, II, 335 *and whan the bed was with the prest i-blessid,* 184 *that every wight was with the lioun frete,* WYCLIFFE, *Lk.* 7, 24 *reed wawid with the wynd,* Ags. *mid winde.* As for *to*, cf. CHAUCER II. 71 *to whom bothe heven and erthe is seene,* IV. 262 *and his comynge unwiste is tevery* (=to every) *wight*, SHAKSPERE, *I am cabin'd, cribbed, confin'd, bound in to saucy doubts and fears.* The gradual rise of *by* over all these variants and the present restriction of *of* to instances where the verb denotes a perception or knowledge rather than actual activity—so that to-day Shaks-perean 'unwhipped of justice' *As.* II. 1, 50 or 'he is received of the most pious Edward', *H.* 4, 3, being notions of external influence upon the person affected, are as impossible as Frois-sart's *'cil furent encore rencontré de chiaus de Laon'* is in modern French—belong to the domain of more recent syntax.

14. None of the other Germanic dialects present a line of chronological development similar to that we have given in our hasty sketch of ENGLISH. Neither GOTHIC nor OLD HIGH GERMAN evidence any regular progressive tendency in this regard. NORSE has but one auctorial preposition, *af*. This word is not yet found in the Eddic poems in the function of a logical subject of passive verbs. The two ex-amples sometimes cited are unreliable: *Gþr.* II. 34, 2 *þann*

munk kjósa af konungum ok þó af niþjum nauþug hafa can
be with ease interpreted in the light of the original local
signification of the preposition, 'though coerced on the part
of my relatives,' or even causally, 'him will I, even though
constrained, choose among kings and have because of my
relatives'; similarly must be construed *Hdl.* 43, 3, where we
likewise have *af* combined with an adjective, *varþr Loptr
kviþogr af kono illre* 'because of the woman', somewhat like
MHG. *sî wart swanger bî ir bruoder, Greg.* 229. This complete
absence of *af* with passives in the early stage of Norse literature represented by the Edda[14] will rule out, for instance, the
Rask-Copenhagen ed.-Munch-Ettmüller interpretation of the
Cod. Reg. version of *Gþr.* II. 4, 4 *oll voru sopuldýr sveita stok-
kin ok of vaniþ vási und vegondum* as *af vegondum,* or Bugge's
exchange of *af* for *at* in Ls. 34 *gisls um sendr at goðom.* The
unaided dative-instrumental (or the *dat. commodi* > *dat. auc-
toris*) alone expresses agency in the Eddic poems. In the
subsequent literary monuments however *af* is the regular device thus employed, perhaps partly due to Latin influence
filtering down to popular usage through the medium of the
learned style;[15] e. g. *Hom.* 40, 12 *hér doemask opt góðir af
illum, enn í oðru lífi fyridoemask ávalt illir af góðum, Hkr.*
542, 35 *varð mjok búizt af skyndingu, Mariusaga,* 904, 11
hann var þangat færdr af tveim ungum mönnum.— It is in
order now to explain some of the more particular features
of the preceding survey, especially the semantic changes
whereby the various prepositions came to acquire their function
of agency.

15. Too much stress cannot be laid on the fact the personal
agent is merely a derivative of some other functional type
having a basic connotation essentially cognate with its own.
For the synthetic expression of this agent Delbrück has inti-

---

[14] Gebhardt, too, in his *Beiträge zur Bedeutungslehre der altwest-
nordischen Präpositionen, Diss. Leipzig,* 1896, fails to produce any
good example. Surely *Hym.* 38, 5 *hver af hraunbúa hann laun um
fekk,* p. 84, cannot seriously be offered as an instance of personal
agency.

[15] Falk og Thorp, *Dansk-Norskens Syntax,* p. 170.

[16] *Syntaktische Forschungen,* V. 135, and *Vergleichende Syntax,* I. 268.

mated in the case of the Sanskrit *kartar*,[16] that it was from
the instrumental of means with an active verb that the instrumental of agency with the passive had risen, i. e. that to
a great extent the personal agent owes its provenience to the
material instrument with which a deed is accomplished. The
distinction, I imagine, would be somewhat that between living
beings and inanimate objects, since persons as well as objects,
lifeless or personified, may be thought of as instruments of
action, cf. SANSKRIT *agnē jayati tvāyā dhānam* 'he attains
through thee, Agni, all good.[17] That this is quite as logically
permissible in the passive as in the active construction, stands
to reason; so that an example like 'he is praised by the singers'
is but a natural step from 'he is praised with, by words'.

16. That this step is not the only one separating the two
extremes must also be clearly understood. The idea of causality
is so very nearly bound up with that of mere instrumentality
that very often no firm division is possible between them:
a spiritual something, an event, a circumstance, an abstraction
can also serve as the means. In GOTHIC *dauþau afdauþ-
jaidau, Mk.* 7, 10, or HOMERIC φερόμην ὀλοοῖς ἀνέμοισιν, φ 524,
or SLAVIC *trīstī vĕtromŭ dvižema Lk.* 7, 24, χάλαμος ὑπὸ
ἀνέμου σαλευόμενος, we can no more speak of material instrument; they are instances of a dematerialized, personified instrument of action, the nearest step to the personal agent
itself. Other examples may be given, GOTHIC—*gasiglidai
waurþuþ ahmin gahaitis* τῷ πνεύματι τῆς ἐπαγγελίας *Eph.* 1, 13;
ANGLO-SAXON—*Beow.* 3117 *þonne strǣla storm strengum
gebǣded,* (1018 *Heorot innan wæs frēondum āfylled*); OLD
NORSE—*dýrkalfr doggo slungenn, HH.* II. 37, 3, *í garð þanns
skriþinn vas innan ormum* 'perreptatum anguibus', *Akv.* 34, 2.
A series of gradations might then thus be erected.

(a) material means, pure and simple as let us say, LATIN
'*myrto vinctus et ipse caput;*'

(b) personal instrument, intermediary, as '*non per me
nunc hoc locutum*'

(c) personified means, often of causal tenor, as (of Troy)
'*tardaque nocturno tela retexta dolo*';

---

[17] Brugmann, *Grundriss*[2] II, 526.

(d) personal agent, as '*Tros Tyriusque mihi nullo discrimine agetur.*'

It will be seen that in the following discussion the development of the analytic agent may to a great extent be subsumed under this natural scheme.

17. PREPOSITIONS of rest: (1) *bi[18]—GOTHIC *bi*, AGS. *bi, be*, OHG. *bi*; SKR. *abhí*, OBg. *obŭ*—is originally a local preposition denoting proximity. 'at', 'near', 'at the side of', as *Beow.* 2538 *arās bî ronde oretta* 'arose the champion by his shield'. Neither High German nor Gothic seem to have expanded this meaning into agency. Instrumentality in a higher sense may be found in GOTHIC, as 2 *Cor.* 12, 7 *jah bi filusnai andhuleino ei ni ufarhafnau* τῇ ὑπερβολῇ τῶν ἀποκαλύψεων, but I could not locate a personal agent with passives. In HIGH GERMAN, too, there are not only local instances like *Parz.* 310, 11, *si gieng im bî*, but decisively causal relations, *Notker Cap.* 353 *Alcmene in guan be Jove*, *Nib.* 622, 2 *si hete bî Gunther einen sun getragen*, *Wigal.* 1023 *si wart swanger bî im eines kindes,*—ideas since entrusted to 'von', just as English *by* auctorial developed from *by* local. Nor is the intermediate person absent, *Not.* 77, 49 *scaden santa er in be dien tiefelen, Iwein* 132 *si sande bî ir dan vrischiu cleider,* but for a full evolution we must look to English.

18. Einenkel in his *Streifzüge*[19] gives credit to the influence of Old French *par* for the auctorial use of *be*, 'Im AE (he means Anglo-Saxon) ist von diesem Gebrauche kaum ein Spur zu entdecken. Dagegen ist altfranz. *par* im vermittelnden wie unmittelbar ursächlichen sinne sehr gebräuchlich, und daher wird auch wohl der ME. und NE. gebrauch des *by* stammen.' Accordingly an OF. *que ia par toi n'iert reconté, Chev. Lyon* 5127 should be the source of the modern 'it is related by him.' That this view is one-sided, is reasonably well proven by facts bearing upon our above categories. Undeniably Thorpe's insertion of auctorial *bi* into *Beow.* 1068 *Finnes<bi>eaferum hæleð Healf-Dena feallan scolde* is,

---

[18] Of non-Germanic cognates only a few are given, in the Germanic dialects only those discussed are represented.

[19] *Streifzüge durch die me. Syntax*, Münster, 1887, pp. 123 and 132.

as I have elsewhere remarked,[20] entirely premature; at the
same time we find already in Old English (a) *be* used to
designate material and advanced means, *Mt.* 4, 4 *ne leofað se
man be hlāfum ānum, Lk.* 6, 44 *ælc treow ys be his wæstme
oncnāwen,* so *Mt.* 7, 20; then ÆLFRED, *Bo.* 29 *hangað nacod
sweord ofer þam hlāfde be smalan þrǣde,* also *C. P.* 168, 15; *Bl.
Hom.* 101, 5 *gesælig bið mæg hine sylfne be þǣre bysene lǣren,*[21]
161, 5 *be þissum (weorcum) we witan magon,* 209, 35 *be heora
handum gebundene, Cod. Exon.* 118, 23 *bi hwon scealt þu
lifgan, Laȝ.* 10501 *he doeþ þe wel to writen ba bi worden and
bi writen;* (b) despite Einenkel, *op. cit.* p. 131, that *be* is
not found before CHAUCER denoting the personal means,
as in V. 343 *and by the gayler gotten hath a barge,* there are:
ÆLFRIC II. 170, 14[22] *sum eawfæst man sende ðam halgan
were twegen butrucas mid wine to láce be anum cnapan,
Sax. Chron.* E 675 *ðas writ seonde seo papa Agatho . . .
bi Wilfred . . . to Engla lande,* 1095 *be him sende,* 1128
ealle . . . be him senden to Ierusalem, WULFSTAN, *Hom.*
292, 14 *ða sende se ælmihtiga god án ærendgewrit . . .
be anum halgan engle.*[23]   These examples vouch for the
early authenticity of the formula '*sendan be*'; (c) causality,
in ÆLFRED, *Be.* 490, 25 *hi be idlum ðingum weoruldgestreon
sece,* ÆLFRIC, II. 226, 5 *hwilc eower ðreað me be synne?
Bl. Hom.* 202, 2 *hi wiston be þæs engles sægenum* 'by the
angel's promises'.   These three classes naturally connect
themselves with the basic idea of close co-existence by means
of the link 'according to', as in *Sax. Chron.* 634 *se Birinus
com hider be Honorius wordum,* CÆDMON, *Gen. fērde tō
þam lande be his hlāfordes hǣse,* ÆLFRED, *C. P.* 240, 5 *be
ðæm ryhtlice be Judeum wæs gecweðen ðurh ðone witgan;*
(d) there is no lack of examples with verbs of *begetting,* cf. §17,
which border on personal agency, as CÆDMON, *Gen.* 2326 *þu
scealt sunu agan, bearn be bryde þinre,* ÆLFRED, *Or.* 56, 25
bi eallum heora wifum bearna striendon.   (d) Finally we have

<hr/>

[20] *Dative of Agency,* p. 98.

[21] Flamme, *Syntax der Blickling Homilies,* Diss. Bonn, 1885, p. 60.

[22] Cf. Gottweiss, *Die Syntax der Präp. æt, be ymb in den Ælfric-
Homilien, Anglia,* 28, 353.

[23] Cf. Bødtker, *Critical Contributions,* p. 37.

sufficient, though not ample, evidence of the personal agent with passive verbs, CÆDMON, *Gen.* 598 *þæt wurde þegn swā monig forlædd be þam lygenum,*[24] ÆLFRED, *Be.* 637, 3 *be ðisses B.' lifes stealle foreweardum we sculan feawum wordum gemynegan, ða ðe be him gedóne wæron,*[25] both Miller's translation 'what befell him' and Bødtker's[26] 'with regard to' being somewhat gratuitous; ÆLFRIC, I. 518, 31 *þæt is gedón be Godes fadunge,* 487, 17 *be ðam þe is gecweden, Bl. Hom.* 163, 27 *þæt . . . . . þæs bearnes weorþe ongyten wære be þyson eallum oþrum mannum* 'understood by all these other men', although 'measured by, according to, all these men'[27] is not impossible.

19. It will be seen that to assert that the construction was altogether due to borrowing from Old French, is out of question. Anglo-Saxon had a latent capacity for the use of *be* as author's preposition and even attests an actual development of it. If it is a Gallicism, it is such not in the sense that the phrase in question was so alien to the spirit of Ags. that we do not expect to see it where we find it, but rather that a homogeneous French locution might analogically have influenced the larger extension of an already existent and rapidly spreading native construction, sufficient instances of which are lacking either because of the defectiveness or because of the insufficiency of the literary material transmitted to us.[28] The expression is natural enough to have sprung up, with a proper foundation, simultaneously in both languages. On the other hand, Mätzner's statement[29] that the diffusion of *by* as an aid to authorship is to be ascribed to the progressive supersession of the other prepositions—*þurh, fram, of*

[24] Cf. Dusenschön, *Die Präp. æfter, æt und be in der ae. Poesie,* Diss. Kiel, 1907.

[25] Wülfing, II. 338: 'paucis quae sunt gesta memoremus'.

[26] *Op. cit.* p. 37.

[27] Cf. Bødtker, *loc. cit.*

[28] Cf. Jesperson, in *Eng. Studien,* 34, 163 'fürs Altenglische kommt noch in betracht, dass die art der überlieferten texte uns zu der annahme drängt, dass eine ganze menge von den im täglichen leben gewöhnlichsten redewendungen und syntaktischen verbindungen nicht zu uns gekommen ist.'

[29] *English Grammar,* II, 398.

—can be understood much better in the light of acceleration by a similar French model.

20. A suitable support for the evolution of *be* may be found in another preposition of rest, (2) *at,—GOT. and ON. *at*, AGS. *æt*, OHB. *az;* LATIN *ad*. Its fundamental meaning of propinquity, in a less comprehensive degree than that of *be*, is seen in the following, GOTHIC—*so aqizi at waurtim bagme ligiþ* ἡ ἀξίνη πρὸς τὴν ῥίζαν τῶν δένδρων κεῖται, *Lk*. 3, 9; AGS.—*and æt hire heafdan sæt se eadiga Petrus,*[30] *Bl. H*. 145, 26; OLD NORSE—*tveir at hǫfþom*, *Sg*. 66, 3; OHG.—*sitzi azs zesuûn halp miin*. From this local relation we have in ANGLO-SAXON and in GOTHIC *at in the sense of the personal agent. Consider, 1 *Thess*. 4, 9 *unte silbans jus at guda uslaisidai sijuþ* θεοδίδακτοί ἐστε,[31] 1 *Tim*. 6, 5 *at þaimei gatarniþ ist sunja* καὶ ἀπεστερημένων τῆς ἀληθείας, *Lk*. 10, 7 *driggkandans þo at im*, sc. *gibanona* πίνοντες τὰ παρ' αὐτῶν, the *Skeireins* version of *Jh*. 6, 13 *þatei aflifnoda at þaim <matjandam>* τοῖς βεβρωχόσιν. ANGLO-SAXON—*Ælfric*, I, 50, 2 *witodlice Stephanus wæs to diacone gehádod æt ðære apostola handum,*[32] II, 480, 19 *seðe wæs ǽr gebletsod æt þæs apostoles handum*, II, 48, 2 *he forgeaf þæt folluht Johanne, and wæs eft gefullod æt Johanne,*[33] *Orrm*. 10663 *þu cumesst her att me to wurrþenn fullhtned*, 10654 *fullhtnedd beon att Sannt Johannes hande;* so also 18232 *att teggre maggstre*.

21. The transition from the notion of rest seems to have been through the verbs of *asking, expecting, receiving, taking, hearing, finding et sim.,*[34] in that the place 'where' one asks etc. is emphasized instead of the customary 'wherefrom', similarly to German 'ich kaufe etwas bei ihm' or 'von ihm', French 'boire dans un verre', English 'to receive at the

[30] Curious is the tendency of *of* to take over this function of *æt*, *Sax. Chron*. E 1123 *he wæs borenn of Luuein*.

[31] Cf. §36 for the expression of this idea by means of an auctorial adnominal genitive in *Jh*. 6, 45.

[32] Wülfing, II. 323.

[33] Cf. Belden, *The prepositions in, on, to, fore, and æt in Ags. prose*, Diss. Baltimore, 1897, p. 76; Gottweiss, in *Anglia*, 26, 326.

[34] Cf. Winkler, *Germanische Kasussyntax*, Berlin, 1896, p. 181, and Wülfing, II. 318.

hands'. This usage is Germanic, OLD NORSE—*nam ek (orþ) at mǫnnom, Hrbl.* 113; ANGLO-SAXON—*þā þing þe ic gehȳrde æt mīnum Fæder, Jh.* 15, 15, *Wycliffe*, 'I herde of my fadir'; GOTHIC—*hvazuh nu sa gahausjands at attin* παρὰ τοῦ πατρός, *Jh.* 6, 45; OHG. *so chindôt Mercurius pe Venere, Not. Cap.* 289 must also be correlated here. Some light may be thrown upon this double usage by the fact that in Gothic *niman* appears with *at* but once, *Jh.* 10, 18 *þo anabusn nam at* παρὰ *attin meinamma*, otherwise either *af* is used, as *Jh.* 10, 18 *ni hvashun nimiþ þo af mis* ἀπ' ἐμοῦ, or a personal dative (of the person from whom something is taken away), which is a *dativus incommodi, Mk.* 4, 25 *afnimada imma*. OLD HIGH GERMAN has this dative, *Otfr.* I. 4, 56 *uns ist iz binoman.* In the *Heliand* we find a curious use of *te,* l. 3513 *nam is mêda fulla te is frôion* 'from his lord'. According to Delbrück[35] the Pregermanic said at first **af *immōt* (abl.) **nimiþi,* then also **af *nimiþi *immai* (dat.)

22. When now this person 'at' whom such action takes place, happens to be the logical subject of a passive verb, *at, æt* becomes an auctorial preposition, just as *be,* of similar basic meaning, comes to be the equivalent of modern German 'von'. A few GOTHIC examples with other verbs may be subjoined, in that they stand at the threshold of agency, *Coloss.* 4, 16 *ussigwaidau at izwis so aipistaule* 'among you', *Philp.* 4, 6 *bidos izwaros kunþos sijaina at guda* πρὸς τὸν θεόν, 2 *Thess.* 3, 1 *(waurd) þragjai jah mikiljaidau, swaswe jah at izwis* καὶ πρὸς ὑμᾶς; cf. also *Lk.* 18, 27 *þata unmahteigs at mannam* παρὰ ἀνθρώποις *mahteig ist at guda* παρὰ τῷ θεῷ, to which both 'is in the power of' and 'can be accomplished by' may be applied.

23. (3) **In*—GOT., AGS., OHG. *in,* ON. *í;* LATIN *in* < OL. *en* = Gk. ἐν—is the actual exponent of locality. Wherever employed as the preposition of agency, it may be explained from its derived signification of 'at', 'by'. Thus, already in turns like the following, we cannot talk of a relation of in-clusion, ON. *fugl sat í limunum, HHv.* 12; GOTHIC,

<hr>

[35] *Synkretismus,* Strassburg, 1907, p. 231.

*jainar hairda sweine managaize haldanaize in þamma fair-
gunja* ἐν τῷ ὅρει, *Lk.* 8, 32; AGS. *ne hafn ic in heáfde hwîte
loccas, Rid.* 41, 98. There is not even an idea of actual location in *bigitaidau in imma, Philp.* 3, 9 or *gaskapanai in
Xristau Iesu, Eph.* 2, 10. On the other hand, the notion of
means appears in AGS. *ðu reces hie in gerde iserre, Vesp.
Ps.* (825) 2, 9; OHG. *geseret habest du mir min herza in
einemo diner oigen, Will.* 4, 9; ON. *i dreyra drifenn, Grm.*
52, 4; GOT. *in þammei gasiglidai sijuþ, Eph.* 4, 30. Consider
these four versions of *Mk.* 1, 8: GOT. *ik daupja izwis in watin,
iþ is daupeiþ izwis in ahmin weihamma,* CORPUS GOSP.
on wætere . . . on Hâlgum Gâste, WYCLIFFE, *in water
. . . in the Holy Goost,* TYNDALE, *with water . . . with
the Holy Goost.*

24. The 'place where' may also be regarded in the light
of mediative instrumentality, *Mt.* 9, 34 *in fauramaþlja un-
hulþono usdreibiþ unhulþons* ἐν τῷ ἄρχοντι τῶν δαιμονίων, Tyndale, 'by the power of the chefe devyll'. The Scandinavian
languages would use 'ved' here. OHG. *oba ih in gotes fingare
uuirphu diuuala T.* 62, 5, *thaz uuurdi arougit gotes uuerc in
imo,* 132. Causality is expressed in 2 *Cor.* 9, 13 *mikiljandans
guþ in ainfalþein gamainduþais* ἁπλότητι τῆς κοινωίας, 10, 15
hvopandans in framaþjaim orbaidim ἐν ἀλλοτρίοις κόποις. Personal agency, too, is found most frequently in GOTHIC.
An OHG. instance like *T.* 59 *got is giberehtot in imo,* and
'personal' references to single books of the Testaments etc.
as *Mk.* 1, 2 *swe gameliþ ist in Esaïin praufetau* ἐν τῷ Ἡσαΐᾳ,
Corpus, béc Isaîam, but Wycliffe, *in Ysaie,*—which are perhaps
felt stronger than a mere ON. *svá sem segir í Vǫlsungakviþu
inni fornu, HH* II. 12 pr. 10,—are of mere collateral interest;
but there is a decided agency in examples like *Gal.* 2, 17
garaihtai domjaindau in Xristau δικαιωθῆναι ἐν Χριστῷ, Purvey, 'justified in Crist', 1 *Cor.* 7, 4 *weihada ist qens so un-
galaubjandei in abin, jah gaweihaids ist aba sa ungalaujands
in qenai* ἡγίασται . . . ὁ ἀνὴρ . . . ἐν τῇ γυναικί, καὶ
ἡγίασται ἡ γυνὴ . . . ἐν τῷ ἀνδρί, Purvey, 'for the vnfeithful hosebonde is halewid bi the feithful womman, and the
vnfeithful womman is halewid bi the feithful hosebonde';

Eph. 1, 13 *in þammei galaubjandans gasiglidai waurþuþ* ἐν
ᾧ καὶ πιστεύσαντες ἐσφραγίσθητε, Purvey, 'in whom (Christ)
je bileuynge ben merkid with the Hooli Goost.' Just how
much the influence of the Greek prototype may have contributed to this meaning of the Gothic preposition, or that of
the Itala to the Anglo-Saxon, is an open question. It is
important, however, to see that often Purvey feels impelled
to render Latin *in* by *bi.*

25. Of the PREPOSITIONS OF MOTION, those denoting separation all agree in that transfer of thought which
makes the point of origin or separation whence the action
proceeds, at the same time the cause of the departure or act;
it is needless to say that this cause, when a person, becomes
the actual agent. Let us see this process in detail. (1) *Fram
—GOTHIC *fram,* AGS. *fram, from,* ON. *frá,* OHG. *fram;*
SKT. *paramam*—will be found connected in the Germanic
dialects with a dative of ablatival function.[36] Its basic meaning is 'ahead', 'forward', i. e. not merely separation, but
separation from a distant object in its relation to the subject.
This representation of 'coming from a place' yields to that
of causality as soon as the place stands no more for the origin
of the action but becomes identical with the causer and doer
thereof.

26. This agent appears only in GOTHIC and ANGLO-
SAXON. The very word *fram* occurs but once in the *Heli-
and, imu mahlidin fram mōdaga wihti,* 3931, and then as an
adverb. Only two instances exist in OHG., *sela fram hello
kihalota, Ic.* and *nalles fra unfrumon, B.,* the latter to render
'non pro dispendio'.[37] Again, in OLD NORSE the idea of
descent is the nearest abstract conception of locality attained
by this preposition, as the *Flateyjarbók* version of *Hdl.* 25, 2
allir bornir frá Jǫrmunrekki.[38] This, of course, is not un-

[36] For the formal confusion of the two cases cf. Delbrück's *Synkretismus,* p. 229 ff.

[37] Graff. *Die ahd. Präpositionen,* Königsberg, 1824, p. 241.

[38] Detter-Heinzel, *Sæmundar Edda,* II. 627, "Die Construction mit
'frá' statt des nackten Dativs deutet vielleicht an, dass sie nicht Söhne,
sondern Enkel, Urenkel Jörmunreks waren. S. oben 8 *koma frá,* unten
25 *uera frá.* Aber *koma frá* wird unten 38 von directer Descendenz
gebraucht."

common in Got. and Ags., ÆLFRED, *Or.* 40, 40 *ealle ða men cómon fram twam gebroðran, Jh.* 16, 27 *galaubideduþ þatei ik fram guda urrann.*

27. As outspoken examples of agency in the two dialects may be cited, GOTHIC—*jah gasaihvans warþ fram izai* καὶ ἐθεάθη ὑπ' αὐτῆς, *Mk.* 16, 11, *jah daupidai wesun allai in Iaurdane ahvai fram imma ὑπ' αὐτοῦ, Mk.* 1, 5 *þata qiþano fram aggilau* τὸ κληθὲν ὑπὸ τοῦ ἀγγέλου,—*fram,* Grimm's ideal preposition with passives [39] rendering mostly always Greek ὑπό. In AN-GLO-SAXON, add to those in §§10 and 11, *Sax. Chron.* 627 *Eādwine cining was gefulwad fram Pauline, Mk.* 1, 5 *wæron fram hym gefullode,* ÆLFRED, *C. P.* 106, 23 *ac wile ðæt simle se oðer beo arǣred from ðæ oðrum,* 'alter regatur ab altero'.

28. The original sense of this auctorial *fram,* so noticeable with adjectives and substantives, as *Beow.* 419 *þā ic of searwum cwōm, fāh from fēondum, Mk.* 10, 27 *fram mannam unmahteig ist, ni fram guda* παρὰ θεῷ,[40] is particularly evident in its connection with such a verb of motion as *sandjan, sendan.* GOTHIC, *insandiþs was aggilus Gabriel fram guþa* ὑπὸ τοῦ θεοῦ *Lk.* 1, 26; 2 *Cor.* 1, 16 *fram izwis gasandjan mik* ὑφ' ὑμῶν προπεμφθῆναι; ANGLO-SAXON, *fram Drihtne, Lk.* 1, 26, *Ælfred, Be.* 475, 8 *eac Vespassianus fram him sended wæs* 'ab eo missus.' *Bo.* 150, 13 *ne wurde þu þeah na adrifen from Ðeodrice*—all as plainly locative as any non-auctorial expression, such as CÆDMON's *Drihten sende regn from rōderum.*

29. Another subtype of the agent in which the local side is transparent is the connection of *fram* with active verbs in passive meaning. Consider *Lk.* 16, 22 *warþ* . . . *briggan fram aggilum* ἀπεχθῆναι ὑπὸ τῶν ἀγγέλων, Wycliffe, 'was borun of aungels', Tyndale, 'by the angelles'; *Lk.* 3, 7 *atgaggandeim manageim daupjan fram sis* βαπτισθῆναι ὑπ' αὐτοῦ, *Corpus, ðæt hī wæron gefullode fram him; Mk.* 8, 31 *uskiusan skulds ist fram þaim sinistam* ἀποδοκιμασθῆναι ἀπὸ τῶν πρεσβυτέρων, so *Lk. 9, 22* and *17, 25* ἀπό. Noteworthy is the Greek preposition

---

[39] *Deutsche Grammatik,*[1] IV. 947.

[40] 2 *Cor. 2, 6 andabeit þata fram managizam* ἡ ἐπιτιμία αὕτη ὑπὸ τῶν πλειόνων 'quae fit a pluribus' is quite like agency.

also in *Mt.* 11, 19 *gadomida warþ handugei fram barnam seinaim* ἐδικαιώθη ἡ σοφία ἀπὸ τῶν τέκνων αὐτῆς, *Ags. wīsdōm ys gerihtwīsod fram heora bearnum,* Wycliffe 'of her sonys', very much like *Elene* 190 (cf. §10.) *swā fram Siluestre lǣrde wǣron,* where the locative idea is at least as strong as the acquired notion of authorship. The presupposed causal chain is completed by instances like *Mk.* 12, 11 *fram fraujin warþ sa* παρά, *Lk.* 9, 7 *waurþanona fram imma; Psalms,* 106, 38 *oft hī fea wurdan feondum geswencte fram þǣre costunge,* ÆLFRED, *Or.* 206, 7 *on þære firran Ispanie forwearð Emilius se consul mid eallum his folce from Lusitaniam þære þeode,*— and such personified means as *Mt.* 8, 24 *þata skip gahuliþ wairþan fram wegim* καλύπτεσθαι ὑπὸ τῶν κυμάτων.

30. (2) **Aba, *af*—GOTHIC *af*, AGS. *of, af*, OHG. *aba, ab;* LATIN *ab*, GREEK ἀπό, SKT. *ápa*—with ablatival dative,[41] denotes a separation rather away from some fixed point than out of it, as does *fram*. So, GOTHIC *ushauhjada af airþai* ὑψωθῶ ἀπὸ τῆς γῆς, *Jh.* 12, 32; OLD NORSE, *hǫfoþ hǫggva monk þér halse af* 'away from your neck', *Skm.* 23, 3; OHG. *sendost aba himele, N.* 103, 3 (in 17, 17 *er santa fon himele*). In Anglo-Saxon a careful distinction is sometimes impossible, since the two prepositions meet at more points than Gothic *fram* and *af.* Sometimes even the above criteria are found interchanged, as ÆLFRED, *Or.* 36, 23 *Moyses lædde Israhela folc of Egyptum* is plainly 'out of', whereas 1, 16 *Moyses lædde Israhela folc from Egyptum ofer þone Readan Sæ* is 'away from'.[42] This use of *of*, I may add, is older than ÆLFRED; we have already *Beow.* 1162 *byrelas sealdon wīn of wunder-fatum* 'out of wondrous jugs' and, in the sense 'out of', 662 *Hrōðgār gewāt . . . ūt of healle.* ÆLFRIC's union of *acennan* with *of* seems also to be based on this signification, similarly that of the *Blickling Homilies,* as in 31, 28 *man biþ acenned of Iudan.*[43] Clear is the meaning of ÆL-FRED, *Be.* 495, 21 *ne wæs acenned of unrihthæmede ne ðurh*

---

[41] A constituent of OHG. *fona* and OS. *fana, Bezzenberger's Beiträge,* 27, 177.

[42] Cf. Wülfing, II. 421 and Bødtker, *op. cit.* p. 6.

[43] Cf. Fischer, *op. cit.* p. 87.

dyrne forligenysse ac acenned wæs of ælicum gesinscype 'sed de legitimo conjugio natus fuerat.'

31. As in the case of *fram*, so here the point from which an action originates may be considered the agent from whom the action proceeds: *af* thus becomes the preposition of agency in Old Norse and its descendants, in Middle English and, to a limited extent, in Gothic also. Examples: GOTHIC—*ni gajiukaizau af unþiuþa* μὴ νικῶ ὑπὸ τοῦ κακοῦ, *Rom.* 12, 21, *ingaleikonda af wulþau in wulþu, swaswe af fraujins ahmin* καθάπερ ἀπὸ κυρίου πνεύματος, Purvey, 'as of the spirit of the Lord'. OLD NORSE [44]—*Fornm.* X. 384 *hón var af Most kynjuð ok fædd, Flat.* I.16 *Nordimbraland er kallatt af Nordmonnum*, as against the old instrumental form in *Fornm.* I. 23 *Norðimbraland var mest byggt Norðmǫnnum, Stjórn.* 458 *hann var virðr minnzt af þeim* as against older form in *Hitd.* 4 *virðist konunginum hann afbragðsmaðr.* Interesting are the following later examples, *hine bleffue bidne ihiel aff gresshopper, Bible* 1550, *derfor var hannom giffuet skiold oc hielm aff kongen, Abs. Pedersen,* 16th c., *saaledis er den gode Enoch hentagen, aff Gud, Vedel's Saxo,* 1575, *Jesus som var undfangen af den Helligaand,* 17th century. ANGLO-SAXON—*Sax. Chron.* 640 *þā syððan warðen gemartrode of Ðunore, Lk.* 6. 18 *þā þe wæron of unclænum gāstum gedrēhte,* Wycliffe, 'trauelid with vnclene spiritis', MOD. ICELANDIC, *er þjáðir voru af óhreinum öndum;* so SWEDISH and NORWEGIAN *af,* even LANDSMAAL, *var plaagad av ureine Andar; Mt.* 14, 24 *scip of þam yþum totorfod,* Wycliffe 'throwen with waves', ÆLFRED, *Or.* 42, 18 *hu hreowlice he wearð adræfed of Othinentium his agenra þeode,* 154, 28 *seo burg wæs getimbred of Lœcedemonium* 'ex Lacedaemoniis conditam civitatem', *La₃.* III 289 *selehðe him wes ₃iueðe of seoluen ure drihten.*

32. In the interpretation of either Gothic or Old Norse *af* it is clear that in the idea of separation the point of departure is equated with the author of the action. Examples like *Nj.* 60 *ek em sendr af Starkaði, Pedersen's Nye Testamenta,* 1529 *it menniske vor udsent aff Gud,* show this well,

---

[44] For *af* in the Edda cf. §14.

also connections with nouns and adjectives, as *Rom.* 9, 3 *ana-þaima wisan silba ik af Xristau* ἀπὸ τοῦ Χριστοῦ, *Egilss.* 162 *hann var harmdauði af mönnum* (modern, *hans dǿd bekla-gedes af . . . . .*), *Alex.* 8 *auðkenndr af öllu fólkinu,* where the underlying concept of agency is felt without an expressly passive moulding.[45] In the English field however the question of Old French analogy has been raised, as in the similar use of *by.* According to Einenkel, *Streifzüge,* p. 162, the exten-sive use in Middle English of our particle as an author's preposition, cf. CHAUCER VI. 309 'thi wille fulfillid be of thi sone', MAUND. 5 'she was buryed of the aungels', is to be attributed to the influence of Old French, as in *Joinv.* 232 *il estoient si pressei des Turs que. . . . .* In reply, it true that aside from few exceptions among which *acenned of, geboren of* is to be emphasized (cf. *Jh.* 3, 6 *þæt þe of Gāste is ācenned, þæt is gāst, Laȝ.* II. 237 *þus wæs Marlin biȝeten & iboren of his moder*) where the concept of origin is paramount, the Ags. preposition of the agent is in later times regularly *fram,* whereas OF. uses *de* with passives—after *né* naturally, as *Ch'est ou Dieus fu de vierge nés, Vrai aniel,* 347—reserving *par* for instances which demand an energetic stress upon the subject. But this does not do away with the fact that in Ags. also we have that progressive development of *of* towards the auctorial which, despite the similar OF. usage, betokens a no inconsiderable degree of independence. Jesperson, in *Eng. Studien,* 34, 163, points out a pertinent instance of how a certain classic example of English relative construction ap-pearing in Dickens' 'I knows a lady, which her name is Harris' and away back in Ags. *se god ðe ðis his beacen wæs,* can be found not only in French, Spanish, Portuguese, but even in New Greek, Lithuanian and Malayan.

33. The French influence, although absolutely plausible, again cannot simply be saddled on the Middle English phrase. The insufficiency of linguistic documents, deplored in §19,

---

[45] There would be no doubt to the Gothic mind, as Grimm[2] IV. 781 remarks, between *afnimada fram imma* and Lk. 8, 18 *afnimada af imma.* Similarly in 2 *Thess.* 3, 2 *jah ei uslausjaindau af gastojanaim jah ubilaim mannam* the meaning is clearly 'deliverance from' and in Lk. 18, 34 'concealment from.'

does to be sure do away with positive proofs of refutation, but this does not in itself preclude the possible existence of *of's* auctorial uses. The French construction may well have aided the English to attain a predominant value and a general currency in its epoch,[46] but we have at least two incontestable proofs in favor of Ags. *of,* viz. that numerically it shows a marked gain over *fram* already in the Saxon Chronicle (cf. §12), and that we can find in Anglo-Saxon those presuppositions which we observed in the case of other prepositions to have been conducive to the personal agent with passives.

34. Let us instance the latter. As in ON. *gørþer þik frǽgjan af firenwerkom, HH.* I. 43, 5, so we have in AGS. expressions of means real as well as nearer the efficient cause, *Bl. Hom.* 11, 9 *weorþian wē ða clāþas his hādes, of ðǽm wæs ūre gecynd geedneówod,* ÆLFRED, *Be.* 493, 9 *þæt ðǣre menniscan gecynde of ælmihtiges Godes gyfe gehealdan wæs* 'quod naturae humanae ex omnipotentis Dei dono servatum est', ÆLFRIC, I. 2, 402 *of ðǽre lafe wǣron gefyllede seofan spyrtan,* where we see an actual competition with *mid,* I. 2,400 *gereordiað of Drihtnes hlāfum,* Orrm. 10137 *off þiss kirrtell mahht tu ʒèt deoplikerr unnderrstanndenn.* The cause or reason is evident in ÆLFRED, *C. P.* 156, 24 ðonne *hie of yflum willan ne gesyngað ac of unwisdome & ungewisses oððe ungewaldes oððe of flǽslicum gecynde oððe of wácmodnesse & of unbieldo oððe of untrymnesse modes oððe lichoman,* Orrm. 5548 *þatt hemm baþe beo þe bett off þatt teʒʒ neh te biggenn, Laʒ.* 24227 *heore ʒeolp makeden of muchele biʒeten. Saxon. Chron.* 1083 *þa wǣron þa munecas swiðe áferede of heom* and *Reg. Ben.* 23, 35 *of domesdaʒ beon ofdrad and of hellewite agrisan* are right on the threshold of agency. Similar causality can be gathered from GOTHIC and OLD NORSE, *Jh.* 14, 10 *þo waurda þoei ik rodja izwis, af mis silbin ἀπ' ἐμαυτοῦ ni rodja, Lk.* 8, 14 *jah af saurgom ὑπὸ μεριμνῶν . . . . . gaggandans afhvapnand; Háv.* 57, 1 *brandr af brandi brenn unz brunninn er, funi kveykisk af funa, Hom.* 12, 13 *hirð eigi þu yfir at stígask af illu* 'noli vinci a malo'. Moreover,

[46] It must be recalled that *fram* is at this time not yet extinct, *R. of Gl.* 5500 *fram God ycham ysend.*

the original local idea, which is entirely natural to Anglo-
Saxon, may be frequently found in examples of the agent,
e. g. ÆLFRED, *Or.* 126, 2 *þæt gefeoht wæs gedón mid micelre
geornfulnesse of þæm folcum bæm,* ÆLFRIC, I. 94, 59 *of
marian werode wæs þus geclypod, Bl. Hom.* 55, 28 *þæt him
ær of þæs lareowes muþe wæs bodad, Orrm.* 19185 *all mann-
kinn iss borenn her off faderr annd off moderr*—all with a
manifest concept of 'a parte', 'seitens'.

35. A curious coincidence must be pointed out *en passant*
between that use of *of* which came to express not only the
agent but the possessive genitive as well, and an old development of the possessive genitive into agency which we observe
in the synthetic stages of some Indo-European languages.
We allude to a primitive formula **deiuosio *dətós,* where the
genitive is adnominal; SANSKRIT, *asya* in *RV.* 10, 160, 4
'conspicitur ille ab eo, eius'; AVESTAN, θwahyā bərəxδąm
vīdušō 'esteemed of him that knows thee', *Y.* 34, 9, aiwiγnixta
sūnō Vd. 7, 29 'gnawed by dogs', really 'the gnawed of dogs';
GREEK, σφαγεὶς Αἰγίσθου 'slain of A.' *Eurip. El.* 123, διός̇δοτος
'the presented of Zeus'; LITHUANIAN *karáliaus siústas* sent
by the king'.[47] The same is probably seen in LATIN, *legati
Romanorum, eius dicta, malevoli veteris poëtae male dictis,*
Terence, *Andr. prol.* 7; GERMANIC, *gedo me lufiende &
onfundne þines wisdomes, Ælfred, So.* 171, 3; *druhtines
giscefti* 'what God created' *Otfr.* II. 1, 7, cf. ed. Erdmann,
p. 383; *jah wairþand allai laisidai guþs* διδαχτοὶ θεοῦ, *Jh.* 6, 45.

36. (3) **Fon(a)*—OLD SAXON *fon, fan,* OHG. *fona,
fon*—a purely Westgermanic preposition connected with an
ablatival dative, is most likely composed of two parts, *af* and
ana, with the initial vowel lost by apocope,[48] cf. Italian
da < *de+ad.* It emphasizes the starting point and as such
can be traced evolving into a preposition of agency.[49] Actual
locality, *T.* 81 *nidarstiganter for themo skefe, N.* 43, 22 *ziu
uuendest du fone uns din anasiune, Nib.* 494, 4 *si vuoren von*

---

[47] Cf. in this connection this interesting instance, 'Er emfängt durch
einen von ihm Abgesandter die Wohltat des heiligen Kommunion,'
p. 212 of *Dichtungen und Dichter,* by Otto Pniower, Berlin, 1912.
[48] Cf. Persson, *IF.* 2, 25, 237.
[49] Graff. *Die ahd. Präpositionen,* pp. 217-240, and *Sprachschatz,* III 523.

dem lande. In a transferred sense, *T.* 97 *arstuont fon to-*
ten, Parz. 480, 15 *einem helfen von der nôt;* so, too, descent,
gl. K. fona herostin, Ra. fona drume 'a stirpe, *Nib.* 643, 1
Hagene von Troneje. Causality, in the sense of modern 'er
fiel von einer Kugel', *T.* 62, 12 *fon thinen uuorton uuirdis tu*
girehfestigot, inti fon thinen uuorton uuirdis tu fornidarit,
Parz. 211, 20 *ieweder ros von müede dampf, Walth.* 3, 26 *sîn*
kraft von dîner kraft verzaget. The thinking agent working
to a definite end, *Is.* 4, 7 *quhad fona dhem angilum, T.* 13, 6
nalles fon bluote ouh fon gote giboranê wârun—in which the
local notion is transparent, as also in *Is.* 11, 13 *fona fater*
ward chiboran, Not. ps. 353-b *keboren fone magede—N.* 36, 23
fone gote uuerdent kerihtet, which has the same force as
the transitional *N.* 32, 6 *sine himela gefestenot fona gotes*
uuorte. Miscellaneous MHG. examples: *ir wart von mir*
gnâde gesagt, Iw., von ir gevidere wart diu linde bedaht,
ibid., do wart genomen bî der hant von wœtlîchen recken
manic wîp wolgetân, Nib. der rede wart gelachet dâ von
maniger edeler muoter kinde, Gudr. From LOW GERMAN,
fon waldandes worde gibiudid, Hel. 1074, *thiu thâr werðad*
ahlûdid fon thero hêlogun tungun, fon them galme godes, Hel.
1071,[50] *ik geuuisso gasazt bin kuning van himo* 'constitutus
sum rex ab eo', *Ps.* 2, 6,[51] *mistrôt bin fan stimmon fiundes in*
fan arbeide, 54, 3 *tedeilda sint fan abulgî ansceines sînis* 'divisi
sunt ab ira vultus ejus', 54, 22.

37. The relation of the *von*-phrase, to designate the agent
with passive expressions, to the pure dative in the same
function, indifferently termed the dative of interest or the
dative of agency, is of great importance because of the development of the Germanic dative itself. The case of this dative
is usually stated[52] as that after the gerundive infinitive
and after verbal adjectives in *-bar* and *-lich* and some past participles, felt as adjectives, such a dative may be considered as
one expressive of agency, on the assumption that the person for
whom the action may or must take place or is an accomplished

---

[50] Cf. also *Hel.* 5026 *it was bi thesun liudin giduan.*

[51] From Heyne, *Kleinere altniederdeutsche Denkmäler*[2] 1877.

[53] Cf. Curme, *A Grammar of the German Language,* p. 536, and Blatz.
Neuhochdeutsche Grammatik, II, 423.

fact, is the very same that performs the action. Still in other words, 'was von jemand gethan wird, wird in irgend einem sinne für ihn gethan.'[53]   Accordingly 'alles ist dem Auge erreichbar' is similar in force to, though not as subjective as, 'es war für mich zur Zeit unausführbar' and to 'anderen Sterblichen schön, kaum noch gesehen von mir'. The same category of sheer interest would embrace also 'eine Seele, die der List und der Liebe gleich unbetretbar war', 'wer sich der äusseren Wirkung ergibt, wird Feinden gefangen', *i. e.* 'den Feinden zum Vorteil', 'uns ist die Schlacht gewonnen', 'neue Gedanken fühl' ich, von denen mir vordem keiner gedacht war.'

38.   However, the syncretistic character of the Germanic dative, in that it represents functionally an older instrumental as well, (to omit the ablative and the locative here), does not allow of this simple conception of our dative as merely a species of the dative of interest. Whilst there is no difficulty in the diagnosis of the dative 'governed' by *von* as an original ablative,[54] the formal confusion of the dative and of the instrumental into what is termed 'dative', cf. §8, would tend to postulate some recognition for the instrumental ingredients of this 'dative'. Narrowed down to fundamentals, it is the case of the Greek dative transplanted to the Germanic soil. With the aid of kindred phenomena in other Indo-European languages, we are in a position to observe in Greek this instrumental constituent from its basic meaning of concomitancy right up to the function of agency, as in examples like *Soph. Ai.* 539 προσπόλοις φυλάσσεται or Isee. ἀπὸ τοῦ ὠφλημένου Σωπόλιδι ἀργυρίου "of the money owed by (not 'due to') Sōpolis".[55]   Regardless of this evidence, however,[56] grammarians as a rule persist in ignoring the lesson of parallel procedure that can be drawn from the Sanskrit, Avestan and Slavic extension of the material use of the instrumental to

[53] Winkler, *Germanische Casussyntax,* p. 80.

[54] Old High German combinations of *von* with instrumental forms like *thiu* and *thisiu* are comparatively young possibilities, where such forms were in all likelihood petrified and adverbial in force.

[55] Cf. Meisterhans, *Gr.*[2] 156, 172.

[56] Cf. *Dative of Agency,* p. 72 ff.

the personal, and will render a *Homeric* δόρυ μακρόν, ὅ οἱ κλισίηφι λέλειπτο, *N*. 168, by 'which for him was left in the tent',[57] as if it were universally established that what one forgets to take along with him, is left somewhere *for* him.

39. It is the existence of such a dative-instrumental of agency that one is inclined to vindicate for OLD HIGH GERMAN also.[58] Language, to be sure, seems to have found a formal means of distinguishing between the various case-forces amalgamated in the 'dative', for such functions as, through a comparison with related languages, can be reduced to an original locative, ablative or instrumental, are in general replaced by and restricted to equivalent prepositional phrases. Old High German has already to a great extent completed this refinement, consequently we feel today that all that has not assumed this new form, belongs to the domain of the real dative, for which Germanic has had a decided predilection. This is the reason why we cannot decide by their own evidences an OTFRIDIAN *fatere giboranan ebanewigan,* an EDDIC *vasat hann ásom alinn,* an ANGLO-SAXON *þǣm eafera wæs æfter cenned geong in geardum,* or a GOTHIC *liugada anþaramma.* On the other hand, we may well surmise their real character, despite the dative garb of the logical subjects, when we turn to other languages and meet SANSKIRT *sáhasā yó mathitó jáyatē nrbhiḥ* 'begotten by men', instrumental, and, for marital relations, SLAVIC *jako oženi sę jeja* ὅτι αὐτὴν ἐγάμισεν, *Mk*. 6, 17, instrumental; and when we see in OLD NORSE *var af Most kynjuð ok fædd, Fornm*. 10, 384, and similarly in ANGLO-SAXON, linguistic feeling further defined and amplified in later prepositional expressions that would never have come about had these datives been pure datives of interest—CÆDMON, *El*. 775 *sē-ðe on rōde wæs ond þurh Mārian in middangeard ācenned weard,* or *Bl. Hom*. 31, 24 *sē ilca sunu wæs ær eallum tīdum acenned fram God Fæder, sē Ælmihtiga from þon Ælmihtigan* or *Jh*. 3, 6 *þæt þe of gaste is acenned.* And this amplification in expression occurs when prepositionless dative-

---

[57] Monro, *A Grammar of the Homeric Dialect²*, §143, 5.
[58] Cf. §4 for the other Germanic dialects.

instrumentals of agency appear simultaneously, cf. for CÆDMON, §4, and p. 103 of *Dative of Agency*.

40.   Withal, we hasten to add, sight must not be lost of the fact that the dative of interest—broad enough to be felt as a logical subject when connected even with a noun, as Plaut. *Poen,* 5, 5, 29 *quid tibi hanc rem tactio est*=*quid hanc rem tangis*—contains in itself the potentialities of an eventual transition to the function of agency, as attested by Latin. But this does not exclude the possibility, in addition, of a dative-instrumental of agency, nor even the partial non-conversion of the latter into the later prepositional phrase, because of attraction or analogy to that dative of interest with which it bore absolutely the same outward form.   In fact, seeing the remains of an original *Indo-European function of the instrumental case thus obscured by that fortuitous circumstance which brought the dative to the fore, we might ask if, had the reverse case-substitution occurred and the instrumental remained constructional, as in Indo-Iranian and Slavic, and entrusted with the functions of the dative, we could claim an exclusively instrumental connotation for all instances hereto pertaining that might be found in Germanic.   And if not, is there not, in this case at least, some fallacy in the reasoning which, in deciding the value of constructions belonging to the dawn of authentic literature, would recognize as sole criterion modern *Sprachgefühl*, and that in the face of cogent evidence contemporaneous with or even antedating such constructions.

41.   One moot point in this connection is the nature of the passive verb in Germanic.   Grimm [59] remarks that, since the passive inflection is lost, really the preterite participle alone stands for the verb.   That thus these participles must be considered as adjectives—for to this they would be changed, if the accompanying dative of the logical subject were a mere dative of interest—especially when connected with the substantive verb, one cannot well believe, because then we could not, save in the spare synthetic remnants of Gothic and the younger reflexives of Old Norse, speak of a Germanic

[59] *Deutsche Grammatik*[2], IV 714.

passive at all, and the periphrasis of Slavic, Sanskrit and Avestan, similar to the Germanic combinations with **wesan* and **werþan*, would mean the absence of finite passive verbal relations in those languages as well. And yet we have in these very tongues evidence of the bare participle, without the copula so essential in Germanic, connected with instrumental forms in instrumental function to denote the logical subject. So we see[60] in SANSKRIT, *RV.* 1, 163, 2 *yaména dattáḥ* 'which is given by Yama', AVESTAN, *Yt.* 10, 38 *frazinte anašitå maēθanyå* 'the houses which are not inhabited by posterity', but especially in SLAVIC, with the bulk of its finite passives expressed solely by the participle, *pravimŭ dĭvěma aggeloma, Supr.* 124, 26, 'qui a duobus angelis ducitur' (so reminiscent of Eddic *vask þrimr verum vegin at húsi, Ghv.* 10, 2), a turn which some grammarians would not hesitate to render, if paralleled in Germanic by a dative-instrumental of agency, as 'zwei Engeln geführt'.

42. Admitting moreover that the participles were, according to their origin, adjectives and in the periphrases with **wesan* and **werþan* would surely be felt at first as such, already Old High German bears out the fact that they early combined with auxiliaries to form a unit, so that they were not independent predicate adjectives, but, inseparable from the auxiliaries, part of a well-defined verbal predicate, especially with **werþan*, which expressed an entrance into the state denoted by the participles.[61] Thus, *Otfr.* 2, 21, 44 *gizelit sint themo, 2, 2, 30 nu sint fon gote erborane, 3, 22, 19 ir ni giloubet thoh thiu halt, thaz ist in ofto gizalt, 1, 17, 73 si wurtun slafente fon engilun gimanote, 4, 16, 13 thi uns giscriban ist* and many others are shown by the context to be distinctly compound past tenses into which the adjectival force need not be read, and even cannot because of the presence of a logical subject or of an adverb. Moreover, already in OHG. the personal periphrasis in the passive was the equivalent of an active verb with an accusative, as *Otfr.* 4, 4, 9 *wirdit fon iu funtan ein esilin gibuntan,* for Latin

'invenietis asinam alligatam.[62] It does not seem to be an open question that the formation of the younger compound passives, *ich bin, was gebunden* and *ich bin, was gebunden gewesen*, in use since the 14th and 15th centuries,[63] has largely been responsible for the modern revival of the original adjectival meaning of the participle; such random instances as *ich bin begraben gewesen*, Konr. v. Würz. *Troj.* 16937, *es ist offt durch Concilia etwas furgewant, aber durch etlicher menschen list behendiglich verhindert und immer erger worden*, Luther, show that *worden* really belongs first of all to the adjective and that, in attaching itself to the participle, levels the latter to the rank of an adjective. In this process, participles like *betrübt, bekannt*, that had long been adjectives, must have been of material aid.

43. This then is the situation in general terms. The writer would accordingly be the first to discountenance any attempt to secure from modern German a tabulation of such auctorial datives as may show a possible instrumental connotation, as against the large mass of genuine datives; a delimitation would simply prove unfeasible. But when he sees the absolute need—*and possibility*—in the other Germanic dialects of a partly instrumental conception of this dative and when he finds OLD HIGH GERMAN itself offering actual instrumental forms [64] expressive, upward of the original comitative function, not only of real means, *Hild.* 53 *suertu hauwan*, 40 *wili mih dinu speru werpan*, *Murb. Hym.* 19, 2, 3 *fuazziu katretanti*, but also of efficient cause *Musp.* 53 *suilizôt lougiu himil*, *Otfr.* 2, 22, 22 *thu hungiru nistirbist*, *Pa.* I. 40, 25 *ubilu cadungan*, *Is.* 15, 2 *druhtines uuordu sindun himila chifestinode*, 15, 3 *sines mundes gheistu standit al iro megin;* also OLD SAXON *ik bithuungan uuas thurstu endi hungru*,

---

[62] Cf. Erdmann-Mensing, *Grundzüge der deut. Syntax*, I. 89, and Cuny *Der temporale Wert der passiven Umschreibungen im Ahd.* Diss. Bonn, 1905; Öberg, *Über die hochdeutsche Passivumschreibung, Lund,* 1907; Löffler, *Das Passiv bei Otfrid und im Heliand, Diss, Tübingen,* 1905, p. 15—.

[63] Cf. Wunderlich, *Der deutsche Satzbau²*, I. 144, and Wilmanns *op. cit.* 3¹, §76, Grimm², IV, 16.

[64] Cf. Ehret, *Der Instrumentalis im Ahd.* Diss. Heidelberg, 1907.

Hel. 4400, cf. *Otfr.* 1, 1, 35 *mit regulu bithuungan*—then
surely he feels justified to postulate at least for the older
period of German, before the formation of the new passives
above alluded to, and for reasons firmly rooted in the ob-
servable facts of historical development, the old inherited
force of the instrumental of agency for all datives employed
as logical subjects whose connotation is not palpably one of
mere subjective interest. The number of these—a suitable
collection is still a desideratum—will not be found to be
great. The reason for this is to be sought not only in the prepositional usages of men like NOTKER, but also in the predilection of writers like OTFRID for the so-called indefinite passive,
i. e. one whose psychological subject is not expressed—a
trait common also to the *Heliand.*[65] With prose writings,
on the other hand, that are sheer translations, like ISIDOR
and TATIAN, care must be exercised to ascertain the extent
of Latin influence.[66] It is encouraging, however, to have
Grimm[2] insert a passage, p. 857 of vol. 4, 'Beim passiv dat.
pro instr.' and quote 'dat *mi* liever ontboren ware (das
besser *von mir* unterlassen wäre) Ferguut 2921; mhd. daz
ist *mir* ungetân, vgl. ahd. *slâfe* antsuebit (somno sopiti) Diut.
1, 505[b] . . . . . ' Could not *Otfr. V.* 1, 27 *mit thiu ist thar
bizeinit, theiz imo ist al gimeinit, Tat.* prol. 3 *uuas mir
gisehan* 'visum est mihi',[67] 35, 2 *zi thiu thaz thu mannun
ni sis gisehan fastenti* 'ne videaris hominibus ieiunans',[68]
126, 18 *quid uns, uuaz thir gisehan si*, 197, 3 *niouuiht wirdic
tode ist imo getân*, be considered in this connection?

44. With respect to (4) *uz—GOTHIC *us* concerns us
only, since ON. *'ør*, OHG, *ur* do not seem to appear in auctorial phrases—it is but another local preposition, combined
with a dative-ablative, with which the 'place' develops into
a concept of authorship, 'out of' yielding to 'away from'
and 'done by', as in the case of *von.* We shall here content

[65] Cf. Löffler, *Das Passiv bei Otfrid und im Heliand,* Diss. Tübingen,
1905, p. 11 ff.

[66] Cf. Kaufmann, *Über Genera Verbi im Ahd.* Diss. Leipzig, 1912, p.
91 ff.

[67] But *225,5 inti gisehan uuas fon in* 'visus esset ab eis'.

[68] But 'ut pareant hominibus,' 35.1 is *thaz sie sih offonon mannun.*

ourselves with enumerating the few examples of agency that could be found in GOTHIC: *Rom.* 9, 12 *ni us waurstwam, ak us þamma laþondin qiþan ist izai* ἐκ τοῦ καλοῦντος ἐρρέθη, to which cf. *Gal.* 5, 8 *so gakunds ni us þamma laþondin izwis ist;* 2 *Cor.* 2, 2 *hvas ist saei gailjai mik, nibai sa gaurida us mis?* ὁ λυπούμενος ἐξ ἐμοῦ, 2 *Cor.* 7, 9 *ei waihtai ni gasleiþjaindau us unsis* ἵνα μηδενὶ ζημιωθῆτε ἐξ ἡμῶν, *Philp.* 1, 23 *aþþan dishabaiþs* <*im*> *us þaim twaim* συνέχομαι δὲ ἐκ τῶν δύο; similarly to *Ags. of, Jh.* 3, 5 *us watin, us ahmin gabairada.* Causality appears in 2 *Cor.* 13, 4 *aþþan jabai jah ushramiþs was us siukein* ἐσταυρώθη ἐκ ἀσθενείας, *akei libaiþ us mahtai gudis* ἀλλὰ ζῇ ἐκ δυνάμεως θεοῦ. For means, cf. *Rom.* 9, 32, *Gal.* 2, 16, 2 *Cor.* 8, 11; interesting is, with reference to §42, *Lk.* 6, 44 *huarjizuh raihtis bagme us swesamma akrana uskunþs ist* ἐκ τοῦ ἰδίου καροῦ γινώσκεται, *AGS. be his wæstme,* Wycliffe, of his fruyt'.

45. This brings us now to the one PREPOSITION OF ACCOMPANIMENT here discussed, *með, *miði—GOT. *miþ,* ON. *meþ,* AGS. OS. *mid,* OHG. *mit;* GREEK μέτα. Originally of a locative significance, cf. *Homeric* μετὰ γναμπτῆσι γένυσσιν, it is the sociative-comitative preposition par excellence of the Germanic dialects, as GOT. *Mt.* 5, 41 *gaggais miþ imma* ὕπαγε μετ' αὐτοῦ, OHG. *Georgsl.* 1, 2 *fuor mit mikilemo herigo,* . . . . . *folko,* AGS. *Cri.* 837 *gefeaht Æ. wið Deniscne here mid Dornsætum.* What is of interest in this sketch is the circumstance that this preposition and its later substitute in English, *with,*[69] attest exactly the same upward development towards the auctorial function as the bare instrumental, itself expressive at first of mere association, whose development we have studied before, §§4 ff. and 43.

46. In OLD HIGH GERMAN we have sufficient testimony only with respect to the earlier stages of this process, such as—to offer solely examples with instrumental forms—concomitation, *Is.* 41, 5 *sitzit pardus mit gheizssinu,* means, *Otfr.* III. 25, 17 *mit uuafanu thuingent*—the transition being some such instance as *T.* 236, 7 *mit ferennu quamun*—and potential agency, *T.* 22, 2 *mit missalihhen suhtin bifangene,* 52, 2 *thaz*

[69] Cf. Erla Hittle, *Zur Geschichte d. ae. Präp. 'mid' und 'wið.* Diss. Heidelberg, 1901.

skef uuard bithekit mit den undon, cf. also *Iw.* 3607 *wan daz er was bedwungen mit selher siecheite,* Servat. 1781 *mit dem tôde teun,* but instances of personal agency, as in the later isolated case from *Eckhart, in wart ze tische gedient wol mit* (=von) *getwërgen,* are wanting. This is also characteristic of OLD SAXON. In OLD NORSE, *viþ, the* preposition which in English fuses with *mid,* stands in the *Eddic* poems only for the means through which something is accomplished, as *Grm.* 45, 2 *sviþom hefk nú ypt fyr sigtíva sunom, viþ þat skal vilbjǫrg vaka.* In the modern dialects, as e. g. DANISH, *ved* is used only for the intermediate agent, *af* being the real auctorial particle, as *Jh.* 1, 10 *verden er giort ved ham* 'mundus per ipsum factus est'; *Rom.* 11, 36 *af ham og ved ham og til ham ere alle Ting,* 'ex ipso et per ipsum et in ipso sunt omnia'; *Bogen er udgivet af Litteraturselskabet ved N. N.*

47. In ANGLO-SAXON and ENGLISH, however, we see the development in its full form. Instrumentality, *Gen.* 251 *mid his handum gesceóp, Oros.* 288, 1 *weard J. mid ðæm bræðe ofsmorod, Mt.* 12, 44 *geclænsod mid besemum.* Efficient agency, *Be.* 587, 7 *þa wæs he gehrinen mid untrumnesse* 'arreptus infirmitate,' *C. P.* 180, 11 *mid ðy storme & mid ðære yste onwend & oferworpen, Metr.* 20, 105 *wæstm . . . . . todrifen siððan wide mid winde;* personal, *Chad.* 158 *gelededu mid engla ðreatum to ðam ecan gefean,* where the basic idea of association is still apparent, *C. P.* 415, 18 *ða wæs his mod gehæft mid ðæm mædene* (modern, 'to be taken with her'), *Be.* pref. *he me sæde of Theodores and Adrianus . . . . . forðon he swyðost wæs mid him gelæred.* It is indeed not surprising that, with the loss of *mid,* the preposition *with* supplanting it, the latter, though fundamentally adversitive,[70] is also found in auctorial expressions, CHAUCER, II. 84 'with twenty knightes take', i. e. to be taken, P. PLOUGH. 353 'that robbed was with theves', TOWN. M. 290 'stolne is he with Jues', SHAKSPEARE, *Ado,* II, 1, 51 'he is attended with a desperate train', *Caes.* III. 2, 197 *Aed.* 'He's coming.' *Brut.* 'How accompanied?' *Aed.* 'With old Menenius.' It will be seen

---

[70] Cf. Hittle, *op. cit.,* p. 166 ff.

that the idea denoted by *with* may be felt as mere participation in something by a person, intensified to agency.
SHAKSPERE, by the way, still employs *with* even in the
function of the intermediary, something which has since become
rare, *Err. V.* 1, 230 'he did arrest me with', i. e. by means of,
an officer, *Hy* 6, B. I. 3, 33 'send for his master with a pursui-
vant'.[71] Nor is the immediate author, as in Tennyson's 'vex'd
with a morbid devil in his blood', usual; cf. the biblical *Lk.*
7, 24—GOT. *raus fram winda wagid*, AGS. *hreod ðe byþ mid
winde āstryred*, WYCLIFFE, 'wawid with the wynd',—
SCANDINAVIAN *af*: ICEL. *af vindi skekinn*, SWED. *af
wädret*, DAN. *af Veiret*.

48.   It will have been noticed that in the foregoing paragraphs the chief care has been to locate the original force
of the prepositions and to trace their evolution into the proximate agent; what specific case-forms each combined with to
express this function, was held only of secondary importance.
Thus, it is irrelevant to the discussion that Anglo-Saxon *mid*
may 'govern' not only the dative and the instrumental, but
the accusative as well.   On the other hand, attention was
drawn to the fact that the prepositions were originally local
in application and that according to the nature of this locality
they became connected with a dative representing either an
ablative or an instrumental, or even with survived instrumental forms.   The DIRECTIVE PREPOSITION (1) *þurh,
next to be considered, is one which has largely accusatival
connections; that in Anglo-Saxon, for instance, we find also
the dative and genitive with it, is immaterial at this point.
GOTHIC *þairh*, AGS. *þurh*, OHG. *duruh*, mod. *durch*, denotes
at first simple entrance, passing, piercing through a resisting
space or object, as *T.* 113 *ingangan thuruh thia engun phorta,
Mk.* 10, 25 *þairh þairko neþlos galeiþan* διὰ τῆς τρυμαλιᾶς
τῆς ῥαφίδος εἰςελθεῖν, ÆLFRIC, *Gr.* 47 *ðurh ða duru wē
gād*.   Once conceived causally, it comes to express not only
the instrument of the action, as AGS. *Gen.* 453 *hē gefērde
þurh feóndes cræfte, Beow.* 557 *fornam . . . . . þurh mīne
hand*, GOT. *Mk.* 6, 2 *ei mahteis swaleikos þairh handuns is*

[71] **Franz,** *Shakespeare-Grammatik²*, p. 419.

wairþand, but the intermediate person responsible for the action, as well as the actual agent with passives. We meet thus in GOTHIC with examples like *Jh.* 14, 6 *ainshun ni qimiþ at attin, niba þairh mik* δί έμοῦ, 1, *Cor.* 15, 2 *þairh þatei jah ganisiþ* δι᾽ οὗ καὶ σώζεσθε, but also *Mt.* 27, 9 *þanuh usfullnoda þata qiþano þairh Iairaimian praufetau qiþandan* τὸ ῥηθὲν διὰ Ἰερεμίου προφήτου, *Mt.* 8, 17 *þata gamelido þairh Esaïan praufetu qiþandan, Lk.* 18, 31 *þata gamelido þairh praufetuns,* 2. *Cor.* 1, 11 *so . . . . . giba þairh managans awiliudodau* διὰ πολλῶν εὐχαριστηθῇ. HIGH GERMAN instances of agency, *T.* 112 *thiu dar giscriban sint thuruh thie uuizagon,* 13, 5 *uueralt uuard thuruh inan gitan;* so *T.* 5, 9, *Is.* 2, 1, *Is.* 3, 3 etc.[72] Also *Nib.* 527, 3 *der Guntheres sal wart bezimbert durch manegen fremden man, Brant, Narrensch.* 13, 60 *Danae entpfing nit durch das gott, Luther,* 2 *Chron.* 23, 18 *durch David getihtet.* ANGLO-SAXON—*Cynew. El.* 1153 *wæs se witedom þurh fyrnwitan sungen, Sax. Chron.* 1014 *wearð þæt earme folc þus beswicen þurh hine,* 1123 *ðis wæs eall ear gedon ðurh se bisceop of Seresbyrig & þurh se biscop of Lincolne, Wulfst.* 54, 12 *ðurh deofol forlæred, Ælfred, Or.* 10, 23 *ac heo wearð gescild þurh þone cristnan casere, Ælfric* (Kluge, *Les.* 57, 145.) *hi wurdon gehælede þurh þone hálgan wer,* and later, *Orrm.* 16084 *þatt wass don þurrh Jesu Crist, Laз.* I. 13 *þorh him heo sculden deiзen, RG.* 9779 *þe churche was ifounded þoru Henri, Town. M.* 273 *what thyng is done . . . . . thrughe wykyd Jues.* Finally, a comparison of *Mt.* 2, 5—*þurh ðone witegan* in Corpus, *bi a prophete* in Wycliffe—gives the following for the SCANDINAVIAN dialects, Danish and Norw. *ved,* Swed. *genom Propheten,* but Icelandic, *er ritað af spámanninum; Mt.* 2, 17 *af* in all, but Icelandic, *sem mælt er fyrir Jeremías;* however, 8, 17, Dan. Norw. *ved,* Swed. *genom,* Icel. *fyrir;* again *Lk.* 18, 31 Dan. *ved,* Swed. *af Propheterna,* Norw. *ved,* Icel. *af spámönnunum,* —showing how opinions diverge in some instances as to the conception of a mediate or of a proximate agent.

49. (2) *To—English *to* is the only one to interest us.

---

[72] Incidentally I fail to see any compelling reason for the change in *Is.* 25, 21 (ed. Weinhold) of *fona* to *sô êr bifora uuardh chichundit DHURAH dhen forasagun.*

I am not disinclined to hold the combination of the passive
verb with a prepositional phrase of agency introduced by *to*, to
be an analytic restatement of the older synthetic dative of
interest in the function of the agent. Instances like CHAU-
CER, II. 71 'to whom bothe heven and erthe and see is
sene', IV. 262 'and his comynge unwiste is tevery, i. e. to
every, wight', would thus be based on earlier native usage.
It is with respect to the fixation of the term 'early native
usage' that a few words remain to be said, since it would mislead one as to the nature of the dative of agency. Einenkel[73]
evidently is still on the working basis of the old dative of
interest, hence in the danger of gathering too much under
that category. After what has been said in §4 ff., we might
pass over this point with the remark that the GOT. *þatei
razn mein razn bido haitada allaim þiudom*, cited by him
as a parallel, may indeed be a dative of interest at bottom,
but that care must now be exercised in differentiating from
similar examples those datives of agency which derive their origin from the lost instrumental, among which one must class,
because of testimony in §§9 and 10, *Wulfst., for þara gebeorge,
þe him (Gode) syn gecorene*, cited by him for one of the
former variety. With this proviso in mind, we can here suggest two distinct, though related, sources of the later *to*-
phrase. There are to be found, namely, not only personal
datives of the type of *Beow. feor-cyðde beoð selran gesohte
þæm þe him selfa deah, Wulfst. þonne bið us gesawen þæt
us ær gesæd was, Cyn. El. þa weard on slæpe . . . . . sigero-
fum gesegen swefnes woma*, ibid. *bið þæt beacen gode halig
nemned*, cf. also GOTH. *Mk.* 11, 17 above and *Rom.* 7, 10
bigitana warþ mis anabusns—but there are also combinations
of such datives with gerundives, conceived of as passives
because of the context, e. g. ANGLO-SAXON, *Oros.* 292, 28
se ealdormon hie betæhte lyþrum monnum to healdonne,
296, 1 *he hie betahte his twæm ealdormonnum to bewitanne,
C. P.* 276, 17 *to wundianne his feondum, Ps.* 38, 10 *þu me
sealdest to bysmrianne þam unrihtwisan*. There are similar
instances in OHG. also, *Otfr.* 2, 9, 55 *in thiu wari follon zi*

---

[73] *Streifzüge*, p. 219, and *Syntax in Pauls Grdr.*² I, 1086.

erkennenne mannon, 2, 8, 27 thâr stuantun wazarfaz thên mannon sih zi wasganne, T. 68, 3 *thiu erloubit ni uuarun imo zi ezzane, nibi then einun heithaftun mannon;* so the GOTHIC, *Mk.* 2, 26 *þanzei ni skuld ist matjan niba ainaim gudjam,* AGS. *þe him ne ālȳfede nǣron tō etanne, būton sācerdon ānum,* to which cf. *Ps.* 16, 14 *hi eton swynenflǣsc, þæt Judeum unalyfedlic ys to etanne.* Other GOTHIC instances, *Mt.* 6, 1 *du saihuan im, Lk.* 2, 6 *usfullnodedun dagos du bairan izai.* The dative, no doubt, belonged originally to the predicate of the sentence, but became in a natural way, through the ἀπὸ κοινοῦ construction, attached to the infinitive and became its logical subject.

50. As to the transition of this dative, of either source, into the Middle English *to*-phrase, one only has to think of the many past participles that could be used for adjectives and of the adjectives that had a semi-verbal force. If MILTON can say, *P. L.* 3, 54 'invisible to mortal sight', 9, 1086 'highest words impenetrable to star or sunlight', just as we say today, 'inaccessible to wrong', 'impassable to the wicked', so already in AGS. we find *Sax. Chron.* 1011 *þæt wæs unāsęcgendlic ǣnigum męnn, Oros.* 214, 21 *hit is us uncuð & ungeliefedlic, Be.* 549, 15 *gesynelice eallum mannum,* 552, 17 *menniscum eage ungesewenlice,* verbal adjectives as against *Wulfst. þonne bid us gesawen,* an adjectival participle. The same idea is expressed by means of the identical verbal root in two ways in *Be.* 504, 30 *forþferde ða Gode se leofe fæder Agustinus, but* 3, 14 *he wæs fram eallum monnum lufad,*[14] and *Beow.* 1255 *þæt gesyne wearþ, widcuþ werum, but Mt.* 6, 18 *þæt þū ne sȳ gesewen fram mannum fæstende.* Interesting is *Lk.* 8, 27 *Gode synd mihtelīce þā þing þe mannum synd unmihtelīce,* when *Lk.* 1, 37 has *nys ælc word mid Gode unmihtelīc.*

51. This ends our investigation. The concrete results thereof lie, of course, in the details of the discussion which treats of the inner development and outer history of the individual prepositions. For the former, it must again be

---

[14] *Ælfric, wearð ða him inweardlice gelufod, Sweet's Reader*[4], 14 A. 16, is instrumental dative.

emphasized that, just as the instrumental and causal domains border hard on each other and partly pass into each other, so causality and authorship are distinctions but of degree and not of kind. This may be regarded as absolutely axiomatic. As for the latter, namely the varying fortunes of the auctorial prepositions, especial attention is requested to the question of foreign influence on Middle English and to the attempt made to fix the status of the bare dative of agency in Old High German with respect to the phrase introduced by the preposition *fona*. To these may be added a further, and somewhat obvious, observation, viz. the extraordinary tendency in English not only to multiply the uses of prepositions but, conversely, to multiply the prepositions in a given use. We have noted fully seven prepositions, employed either simultaneously or divided at no distant periods, to express the logical subject of passive verbs. This is a fact; the *why* and the *wherefore* of it, however, is shrouded in that will-o'-the-wisp play and counterplay of psychological forces which, for want of better understanding, we term 'processes of linguistic consciousness.' Whence the necessity of supplanting *þurh* with *fram*? Why the substitution of *by* for *of*? Wherein lies the superior service of one over the other? These are questions we must perforce leave here unanswered. One assumption however, gathered in the course of study, may be risked with reasonable certainty: just as the loss of the traditional distinctions between, let us say, the dative, ablative and instrumental qualities in Latin *equō* necessarily brought about the clearer presentation of these respective ideas by means of satisfactory prepositions, so the confusion resulting from the co-existence of the several auctorial phrases must of itself have demanded a gradual clearing-up. Undoubtedly, the same syntactic notion being, as we have seen, variously expressed by various prepositions gave rise to different determinations of the same idea, all depending upon the viewpoint embodied in the original signification of the prepositions, —yet, were not the final results absolutely identical? It is here that the economy of expression we mentioned in the introductory remarks, stepped in and reaffirmed the progressive tendency of language by the destruction of synonymity and the creation of clearness out of chaos: first þ*urh* begins to lose ground, then *fram* follows suit, and then *of* gives way to *by*, which becomes the modern preposition of agency through the gradual supersession of all its competitors. It is no mere empty phrase that in language, too, we have a struggle for existence and a survival of the fittest. Only, it must ever be remembered that 'language' means the mentality of the people speaking it and that the human mind abhors abstruseness.

ALEXANDER GREEN.

University of Illinois.

THE PARDONER'S TAVERN

Of late certain oracular critics have lost no opportunity to accuse present-day Anglistic scholarship of an undue devotion to medieval themes; and valiant defenders have arisen to protest against this charge of exclusive absorption in a supposedly narrow phase of the past. To the present writer the charge seems distinctly "not proven," inasmuch as nothing is rarer among professed medievalists than the medieval perspective. By many reputable students of the literature of the Middle Ages any demonstration of the point of view of that period is greeted with shocked incredulity, because it must inevitably clash with the conceptions of our own time. From this unimaginative outlook, from this inability of the Peter Bells of scholarship to "fancy another situation from that in which they stood," no one has suffered more than Chaucer. Every fact of his life has been exploited, every line of his verse has been weighed, every source of his inspiration has been sought. All that has been missed is the one thing that seems absolutely essential to the proper interpretation of his poetry, his horizon, that is, his strict confinement within the bounds of fourteenth-century thought. "Chaucer, temp. 1890 or 1900 or 1914" has been studied to repletion. "Chaucer, temp. 1390" has been almost disregarded.

It is our present duty to remedy this neglect, else we shall never read rightly. One of the chief scholars of England, in giving hearty assent to my recently broached thesis of Chaucer's architectonic use of the motif of the Deadly Sins,[1] points out one phase of this unfortunate modernism:— "Of course your view will by many be regarded as fanciful, because it is difficult for us moderns to keep fully in mind the large place that theology had in the intellectual interests of cultured lay Englishmen in the fourteenth century, and indeed much later. Even very able scholars have, I think, sometimes reasoned in a way that shows imperfect apprehension of this." And so when Chaucer follows what this

[1] *Publications of Modern Language Association,* March 1914.

same clear-eyed scholar calls, "the line of least resistance by falling into the well-worn *exempla* track," there are some who are sadly puzzled by a design so different from their twentieth-century conception of a poet's province. Is it permitted me to regard as a happy augury the readiness of certain eminent specialists and Chaucer-lovers to approve my carefully considered effort to walk within the only pales that Chaucer knew? It seems to them as to me that, as scholars, we must always ask this question, "What did our medieval thinker mean by this?" and not, "What is the obvious meaning to the casual reader of to-day, who has made no attempt to plumb the depths and shallows of medieval thought?"

Before we turn to the tale that is our chief concern, let me cite several instances in which Chaucer's intent has been altogether lost. I have already commented at length upon the delicious irony of a long harangue against Pride in the tale of the proudest figure among the pilgrims, the Wife of Bath. Such a sermon is quite in accord with that just knowledge of human nature which makes each wayfarer assail his individual fault or the notorious weakness of his type. But the homily must fit the story as well as the storyteller, if the author is an artist. And the place of this preachment in the tale has been as thoroughly ignored as its relation to the Wife. No one has suggested in this connection—no one with only the modern outlook could suggest—that the Loathly Dame's discourse on Pride introduces a common element in the conception of courtly love. It is this Vice against which the God of Love warns the "gentle lover" of the *Romaunt of the Rose* (2245 f.) :—

> For pryde is founde in every part
> Contrarie unto Loves art.
> And he that loveth trewely
> Shulde him contene jolily,
> Withouten pryde in sondry, wyse.[1]

The verbal parallels between the Dame's exhortation to "gentilesse" (D 1109f.) and the God of Love's command, *Romaunt of the Rose*, 2187f., have been often noted with never a thought of the bearing of this relation upon the

[1] See Dodd's *Courtly Love in Chaucer and Gower*, p. 26.

essential purpose of the Wife's Tale of obedience in love.
Troilus, who, like the knight of the Wife's Tale, is an ''obe-
dient'' lover in a courtly story, divests himself utterly, under
Love's influence, of the Sin of Pride (I, 1079f.) :—

> For he bicom the frendlyeste wight,
> The gentileste, and eek the moste free,
> The thriftieste and oon the beste knight,
> That in his tyme was, or mighte be.
> Dede were his japes and his crueltee,
> His heighe port and his manere estraunge,
> And ech of tho gan for a vertu chaunge.

So far from being ''irrelevant,'' the sermon of the Wife's
story is not only, like all the homilies in the Sins tales, in
ironical accord with the character of the narrator, but is
admirably suited to the context of romantic love.[2a] How
obvious all this must have been to the medieval reader!

Or to take another illustration of the wide gap between
our critical viewpoint and fourteenth-century literary design.
To our way of thinking nothing could be less apposite than
the Poverty prologue, which introduces the Man of Law's
Tale of Constance. But every man of the Middle Ages must
have recognized at once the inherent fitness of prefacing
a tale of Envy—for Chaucer here is in Gower's wake[3]—with
stanzes illustrating such a dominant phase of Envy as
''grucchyng'' against one's wretched lot and ''sorwe of other
mannes wele'' (see *Parson's Tale*, 483, 498) or, more precisely,
that Impatient Poverty which is traditionally associated with
Envy even as late as the middle sixteenth century.[4]

The last word has not been said on the subject of Chaucer's
direct sources, despite the energy of hunters. Patristic or-

[2a] To Chaucer as to his great exemplar, "Amore e 'l cor gentil sono
una cosa."

[3] As I have already shown in my *Publications* article, Chaucer uses
four of Gower's stories to illustrate the same Sins. No one has noted
that our poet's independent development of *exemplum* themes suggested
by his contemporary recalls the very similar indebtedness of *The Legend
of Good women* to Boccaccio's topics rather than to his stories.

[4] I discuss in *The Nation*, July 9, 1914, the light cast by the morality,
"Impatient Poverty", circa 1560 (*"Lost" Tudor Plays*, edited by Farmer),
upon the time-honored relation between this form of Poverty and Envy.

igins of large portions of the Summoner's and Physician's
Tales have been entirely disregarded, as I show in an article
now in press.   Moreover far too little has been made
of the parallels between our poet's motives and those of his
contemporaries, Gower, Langland, Wyclif.   But the source-
hunter, hard on the trail of obvious plunderings, is in danger
of forgetting that a far larger significance than unquestioned
liftings can possibly possess often attaches to close resemblances between two authors who are giving and taking nought
directly but who are both repeating current fancies.   Such
parallels constitute the highest evidence for an established
tradition and hence are our safest guides to a proper perspective.   Let me illustrate the value of such a study of
tradition by a comparison between some of Chaucer's familiar
conceptions and the stock figures of that remarkable summary
of the typical weaknesses and weaklings of medieval society,
the *Ship of Fools*.

   Among the many social types preserved in Barclay's early
sixteenth-century version of the famous satire[5] are the Proud
and Shrewish Wife and the Drunken Cook.   The picture
of the woman as sometimes wise, but often foolish of counsel, largely given to chiding, so wrathful that "she passyth
all the cruel bestis of Inde"—even the tiger robbed of her
whelps,—ever devising scorn, full of guile and falsehood, and
emptying by her proud apparel her husband's purse, acknowledging Pride as lady and mistress, well images a conception
of the sex which Chaucer turned to large account and which
long persisted in literature.[6]   Indeed the sketch of the Wife
of Bath owes quite as much to this tradition as to the
Romaunt of the Rose or to the *Miroir du Mariage*.   To the
proverbial drunkenness of Cooks, which is as old as classical
comedy, Barclay devotes an entire section (II, 91-93).   The

---

[5] Barclay's *Ship of Fools*, edited by Jamieson, 1874, 2 vols.
[6] Such sixteenth-century products as "The Proude Wyves Pater
Noster," "The Wife Lapped in Morrelles Skin," "The Pride and
Abuse of Women," "A Glasse to Viewe the Pride of Vaineglorious
Women," (Hazlitt, *Remains of Early Popular Poetry*, vol. IV.), all
continue the tradition that feminizes the First of the Deadly Sins in
Langland, Chaucer and the example-books, and much later in Spenser.

foolish and bawdy Cook, the very type of glutton and rioter, consuming wine and ale till all the best be gone and his master's good be consumed, must have been a well-known figure long before he invited on the Canterbury Road the chiding of his superior officer, the Manciple.[7] But the satirist devotes the largest space in his *Ship* to the tavern-revelers—drinkers, lechers, dicers, blasphemers—who are revealed so grimly in the "moralities" of the *Pardoner's Tale*. To this wretched crew we shall soon give full attention.

It seems to me that everything that is really essential in the setting of the *Pardoner's Tale* has been entirely disregarded in the many elaborate discussions of the rascal's contribution, simply because commentators have failed to realize that the great master of irony selects a tavern for his ribald's sermon against tavern-revels, the home of Gluttony as the scene of violent tirades against Gluttony and its accessory faults. It is my present purpose to show two things: first that the tavern is the stage of the Pardoner's harangues; and secondly, that these harangues are directed against those vices which are ever associated with taverns in medieval tradition. Of the other and perhaps more important phase of the Pardoner's character and discourse, his thorough-going revelation of Avarice by positive practice and negative precept, it is needless to speak now.

No long argument is necessary to show that the Pardoner and his fellows do not leave the tavern-benches just after the corny ale has been quaffed and his prologue is complete. Jusserand has rightly observed:[8] "On the further bench of the tavern the Pardoner remains still seated. There enter Chaucer, the Knight, the Squire, the Friar, the Host— old acquaintances. We are by ourselves, no one needs be afraid of speaking, the foaming ale renders hearts expansive; here the secret coils of that tortuous soul unfold to view; he gives us the summary of a whole life, the theory of his existence, the key to all his secrets." But the observant

---

[7] It has not been recognized that the quarrels of the Canterbury pilgrims are as professional and typical as the characters themselves. But more of this in another place.

[8] *English Wayfaring Life in the Middle Ages*, pp. 332-333.

French scholar does not record that the pilgrims are still seated in the ale-house, when, at the conclusion of his tale, the wonderful scoundrel bids them (C 925-926) :

> Cometh forth anon and kneleth heer adoun,
> And mekely receyveth my pardoun.

Will anyone dare suggest that the company are now ahorse and that the Pardoner proposes to them to dismount that he may confer absolution? Nor can it be alleged that the Pardoner is here merely rehearsing a sermon without thought of his present company or surroundings—as indeed he is doing some lines above when he calls, "Cometh up, ye wyves, offreth of your wolle!" and adds, "Lo, sirs, thus I preche." He now not only alludes to the story that he has just told, "But, sirs, o word forgat I in my tale," but proceeds to discuss the pilgrims' wayfaring through town's end and countryside in the high honor and worth of his illustrious companionship. We are explicitly told at the end of the epilogue (C 968) that the pilgrims "riden forth hir weye" —a phrase that is elsewhere used (A 856) to indicate a similar resumption of the journey after a stop. What infinite zest it adds to the Pardoner's arraignment of tavern follies to realize that every count of his indictment is pronounced amid huge creature-comfort in the joys of an ale-house—the clink of canakins, the laughter of tap wenches, the rattle of dice, the sound of oaths! The irony of the environment is as delicious as the mockery of personality—both utterly at variance with the tenor of the Pardoner's sentences, so gravely pronounced. How much of Chaucer's fun we moderns miss!

The purport of the Pardoner's sermonizing is altogether lost, if we pass over it lightly as "a long discussion on the sins of swearing, gluttony, dicing and other of the deadly sins." We have double evidence of the strongest that the Pardoner is exemplifying only the vices of the tavern. First, Chaucer, here, as in other Sins tales, derives his application —else no artist he—directly from the substance of his story. His moralities follow immediately his picture of the tavern, that abode of Gluttony in all its phases—drinking, lechery, hazardry, and great oaths. In this "devil's temple" his young folk

> pleye at dees bothe day and night,
> And ete also and drinken over hir might.
> ....
> Hir othes been so grete and so dampnable.

Among them is kindled and blown

> the fyr of lecherye,
> That is annexed unto glotonye.

It is significant that in the poet's other picture of tavern revel, the contribution of the wine-bibbing Cook (A 4365f.), drinking, wenching, dicing, find a large place.

All this is undeniable. Our other evidence, that of tradition, needs larger illustration. In accounts of the Deadly Seven we find that Gluttony includes "Sins of the Tavern," and moreover that these sins are the very vices enumerated by Chaucer. Langland's sketch of Gluttony is a tavern scene (*Piers Plowman*, B, V, 304f.). Dan Michel, in his *Ayenbite of Inwit* (pp. 56-57), following *Le Mireour du Monde* (pp. 170-171), discusses, under the head of Gluttony, "the zennes thet byeth ydo ine the taverne," and then proceeds much in Chaucer's wise:—"The tauerne ys the scole of the dyeule huere his deciples studieth, and his oȝene chapele ther huer me deth his seruese and ther huer he maketh his miracles zuiche ase behoueth to the dyeule . . . . . Ac the dyeuel deth al ayenward ine the tauerne. Vor huanne the glotoun geth in to the tauerne ha geth opriȝt; huanne he comth ayen, he ne heth uot thet him moȝe sostyeni ne bere." Likewise the anonymous author of *Jacob's Well*[9] writes under the caption, "De Gula" (p. 147): "At the tauerne often the glotonye begynneth; for the tauerne is welle of glotonye, for it may be clepyd the develys scolehous & the develys chapel, for there his dyscyples stodyen & syngyn, bothe day & niȝt, & there the deuyl doth meraclys to his seruantys, etc."[10] And Bar-

---

[9] *Early English Text Society*, 115 (1900).

[10] Compare Royster, *A Middle English Treatise on the Ten Commandments, Introduction*, pp. ix-x. "Devil's Chapel" is still a potent phrase on the "temperance" platform.

clay, in the *Ship of Fools* thus speaks of the Sin of Gluttony
(I, 93) :—

> The people that are acloyed with this synne,
> On no thynge els theyr myndes wyll aply:
> Saue to the wyne and ale stakes to renne
> And there as bestes to stryue and drinke auy.

How then, in the light of medieval perspective, could Chaucer
more accurately illustrate the Sin of Gluttony than by a tavern
picture drawn by a tavern reveler seated in the very hour of
his sermonizing on a tavern bench?

Moreover the sins assailed by the Pardoner are those conventionally associated with Gluttony and the tavern. I have
already demonstrated at sufficient length in my *Publications*
article (pp. 105-106) that the close relation between Lechery
and Gluttony, based upon Ephesians V, 18, is a common-
place of all medieval descriptions of Gluttony and that, in
many sketches of this Sin, the *exemplum* of Lot and his
daughters (Genesis XIX) finds mention. This traditional
relation is still strong in the *Ship of Fools*:

> But namely dronkennes and wretchyd Glotony
> By their excess and superfluyte
> Engendreth the rote of cursed Lechery.

It was therefore inevitable in the irony of things that the
companion Sin should be assailed by this typical Glutton who
has "a jolly wench in every town."[11]

The two other accessories of Gluttony—Hazardry and Blas-
phemy—are always closely associated in medieval literature.
One of the most famous of all *exempla* is that of the unlucky
dicer who blasphemes the Virgin and loses his eyes.[12] Miss
Petersen[13] finds a close parallel to the setting of the Pardoner's
Tale in the account by Thomas Cantipratensis of a Brabant

---

[11] In the English Moralities wenching is ever associated with the
life of taverns. In the *Digby Play* Mary Magdalene is led by Lechery
to a tavern where she is tempted and falls. In *Nature* Sensuality
conducts Man to a tavern and to the society of Margery. In the
Interlude of Youth Riot suggests to his victim that they repair to
the tavern for a surfeit of wine and a kiss from a pretty wench.

[12] See Herolt, s. v. "Blasphemia"; Herbert, *Catalogue of Romances,*
III, 360, 608, 624, 648, 665.

[13] *The Sources of the Nonne Prestes Tale,* p. 98.

"cellarium in quo perditissimi adolescentes ad ludum tessarum sedentes blasphemiis et juramentis ad invicem contendebant." So Bromyard, in his *Summa Predicantium,* combines under "Gula" with drinking and wenching illicit oaths and forbidden games.[14] In Barclay's account of Card Players and Dicers (II, 71-72) we learn that

> the woundes of God ar sworne,
> His armys, herte and bonys, almoste at every worde;
> Thus is our Sauyour amonge these caytyfs torne.

Similarly under "Blasphemers and Sweres":—

> The tables, tenys, cardis or the dyce
> Ar chefe begynnynge of this vnhappynes,
> For whan the game wyll nat well aryse
> And all the players troubled by dronkenes,
> Than suche caytyfs as joy in this exces
> At eche worde labour our Sauyour to tere
> With othes abhomynable whiche they ungoodly swere.

Occleve's Beggar confesses (*Regement of Princes,* ll. 626f.) that, playing dice all night at the tavern, he dismembered with great oaths and rent limb from limb "the former of every creature." Finally our chief authority, the Pardoner himself, tells us very plainly (C 650f.) that Cursing arises over the dice.

Hasardry, though it has already received treatment under Avarice (as in the Parson's Tale), is one of the subheads of Gluttony in the *Ayenbite of Inwit* (p. 52); and "Great Oaths" is subordinate to Gluttony in both Bromyard and Langland (B, VI, 92, V, 314, XIII, 400). Indeed Langland's Glutton thus makes his shrift (B, V, 374f.):—

> "I glotoun," quod the gome, "gylti me gelde,
> That I have trespassed with my tonge, I can nougte telle how ofte,
> Sworen 'goddes soule' and 'so god me help and halidom,'
> There no nede ne was nyne hundreth tymes."

Moreover it is under Gluttony (I, 96) that Barclay writes:—

> Some swereth armys, nayles, herte and body,
> Terynge our lord worse than the Jowes hym arayed.[15]

---

[14] See my *Publications* article, pp. 105.

[15] An interesting *exemplum* of the danger of Great Oaths—not included in Skeat's elaborate notes upon this rending of the Christ (V, 275-276, 284)—is "The Tale of the Bleeding Child", *Handlyng Synne,* 665-800, and *Gesta Romanorum* (English version), No. LXXXVIII (*E. E. T. S., Extra Series,* 33, pp. 409, 506).

How could a medieval poet better illustrate the Sin of Gluttony than by due discussion of each of its traditional phases or accessories? There is nothing confused or heterogeneous in the Pardoner's summary of sins in the application at the close of his tale (C 895-899). It is an orderly exposition in the true *exemplum* manner of the two Deadly Sins illustrated by his story and by his own practice and assailed in his sermons: first, cursed Avarice, that leads to homicide; then Gluttony and its three accessories, Luxury, Hasardry and Blasphemy. Indeed it is as clear-cut as Langland's famous feofment (B, II, 92-93) :—

> Glotonye he gaf hem eke and grete othes togydere,
> And alday to drynke at dyuerse tauernes.

In his use of Deadly Sins material in the Pardoner's moralities, as in his other *exempla* of the Vices, Chaucer is largely indebted to the material of his Parson's Tale. This relation has already been so fully indicated by scholars[16] that it need not long detain us. It is interesting that the Parson, like Peraldus, includes Hasardry under Avarice and Great Oaths under Wrath. This arrangement, however, does not debar the poet, when fashioning the Pardoner, from combining Dicing and Swearing in the traditional conception of the Glutton as a lord of tavern revels and misrule rather than as a mere slave of food and drink. Even the Parson, who unlike Dan Michel, Langland, Bromyard, and Barclay, views Gluttony in its narrower aspect, recognizes its close bond with Lechery (I, 836), "for thise two sinnes been so ny cosins that ofte tyme they wol nat departe;" and expressly indicates the tie between Hasardry and Blasphemy (I, 792), "Now comth hasardrye with hise apurtenances, as tables and rafles; of which comth deceite, false othes, chydinges, and alle ravines, blaspheminge and reneyinge of God, etc."

If the Pardoner's relation to his background has been ignored, the variance of his gluttonous practice from his sober precept disregarded, the tenor of his precept misunderstood, so his clash with one of the other pilgrims has been entirely

[16] See Koeppel, *Herrig's* Archiv, LXXXVII, pp. 33-54; Notes to Skeat's edition; Miss Petersen, *Sources of the Parson's Tale*, passim; my *Publications* article, 105, 115.

unapprehended. The reader has only to compare the oaths which the Pardoner places under the ban (C 651-652) :—

> By Goddes precious herte and by his nayles
> And by the blode of Crist, that it is in Hayles.

with the very recent blasphemy of the Host's link between the tales of the Physician and the Pardoner, "by nayles and by blood!" (C 288) and "by Corpus bones" (C 314), in order to recognize that our specious rascal convicts the Landlord of sin long before he further invites his wrath by summoning him to "kisse the reliks everichon" (C 946). And here it is necessary to note that the Host's swearing, for which he is so ready to take up the cudgels against Lollards (B 1172-1173),[17] is typical of his profession. If the tavern is the breeding-place of oaths, it is inevitable that the taverner should be an adept in blasphemy. Barclay, in a single line (I, 12), gives ample evidence that the Host's cursing is traditional, "Blasphemers of Christ, hostlers and taverners." It is of course a striking feature of the situation that the Pardoner himself, professed champion of the Second Commandment, is a constant offender against its decree: D 164, "by God and by Seint John"; C 320, "by Seint Ronyon" (where he repeats the oath of the Host); C 457, "by God".

Fortunately contemporary interpretation of the character of the Pardoner is no mere matter of surmise. That he— and not the Friar, who "knew the tavernes wel in every toun" (Prologue, A 240)—was deemed the typical tavern-reveler of the company, fond of both his glass and his lass, is put beyond all question by the "Prologue of the Merry Adventure of the Pardoner with a Tapster at Canterbury", which prefaces the pseudo-Chaucerian sequel to the Tales, the *Tale of Beryn*. No sooner are the pilgrims installed at the "Cheker of the Hope" inn at the cathedral city than the Pardoner "as a man i-lernyd of such kyndnes" makes warm

---

[17] The citation by a contemporary, Knighton, Anno 1388 (*Rolls Series*, 92, II, 262) of Wycliffite opinions is not inapposite here: "Item quod non licet aliquo modo jurare. Nota ibi isti firmandus, nam sequela cujuslibet dicti eorum talis erat, 'I am sykyr, it is soth,' vel sic, 'Withoute doute, it is so.'" See Trevelyan, *England in the Age of Wycliffe*, p. 317; and Arnold, *Wyclif's Works*, III, 332.

friends with Kit the Tapster, embracing her by the middle, chucking her under the chin and tempting her with a groat. The outcome of the intrigue is as sorry as anything in Smollett. The Pardoner seeks to secure the Tapster for his own, but, in the old phrase, he "drinks without the cup," though she feigns full consent. After ordering for his newly found love and himself "a cawdle of wine and sugar", the Pardoner returns to the company. Light-hearted with song, he leaves them at bedtime and goes in search of his lowly lady. Then follows the horse-play. The Pardoner scratches and whines at the locked door of the Tapster; but he is soundly thrashed by the Tapster's Paramour, and is chased and chevied by Jack the Hostler, a creature of Host-like oaths. He is finally forced to lie down in the litter of a great Welsh dog, which bites him in the thigh. The poor wretch finds nought save curses to assuage his anger and despair. On the morrow the unhappy Pardoner washes the blood off his cheeks, binds up his head and rides away singing in the midst of the company.

Now whence was this conception of the Pardoner derived? Certainly not from the General Prologue, where we hear nothing of potent potting or of amorous adventures. Nor is this the hypocritical exponent of Avarice known to every reader. This *picaro* is the gluttonous Pardoner of his prologue and tale, lickerish, lecherous, blasphemous, unable ever to resist the lure of ale-stake or of petticoat, bibulously preaching sermons against Gluttony from a tavern-bench.[18] Moreover what convincing testimony to the Pardoner's repute in the company is given by the cry of the gentles (C 324), when the Host heralds this "noble ecclesiaste:" "Nay, let him telle us of no ribaudye!"[19] It must be remembered that

[18] Furnivall has noted, in his Introduction to the *Tale of Beryn* (*Chaucer Society*, 1887, *Early English Text Society*, 1909), how well the anonymous author preserves the traits of Chaucer's pilgrims.

[19] Indulgence in ribald tales is yet another trait of medieval Gluttony. Langland's Glutton says of himself (B. V, 383), "For loue of tales, in tauernes to drynke the more I dined," and (C. VII, 433), "ich fedde me with ale out of reson among rybaudes here rybaudrye to huyre."

the Wife of Bath has already (*contra* the Chaucer Society, her tale certainly precedes the Pardoner's) suggested (D 170-171) that he is over-fond of ale. Hence both internal and external evidence shows that the chief tavern-haunter of the fellowship is selected to inveigh against the evils of "the devil's temple"—in due accord with the design that makes each pilgrim denounce his peculiar weakness.

This article is an implicit plea not only for the imaginative insight which enables us to enter into the life of another age and to read its poet's words aright, but also for that humbler every-day quality of accurate observation which alone makes it possible for us to read a poet's words at all. I have encountered from scholars of repute such objections as this: Despite the Manciple's lengthy chiding of the Cook (H 25f.)—if anyone is so incautious as to admit that he really does chide the Cook—he certainly cannot be deemed a Chider. And why not? Because, forsooth, he is called in the General Prologue (A 567), to which many of us apparently confine our reading, "a gentil Maunciple." Just as though our wrathful Summoner were not described in the same General Prologue (A 647) as a "gentil harlot and a kinde", and as though "the lost soul" of our present discussion were not "a gentil Pardoner" (A 669). Likewise the Man of Law is absolved from all Envy by the staunch adherent of the General Prologue, who overlooks entirely the Impatient Poverty (Envy) prologue, with which he prefaces Gower's Envy tale. So the Pardoner must not be considered a typical glutton or tavern-reveller—once more the negative evidence of the General Prologue!—though this lover of "cakes and ale" is so proclaimed by his own confession, by his perverse sermonizing, by the pot-house setting of his story and by his contemporary reputation. It will be a happy day for our contemplation of the great works of our medieval literature, when the critical astigmatism that either disregards the text altogether or sees it blurredly through the medium of modern lenses yields to the undimmed vision that views the poet's thought in the large light of the poet's own perspective.   FREDERICK TUPPER.
University of Vermont.

WHAT IS THE PARLEMENT OF FOULES?

Professor Manly's article with the above title (Morsbach *Festschrift*, p. 278) is noteworthy, if for no other reason, as perhaps the strongest statement possible by a disbeliever in the historical basis for Chaucer's *Parlement of Foules*. Let us see what the most radical skepticism may say against Koch's theory. And first, putting aside for a time Professor Manly's objections to the accepted symbolism of the poem, what does he put in its place? He does not deny that the poem was written about the time usually assigned to it. He admits that the theory is more plausible in its present form than when originally proposed by Professor Koch. But, after emphasizing that the poem is of the vision type, with a love debate, or *demande d'amours,* and that the assembly of birds was held on Valentine's day, he proposes as his new theory that the poem was merely a Valentine day exercise for some possible Valentine society of the time.

Now it may be said at once that no one denies, or need deny the three points in Professor Manly's analysis of the poem. It is a vision poem, it is a love debate, and the time is Valentine's day. Not one of these things interferes with the interpretation of the poem now so long and so generally accepted. Professor Manly has missed the point, or at least has not met it so far. It is the coincidence in time and many particulars between Chaucer's poem and the incidents of the royal courtship itself, which makes for the interpretation of Professor Koch. This striking coincidence Professor Manly has not explained away.

Yet there is, apparently, an implication in the suggestion of Chaucer's using well-known conventions, that he could not have used them for a particular purpose. Now the practice of pointing out the conventional in a work, as if it were a complete explanation of that work, has been ridden very hard of late years. It has too often been assumed that the use of a conventional form precluded any origination on the part of the poet, or even adaptation to a particular end. This is neither logical nor complete criticism. There is much that is conventional in all poetry, even that of late times. But that we have completely eliminated the personality of the poet as anything more than a mere imitator, by the process of finding some indebtedness to others is far from true. Or that, if Chaucer in this particular case used a conventional form, he could not have applied it to a particular purpose or occasion is of course in the last degree untenable.

Indeed, if Chaucer had been specifically planning a poem on the royal courtship, he would naturally have used some form with which he had previously become acquainted. The vision form he had already used in another poem of occasion, the *Book of the Duchess.* He had also used the Valentine day setting in the *Complaint of Mars,* as Professor Manly points out here, referring to his article in *Harvard Studies and Notes* V, 107.[1]

Again, if Chaucer had been planning a poem on the royal courtship he would naturally have used the love-debate, since that was inherent in the subject itself. The use of one or more of these forms, therefore, does not prove that Chaucer may not have used them for a particular purpose, as in shadowing forth an important event in English court life. Again I emphasize the real point, the use of these conventions at such a time and with so many similarities of incident that they suggest to us, as they presumably suggested to hearers of the poem in Chaucer's time, a relation to the courtship of Richard and Anne. The most effective way in which to overthrow the present theory would be to show that the *Parlement of Foules* was made at some different

---

[1] Yet the language of Professor Manly in the *Festschrift* seems to imply too much. "That Chaucer himself took part in the literary features of such social entertainments is indicated by his *Complaint of Mars,*" begs the question. Until we have further proof that there were such literary and social entertainments, they cannot be used for purposes of argument. Professor Manly uses the language of one who has won his case. All we know of the *Complaint of Mars,* so far as this point is concerned, is that Chaucer used the Valentine day setting for his poem, but nothing regarding the occasion of its delivery.

time, and for some different set of circumstances than those usually supposed to be indicated.

Professor Manly makes no attempt to indicate a different time for the composition of the poem, as was earlier done by Tyrwhitt, followed by Godwin, who thought it applied to the marriage of John of Gaunt in 1359,[2] or by a writer in the *Saturday Review* of April 15, 1871, who applied it to the marriage of Lord De Coucy in 1364.[3] If such a time can be successfully brought forward, we must all, give up the accepted theory. Nor does Professor Manly propose a different set of circumstances to which the incidents of the poem may be in some sense parallel. He merely opposes altogether any such parallelism. On the other hand he does propose an occasion which, he thinks, sufficiently accounts for the poem, without connecting its incidents with contemporary life.

Yet it must be noted that, if Professor Manly could prove there were literary entertainments in England in honor of Saint Valentine as early as 1380 or 1382, he would not yet have overthrown the theory of Koch, as he seems to think. There is no reason why, if Chaucer had been planning to write such a Valentine poem about that time, he should not have chosen as subject the royal courtship, then in everybody's mind. That is, Professor Manly has proposed in his hypothesis only a new occasion for the delivery of such a poem. In so doing, however, he has not provided any new interpretation of the poem which precludes its reference to the circumstances usually supposed to be symbolized. In a similar way the *Complaint of Mars* may have been intended as a literary feature of such a social entertainment as Professor Manly thinks possible some score of years before it is known to have been in existence. Yet this would not

---

[2] Tyrwhitt's note is in *Appendix* to his *Preface*, C, note e. Godwin discusses the subject in his *Life of Chaucer*, ch. xxi (vol. II, p. 68).

[3] See Furnivall's *Trial Forewords*, p. 70. That Tyrwhitt, as early as the late seventies of the eighteenth century, first connected the *Parlement of Foules* with an important marriage in England is significant indication of the appeal made by the poem's symbolism.

prevent its reference to some incident of court life, as that to which Shirley refers in his manuscript note.

But Professor Manly has not furnished anything like adequate proof of the occasion which he proposes. This vital suggestion of his paper remains at best an unsupported conjecture. He would have us believe that the *Parlement of Foules* was written as a mere imitative exercise for a society, of which none is known to have been in existence for twenty years, and then only in a country which certainly did not usually adopt its social or literary customs from England. The hypothesis would suit admirably if its author could prove that the *Parlement of Foules* was written after 1400, when the French society of the Valentine cult was in existence,—and Chaucer was in his grave. As it stands, Professor Manly's extraordinary skepticism in the one case, and far more extraordinary faith in a society to suit his purpose seem somewhat at variance.

I say this, too, without any special prejudice in favor of Koch's theory. Professor Manly admits its greater plausibility with the modification it was my good fortune to make.[4] Yet if there be a better explanation of the poem than Professor Koch proposed, no matter how it conflicts with previous views, it is the part of common sense to adopt it. The new hypothesis, however, must not place a greater strain upon belief than the one which it displaces.

[4] It is not uninteresting, I think, and not undeserving of record that two others had already made the discovery of Charles of France as one of the suitors in the poem, by the time my article was published in *Modern Philology* VIII, 45. These are Dr. Samuel Moore, now of the University of Wisconsin, and Dr. T. S. Graves of Trinity College, North Carolina. I presume they will have no objection to my referring to statements made to me in conversation some years ago. Besides, I noticed only recently that Coulton in *Chaucer and His England* refers to Charles and his wish to make Anne his wife, without however suggesting the relation to the *Parlement of Foules*. On p. 204 he speaks of "how Richard offered an immense sum for her [Anne of Bohemia] in order to outbid his royal brother of France." This statement I did not see until sometime after printing my article.

But Professor Manly urges some special objections to Koch's theory which must be examined. "To whom", he asks, "was the poem intended as a compliment? To Richard, or Anne, or both? The critics are in general not specific on this point." He then argues that, if written after Anne's arrival in England, the poem was not complimentary to her. If written before, it was not complimentary to Richard. These objections seem to me greatly magnified, if indeed they have any foundation. Frankly, I take it the critics have not been "specific on this point" because they have not thought it necessary. Nor can it be regarded as necessary except by great emphasis on extremely minor details.

In fact, Professor Manly's premise that the poem is un-complimentary in its present form to either or both of the royal personages rests, it seems to me, on no solid basis. That Chaucer might have made it more flattering to either or both is doubtless true. Why he did not do this we shall perhaps never know. But that these young people, not quite "children" in any real sense, would not have enjoyed this beautiful poem, as others must have enjoyed it, seems to me impossible. Neither Richard nor Anne was likely to find fault with such consummate artistry. Neither would have thought of dis-secting it minutely, to see whether it sufficiently fitted his particular case.

But Professor Manly thinks Anne would have been offended that she is represented as "undecided in her choice", or "unable to decide." Such expressions, however, are quite too strong for the case. The formel eagle is represented as ask-ing what all young ladies were supposed to desire, or what they were conventionally supposed to demand, the year of "respite for to avysen me." The best evidence that this could not have been derogatory to Anne is found when we compare the situation here with that in another of Chaucer's poems. In the *Book of the Duchess*, Blanche of Lancaster is represented as putting off her princely lover for a similar period. The first offer of marriage by a prince of the realm was quite as desirable for the daughter of Henry of Lancas-ter, as was that of Richard for Anne, considering the latter's other offers at the time. Yet it was only when John of Gaunt renewed his proposal "another yere" (1. 1258) that Blanche gave him "the noble yift of hir mercy." The parallel is even more favorable to Anne. The "man in blak" tells the story of an absolute rejection. The formel eagle merely asks time to reflect.[5]

Again, in his development of a supposed dilemma, Professor Manly thinks that, if the poem had been written before Anne's arrival in England, it must have been intended as a compliment to Richard.[6] In this he believes it fails because the young king was not immediately preferred to his rivals. This rivalry Professor Manly minimizes by calling Friedrich an "insignificant princeling", and the young Charles "nostre adversaire" instead of heir to the French throne. However no one will be misled by this clever use of names. Friedrich of Meissen was originally considered a worthy match for Anne of Bohemia,[7] and the heir to the French throne was certainly so. In any case the rivalry was a real one for Richard, and it was only a combination of circumstances, political and religious, which finally turned

[5] It matters little whether the allusion in the *Book of the Duchess* is based on fact or not. The use of it by Chaucer made it public property, and the reference to it in the poem by the lover himself shows that he did not regard it as a slight.

[6] To one statement of Professor Manly a footnote seems sufficient. He says: "If the poem was written before Anne's arrival in England, in December 1381, it is difficult to see how it can have been intended for her. She could not have known of it unless Chaucer had sent it to her in Bohemia, and this, while possible, is highly improbable." Is it impossible that the poem could not have been written in anticipation of Anne's coming, and have been read or recited on her arrival in England? Compare the similar situation in the writing of Dunbar's *Thissel and Rose,* to which I later call attention.

[7] In a footnote to p. 280 Professor Manly seems to imply that I had made too much of Friedrich's after greatness. That was not my intention, but the implied slight to the young prince as a suitor may be easily answered. He was thought worthy of Anne, not as an "insignificant princeling", but as heir to an important German principality, and as what he was likely to become. The kinsmen of Anne could not have been entirely blind to their own or her advantage.

the scale in his favor.[8] Besides, Richard must by this time have become somewhat accustomed to meeting obstacles to' his marriage. Negotiations for · a marriage with Princess Mary of France had twice come to nought,[9] and at least two other matches for him had been proposed and put aside for various reasons.[10] It is inconceivable that Richard should not have known of these things, and certainly they were known to the courtiers who heard the poem read or recited. Had Chaucer therefore tried to minimize the rivalry, in order to flatter Richard, he would not only have been untrue to the facts, but would have been in danger of rendering his effort at sychophancy ridiculous.

Even if this were not so, does not Professor Manly greatly magnify the young Richard's feelings? The marriage of a prince is a conventional matter at best. Richard especially was too young to take the maturer interest of a man deeply in love, and must have looked on the various stages of the negotiations with curious rather than passionate eyes. When, too, the young bride did arrive, he was quite too much pleased and satisfied, to care whether a pretty poem that seems to refer to his affairs had put everything exactly to his liking.

But apart from these suggestions in refutation of Professor Manly's objections, is the poem uncomplimentary to either of the royal personages? I put aside for the present the question why Chaucer did not represent the successful conclusion of the courtship. Taking into account only what was attempted on the accepted theory, why is the poem uncomplimentary to either Richard or Anne?

As to Richard, the "royal tercel" of the usual interpretation, he is given the first choice of a mate; he is affectionately called "my sone" by the presiding goddess Nature,

---

[8] This has been made plain, I think, in my two articles, with their numerous references to documents of the time: *A New Note on the Date of the Knight's Tale*, Hart anniversary volume, p. 203; and the *Suitors in Chaucer's Parlement of Foules*, already referred to.

[9] Froissart, *Chroniques* (De Lettenhove) VIII, 383, 385; Longmans, *Life and Times of Edward Third*, II, 271f.; Skeat's *Chaucer*, I, xxvii.

[10] Froissart, *Chroniques*, IX, 212.

who specifically asks him to make his choice; his is the only speech to make any recognized impression on the "formel egle"; he is indicated to the latter in no uncertain terms by the "tercelet of the faucon", after the suitors had misunderstood the proposal of "batayle" for supremacy; and finally, as clearly foreshadowing the conclusion of the matter, Dame Nature advises the formel eagle in the most explicit language, "I counseyle yow the royal tercel take." Would not these several and favorable allusions be sufficiently flattering to the young king? Would he have been better pleased with a more abject adulation?

Or could Anne fail to feel complimented by the allusions in the poem to her? She could scarcely have been praised more highly when the formel eagle is first introduced (11. 372-78). She could not have been treated more kindly than when Nature covers her confusion at the professions of her young lover, and gently soothes her with "Doghter, drede yow noght, I yow assure." (1. 447). She was given the special privilege of choice (1. 409), a privilege unknown to bird life and none too common among marriageable women of the time. This privilege, too, Nature emphasized a second time (11. 626-7), although she immediately after gave advice that was intended to settle the formel eagle's choice upon the royal tercel. She was at last allowed to have her own way—what more pleasing to a woman—in the choice of a period for deliberation,

> "And after that to have my choys al free."

This period she asks for herself alone:

> "I wol noght serven Venus ne Cupyde
> For soothe as yet."

She is not one to play with her lover's affection, or send him on a useless and dangerous quest, for like Blanche of Lancaster in the *Book of the Duchess* (11. 1015-33).

> "She ne used no suche knakkes smale."

Finally, her decision is received by Nature and the bird parliament as an entirely fitting ending of the love debate.

Surely this did not indicate that Anne was "unable to decide", but rather that she thought it unmaidenly and unconventional to make her choice so quickly. Especially the fact that Nature and the whole bird family take the conclusion as entirely right—it was utterly at variance with what could happen in bird life—must indicate that it was not intended in any sense to show a vacillating character in Anne of Bohemia. It is Professor Manly only, so far as I now remember, who feels any dissatisfaction for the formel eagle, or any doubt as to what she really wished to do—at the proper time.[11]

I would press this last matter one point further. If the bird parliament is nothing more, as Professor Manly supposes, why this introduction of a convention—the putting off of the lover for a time—never known in the realm of animal life, but characteristic of human marriage arrangements in the period of Chaucer's *Parlement of Foules?* What is the meaning on Professor Manly's hypothesis of this vital element of the poem? Indeed, is not the conclusion on his basis far more lame, than he thinks it on the accepted theory?

Another objection is urged by Professor Manly in these words:

"Some stress has been laid upon the accuracy with which the descriptions of the suitors in the poem fit the three candidates. This appearance of accuracy is obtained by emphasizing certain phases of the situation and disregarding others. If the poem be taken not seriously, as an intended compliment to Richard and Anne, but as a bit of merriment intended to amuse the adults at the expense of these royal children, the descriptions fit well enough. But if this is the case, the poem is not a compliment to Richard and Anne, but makes sport of them."

It will be seen from this second use of it that Professor Manly is fond of the logical dilemma. Nor will anyone object to his putting the best face possible on the case. Granting the premises on which he rests the dilemma argument, the case is his. But are the premises sound?

Now I have tried to show—I purposely avoid the special

[11] Even the late Henry Morley accepted the symbolic character of the poem, though he preferred to go back to Tyrwhitt's long discarded hypothesis as to the occasion intended. Von Westenholz (*Anglia, Beiblatt* XII, 167) can hardly be classed here, though as early as 1901 he suggested a mild skepticism regarding Koch's theory.

pleader's "I have shown" too much used of late [12]—that Professor Manly has taken quite too seriously the first horn of his argument. I cannot believe that the poem can be reasonably regarded as uncomplimentary to the royal lovers of 1380 and 1381. Yet has the other horn of the dilemma— a mixed figure seems absolutely necessary—any firmer foundation? It largely rests on a misconstruction of a part of my paper on the *Suitors in the Parlement of Foules*. When the discovery was made that another suitor might better take the place of the Prince of Bavaria in Koch's earlier interpretation, it was natural to see whether the new claimant would fit into the speeches assigned by Chaucer to the three tercel eagles. If no fit place had been found for him there, it would have been an argument against admitting Charles of France as one of the suitors. It was with some pleasure, I admit, that I found the parallelism between the speeches and certain known facts to be more considerable than they had been in the older form of the theory. Yet I cannot believe that these coincidences were too much magnified in this conservative statement:

"It must be admitted that the notes of time in the speeches of the last two suitors have significant parallelism in

---

[12] It may be permissible in this connection to call attention to Professor Manly's use of this expression in the Kittredge *Anniversary Papers*. In his article *What is Chaucer's House of Fame*, he says: "Neither the *Boke of the Duchesse* nor the *Legend of Good Women* has the slightest claim to be regarded as allegorical; and the *Parlement of Foules*, as I have recently shown (Morsbach *Festschrift*) is a Valentine poem, presenting a *demande d' amours* in the setting of a bird parliament."

I agree entirely that allegory and allegorical are often too loosely used. But they are so used by very good critics—see Legouis's chapter on the Allegorical Poems of Chaucer—and Professor Manly's statement is far too strong. Besides, if he also means by his sentence that he "has shown" the *Parlement of Foules* is not allegorical in the accepted sense, more accurately a poem of occasion, he is himself using language somewhat unwarrantedly, it seems to me. I have in mind the words of Professor Kittredge in his *Chaucer's Alceste* (*Mod. Phil.* VI, 435) that "when a particular suggestion of this kind has been put into type, it becomes a kind of dogma."

the long betrothal of Friedrich of Meissen, and the short period during which Charles VI was considered a suitor."[13]

But Professor Manly charges that the parallelism "is obtained by emphasizing certain phases of the situation and disregarding others." The specific instance to which he points (see his footnote 1 to p. 281) is due to an entire misunderstanding of one of my footnotes to the "Suitors" article.[14] I had thought the suggestion there put had sufficient clearness not to be wholly missed, and sufficient delicacy not to offend. It amounts to nothing in the argument, was not stressed as a part of it, and may be wholly disregarded without injuring the case. That Professor Manly has so completely misunderstood its import almost makes me regret using it. But he should hardly have assumed that I knew so little of fourteenth century history as to believe Richard was considerably more important in the affairs of England, than Charles VI in those of France, or any less "helpless in the hands of his uncles." I referred to a quite different kind of "prowess."

Again Professor Manly seems to criticise my reference to what he calls "two equally good explanations of the 'half a yere' of line 475." His criticism might be justified, perhaps, if I had asserted that the "half a yere" must apply to one or the other of these periods. Even that might be possible if we knew to a day the time of Chaucer's writing the poem. But I had no idea of anything so minute, and I have prefaced the discussion of the speech of the third tercel eagle by the sentence: "I recognize that we must not try to see too much, and the main point is made in emphasizing the rivalry of Charles VI and Richard II." Further the discussion is closed, not by stressing these matters, but by again resting the case on the aptness of the parallelism in the time references of the last two speeches.

Professor Manly objects also to applying certain lines of the poem (548-51) to Richard, since he was too young to be "worthieste of knighthode" and so "sittingest for hir." It is difficult to be serious with this sort of objection. Even

[13] *Modern Philology* VIII, 58.
[14] *Modern Philology* VIII, 58, footnote 3.

though the critic admits that "'allegories need not go on all fours", he here presses the matter as if we must not only find the "all fours" of the allegory, but also the hair and teeth. On such a basis how much of symbolic poetry would be left? How absurd, for example, for Spenser to picture Sidney as killed by a wild boar when everyone knew he was wounded in a fair fight with his enemies! Or how ridiculous for Milton to picture his dead friend, who probably knew nothing about sheep, as a shepherd of so little judgment in his sheep-tending as somehow to get mixed up with the sea; and how unthinkable that the poet should have introduced in this inappropriate imagery of a by-gone age an historical allusion to the church of England,[15] especially under such

---

[15] Professor Manly's skepticism regarding the historical basis of the *Parlement of Foules* also extends to my article on the *Date of the Knight's Tale* in the J. M. Hart anniversary volume. Now I cannot expect to convince all of such a conjectural interpretation. Everyone who proposes such an explanation of a few lines knows that its final acceptance or rejection rests not with himself, but with others. Still Professor Manly should not dismiss the article with the statement he has seemed to think sufficient. It is not true that historical "allusions can be found almost anywhere". Nor need it have been implied that Professor Lowes, with whose article on l. 26 of the *Knight's Tale* he couples mine, or myself had "diligently sought" to discover something that might be tortured into a reference to a contemporary event. Such a remark, to say the least, is not an answer to a reasoned case.

Yet let me meet directly Professor Manly's specific objection to my article. More than once in this contribution to the Morsbach *Festschrift* he reiterates his reference to Anne and her suitors as "children." The term is too strong for two who were regarded as old enough to marry, and whose training as princes would surely have given them greater maturity of mind than usually accompanies such ages as theirs. In combatting my other article, however, he implies a maturity of feeling regarding his kingly prerogative quite unlikely in Richard, a boy of thirteen or fourteen, especially if, as he rightly says in another place, "Richard was almost as helpless in the hands of his uncles as Charles was in the hands of his." Under such conditions of helplessness, and the outstanding importance of John of Gaunt as English prince and claimant of the Spanish throne, it is doubtful whether the boy Richard could have felt any lack of consideration in the possible allusion to him as a "kinges brother sone." In other words, Professor Manly should not reason in the one case that the princes were younger than the facts would warrant, and in the other that Richard would have

an impossible metaphor as "blind mouths." Or still again, how ludicrous, as good Doctor Johnson pointed out, for Gray to ask Father Thames to tell him the names of the youngsters who sported on his banks at Eton. As the wise critic said, Father Thames had "no better means of knowing than himself." If Professor Manly presses so hard the allusion to Richard II in the *Parlement of Foules,* he must have great difficulty with many passages in English poetry.

But the main difficulty with Chaucer's *Parlement of Foules* as a poem of historical reference, a difficulty which all must feel at times, is its conclusion. This is really at the basis of Professor Manly's contentions. Why did not Chaucer carry the royal courtship to what would seem to us a more satisfactory close in the full acceptance of Richard by Anne, or even, if he wrote so late, in a description of the royal marriage?[16] I do not flatter myself that I can answer the question satisfactorily, but I may point out its relation to the controversy. That Chaucer did not complete the poem as we should have supposed he would, or might have done, does not invalidate the many resemblances between it and actual events of the time. We may wonder that he did not go a step further, but that need not take from our admiration that he went so far.

On the basis of such criticism as Professor Manly's we might make difficulties with a good many other poems. Who can explain, for example, why Chaucer chose to write a poem on the death of Blanche of Lancaster, rather than on Queen Philippa who died a month before and was so much more important to England? On most if not all grounds Chaucer,

---

had the feelings of a man, ruling in person a great kingdom. Besides, instead of refuting my main argument, Professor Manly has again chosen to oppose a quite minor point in my article.

[16] Professor Lounsbury (*Studies in Chaucer* III, 321) is satisfied with attributing the conclusion as it stands to imperfect art. Coupling the poem with the *Book of the Duchess,* he says: "There is a sense of incompleteness about the two poems which detracts from their perfection as works of art." Later, (p. 431), he speaks of them as terminating "so abruptly as well as so tamely that it can be fairly said of them that they are broken off rather than ended."

a squire in the household of the king, a man looking for advancement through personal favor—the only means of advancement in his time—would certainly have seen the greater opportunity. Yet it would be foolish to deny that the *Book of the Duchess* does refer to Blanche of Lancaster, because a sensible poet would have preferred Queen Philippa as a subject for his elegy. Or would it be reasonable to deny that the ''man in blak'' can be John of Gaunt, because he could not have been pleased with a proclamation to the world that Blanche of Lancaster, merely a subject of his royal father, had refused his proffers as a lover for a full year? Similar examples might be found in every period of our literature.

Such analogies merely point the possibility of Chaucer's having a reason that seemed good to him, for doing what seems not wholly clear to us. On the other hand, might it not be contended with much force that the close of the *Parlement of Foules* was not unsatisfactory for the time. The year of respite asked by the formel eagle, and thought by Professor Manly to be derogatory to Richard, was common enough. If it was more commonly a sending of the lover on some expedition to prove his worth, as described by Gower in the *Confessio Amantis* (IV, 1620f.),[17] it is to Anne's credit that she required no such sacrifice. But that such putting off of the lover could not have been regarded as a slight, should be clear from Chaucer's use of it in the *Book of the Duchess,* already mentioned. Besides, we have a parallel to the maidenly modesty of Anne in the maidenly modesty of Emelye of the *Knight's Tale,* as she prays in the temple of Diana.

Moreover, the conclusion was accepted without a murmur by all the characters of the poem. The tercel eagles who were only too willing to engage in combat for their love, as shown by one of the most dramatic bits of the poem (1. 540), have no word of complaint. As already noted this is inconceivable in the conduct of birds, if birds only are meant. Yet the eagles, who have been so passionate in their first

---

[17] See the references given by Skeat, *Chaucer's Works* I, 485.

speeches, receive the decision without objection, and seem wholly content with Nature's,

"A yeer is not so longe to endure."

In the same way the other birds, who had been only too ready to jangle and waste their time in profitless discussion when given a chance—how delightfully Chaucer makes it give us pleasure as we hear them—

"Assented were to this conclusioun."

Now I submit that what is represented as so wholly satisfactory to the characters of the poem, so wholly satisfactory to the poet himself we must assume, could not have been wholly unsatisfactory to hearers or readers at the time. We must not condemn the conclusion of a work, otherwise so charming, simply because we cannot wholly understand its relation to the plot. Moreover, if the poem otherwise suits so admirably a symbolic representation of the royal courtship, we may not deny its symbolism in other respects because we cannot fully appreciate the relation of its conclusion to the series of historical circumstances. Indeed, the full acceptance of the conclusion by all most intimately concerned strengthens, rather than weakens, the symbolic interpretation which so long has been placed on this beautiful poem.

One word further may be added. It is well known that Dunbar wrote his *Thissel and the Rose* in imitation of Chaucer's *Parlement of Foules*. In it Dame Nature presides over beasts, birds and flowers, and appoints the lion, eagle and thistle as king of each class of living things. Then she crowns the Rose as Thistle's queen. The occasion of the poem is known to have been the marriage, August 8, 1503, of James IV with Margaret, eldest daughter of Henry VII of England. But Dunbar wrote in the preceding May, as he tells us in the last line of the poem, and the imagery is wholly of that period. Now I do not mean to suggest that Dunbar must have imitated Chaucer's poem because he had heard it had been written for a similar occasion, though there may be something even in that. Chaucerian imitation in Scotland began within a quarter century of Chaucer's death, and Chaucerian tradition may have been accurately preserved in that country for a century. What I do wish to suggest is a certain parallelism between the poems in other respects.

As already noted Dunbar chose to write his poem three months before the marriage of the king. He thus chose, as perhaps Chaucer did, not to describe the marriage itself, the greater occasion one would have thought. All he does, therefore, is to picture Nature as crowning the Rose as the most beautiful of the flowers, and to represent the birds as singing her praises. Does Professor Manly think this would have been sufficiently complimentary to the daughter of Henry VII of England? To be crowned queen of the May was a yearly occurrence in every village. Could Margaret have thought it worthy of her new position as queen of Scotland? Or would James IV have been any better pleased with the poem? Lines 134 to 140 give him some advice on his none too virtuous life, and he is asked in no uncertain terms to "lat no nettell vyle and full of vyce" and "no wyld weid" take the place in his affections of "the fresche Rose". Would the king be pleased with such allusion to him as a light of love? Or would the queen enjoy this public reflection upon the character of the prince she was marrying? Have we not here another of Professor Manly's dilemmas—with this difference, that we know the subject of Dunbar's poem, know when it was written to a day, and know also that he suffered no loss of favor because of what Professor Manly would certainly think slighting references to Scotland's king and queen.

To return to the main question, there is no inherent reason why Chaucer should not have written a poem upon the courtship of Richard and Anne. Except for the lyrist Minot, whose small body of verse was wholly in praise of his king, Chaucer more than any poet up to his time or long after dealt with contemporaries or contemporary life. The *Book of the Duchess* is accepted by all as a poem of a particular occasion. The *Complaint of Mars* may have had some basis in facts of the time. The *Legend of Good Women* was written for Queen Anne, since lines 496-97 of the *B. Prologue,* now generally believed to have been the first written, are a virtual dedication of the poem to her. The envoy to *Fortune* is addressed to the English princes, probably the uncles of the king, whatever be the interpretation of "the beste frend" of that poem. *Lack of Steadfastness* is directed to a prince, usually supposed to have been Richard himself, at some crisis of his affairs. The poems *To Scogan, To Bukton* are to friends of the poet, the first playful, the second bearing upon court influence which Chaucer hoped might be exerted in his behalf. The envoy to the *Complaint of Venus* is directed to a princess at least, perhaps Isabel of York, and it also mentions by name a contemporary French poet known and honored in England. The *Complaint to his Purse* is an appeal to the new king of England, who heeded the witty request of the aged poet and bestowed a fitting reward. Even Adam Scriveyn is embalmed to an immortality he would doubtless have preferred to escape. And just the other day it seems to have been shown that Chaucer's incomparable *Truth* is not of mere general nature, but was dedicated in its envoy to a nobleman of England, who must also have been Chaucer's friend.

What more reasonable, therefore, as following a practice characteristic of the great poet, that the *Parlement of Foules* should have had its occasion in one of the most interesting incidents in the life of Chaucer's king and queen.

OLIVER FARRAR EMERSON

Western Reserve University.

IMAGINATIF IN PIERS PLOWMAN

Those who are interested in the history of the word *imagination* should not overlook the character, Imaginatif, who speaks at length in Piers Plowman. If, dissatisfied with Professor Skeat's brief note—"By *ymaginatif* is represented what we should call Imagination or Fancy"—the curious should turn to mediæval psychology as it took shape under Platonic, neo-Platonic, and Artistotelian influences, they would find themselves in touch with ideas and systems of great significance in the history of human thought and indispensable to an understanding of mediæval allegory. More particularly, they would see the character in Piers Plowman in its true light.

This character, it will be remembered, is a spokesman for Reason as a faculty consecrated to the service of God. He has often moved the poet to think of the end of life—(B. XII, 4) to prepare himself against the wrath to come. More than that, it is Imagination that recommends an accommodation of Kynde Witte to Clergye. In a chiastic line he writes:—

Clergye and Kynde Witte comth of siȝte and techynge.

And further down:

Of *quod scimus* cometh clergye and connynge of hevene
and of *quod vidmus* cometh kynde witte of siȝte of dy-
verse peple.

But this natural wit—this wit of bodily knowing[1]—is near akin to the *quod scimus* of clergy, to the "connynge of hevene":—

"For-thi I conseille the for Cristes sake. Clergye that
thow lovye
For Kynde Witte is of his kyn and neighe cosynes bothe
to owre lorde, leve me; for-thi love hem, I rede;

---

[1] In the *Promptorium Parvulorum* (E. E. T. S. ed. col. 531) we find *wytte of understondynge* glossed *by ingenium; wytte of bodely knowynge,* by *sensus.* In Chaucer's Boethius *wit* regularly translates the Latin *sensus.* Compare the following passage alluded to later on:— Ipsum quoque hominem aliter sensus aliter imaginatio aliter ratio aliter intelligentia contuetur. (De Consolatione. Bk. V, Prose IV, 79 ff.) Chaucer translates this: And the man himself otherweys wit beholdeth him, and otherweys imaginacioun, and otherweys resoun, and otherweys intelligence.

For bothe ben as miroures to amenden owre defautes,
And lederes for lewed men and for lettred bothe.'' (B-text)
Both Kind Wit and Clergy, then, aid us in our ascent to
God. But a kind-witted man without Clergy is like a blind
man in battle. Unless clerks help him this man ''for all
his kind wits'' cannot be saved. Elsewhere *Imaginatif* speaks
as one who knows about future rewards and punishments,
—of the thief at the crucifixion, (B. XII, 196 ff.) of Jews,
of Saracens (B. XII, 278 ff.); and he makes very clear the
distinction between mere secular curiosity about the natural
world and the use of its phenomena as similitudes of spiritual
truth (B. XII, 236 ff.). To sum up, it appears that *Imaginatif* is not only the spokesman of Reason but is gifted with
a vision of joy and sorrow to come, and is entitled to speak of
the relation of Kind Wit and Clergy, and the uses to which
in our spiritual education we should put the images, the
phenomena, of the physical world.

Now these characteristics of *Imaginatif* are clearly accounted for by mediæval Christian psychology. The details
are obvious in a twelfth century allegory by Richard of St.
Victor, that was translated into English in the fourteenth
century.[2] This treatise, the Benjamin Minor, presents Benjamin—adolescentulus in mentis excessu—as the embodiment of the highest stage of mystic contemplation, and ac-
commodates to this symbolism the whole family of Jacob with
the result that the growth of that family is made to typify
the progress of the human soul along the mystic way. Jacob
is God; his wives, Leah and Rachel, are respectively Affection
and Reason; Zilpah, Jacob's concubine and Leah's maid is
Sensuality; his other concubine, Bilhah, who is Rachel's
maid, is Imagination. The sons of Jacob and Leah are Dread
of Pain (Reuben), Sorrow of Sin (Simeon), Hope of For-
giveness (Levi), Love of Righteousness (Judah), Joy in Inward Sweetness (Issachar), Hatred of Sin (Zebulum), Ordained Shame (Dinah). The sons of Jacob and Zilpah are
abstinence (Gad) and Patience (Asher). The sons of Jacob

[2] *Patrologia*, 196, Iff.   Horstman, *Richard Rolle of Hampole*, I,
162 ff. *The Cell of Self-knowledge*, with introduction and notes by Edmund G. Gardner (London and New York, 1910), 3 ff.

and Rachel are Discretion (Joseph) and Contemplation (Benjamin). The sons of Jacob and Bilhah are Sight of Pain to Come (Dan) and Sight of Joy to Come (Naphtali).

Of this numerous progeny, the children of Leah were born first, because the first step in the life of contemplation is to surrender one's affections to God. Here, at the very threshold of the religious life appear contrition, hope, and the other symptoms of conversion. The stage here described corresponds to Langland's Vision of the Seven Deadly Sins, which immediately precedes that of Dowel. In the latter vision we pass from the theme of repentance to that of Wit, Study, Clergy, and Reason, as aids in the religious life. That is we turn from the general subject of the affections of man in the service of God to that of the mind of man in the service of God.

Now, according to Richard's allegory, it is Imagination that conducts man from the lower to the higher plane. In his allegory this is figured forth in the birth of Dan and Naphtali, Jacob's children by Bilhah (Imagination) after Leah had borne her seven sons. "For it falleth", says Richard,[3] "to a perfect soul both to be inflamed with the fire of love in the affection, and also to be illumined with the light of knowing in the reason. Then when Judah waxeth, that is to say, when love and desire of unseen true goods is rising and waxing in a man's affection; then coveteth Rachel (Reason) for to bear some children;[4] that is to say, then coveteth Reason to know these things that affection feeleth; for as it falleth to the affection for to love, so it falleth to the reason for to know. Of affection springeth ordained and measured feelings; and of reason springeth right knowings and clear understandings. And ever the more that Judah waxeth, that is to say love, so much desireth Rachel bearing of children, that is to say reason studieth after knowing. But who is he that woteth not how hard it is, and nearhand impossible to a fleshly soul the which is yet rude in ghostly studies, for to rise in knowing of unseeable things and for to set the

---

[3] I use Mr. Gardner's version.

[4] Just as the dreamer in Piers Plowman strove unsuccessfully to derive help from Reason before he is instructed by Imagination.

eye of contemplation in ghostly things? For why, a soul that is yet rude and fleshly, knoweth nought but bodily things, and nothing cometh yet to the mind but only seeable things. And, nevertheless, yet it looketh inward as it may; and that that it may not see yet clearly by ghostly knowing it thinketh by imagination. And this is the cause why Rachel had first children of her maiden than of herself. And so it is that, though all a man's soul may not yet get the light of ghostly knowing in the reason, yet it thinketh it sweet to hold the mind on God and ghostly things in the imagination''. ''Without imagination'', says Richard in the Prologue to the Benjamin Minor, ''reason may not know''. From the above it is perfectly clear that Imagination, the maid of Reason, with the ''two beholdings'' for her children, bearing children before her mistress but after Leah (Affection), is the same Imagination who took the dreamer of Piers Plowman in charge after the confession of the Deadly Sins and after he had impatiently sought to know by reason alone.[5]

This imagination, to be traced to the Aristotelian φαντασία,[6] played a prominent rôle in scholastic psychology from the time of Augustine. Its function was that of recording the images of the phenomenal world, not simply of noting but of retaining the multiple messages that come through the channels of the several senses to the unifying *sensus communis*.[7] The *cella fantastica* was the repository of its records as the *cella rationalis* was the abode of the higher faculty.[8]

---

[5] The opening passus of Piers Plowman in its transition from the theme of conversion to that of Reason—with her associates, Wit, Study, etc., and her sponsor, Imagination—follows then the way of mystic discipline. It is interesting to note that the dreamer goes off with *Activa Vita* after Reason is discredited.

[6] Freudenthal, Ueber den Begriff des Wortes Φαντασία bei Aristoteles, Göttingen, 1863. Grote, Aristotle, II, 211 ff. Lutz, Die Psychologie Bonaventuras, Münster, 1909, (Beiträge zur Geschichte der Philosophie des Mittelalters, VI). Mignon, Les Origines de La Scolastique, I, p. 113.

[7] Lutz, *op. cit.* p. 97.

[8] In connection with that detail of Richard's allegory which represents the children of Imagination as Vision of Joy to Come and Vision of Sorrow to Come we might note what Bonaventura says in the Itinerarium (Chap. III) about Memory, which is often synonymous with Imagination: Operatio autem memoriae est retentio et representatio, non solum prae-

From all this it is clear that imagination was often equivalent to memory. But the point to be noted here is that in mediæval psychology imagination was not only a faculty of lower grade than reason but that in man's mental processes and the growth of his mind it mediated between the world of senses and the intellectual world.

The rôle of Imagination and its relation to Reason, set forth in a conveniently clear-cut manner in Richard of St. Victor's *Benjamin Minor*, receive more broadly philosophical treatment in the same writer's *Benjamin Major*.[9] There we have distinguished six kinds of contemplation:[10] 1. In imaginatione et secundum solam imaginationem. 2. In imaginatione secundum rationem. 3. In ratione secundum imaginationem. 4. In ratione et secundum rationem. 5. Supra sed non praeter rationem. 6. Supra rationem et videtur esse praeter rationem. In connection with *Imaginatif's* discouragement of scientific curiosity and debate (B. XII, 217 ff.) we may note the following explanation of the first kind of contemplation: Tunc autem contemplatio nostra in imaginatione versatur, et secundum solam imaginationem formatur, quando nihil argumentando quaerimus vel ratiocinando investigamus; sed libera mens nostra huc illucque discurrit, quo etiam in hoc spectaculorum genere admiratio rapit.

That Richard, as we should have supposed, has drawn his psychology from his master Hugo of St. Victor becomes interestingly clear in Dr. Ostler's excellent study of the latter's system.[11] Dr. Ostler, moreover, traces the details of the psychology through the mazes of patristic speculation. Among other things he makes clear the essential similarity between the psychology of the Victorine and the following passage in the *De Consolatione Philosophiae*:— ''A man himself is dif-

---

sentium, corporalium, et temporalium, verum etiam succedentium, simplicium et sempiternalium. Retinet namque memoria praeterita per recordationem, praesentia per susceptionem, futura per praevisionem.

[9] Migne, 196, 63 ff.

[10] *Op. cit.* Ch. VI.

[11] Ostler, Heinrich, *Die Psychologie des Hugo von St. Viktor,* Münster, 1906 (Beiträge zur Geschichte des Philosophie des Mittelalters, Band VI, Heft. 1.)

ferently comprehended by the senses, by imagination, by
reason, and by intelligence. For the senses distinguish the
form as set in the matter operated upon by the form; imagination distinguishes the appearance alone without the matter. Reason goes even further than imagination; by a general
and universal contemplation it investigates the actual kind
which is represented in individual specimens. Higher still
is the view of the intelligence, which reaches above the sphere
of the universal, and with the unsullied eye of the mind gazes
upon that very form of the kind in its absolute simplicity.''
Similar accounts are given by St. Augustine in *De Anima
et ejus Origine,* by William of St. Thierry, Isaac of Stella,
Alcher of Clairvaux and Peter of Poitiers.[12] Bonaventura
too, in the *Itinerarium Mentis ad Deum,* having divided
the soul into *Sensualitas, Spiritus,* and *Mens,* attributes to
Sensualitas, sensus and *imaginatio* and to *spiritus, ratio* and
intellectus. Throughout we find the Imagination—what
Hobbes calls ''the decaying sense''—mediating as the character in Piers Plowman between the senses and the reason.

And this is, of course, the place of imagination, φαντασία,
in the Aristotelian psychology as set forth in the *De Anima.*
Distinguishing between the reproductive and the productive
imagination, Aristotle in each case considers the faculty a
function of the bodily organism and directly dependent upon
sense perceptions. On the other hand, its operations are
sufficiently similar to and closely enough connected with those
of reason to justify our consideration of it as an intermediate
faculty. Imagination is essential to the operation of the noëtic
soul, just as the senses are necessary to the imagination.
Aristotle uses expressions that are very closely paralleled in
a sentence already quoted from Richard of St. Victor—''Without imagination reason cannot know''. Aristotle says: οὐδέποτε
νοεῖ ἄνευ φαντάσματος ἡ ψυχή. (De Anima, VII, p. 431, a. 16)
and νοεῖν οὐκ ἔστιν ἄνεν φαντάσματος. (De Memoria et Reminiscent.) 1, pp. 449, 631.[13]

H. S. V. JONES.

[12] Ostler, *op. cit.* 119 ff.
[13] Quoted by Grote, *op. cit.,* p. 211.

THE CORPUS CHRISTI PROCESSION AND THE COR-
PUS CHRISTI PLAY

The following article was begun as a review of Dr. M. Lyle Spencer's *Corpus Christi Pageants in England*, New York, 1911. It devotes itself, however, to a discussion of some of the points arising out of the perusal of the earlier chapters of Dr. Spencer's book and not to the possibly more profitable end of reviewing the book itself. There can be no question of the value of Dr. Spencer's study as a whole, and, particularly, I think, of his chapters on pageants, staging and Corpus Christi conventions, which seem to me to be unusually sound and valuable.

It is now pretty generally agreed that the English religious plays grew from their liturgical origins on English soil and were not translated from the French.[1] The older view, (Warton, *History of English Poetry*. i., 248; Hone, *Ancient Mysteries Described*, 201 ff.; Ten Brink, *History of English Literature*, ii., 1, 237 *et passim;* Ward, *English Dramatic Literature*, i., 9 ff., 76 ff.) which believed in special authorship and foreign originals, was based upon the well-known Chester tradition pointing to the year 1328 as the year of translation and to Randall Higdon, who was "thrice at Rome before he could have leave of the Pope to have them in the English tongue", as the translator.[2] Another entry pointing the same way is the altogether impossible one from the Coventry manuscript Annals where it states that the plays were invented in 1416. Translation from the French is now disallowed except, possibly, for the Chester Plays where the parallel with the *Mystère du Viel Testament* and other French plays is obvious,

---

[1] Chambers, *The Mediæval Stage*, vol. ii., pp. 108, 146-7; Creizenach, *Geschichte des neueren Dramas* (new edition), i., 187 ff., 359 ff.; Davidson, *Studies in the English Mystery Plays*, 171 *et passim;* Schelling, *The Elizabethan Drama*, i., 12 ff.

[2] Morris, *Chester in Tudor and Plantagenet Times*, 317; Furnivall, *The Digby Plays*, quotations from the Breviary of Chester, p. xviii. ff.; and especially Chambers, ii., 348 ff., where so much has been done to render the confused traditions intelligible.

but even there actual translation is not probable.[3] It is far
more likely that we have back of this parallelism a somewhat extensive Latin play. I have suggested that the corrupt and imperfect Benedictbeuern Christmas play is of the
same type and composition as one of the forerunners of the
Chester plays.[4] The French employed in the Chester cycle
and others does not point to a French original, but to its
deliberate use on the part of the writers of the plays with
intent to caricature persons of high estate; such as Pilate
and Herod. England had the same liturgical inheritance as
had France, Germany, and Italy; but, allowing for that, the
dramas preserved are surprisingly national, or rather local,
in their characteristics. They passed from Latin to English
by a method of repeating and amplifying the Latin texts
in the vernacular. There are examples of this in the religious
dramas of all countries.[5]

Another matter that has been emerging into clearness is
that the Corpus Christi play, as we know it in the four full
cycles, the fragments of lost cycles and in the records, occupied a comparatively restricted area and was a separate
dramatic form with certain definite characteristics. Corpus
Christi plays seem to have belonged mainly to the north and
east of England. There were plays of the Corpus Christi
type at Newcastle, Kendall, Preston, Beverley, York, Chester,
Lincoln, Louth, Norwick, Ipswich, Coventry, Worcester; and
more doubtfully, at about as many more places. There was
a procession and, almost certainly plays also, at Dublin; and
also, no doubt, at some places in Scotland. Corpus Christi
plays are by no means the only plays on biblical subjects in
England. In fact dramatic activities were much more varied
than the current histories of the religious drama indicate.

[3] H. Ungemacht, *Die Quellen der fünf ersten Chester Plays;* Hemingway, *English Nativity Plays*, pp. xxiv ff., 217 ff. To the parallels pointed
out by these writers add also the very significant one of the Balaam play
in the *Mystère*, which follows, as at Chester, immediately after the
scene of Moses and the Tables of the Law.

[4] *The Origin of the Old Testament Plays, Modern Philology*, x., 486-7.

[5] Chambers, ii., 69 ff.; Creizenach, i., 100 ff. See a particularly good
example of this transitional stage in the Shrewsbury Fragments, Manly,
Specimens of the Pre-Shakspearean Drama, i., pp. xxvii ff.

The histories are based upon the records of the Corpus Christi plays, which are many times more numerous and extensive than the records of other plays.

In order to arrive at some sort of classification of the plays on religious subjects, it is necessary to recognize the Corpus Christi plays as a separate class.

First of all, in the matter of terminology, "Corpus Christi play" is used dozens of times, and used discriminately to denote the type of play we have in mind. Consider a few of the more familiar references:

Heywood, *The Foure PP.* 831:
"Oft in the play of Corpus Cristi
He had played the deuyll at Couentre."
The *C Mery Talys, lvi:*

"Yf you beleue not me, then for a more suerte and suffycient auctoryte, go your way to Couentre, and there ye shal se them all playd in Corpus Christi playe."
Newcastle-on-Tyne, fifteenth century craft ordinaries:[6]

"Whensoever the generall plaies of the town of Newcastle, antiently called the Corpus Christi plays, shall be plaied, etc."
Weever's Funeral Monuments, Folio, p. 405:[7]

"Richard Marlow was Lord Maior [of London] in 1409 in whose Maioraltie there was a play at Skinners Hall, which lasted eight dayes (saith Stow) to heare which most of the greatest Estates of England were present. The subject of the sacred Scriptures, from the creation of the World: They call this Corpus Christi Play in my countrey which I have seene acted at Preston, and Lancaster, and last of all at Kendall, in the beginning of the raigne of King James; for which the Towns-men were sore troubled; and upon good reasons the play finally sup-prest, not onely there, but in all other Townes of the Kingdome."

Weever was from the north and was born in Lancashire in 1576. He wrote about 1631, and he seems to recognize that the Corpus Christi play was a northern rather than a southern institution.

So definite was the term that even when, as at some places, the play was no longer acted as Corpus Christi, it was still referred to as a Corpus Christi play. At Chester, where the plays were acted at Whitsuntide, the Bakers' Charter in 1462 speaks of the "play and light of Corpus Christi;" the Sad-dlers' Charter in 1471 of "paginae luminis et ludi Corporis Christi." These references may or may not be after the transference of the plays to Whitsuntide, but references of

---

[6] Quoted by Chambers, ii., 385.

[7] Quotation derived from Sharpe, *Dissertation*, 133.

the sixteenth century make it clear that they were always known by their old name. The "White Book" about 1544 speaks of "pagyns in the play of Corpus Xpi." [8] From Norwich, where likewise the plays were at Whitsuntide, comes the jocular reference by J. Whetley in a letter to Sir John Paston[9] of Lord Suffolk how "ther was never no man that playd Herrod in Corpus Christy play better and more agreable to hys pageaunt than he did." Finally, there is an entry from Lincoln at the time of the Marian reaction. The Corporation Register for July 6, 1554, contains this entry: "Agreed at a Secret Council that St. Anne's guild with Corpus Christi play shall be brought forth and played this year, and that every craft shall bring forth their pageants as it hath been accustomed, and all occupations shall be contributory as shall be assessed."[10] This is an obvious association of the Lincoln Corpus Christi play with the St. Anne's day procession, an association possible also from the content and nature of the latter play as revealed by various records.[11]

On the other hand, where the plays were of another kind, they seem to have been called by other names. At New Romney in Kent[12] there is mention of a "Resurrection" play in 1456 and a "play of the Interlude of our Lord's Passion" in 1463. It was a stationary play of considerable extent, and the circumstances of its representation lead one to conclude that it was of the type familiar in the passion plays of the continent. There was much dramatic activity in that part of England, and the free interchange of performances among the towns leads one to think that they must have had stationary plays and not cyclic Corpus Christi plays. At Aberdeen, where the passion group and the nativity group were not united, the passion, which was performed at Corpus Christi day, was called the "Haliblude play." Similarly, at

---

[8] Chambers, ii., 348 ff.

[9] *Paston Letters*, ed. Gardiner, iii., 227.

[10] Hist. MSS. xiv., 8, 47.

[11] See Hist. MSS. as above pp. 25-58; also A. F. Leach, *Some English Plays and Players* in the Furnivall Miscellany, pp. 222-228, and Chambers, ii., 377 ff.

[12] Hist. MSS., v., 533.

Leicester there is mention in 1477 in the Hall book of the Corporation of a "passion play" with no ground for connecting it with Corpus Christi, though unfortunately details which might define it more closely are lacking. There is also the example of the Cornish *Creation, Passion and Resurrection* which is not a Corpus Christi play. Finally, there are a few small pieces of evidence to show that the plays of London were possibly of the same general form as the Cornish plays; they were certainly not Corpus Christi plays. I refer to the record in the Issue Roll of the Exchequer for Easter to Michaelmas, 1391, of a payment to "the Clerkes of the Parish Churches and to divers other clerkes of the City of London", as a gift from the king, "on account of the play of the Passion of our Lord and the Creation of the World by them performed at Skynner Well, after the Feast of Bartholomew last past." The entry of 1391 in Malvern's continuation of Higden's *Polychronicon*, with which Chambers connects this payment, says merely, "Item xviij° die Iulii clerici Londonienses fecerunt ludum satis curiosum apud Skynnereswell per dies quatuor duraturum, in quo tam vetus quam novum testamentum oculariter ludendo monstrabant." There is also the reference in Machyn to a "stage play at the Grey freers of the Passyon of Cryst" during the reign of Queen Mary in 1557.[13] There were then at least two major types of cyclic plays, and a Corpus Christi play was a different kind of play from a passion play.

Besides these, every possible kind of religious play and stage of development was probably represented in England. Smaller towns and special communities presented a variety of dramatic forms, for the simpler stages did not disappear with the establishment of the great cycles. There were Resurrection plays at Bath (?), Kingston-on-Thames, Leconfield in Yorkshire, Leicester, Morebath in Devonshire, Magdalen College, Oxford, and possibly also at Reading, which last, however, may have been a part of a full cycle. Nativity plays were acted separately from resurrection plays at Aberdeen, as

---

[13] On the whole matter of the London plays see Chambers, ii., 379 ff., and the references given there.

already pointed out, at Leconfield and at Leicester. There was possibly also a Christmas play of some sort at Lincoln. It is referred to in the Chapter *computi* in 1406, 1452 and 1531, according to Canon Wordsworth, (*Lincoln Statutes,* ii. lv) as follows: ''In serothecis emptis pro Maria et Angelo et Prophetis ex consuetudine in Aurora Natalis Dni hoc anno.''[14] Chambers in the *Mediæval Stage,* volume ii, Appendix W, from which I have drawn the foregoing materials, gives references which indicate a variety of forms of the religious drama, and his list is by no means complete. The Digby plays are also a case in point, since you have there four plays none of which belongs to Corpus Christi cycles. The Massacre of the Innocents is a part of an elaborate Nativity cycle, and the Burial and Resurrection is apparently an independent resurrection play.

Corpus Christi plays were characterized, in the first place, by completeness of cyclical content. They extended from the Creation to Doomsday, and they included plays of the Nativity, as well as of the Passion and Resurrection. They seem all to have been acted by craft guilds, with local differences as at Norwich, and to have been, to a greater or less degree, under municipal control. The plays of the Corpus Christi type were probably all acted, as the name indicates, originally at Corpus Christitide, and it is natural to think that they came into existence in connection with the observance of the festival of Corpus Christi; but there is very little actual evidence to connect the plays, as is usually done, with the Corpus Christi procession.

The Corpus Christi festival, and with it the procession, made its way very quickly over England. It was reaffirmed in 1311, delayed for some years, and reissued by Pope John XXII in 1316 as part of the Canon Law. The papal decree

---

[14] It is natural to connect with this an entry imperfectly given by the same author (C. Wordsworth, *Notes on the Mediæval Services in England,* 126.): "In 1421 tithes to the amount of 8s 8d were assigned to Thomas Chamberleyn for getting up a spectacle or pageant ('cuiusdam excellentis visus') called *Rubum quem viderat* at Christmas.

ordered not only the celebration of the festival of Corpus Christi but an attendant procession. The festival was declared a principal feast of Canterbury in 1317, and there is mention of special services appointed for the festival. (Hist. MSS. Eighth Report, vii., 321.) There is another significant entry in *Historia Monasterii Sancti Petri Gloucestriae*,[15] where you have: "Nota de festivitate Corporis Christi (1318). Anno Domini Millesimo trecentesimo decimo octavo incoepit festivitas de Corpore Christi generaliter celebrari per totam ecclesiam Anglicanam." The same immediacy of its introduction into England is borne out by the reference to Sprott's *Chronicles* which states that the festival was a confirmed institution in England by the year 1318.[16] In considering the processional feature of the Corpus Christi festival, it is important to note the wide latitude allowed each diocese or parish as to the extent and manner of the procession. A Council at Paris in 1323 speaks of it in these words: "As to the solemn procession made on the Thursday's feast, when the Holy Sacrament is carried, seeing that it appears to have been introduced in these our times, by a sort of inspiration, we prescribe nothing at present and leave all concerning it to the devotion of the clergy and the people."[17]

At Ipswich the Gild Merchant was reconstituted as a Gild of Corpus Christi in 1325, and the Constitution provides for a procession on Corpus Christi day.[18] At London the fraternity of Skinners had a procession once every year on Corpus Christi day afternoon; this guild dates from 1327.[19] The Tailors' Gild of Lincoln, founded in 1328, had a pro-

---

[15] Rolls Series, *Chronicles and Memorials of Great Britain and Ireland during the Middle Ages*, ii., 44.

[16] Mr. M. Lyle Spencer, *Corpus Christi Pageants in England* page 11, cites Sprott but gives no further information as to the introduction of the festival into England. I owe the two important citations given above to a University of Minnesota unpublished Master's thesis on the *Origin and Theological Significance of the Corpus Christi Festival* by Mr. Paul E. Kretzmann.

[17] Gueranger, *The Liturgical Year*, vol. vii., part 1, p. 287 ff.

[18] Hist, MSS. ix., 1, 245.

[19] Stow, *Survey of London*, 87.

cession of the brethren and sisters on the feast of Corpus
Christi. Similarly there are records of processions at Coventry
in 1348.[20] Leicester in 1349-50,[21] Beverly between 1330 and
1350.[22]

The earlier part of the fourteenth century, after 1318,
would be the probable time for the invention of the Corpus
Christi play, if it arose definitely in connection with the observance of Corpus Christi day. The earliest records of
Corpus Christi plays are from Beverley in 1377, where in
1390 they are spoken of as "antiqua consuetudo"; from York
in 1378, where in 1394 the pageants are to play at places
"antiquatus assignatis"; from Coventry in 1392, and others
in the early fifteenth century.[23] We may fairly take the
Cambridge reference of about 1350 to a certain William de
Lenne and his wife who joined the gild of Corpus Christi
and spent a mark "in ludo filiorum Israelis", as partly bridging the long gap from the traditional date of 1328 at Chester
to the earliest Beverley record in 1377. In that case we
should understand the "ludum filiorum Israelis" as being
a play of the Slaughter of the Innocents, and therefore, an
ordinary member of a Corpus Christi cycle. The play of the
sons of Jacob, which Creizenach takes this to mean, is otherwise unknown in England, and the play of the Slaughter of
the Innocents is several times called the Children of Israel.[24]
A lost play on the subject at Beverley was so called; so
also apparently a pageant in the Dublin procession; in the
Norwich list the "Children of Israel" refers to Moses and
his host in the Pharoah play. At any rate the Cambridge
reference probably indicates a Corpus Christi play. The Chester tradition has been frequently discussed of late years,
and the general effect has been to render it credible, as

[20] Smith, *English Gilds*, 182, 232.

[21] W. Kelly, *Notices of the Drama*, 36.

[22] A. F. Leach, *Beverley Town Documents*, p. ix.

[23] Chambers, ii., Appendix W.

[24] Chambers, ii., 344 and other entries in Appendix W; *Retrospective
Review*, xii., 7 quoting Masters, *History of C. C. C. Cambridge*, i., 5;
Creizenach, i., 69.

it certainly is on *a priori* grounds.[25]   The paucity of records during the fourteenth century must be due to the fact that the plays had not yet emerged from parochial control; as they did so they became more and more affairs of municipal importance and were noted in the records of towns and cities.

There is no evidence that the plays had been combined into cycles before the early part of the fourteenth century. Such combinations had been made on the continent but probably not in England.   The scanty records of the thirteenth century point to a condition where the plays were in their original groups.   The Cathedral Statutes of Bishop Hugh de Nonant (1188-98) of Lichfield provide for *Pastores* at Christmas and Resurrection and *Peregrini* at Easter.[26]   A thirteenth century continuation of the life of St. John of Beverley records a recent (about 1220) miracle wrought in the minster while the crowd was watching a performance of a play of the Resurrection beside the church.[27]   The denunciations of plays by Grosseteste (1244) and other ecclesiastics of the century point to a close connection between the plays and the church itself.   Denunciations grew less frequent and more specific after the plays became clearly secular.[28]   The Statutes of York Cathedral about 1255 provide for *Pastores* and *Stella*.[29]   The Shrewsbury Fragments may be a case in point, but it is impossible, with the information available, to tell anything about the date of the manuscript.   It is of course believed on linguistic and metrical grounds that many of the plays go back to the thirteenth century.   There is no evidence that the plays were written at the time of the establishment of the festival of Corpus Christi.   They had for the most part been in existence long before that time.   The invention of the cyclic play was also at least one hundred years old, and the idea was no doubt borrowed from the

[25] Chambers, ii., 348 ff.; S. B. Hemingway, *English Nativity Plays*, xix ff.; M. L. Spencer, *Corpus Christi Pageants in England*, 12 ff.

[26] Wordsworth, *Lincoln Statutes*, ii., 15, 23.

[27] *Historians of the Church of York*, i., 328, Rolls Series lxxi.

[28] H. S. Symmes, *Les Debats de la Critique dramatique en Angleterre*, 6-12.

[29] *Lincoln Statutes*, ii., 98.

continent; but not, I think, the actual form of the English Corpus Christi play; there are no extant parallels among the cyclic plays of the continent, although there are fairly close approximations. What seems to have been done was to transfer to Corpus Christi day and to arrange, in the extensive cyclic form, plays already of considerable development.

An indication of this special establishment is perhaps to be found in the subjects played by the various gilds in the cycles. The way they fit together seems to point to deliberate assignment. The bakers at Beverley, Chester and York played the Last Supper, probably because it seemed appropriate to some one for them to furnish bread; the cooks of Beverley and Chester played the Harrowing of Hell, because, we may suppose, they could handle fire; the watermen at Beverley and Chester, and the shipwrights of York and Newcastle played Noah's Ark for obvious reasons, and so on. It is pretty obvious from records at Coventry and Beverley and other places that a gild often played a play having to do with its patron saint. All these familiar facts indicate that, at one time in the history of the plays, there was a freedom to choose, or to be assigned a desirable or appropriate subject as a part in the cycle. The cases are so numerous as to preclude the possibility of their being the result of chance or gradual adaptation; they can hardly be the result of choosing in pre-cyclic times. The cases of Leicester in 1477, where there was a debate as to putting their passion play to the crafts, and Norwich in 1527, where the plays were shifted from St. Luke's gild to all the gilds, are both in point.

This set of circumstances, the general recognition of the play as a dramatic species, its cosmic form, its geographical location, its connection with the crafts, its complete establishment during the fourteenth century, so that by the end of the century it had become an ancient custom, together with the evidences that the parts of the play were still uncombined in the thirteenth century, to take the English records alone, constitute a fair ground for believing that the Corpus Christi play was invented about the end of the first quarter of the fourteenth century at some place probably in the north or

east of England, and spread thence to other places in the
island. The same cycle was not borrowed, but other places
constructed out of their own local plays similar cycles.

It yet remains to be asked why such an invention should
have been suggested by the festival of Corpus Christi. There
is nothing deliberately descriptive of the great cosmic theme
either in the bull of Pope Urban IV., the order of the Council of Vienna, the confirmation of the decree in the Canon
Law, or the service of Corpus Christi day, although they were
all written with the idea that this service was theologically
and ritualistically a consummation of the entire plan of salvation. Indeed the service may be said to portray the entire
plan of salvation, culminating in sacrifice and everywhere
conscious of the types of Christ among the patriarchs and
of prophecy and its fulfillment. It is the same great story of
the fall and redemption of man as that which we have in
epics, sermons, commentaries, and cyclic plays both of the
Corpus Christi type and the passion play type; it may almost
be said to be the whole service of the year in miniature.
There is not, however, any suggestion of historical sequence.

Since there was such latitude in the matter of the procession and since some of the plays are themselves processional,
it has been suggested that the plays began as dumb-show
pageants in the Corpus Christi procession and developed into
drama from dumb-show, or had added to them the traditional
materials from the already secularized liturgical plays.[80]
There are some serious objections to this theory in either
form. In the first place, it makes a mistake as to what the
nature and purpose of the Corpus Christi procession was.
It was a very much commoner thing than were the plays,
and was entirely independent of them. This is interestingly
illustrated by the substitution of the *Credo* play for the
Corpus Christi play at York in 1535 and 1568 and of the
Pater Noster for it in 1558 without apparently affecting the

---

[80] C. Davidson, *English Mystery Plays;* Creizenach, i., 169 ff.; Chambers, ii., 173 *et passim;* M. L. Spencer, *ut sup.,* 61 ff.

procession.[31]   A Corpus Christi procession was a march of
ecclesiastics and laity, usually the whole body of citizens,
through the streets of the city; it was part of a religious
service and usually comprehended a return to the place of
setting out.   The citizens marched by crafts and in livery;
and since they were themselves the spectators and actors of
the plays, it is hard to see how plays could ever have been
acted as part of the procession.   It is doubtful, particularly
in the earlier days of the procession, if the acting of plays
would have been suitable or acceptable, even if it were possible to act them as the procession moved.   There is none
except very late evidence to connect the pageants with the
Corpus Christi procession; they did not always appear in it,
and if they did appear, it was not always in any very orderly
way.   The processional lists from Hereford and Dublin and
the gear from the procession at Dundee are indications of
defunct cycles rather than mimetic pageants about to develop
into cycles.[32]   Moreover, the narrow, crooked streets of mediæval English towns would have made acting as the pageants
moved a very impracticable thing both for actors and spectators.

More important still, a series of pageant tableaux on so
extensive and so orderly a scale, as must have been, from its
very beginning, every Corpus Christi play of which we have
any record, could hardly have come into existence at all
until after the community had been educated by familiarity
with the plays.   We should never have arrived at the uniform
definite result that we have, Corpus Christi cycles with their ·
general similarities, their local differences and their constant
dependence upon their liturgical predecessors, if a beginning
had been made from a set of ideally constructed pageant

[31] Davies, *Municipal Records*, 256-8.   An entry in the Corporation
Register of Lincoln of December 31, 1521, indicates a similar independence on the part of the St. Anne's procession at Lincoln: "Every
alderman to make a gown for the kings in the pageant on St. Anne's day,
and the *Pater noster* play to be played this year."   Hist. MSS., xiv., 8,
29.   The Sacrament was carried in the St. Anne's procession and it
seems to have been a Corpus Christi procession, although held on St.
Anne's day.

[32] Chambers, ii., App. W; M. L. Spencer, 71 ff.

tableaux. In other words, the particular set of subjects treated in the Corpus Christi plays are there, not because they were chosen to suit the idea of Corpus Christi, or because they were attractive in themselves, but because they were the liturgical themes handed down for centuries and ready to be combined into cycles for that occasion. The idea that a pageant antedates a play puts the cart before the horse. The ceremony at Beverley, recorded in 1355, connected with the feast of the Purification, and cited by Mr. Spencer as an example of a mimetic pageant,[33] is not necessarily dumb-show. The regular play on this subject must have had an independent existence for a long time. It has no fixed place in the cycles and shows evidence in every single case of being outside the parent cycle.

If we reduce a Corpus Christi cycle, say the Chester Whitsun plays, to its lowest terms, so to speak, and cut out from it every play which might by any chance be a later addition, or the result of development during the history of the cycle as a whole, as well as all useless homiletic materials, comicalities and excrescences, we yet have a drama of very considerable extent, perhaps one-third to one-half the whole, as it now stands; therefore, a drama that would require for its presentation, even at a very limited number of stations, a considerable amount of time. The Chester cycle would demand the treatment of the following topics: Fall of Lucifer, Creation, Fall of Man, Cain and Abel, Noah, Abraham and Isaac, *Processus*, Nativity with much special material, *Pastores, Stella,* Slaughter of the Innocents with Flight into Egypt, Temptation, Lazarus, Woman taken in Adultery (?), Entry, Conspiracy, Last Supper, Capture, Trial, Crucifixion, Death and Burial, Harrowing of Hell, Setting of the Watch, Resurrection, *Hortulanus, Peregrini,* Doubting Thomas, Ascension, Pentecost, Antechrist, Doomsday. No matter how briefly such topics were treated in the beginning, the skeleton itself is so extensive that it would have required a number of hours to present it. If we grant, for the purpose of getting the plays on the road, that the plays started out with the Corpus

[33] Smith, *English Gilds,* 149-50; M. L. Spencer, *loc. cit.,* 70 ff.

Christi procession, bearing in mind, however, that there is no evidence for it, and stopped at various places to act the scenes one after another, then it follows from the amount of time required, even from the first, that the Host, the clergy, the mayor and the city fathers must have preceded the gilds with their pageants; for otherwise they would have had to halt in the street at the first station for three or four hours.

Mr. Spencer states that in the earliest times the craftsmen led the procession and the ecclesiastics followed, but in this matter I think he has been misled.[34] The oldest and best case, that of Ipswich, is precisely the other way about.[35] So also at Beverley and York. Sharp states[36] that it seems reasonable to infer that the laity preceded the Host at Conventry; but it is not absolutely certain that this was the case, and if it was, it is the exception rather than the rule.

There were some places, where for all we know, the plays were just as ancient, in which the pageants were not carried about the streets, but the plays were acted on fixed stages. A connection with the Corpus Christi procession is not absolutely necessary to account for the processional idea. It is certain that the Corpus Christi play originated, not in dumb-show, but by the union of preëxistent plays, in cyclic combination for the most part, extensive in scope, long familiar to the people, and of native growth.

HARDIN CRAIG.

University of Minnesota.

[34] *Loc. cit.,* p. 77.
[35] His. MSS. ix., 8, 245.
[36] *Dissertation,* 125.

REVIEWS AND NOTES

GRUDZINSKI, HERBERT: SHAFTESBURYS EINFLUSS
AUF CHR. M. WIELAND. Mit einer Einleitung über
den Einfluss Shaftesburys auf die deutsche Literatur bis
1760. Breslauer Beiträge zur Literaturgeschichte. Stuttgart 1913. Metzlersche Buchhandlung. 104 pp. M. 3:00.

ELSON, CHARLES: WIELAND AND SHAFTESBURY.
Columbia University Germanic Studies. Columbia University Press. New York, 1913. 143 pp.

Diese zwei Arbeiten ergänzen sich in erfreulicher Weise.
In seiner Dissertation definiert Grudzinski zuerst Shaftesburys Philosophie. Der Grundzug derselben besteht darin,
Welt and Leben aesthethisch zu erfassen und zu gestalten.
Daher lehnt Shaftesbury die Metaphysik ab und strebt nach
Lebensweisheit. Die Grundlage dieser Lebensweisheit aber ist
sein aesthetischer Begriff der Harmonie, der dann direkt zur
aesthetischen Theodizee führt. Denn die Natur erscheint ihm
—wie einem Platon, einem Plotinus, einem Bruno—als schön-
heitsvolle Harmonie und Ordnung. Shaftesbury überträgt
nun diesen Harmoniebegriff auf die Sittlichkeit und gelangt
auf diese Weise zum Gedanken einer aesthetischen Bildung,
zur Verwerfung jeder Verkümmerung durch Pflichtgebote,
und zur Begründung des sittlichen Handelns auf dem Geschmack. Wie gewaltig diese Gedanken im achzehnten Jahrhundert besonders auf Schiller gewirkt haben, bis Kant mit
seinem kategorischen Imperativ ein preussisch-spartanisches
Ideal aufstellte, brauche ich wohl kaum zu betonen. Ferner,
dass Goethe auch auf diesem Gebiete mit Shaftesbury über-
einstimmt statt mit Kant, und dass sich in der Romantik,
wie Walzel (Euph. XIX S. 376) hervorgehoben hat, unter
dem Einfluss Shaftesburys kräftig lebensbejahende Stim-
mungen finden, darauf sei hier nur nebenbei hingedeutet.
Mit seiner allgemeinen Weltbetrachtung hängt nun Shaftesburys Ideal des "virtuoso" zusammen, des "real fine gentleman", der Liebe zur Wissenschaft mit weltmännischem
Auftreten verbindet. In der harmonischen Entfaltung der
Persönlichkeit, auf die Shaftesbury immer wieder das Haupt-
gewicht legt, spielen die altruistischen Regungen ("natural
affections"), im Gegensatz zum theoretischen Egoismus eines
Hobbes und La Rochefoucauld, eine bedeutende Rolle. Aus
Shaftesburys aesthetischer Auffassung der Moral folgert
logisch, dass der Mensch durch sittliche Arbeit an sich selbst
zum Künstler wird. Daher ist die harmonische Seele die

höchste irdische Schönheit ("moral grace", "moral Venus").
Wer dächte nicht sofort an Goethe's griechisch-Shaftes-
burysches Ideal? Die Pflicht des Dichters ist es nun, nach
Shaftesbury, die Schönheit im Sinne des aesthetischen Optimismus zum Ausdruck zu bringen. Der Künstler wird
auf diese Weise zum Schöpfer: "a veritable Prometheus
under Jove". Wir erinnern uns bei dieser Gelegenheit
der Ausführungen Walzels in "Das Prometheussymbol von
Shaftesbury zu Goethe", Leipzig und Berlin 1910, einer
Schrift die auch G. zitiert und in der mit Gründlichkeit
und Geist die Benutzung des Prometheusmythus bei den
verschiedenen deutschen Dichtern des 18ten Jahrhunderts
nach dem Erscheinen der Werke Shaftesbury's verfolgt wird.
Der feine englische gentleman Shaftesbury, dem an der
Harmonie der Seele liegt, wehrt sich mit aller Gewalt gegen
jede Art von Übertreibung und vor allem vor unbeherrschter
Begeisterung. Daher erscheint ihm "enthusiasm" ("Schwärmerei"), der sich im siebzehnten Jahrhundert auf reli-
giösem Gebiete als gefährlich erweisen hatte, als die wider-
lichste aller Verirrungen. Aus seiner ganzen Weltbetrachtung
folgert weiter—und auch hierin wird Shaftesbury einer der
Führer der neuen geistigen Bewegung des achzehnten Jahrhunderts—, dass selbst die Religion der wissenschaftlichen
Kritik unterbreitet werden muss. Er nimmt der Religion
daher ihren Jenseitscharakter und legt den Hauptnachdruck
auf das sittliche Leben.

Wenn ich hier G.'s Ausführungen etwas im Detail wieder-
gegeben und somit manches Bekannte wiederholt habe, so
geschah das nur, weil meines Wissens in der grossen Literatur über Shaftesbury nirgends die Hauptgrundzüge seines
philosophischen Systems so knapp und klar dargelegt worden
sind, wie bei G. Und wir sind uns ja erst in den letzten
Jahren, vor allem durch Dilthey und Walzel, über die ge-
waltige Bedeutung Shaftesburys für das ganze Lebens-
ideal unserer Klassiker klar geworden. Denn Shaftesbury
fand sofort, wie G. weiter ausführt, lebhaften Anklang,
Zuerst selbstverständlich in England (Hutcheson, James
Thomson, Richardson, u. A. m.), dann aber in Deutschland.
Sein Optimismus wirkte im Gegensatz zum finsteren Pessimismus des siebzehnten Jahrhunderts auf lebensfrohe
Dichter wie Hagedorn. Sein Geselligkeitstrieb förderte den
Zug der allgemeinen Menschenliebe, der sich im ganzen
achzehnten Jahrhundert in Deutschland zeigt. Man denke
an den Freundschaftskultus der Gleim und Klopstock, an
Goethe's "Zueignung" ("Für andere wächst in mir das edle

Gut''), an die Ode ''Edel sei der Mensch'', and den zweiten Teil von ''Faust''. Shaftesburys Ideal, der harmonischen Entwicklung der Triebe aber beeinflusste lange vor Goethe Männer wie Uz, Justus Möser, Mendelssohn, Sulzer, wird weiter entwickelt von der Humanitätsphilosophie und der Frühromantik, und findet seine höchste Ausprägung in Schiller's Ideal der schönen Seele. Ferner wurde wichtig für Deutschland Shaftesburys Nachdruck auf die Bedeutung des Ästhetischen für die menschliche Kultur. Dem Hang zum einseitigen Gelehrtentum, der das ästhetische Moment bewusst oder unbewusst vernachlässigt und der sich in der deutschen Wissenschaft des siebzehnten und angehenden achzehnten Jahrhunderts—wie übrigens leider auch seitdem,—oft gezeigt hat, wirkt Shaftesburys oberflächlichere, aber auch kultiviertere Auffassung des Geisteslebens entgegen. Wie viel Goethe bei aller germanischen Tiefe mit dieser englisch-romantischen Richtung gemein hat, fällt sofort ins Auge.

Unter allen Jüngern Shaftesburys in Deutschland ist nun bei weitem der bedeutendste und einflussreichste Wieland. Durch ihn, den gehätschelten Lieblingsschriftsteller der höheren Kreise, werden die Shaftesburyschen Gedanken in Deutschland eingebürgert. Die ungesunde Mystik, die sich in der Tübinger-Biberacher Zeit bei Wieland zeigt, weicht bei ihm mehr und mehr einer Shaftesburyschen Lebensfreude. Schon im ''Cyrus'' (1757-59) zeigt sich der Einfluss des englischen Philosophen. Die Natur siegt mehr und mehr über die Schwärmerei und das Virtuosoideal findet einen abschliessenden Ausdruck in der ''Musarion'' (1768). Dass ein so begeisterter Bewunderer Shaftesburys sich mit aller Energie gegen Rousseaus kulturfeindliche Lehre wendet, ist geradezu selbstverständlich. In wie weit Shaftesburys Einfluss auch andere vor unkritischer Abhängigkeit bewahrt hat, harrt noch der näheren Untersuchung. In den letzten Jahren seines Lebens kommt Wieland seltener auf Shaftesbury zurück. Aber sogar der ''Aristipp'' (1800-1802) und andere Werke und Aussagen des Greisenalters beweisen, dass dem heiteren Schöpfer des ''Agathon'' sein Liebling Shaftesbury nie fremd geworden war.

Zu denselben Resultaten wie G. gelangt nun Elson in seiner Schrift, die freilich die eben besprochene an Reichhaltigkeit des Materials bei weitem übertrifft. E. hat sich in allen Ecken und Winkeln der Wielandschen Gedankenwelt umgesehen und fördert daher unsere Kenntnis des Shaftesburyschen Einflusses auf Wieland in höchst dankenswerter Weise. Da er aber keine Einleitung über Shaftesbury in Deutsch-

land vor Wieland gibt, noch aber seinem Stoff in so lichtvoller
Weise gliedert wie G., so ergänzt er zwar G.'s Schrift, macht
sie aber trotz seiner Gründlichkeit durchaus nicht überflüssig. Erst nach der Lektüre von G.'s Dissertation kann
der Leser die Resultate der Elsonschen in fruchtbarer Weise
ausnützen.

So haben wir allen Grund, uns über diese zwei Untersuchungen zu freuen, die, jede in ihrer Art, zum Verständnis der tiefen Bedeutung Shaftesburys in tüchtiger Weise
beitragen.

Nur eins hätte ich an der Methode auszusetzen. Man gewinnt sowohl bei G. wie bei E. den Eindruck, als ob Wieland
erst durch Shaftesbury zu einer Wandlung in seinen Anschauungen gekommen wäre. Wir sollten mehr und mehr den
Anschein vermeiden, als wenn wir glaubten, dass ''Einflüsse''
auf rein mechanische Weise das Weltbild irgend eines Menschen gewandelt hätten. Natürlich lag bei Wieland schon in
der Jugend der Keim zum Umschlag. Allerdings bedurfte
es äusserer Anregungen, bis aus dem Verfasser ''Der Empfindungen eines Christen'' der Dichter des ''Don Sylvio''
werden konnte. Shaftesburys Werke gaben einen, und
wahrscheinlich den mächtigsten, Anstoss. Es hätte sich nun
der Mühe verlohnt, Inkonsequenzen und Ansätze zu neuen
Anschauungen in den Jugendwerken und -Briefen Wieland's
aufzudecken und so dem ''Einfluss'' Shaftesburys in noch
kritischerer Weise nachzuspüren.

CAMILLO VON KLENZE.

Brown University, Providence, R. I.

DASS GERETTETE VENEDIG, eine vergleichende
    Studie von Fritz Winther. University of California
    Publications in Modern Philology. Vol. 3. No. 2. pp.
    87-246. Feb. 12, 1914.

Es wird heutzutage der vergleichenden Literaturgeschichte
zum Vorwurf gemacht, dass es ihr an psychologischer Vertiefung mangle. In dem eintönigen Versuch, den Einfluss
eines Dichters auf einen anderen festzustellen, zählt sie Entlehnungen über Entlehnungen, Anklänge über Anklänge
auf. Sie lässt dabei gewöhnlich ausser acht, dass die
Übernahmen eben so gut unbewusst wie bewusst sein
können, und dass durch die blosse Aufhäufung von Paral-
lelen der Originalität eines Dichters kein Eintrag getan
wird. Es wäre eine grössere und lohnendere Aufgabe, der

Empfindungsweise und der Gedankenwelt der Dichter verschiedener Nationen und Epochen nachzugehen, die bedeutendsten und kräftigsten Ideen, die sie bewegen, hervorzuheben. Denn hier treten wirkliche Zusammenhänge zutage, die von grosser Bedeutung sind, sowohl für die allgemeine Geschichte des menschlichen Geistes wie für das richtige Verständnis der betreffenden Dichter. Nach dieser höheren Auffassung der vergleichenden Literaturgeschichte verfährt Fritz Winther in seiner Untersuchung des Motivs ''Das gerettete Venedig'' in den gleichnamigen Dramen von Otway, La Fosse und Hofmannsthal.

Otway, das englische Vorbild des französischen und des deutschen Dichters lebte von 1651-1685. In den kurzen Jahren seinen Daseins durchlebte er ''das letzte Tosen der Renaissance, das satirische Gezänk der Restauration und die Arien des französischen Klassizismus.'' Sein ''Venice Preserved'' ist sogar das bedeutendste englische Drama zwischen Shakespeare und Shelly. Otway's persönliche Erlebnisse trugen dazu bei, ihm jene düstere Weltanschauung aufzuprägen, die den einzelnen Menschen als zufälligen Federball roher und feindlicher Mächte betrachtet. Seine Menschen geben sich ihrem ungezügelten Treiben hin, ihr ganzes Tun wird nur von Leidenschaft und Phantasie bestimmt und sie stürzen ins Verderben ohne Rücksicht auf die höheren Geistsfähigkeiten.

Der französische Dramatiker La Fosse lebte von 1653-1738, in der Zeit zwischen Racine und Voltaire, als der Rationalismus seinen Höhenpunkt erreichte. Er steht ganz unter dem Zeichen des französischen Klassizismus und wurde sogar zum Fürsprecher der französischen Aristokratie, in der sich die Ideale des Klassizismus verkörperten. Verstand und Vernunft sind die Merkmale seiner Dichtung und seine Menschen bleiben immer im steifen Rahmen der formelhaften Wiederbelebung der Antike.

In scharfem Gegensatz zu La Fosse und gleichsam auf einer Mittelstufe zwischen ihm und Otway steht der deutsche Dichter Hugo von Hofmannsthal. Früh wandte er sich mit Ekel vom Naturalismus und der banalen Alltäglichkeit seiner Mitwelt, um sich in die Spätrenaissance, die Zeit freien, künstlerischen Schaffens, und grosser, selbstbestimmender Persönlichkeiten zu versenken. Als Sohn seiner Zeit aber hat er sich dem rationalistischen Einfluss des neunzehnten Jahrhunderts nicht ganz entziehen können. Er neigt also einerseits zu den impulsiven tatkräftigen Menschen der Shakespeareschen Bühne, andererseits den vernünftigen, intellektuellen Menschen der französischen Bühne hin. Als Folge eines unausgeglichenen Kampfes zwischen Verstand und Leidenschaft entsteht bei Hofmannsthal ein Menschentypus, der sich von der Gestalten des Shakespeareschen Dramas wie von denen der französischen unterscheidet, eine Menschenart, die ihre Gefühle und Ideen in sinnlichen metapherreichen Wortgebilden ausdrückt, die aber nicht die Kraft besitzt, ihr Wollen in Handlung umzusetzen.

Auf der breiten Grundlage des persönlichen Erlebnisses und der Zeitströmungen prüft Winther die drei Bearbeitungen "des geretteten Venedigs" auf ihrem geistigen Inhalt. Er teilt sein Hauptkapitel "Unterschiede in der Darstellungsweise" in folgende Abschnitte ein: 1. Verstand, Phantasie, Leidenschaft; 2. Einzelne Charaktere; 3. Freundschaft; 4. Ehe; 5. Der Übergang vom Verchwörer zum Verräter; 6. Motive des Handelns; 7. Orient und Renaissance; 8. Lyrische Elemente; 9. Sprache und Technik. Der Hauptverdienst der Wintherschen Arbeit liegt gleich im ersten Abschnitt. Mit psychologischem Scharfsinn und umfassender Kenntnis des Zeitgeistes betont er das Vorherrschen des Verstandes, der Phantasie, oder der Leidenschaft in den drei Dramen. Das Ergebnis dieses Teils seiner Untersuchung lautet folgendermassen: "Bei La Fosse finden wir ein Maximum des Verstandes und ein Minimum der Phantasie; bei Otway ein Minimum des Verstandes und ein Maximum der Phantasie; bei Hofmannsthal hat sich das Problem verwickelt; wir haben Stellen, wo der Verstand der Phantasie untergordnet ist, entweder so dass er ganz ausgeschaltet zu sein scheint, oder so dass er ganz in den Dienst der Phantasie gestellt wird, also ähnliche Verhältnisse wie bei Otway; anderswo sind Verstand und Phantasie ziemlich gleichgestellt und dann finden wir den besonders die Moderne auszeichnenden Fall, dass der Verstand sich die Phantasie dienstbar macht."

Besonders einleuchtend ist der Abschnitt über die Ehe. Winther leitet die Auffassung des Verhältnisses zwischen Mann und Weib sowohl von der gesellschaftlichen Stellung der Dichter wie von den Kulturzuständen des Zeitalters her. Otway's Belvidera verkörpert die Ideale des englischen Bürgertums, dem der Dichter selbst entsprungen ist. Ganz Demut opfert sie sich ohne Widerstand den höheren Interessen ihres Mannes. Die Valerie von La Fosse ist aber die vornehme und selbstbewusste Aristokratin, die ihrem Manne geistig und gesellschaftlich gleichgestellt ist. Stolz und Ehrgefühl sind die Triebfedern ihrer Handlungen. Als geborener Aristokrat bevorzugt Hofmannsthal die französische Heroine. Stolz und Verachtung der sozial Tieferstehenden

gegenüber hat sie mit der französischen Valerie gemein.
Aber das Herbe und Amazonenhafte der La Fosseschen
Heldin wird wesentlich gemildert durch das starke Heraus-
arbeiten des weiblichen bezw. mütterlichen Elements. Winther
sieht weiter in Belvidera eine Verwandte des modernen starken
Frauentypus. Dieser Ansicht kann ich nicht beistimmen.
Sind doch Belvideras Hingabe an ihren Mann und ihre Liebe
zu ihren Kindern Beweise dafür dass sie sich viel mehr dem
entgegengesetzten Typus nähert. Meines Erachtens schiesst
Winther auch ganz fehl, indem er behauptet, gerade solche
starken Frauennaturen pflegten sich in die Schwäche eines
Mannes zu verlieben.

Im sechsten Abschnitt "Motive des Handelns" seziert
Winther mit dem Eifer eines Anatomen das Gehirn der dramatis personæ. Er zeigt ausführlich wie die Motive bei
La Fosse allgemeiner, abstrakter Art, bei dem Engländer und
dem Deutschen konkreter, selbstischer Natur sind. Bei La
Fosse wiegen Vaterlandsliebe, Tugend, und Ehre, bei den
anderen Egoismus und sexuelle Momente vor. Hinsichtlich
des Gewissens zieht Winther folgende Schlüsse: "Bei Otway
finden wir das Gewissen sozusagen im Erwachen begriffen;
als Motiv des Handelns betrachtet ist es eine Kraft neben
anderen. Bei La Fosse haben wir einen hohen Grad von
eigentlich abstrakt raisonnierendem Gewissen, also Gewissen
im eigentlichsten Sinne des Wortes. Bei Hofmannsthal finden
wir beinahe jenen Standpunkt jenseits von Gut und Böse,
den Stendahl, Burkhard und Nietzsche uns in der italienischen
Renaissance sehen gelehrt haben."

Der Abschnitt "Orientalismus und Renaissance" beschäftigt sich fast ausschliesslich mit Hofmannsthal, denn er allein
von den drei Dramatikern hat sich den Zeitgeist der Spätrenaissance zu eigen gemacht. In der Mullattin, der Dienerin
der Kurtisane Aquilina verkörpert Hofmannsthal jene sinnliche Mystik des Orients, die sich in der Renaissance geltend
machte; in Aquilina selbst das unsittliche Element, welches
der Kurtisane den Umgang mit den Ersten der Republik
ermöglichte; in dem Verschwörer Capello ein mit oriental-
ischer Grausamkeit vermischtes Geckentum; und schliesslich
in den Senatoren Dolphin und Priuli die ungeheuerliche
Selbstschätzung der übermenschlichen Herrschernaturen der
Renaissance.

Eine Untersuchung, wie diese von Winther, hat natürlich
nicht die Pflicht, den künstlerischen Wert eines Dramas
festzustellen. Aber die Frage drängt sich doch dem Leser
auf, ob man den allgemein anerkannten Wert eines Dramas

nicht in Betracht ziehen sollte, ehe man denselben einer so tiefgehenden Untersuchung würdigt. Als bühnengerechtes Drama is bekanntlich Hofmannsthals Stück von dem Publikum und der Kritik abgelehnt worden. Es leidet nämlich an Retardierung der Handlung durch weitläufige Milieuschilderung und Zersplitterung des Interesses zwischen den zwei Helden Jaffier und Pierre. Vom Standpunkt des Dichters ist Jaffier der psychologisch konsequent durchgeführte Held. In der Tat aber ist er ein kleinlicher, schwacher Mensch ohne innere Grösse, der sich in ein Unternehmen einlässt dem er nicht gewachsen ist, und durch seine Gattin bestimmt, das Werk und seinen Freund verrät. Der eigentliche Held ist der Hauptverschwörer Pierre, der der volkstümlichen Auffassung des Heldenhaften völlig entspricht. Man hat das Gefühl dass die relative Bedeutung dieser Menschen verkehrt ist. Es ist gerade als wenn Goethe Werslingen statt Götz zum Helden seines Dramas gemacht hätte.

Ich möchte durch diese Bedenken keineswegs die Bedeutung der Wintherschen Arbeit unterschätzen. Schade nur dass er kein wichtigeres Drama zum Gegenstand seiner Untersuchung gewählt hat. Seine Arbeit ist und bleibt ein wertvoller Beitrag zur vergleichenden Literaturgeschichte. Es kann sein, dass manches psychologische Detail ausgeklügelt und weit hergeholt ist. Diesen Mängeln nachzugehen, überlasse ich dem fachmännischen Psychologen. Die Grundlinien seiner Studie sind mit fester und kräftiger Hand gezeichnet und sollten als Vorbild dienen für weitere Untersuchungen auf diesem Gebiet.

GEORGE M. BAKER.

Philadelphia.

RECENT BOOKS ON THE MEDIÆVAL RELIGIOUS DRAMA

Friedrich Krage has published in the *Germanische Bibliothek* a very welcome new edition of the fifteenth century Low German play, Der Sündenfall. The only edition hitherto available is the one by Schönemann of the year 1855, which offers a very inaccurate text and has also long been out of print. The introduction of the new edition begins with a study of the language of the play and a utilization of the results in fixing the home of the poet in the Göttingen-Grubenhagen district, probably either in the town of Einbeck, whose famous beer is served and praised by Solomon in the play, or in Alfeld, where the name Arnold Immessen is found in a

document of the year 1486. For most of the play Arnold
seems to have had no important source except the Vulgate.
His version of the sending of Seth into Paradise is taken from
another source. Schönemann thought he used the Low German Hartebok der Flanderfahrer. Krage shows, however,
that Arnold did not use the Hartebok but used its Netherland
source Dboec van den houte and used it also with intelligence
and skill.[1]

Arnold covers in his play the time from the creation of
the world to the presentation of the three-year-old Mary in
the temple. This does not seem a natural place to end and
the question has often been raised as to whether the play
with its 3962 lines is complete. Krage considers the question
and answers it in the affirmative. The introduction ends with
a brief metrical study and a list of text emendations and
deviations from Schönemann. After the text come some
pages of notes and a glossary of the Low German words that
might give one trouble. The note on "an sinen dank"
(l. 1626) seems awkward and even incorrect; the expression
as used here means "against his will" or "without his being
able to help it". Krage's edition, with its apparently accurate text and all these other aids, is a valuable and service-
able addition to the literature of this field.

In Rudolph Höpfner's investigation of three related Easter
plays he devotes about two-thirds of his book to a study of the
language of the plays and attempts to determine in this way
the home of the respective poets as well as the scribes of the
manuscripts. All three plays have long been known to be
of Middle German origin. Höpfner establishes a probability
of the Innsbruck play having been written in the Henneberg
district, possibly in Schmalkalden, and he dates it, or at least
a certain part of it, between 1323 and 1347. The Berlin
play, of which only a fragment of two pages has been preserved, he assigns to Thuringia. The Vienna play he places
further East in Silesia and thinks it was written in the
second half or towards the end of the fourteenth century.

---

[1] Arnold Immessen, Der Sündenfall. Mit Einleitung, Anmerkungen
und Wörterverzeichnis neu herausgegeben von Friedrich Krage (Germanische Bibliothek, hrsg. von W. Streitberg, II, 8.). Heidelberg, 1913.
Carl Winters Universitätsbuchhandlung. M. 6:40; bound M. 7:40.

Untersuchungen zu dem Innsbrucker, Berliner und Wiener Osterspiel
von Rudolph Höpfner (Germanistische Abhandlungen 45). Breslau,
Verlag von M. & H. Marcus, 1913. M. 5:60.

Die Prophetensprüche und -zitate im religiösen Drama des deutschen
Mittelalters, von Dr. Phil. Joseph Rudwin (Purdue University, Indiana).
Leipzig und Dresden, 1913. Kommissionsverlag von C. Ludwig Ungelenk.
50 Pf.

The last third of Höpfner's work is devoted to a study of the literary relations of the plays to each other and to other plays. The net results are not great, although a good many interesting matters of detail are brought out. Recent years have seen a number of detailed studies of plays, such as this of Höpfner, and they are important steps towards a better knowledge of the history of the mediæval religious drama.

The little work of Dr. Rudwin on the Prophetensprüche discusses briefly the prophet scenes in the mediæval religious drama of Germany, their importance and widespread occurrence, their purpose, the external appearance of the prophets and the Biblical sources of their prophecies, the development from the simple prophet scenes to disputation scenes between prophets and Jews, and finally into disputation scenes between Ecclésia and Synagoga. The limitation to Germany is unfortunate. The early forms of the mediæval religious drama and especially its Latin beginnings cannot be profitably discussed without overstepping national lines. Within the limited field there are omissions; there is no mention of the prophets and their prophecies in the Brixen Passion play or of the Shrovetide play "Die alt und neu Ee" with its survival of the Ecclesia-Synagoga dispute. Important literature on the subject is apparently unknown or unused, notably Paul Weber's Geistliches Schauspiel und kirchliche Kunst in ihrem Verhältnis erläutert an einer Ikonographie der Kirche und Synagoge (1894). A few inaccuracies were noticed in matters of detail. In the first sentence in the book the first statement is misleading in that it is true only of Germany, while the second statement is quite contrary to fact. At the bottom of page 12 there is a comedy of errors, the statement regarding the introductory speech of Augustinus in the St. Gallen Passion play is wrong, the date of the play is wrong, and the footnote on the play is wrong, as Froning has no edition of the St. Gallen play. Aside from a few omissions and inaccuracies Dr. Rudwin gives a very good popular account of the development, but his little book cannot be considered as having scholarly value as a contribution to the knowledge of the subject.

N. C. BROOKS.

University of Illinois.

POETASTER AND SATIROMASTIX, edited by Josiah H. Penniman. The Belles-Lettres Series. Boston. D. C. Heath and Company. 12mo., pp. lxx, 456. 1913.

It was a happy idea to bring into one volume *Poetaster* and *Satiromastix*. Neither play can be properly studied without the other; and a knowledge of both is essential to an understanding of "that terrible Poetomachia" which so profoundly disturbed the dramatic world during the later years of Elizabeth's reign. *Poetaster*, it is true, has long been accessible in more than one satisfactory edition, but hitherto *Satiromastix* has been inaccessible to most readers; it has, indeed, been properly edited only once, by Dr. Hans Scherer in Bang's *Materialien*. In placing an accurate text of these two plays within the easy reach of all students, Professor Penniman has rendered a valuable service to the study of the Tudor drama.

In addition to the texts, the volume contains a short Biography of each of the two playwrights, a long Introduction on the War of the Theatres, elaborate Notes, and a Glossary. But to this editorial work, I regret to say, unstinted praise cannot be given; the volume has too many faults, both of commission and of omission, to satisfy the highest standard of scholarship.

For the purpose of testing the general accuracy of the editorial work, I selected the Biography of Dekker, in the main a catalogue of Dekker's numerous dramatic and non-dramatic works. The first paragraph of this catalogue (p. ix) I checked up with Henslowe's *Diary*, on which it is supposedly based, and discovered the following errors:

Four plays are entirely omitted: *Wars of Henry I*, 1598, with Chettle and Drayton; *Pierce of Winchester*, 1598, with Drayton and Wilson; *Second Hannibal and Hermes*, 1598, with Drayton, and *Fair Constance of Rome*, Part II, with Drayton, Hathaway and Munday.

The Golden Ass is wrongly attributed to Dekker, Munday, Drayton and Hathway. It was written in collaboration with Chettle and Day.

Of *Chance Medley* Professor Penniman says: "To this Chettle or Munday also contributed." There is no doubt as to Munday's share; he received 25 s. for the play. The doubt applies to Dekker himself. Mr. Greg says: "It is not clear whether it was Dekker or Chettle that was engaged on this piece."

The play called *Two Harpies*, (Malone's guess for Henslowe's indecipherable scrawl) Mr. Greg has identified as "beyond doubt" *Caesar's Fall,* and it should, perhaps, have been so entered.

Finally, the name of Chettle is omitted from the list of collaborators in the two parts of *Lady Jane Gray,* and in *Christmas Comes but Once a Year.*

The inaccuracies here noted do not inspire one with confidence; nor have I found painstaking accuracy an invariable characteristic of the editorial material. Professor Penniman seems to have made little use of Greg's scholarly edition of Henslowe's *Diary.* That he sometimes relied on unauthoritative sources is indicated elsewhere; for example, when, in his note to p. 325, ll. 275-6, he says, following Fleay: *"Gammer Gurton's Needle,* a play by Bishop Still, was acted in 1562-63 at court, and at Cambridge in 1566"; and again when in his note to p. 349, l. 122, he says: *"Alexander and Lodowick.* The name of a play by Martin Slaughter."[1]

I have made no attempt to verify other statements contained in these two Biographies; yet in rapidly glancing over the account of Jonson, I observed that the duel with Spencer is wrongly dated 1599 (probably through a printer's error); and the impression is given that this duel led to a permanent breach with Henslowe—at least the fact that in 1599 Jonson was again writing for the Admiral's Men is omitted. Since at this time Marston and Dekker were also writing for the Admiral's Men, and since Jonson was collaborating with Dekker, and possibly with Marston, the fact has special significance for the impending animosity of these playwrights.

But let us turn to Professor Penniman's more serious labors—his Introduction, Texts, and Notes.

The Introduction fails to give what one would most naturally expect—a clear and well-ordered account of the War of the Theatres; instead, it leaves the reader confused and perplexed. A brief summary, based on the facts actually known, and narrating in a simple and straightforward manner the history of the quarrel between Jonson and the Poetasters, would be desirable in a work of this nature, intended for the college student and the general reader as well as for the scholar.

Professor Penniman spends most of his time in seeking to identify characters in various plays with real persons. In some cases, of course, the identification is patent enough—

---

[1] *Gammer Gurton's Needle* was written by William Stevenson, and was acted at Christ's College, first in 1553-4 according to Professor Bradley, in 1550-53 according to Professor Wallace; and again in 1559-60. There is no evidence that it was ever presented at court. Martin Slaughter was an actor and not a playwright.

even acknowledged by the authors. But Professor Penniman, like other scholars who have written on the subject, does not hesitate to indulge in the purest speculation. In many cases the evidence that he adduces to establish his identifications is trivial, and in some cases worse. Those who seek to prove that Bacon wrote the plays of Shakespeare, or that Mistress Davenant was the Dark Lady of the *Sonnets,* employ reasoning hardly less astonishing. For example, Samuel Daniel, who was so highly praised by Spenser, Barnfield, Lodge, Meres, and others, the tutor to William Herbert, Earl of Pembroke, and to Lady Anne Clifford, whom Jonson himself described as "a good honest man," Professor Penniman identifies with Mattheo, the town gull in *Every Man in His Humour,* with Fastidious Brisk in *Every Man Out of His Humour,* with Hedon in *Cynthia's Revels,* with Gullio in *Parnassus,* and with Emulo in *Patient Grissel.* This remarkable series of identifications mainly hinges on the identification of the foolish Gullio, in *The Return from Parnassus,* Part I, with Daniel. In establishing this identification the editor makes much of the fact that Gullio is represented as a plagiarist, and he cites the Second Part of the *Return from Parnassus* as proof that Daniel was commonly thought to be a plagiarist. The passage referred to, however, serves rather to reveal the high opinion the author of the Parnassus plays had of Daniel, and to make quite improbable any attack upon him in the silly and contemptible character of Gullio:

> Sweet hony dropping *Daniell* doth wage
> Warre with the proudest big Italian
> That melts his heart in sugred sonneting.
> Onely let him more sparingly make use
> Of others wit, and use his own the more
> That well may scorne base imitation.

The charge here may be that of "imitation" rather than plagiarism. But assuming that Daniel was known to be guilty of plagiarism, Professor Penniman adduces the following proof that Gullio was intended for Daniel: "Gullio quotes, as his own, lines from Shakespeare, and 'will runne through a whole booke of Samuel Daniell's.'" To me, however, the fact that when Gullio begins to quote, as his own, scraps of verse from well-known poets, the sarcastic Ingenioso remarks "I think he will runne through a whole booke of Samuel Daniell's," refutes the theory that Gullio was intended for Daniel. Does not the remark of Ingenioso really compliment Daniel in implying that his books were popular, and hence apt to be quoted? Let any one who is in doubt turn to Macray's edition of *The Return from Parnassus* and read page 52, which introduces, and fully characterizes, the person of Gullio.

But Professor Penniman, having decided the identity of Gullio, remarks: "The identification of Gullio with Daniel fixes the identity of several other precisely similar characters"; and he then proceeds to establish these identifications. His arguments run like this: "Hedon keeps 'a barber and a monkey,' Gullio writes 'an epitaph on a [his mistress'] monkey'," etc. See pages xxxix-xl.

Jonson wrote his own protest against this, and I cannot do better than to let him speak for himself: "My works are read . . . . look into them . . . . . where have I been particular? Where personal? except to a mimic, cheater, bawd, or buffoon, creatures, for their insolence, worthy to be taxed? . . . . . I know that nothing can be so innocently writ or carried, but may be made obnoxious to construction . . . . . Application is now grown a trade with many; and there are that profess to have a key for the decyphering of everything; but let wise and noble persons take heed how they be too credulous."[2]

In the case of *Satiromastix*, likewise, the temptation to discover real persons in the characters is stronger than scholars have been able to resist. Dekker is very explicit, and, apparently, absolutely sincere in his statement to his readers: "Thus much I protest (and sweare by the divinest part of true poesie) that (howsoever the limmes of my naked lines may bee, and I know have been, tortur'd on the racke) they are free from conspiring the least disgrace to any man, but onely to our new *Horace*." Yet Mr. H. C. Hart identifies the ignorant city gull, Asinius Bubo, with the poet Michael Drayton. Professor Penniman gives Mr. Hart's identification (pp. 400-401) apparently with approval—he refers to it often —certainly with no disapproval. Yet who can believe that these lines were intended to satirize "Draiton, diligent and formall"?—

Hor. Good Bubo, read some booke, and give us leave—
Asin. Leave have you, deare ningle. Marry, for reading any book, he take my death upont (as my ningle sayes) tis out of my element. No, faith, ever since I felt one hit me ith teeth that the greatest clarkes are not the wisest men, could I abide to goe to schoole; I was at *As in presenti* and left there: yet, because Ile not be counted worse foole than I am, Ile turne over a new leafe.

[2] Dedication prefixed to *Volpone*, 1607.

Or who can believe that when Sir Vaughan, at the end of the play, makes Bubo take the following oath as to his future conduct, he is referring to Drayton?—

> You will not hyre Horace to give you poesies for rings, or hand-kerchers, or knives, which you understand not, nor to write your love-letters which you (in turning of a hand) set your markes upon, as your owne; nor you shall not carry Latin poets about you, till you can write and read English at most.

Is neither Dekker nor Jonson to be allowed to represent a gull without being accused of satirizing some eminent poet? For my part, I am willing to accept the statements of the play-wrights, so earnestly made, until better evidence is advanced by those who attempt to prove the contrary.

After all, was not the War of the Theatres a much simpler thing than most scholars seek to make it? In the works of Samuel Daniel no one has yet been able to discover the slightest echo of this War. Jonson is very specific as to his share in it. He asserts that he took no notice of his enemies before he wrote his acknowledged reply in *Poetaster*:

> *Hor.* I take no knowledge that they doe maligne me.
> *Tib.* I, but the world takes knowledge.

And in his Apologeticall Dialogue, he reiterates the state-ment that *Poetaster* was his first answer to their attacks:

> But sure I am, three yeeres
> They did provoke me with their petulant styles
> On every stage: And I at last, unwilling,
> But weary, I confesse, of so much trouble,
> Thought I would try if shame could winne upon 'hem,
> And therefore chose Augustus Caesars times.

Dekker's share in the War was limited to *Satiromastix*. And a short time after the appearance of *Satiromastix*, both Mars-ton and Dekker were on the best of terms with Jonson.

For his text of *Poetaster* Professor Penniman has wisely reproduced the folio of 1616. He has undertaken to give a faithful reprint, with certain minor exceptions to which no one can object. Since Jonson himself edited the folio of 1616 with great care, the importance of preserving the original spelling and punctuation is obvious. The editor has pains-takingly collated several copies of the first folio, the quarto of 1602, and several copies of the folio of 1640, including the large-paper copy in the British Museum, and has con-veniently recorded all variants in footnotes.

I have carefully compared ten pages of the reprint with copies of the 1616 and the 1640 folios in my own possession, without discovering a single error; and all the variants I

have found duly recorded. Unfortunately, however, the Induction and the Prologue were not so carefully printed. In
these I noted the following errors:

P. 5, l. 1. After *thee* a semicolon for a comma.

P. 5, l. 11. After *stay* a colon for an exclamation.

P. 5, l. 14. After *not* the comma has been dropped; and
the word *these* has been unnecessarily capitalized.

P. 5, l. 16. After *lights* the comma has been dropped.

P. 6, l. 22. *riffe* for *risse*.

P. 8, l. 12. *fence* for *sence*.

Satiromastix is printed from the only text, the quarto of
1602. The editor says: "As the quarto was carelessly printed,
an attempt is made here to give a correct text, changes being
indicated in the footnotes. Obvious misprints have been
silently corrected and the punctuation modernized." The
text, so far as I have been able to discover, has been reproduced with scrupulous accuracy; but the "modernized" punctuation is far from satisfactory. Although Professor Penniman has used the greatest freedom in altering the original
punctuation and capitalization, he has done his work so
half-heartedly that he has produced a text which, like Fal-
staff's otter, is neither fish nor flesh; it fails to reproduce the
original, and it cannot be fairly described as a modernization.
I cite a few illustrations:

293. 342. "By Jesu, within this hour, save you, Captayne
Tucca." This should be: "By Jesu, within this hour. —Save
you, Captayne Tucca." In the first clause, Horace promises
Blunt to have the poem ready within an hour; in the second
clause, he suddenly recognizes Tucca, who has just entered.

313. 48. "Away, and, stay: here be epigrams" . . . . .
This should be punctuated: "Away, and—Stay, here be
Epigrams" . . . . .

322. 183. "*Tuc.* Why well said, my nimble Short-hose."
This punctuation spoils the sense. The first clause, "Why well
said," was addressed to Mistress Miniver; the second clause,
"My nimble Short-hose," was spoken aside to Short-hose.
One could readily multiply examples, but the reader will find
them on almost every page.

The Notes to *Poetaster* are full, and in the main scholarly.
The play, it is true, had already been carefully edited by
Whalley, Gifford, Cunningham, Nicholson, Mallory, and Hart,
so that little matter of great importance could be added; but
Professor Penniman has shown good judgment in selecting
from different interpretations, and has added fresh material
when he could. The Notes to *Satiromastix* are less satisfactory. This play, of course, had not received the careful

attention that had been given by many scholars to *Poetaster*. Professor Penniman, however, has corrected a number of errors made by Doctor Scherer, and has contributed many valuable notes of his own.

The inclusion of certain explanatory material in a Glossary at the end of the volume is a constant source of annoyance. For this, of course, the editor is not to blame; it is the fault of the series. Yet he has aggravated the annoyance by inserting in his Notes many words that logically should be in the Glossary; for example, 267.14; 273.48; 273.52; 273.64; 284.124; etc. Such inconsistency is hard to understand. And equally hard to understand is the failure of the editor to explain in the Glossary many words that clearly demand explanation. A few cases may be cited: 91.45 "minsitive," (the *N.E.D.* records this as the only occurrence of the word as an adjective, and records only one occurrence of the noun); 115.10 "everts" (which the *N. E. D.* describes as rare, and can give only two other occurrences); 383.164, "place-mouth"; 339.146, "scowring-sticke"; 370.61, "posted off"; 309.219, "repaires"; 328.340, "tall." The same thing is true, though to a less extent, of passages that call for explanatory notes. For example, 321.151-52: "She has a vizard in a bagge will make her looke like an angell," meaning, her wealth will transform her ugly face into that of an angel; 305.138-39: "above a hundred merie tales," referring to the popular jest-book of that name. Of course the standard of what is to be included and what excluded varies in different annotated editions; but I have kept in mind the standard that this particular volume sets for itself, and judged by its own standard, there are many omissions, in both the Notes and the Glossary.

Below are recorded some of the corrections and additions suggested by an examination of the Notes.

5.3. In giving references, the editor might well have recorded the article by W. J. Lawrence, *Title and Locality Boards on the Pre-Restoration Stage*, printed in the *Shakespeare-Jahrbuch* for 1909 (xlv. 146), and subsequently reprinted in his *The Elizabethan Playhouse*.

10.5-6. *Songs and Sonnets.* "This was the title of Surrey's Poems 1557." To be exact, it was the title of Tottel's Miscellany, in which appeared poems not only by Surrey, but also by Wyatt, Grimald, Vaux, Heywood, Somerset, "and other," as the titlepage states. For "H. E. Hart" read "H. C. Hart." An apter reference than those noted is Master Slender, in Shakespeare's *Merry Wives* I. i.

11.33. *Pantilius Tucca.* For an interesting surmise as to the origin of this name, see Wm. Hand Browne, *Mod. Lang.*

Notes, 1905, xx. 216. Professor Browne's surmise is supported by a passage in *Lady Alimony* (Hazlitt's Dodsley, xiv. 284).

16.62. Tucca says of the players: "They forget they are i' the statute, they are blazond there, there they are trickt, they and their pedigrees; *they neede no other heralds, I wisse.*" The last clause the editor paraphrases thus: "The Statute describes players so clearly that no other description or announcement concerning their low position is needed." But obviously Tucca refers, not to an "announcer," but to the College of Heralds; he means that the players need no other herald than the Statute to establish their pedigree. The Statute names the players along with fencers, bearwards, jugglers, pedlers, tinkers, and petty chapmen, and classifies them all as "rogues, vagabonds and sturdy beggars." Cf. *Histrio-Mastix*, III. 272. Philarchus says of the players: "Blush not the peasants at their pedigree?"

19.137. *sing with angels.* This is a punning reference to the fact that an angel was commonly called "the lawyer's fee." Thus Stubbes, discussing the lawyers in *The Display of Corruptions*, says: "It is no meruaile if they be rich and get much, when they will not speak two words under an angell (for that is called a counsellers fee)."

19.148. *Three bookes will furnish you.* In *Stukeley* (Simpson, *School of Shak.* I. 166) these are "Littleton, Stamford, and Brooke."

21.187. Tucca calls Ovid Senior "old stumpe." The editor thinks this may be "an allusion to the fact that the character was acted by a boy," or "to the fact that Ovid walked 'stiffly as an old man,' as Dr. Mallory suggests." The words "old stumpe" do not suggest either littleness or stiffness; probably Tucca is merely referring to the age of Ovid Senior.

23.227. *This chain.* The editor rejects Dr. Mallory's plausible suggestion that the chain worn by Ovid Senior was such as in Jonson's day were worn by aldermen and wealthy citizens. He contends that since Ovid Senior was a Roman, the reference is to the *torquis,* an ornament of twisted gold worn in classical times on the arm, attached to the breast, or less frequently about the neck. But Jonson's actors did not attempt to reproduce Roman costumes closely; note the hat and feather of Crispinus, the cap of Chloe with its silver bodkin, and the long description of contemporary woman's headdress. Jonson would hardly stickle on this point. On page 24, Tucca says to Ovid: "Jove Keepe thy chaine from pawning." This refers to the Elizabethan custom, so often mentioned in the drama, of men pawning their gold chains. As to the value of these chains, see *The Puritan*

Widow I. iv. 122-6: "Wilt soon at night steal me thy master's chaine? . . . . . I know it to be worth three hundred crowns."

43.107-10. I cannot agree with the editor's note on this passage. Johnson is merely satirizing the custom of certain persons in going to see plays for the purpose of storing up high-sounding phrases. The custom is often satirized; note *Cynthia's Revels* III. i: "O, that piece was excellent! If you could pick out more of these play-particles, and, as occasion shall salute you, embroider or damask your discourse with them, persuade your soul, it would most judiciously commend you."

66.1-3. It should be observed that the use of the terms "bloudhound," "mungrels," "curres," bandogs," etc., applied to the lictors here and throughout the play, is based on the use of the cant term "dog," meaning "constable."

73.329. *Accommodate it unto the gentleman.* The editor remarks: "evidently an affected word." Jonson himself says as much in *E. M. I. H.* I. iv, and at the same time explains it: "Hostess, accommodate us with another bed-staff here quickly. *Lend* us another bed-staff—the woman does not understand the words of action."

88.396-402. In connection with this ridicule of Peele's *Battle of Alcazar*, it should be noted, that although originally produced "before 1589," the play was revived by the Admiral's Men shortly before *Satiromastix* was written, and hence was fresh in the minds of the audience. For the Plot of the revival, see Greg's *Henslowe Papers*, pp. 138-141. Much popular interest in the Battle of Alcazar was aroused in England about this time by the news of the appearance of a Pretender to the Portuguese throne, claiming to be King Sebastian who was slain in that famous battle. This interest is reflected in the revival of Peele's play, in the revival of *Stukeley,* in Munday's pamphlet *The Strangest News That Ever Happened* (1602), and in a new play by Dekker and Chettle entitled *Kinge Sebastian of Portugall* (1602).

105.11. The Banquet of the Gods was inspired by Lucian, rather than by Homer, although Jonson has borrowed from both. See *Mod. Lang. Notes*, January, 1912, vol. xxvii. p. 30.

152.343. *Thou motley gull.* Professor Penniman says: "i. e. Tucca." But it seems clear to me that Horace is addressing himself to Demetrius Fannius.

269.62. The editor's note indicates that he failed to understand the passage. Dekker means simply: "This play would not have appeared in print, had not," etc.

273.53. *lead apes in hell.* The best explanation of this
difficult expression has been made by Prof. G. C. Moore
Smith, in *Mod. Lang. Review*, April, 1904, vii. 6.

282.54-5. A glance at the horn joke.

282.71. Asinius refers to his pipe.

294.351. *Caine.* Tucca, addressing Asinius, makes a pun
on "cane" tobacco.

296.415. *Gorboduck.* The editor thinks this a reference to
the tragedy in the Senecan manner, written by Norton and
Sackville, and acted by the lawyers in 1560. But it is far
more likely that Tucca is referring to plays fresh in the
minds of the audience. From Henslowe's *Diary* we learn
that in 1600 Haughton wrote a play on the same theme, called
Ferrex and Porrex. For the same reason I believe that
Tucca's reference to *Damon and Pithias*, l. 406, is to Chettle's
play written for Henslowe in 1600, rather than to the early
play of the same name by Edwards, 1564.

296.419. *heyre apparant of Helicon.* The editor is wrong,
I think, in supposing that Tucca refers to Jonson. The
phrase is applied to Crispinus-Marston, "the new poet."
Dekker pays him another compliment on page 382, lines 125-6.

297.437. *When thou ranst mad for the death of Horatio.*
The editor says: "There were two plays in which Jeronymo
appears. One is *The Spanish Tragedy*, and the other, earlier,
is referred to by Jonson in the Introduction to *Cynthia's
Revels* as 'Hieronimo as it was first acted.'" These are not
two plays, for Jonson is referring to Kyd's *Spanish Tragedy*
as it was before "additions" were made to it by later writers.
Jonson himself, in 1601, was hired to make such additions.
The editor makes the same confusion in his note to 321.176.

313.50-4. *Fannius his play-dresser, who . . . . . cut an
innocent Moore i' th middle, to serve him in twice.* Professor
Penniman says: "We do not know what Dekker refers to
when he says that Jonson 'cut an innocent Moore i' th middle'
etc." Dekker does not accuse Jonson of this, but himself.
Professor Penniman adds: "Mr. Fleay offers the only plausible explanation thus far discovered," and quotes Fleay's
theory that Dekker had "patched up the play" of *Stukeley*
"with half of one by Peele on the Moor Mahomet." But this
theory is not very plausible, for the passage seems to mean
that Dekker took a single play, made it into two, and thus
served it in twice; in *Stukeley* we have two plays condensed
into one.

317.56. The editor's note indicates that he did not understand this passage; the latter part of his note is wholly ir-

relevant. Sir Vaughan dubs his man "Peter Salamander" because of Peter's violent red nose and face—a frequent make-up for the Elizabethan clown, for example, Bardolph in *Henry IV*.

326.316. *Alexas Secrets.* "Alexas is an attendant on Cleopatra in *Antony and Cleopatra*. The reference is perhaps to the scene with the Soothsayer (I. ii)." But Shakespeare is supposed not to have written *Antony and Cleopatra* until 1607-8.

328.346. Tucca, speaking of Horace-Jonson, says: "Ile love the little atheist." The editor comments: "Actors were regarded by many (e. g. Gosson) as immoral and profligate characters." However true this may be in general, it hardly applies here. Dekker is not satirizing Jonson as an actor; instead he is taking up the cudgels for the actors against their enemy Jonson. Apparently Dekker is referring to Jonson's religion, or is trying to brand him with atheism. Note that the charge is repeated, p. 394, l. 10: "That *hereticall libertine* Horace."

340.165-6. *banisht thee into the Ile of Dogs.* The word "banisht" and Tucca's habit of referring to famous plays make it almost certain that he is here glancing at Nash's *Isle of Dogs*.

349.128-30. *Thou'll shoot thy quills at me . . . . . wilt not, porcupine?* Topsell, in *The History of Four-footed Beasts* (1608), p. 588, says that the porcupines shoot their quills "with such violence that many times they stick into trees."

358.106-7. *Like the poore fellow under Ludgate.* The editor's note about the debtors' prison is not to the point. Dekker probably refers to a particular beggar at Ludgate, and not to the general practice of prisoners begging through the grates, which, according to Thomas Heywood, had been rendered unnecessary at Ludgate by the generosity of Agnes Foster. See Heywood, ed. 1874, I. 277, 380.

358.126. *Peter is never burnt.* A pun, referring to (1) the fact that salamanders are not injured by flames, and (2) the French disease.

358.130-1. *That's treason: clip? horrible treasons.* The note should explain that to "clip" meant to mutilate the coin of the realm by paring the edges.

361.210. *When.* "Used absolutely, meaning 'ready,' 'now,' 'then!' " Dr. Scherer says: "When=vorwärts." The word was used merely as an expression of impatience. Cf. *Julius Caesar* II. i. 5.

375.54. *mistery.* Professor Penniman explains this as a pun: "A 'mystery' was a play based on a subject taken from the Bible." But the word "mystery" in this sense seems to have been first used in England by Dodsley in his Preface to his collection of *Old Plays*, 1744. See E. K. Chambers, *The Mediæval Stage* II. 105, and A. W. Pollard, *English Miracle Plays*, xix-xx.

382.137. *Call in that selfe-creating Horace.* For "selfe-creating" read "self-created" ? Cf. p. 387, ll. 269-70.

388.283. *inpudentlie.* An error for "impudentlie," which is correctly printed in the quarto.

388.294. *Thee.* Read "the."

390.340-1. *Sit in a gallery.* "The gallery was the best place in the theatre, the price of admission being commonly two-pence." The price of admission to the "best place" in the theatre was at this time (1601) more than two-pence. It is probable that two-pence admitted one to the topmost gallery, but for the best places in the other galleries, six-pence, a shilling, and even more was charged. The editor was probably misled by Dr. Scherer's comment. He states the facts correctly in his note to 75.238.

395.142-3. *Good lord blesse me out of his majesties celler.* For "celler" read "coller" i. e. choler. Cf. 306.159,161.

Although Professor Penniman by his Notes has added much to the elucidation of *Satiromastix*, the play presents unusual difficulties, and needs close scrutiny by many scholars. I hope shortly to publish in a separate article additional notes to both plays, which my study of this edition has suggested, and which could not be given here without unduly lengthening this review.

JOSEPH QUINCY ADAMS, JR.

Cornell University.

THE MIDDLE ENGLISH PENITENTIAL LYRIC, by Frank Allen Patterson. The Columbia University Press, New York, 1911; pp. IX and 203.

The Middle English Penitential Lyric, by Dr. Frank Allen Patterson, which appears as one of the Columbia University Studies in English, is an important contribution to the history of early religious verse. The book is divided into three parts: an introduction, of forty-five pages; a corpus of texts, of one hundred and eight pages; and forty-six pages of notes and bibliography.

The Introduction is admirably clear and concise. Since the religious lyrics in Middle English are essentially mystical, Doctor Patterson makes mysticism the point of departure in classifying the lyrics. He first enumerates the three stages recognized by the mystics in the progress of the soul toward God, *purificatio, illuminatio,* and *contemplatio,* and then, since the distinction between the illuminative experience and the contemplative experience is only a matter of degree, classifies the lyrics as Poems of Purification and Poems of Divine Love-longing. The study is then limited to the poems of the first class. Since the chief acts of purification are those connected with penitence, Penitential Poems, as a more self-evident term, is chosen in preference to Poems of Purification. As penance consists of contrition, confession, and satisfaction, and as satisfaction—penitential works—is not adapted to lyrical expression, the penitential poems may all be classed as poems of contrition or poems of confession.

Such a classification is then made, as follws:

A. Poems of Confession
  I. Liturgical
    a. Public
    b. Extended
  II. Non-Liturgical
    a. Informal

B. Poems Expressing Contrition
  α. Sorrow for Sin
    I. Liturgical
      a. Paraphrases and Translations of Portions of Service
      b. Poems built upon the Litany
      c. Other Poems showing strong Liturgical Influence
    II. Non-Liturgical
      a. Prayers to the Deity
      b. Prayers to the Virgin Mary
      c. Timor Mortis Poems
  β. Prayers to be Kept from Sin and for Aid
    I. Liturgical
      a. Translations and Paraphrases
    II. Non-Liturgical
      a. Resolves to Reform
      b. General Prayers to the Deity for protection from Sin
      c. Prayers to Christ
      d. Prayers to Virgin Mary

The second part of the Introduction deals with the influences that brought about the development of the vernacular lyric; these are found to be principally in the liturgy and in the patristic writings.

The third part considers the French influence, as exerted by such types as the *chanson d' amour*, the *chanson à personnages*, the *serventois* and the *ballade*.

Dr. Patterson has established an excellent precedent in this new classification, organic and fundamental, of the Middle English religious lyrics, and greatly simplifies the task of those scholars who may take up the detailed study of other phases of the lyrics. The study has been conducted with much sympathy, and the writer's appreciation of the beauty of these fervent poems, so full of the mystic ardour of the Mediæval Church, is in gratifying contrast to the spirit of condescension in which they are too often approached.

If the second and third parts of the Introduction contain little that is really new, they yet give a more systematic and succinct statement of the facts involved than elsewhere is to be found.

The *corpus* of texts is intended to be complete, and this intention has very nearly been realized. However, not questioning, for the moment, the author's judgment in determining what types of lyrics to include, there are a few poems of the accepted types that have been overlooked. The most conspicuous omission is the poem *Parce mihi Domine*, beginning "By a forest side walkyng as I went", which is very similar to No. 5, "As I wandrede her bi weste". Three copies of this lyric are extant, in Mss. Ashmolean 189, f. 105; Cambridge 601 (R. 3. 20), f. 34; and Cambridge 1450 (O. 9.38), f. 24. This omission is the more surprising as the antiphon "Parce Domine, parce populo tuo", the liturgical basis of this poem, is noted under No. 2, v. 5 (p. 160). Of this same type is the poem *Salvum me fac Domine*, Ms. Ashmolean 189, f. 105. Similar to No. 48, "A morning thanksgiving and prayer to God", is the morning hymn, "Ihesu, Lord, blyssed yu be", and the evening hymn, "Ihesu, Lord, well of all goodness", Ms. Ashmolean 61, f. 22.

There is of course room for difference of opinion as to just what types of lyrics should be regarded as penitential. In general, Dr. Patterson has drawn the line with care, yet I cannot see why the translations of the penitential psalms should be omitted, especially as the *paternoster* is included. These psalms are translated with much freedom and feeling and have a marked personal note. Such translations as those in Ms. Ashmolean 61, fs. 108-118ᵇ, and Ms. Cambridge 600 (R. 3. 20), f. 197—ascribed to Thomas Brampton, would seem to have a claim upon this *corpus.*

Another class of lyrics that one would expect to find included are the exhortations to contrition, in which sinful man is called upon to repent, such as the Virgin's doleful exhortation in Ms. Ashmolean 189, II, f. 109, beginning,

> Thou synfulle man of resone,
> þat walkest here up and downe.

On the other hand, No. 68, "The Five Joys of the Virgin, is not primarily a poem of contrition. To be sure, it ends with a prayer, "help os at ore lynes ende", etc., but we can scarcely regard this as more than a conventional device for closing a poem, a device that was employed in many and many a carol to give it a good ending, as in the following characteristic stanza that concludes the carol *Puer nobis natus est*:

> Mary, modur and leve virgin,
> That bare a child withouten sin,
> Kepe us all fro helle pin!
> De virgine Maria.

It certainly has no more claim than the poem, "The Arms of Christ", a poem which concludes a description of the instruments of Christ's passion with the following prayer:

> Lord, graunt me, ere þat I dye,
> Sorowe of hert with teres of ey;
> Clen clensed for þy mercy,
> Ere þat I in my grave lye.
> So þat I may or domes day
> To þat dom cum with owt afray,
> And wend to blys in cumpany,
> Ther as men schall nevyr dye;
> But dwell in blys with þe, Lord bryȝt,
> Wher evyr is day and nevyr nyȝt;
> And lest schall with owt hend.
> Ihesu Crist uus þether send!
>   Amen.

Of this poem two excellent versions are extant, one in the library of the Catholic College of Blairs, Ms. 13, and the other in the library of Stonyhurst College, Ms. 32.

The notes are excellent, and give the maximum of pertinent information in the minimum of space. They are especially valuable in showing the relation of the lyrics to the liturgy. In a very few instances some of the variants of poems have been overlooked. Thus the poem *Deus in nomine tuo*, No. 21, of which it is stated that there is no variant, is also to be found in Ms. Ashmolean 59, f. 69. Among the variants of No. 52, the *Oratio magistri Richardi de Castre*, should be noted the very fine version in Ms. Sidney Sussex 80 (Δ. 4.

18), and among the variants of No. 60, "Mary moder welle the be", the version in Ms. Ashmolean 750, f. 100.

The usefulness of the book would have been enhanced by an index of first lines, and by an index of manuscripts.

The defects that have been noted are relatively slight, and this book maintains the standard of excellence of a noteworthy series.

FREDERICK MORGAN PADELFORD.

University of Washington.

LOHMANN, HANNA: JOHN WOODWARD, THE LIFE AND TRAGEDY OF THE ROYAL LADY MARY, LATE QUEEN OF SCOTS. Berlin, 1912; pp. 138.

This monograph, a University of Berlin dissertation, presents in admirable form and with more than adequate critical apparatus, a text of John Woodward's poem, which Dr. Lohmann has chosen as the excuse for her dissertation.

The poem in itself is thoroughly pedestrian. All the defects of the ordinary stall ballad are here rendered doubly oppressive by the prolixity—there are one hundred and eighty-six seven-line stanzas—which the balladist usually avoided. Finding the poem as it was, however, Miss Lohmann has treated it admirably, and has made it the occasion for a discussion of various matters of interest.

The text as here printed is based on a hitherto unpublished MS. in the Advocates' Library, and the occasional lacunae are supplied from the only other discovered MS. in the British Museum. Recording in the footnotes all variant readings, Miss Lohmann has treated the poem as if it were a newly discovered fragment of Chaucer, but has made the mistake of retaining in her text the original punctuation ("Die interpunktion habe ich beibehalten"), thereby rendering it needlessly difficult to understand Woodward's verse.

The most contributory section of the monograph is that entitled "Frühere Dichtungen über Maria Stuart." In these thirty pages the author has collected material of undoubted, if limited, interest. Other sections, dealing with the relation of the poem to history, and its debt to the *Mirror for Magistrates,* are less valuable.

Taken as a whole, the dissertation is an admirable exercise in editing. It is unfortunate that the poem which occasioned the study was not more worthy of reclamation from the limbo of the deservedly forgotten.

FRANKLYN BLISS SNYDER.

Northwestern University.

VERLAG DER WIEDMANNSCHEN BUCHHAND-
LUNG IN BERLIN.

Soeben erschienen:

Vom Mittelalter
zur Reformation

Forschungen zur Geschichte der deutschen Bildung

Im Auftrage der Königl. Preussischen Akademie der
Wissenschaften herausgegeben von

Konrad Burdach

Zweiter Band

Briefwechsel des Cola di Rienzo

Herausgegeben von

Konrad Burdach und Paul Piur

Dritter Teil. **Kritischer Text, Lesarten und Anmerkungen.**
Mit 3 Faksimilebeilagen. Gr. 8°. (XXIII u. 471 S.)
Geh. 16 M.

Vierter Teil. **Anhang.** Urkundliche Quellen zur Geschichte
Rienzos. Oraculum Angelicum Cyrilli und Kommentar
des Pseudojoachim. Gr. 8°. (XVI u. 354 S.) Geh
12 M.

Die vorliegenden beiden Teile bieten den erhaltenen Bestand aller
von Rienzo und an ihn ergangenen Briefe, sowie aller seine Person betreffenden gleichzeitigen urkundlichen Quellen in kritischer Herstellung
und eine Übersicht der zu Grunde liegenden handschriftlichen Überlieferung.

Die vorangehenden Teile folgen später.

Verlag von Vandenhoeck & Ruprecht in Göttingen.

Hesperia

Schriften zur germanischen Philologie

herausgegeben von

Hermann Collitz

Professor of Germanic Philology, Johns Hopkins University, Baltimore.

Diese Sammlung von Schriften ist aus den Bedürfnissen der germanischen Philologie in den Vereinigten Staaten erwachsen. Ihre Mitarbeiter werden in erster Linie Philologen sein, die an amerikanischen Universitäten wirken oder an solchen ihre Ausbildung erhalten haben. Mit Rücksicht hierauf hat sie den Namen „Hesperia" erhalten, dessen Verwendung uns durch Professor Gildersleeves Schrift: „Hellas and Hesperia" nahegelegt war.

1. **Hermann Collitz, Das schwache Präteritum und seine Vorge-** schichte. XVI, 256 S. 1912. Geh. 8 M; Leinwdbd. 8,80 M.

Der herkömmlichen Ansicht gegenüber, welche in dem schwachen Präteritum eine Zusammensetzung mit dem Zeitwort „tun" sieht, wird hier die Auffassung begründet, daß das schwache Präteritum als eigenartige Entwicklung des indogermanischen medialen Perfekts anzusehen sei. Die Einleitung gibt Auskunft über die bisherigen Versuche, die Entstehung des schwachen Präteritums zu erklären. Ein Anhang enthält Bemerkungen zum lateinischen Perfekt und eine neue Theorie des griechischen Passivaoristes.

2. **Hans Sachs and Goethe. By M. C. Burchinal, Ph. D.** IV, 52 S. 1912. Geh. 1,80 M; Leinwdbd. 8,80 M.

8. **Wörterbuch und Reimverzeichnis zu dem „Armen Hein-** rich" Hartmanns von Aue. Von Guido T. L. Riemer, Prof. a. d. Bucknell-University, Lewisburg. IV, 162 S. 1912. Geh. 8 M; Lwbbd. 3,70 M.

4. **Nature in Middle High German Lyrics. By B. Qu. Morgan,** Ph. D., University of Wisconsin, Madison. VIII, 220 S. 1912. Geh. 7 M; Leinwdbd. 7,80 M.

Hesperia Ergänzungsreihe:

Schriften zur englischen Philologie

Herausgegeben von

Hermann Collitz und James W. Bright

Professoren an der Johns Hopkins University in Baltimore.

Da das Studium des Englischen ein Arbeitsgebiet für sich bildet, schien es zweckmäßig, die Monographien, die sich vorwiegend auf die englische Sprache und Literatur beziehen, zu einer besonderen Abteilung zusammenzufassen.

Some Parallel Formations in English. By Professor Francis A. Wood, University of Chicago. 1913. 2,40 M; geb. 3 M.

2. Heft: **Historia Meriadovi and de Ortu Waluuanii. Two Ar-** thurian Romances of the XIIIth Century in Latin Prose. By Professor F. Douglas Bruce, University of Tennessee. Second Edition. Texts revised and corrected. Introduction re-written and enlarged. 1913. Etwa 4 M; geh. etwa 4,80 M.

Verlag von W. Kohlhammer,

Stuttgart, Leipzig und Berlin.

Zeitschrift
für deutsche Philologie.

Begründet von Julius Zacher im Jahre 1868.

Herausgegeben von Hugo Gering und Friedrich Kauffmann.

Die Zeitschrift gliedert sich in zwei Teile, von denen der eine Abhandlungen und Aufsätze oder auch ungedruckte Texte kleineren Umfangs, der andere kritische Referate und Rezensionen bringt. Ihr Inhalt umspannt das **Gesamtgebiet der deutschen Philologie;** sie berücksichtigt in gleichem Maße die Sprache und die Literatur, und zwar sowohl nach ihren volkstümlichen wie nach ihren künstlerischen Ausdrucksformen (**Stilgeschichte und Versgeschichte),** nach ihren heimischen Quellen wie nach ihren fremdsprachlichen Beziehungen, nach ihren älteren wie nach ihren jüngeren Denkmälern. Ferner läßt sie sich die der Pflege besonders bedürftige **deutsche Altertumskunde** angelegen sein und wahrdadurch den Zusammenhang mit der deutschen Geschichtswissenschaft (Kulturgeschichte, Kunstgeschichte).

Es ist dafür Sorge getragen, daß alle wichtigen wissenschaftlichen Publikationen, die auf dem Büchermarkt erscheinen, bibliographisch zusammengestellt und von sachkundigen Referenten besprochen und beurteilt werden. Über die Verhandlungen der Philologenversammlungen, wird ausführlich Bericht erstattet; außerdem werden die Leser durch Aufnahme biographischer Einzelschreiben oder zusammenfassender Charakteristiken der namhafteren Forscher mit den äußeren Vorgängen in der germanistischen Wissenschaft auf dem Laufenden erhalten.

Der feste Stamm von Mitarbeitern setzt sich aus Professoren und Dozenten der Universitäten und höheren Lehranstalten Deutschlands, Österreichs, Hollands, Skandinaviens und der Schweiz zusammen; die Redaktion läßt es sich aber auch angelegen sein, jüngeren Gelehrten für ihre Erstlingsarbeiten Raum zu gewähren.

Die Zeitschrift erscheint viermal jährlich in Heften von ca. 8 Bogen. Der Abonnementspreis beträgt jährlich 20 Mark.

Bestellungen nimmt jede Buchhandlung entgegen.

www.ingramcontent.com/pod-product-compliance
Ingram Content Group UK Ltd.
Pitfield, Milton Keynes, MK11 3LW, UK
UKHW041643280426
12128UKWH00013B/23